V. I. LENIN

An annotated bibliography
of English-language sources
to 1980

DAVID R. EGAN &
MELINDA A. EGAN

with the assistance of
JULIE ANNE GENTHNER

THE SCARECROW PRESS, INC.
Metuchen, N.J., & London • 1982

Library of Congress Cataloging in Publication Data

Egan, David R., 1943-
    V.I. Lenin, an annotated bibliography of English
language sources to 1980.

    Includes indexes.
    1. Lenin, Vladimir Il'ich, 1870-1924--Bibliography.
I. Egan, Melinda A. II. Genthner, Julie Anne.
III. Title.
Z8500.8.E36 [DK254.L4] 016.947084'1   82-659
ISBN 0-8108-1526-5   AACR2

TABLE OF CONTENTS

INTRODUCTION

Purpose

The goal of this bibliography is to provide a central listing of English language publications about V. I. Lenin. Since many of these publications are from Soviet English language periodicals or are translations from the Russian language, this bibliography is very much an international listing of Lenin sources, with nearly a balance of critical, non-critical and hagiographic entries. Serious research on Lenin must, of course, not be limited to English language materials; nonetheless, a reference work such as this one should be a useful tool for the specialist and non-specialist alike.

Scope

Included through 1979 are books, essays, chapters from general studies, periodical articles, reminiscences, interviews, addresses, doctoral dissertations, reviews of major Lenin studies, and introductions to Lenin's works. Additionally listed are major studies which include significant discussion of Lenin, but do not contain a separate chapter on him.

Excluded are textbooks, newspaper articles, encyclopedias, correspondences, fiction, master's theses, and works by Lenin.

Format

Entries have been arranged alphabetically under the topic most central to their content. Because many sources discuss equally several facets of Lenin's career, the selection of a main listing has been a difficult and somewhat arbitrary process. Consequently, no one section contains all the useful sources on the topic listed, but rather only through full use of the subject index can a complete list of writings be compiled for any one facet of Lenin's life, work, or thought. When entire sections overlap significantly (for example, Nationality Doctrine and National Liberation Movements), they have been cross-referenced by way of a note at the end of the sections concerned.

For the reader's convenience, Library of Congress call numbers have been included for books and essays. Also, articles which have appeared, wholly or in part, in more than one periodical, or essays which have been published under separate covers, have been so noted to assist in their location.

Annotations

Annotations have been included for books, essays, chapters from general studies, and for periodical articles whose focus is obscure by title alone. The annotations are descriptive, rather than critical, and therefore merely indicate scope and emphasis for non-interpretive sources and thesis or judgment for those sources where one is clearly discernible. Although no attempt has been made to assess the accuracy of information or validity of interpretation of any one source, asterisks have been provided for those which are scholarly, comprehensive, or particularly interesting, or which have been influential.

Anthologies

The component parts of anthologies have been listed individually beneath appropriate subject headings. Anthology titles have been abbreviated, with the word "anthology" appearing in parentheses after the abbreviation. For example, Lenin and Leninism would be listed as LAL (anthology). All abbreviated anthology titles have been listed alphabetically in one section (that which follows periodical abbreviations), where editorship, complete publication data, and a general annotation appear.

Spelling

Authors' names have been spelled the same way as they appear on the title page of their respective publications. Consequently, there are alternate spellings for some entries (Gorki/Gorky; Krupskaia/Krupskaya, etc.). Spelling has been standardized in the annotations and author/subject indexes.

ABBREVIATIONS / PERIODICALS

ACEN News	Bulletin of the Assembly of Captive European Nations
ASEER	American Slavic and East European Review
Acta Soc	Acta Sociologica
Am Anthro	American Anthropologist
Am Hist R	American Historical Review
Am Merc	American Mercury
Am Pol Sci R	American Political Science Review
Am R	American Review
Am Sociol R	American Sociological Review
America	America
Analysis	Analysis
Anglo-Sov J	Anglo-Soviet Journal
Ann Ukr Acad Arts Sci	Annals of the Ukrainian Academy of Arts and Sciences
Annals AAPSS	Annals of the American Academy of Political and Social Science
Antioch R	Antioch Review
Arch Eur Soc	Archives Européenes de Sociologie (European Journal of Sociology)
Arch J	Architects' Journal
Arch R	Architectual Review
Army Q	Army Quarterly
Art A	Art and Artists
Aryan P	Aryan Path
Asia	Asia (New York)
Asian S	Asian Survey
Atlan Mo	Atlantic Monthly
Atlantic	Atlantic
Aust J Phil	Australian Journal of Philosophy
Aust J Pol Hist	Australian Journal of Politics and History
Aust O	Australian Outlook
Australasian J Phil	Australasian Journal of Philosophy
Ave Maria	Ave Maria
B Inst St USSR	Bulletin for the Institute for the Study of the U.S.S.R.
B Rus Info Bur	Bulletin of the Russian Information Bureau in the U.S.
Belorus R	Belorussian Review
Berkeley J Sociol	Berkeley Journal of Sociology
Bihar Info	Bihar Information
Bk R D	Book Review Digest

Black Sch	Black Scholar (California)
Booklist	Booklist
Bookman	Bookman
Books	Books
Boston Coll St Phil	Boston College Studies in Philosophy
Bul Ch GV	Bulletin of the Chunilal Gandhi Vidyabhavan
Bulletin	The Bulletin of the Workers League for a Revolutionary Party (New York)

Cahiers B	Cahiers Bruge
Cahiers du Monde	Cahiers du Monde Russe et Sovietique
Cahiers H M	Cahiers d'Histoire Mondiale
Call	Call (India)
Campaigner	Campaigner
Can Am S S	Canadian American Slavic Studies
Can Dim	Canadian Dimension
Can Forum	Canadian Forum
Can Hist R	Canadian Historical Review
Can J Hist	Canadian Journal of History
Can J Pol Sci	Canadian Journal of Political Science
Can S P	Canadian Slavonic Papers
Can S S	Canadian Slavic Studies
Cath D	Catholic Digest
Cath E	Catholic Educator
Cath Hist R	Catholic Historical Review
Cath Int O	Catholic International Outlook
Cath W	Catholic World
Cauc R	Caucasian Review
Cent M	Century Magazine
Century	Century (India)
Chambers J	Chambers Journal
Chin St Hist Phil	Chinese Studies in History and Philosophy
Chin St Phil	Chinese Studies in Philosophy
China Q	China Quarterly
China Rep	China Report
Choice	Choice
Chris Cent	Christian Century
Chris Order	Christian Order
Chris Today	Christianity Today
Church Hist	Church History
Civ Aff	Civic Affairs
Clio	Clio
Co-existence	Co-existence
Colliers	Colliers
Columbia	Columbia (Connecticut)
Columbia U Forum	Columbia University Forum
Com Int	Communist International
Com R	Communist Review
Com V	Communist Viewpoint
Commentary	Commentary
Commerce	Commerce
Commonweal	Commonweal
Communist	Communist (New York)

Comp Ed R	Comparative Education Review
Comp St Soc Hist	Comparative Studies in Social History
Congreg Q	Congregational Quarterly
Contemp Ind Lit	Contemporary Indian Literature
Contemp R	Contemporary Review
Contemporary	Contemporary (India)
Contract S	Contract Social
Convergence	Convergence
Cornhill	Cornhill
Cr Cur	Cross Currents
Critique	Critique
Cult Life	Culture and Life
Cur Hist F	Current History and Forum
Cur Hist M	Current History Magazine
Cur Op	Current Opinion
Dalhousie R	Dalhousie Review
Dar Int	Darshana International
Dialec Hum	Dialectics and Humanism
Dissent	Dissent
Dublin R	Dublin Review
Duquesne R	Duquesne Review
E Eur	East Europe
Ec Pol W	Economic and Political Weekly
Ec Soc	Economy and Society
Economica	Economica
Economist	Economist
Edinb R	Edinburgh Review
Encounter	Encounter
Eng Hist R	English Historical Review
Eng R	English Review
Eur J Sociol	European Journal of Sociology (Archives Europeennes de Sociologie)
Eyewitness	Eyewitness
Far East Eco R	Far East Economic Review
Far East S	Far East Survey
Films F	Films and Filming
Filosofia C	Filosofia Casopis (Italy)
Flinders J Hist Pol	Flinders Journal of History and Politics (Australia)
For Aff	Foreign Affairs
For Aff Rep	Foreign Affairs Report
Fortn R	Fortnightly Review
Forum	Forum
Fourth Int	Fourth International
Freeman	Freeman
GK's W	GK's Weekly

G Pol Sci As J	Georgia Political Science Association Journal
Gal-Jul Q	Galdeman-Julius Quarterly
Gandhi M	Gandhi Marg
Ger For Pol	German Foreign Policy
Gov Opp	Government and Opposition
Great S B	Great Speckled Bird
Harper	Harper
Harv Sl St	Harvard Slavic Studies
Helix	Helix
Herald Lib Sci	Herald of Library Science
Hibbert J	Hibbert Journal
High Sch J	High School Journal
Hist J	Historical Journal
Hist Today	History Today
Historian	Historian
History	History (London)
Horizon	Horizon
Horizons	Horizons: The Marxist Quarterly
Hound and Horn	Hound and Horn
Hum Events	Human Events
Humanist	Humanist
Illus Wk India	Illustrated Weekly of India
Independent	Independent
India Q	India Quarterly
Indian Eco R	Indian Economic Review
Indian J Pol Sci	Indian Journal of Political Science
Indian Lib	Indian Librarian
Indian Lit	Indian Literature
Indian Pol Sci R	Indian Political Science Review
Indian R	Indian Review
Indian Soc B	Indian Sociological Bulletin
Indo-As C	Indo-Asian Culture (now: Indian Horizons)
Inquiry	Inquiry (Oslo)
Insurg Soc	Insurgent Sociologist
Int Aff	International Affairs (Moscow)
Int J	International Journal
Int Labor R	International Labor Review
Int Lit	International Literature
Int R Hist Pol Sci	International Review of History and Political Science
Int R Soc Hist	International Review of Social History
Int Soc R	International Socialist Review
Int St	International Studies
Irish Mo	Irish Monthly
Iss St	Issues and Studies (Taiwan)
J Am Psy Asso	Journal of the American Psychoanalytic Association

J Asian St	Journal of Asian Studies
J Baltic St	Journal of Baltic Studies
J Black St	Journal of Black Studies
J Chin Phil	Journal of Chinese Philosophy
J Contemp Asia	Journal of Contemporary Asia
J Contemp Hist	Journal of Contemporary History
J Crit Anal	Journal of Critical Analysis
J Hel D	Journal of the Hellenic Diaspora
J Hist Ideas	Journal of the History of Ideas
J Hist Phil	Journal of the History of Philosophy
J Mod Hist	Journal of Modern History
J Phil	Journal of Philosophy
J Pol	Journal of Politics
J Pol Ec	Journal of Political Economy
J Roy U Serv Inst	Journal of the Royal United Service Institution
J Rus St	Journal of Russian Studies
J Sport Hist	Journal of Sport History
Jahr Ges Ost	Jahrbücher für Geschichte Osteuropas
Journalism Q	Journalism Quarterly
Kurukshetra	Kurukshetra (India)
Kurukshetra U Res J	Kurukshetra University Research Journal
Kyoto Un Ec R	Kyoto University Economic Review
Labor H	Labor History
Labour Mo	Labour Monthly
Latin Amer	Latin America
Lib J	Library Journal
Lib M	Liberty Magazine
Liberation	Liberation
Liberator	Liberator
Life	Life
Link	Link (Indian)
Listener	Listener
Lit D	Literary Digest
Lit Ideol	Literature and Ideology
Lit R	Literary Review
Liv Age	Living Age
Lon M	London Magazine
Look	Look
Lotus	Lotus: Afro-Asian Writings
Luth Stand	Lutheran Standard
Mainstream	Mainstream
Majallah	Majallah
Mankind	Mankind
Mel Hist J	Melbourne Historical Journal
Metaphilosophy	Metaphilosophy
Mich Q R	Michigan Quarterly Review
Midstream	Midstream

Midwest J Pol Sci	Midwest Journal of Political Science
Military R	Military Review
Millennium	Millennium
Millgate	Millgate
Minor	Minor (India)
Mod Age	Modern Age
Mod Asian St	Modern Asian Studies
Mod China	Modern China
Mod Mo	Modern Monthly
Mod R	Modern Review
Mod Q	Modern Quarterly
Mod W	Modern World
Month	Month
Monthly R	Monthly Review
Movement	Movement

N Cent	Nineteenth Century and After
NY R Books	New York Review of Books
NY Times Bk R	New York Times Book Review
NY Times M	New York Times Magazine
Nat Ath	Nation and Atheneum
Nation	Nation
National R	National Review
Nations Bus	Nation's Business
New Cath W	New Catholic World
New Direc	New Directions
New Eur	New Europe
New Int	New International
New Leader	New Leader
New Left R	New Left Review
New Lugano R	New Lugano Review
New Masses	New Masses
New Pol	New Politics
New R	New Review
New Rep	New Republic
New Rus	New Russia. A Political and Economic Weekly Review
New Soc	New Society
New Sta	New Statesman
New Sta Nat	New Statesman and Nation
New Times	New Times (Moscow)
New World R	New World Review
New Yorker	New Yorker
New Z J Hist	New Zealand Journal of History
New Z Slavonic J	New Zealand Slavonic Journal
News USSR	News from the USSR
Newsletter Comps St Com	Newsletter on Comparative Studies of Communism
Newsweek	Newsweek
No Dakota Q	North Dakota Quarterly

Occidente	Occidente

Orbis	Orbis
Outlook	Outlook
P Star	Polar Star
Pakistan Phil Cong	Pakistan Philosophical Congress
Pan Am M	Pan American Magazine
Partisan R	Partisan Review
Peo Dem	People's Democracy
Phil E W	Philosophy East and West
Phil Phen Res	Philosophy and Phenomenological Research
Phil Pub Aff	Philosophy and Public Affairs
Phil R	Philosophical Review
Philosophy	Philosophy
Phylon	Phylon
Pitt Mo B	Pittsburgh Monthly Bulletin
Poetry	Poetry
Pol Aff	Political Affairs
Pol Ger	Poland and Germany
Pol Q	Political Quarterly
Pol Sci	Political Science
Pol Sci Q	Political Science Quarterly
Pol Sci R	Political Science Review
Pol Soc	Politics and Society
Pol St	Political Studies
Polish R	Polish Review
Polity	Polity
Poznan St	Poznan Studies
Pr Sch	Prairie Schooner
Praxis	Praxis
Presb J	Presbyterian Journal
Prob Com	Problems of Communism
Prob Ec	Problems of Economics
Prob Peoples USSR	Problems of the Peoples of the USSR
Proc Brit Acad	Proceedings of the British Academy
Pub Op Q	Public Opinion Quarterly
Quar R	Quarterly Review
Queen's Wk	Queen's Work
RR	Review of Reviews
R Int Aff	Review of International Affairs (Yugoslavia)
R Meta	Review of Metaphysics
R Pol	Review of Politics
R Rad Pol Ec	Review of Radical Political Economics
R Roum Etudes	Revue Roumaine d'Etudes Internationales (Rumania)
R Sov Med Sci	Review of Soviet Medical Science
Rad Amer	Radical America
Rad Phil	Radical Philosophy (London)
Ramparts M	Ramparts Magazine

Ratio	Ratio
Rev W	Revolutionary World
Review	Review
Rus Hist	Russian History
Rus Info R	Russian Information and Review
Rus Lang J	Russian Language Journal
Rus R	Russian Review
SEER	Slavonic and East European Review
Sarvodaya	Sarvodaya (India)
Sat Night	Saturday Night
Sat R	Saturday Review
Sat R Lit	Saturday Review of Literature
Sci Mo	Science Monthly
Sci Soc	Science and Society
Science Q	Science Quarterly
Scrib M	Scribner's Magazine
Senior S	Senior Scholastic
Sign	Sign
Silent Picture	Silent Picture (New York)
Slav R	Slavic Review
Slav Y	Slavonic Yearbook
Slavonic R	Slavonic Review
So Eco	Southern Economist
Soc Justice R	Social Justice Review
Soc Praxis	Social Praxis
Soc St	Social Studies
Soc Theo Prac	Socialism: Theory and Practice
Socialist Com	Socialist Commentary
Socialist Cong	Socialist Congressman (India)
Socialist R	Socialist Review
Socialist Reg	Socialist Register
Socialist Rev	Socialist Revolution (San Francisco)
Sociol Q	Sociological Quarterly
Sociol R	Sociological Review
Sov Armed For R An	Soviet Armed Forces Review Annual
Sov Doc	Soviet Documents
Sov Ed	Soviet Education
Sov Film	Soviet Film
Sov Land	Soviet Land (India)
Sov Life	Soviet Life
Sov Lit	Soviet Literature
Sov Mil R	Soviet Military Review
Sov R	Soviet Review (irregular publication of the Soviet Embassy in India)
Sov Rev	Soviet Review (United States)
Sov Soc	Soviet Sociology
Sov St	Soviet Studies
Sov St Hist	Soviet Studies in History
Sov St Phil	Soviet Studies in Philosophy
Sov Sur	Soviet Survey
Sov Un R	Soviet Union Review
Spectator	Spectator

St Anth P	St. Anthony's Papers
St Comp Com	Studies in Comparative Communism
St Int Filosf	Studi Internazionali di Filosofia (International Studies in Philosophy)
St Left	Studies on the Left
St Sov Phil	Studies in Soviet Philosophy
St Sov Tho	Studies in Soviet Thought
St Sov Un	Studies on the Soviet Union
Strat Mo	Stratford Monthly (Boston)
Strug Rus	Struggling Russia
Studies	Studies
Studio	Studio
Sun Times M	Sunday Times Magazine (London)
Survey	Survey
Swarajya	Swarajya (India)
TLS	Times Literary Supplement
Tablet	Tablet
Telos	Telos
Texas Q	Texas Quarterly
Theo Soc	Theory and Society
Theology	Theology
Thought	Thought
Time	Time
Trans Asso Rus-Am Sch	Transactions of the Association of Russian-American Scholars
Twent Cent	Twentieth Century
UNESCO C	UNESCO Courier
UN Mo Chron	U. N. Monthly Chronicle
US News W Rep	U. S. News and World Report
USAF Translations	UASF Translations
USSR	USSR
USSR Info B	USSR Information Bulletin
U Asia	United Asia
Ukr Q	Ukrainian Quarterly
Ukr R	Ukrainian Review
Va Q R	Virginia Quarterly Review
Vital S	Vital Speeches
W Aff	World Affairs
W Marxist R	World Marxist Review
W Music	World of Music
W Pol	World Politics
W Today	World Today
W Tomorrow	World Tomorrow
W's Work	World's Work
West Geo Col R	Western Georgia College Review
West Pol Q	Western Political Quarterly

Anthologies are not listed themselves by title but rather the sources within them have been extracted, annotated individually and placed within the appropriate section in accord with the following abbreviations.

AL   About Lenin. Moscow: Progress Publishers, n. d. ;
     221pp. Fourteen recollections, by observers, friends,
     and family of Lenin, providing mostly biographical
     information on Lenin. [DK254. L4R2313]

CFOLI   Romanian Academy of Social and Political Sciences.
     The Creative Force of the Leninist Ideas. Buchar-
     est: Publishing House of the Academy of the So-
     cialist Republic of Romania, 1970; 305pp. Seventeen
     essays dealing with various aspects of Lenin's thought
     and policies and their influence on Rumanian commu-
     nism. [HX312. L43C4513]

DORT   Development of Revolutionary Theory by the CPSU.
     Moscow: Progress Publishers, 1977; 379pp. Twelve
     essays "on the creative development of Marxist-
     Leninist theory in the documents and practical ac-
     tivity of the CPSU. " Only those essays containing
     significant information on Lenin have been annotated
     individually. [HX314. R3913]

GTSE   Gandhi through Soviet Eyes. Lenin through Indian Eyes.
     New Delhi: Indo-Soviet Cultural Society, an ISCUS
     publication, 1971; 85pp. Six essays which favorably
     assess Lenin's teachings and policies on revolution,
     the national liberation movement, and foreign policy,
     and present him as a leader with immense influence
     on India. [DS481.G3G265]

HDASP   Kirko, V. M. et al. Historical Development and Social
     Progress in Africa. Moscow: Novosti Press, 1970;
     150pp. Ten essays on the Marxist revolutionary
     movement in Africa, five of which deal with Lenin
     and have been annotated individually. [HX438. 5. H5713]

IAL   Gupta, Anand, ed. India and Lenin. A Collection.
     New Delhi: New Literature Press, 1960; 96pp. A
     collection of short articles intended to illustrate how

the people of India reacted to Lenin's thought and to acquaint the reader with Lenin's works on the national liberation struggle. [DK254. L4G85]

L   Silverman, Saul N., ed. Lenin. Englewood Cliffs: Prentice-Hall, 1972, 213pp., bib. 205-08. A collection of excerpts, as part of the Great Lives Observed Series, from the writings of Lenin, twenty of his contemporaries, and four modern analysts, which provide insight into and assess Lenin, his thought and activities. [DK254. L3A5785]

LAB   Okorokov, A. Z., comp. Lenin and Books. Moscow: Progress Publishers, 1971; 198pp. A series of articles and reminiscences dealing with Lenin's reading tastes, research habits, philosophy of literature, and literary criticism. [DK254. L3L3413]

LACW   Jain, Vijender, ed. Lenin and the Contemporary World. New Delhi: Institute for Socialist Education, 1970; 127pp. Twenty-nine inspirational speeches on Lenin and his influence presented to the All India Youth Seminar on Lenin and the Contemporary World. [HX312. L43A27 1970]

LAG   Institute of Marxism-Leninism. Lenin and Gorky. Moscow: Progress Publishers, 1973; 429pp. An abridged version of the Russian language collection of the correspondence between Lenin and Gorky and letters by Lenin and Gorky to third persons. The 250 plus correspondences are a significant source of information about Lenin. The lack of a subject index makes this work somewhat difficult to use, though the editors do include an author index and a substantial set of notes (378-408) defining terms, discussing events, and providing general historical context. The editors append twelve reminiscences, by the family and friends of Lenin, dealing with his relationship with Gorky. [DK254. L4A46913 1973]

LAI   Adhikari, G., M. B. Rao and Mohit Sen, eds. Lenin and India. New Delhi: People's Publishing House, 1970; 236pp. Ten essays written by Indian political leaders to commemorate the Lenin centenary. The essays positively assess Lenin's views on the party, state, revolution, and the national and women questions, and his influence on India. [DK254. L447L42]

LAL   Eissenstat, Bernard W., ed. Lenin and Leninism. Lexington: D. C. Heath and Company, 1971; 322pp. Seventeen essays (originally presented at a 1970 Lenin centennial conference at the University of Oklahoma, Stillwater) written by an international field of experts on Lenin and Leninism. The collection consists of five parts: Lenin, Philosophy and Ideology; Lenin, Law and Legality; Lenin and Economics; Lenin, Myth and Culture; and Lenin, Leninism and the Present. [HX312.L43L44]

LAMCP   Sladkovsky, M., ed. Leninism and Modern China's Problems. Moscow: Progress Publishers, 1972; 254 pp. Eleven essays on the applicability of Lenin's teachings to problems existing in contemporary China and on Maoist distortions of Leninism. [HX387.S5713]

LANLIE   Gafurov, B. G. and G. F. Kim, eds. Lenin and the National Liberation in the East. Moscow: Progress Publishers, 1978; 468pp. Fourteen essays on Lenin's writings on nationality, self-determination, and national liberation movements, and their influence in Asia and the Middle East. [DK254.L46L39213]

LARIE   Lenin and Revolution in the East. Moscow: Novosti Press, 1969; 119pp. Five articles, by Soviet foreign policy specialists and journalists, dealing with the world impact of Lenin's views and policies on national liberation movements. [DK254.L46L35]

LATU   Frantsov, Y. et al. Leninist Approach to Unity of the World Communist Movement. Moscow: Novosti Press, 1970; 102pp. Four articles from the Soviet press dealing with the contemporary world communist movement and Lenin's influence upon it.

LAWRWM   Kuskov, Y. et al., eds. Leninism and the World Revolutionary Working-Class Movement. Moscow: Progress Publishers, 1971; 497pp. Ten essays, written by Soviet and foreign Marxists, on the nature and impact of Lenin's thought and policies on the international communist and national liberation movements. [HX44.L39713]

LCAM   Bychkova, N., R. Lavrov and I. Rusanova, comps. Lenin. Comrade and Man. Moscow: Progress Publishers, n.d.; 193pp. A collection of some 160 notes, letters, telegrams, instructions, and minutes written by Lenin precedes a series of 40 recollections from various people who knew, met, or observed him. The more noteworthy of these reminiscences have been annotated individually. [DK254.L4A423]

LCIA   Lenin's Comrades-in-Arms. Episodes from the Lives of Foreign Comrades-in-Arms and Contemporaries. Moscow: Progress Publishers, 1969; 337pp. Sixteen essays about foreign communists and the "paths that led (them) to Lenin; how they met him; details of their conversations, their correspondences, their arguments, and how all this affected the life of all these followers of Lenin. " [DK254. L46L42532]

LDMORP   Page, Stanley W. Lenin. Dedicated Marxist or Revolutionary Pragmatist? Lexington, Mass.: Heath, 1970; 113pp., bib. 111-13. Sixteen writings, by Soviet and Western authors, which present conflicting interpretations and impressions of Lenin as a theorist, revolutionary, and political leader. [DK254. L46P3]

LGT   Iskrov, M., ed. Lenin, the Great Theoretician. Moscow: Progress Publishers, 1970; 391pp. Fourteen essays, by various Soviet scholars, dealing with Lenin's views on Marxism, capitalism, socialist revolution, strategy and tactics, the party, dictatorship of the proletariat, economic theory, national and colonial questions, and the world communist movement. The essays summarize Lenin's thought, link it to Marxism, and attack his socialist and bourgeois critics. [HV40. V213]

LHIII   Kaushik, Devendra and Leonic Mitrokhin, eds. Lenin. His Image in India. Delhi: Vikas Publications, 1970; 166pp. A collection of articles and excerpts from writings about Lenin by 66 prominent Indian leaders, writers, poets and journalists which deal favorably with a wide array of his writings, policies, and accomplishments as well as with episodes in his life. [DK254. L46K33]

LIOL   Sdobnikov, Y., ed. Lenin in Our Life. Moscow: Progress Publishers, 1967; 319pp. Sixteen articles about the direct and indirect influence Lenin had upon his contemporaries. The editor states that he has combined in one volume intimate and distant recollections so as to illustrate that Lenin was interested in and influenced not only his comrades but those who never met him. [DK254. L42L3813]

LIOR   Marx-Engels-Lenin Institute. Lenin in the October Revolution. Reminiscences of Participants. Moscow: Cooperative Publishing Society of Foreign Workers in the USSR, 1934; 88pp. Eleven reminiscences by party leaders and others who knew and observed Lenin during the October Revolution.

LIOUS   Mason, Daniel and Jessica Smith, eds. Lenin's Impact on the United States. New York: New World Review Publications, 1970; 224pp. A collection of articles, reminiscences, and poems, originally published in

the Winter issue of the New World Review (1970),
dealing favorably with Lenin and his thought, accomplishments, and influence. [DK254.L46L42]

LIPOY   Lenin in the Practice of Yugoslavia. Belgrad: Meduna-
rodna Politika, 1970; 44pp. Six articles, by Yugo-
slav Marxists, commemorating the Lenin centenary
by discussing the Leninist qualities of communism in
Yugoslavia. [DK254.L447L4813]

LITW-1   Lenin's Ideas Transform the World. Volume I. Moscow: Novosti Press, 1971; 324pp. A collection of
speeches, by more than 80 foreign communist
leaders, commemorating the Lenin centenary by
discussing Lenin's accomplishments and his influence
throughout the world. [HX44.L3975]

LITW-2   Lenin's Ideas Transform the World. Volume II. Moscow: Novosti Press, 1971; 248pp. Nineteen articles
written for Pravda, by foreign leaders of communist
and workers' parties, on the occasion of the Lenin
centenary illustrating the world impact of Lenin's
thought and work. [HX44.L3975]

LKAL   Simsova, S., ed. Lenin, Krupskaia and Libraries.
London: Archon Books and Clive Bingley, 1968;
73pp., bib. 66-69. A compilation of the thoughts
of Lenin and Krupskaya on libraries, accompanied
by a series of short articles and excerpts about
Lenin's views on and policies toward libraries.
[Z819.A1S55]

LMAHW   Williams, Albert Rhys. Lenin. The Man and His
Work. Includes The Impressions of Colonel Raymond Robins and Arthur Ransome. New York:
Scott and Seltzer, 1919; 202pp. An early Western
attempt to present an accurate image of Lenin for a
world, which in 1919, had only biased, critical, and erroneous sources based on "rumor, phantasies and
pure fiction." The impressions of Williams, Robins,
and Ransome have been annotated separately as have
the samples, appended to the book, of conservative
and adverse opinions of Lenin. [DK254.L4W5]

LMTL   Schapiro, Leonard and Peter Reddaway, eds. Lenin.
The Man, the Theorist, the Leader. A Reappraisal.
New York: Praeger, 1967; 317pp., bib. 297-304.
Twelve essays, originally presented as papers at the
London School of Economics and Political Science,
written by an international field of Lenin scholars.
Collectively the essays assess Lenin as a philoso-
pher, tactician, civil war leader, and economist, and
analyze him in connection with the intelligentsia, arts

Marxism, religion, the peasants, law, and the nationalities question. [DK254.L4A153]

LOSS   Lenin on the Socialist State. Moscow: Novosti Press, 1969; 63pp. Three essays, by Soviet specialists, on Lenin's theory of the state in its capitalist and socialist forms. [HX312.L43L45]

LR   Filatov, V. P., ed. Lenin the Revolutionary. Moscow: Progress Publishers, 1979; 215pp. Thirteen Soviet essays dealing with various aspects of Lenin as a revolutionary. The essays are arranged under four headings: "The intellectual basis of revolution," "Creating a revolutionary party," "Lenin and the revolution," and "Architect of the Soviet state."

LT   Sweezy, Paul M. and Harry Magdoff, eds. Lenin Today. Eight Essays on the Hundredth Anniversary of Lenin's Birth. New York: Monthly Review Press, 1970; 125pp. Eight essays, originally published in the Monthly Review (April 1970), dealing with Lenin's theories on the party, imperialism, the state, and revolution as well as with his influence on the modern world. [DK254.L4A185]

LTCOA   Leninism Today. A Collection of Articles. Moscow: Novosti Press, 1970; 263pp. Fourteen articles dealing with Lenin's thought, accomplishments and influence originally published in the Soviet press for the Lenin centenary. [HX44.L3947]

LVI   Leninism versus Imperialism. The Present Stage. Moscow: Novosti Press, 1969; 136pp. Four articles, by Soviet specialists in foreign affairs, on Lenin's theory of imperialism and its applicability to the contemporary world. [HX312.L43L47]

LYAWT   Lenin, Youth and the World Today. Moscow: Novosti Press, 1970; 182pp. Six essays based on materials presented at the International Youth Seminar (1969) on Lenin as a revolutionary, scholar, organizer, and leader of the Communist Party, and as a man deeply interested in and an influence on socialist youth. [HX547.I55]

NBPA   Deutscher, Tamara, ed. Not by Politics Alone-the Other Lenin. London: George Allen and Unwin, 1973; 256pp. A collection of 37 documents (mostly letters) by Lenin and reminiscences of him designed to illustrate that he did not live by politics alone. These sources, many translated here for the first time, represent a valuable and favorable body of information on his personal likes, dislikes and habits.

Deutscher includes a lengthy introduction on the "personal Lenin" and an extensive subject index.
[DK254. L4D48]

OL   Our Lenin. Reminiscences, Stories, Articles and Poems about V. I. Lenin. Moscow: Ministry of Defense, 1970; 261pp. A collection of 29 reminiscenses and fictional writings about Lenin, many of which deal with military related matters.
[DK254. L4O83]

PHVIL   Milovidov, A. S. and V. G. Kuzlov, eds. The Philosophical Heritage of V. I. Lenin and Problems of Contemporary War. A Soviet View. Moscow: Military Publishing House, 1972; 292pp. Nineteen essays, written by Soviet specialists in military philosophy, on Lenin as a military theorist and founder of the Soviet army. The volume is "designed for officers, generals and all students of Lenin's military and theoretical heritage" and has been widely read within Soviet military circles.
[B4249. L384F5413]

POLFP   Principles of Lenin's Foreign Policy. Moscow: Novosti Press, 1970; 96pp. Four articles, previously published in the monthly, International Affairs, by Soviet foreign policy specialists, dealing with Lenin's views on diplomacy, proletarian internationalism, and peaceful coexistence. [DK254. L46P74 1970]

ROL   Recollections of Lenin. Moscow. Foreign Languages Publishing House, 1962; 96pp. A collection of articles, by acquaintances of Lenin and workers who listened to his speeches, discussing his work habits and mannerisms and the impression he made on those who met or observed him. [DK254. L42R4]

ROLBHR Moscow Institute of Marxism-Leninism. Reminiscences of Lenin by his Relatives. Moscow: Foreign Languages Publishing House, 1956; 232pp. A collection of reminiscences from four of Lenin's relatives: Anna I. Ulyanova-Yelizarova (sister), Maria I. Ulyanova (sister), Dmitry I. Ulyanov (brother), and N. K. Krupskaya (wife). Krupskaya's recollections (180-224) are excerpts from her Reminiscences of Lenin and have been annotated under that title; the other three sets of reminiscences have been annotated individually. [DK254. L42M633]

SOL   Stalin, Joseph. Stalin on Lenin. Moscow: Foreign Languages Publishing House, 1946; 95pp. Eight of Stalin's writings, speeches, and interviews dealing with Lenin. The collection includes Stalin's article

on Lenin as the organizer and leader of the Communist Party; his two speeches (26 Jan. and 28 Jan.
1924) upon Lenin's death; interviews with the First
American Labor Delegation, and with Emil Ludwig;
and two speeches (11 Dec. 1937 and 17 May 1938)
on Lenin's legacy. [DK254. L4S715]

TKL   Bezveselny, S. F. and D. Y. Grinberg, comps. They
Knew Lenin. Reminiscences of Foreign Contemporaries. Moscow: Progress Publishers, 1968;
287pp. A collection of comments on and impressions
of Lenin by 41 people from various nations and back-
grounds who either met, knew, or observed him.
The articles are relatively brief, anecdote-oriented,
and most frequently concern Lenin's character and
personality rather than his work and writings.
[DK254. L42O23]

UF   Baranov, I. , ed. The Ulyanov Family. Moscow:
Progress Publishers, 1969; 132pp. Six essays,
written by staff members of the Ulyanovsk Branch
of the Central Lenin Museum, on the Simbirsk
period (1869-1887) in the life of the Ulyanovs. The
authors' stated purpose is to provide, through a discussion of Lenin's home life, a means of presenting
"some of the most important circumstances which
were responsible for the development of Lenin's
revolutionary world outlook. " [DK254. L43S43]

VILIL Karachan, N. B. V. I. Lenin in London. Leningrad,
1969. A discussion of Lenin's life in exile in England, followed by a collection of excerpts from
reminiscences by nine British writers and Marxists
who met or were acquainted with him.
[DK254. L446K35]

WHML   We Have Met Lenin. Moscow: Foreign Languages
Publishing House, 1939; 75pp. A compilation of
articles, reminiscences and notes by foreign communists who knew and admired Lenin. Only the
most noteworthy of these sources have been annotated individually. [DK254. L4W3]

WLMTU Gupta, Anand, ed. What Lenin Means to Us. Delhi:
New Literature, 1970; 68pp. Eleven articles, written
by Indian scholars to commemorate the 100th anniversary of Lenin's birth, dealing with Lenin's influence
on the authors personally and India in general.
[DK254. L447W4]

REFERENCE SOURCES

Access; the Supplementary Index to Periodicals. Syracuse: Gaylord
    Professional Publications, 1975+.

Agricultural Index. New York: Wilson, 1916-1964. Superseded by
    Biological and Agricultural Index.

Alternative Press Index. Northfield, Minnesota: Radical Research
    Center, 1969+.

America: History and Life. A Guide to Periodical Literature.
    Santa Barbara: Clio Press, 1964+.

American Bibliography of Russian and East European Studies, 1956-
    1966. Bloomington: Indiana University Press, 1957-1967. Con-
    tinues as American Bibliography of Slavic and East European
    Studies.

American Bibliography of Slavic and East European Studies, 1967+.
    Various publishers.

American Correspondents and Journalists in Moscow, 1917-1952:
    A Bibliography of Their Books on the USSR. Washington: U.S.
    Department of State, Division of Library and Research Sources,
    1953.

Besterman, Theodore. A World Bibliography of Bibliographies,
    5 vols. Lausanne: Societas Bibliographica, 1966. Supplement,
    Alice Toomey.

Bibliographic Index. A Cumulative Bibliography of Bibliographies.
    New York: Wilson, 1937+.

Biography Index. New York: Wilson, 1946+.

Biological and Agricultural Index. New York: Wilson, 1964+. Pre-
    ceded by Agricultural Index, 1919-1964.

Book Review Digest. New York: Wilson, 1917+.

Book Review Index. Detroit: Gale, 1965+.

Book Review Index to Social Science Periodicals. Ann Arbor:
    Pierian Press, 1978+.

Brewster, John M. and Joseph A. McLeod. Index to Book Reviews in Historical Periodicals. Metuchen: Scarecrow Press, 1972-1977.

British Education Index. London: British Library, Bibliographic Service Division, 1954+.

British Humanities Index. London: Library Association, 1962+. Preceded by Subject Index to Periodicals.

British Museum, Department of Printed Books. General Catalogue of Printed Books. 263 vols. London: Trustees of the British Museum, 1959-1966. Coverage up to 1956. Ten-year supplement (1956-1966) issued in 1968, 50 vols.; five-year supplement (1966-1970) issued in 1971-1972, 26 vols.

British National Bibliography, 1950+. London: Council of British National Bibliography, 1950+. Cumulated Subject Catalogue (1951-1954) published in 1958.

Canadian Essay and General Literature Index, 1973+. Toronto: University of Toronto Press, 1973+.

Canadian Index to Periodicals and Documentary Films, 1948-1959. Ottawa: Canadian Library Association, 1962; 1180pp. Superseded by Canadian Periodical Index, 1960+.

Canadian Periodical Index. Toronto: Public Libraries Branch, Ontario Department of Education, 1928-1947.

Canadian Periodical Index, 1960+. Ottawa: Canadian Library Association, 1964+. Preceded by Canadian Index....

Catholic Periodical Index. New York: Catholic Library Association, 1939-1967. Superseded by Catholic Periodical and Literature Index.

Catholic Periodical and Literature Index, 1967+. Haverford, Penn.: Catholic Library Association, 1968+. Preceded by Catholic Periodical Index.

Combined Retrospective Index to Journals in Political Science, 1886-1974. Washington: Carrollton Press, 8 vols., 1977.

Comprehensive Dissertation Index, 1861-1972. 37 vols. Ann Arbor: University Microfilms, 1973+. With annual supplements.

Cumulated Magazine Subject Index, 1907-1949. Boston: G. K. Hall, 1964. A cumulation of the F. W. Faxon Company's Annual Magazine Subject Index.

Cumulative Book Index (CBI); A World List of Books in the English

Language, 1928/32+. New York: Wilson, 1933+. Published 1898-1928 as United States Catalog.

Cumulated Subject Index to Psychological Abstracts, 1927-1960. Boston: G. K. Hall, 1960. With supplements.

Cumulated Subject Index to the Public Affairs Information Service Bulletin, 1915-1974. Arlington: Carrollton Press, 1978.

Cumulative Index to Periodical Literature, 1959-1970. Princeton: National Library Services Corporation, 1959-1970.

Current Book Review Citations. New York: Wilson, 1976+.

Dossick, Jesse J. Doctoral Research on Russia and the Soviet Union. New York: New York University Press, 1960. Updated 1960-1975 in a supplementary volume; annual updates since 1976 in December issue of Slavic Review.

Education Index. New York: Wilson, 1932+.

English Catalogue of Books, 1801-1965. London: Circular Limited, 1906-1966.

Essay and General Literature Index. New York: Wilson, 1934+.

Foreign Affairs Bibliography. New York: Bowker, 1919+.

Foreign Affairs Bibliography. 50-Year Bibliography. New Evaluations of Significant Books on International Relations, 1920-1970. New York: Bowker, 1972; 936pp.

Goode, Stephen H. Index to Commonwealth Little Magazines. New York: Johnson Reprint Corporation, 1966+.

Gray, Richard A. A Guide to Book Review Citations: A Bibliography of Sources. Columbus: Ohio State University Press, 1969; 221pp.

Gray, Richard A. and Dorothy Villmow. Serial Bibliographies in the Humanities and Social Sciences. Ann Arbor: Pierian Press, 1969; 345pp.

Grierson, Philip. Books on the Soviet Union, 1917-1942. London: Methuen, 1943; 354pp.

Guide to Indian Periodical Literature. Guragon: Indian Documentation Service, 1964+.

Guide to Social Science and Religious Periodical Literature. Flint,
Michigan: National Library of Religious Periodicals, 1969+.
Preceded by Religious and SemiReligious Periodical Literature.

Historical Abstracts. Santa Barbara: International Social Science
Institute, 1955+.

Horak, Stephan. Russia, the USSR, and Eastern Europe. A Bibliographic Guide to English Language Publications, 1964-1974.
Littleton, Colorado: Libraries Unlimited, 1978.

Horecky, Paul L. Russia and the Soviet Union. A Bibliographic
Guide to Western Language Publications. Chicago: University of Chicago Press, 1965; 473pp.

Humanities Index. New York: Wilson, 1974+. Preceded by
Social Sciences and Humanities Index.

Index to Book Reviews in the Humanities. Detroit: Philip Thomson,
1960+.

Index India. Jaipur: Rajasthan University Library, 1967+.

Index to Legal Periodical Literature. Boston: Chipman Law Company, 1917+.

Index to Psychoanalytic Writings. New York International Universities Press, 1956-1969.

Index to Religious Periodical Literature. Berkeley: American
Theological Library Association, 1949-1976. Superseded by
Religion Index.

International Bibliography of Political Science, 1953+. London:
Tavistock, 1953.

International Index to Periodicals. New York: Wilson, 1907-1965.
Superseded by Social Sciences and Humanities Index.

International Political Science Abstracts. New York: Johnson Reprint Corporation, 1952+.

Jones, David L. Books in English on the Soviet Union, 1917-1973;
A Bibliography. New York: Gaylord Publishing Company,
1975.

Kanet, Roger E. Soviet and East European Foreign Policy. A
Bibliography of English and Russian Language Publications,
1967-1971. Santa Barbara: ABC-Clio Press, 1974.

Lachs, John. Marxist Philosophy: A Bibliographic Guide. Chapel
    Hill: University of North Carolina Press, 1967.

London Bibliography of the Social Sciences. 1929+. London: Man-
    sell, 1934-1975. (publisher varies).

MacDonald, K. I. , ed. The Essex Reference Index. British Jour-
    nals on Politics and Sociology, 1950-1973. London: Macmillan,
    1975.

National Bibliography of Indian Literature, 1901-1953. New Delhi:
    Sahitya Akademi, 1962-1970.

National Union Catalog..., 1956+. Ann Arbor: Edwards, 1958-
    (publisher varies). Superseded by U. S. Library of Congress
    Catalog....

Neilson, John G. "Select Checklist of Articles on the Soviet Armed
    Forces in the Western Military Press, " Soviet Armed Forces
    Review Annual, 3 (1979), 346-64.

Nerhood, Harry W. To Russia and Return. An Annotated Bibliog-
    raphy of Travelers' English-Language Accounts of Russia from
    the Ninth Century to the Present. Columbus: Ohio State Uni-
    versity Press, 1968; 367pp.

New York. Public Library. Research Libraries. Dictionary Cata-
    log of the Research Libraries. New York: New York Public
    Library, 1972+.

_____. Slavonic Division. Dictionary Catalog of the Slavonic
    Collection. Boston: G. K. Hall, 1974, 21 vols.

Philosophers' Index. Bowling Green: Bowling Green University
    Press, 1967+.

Philosophic Abstracts. New York: Kraus Reprints, 1966+.

Prpic, George J. Eastern Europe and World Communism. A Selec-
    tive Annotated Bibliography in English. Cleveland: Institute for
    Soviet and East European Studies, John Carroll University, 1966.

Psychological Index. Princeton: Psychological Review Company,
    1903-1935.

Public Affairs Information Service Bulletin (PAIS). New York: PAIS,
    1917+.

Readers' Guide to Periodical Literature. New York: Wilson, 1917+.

Sader, Marion, ed. Comprehensive Index to English Language Little Magazines 1890-1970. Millwood, N.J.: Kraus-Thomson, 1976, 8 vols.

Schultheiss, Thomas. Russian Studies 1941-1958. Ann Arbor: Pierian Press, 1972, 395pp. A cumulation of the annual bibliographies published in the Russian Review.

Seidman, Joel. Communism in the United States: A Bibliography. Ithaca: Cornell University Press, 1969; 525pp.

Shapiro, David. A Selected Bibliography of Works in English on Russian History, 1801-1917. Oxford: Basil Blackwell, 1962.

Social Science Abstracts. Menasha, Wisconsin: Social Science Abstracts, Inc., 1929-1933, 5 vols.

Social Sciences and Humanities Index, 1965-1974. New York: Wilson, 1965-1974. Preceded by International Index to Periodicals; succeeded by Humanities Index and Social Sciences Index.

Social Sciences Index. New York: Wilson, 1974+. Preceded by Social Sciences and Humanities Index.

Sociological Abstracts. Ann Arbor: Edward Brothers, 1953+.

Subject Index to Periodicals. London: Library Association, 1919-1962. Superseded by British Humanities Index.

Sworakowski, Witold S. The Communist International and Its Front Organizations. A Research Guide and Checklist of Holdings in American and European Libraries. Stanford: Hoover Institution, 1965.

Thompson, Anthony. Russia/USSR: A Selective Annotated Bibliography of Books in English. Oxford: Clio Press, 1979.

Toomey, Alice F. A World Bibliography of Bibliographies. Totowa: Rowman and Littlefield, 1977, 2 vols. Supplement to T. Besterman A World Bibliography of Bibliographies.

Ulrich's International Periodicals Directory. New York: Bowker, 1932+.

United States Catalog; Books in Print (1899-1928). New York: Wilson, 1899-1928. Superseded by Cumulative Book Index (CBI).

Vir, Dharna. Gandhi Bibliography. Delhi: Udyog Shala Press, 1967; 575pp.

Walford, Albert J. Guide to Reference Material. London: Library Association, 1966-1970, 3 vols.

Whetter, Lawrence. Current Research in Comparative Communism. An Analysis and Bibliographic Guide to the Soviet System. New York: Praeger, 1976; 159pp.

Whitaker's Cumulative Book List. London: Whitaker, 1924+.

White, Carl M., et al. Sources of Information in the Social Sciences. Chicago: American Library Association, 1973; 702pp.

World Communism: A Selected Annotated Bibliography. Washington: U.S. Government Printing Office, 1964, 1971, 2 vols.

1. GENERAL STUDIES, BIOGRAPHY, AND ASSESSMENTS

A. General Works

1   Adams, Paul. V. I. Lenin. London: Workers Fight Pamphlet, 1976; 17pp.
    A short, primer-like outline of Lenin's career as a revolutionary and political leader. [HX314.Z7A33]

2   *Antropova, T., et al., eds. Lenin. Moscow: Novosti Press, 1970; 31pp., (text by G. D. Obichkin and M. Y. Pankratova).
    A general review of the highlights of Lenin's life precedes an impressive collection of over 175 paintings, photographs, and illustrations portraying him at various stages of his career (see item 39). [DK254.L45L3]

3   Appignanesi, R. and O. Zarate. Lenin for Beginners. New York: Pantheon Books, 1978; 171pp., bib. 170-71.
    An introduction to Lenin's life and writings presented in comic strip form. The authors provide both captions for their humorous illustrations and short explanatory statements for continuity and direction. [DK265.15.A66]

4   Baker, Nina B. Lenin. New York: Vanguard Press, 1945; 257pp., bib. 249-51.
    A favorable and fanciful introduction to Lenin's life, intended as a popular account for young readers. Baker provides most detail on Lenin's personal life, often projecting that which he might have said or felt in a particular situation. [DK254.L4B3]

5   *Balabanoff, Angelica. Impressions of Lenin. Ann Arbor: University of Michigan Press, 1965; 152pp.
    Personal recollections of Lenin by a Russian socialist who knew him well. In the foreward, Bertram D. Wolfe, refers to these impressions as (with the exception of Valentinov's Encounters with Lenin) "the best portrait, at once admiring and critical, of the ambivalent spirit of the founder of Russian Bolshevism." Balabanoff discusses Lenin's views on the party, political strategy, religion, justice, government and other weighty issues, while also describing Lenin's personal appearance, relations with party members, especially Trotsky, and a number of episodes in his life. She both chronicles his opinions and notes his characteristics while at the same time provides critical insights into many facets of Lenin and Leninism. [DK254.L4B3253]

5a   Reviewed in:
           Am Hist R, (Jan. 1965), 460, by H. J. Ellison.
           *Antioch R, 24, no. 2 (1964), 223-36, by B. D. Wolfe.
           *Antioch R, 24, no. 4 (1964), 530-37, by R. D. Warth.
           *Commentary, 38, no. 6 (Dec. 1964), 57-60, by L.
              Schapiro.
           *E Eur, 13, no. 11 (Nov. 1964), by L. Dennen.
           Int Aff, (July 1965), 551, by V. Conolly.
           Listener, (Jan. 1965), 113, by V. Frank.
           New Sta, (22 Jan. 1965), 114, by P. Johnson.
           NY R Books, (1 June 1972), 19, by R. Shattuck.
           *Rus R, 22 (Oct. 1963), 369-76, by L. K. D. Kristof.
           *Rus R, 23, no. 4 (Oct. 1964), 386-89, by R. C. Elwood.
           Slav R, (Mar. 1965), 121, by S. N. Silverman.
           Yale R, (Spring 1965), 426, by C. E. Black.

6   Bell, Thomas. Nikolai Lenin. A Brief Biographical Sketch.
        London: Communist Party of Great Britain, 1925; 14pp.
        Unavailable for annotation.

7   Charnock, Joan. Red Revolutionary. A Life of Lenin. New
        York: Hawthorn Books, 1970; 138pp., bib. 133.
        A general introduction, written for non-specialists, to the
        highlights of Lenin's life and work. Other than noting spe-
        that Lenin failed to establish democracy in Russia, Char-
        nock offers little assessment or criticism of Lenin nor
        does she discuss his theoretical works or polemics with
        rivals. [DK254.L455C5 1970]

8   *Conquest, Robert V. V. I. Lenin. New York: Viking Press,
        1972; 152pp., bib. 145-46.
        A political biography of Lenin depicting him as an individ-
        ual without whom Russia and the modern world would be
        much different today. Conquest states that if Lenin died
        young there would have been no Bolshevik Party; if he died
        in March 1917, the Bolsheviks would not have broken with
        other socialist parties; if he died in July 1917, there would
        have been no Bolshevik Revolution and if he had not lived
        for seven years after the Bolshevik Revolution, the Bolshe-
        viks would have been denied their major accomplishments.
        He examines Lenin's major works and maintains that their
        appeal is due more to his successes as a revolutionary
        and political leader than to any inherent value in them, and
        that, in fact, the very importance of his personal leader-
        ship of the Bolshevik Party contradicts the philosophical es-
        sence of his works. Conquest concludes that while Lenin
        must be viewed as a dedicated revolutionary and masterful
        political tactician, less positive judgments must be made
        on the state and party which he bequeathed.
        [DK254.L4C665 1972]

8a   Reviewed in:
           Am Hist R, 79 (Apr. 1974), 543-45, by R. Thompson.
           Va Q R, (Spring 1973), 77.

9   Dutt, R. Palme. Life and Teachings of V. I. Lenin. New
     York: International Publishers, 1936; 95pp., bib. 93-95.
     The author's stated purpose is to counter bourgeois biog-
     raphers by presenting a study of Lenin which aims "to
     maintain unblunted the 'revolutionary edge' of his life,
     work and teaching; and still more, to maintain that unity
     of theory and practice which was the essence of his out-
     look." Dutt divides his study into two main sections: one
     dealing chronologically with Lenin's revolutionary career
     (1920-1922), the other discussing his writings on imperial-
     ism, world revolution, dictatorship of the proletariat, na-
     tional and colonial liberation, tactics and organization of
     revolution and overall world outlook. Throughout he de-
     picts Lenin as a forceful and dedicated revolutionary leader,
     a consistent Marxist and a great liberator. [DK254. L4D8]
     Also published as Lenin. London: Hamish Hamilton, 1933.

10   *Fischer, Louis. The Life of Lenin. New York: Harper and
     Row, 1964; 703pp.
     A detailed and widely acclaimed study of Lenin's life with
     emphasis placed on the years during which he was the
     leader of the Soviet state. Fischer maintains an objective
     posture as he neither detracts from Lenin's positive quali-
     ties nor uncritically accepts all that Lenin did. Using
     many primary sources, he surveys Lenin's pre-1917 career
     and then turns to a full assessment of his last seven years,
     including his domestic and foreign policies, writings, and
     personal life, with the last 100 pages of the book dealing
     with his thoughts in the months of his failing health, es-
     pecially his so-called "last will and testament." Fischer
     concludes with a brief appendix where he dismisses the
     theory that Stalin poisoned Lenin. [DK254. L4F53] Excerpt
     as "Lenin Built the Soviet State," in L (anthology), 182-88.
10a Reviewed in:
       Am Hist R, (Apr. 1966), 1022, S. W. Page.
       *Antioch R, 24 (Winter 1964-1965), 530-37, by R. D.
         Warth.
       Cath Hist R, (July 1965), 205, by W. H. Webb.
       *Commentary, 38, no. 6 (Dec. 1964), 57-60, by L.
         Schapiro.
       Cr Cur, (Winter 1965), 100, by W. W. Kulski.
       *E Eur, 13, no. 11 (Nov. 1964), 54-56, by L. S. Feuer.
       Int Aff, (Oct. 1965), 730, by V. Conolly.
       Int J, (Autumn 1964), 581, by R. H. McNeal.
       J Mod Hist, (Sept. 1965), 410, by W. Lerner.
       Listener, (21 Jan. 1965), 113, by V. Frank.
       National R, (17 Nov. 1964), 1024-26, by R. V. Allen.
       New Leader, (3 Aug. 1964), 18, by L. S. Feuer.
       New Sta, (22 Jan. 1965), 114, by P. Johnson.
       NY R Books, (11 June 1964), by G. Lichtheim.
       NY Times Bk R, (14 June 1964), 1, by H. L. Roberts.
       New Yorker, (27 June 1964), 111.
       *Rus R, 23, no. 4 (Oct. 1964), 386-89, by R. C. Elwood.

Sat R, (18 July 1964), 31, by P. Viereck.
Slav R, (Mar. 1964), 121, by S. N. Silverman.
*Spectator, (Apr. 1965), 537-38, by G. Katkov.
TLS, (21 Jan. 1965), 42.
Yale R, (Spring 1965), 426, by C. E. Black.

11   Fox, Ralph. Lenin. A Biography. New York: Harcourt,
      Brace and World, 1934; 320pp.
      A general and positive account of Lenin's life with empha-
      sis placed upon the years before the October Revolution.
      Fox both discusses the landmarks in Lenin's career and
      the historical content within which he functioned.   He
      presents an image of Lenin as a man with extraordinary
      courage, intelligence, and energy, simple in taste and
      free of personal vanity or ambition, a man with a in-
      domitable will cast more in the mold of an Abe Lincoln
      than a dictator.   [DK254. L4F6]
11a   Reviewed in:
      Cur Hist M, 39 (Mar. 1934), 4, by P. W. Wilson.
      For Aff, 12 (Jan. 1934), 348, by W. L. Langer.
      Nation, 138 (21 Feb. 1934), 224, by J. Strachey.
      New Sta, 6 (9 Sept. 1933), 302, by B. Webb.
      Sat R Lit, 10 (24 Feb. 1934), 503, by S. Hook.
      Spectator, 151 (8 Sept. 1933), 319, by J. Hallett.
      Survey, 23 (Apr. 1934), 198, A. Kaun.
      TLS, (31 Aug. 1933), 569.

12   *Gorky, Maxim. Days with Lenin. New York: International
      Publishers, 1932; 64pp.
      A widely read series of recollections on Lenin's person-
      ality, character, beliefs and activities in the post-1906
      period.   Gorky recollects Lenin's activities at the 1907
      London Congress of the RSDLP, meetings with him in
      Paris and Capri, and various conversations with and ob-
      servations of him as Soviet leader.   He presents Lenin
      as a man of great will and self-discipline, devoid of ego
      and loyal to comrades, and recollects his interest in mu-
      sic, Russian classical literature, and political writers.
      [DK254. L4G633]   Excerpts in: "Gorky on Lenin," in L
      (anthology), 136-40; "I Met Lenin," USSR, no. 4 (Nov.
      1957), 22-24; "Maxim Gorky's Reminiscences," in LCAM
      (anthology), 150-52; "A Profile on Lenin," Sov Life, 3,
      no. 162 (Mar. 1970), 40-42.

13   *_____. Lenin. Moscow: Centrizdat, 1931; 48pp.
      An account of the author's personal contact with Lenin,
      and an assessment of Lenin's character, personality and
      leadership.   Gorky recounts Lenin's relations with such
      figures as Plekhanov, Martov, Luxemburg, and Bogdanov,
      his contact with Lenin in London and on Capri, and his
      relationship with him after the revolution.   He presents
      an image of Lenin as a man who represented all the best
      qualities of the Russian intelligentsia and who was excep-

tionally great because of his "irreconcilable, unquenchable
hostility towards the sufferings of humanity." Gorky provides numerous examples of Lenin's self-discipline, dedication, simple tastes and devotion to comrades.
[DK254. L4G6335] Excerpt in: "Lenin," Sov Life, 4, no.
103 (Apr. 1965), 6-8.

14   Gourfinkel, Nina. Portrait of Lenin. An Illustrated Biography.
New York: Herder and Herder, 1972; 176, bib. 175-76.
A general non-interpretive survey of Lenin's life and work.
Gourfinkel reviews Lenin's family background, early revolutionary activity, years in exile in the West and Siberia,
his development of the Bolshevik Party, return to Russia
and leadership of the October Revolution, and his policies
up to his 1924 death. Over 60 illustrations accompany
the text, and Lenin's "testament" is appended (166-71) to
the book as is a chronology of the leading events of his
life. [DK254. L4G683] Originally published as Lenine.
Paris: Editions du Sevil, 1961.

15   Hill, Christopher. Lenin and the Russian Revolution. London: English Universities Press, 1961; 245 pp., bib. 240.
A favorable introduction to Lenin's pre-1917 career
and leadership of the revolution and the Soviet state, and
a positive assessment of the historical significance of
both Lenin and the Russian Revolution. The image of
Lenin which emerges is that of a humane, practical, and
pugnacious leader who loved the common man and Russia,
and who bequeathed to the world a highly effective model
for economic development of backward and impoverished
nations. [DK254. L4H5]

16   *Hollis, Christopher. Lenin. Portrait of a Professional Revolutionary. London: Longmans, Green and Company,
1938; 285pp.
A discussion of Lenin's revolutionary career stressing the
radical milieu of late 19th-century Russia as the factor
which most shaped his thought, temperament, and policies.
Hollis sees the fanatic, conspiratorial, and ascetic nature
of the revolutionary tradition in Russia as having influenced
Lenin in his organization of the Bolshevik Party, the
struggle that he waged against both the bourgeoisie and
the Marxist revisionists, and the policies which he pursued
during the 1917 and the Civil War period. He examines
Lenin's early years as a revolutionary, his Siberian exile,
creation of Iskra, "revolt against religion," and, especially, his activities in the 1914-1918 period. [DK254. L4H6]

16a   Reviewed in:
Cath W, 148 (No. 1938), 248.
Commonweal, 28 (15 July 1938), 330, by C. O. Cleve-
land.
*Dublin R, 204 (Jan. 1939), 71-84, by G. Bennigsen.
Economist, 133 (15 Oct. 1938), 118.

Nation, 147 (17 Sept. 1938), 272, by L. Lore.
New Sta, 16 (10 Dec. 1938), 1012, by R. H. S. Cross-
man.
TLS, (12 Nov. 1938), 730.

17   Kerzhentsev, P. M. Life of Lenin. New York: International
Publishers, 1939; 336pp., bib. 330-36.
A sympathetic political biography of Lenin. Although
Kerzhentsev provides some glimpses into Lenin's personal
life, he concentrates on the leading events in Lenin's rise
from Siberian exile to leadership of the Soviet state.
With little concern for Lenin's theoretical works, he discusses Lenin's founding and shaping the party along the
proper course during the years of war, revolution, and
civil war. He gives a brief account of Lenin's economic
program of the early 1920's before eulogizing him as man,
revolutionary, and leader. [DK254. L4K433]

18   Kochan, Lionel. Lenin. London: Wayland Publishers, 1978;
96pp.
An illustrated introduction to Lenin's revolutionary and
political career supplemented by scores of quotes from
Lenin and other sources. The study is simply structured
and written on a level easily comprehensible for secondary
school students. [DK254. L455K58]

19   Krishna, Rao G. V. Nikolai Lenin--His Life and Activities.
Madras, India, 1921. Not available for annotation.

20   *Krupskaya, Nadezhda. Memories of Lenin. London: Lawrence and Wishart, 1970; 318pp.
A diverse and detailed set of reminiscences, by Lenin's
wife, on the period from 1893 to the seizure of power in
October 1917. Krupskaya establishes the character of
Lenin's life in exile, presents much information on his
relations with a wide range of revolutionary personalities,
on the activities of the RSDLP (especially his polemics
with rival socialists), and on his reactions to historical
developments in Russia. To a lesser extent, she provides information on the personal side of her life with
Lenin. [DK254. L42K7213] Excerpt as "Memoirs of
Lenin's Wife," Sov Life, 151, no. 4 (Apr. 1969), 28-31.

21   *_____. Reminiscences of Lenin. New York: International
Publishers, 1970; 523pp.
Reminiscences of various episodes in Lenin's life in the
1893-1920 period, with most information on the pre-1917
period. Krupskaya's recollections range from Lenin's
many feuds with rival socialists, his conversations with
friends, planning and writing of major works, and his
reactions to the historical events in Russia and Western
Europe, to the many habits, tastes, dislikes, and traits
that comprised his personality. The recollections are

arranged chronologically under headings indicating when
and where the Lenins were living at the time. A ten
page index of the names of people appearing in the
memoirs makes for convenient use of this volume.
[DK254. L4K7213] Excerpts in: "Lenin as I Knew Him, "
Illus Wk India, 87, no. 17 (24 Apr. 1966), 21; "Lenin's
Moods, " in L (anthology), 134-36; "N. K. Krupskaya's
Reminiscences, " in LCAM (anthology), 147-150.

22   *Landau-Aldanov, M. A. Lenin. New York: Dutton and
        Company, 1922; 241pp.
        A highly critical, early interpretation, by a Russian so-
        cialist writer, of Lenin's writings, personality and achieve-
        ments. Aldanov surveys Lenin's economic, political, and
        philosophical thought and dismisses it as inherently sound-
        less and shallow, and interesting only for its "soap-box
        polemics" and "narrow-minded sagacity. " He attacks the
        image of Lenin as a prophet, and claims that Lenin never
        predicted revolution but only turned mass discontent "to
        the benefit of his own ideas. " In assessing Lenin's per-
        sonality, character and leadership qualities Aldanov pre-
        sents a more favorable image of Lenin as incorruptible,
        singleminded, and a genius at human psychology: a born
        "handler of men. " He concludes that the heart of Lenin's
        Bolshevism is his belief in the dictatorship of the prole-
        tariat exercised by his party without any moral and popular
        restraints. [DK254. L4A716]
22a   Reviewed in:
        Am Pol Sci R, 16 (Aug. 1922), 523.
        Freeman, 5 (5 Apr. 1922), 92, by J. Macy.
        Independent, 108 (25 Feb. 1922), 201, E. L. Pearson.
        Lit R, (25 Mar. 1922), 524, by A. Nazaroff.
        New Rep, 31 (7 June 1922), 56, W. H. Chamberlin.
        NY Times Bk R, (9 July 1922), 3, H. Bernstein.
        Outlook, 131 (19 July 1922), 499.
        Pitt Mo B, 27 (July 1922), 366.

23   *Lenin. Moscow: State Publishing House of Political Litera-
        ture, 1939; no pp. numbers.
        A collection of over 200 documents, illustrations, letters,
        excerpts from works, sketches and photos from the Cen-
        tral Lenin Museum (Moscow), on a wide range of subjects
        related to Lenin. Substantial captions provide pertinent
        context for the many interesting materials in this volume
        which was compiled for the 1939 New York City World's
        Fair. [DK254. L4M847]

24   Lenin. His Life and Work. Moscow: Novosti Press, 1965;
        44pp.
        A short, general, and heavily illustrated introduction of
        Lenin's life and leading accomplishments. [DK254. L4L335]

25   Levine, I. E. Lenin. The Man Who Made a Revolution.

Folkestone: Bailey Brothers and Swinfen, 1970; 189pp.,
bib. 183-84.
A non-interpretive account of the leading events in
Lenin's life as a revolutionary and political leader of the
Soviet state. The author presents most information on
Lenin's early (pre-1903) revolutionary career and the
events of 1917. [DK254.L455L45]

26 *Levine, Issac Don. The Man Lenin. New York: Seltzer,
1924; 207pp.
An early study of Lenin's life with most emphasis on his
activities in 1917 and 1918. In addition to detailing
Lenin's planning, organization and leadership of the October Revolution and his policies immediately after coming
to power (especially his efforts at concluding peace with
Germany), Levine has several chapters on Lenin's personal characteristics and tastes. He also discusses Leninism not as a theory but as an illustration that a well-
organized minority can seize and hold power in the name
of any "ism." Levine concludes that Lenin was not an
original thinker, but was a genius as a political strategist
who "demonstrated once more the fallacy and emptiness
of political democracy." [DK254.U6L4]

26a   Reviewed in:
Booklist, 21 (Nov. 1924), 66.
New Rep, 10 (17 Sept. 1924), 81, by E. A. R.
NY Times Bk R, (10 Apr. 1924), 21, by K. Karsner.

27 Liversidge, Douglas. Lenin. Genius of Revolution. London:
Watts, 1969; 189pp.
A general, simply-written introduction to Lenin's revolutionary and political career stressing the effectiveness
of his leadership and tactics while criticizing the dictatorial qualities of his party and government. Liversidge
maintains that in spite of Lenin's triumphs he was a
failure because he did not establish a society consistent
with his ideals and, in fact, gave to the Russian people
no more freedom than they had under the tsars.
[DK254.L455L58 1969]

28 Mack, Donald W. Lenin and the Russian Revolution. London:
Longman Group, 1970; 104pp.
A general introduction, designed for young readers, to
Lenin's leadership of the Russian Revolution and Soviet
state. Mack includes numerous illustrations, a glossary
of terms and a list of supplemental activities for students
interested in studying Lenin and the revolution.
[DK265.17.M2]

29 *Marcu, Valeriu. Lenin. New York: Macmillan, 1928;
411pp.
A general and somewhat fanciful account of Lenin's revolutionary and political leadership with most attention given

to the years prior to his seizure of power. Marcu discusses sympathetically the standard highlights in Lenin's
career and provides particular depth on intra-party affairs in the pre-1914 period. [DK254.L4M3]

29a   Reviewed in:

Booklist, 25 (Nov. 1928), 69.
Bookman, 68 (Nov. 1928), 351, by B. C. Vladeck.
Chris Cent, 45 (6 Oct. 1928), 1197, by E. N.
Nat Ath, 44 (22 Oct. 1928), 114, by K. Martin.
New Rep, 57 (16 Jan. 1929), 251, by J. B. S. Hard-
    man.
NY Times Bk R, (4 Nov. 1928), 3, by T. R. Ybarra.
Sat R, 146 (14 July 1928), 51.
Sat R Lit, 5 (8 Dec. 1928), 451, by J. B. MacDonald.
Survey, 61 (1 Nov. 1928), 176, by L. L. W. Wilson.
TLS, (5 July 1928), 495.
Wis Lib B, 24 (Nov. 1928), 304.
Yale R, n.s.18 (Spring 1929), 600, by G. Vernadsky.

30   Maxton, James. Lenin. New York: Appleton, 1932; 180pp.,
    bib. 171-174.
    A sympathetic account of Lenin's life and work with em-
    phasis on his activities as a revolutionary. Maxton pre-
    sents Lenin as "the liberator of Russia" and the "pioneer
    of a new world order," and concludes that even if the
    Communist experiment fails, Lenin must be viewed as a
    great man and leader. [DK254.L4M33]

31   Mikhailov, Nikolai. Stories about Lenin. Moscow: Novosti
    Press, 1970; 32pp.
    A general account of the leading events in Lenin's life as
    a revolutionary and leader of Soviet Russia. Mikhailov
    provides anecdotes about and illustrations of Lenin in a
    variety of situations and capacities. [DK254.L4M42]

32   *Mirsky, D. S. Lenin. Boston: Little, Brown and Company,
    1931; 236pp., bib. 217-22.
    A general and sympathetic biography of Lenin by a Rus-
    sian contemporary. Mirsky briefly scans Lenin's youth and
    then procedes to discuss Lenin's career chronologically as
    a revolutionary, politician and statesman, stressing his
    many accomplishments as leader of the Soviet state.
    Mirsky concludes with an assessment of Leninism as con-
    sisting of five basic propositions: commitment to the
    elimination of exploitation of man by man; faith in only the
    proletariat as the means to ending exploitation; mastery of
    the art and science of revolution; reliance on the "spon-
    taneous discipline" of the proletariat in equaling and sur-
    passing capitalist production; and the creation of a society
    "consonant with the dignity of man and of his further task
    of conquering nature." [DK254.L4M5]

32a   Reviewed in:
    Am Hist R, 37 (Jan. 1932), 344, by R. J. Kerner.

Booklist, 27 (May 1931), 404.
Books, (12 Apr. 1931), 2, by L. Fischer.
Chris Cent, 48 (1 July 1931), 873, by P. Hutchinson.
Cur Hist M, 34, no. 9 (July 1931), by S. Zimand.
Nation, 132 (13 May 1931), 534, L. Fischer.
New Rep, 66 (13 May 1931), by F. L. Shuman.
New Sta, 1 (20 June 1931), 618, by H. Agar.
NY Times Bk R, (12 Apr. 1931), 11, by A. Nazaroff.
Outlook, 157 (22 Apr. 1931), 567.
Sat R, 151 (18 Apr. 1931), 574, by A. P. Nicholson.
Sat R Lit, 7 (6 June 1931), 875, by V. M. Dean.
Spectator, 146, sup. 509 (28 Mar. 1931), by H. W.
  Nevinson.
TLS, (30 Apr. 1931), 335.
Wis Lib B, 27 (Oct. 1931), 221.
Yale R, n.s. 20 (Summer 1931), 810, by S. N. Harper.

33   *Morgan, Michael C. Lenin. Athens: Ohio University Press,
     1971; 236pp., bib. 223-30.
     A general and objective political biography of Lenin based
     on English language sources. Morgan briefly discusses
     the historical circumstances of late 19th century Russia
     before surveying Lenin's conversion to Marxism, creation
     of the Bolshevik Party, reaction to the 1905 Revolution,
     and his years in exile. Receiving more attention is
     Lenin's leadership in both the October Revolution and
     Soviet state. In assessing Lenin's character, Morgan
     states that Lenin had many constructive qualities, was
     dedicated, selfless and simple in tastes, but was possessed
     by "an uncommon, ruthless, and maybe perverting tenacity"
     which greatly influenced the revolution and the character-
     istics of the Soviet state. [DK254. L4M625]

33a   Reviewed in:
         Am Hist R, 79 (Apr. 1974), 543-45, by R. Thompson.
         *Arch Eur Soc, 17 (1976), 366-83, by N. Harding.
         *Hist J, 15 (1972), 794-803, by D. Geary.
         Slav R, (June 1973), 386, by R. D. Warth.
         TLS, (24 Dec. 1971), 1596.

34   Moscow. Institute of Marx-Engels-Lenin. V. I. Lenin. A
     Brief Sketch of His Life and Activities. Moscow:
     Foreign Languages Publishing House, 1942; 326pp.
     An official biography of Lenin as a revolutionary and po-
     litical leader. The authors present favorably the high-
     lights in Lenin's career, while paying much attention to
     his polemics. The lack of a table of contents, chapter
     titles, and an index make this volume difficult to use.
     [DK254. L4M732 1942]

35   Moscow. Institute of Marx-Engels-Lenin. Vladimir I. Lenin.
     A Political Biography. New York: International Publish-
     ers, 1943; 288pp.
     An official history of Lenin's political views and activities

as both a revolutionary and Soviet leader. The authors
discuss the standard landmarks in his creation and development of the Bolshevik Party while consistently
stressing his tireless efforts, tremendous insight into
the historical process, and immeasurable value as leader
of the revolution. [DK254.L4M732]

36   Moscow. Institute of Marx-Engels-Lenin-Stalin. Lenin. A
     Biography. London: Lawrence and Wishart, 1955; 272pp.,
     bib. 267-72.
     An official biography of Lenin's life organized into 13
     chronological (periodized) chapters. The authors present
     the standard landmarks in Lenin's life, all in a positive
     light. [DK254.L4M732 1955]

37   Moscow. Institute of Marxism-Leninism. V. I. Lenin. A
     Short Biography. Moscow: Progress Publishers, 1968;
     146pp.
     As an abridged version of the official party biography of
     Lenin, this volume provides a general sympathetic survey
     of Lenin's pre-revolutionary work and writings, his role
     in the October Revolution and leadership of the Soviet state.
     [DK254.L4M73953 1968]

38   Obichkin, G. D., et al. V. I. Lenin. A Short Biography.
     Moscow: Progress Publishers, 1969; 216pp.
     A translation of the 6th Russian edition of Lenin. A Short
     Biography prepared by the Institute of Marxism-Leninism
     as a general introduction to Lenin's life and work. The
     editors present a praiseful account of Lenin's leadership
     and accomplishments, with a balance of information on his
     pre-revolutionary, revolutionary and post-1917 career.
     [DK254.L40288]

39   _____. Vladimir Ilyich Lenin. A Short Biography. Mos-
     cow: Novosti Press, 1969; 112pp. A condensed, black
     and white version of the Antropova book Lenin (item 2).
     [DK254.L40228]

40   Ossendowski, Ferdinand. Lenin. God of the Godless. New
     York: Dutton, 1931; 419pp.
     A bitter and somewhat fanciful attack on Lenin and his
     policies. Ossendowski presents Lenin as an unscrupulous,
     manipulative and evil atheist who ruined all that was good
     in Russia. [DK254.L407]

41   *Payne, Robert. The Life and Death of Lenin. New York:
     Simon and Schuster, 1964; 672pp., bib. 641-44.
     A general and popular biography of Lenin with emphasis
     on the 1917-1924 period of his life. Payne states that he
     has attempted to divorce Lenin from his legend and to see
     him whole, alive and breathing: "I wanted to know how he
     walked through life, and how he laughed, and what he said

when he was not holding a tight rein on himself, and how he came to those exclusive fanatical dogmas which once threatened to destroy the world." To this end, Payne examines both the inner and outer life of Lenin as he surveys the landmarks in his career and presents an image of him as "an embattled, tormented and variously gifted man who is perhaps the only indisputable political genius to emerge in our time." Payne concludes with a lengthy discussion of Lenin's illness and death, and advances an argument that Stalin had Lenin poisoned. Appended is the official Soviet report of Lenin's autopsy. [DK254. L4P35]

41a   Reviewed in:
*Antioch R, 24 (Winter 1964), 530-37, by R. D. Warth.
Atlan Mo, (July 1964), 133, by W. Barrett.
*Commentary, 38, no. 6 (Dec. 1964), 57-60, by L.
     Schapiro.
*E Eur, 13, no. 11 (Nov. 1964), 54-56, by L. Dennen.
Int Aff, (Oct. 1965), 730, by V. Conolly.
Lib J, (1 Mar. 1964), 1078, by O. Ivsky.
*Life, 56 (19 June 1964), 10+, by F. Barghoorn.
Listener, (21 Jan. 1965), 113, by V. Frank.
*National R, (17 Nov. 1964), 1024-26, by R. V. Allen.
New Leader, (3 Aug. 1964), 18, by L. S. Feuer.
New Sta, (22 Jan. 1965), 114, by P. Johnson.
NY R Books, (11 June 1964), 3, by G. Lichtheim.
NY Time Bk R, (14 June 1964), 1, by H. L. Roberts.
New Yorker, (27 June 1964), 111.
*Rus R, 23, no. 4 (Oct. 1964), 386-89, by R. C. El-
     wood.
Sat R, (13 June 1964), 28, by P. E. Mosely.
Slav R, (Mar. 1965), 121, by S. N. Silverman.
Spectator, (20 Nov. 1964), 684, by D. Footman.
Time, (10 July 1964), 102.
TLS, (22 Oct. 1964), 954.
Yale R, (Spring 1965), 426, by C. E. Black.

42   *Pospelov, P. N., et al. Vladimir Ilyich Lenin. Moscow:
     Progress Publishers, 1966; 590pp.
     Sponsored by the Moscow Institute of Marxism-Leninism, this official biography of Lenin presents a mass of information on Lenin's life and work. To quote the authors, they "have set out to record, besides purely biographical data, Lenin's most important guiding ideas" and to draw "more extensively than previous editions on the rich memoir literature of the period" as a source of "interesting facts revealing to us Lenin the man, leader and comrade." In fulfilling this goal, the authors present an even balance of information on Lenin's pre-revolutionary, revolutionary, and post-revolutionary career. Throughout, they portray Lenin as a tireless revolutionary and political leader with remarkable foresight, a faithful interpreter of Marx, and a defender of Marxism against all shades of revisionism. [DK254. L4M7423]

43 *Possony, Stefan. Lenin: The Compulsive Revolutionary.
    Chicago: Regnery, 1964; 418pp., bib. 401-08.
    A critical interpretation of Lenin's revolutionary and
    political thought and activities. Possony credits Lenin
    with combining Marx with the Russian revolutionary tra-
    dition, forging effective political techniques and organiza-
    tion, and with introducing both "novel combinations of
    violent and non-violent combat" and the concept of "the
    multi-dimensional war of the modern age." He attacks
    the saintly Soviet image of Lenin by presenting consider-
    able information on "unofficial" and questionable aspects
    of his personal life as well as on episodes (the Malinovsky
    affair, relations with the German government) which re-
    flect negatively on his leadership, morality, and scruples.
    Above all, Lenin emerges as a compulsive revolutionary
    characterized by "dogmatism of thought and pragmatism
    of action." [DK254.L4P647]
43a Reviewed in:
       Am Hist R, (Oct. 1964), 254, by S. W. Page.
       Annals, (May 1965), 239, by B. D. Wolfe.
       *Antioch R, 24 (Winter 1964), 530-34, by R. D. Warth.
       *Commentary, 38, no. 6 (Dec. 1964), 57-60, by L.
         Schapiro.
       Commonweal, (26 June 1964), 430, by M. A. Fitz-
         simons.
       Contemp R, (Apr. 1966), 216, by P. Wilkinson.
       History, 5, no. 173 (Oct. 1966), 331-35, by A. J.
         Nicholls.
       Int Aff, (Jan. 1965), 142, by V. Conolly.
       Int J, (Autumn 1964), 581, by R. H. McNeal.
       J Mod Hist, (Mar. 1965), 109, by J. D. Clarkson.
       Lib J, (1 Mar. 1964), 1078, by O. Ivsky.
       Mod Age, (Fall 1964), 420, by R. F. Byrnes.
       *National R, (17 Nov. 1964), 1024, by R. V. Allen.
       New Leader, (3 Aug. 1964), 18, by L. S. Feuer.
       NY R Books, (11 June 1964), 3, by G. Lichtheim.
       NY Times Bk R, (14 June 1964), 1, by H. L. Roberts.
       *Rus R, 23, no. 4 (Oct. 1964), 386-89, by R. C. El-
         wood.
       Slav R, (Mar. 1965), 121, by S. N. Silverman.
       *Spectator, (23 Apr. 1965), 537-38, by G. Katkov.
       Time, (10 June 1964), 102.
       TLS, (24 Mar. 1966), 239.
       Yale R, (Spring 1965), 426, by C. E. Black.

44 Prilezhayeva, Maria. V. I. Lenin. The Story of His Life.
    Moscow: Progress Publishers, 1978; 231pp.
    A sympathetic and fanciful account, "written simply and
    with love," of the leading events in Lenin's youth, revo-
    lutionary career and years as Soviet leader. Designed
    for young readers. [DK254.L4P7423]

45 Roberts, Elizabeth M. Lenin and the Downfall of Tsarist
    Russia. London: Methuen, 1966; 100pp., bib. 96.

As part of the "Methuen Outlines" series, this work provides a general, non-interpretive introduction to Lenin's personal life, revolutionary career, and accomplishments as Soviet leader. Roberts includes separate chapters on Lenin's youth, career as a young Marxist, role in the 1905 Revolution and interpretation of World War I, and on the February Revolution, October Revolution, and postrevolutionary Russia. [DK265.17.R57 1966a]

46   Shaw, Ruth and Harry A. Potamkin, eds. Our Lenin. New York: International Publishers, 1934; 62pp.
This volume combines an illustrated story of Lenin's life published in the Soviet Union under the title Lenin for Children with supplemental biographical information on his childhood largely taken from the reminiscences of his sisters. The story is partly fictionalized, but generally follows the highlights of Lenin's career. [DK254.L408]

47   *Shub, David. Lenin. Garden City: Doubleday, 1948; 438pp.
A detailed study of Lenin's life and work based on Russian sources and on the author's personal contact with Lenin and other revolutionaries. Shub refrains from direct criticism or praise but rather relies on 'the facts speaking for themselves' as he examines the Russian roots of Lenin's politics, his evolution as a revolutionary and his policies as Soviet leader. Shub does not assess Lenin's writings or thought, but instead concentrates on both the personal and political Lenin, presenting numerous direct quotes from him as illustrations of his character and leadership. Lenin emerges from this study as a dedicated, dynamic and ruthless revolutionary who used any and all means to advance his cause. [DK254.L4S482]

47a   Reviewed in:
Am Hist R, 54 (Oct. 1948), 142, by F. L. Schuman.
Booklist, 45 (15 Sept. 1948), 30.
Cath W, 167 (Sept. 1948), 566, by L. J. Schweitzer.
*Commentary, 8 (July 1949), 1-9, by H. Rosenberg.
Commonweal, 48 (25 June 1948), 264, by J. Cournos.
Lib J, 73 (15 Apr. 1948), 653, R. P. Breaden.
New Rep, 119 (16 July 1948), 22, by J. R. Newman.
NY Times Bk R, (25 Apr. 1948), 5, by H. Kohn.
New Yorker, 24 (24 Apr. 1948), 106.
Sat R Lit, 31 (24 Apr. 1948), 11, by A. Brynes.
Yale R, n.s. 38 (Winter 1949), 352, F. C. Barghoorn.

48   *Theen, Rolf H. W. Lenin. Genesis and Development of a Revolutionary. Philadelphia: Lippincott, 1973; 194pp., bib. 183-88.
A study of the development of Lenin as a revolutionary focusing on the years 1887-1900, and continuing in survey fashion up to 1924. Theen concentrates on Lenin "the man, revolutionary and theoretician and political leader" at the expense of a full examination of the historical con-

text within which Lenin developed. He begins with a detailed examination of Lenin's family as a close and disciplined one, though its members had diverse interests and personalities, and emphasizes the impact on Lenin of the 1887 execution of his older brother. Theen traces the gradual development of Lenin as a revolutionary, noting the influence of the writings of Chernyshevsky and Lenin's close relationship with revolutionary neo-Populism, and stresses that by 1900 Lenin had lost faith in the ability of any social class to produce a revolution, and consequently turned to the creation of an elitist and centralized party to lead the workers in the proper direction. [DK254.L4T47] Excerpt as "Lenin as a Speaker," in L (anthology), 141-43.

48a   Reviewed in:
       Am Hist R, 79 (Apr. 1974), 543, by R. Thompson.
       Economist, 251 (11 May 1974), 121.
       Lib J, 98 (Aug 1973), 2287, by G. Charney.
       TLS, (13 Sept. 1974), 983.
       Pr Sch, 48 (Winter 1974-1975), 368.

49   *Trotsky, Leon. Lenin. Notes for a Biographer. New York: Putnam, 1971; 224pp.
     A biography of Lenin hastily put together by Trotsky immediately after Lenin's death because, as Bertram D. Wolfe states in the introduction to the book, "the whole country expected a 'last word' from the man" most expected to be Lenin's successor. The first two parts of the study are divided by the 1917 Revolutions, while the third and most valuable part consists of a series of seven essays, articles, and speeches by Trotsky dealing with Lenin's national characteristics, a critique of H. G. Wells' characterization of Lenin, an attack on Gorky's On Lenin's Portrait, a discussion of a collection of children's writings about Lenin, and separate essays on his wounding, illness, and death. Trotsky treats the theoretical, revolutionary, and political Lenin in parts one and two, while in part three his stated purpose is to provide a characterization of Lenin. Included is an interesting introductory essay by Bertram D. Wolfe on the writing of this book and on Trotsky's relation with Lenin. [DK254.L4T7] Also published as Lenin. London: Harrap, 1925; 247pp.

49a   Reviewed in:
       Lib J, 96 (1971), 1970, by L. Barron.
       NY Times Bk R, (25 Apr. 1971), 52.
       Rus R, 31 (Apr. 1972), 205, by A. Ascher.

50   *Veale, F. J. P. The Man from the Volga. The Life of Lenin. London: Constable and Company, 1932; 288pp.
     A non-interpretive study of Lenin's life and activities as both a revolutionary and political leader. Veale's efforts are evenly divided between the pre-1917, 1917 and post-1917 phases of Lenin's career, though in each he focuses

more on Lenin's political beliefs and tactics (with parallels to tsarist tradition) than on his theoretical works. Veale characterizes Lenin as a man who possessed tremendous sincerity, dedication, energy, and selflessness, more callous than cruel, and willing to use any means (brutal, un-Marxist or otherwise) to advance his cause. [DK254. L4V35]

51 *Vernadsky, George. Lenin. Red Dictator. New Haven: Yale University Press, 1931; 351pp.

A general biography stressing Lenin's revolutionary activities and leadership rather than his theoretical works or personal life. Vernadsky proceeds chronologically dividing his study evenly between Lenin as a revolutionary before 1917 and as a political leader after 1917. He maintains that "the unique quality of Lenin ... consisted ... in the combination of the most abstract intellectual program with an uncommon capacity ... to adapt tactics to the demand of actual conditions." Lenin's fanaticism gave him courage, energy, and won him supporters while his opportunism made him a master at capitalizing on every shift in circumstances which he confronted. Vernadsky also sees Lenin as both a destroyer and a creator, a man possessed of great strength of will, a remarkable orator, and merciless in execution of his plans. [DK254. L4V4]

51a Reviewed in:

Am Hist R, 37 (Jan. 1932), 344, by R. J. Kerner.
Am Pol Sci R, 25 (Nov. 1931), 1074, by V. M. Dean.
Booklist, 27 (May 1931), 406.
Books, (12 Apr. 1931), 1, by L. Fischer.
Chris Cent, 48 (1 July 1931), 873, by P. Hutchinson.
Cur Hist, 34, no. 10 (July 1931), by S. Zimand.
Nation, 132 (13 May 1931), 534, by L. Fischer.
New Rep, 66 (13 May 1931), F. L. Shuman.
New Sta, 1 (20 June 1931), 618, by H. Agar.
NY Times Bk R, (12 Apr. 1931), 11, by A. Nazaroff.
Outlook, (22 Apr. 1931), 566.
Pitt Mo B, 36 (Oct. 1931), 66.
Sat R Lit, 7 (6 June 1931), 875 by V. M. Dean.
TLS, (18 June 1931), 477.
W Tomorrow, 14 (Aug 1931), 265.
Yale R, n.s. 20 (Summer 1931), 809, by S. N. Harper.

52 V. I. Lenin. A Biography. Colombo, Ceylon: Tribune Publications, 1970; 123pp.

A positive, illustrated, and general introduction to Lenin's activities and policies both as a revolutionary and Soviet leader. [DK254. L4V143]

53 *Warth, Robert D. Lenin. New York: Twayne, 1973; 198pp., bib. 183-89.

A short biography of Lenin with emphasis on his activities as opposed to his thought. The author states that his study lacks a particular thesis but rather seeks "to present a controversial subject in a nonpartisan spirit." To this end he reviews the political and revolutionary highlights of Lenin's life and presents his positive qualities as being modesty, simplicity of taste, dedication, enormous will power, keen intelligence, a sense of humor and high personal morals (a puritan among communists). Warth criticizes Lenin for specific errors of judgment as Soviet leader and for the general direction in which he led the infant Soviet state, namely towards a rigid one-party dictatorship. [DK254.L4W27]

53a Reviewed in:

Choice, 11 (May 1974), 500.

Can S P, 17 nos. 2/3 (Summer/Fall 1975), 532-33, by L. D. Calder.

History, 11 (May 1974), 500.

54 White, William C. Lenin. New York: Harrison and Robert Haas, 1936; 172pp., bib. 170.
A general and non-critical biography of Lenin. White reviews Lenin's youth and family life, his turn to the revolutionary movement, and creation of the Bolshevik Party, before discussing in more detail his years in exile prior to the 1917 revolution and the revolution itself. He frequently describes Lenin's personal life and to a lesser extent his party activities, and generally disregards his theoretical writings. [DK254.L4W38]

55 *Wolfe, Bertram D. Three Who Made a Revolution. A Biographical History. New York: Dell, 1964; 659pp.
A highly acclaimed history of the development of Marxism in Russia up to the outbreak of World War I, through the lives of Lenin, Trotsky, and Stalin. Although titled a biographical history, Wolfe's focus is on the intellectual lives of his protagonists, or, in his own words, the work is an "ideological history" as much as a biographical study. He draws upon his personal acquaintance with many of the leading Bolsheviks and uses an impressive number of primary sources to examine the intellectual evolution of Lenin from his youth to the 1914 writings of his Seven Theses against War. Throughout, Wolfe critically analyzes without condemning Lenin's principal thoughts, actions, and accomplishments. [DK254.L4W6]

55a Reviewed in:

Commentary, 8 (July 1949), 1-9, by H. Rosenberg.

Encounter, 40, no. 4 (Apr. 1973), 74-77, by L. Schapiro.

Spectator, (Feb. 1967), 200, by T. Szamuely.

56 Zevin, Vladimir and G. Golikov. Vladimir Ilyich Lenin. A Short Biography. Moscow: Novosti Press, 1972; 167pp.
A general and positive account of Lenin as founder of the CPSU, leader of the revolution, builder of socialism and

a man with immense international significance. In addition to his sympathetic presentation of the highlights of Lenin's life, Zevin includes many illustrations and photos. [DK254.L4Z463]

57 _____. Vladimir Ilyich Lenin. Life and Work. Moscow: Novosti Press, 1975; 177pp.
A heavily illustrated, Soviet introduction to the highlights of Lenin's career as a revolutionary and political leader. The authors include a lengthy section on the international significance of Lenin.

B. Personality, Character, and Biographical Data

1. Youth

58 *Baranov, I. Y. "Lenin's Boyhood," in UF (anthology), 102-
33.
An examination of the influence of Lenin's family in mold-
ing his revolutionary world outlook. Baranov states that
Lenin's parents were "advanced, progressive people of
their time" and instilled in their children respect for
democratic literature and for the common working man.
Lenin's father was "a vivid example of devoted service
to the people" and heavily influenced Lenin with his sympathetic, democratic attitude towards the oppressed.
Baranov states that while Lenin was still a boy, he came
to understand well the phenomena of social inequality and
injustice, and to accept vigorous political action as a
means of social improvement. Baranov also discusses
the revolutionary turn taken by Lenin in response to his
older brother's execution.

59 DeKorostovitz, V. "Portrait of Young Lenin," Cath D, 2
(Nov. 1937), 36-39.

60 *Deutscher, Isaac. Lenin's Childhood. London: Oxford University Press, 1970; 67pp.
A scholarly analysis of Lenin's life up to the age of 17.
Besides presenting many details on Lenin's youth,
Deutscher provides a link between Lenin's turn to revolution and the humanitarian activities of his father as
well as the militant radicalism of his older brother, and,
in the process, sketches the immediate environment and
broader political, social, and economic milieu within which
Lenin grew up. Deutscher intended to produce a definitive
biography of Lenin but died before he could do so. This
study represents only one unfinished chapter of his proposed
work, but nonetheless is extremely valuable.
[DK254. L44D48]
60a   Reviewed in:
Am Hist R, 77 (Apr. 1972), 548-89, by R. H. McNeal.
*Arch Eur Soc, 17 (1976), 366-83, by N. Harding.
Aust O, (Aug. 1971), 239, by J. N. Westwood.
For Aff, (Jan. 1971), 368, by K. G. Stoessinger.
Hist Today, 21 (Feb. 1971), 143, by W. J. Fishman.
J Mod Hist, 43 (Sept. 1971), 534-36, by P. Pomper.
Lib J, 96 (1971), 470, by H. Kublin.

Nation, 212 (15 Mar. 1971), 342-45, by L. Menashe.
New Yorker, (27 Feb. 1971), 108.
*Newsletter Comp St Com, 6, no. 4 (Aug. 1973), 30-39,
by A. Meyer.
Rus R, 31 (Jan. 1972), 85-86, by G. E. Brancovan.
TLS, (20 Nov. 1970), 1348.

61 *Frumkina, E. "With Deep Emotion...." Sov Ed, 12, nos.
3-5 (Jan.-Mar. 1970), 36-52.
A review article on Lenin and Simbirsk (a Russian publication), a collection of documents, materials, and
reminiscences on Lenin's life as a youth in Simbirsk.

62 *Haimson, Leopold H. "Against the Stream: The Youth of
Vladimir Ulyanov," in The Russian Marxists and the Origins of Bolshevism. Boston: Beacon, 1966; 92-114.
A scholarly examination of Lenin's personality and involvement in the revolutionary movement up to 1898.
Haimson first discusses the nature of Lenin's home environment and school years before turning to his political
awakening in response to the execution of his brother
Alexander. In sketching a political profile of the young
Lenin, Haimson stresses the influence of Chernyshevsky
in shaping Lenin's world outlook and thoughts on the revolution, revolutionaries, and the socialist utopia. He presents an image of Lenin as an impatient revolutionary,
scornful of compromise and compromisers and, most importantly, convinced that an individual armed with the
proper (Marxist) philosophy could exert great influence
over the revolutionary movement. [HX313.H3]

63 *Kalachyova, G. I. "Literary Interests," in UF (anthology),
72-83. A presentation of the members of the Ulyanov
family as avid readers devoted to cultural pursuits.
Kalachyova discusses the reading tastes of the family,
and how the Ulyanovs often read aloud literary classics,
such as Tolstoy's War and Peace, and cites as Lenin's
favorite works: Uncle Tom's Cabin, Spartacus, and What
Is to Be Done? (Chernyshevsky). She concludes that the
Ulyanovs' practice of "wisely helping (the children) to
choose the right sort of literature ... inculcated in them
lofty social ideals, love of knowledge and creative work."

64 Kapranova, A. N. "Friends and Acquaintances," in UF (anthology), 84-101.
An account of the Ulyanov family's relations with various
friends and acquaintances in Simbirsk. Kapranova establishes the personal qualities possessed by the Ulyanovs'
friends, and notes the smallness of the group and its
rather select nature. She also notes Lenin's shock and
pain over the cowardice shown by some of these individuals
as they shunned the Ulyanovs after the arrest and execution
of Alexander Ulyanov for involvement in a plot to assassi-
nate Alexander III.

65 Kerensky, A. "Lenin's Youth and My Own," Asia, 34 (Feb. 1934), 68-73.

66 Kosa, John. "The Red Superego," in Two Generations of Soviet Man. New Haven: College and Unity Press, 1964; 24-44.
Lenin is not the focus of this chapter, but it contains an interesting, brief psychological assessment of him as a youth. [HX44.K635]

67 *Kostin, A. "Vladimir Ulyanov in Simbirsk," Sov Lit, no. 4 (1979), 112-24.

68 *Kovnator, Ray. Lenin's Mother. Moscow: Foreign Languages Publishing House, 1944; 34pp.
An account of the influence exerted upon Lenin by his mother (Maria Ulyanova) and of the relationship he had with her until her death in 1916. Kovnator praises Maria both for establishing a home environment which encouraged the young Lenin to be industrious, humane, and to love knowledge, and for her courage and fortitude in holding the Ulyanov household together after the 1886-1887 deaths of Lenin's father and older brother. Kovnator also discusses Maria's support for the revolutionary activity of Lenin and her other children, and how, in frequent letters and periodic visits, Lenin kept in close contact with his mother apprising her of the development of the revolutionary movement while expressing his deep affection for her. [DK254.U4K62]

69 "Lenin," Liv Age, 320 (15 Mar. 1924), 486-87.
A brief note on the discovery of Lenin's secondary school records.

70 "Lenin's Boyhood," Rus Info R, 4 (9 Feb. 1924), 93+.
A discussion of Lenin as a student in 1887 (based upon the opinions of his school's headmaster).

71 *Moleva, A. N. "Learning How to Work," in UF (anthology), 26-50.
A discussion of the high regard for education by Lenin's parents and their instillation in their children of "the habits of regular, persistent labour and ... a thirst for knowledge." Moleva examines the parents' concern for the childrens' school lessons and performance, their creation of a disciplined work atmosphere at home, and the general encouragement given to the children to acquire as much knowledge as they could master. She concludes that Lenin "would not have become what he was if he had not acquired the habit of hard work at school and remained faithful to it all his life."

72 *Moscow Institute of Marxism-Leninism. Reminiscences of Lenin by His Relatives. Moscow: Foreign Languages

Publishing House, 1956.
Unavailable for annotation.

73   *Pollock, George H.   "On Mourning, Immortality, and Utopia,"
      J Am Psy Asso, 23, no. 2 (1975), 334-62.
      An assessment of the connection between childhood loss
      and later utopian ideals, with Lenin's loss of his father
      and older brother and consequent turn to Marxism serving
      as a case study.

74   Shugayeva, L. N.   "A Gifted Teacher and Educationalist," in
      UF (anthology), 7-25.
      Lenin is not the focus of this essay but as an account of
      the educational career of his father, this is a useful
      source of information on the values of an individual who
      greatly influenced him.

75   *Tomul, A. I.   "Sincere Affection and Close Friendship," in
      UF (anthology), 51-71.
      A discussion of Lenin's attitude towards his relatives as a
      model of "genuinely communist morals and ethics." Tomul
      maintains that Lenin acquired his selfless, sincere, and hu-
      mane traits from his parents who created an ideal home
      and family atmosphere. He discusses the qualities possessed
      by Lenin's mother and father as loving and dedicated parents,
      and provides numerous examples of the exceptionally close-
      knit nature of the Ulyanov family.

76   *Trotsky, Leon.   The Young Lenin.   Garden City: Doubleday,
      1972; 224pp.
      A detailed analysis of Lenin's life and work up to 1893.
      Trotsky discusses as the most important early influences
      on Lenin the remnants of serfdom, the revolutionary dis-
      content in the countryside, the influence of a patriarchal
      father, and the tragic execution of his older brother, and
      then turns to Lenin's early years as an impressionable
      young revolutionary. He takes issue with those biographers
      who depict young Lenin as cruel, conceited, and vindictive,
      but rather sees him as a mature, aggressive, and argumen-
      tative youth who, though a ruthless opponent, never con-
      descended to personal attacks on those with whom he
      argued. Throughout, Trotsky shows great admiration for
      Lenin while defending him against attacks by rivals and
      critics. [DK254.L44T79] Excerpt in Horizons, 14 (Sum-
      mer 1972), 110-15.

76a   Reviewed in:
      *Arch Eur Soc, 17 (1976), 366-83, by N. Harding.
      *Int Soc R, 34, no. 4 (1973), 38-43.
      Lib J, 97 (1972), 2182, by R. H. Johnson.
      New Rep, 167 (23 Sept. 1972), 27-30, by G. Charney.
      New Yorker, (16 Sept. 1972), 127.
      *Newsletter Comp St Com, 6, no. 4 (Aug. 1973), 30-39,
          by A. Meyer.

Rus R, 29, no. 4 (Oct. 1970), by A. Parry.
Slav R, 32, no. 4 (Dec. 1973), 816-17, by B. D. Wolfe.
TLS, 3701 (9 Feb. 1973), 144.

77 *Ulyanov, D. I. "Excerpts from the Reminiscences of Lenin,"
    in ROLBHR (anthology), 93-95, 108-33.
    Recollections, by a family member, of Lenin's teenage
    school days, play as a youth, love of chess, 1892 court
    case against a merchant (Arefyev), appreciation of music,
    and his 1900 arrest by police for violating the conditions
    of his release from Siberian exile.

78 *Ulyanova, M. I. "Excerpts from the Reminiscences of Lenin,"
    in ROLBHR (anthology), 95-107, 134-77.
    Lenin's sister Maria recollects his school years, contacts
    with Populists, work habits in the early 1890's (while
    living in Samara), and his many letters to his family, and
    in the process provides insight into Lenin's tastes, moods,
    thoughts, and relations with various people. Ulyanova
    also recounts later events in Lenin's life, most notably
    his evasion of the police hunts for him in July 1917, an
    abortive attempt on his life, and his holiday (summer
    1918) visit to the country home of V. D. Bonch-Bruyevich.

79 Ulyanova-Yelizerova, Anna. Lenin's Boyhood and Adolescence.
    Moscow: Foreign Languages Publishing House, 1955;
    37pp. [DK254. L4F382] Unavailable for annotation.
    Excerpt as "Lenin--Childhood and Youth," in L (anthology),
    133-34.

80 *_____. "Reminiscences of Ilyich," in ROLBHR (anthology),
    11-89.
    Recollections, by Lenin's sister Anna, of incidents in his
    childhood and adolescence, including his school work, re-
    jection of religion, and conversion to radicalism. Ulyano-
    va also recounts her relationship with Lenin in Kazan and
    Samara, the beginnings of his revolutionary work, his ar-
    rest and exile to Siberia, return from Siberia, and de-
    parture for Northern Europe.

81 *Valentinov, Nicolai. The Early Years of Lenin. Ann Arbor:
    University of Michigan Press, 1969; 302pp.
    A highly acclaimed, detailed account of the youth of Lenin
    and the evolution of his revolutionary thought. Valentinov,
    a one time follower of Lenin and an authority on Russian
    intellectual history, provides, in Part I of his study, in-
    sights into Lenin's childhood paying special attention to the
    sources and influences which led him to become a revo-
    lutionary. In the second and more detailed part of his
    work, Valentinov analyzes the intellectual birth of Lenin
    placing great emphasis on the impact of N. G. Chernyshev-
    sky not only on Lenin's commitment to revolution but also
    on his materialism and dialectics, hatred of bourgeois

liberalism, and his belief that the end justifies the means. Throughout, the author delves into the temperament and personality of Lenin, isolates his principal characteristics, and in the process sketches a complex psychological portrait of him.

81a   Reviewed in:
      *Can Am S S, 6, no. 1 (1972), 120-27, by R. H. Theen.
      Can S S, (Spring 1971), 130, by J. Keep.
      Encounter, 40, no. 4 (Apr. 1973), by L. Schapiro.
      Lib J Bk R, (1969), 161, by O. Ivsky.
      Mich Q R, (Winter 1972), 60, by W. Zimmerman.
      *Rus R, 29, no. 4 (Oct. 1970), 457-63, by A. Parry.
      Slav R, 29 (Dec. 1970), 700, by E. Mickiewicz.

82   Veretnnikov, N. "Choosing a Profession," in OL (anthology), 32-33.
      A brief account, by a boyhood friend, of Lenin's decision to study law at Kazan University. Excerpt from Volodya Ulyanov. Moscow: Foreign Languages Publishing House, 51-60.

83   *Wilson, Edmund. "Lenin: The Brothers Ulyanov," in To the Finland Station. A Study in the Writing and Acting of History. Garden City: Doubleday, 1953; 347-71.
      A scholarly examination of Lenin's life up to the age of 23. Wilson describes the personal and intellectual qualities of Lenin's parents, brothers and sisters (especially Alexander and Olga), stressing their industry, austere and orderly life style, and passion for learning. He presents Lenin as an intelligent, spirited and sensitive youth, greatly influenced by the deaths of his father, brother Alexander, and sister Olga. The chapter concludes with an account of Lenin's turn to Marxism and his very first radical activities, with parallels drawn to Chekhov's Ward No. 6. [HX36.W5]

2. Adulthood

84   "An Acquaintance of Lenin's," in LCAM (anthology), 191-93.
      A story, published in Pravda after Lenin's death, illustrating how he personally touched the lives of many common people.

85   Aleyev, Y. "The Elder," in LCAM (anthology), 123-24.
      A brief recollection, by Lenin's aide, of a visit by four peasants from Kostroma, who were impressed by his simple life and concern for their welfare.

86   Alikin, S. N. "Modesty that Came from the Inmost Heart," in LCAM (anthology), 118-19.
      Recollections, by a bodyguard, of Lenin's modesty and how Lenin had all gifts he received sent to homes and hospitals for children and the elderly.

87   *Armand, Inna. "My Memories of Lenin," Sov Lit, no. 3
      (1970), 97-106.
      The daughter of Inessa Armand reminisces on the 1920-
      1922 assistance provided to her, following the death of
      her mother, by Lenin and Krupskaya.

88   "The Attempt on Lenin's Life," Rus Info R, no. 5 (2 Feb.
      1924), 69.
      An eyewitness account of the August 1918 Kaplan assas-
      sination attempt.

89   Avasthi, Ramashankar. "An Intrepid Speaker," in LHIII (An-
      thology), 63.
      A note on Lenin's ability to move an audience.

90   Bagotsky, S. J. "In Cracow and Poronin," in NBPA (anthol-
      ogy), 62-67.
      An account of visits with Lenin and Krupskaya while they
      were in Poland. Bagotsky recounts their love of chess,
      skating, mountain climbing, and Lenin's devotion to his work.

91   Barry, William. "Anatomy of a Bolshevik," N Cent, 85 (May
      1919), 845-61.
      A highly negative assessment of Lenin's theory, character,
      and accomplishments.

92   *Basevi, W. A. F. "Lenin: A Silhouette," Forum, 65 (Apr.
      1921), 379-91.
      A critical evaluation of Lenin as a man driven by both
      personal ambition and an intense hatred of the bourgeoisie.

93   Baturin, P. T. "Unassuming and Warm-Hearted," in LCAM
      (anthology), 140-42.
      A reminiscence, by a member of the Red Guard, of
      Lenin's unassuming manner and concern for others.

94   Bedenkoff, Alexander. "Lenin Wept One Christmas Eve,"
      America, 56 (26 Dec. 1936), 271-72.
      A description of a Christmas eve 1904 secret meeting of
      Bolshevik leaders at the home of Leonid Krassin (the source
      of the account) where Lenin insisted that they cut down
      and decorate a fir-tree. Lenin tearfully recollected his
      happy childhood Christmases and compared them to his
      miserable existence as a hunted revolutionary.

95   *Bell, Daniel. "Ten Theories in Search of Reality: Kto-Koyo--
      the Id and Ego of Bolshevism" in The End of Ideology.
      New York: Free Press, 1967; 326-37.
      An analysis of Nathan Leites book, The Operational Code
      of the Politburo, with much insight into Lenin's psycho-
      logical make-up. [HN57.B45]

96   Bezymensky, Alexander. "Memories of Lenin," New Times,
      16 (21 Apr. 1970), 16-18.
      A recollection of Lenin's qualities as a speaker, 1918-1920.

97   Bhide, Ramkrishna G.   "Man of Simple Habits," in LHIII
      (anthology), 67.

98   *Bradford, Gamaliel.   "The World as Idea: Nikolai Lenin,"
      in The Quick and the Dead.   Port Washington: Kennikat,
      1969 (reprint of a 1931 publication), 149-84.
      A study of Lenin's "soul" based upon what the author
      terms "psychographic methodology."   Bradford character-
      izes Lenin as a classic example of a "doer," meaning a
      man possessed of "astonishing readiness to accept re-
      sponsibility and make critical decisions, a passion for
      dealing with men and the methods of controlling them."
      Such traits made Lenin a formidable revolutionary and
      dynamic leader: "Lenin liked the responsibility for the
      welfare and the ill-fare of others which to more timid
      souls is simply intolerable."   Obsessed by the notion of
      reshaping Russia in an ideal mold, Lenin was a driven
      man with utter contempt for all obstacles, a contention
      the author supports with examples of Lenin's unscupulous
      use of any means that would advance his cause.   Brad-
      ford concludes with an examination of Lenin's private life
      demonstrating how Lenin crushed and uprooted the per-
      sonal side of his life in service of an ideal cause.
      [CT120. B65]

99   Brishkina, S. B.   "Comradely Solicitude," in LCAM (anthol-
      ogy), 153-54.
      Examples of Lenin's solicitude for others by a staff mem-
      ber of the Secretariat of the Council of People's Com-
      missars.

100   Bruk, Michael.   "He Talked to Lenin," Sov Life, 4, no. 103
      (Apr. 1965), 9.
      A report on Lenin's 1921 interview with Dr. A. Hammer.

101   *Bryant, Louise.   "Lenin and His Subordinates," in Mirrors
      of Moscow.   New York: Seltzer, 1923; 3-22.
      A positive assessment, based on the author's first-hand
      experience, of Lenin's personality, character, and leader-
      ship.   Bryant states that Lenin impressed her most be-
      cause of his flawless personal conduct and composed,
      authoritative manner.   She states that while others (Chi-
      cherin, Trotsky) hesitated or lost their composure, Lenin
      always remained calm in energetic pursuit of his goal.
      She recollects his great interest in America, his lack
      of revenge towards political enemies and opponents, se-
      lection of subordinates, lack of vanity, and close relation
      with his wife who Bryant claims had been a tremendous,
      positive influence on his life.   [DK265. B75] Excerpt as
      "My Acquaintance with Lenin," in LIOUS (anthology), 71-
      73.

102   Buck, Tim.   "Audacity: Your Name Was Lenin,"

in Lenin and Canada. His Influence on Canadian Political Life. Toronto: Progress Books, 1970; 127-133.
A discussion of Lenin's personal audacity as resulting from the confidence he gained from minute study of any issue prior to determining a course of action. Buck also states that Lenin's practical application of Marxist principles is an example of his intellectual audacity. [HX102.B8] Excerpt in Com V, 2, no. 2 (Mar.-Apr. 1970), 11-15.

103   Carr. A. "When Lenin Lived in London," Millgate, (Apr. 1936), 381-82.

104   Cash, Anthony. Lenin. London: Jacdaw Publishers, 1972.
A collection of documents and writings by and about Lenin designed for use by secondary school students. [DK254.L45C37 1972]

105   Dmitriev, V. "Lenin's Memory Revered Here," Sov Mil R, no. 8 (Aug. 1969), 13-16.
An account of the high regard for Lenin in places where he stayed while in exile (Geneva, Paris, Cracow, London).

106   Dolzhenko, D. M. "An Episode," in LCAM (anthology), 161-63.
An account of how Lenin took time out from his busy routine to provide clothes for a comrade recently returned from captivity.

107   Drabkina, Y. "Alyosha Kalenov's Drawings," in AL (anthology), 135-44.
A recollection, by a Soviet writer, of Lenin's reaction to a series of drawings done by a 12-year-old boy living in an impoverished district of Petrograd, and how Lenin made arrangements to move the boy and his family to a luxurious home vacated by a Russian emigré.

108   Essen, M. "In Geneva, II," in NBPA (anthology), 60-61.
A brief recollection of Lenin's physical strength, love of exercise, and single-mindedness when faced with a problem.

109   Farner, K. Where Lenin Lived in Switzerland. Moscow, 1957.
Unavailable for annotation.

110   "Fate of Dora Kaplan," Newsweek, 53 (4 May 1959), 36+.

111   Fiertz, Gertrude B. "We Rented to the Lenins," Partisan R, 6, no. 3 (Spring 1939), 26-28.
Reminiscences, by the Swiss cobbler who rented to the Lenins' in Zurich in 1917, of the Lenins' domestic life habits.

112 *Fotiyeva, Lidiya A. Pages from Lenin's Life. Moscow:
Foreign Languages Publishing House, 1960; 195pp.
A series of reminiscences, by Lenin's personal secretary, on Lenin's activities in exile in Geneva and Paris,
and, especially, on his daily work as leader of the Soviet
state. Fotiyeva's recollections of Lenin in exile are
relatively brief and mostly concern inner party matters
and his personal habits. She presents a great deal of
information on the content, extent, and routine of Lenin's
work in the March 1918 to March 1923 period, when she
served as a personal secretary, with separate sections
on "Lenin's Working Day," "Lenin's Office in the Kremlin," "Attempt on Lenin's Life (30 August 1918)," and
"Lenin the Agitator." Fotiyeva organizes the remainder
of her recollections under chronological headings (March-
May 1918 and October 1922-March 1923) in which she
discusses, respectively, Lenin's first month's work through
the Council of People's Commissars and his continuation
of work under the strain of his failing health. In this
last six-month period, her stated aim "was to describe
V. I. Lenin's work of that period day by day with no
omissions, if possible" except for those days when ill
health prevented him from working at all.
[DK254. L4F5713] Excerpts as: "Lenin's Study in the
Kremlin," USSR, no. 1 (Aug. 1956), 19-20; "Thoughtfulness for the Needs of Others" in LCAM (anthology), 115-
18; "The Way He Worked," Sov Life, 1, no. 160 (Jan.
1970), 24-25+; and "The Way Lenin Worked" in OL (anthology), 130-36.

113 "Four Rare Photographs," Sov Life, no. 4 (Apr. 1970), 30-
37.

114 Gandhi, Mahatma. "Noble Examples of Renunciation," in
LHIII (anthology), 3.
A brief statement on Lenin's selflessness and dedication.

115 Ghil, S. "Attempt on Lenin's Life," in AL (anthology), 145-
56.
An account, by Lenin's chauffeur of six years (1917-
1924), of the 30 August 1918 attempt on Lenin's life by the
Socialist Revolutionary Fanny Kaplan.

116 Gil, S. K. "Lenin Robbed," in NBPA (anthology), 90-93.
An account of how, in January 1919, Lenin, his sister-
in-law, and his driver were held up at gun point.

117 Goldman, Emma. The Truth about the Bolsheviks. New
York: Mother Jones Publishing Association, 1918; 12pp.
Lenin is not the focus of this pamphlet, but as an attempt
to "dispell the attitude of dense ignorance and stupidity
toward the Bolsheviks" it presents a sympathetic account
of his character, accomplishments, and goals.

118   Goldstick, Danny. "Lenin on Truth and Duty," Com V, 3,
            no. 3 (1971), 36-44.

119   Gopner, Serafina. "Lenin in Paris," in Sov Life, 9, no.
            156 (Sept. 1969), 46-48.
            Reminiscences on Lenin's life and character while in
            exile in Paris.

120   Gorki, Maxim. "Lenin the Man," Nation, 119 (26 Nov. 1924),
            584-85.
            Excerpts from Gorky's article on Lenin published in a
            German magazine.

121   Gorky, Maxim. "Maxim Gorky on Lenin," Contemp R, 118,
            no. 158 (Nov. 1920), 728-33.
            A reprint of Gorky's appreciations of Lenin published in
            l'Humanité. Gorky depicts Lenin as the "source of en-
            ergy" without which the Russian Revolution would have
            been much different, and characterizes him as simple,
            fearless, politically astute, and a humanitarian at heart.

122   *_____. "Prophet of Bolshevism," Liv Age, 307 (9 Oct.
            1920), 69-73.
            A brief and favorable assessment of Lenin's accomplish-
            ments.

123   _____. "V. I. Lenin," Int Lit, no. 2 (Jan. 1939), 53-67.
            Recollections of Lenin's great interest in and appeal to
            workers, his relations with Plekhanov and Bogdanov, and
            his love of music.

124   *Greenberg, H. "Lenin--Portrait of a Bolshevik," in Jewish
            Frontier Anthology, 1934-1944. New York: Jewish Fron-
            tier Association, 1945; 523-31.
            A discussion of Lenin's asceticism and denial of the spiri-
            tual and artistic side of his personality. Greenberg cri-
            ticizes Lenin for being so possessed by a compulsive de-
            sire to help people that he would destroy entire classes
            in unemotional pursuit of his goal. [DS149.J3]

125   Gryaznov, Alexei. "Where He Worked," Sov Life, 2, no.
            161 (Feb. 1970), 46-47.
            A description of Lenin's apartment in the Kremlin.

126   Herrick, William. "On Handel's 292nd Birthday. A Letter
            to Lenin," New Leader, 60 (28 Mar. 1977), 10-11.
            A humorous note to Lenin juxtaposing his somber realism
            to the loftiness of human spirit as embodied in music.

127   Ivanov, A. V. "In Lenin's Own Hand," in LCAM (anthology),
            137-40.
            A recollection of Lenin's assistance in helping the author
            to locate the luggage which he lost in his haste to bring

to Lenin news about difficulties in the grain-producing region of Kazan.

128 *Jackson, George D. "Lenin and the Problems of Psychohistory," Can S P, 19, no. 2 (June 1977), 207-22.

129 Kamenev, L. B. and G. E. Zinoviev. Lenin. Moscow, 1920; 16pp.
Not available for annotation.

130 *Karachan, N. B. V. I. Lenin in London. Leningrad, 1969.
An account of Lenin's five stays in London (1902-1908) with most information on the April 1902 to May 1903 period. Karachan discusses Lenin's mastering of the English language, the many meetings and gatherings of workers which he attended in London's East End, his frequent walks with Krupskaya through London's suburbs, work in the British Museum, and especially activities at the three RSDLP Congresses held in London. Karachan appends a series of reminiscences of Lenin by British contemporaries. (Those reminiscences which are not part of a work already annotated have been annotated individually.) [DK254. L446K35]

131 Karpinsky, V. A. "Heart-to-Heart Chat," in LCAM (anthology), 179-80.
A recollection of Lenin's enjoyment of the reception days at the Kremlin when peasants came to seek solutions for various problems and of how the peasants warmed to his friendly concern.

132 Katayama, Sen. "With Comrade Lenin," in WHML (anthology), 11-15.
An account of the author's three meetings with Lenin, with most information on Lenin's character and his qualities as a speaker.

133 Kausakyayan, Bhadant A. "Lenin as a Man," in WLMTU (anthology), 30-35.
A presentation of quotes from Gorky's speech on Lenin's 50th birthday and an account of a meeting between Lenin and a peasant who came to get information on the land decree. Kausakyayan uses both sources to advance an image of Lenin as a selfless leader sincerely interested in the common man's happiness.

134 Kirov, S. M. "Man and Comrade," in LCAM (anthology), 109.
A brief statement praising Lenin for his warm and human qualities.

135 Kisch, Egon E. "Lenin's Furnished Room," Int Lit, no. 4 (Apr. 1943), 33-34.

A reminiscence of Lenin's leaving of his Zurich flat for
Russia in 1917.

136   Kokorev, S. Y.   "A Man with a Great Heart," in <u>LCAM</u> (anthology), 176-77.
An army student on guard duty at the Kremlin gives examples of Lenin's concern for others.

137   Kollontai, A.   "A Giant of Spirit and Will," in <u>AL</u> (anthology),
9-11.
A brief characterization of Lenin as a representation of
all that was great about the revolutionary epoch: "steel-
willed, powerful, mercilessly destructive and stubbornly
creative in revolution."

138   Kolobyakov, A. F.   "On Guard Duty in the Kremlin," in
<u>LCAM</u> (anthology), 169-71.
Examples, by a Kremlin guard, of Lenin's attention to
the needs of others and his simple lifestyle.

139   Korichev, S. A.   "An Unforgettable Visit," in <u>LCAM</u> (anthology), 184-86.
A recollection of Lenin's assistance to the people of Chu-
vash who were suffering from food shortages.

140   Krivov, T. S.   "On Lenin's Orders," in <u>LCAM</u> (anthology),
187-88.
An account of Lenin's concern for the health of former
tsarist political prisoners and his order that they be
examined by two eminent physicians.

141   *Krupskaya, N.   "His Wife Describes Lenin," <u>Sov Life</u>, 2,
no. 161 (Feb. 1970), 44-45.
A response to a 1935 questionnaire, from the Institute
of the Brain in Moscow, on Lenin's mental and psychological reactions to various stimuli.

142   *_____.   "How Lenin Approached the Study of Marx," in
<u>LAB</u> (anthology), 137-44.
An account, by Lenin's wife, of how Lenin used Marx as
a guide or a reference for his ideas and writings.

143   *_____.   "How Lenin Studied Marx," Labour Mo, 15, no.
3 (Mar. 1933), 170-81.   An account of Lenin's consulta-
tion of the works of Marx and Engels as part of his study
of any question.

144   _____.   "Lenin as a Man," in Communist Morality, N.
Bychkova, R. Lavrov and V. Lubisheva, comps.   Moscow: Progress Publishers, n. d.; 150-52.
A brief characterization of Lenin as a man who was devoid of "petty envy, anger, revengefulness and vanity"
and who possessed great compassion (especially for com-

rades), kindness, and strength of will. Krupskaya states that successful work delighted him as did close contact with the workers he so loved.

145 * _____. "Lenin in Siberia," Liv Age, 332 (1 May 1927), 817-24.

146 _____. "Lenin on Communist Morality," in Communist Morality, N. Bychkova, R. Lavrov and V. Lubisheva, comps. Moscow: Progress Publishers, n.d.; 153-55. Lenin's wife recollects his ascetic lifestyle and his disgust with bourgeois morality. In spite of his love of music, physical exercise, and the beauty of life in general, Lenin, Krupskaya states, subordinated all of this to the struggle to improve the lot of the masses. She claims that to Lenin the essence of Communist morality was tireless work and conscious self-discipline in pursuit of the cause.

147 Krzhizhanovsky, Gleb. "About Vladimir Ilyich," Sov Lit, no. 3 (1970), 7-10.
A positive assessment of Lenin's personality, character, and work habits.

148 _____. "The Siberian Deportee," in NBPA (anthology), 49-51.
Reminiscences of Lenin's physical and spiritual strength, abundance of energy and tremendous capacity for work, all while in Siberian exile.

149 Krzhizhanovsky, G. M. et al. Recollections of Lenin. Moscow: Foreign Languages Publishing House, 1962; 95pp. Not available for annotation. Excerpt as "As We Saw Him," Sov Life, 7, no. 154 (July 1969), 28-30+.

150 *Kunetskaya, L. Lenin in the Kremlin. Moscow: Novosti Press, 1970; 72pp.
A description of Lenin's apartment and study in the Kremlin, an account of the various people who came there to visit him, and of the policy decisions which he reached while living there. Kunetskaya also examines the contents of Lenin's private library and discusses his reading tastes and the type of research he engaged in while a resident of the Kremlin. [DK254. L446K86]

151 Kunetskaya, L. and K. Mastakova. "Meetings and Discoveries," Sov Lit, no. 1 (1970), 105-14.
A tour of Lenin's study and flat in the Kremlin and an account of the books he read.

152 Kuprin, Alexander. "Lenin," Atlan Mo, no. 127 (Jan. 1921), 114-18.
A portrayal of Lenin as an intelligent, honest, realistic,

and dedicated leader devoid of emotion and willing to use any means to reach his goals.

153   Kurella, Alfred. "Humane in All Things," W Marxist R, 13, no. 6 (June 1970), 43-45.

154   Lakova-Abramova, Y. N. "Five Years with Lenin," in LCAM (anthology), 154-56.
       Reminiscences of Lenin's concern for others, by a telephone operator in his private office.

155   Larionova, A. "Ilyich's Thoughtfulness," in LCAM (anthology), 144-45.
       A brief comment, by a clerk, on Lenin's consideration for the comrades working at Lenin's office.

156   Lavrentyeva, A. N. "If People Only Knew Who the Present Was From!" in LCAM (anthology), 145-47.
       A cleaning woman at the Kremlin relates incidents showing Lenin's concern for her and other workers at the Kremlin.

157   "Lenin. A Biographical Sketch," Sov Life, 4, no. 91 (Apr. 1964), 1-4.

158   "Lenin a Great Leader of Our Age," in LHIII (anthology), 82-85.

159   "Lenin as We Knew Him," Int Lit, no. 1 (Jan. 1939), 74-83.
       A series of recollections on Lenin as a modest, concerned, and dynamic leader (1917-1921).

160   *Lenin in Profile, World Writers and Artists on Lenin. Moscow: Progress Publishers, 1975; 442pp.
       Not available for annotation.

161   "Lenin: The Man of Many Mysteries in the Plotting at Petrograd," Cur Op, 64 (Feb. 1918), 95-96.
       A discussion of Lenin's aliases and disguises while in exile, his physical appearance and personal characteristics, and qualities as a speaker; and a restatement of some of the misconceptions in biographical information on Lenin.

162   "Lenin through the Eyes of His Contemporaries," USSR, 3, no. 4 (Apr. 1960), 6-14.
       Excerpts on Lenin's personal habits and style of work from various people who knew or observed him.

163   *Lenin, V. I. Interviews Given to Foreign Correspondents. Moscow: Progress Publishers, 1970; 66pp.
       Not available for annotation. [DK266.5.L2813]

164   "Lenine: The Man and His Ideas," Cur Hist M, 7, part 2
        (Jan. 1918), 14-17.

165   "Lenin's Magnetic Spell," in LHIII (anthology), 52.
        A note praising Lenin as a speaker.

166   Lepeshinsky, P. N.   "The Sportsman," in NBPA (anthology),
        56-57.
        A recollection of Lenin's sportmanship (especially his
        love for shooting and hunting) and skill at chess.

167   Lepeshinskya, O.   "The Siberian Deportee," in NBPA (anthol-
        ogy), 52-53.
        Notes on Lenin while in exile with him in Siberia.   Le-
        peshinskya discusses Lenin's reading tastes and his rou-
        tine of physical exercise during his "rest periods" from
        work.

168   "Lovable Lenin," Time, 97 (4 May 1962), 27.
        A critique of a Pravda article on Lenin's humanitarianism
        and kindness.

169   *Lunacharsky, Anatoly V.   "Lenin," in Revolutionary Silhouet-
        tes.   New York: Hill and Wang, 1967 (translation of the
        1923 edition); 35-58.
        A 1918 account of the author's personal relations with
        and impressions of Lenin.   Lunacharsky, the first Com-
        missar for Education and long-time friend of Lenin, be-
        gins with his 1903 meeting of Lenin amidst the divisions
        within the RSDLP.   There follows a somewhat disjointed
        though illuminating series of events and episodes in Len-
        ins's life up to the October Revolution.   Throughout,
        Lunacharsky characterizes Lenin as having an extremely
        powerful will, astonishing vitality, impressive intellect,
        and incredible political insight.   [DK253.L813]

170   _____.   "Man of a New World," Sov Lit, no. 4 (1977),
        3-7.
        Lunacharsky reminisces on Lenin's personality.

171   Malkov, Pavel.   "Notes of a Kremlin Commandant (excerpts),'
        Sov Lit, no. 3 (1970), 47-54.
        Reminiscences of conversations and dealings with Lenin
        and Krupskaya during their stay at the Smolny Institute
        in Petrograd.

172.   Mann, T.   "A Man of Extraordinary Ability," in VILIL (an-
        thology), 80.
        A brief recollection of a talk with Lenin.   Mann notes
        the depth of Lenin's insight into Russian and world af-
        fairs and confidence in his ability to cope with problems.

173   *Mazlish, Bruce.   "Lenin," in The Revolutionary Ascetic.

Evolution of a Political Type. New York: Basic Books, 1976; 111-56.
A discussion of the revolutionary personality of the "ascetic type," drawing upon Max Weber's study of asceticism in service of capitalism and Sigmund Freud's analysis of leadership as possessing "few libidinal ties." Mazlish constructs a model of an ideal revolutionary who has a "displaced libido with traditional ascetic traits" and then applies it to Lenin as a "prototypic revolutionary ascetic, the closest figure in actuality to our ideal type." In the process, Mazlish analyzes Lenin's relationship with family and friends as he came to free himself from all ties, emotional and otherwise, that would diminish his ability to create and lead a revolutionary party. [D210.M34]

174   *"Men of Letters on Lenin," Int Lit, no. 1 (Jan. 1939), 68-72.
Excerpts from reminiscences of Lenin by I. Ehrenburg, F. Gladkov, and G. B. Shaw.

175   Mendelevich, Georgi. "Charles P. Steinmetz: 'I Wish You the Fullest Success,'" Sov Life, 6, no. 165 (June 1970), 12+.
A review of Steinmetz's correspondence with Lenin.

176   Meshcheryakov, Nikolai. "Excerpts from 'Reminiscences of Lenin,'" Sov Lit, no. 3 (1970), 40-46.
Reminiscences of Lenin's life in exile in London, leadership of the Bolshevik Party, and his post-1917 plan to electrify the entire nation.

177   *Mihajlov, Mihajlo. "On Responsibility. Marx and Lenin in Their Personal Lives," in Underground Notes. Kansas City: Sheed Andrews and McMeel, 1976; 37-42.
A plea for objectivity and sensitivity in the study of Lenin's personal life. Mihajlov questions Soviet interpretations that canonize Lenin as well as those which criticize him for neglecting friends and family for the sake of "the cause," and states that almost all men who have been innovators have had to choose between their goal and "caring for their families, everyday earnings, public opinion and generally accepted moral standards...." [DK276.M483]

178   Minor, Robert. "We Have Met Lenin," in LIOUS (anthology), 77-82.
An anecdotal account of Lenin's many efforts to meet and converse with foreigners.

179   Mitin, M. B. "Lenin and Humanism," St Sov Phil, 7, no. 1 (1968), 3-13.
A presentation of Lenin as a revolutionary humanist in

leading the masses to revolution and in constructing a socialist society free of oppression.

180   Moiseyev, Grigori. "Where Does the Name Lenin Come From," Sov Life, 3, no. 162 (Mar. 1970), 56-57.
A discussion of "Lenin" as a pseudonym.

181   "Mother and Son," Sov Life, 1, no. 160 (Jan. 1970), 23.
A discussion of various letters between Lenin and his mother.

182   Nagy, Jeno. "Meetings with Lenin," W Marxist R, 16, no. 8 (Aug. 1973), 119-22.
Recollections of two brief meetings with Lenin when the author served as a Kremlin sentry.

183   Nechkina, Y. A. "Recollections of a Nurse" in LCAM (anthology), 189-90.
Recollections, by the nurse who attended Lenin after the Kaplan assassination attempt, of Lenin's courage, interest in others and kindness toward her.

184   Nehru, Jawaharlal. "A Great Leader with Love and Sympathy for the Poor," in LHIII (anthology), 9-10.

185   *Ogden, Dennis. "What They Said Then," Anglo-Sov J, 30, no. 3 (Apr. 1970), 19-26.
A survey of statements in the British press on Lenin from 1917-1924.

186   Okhrimenki, P. "A Note Written by Lenin," in LCAM (anthology), 167-68.
An account of the assistance given by Lenin to a young, penniless and homeless translator who came to his attention.

187   Otsup, Pytor. "How I Photographed Lenin," Sov Life, 10, no. 157 (Oct. 1969), 34-35.

188   Ovsyannikova, K. S. "He Was Attentive to People," in LCAM (anthology), 177-78.
A reminiscence illustrating how Lenin valued and listened to what the common people said and felt.

189   Petrov, Andrei. "A Game of Chess on Capri," Sov Life, 12, no. 159 (Dec. 1969), 41.
A brief note on Lenin and Gorky playing chess on Capri.

190   _____. "Lenin in Gorki," Sov Life, 3, no. 152 (Mar. 1970), 43-46.
An account of Lenin's love for the city of Gorki and his trips there to relax and convalesce.

191 _____. "Vladimir Lenin Was Filmed by an American:
Who Was the Cameraman?" Sov Life, 7, no. 154 (July
1969), 32-33.
An account of the rediscovery in America of six photos
of Lenin taken during an interview with an American correspondent.

192 Plesums, P. P. "Recollections of a Former Red Army Man,"
in OL (anthology), 107-109.
Personal reminiscences of a private in the Lettish Re-
serve Regiment who while on guard duty at the Smolny
observed Lenin on a number of occasions. He describes
Lenin's dress, his interest in the soldiers, long work
hours, and how Lenin suffered the same privations as
every other party member.

193 Polevoi, Boris. "Lenin in Life," Sov Mil R, no. 3 (Mar.
1970), 17-20.
Examples of Lenin as a man of action, simplicity, courage, diligence, and honor.

194 Popoff, G. "Lenin's Last Speech," Liv Age, 318 (7 July
1923), 15-19.
Lenin's last speech serves as a springboard for a description of his qualities as a speaker in general.

195 R., G. K. "Life of Lenin," Illus Wk India, 91, no. 17
(n. d.), 8-13.

196 *Ransome, Arthur. "Lenin in 1919," in LMAHW (anthology),
167-87.
A series of recollections on Lenin's personality and
character as well as on such diverse subjects as his
enthusiastic reception at the 1919 Third Comintern Congress, his thoughts on the likelihood of revolution in England, and his opinion of George Bernard Shaw, Raymond
Robins, and Daniel DeLeon.

197 *Rothstein, Andrew. Lenin in Britain. London: Communist
Party Pamphlet, 1970; 32pp.
An account of Lenin's attitude toward Britain prior to
his first visit, his reasons for coming to Britain, work
at the British Museum, and his activities while living
there. Rothstein provides most information on Lenin's
role in the two RSDLP Congresses in London and on his
Iskra publications. [DK254. L446R68]

198 No entry.

199 Roy, M. N. "Nothing of a Dictator," in LHIII (anthology),
32-35.
An account of a meeting with Lenin in which Roy was

struck by Lenin's personality, finding him more "human" than he had expected.

200   Rubakin, N.   "Lenin-Ulianov--the Man and the Revolutionary," in LKAL (anthology), 53-54.
A brief description of Lenin's character stressing his being a man of emotional extremes (intense hatred for the bourgeois society and intense love for those close to him) who was totally dedicated to and confident in his cause.

201   Salvadori, M.   "History Lesson; Letter," National R, 22 (14 July 1970), 721.
A brief attack on a Manchester Guardian article for presenting Lenin as a humane leader.

202   Semashko, N. A.   "Lenin and Children," in LCAM (anthology), 112-14.
A discussion of Lenin's love for children and the policies he instituted for their education, protection, and general welfare.

203   _____.   "Lenin's Concern for People," in LCAM (anthology), 109-12.   Recollections, by the People's Commissar of Health, of instances when Lenin showed sympathy for or assisted strangers and friends alike.

204   Serafimovich, Alexander.   "A Visit to Lenin," Sov Life, 12, no. 159 (Dec. 1969), 40.

205   Shaginyan, Marietta.   Retracing Lenin's Steps.   Moscow: Progress Publishers, 1974; 224pp.
A collection of four articles (originally published in the Soviet press) which "retrace Lenin's steps" as an exile by discussing his stays in a number of European countries, concentrating on France, Britain, and Italy.   The author describes her search in these countries for any information dealing with Lenin's visits, contacts, and residences, and notes consistently the high regard and warm feelings toward him in the many places she visited. [DK254. L46S4813]

206   Shulzhenko, I.   "In the Kremlin," in LCAM (anthology), 171-72.
Examples of Lenin's concern and kindness toward others as told by an army student on guard duty at the Kremlin.

207   Stalin, J.   "Notes," in SOL (anthology), 23-26.
A September 15, 1922 Pravda article in which Stalin give his impression of Lenin's "doctor's orders" vacation. Stalin describes Lenin's initial thirst for information and a nervous craving for work giving way to renewed vigor,

calm, and self-assurance, and cool-headed assessment of Russia's present condition.

208   "Stalin's Memories of Lenin," USSR Info B, (22 Jan. 1947), 6-7.

209   Stasova, E. D. "Care for Comrades," in LCAM (anthology), 115.
A brief account of Lenin's concern for his "comrades" and his attention to even the smallest detail of their welfare.

210   _____. "Teacher and Friend," in ROL (anthology), 73-80.
A recollection of Lenin's interest in recruiting young workers for the revolutionary movement, and of his modesty and comradely concern for the welfare of his fellow Bolsheviks. Stasova also describes Lenin's skills as an orator as demonstrated at the 1905 Party Congress.

211   Subbotina, Z., et al. Lenin--Great and Human. Moscow: Progress Publishers, 1970; 162pp.
This book "deals with the memorable places in the Kremlin associated with Lenin, tells of the creation of the museum and the stories behind its various exhibits. Drawing on a wealth of documentary material, the reminiscences of veteran Communists and visitors to the museum, they describe some of Lenin's work methods, his close contact with the masses and his family style."
[DK254. L4S8613]

212   No entry.

213   Sukhotin, Yakov. "Ulyanov Is Charged with the Defense," Sov Life, 1, no. 160 (Jan. 1970), 23.
A brief account of Lenin as a lawyer.

214   Takho-Godi, A. A. "Daghestan Bolsheviks Visit Lenin," in LCAM (anthology), 180-83.
An account of a visit to Lenin by three peasants from Daghestan during which he showed interest in the welfare of the people and political climate of the countryside.

215   Thomson, Carl. Lenin Visits Denmark. Copenhagen: Royal Library, 1970; 18pp.
A pamphlet on Lenin's stays in Denmark, his interest in various Danish affairs and, especially, his activities at the 1907 RSDLP Congress. [DK254. L446T47]

216   *Trotsky, Leon. "Vladimir Ilyich Lenin," in Portraits. Political and Personal. New York: Pathfinder Press, 1977; 48-54.
A description of the leading features of Lenin's speaking

style. Trotsky discusses Lenin's appearance as a speaker, the sense of purposefulness he always projected, the clearness of his thought in spite of elaborate sentence structure, his mastery of polemics, and strategic sense of humor. [HX23.T74] Originally "Lenin on the Platform," in Socialist Appeal., (25 Jan. 1941).

217 "Two Adverse Opinions," in LMAHW (anthology), 196-97.
Two brief critical opinions of Lenin, one by John Spargo charging Lenin with being totally unscrupulous, and the other by Princess Radziwill asserting that personal ambition and desire for wealth motivated him.

218 Ulyanova-Elizarova, Anna. "Vladimir Ilyich Lenin," in Makers of the Russian Revolution. Biographies of Bolshevik Leaders, Haupt, Georges and Jean-Jacques Marie, eds. Ithaca: Cornell University Press, 1974; 48-64.
A general biography of Lenin, by his sister Anna, which, to quote the editors, "is considered by most Lenin biographers to be a useful source for the study of the milieu in which the leader spent his youth, in which he was shaped and took his first revolutionary steps" but "inadequate on and gives no insight into Lenin's development on the ripening of his theoretical views in the 1917 Revolution and after the establishment of Soviet power." [HX313.H3613 1974a]

219 Usmani, Shaukat. "Visit to the Kremlin," in LHIII (anthology), 115.
A brief anecdote on Lenin describing him as self-sacrificing.

220 Vaillant-Couturier, Paul. "Memories of Lenin," in Int Lit, nos 4-5 (Apr.-May 1940), 78-80.
A recollection of a 1921 meeting with Lenin. The author describes Lenin's appearance, capacity for work, and identity with workers.

221 *Vinogradskaya, S. "Anniversary," in AL (anthology), 203-21.
A recollection, by the assistant to Lenin's sister, of an anniversary party held on the occasion of Lenin's 50th birthday. Vinogradskaya remembers Lenin's opposition to such affairs and then recounts the eulogies and festivities of that evening.

222 Vorontsova, N. N. "When I Am Downhearted I Think of Him," in LCAM (anthology), 128-31.
A reminiscence of Lenin, by a waitress at the CPC dining room, who originally felt he was the anti-Christ but changed her opinion after seeing his kindness and concern for others.

223 Vorovsky, V. "V. I. Ulyanov-Lenin," in AL (anthology),
    17-22.
    A recollection of Lenin's "tremendous power of thought,
    strength of will and depth of feeling" as well as his
    blending of theory and historical reality to give him "an
    astonishing gift of political foresight."

224 Ward, Harry F. "The Lenin Spirit," in LIOUS (anthology),
    86-91.
    A January 1945 address, to a Lenin memorial meeting,
    stressing Lenin's concern for and fraternization with
    workers.

225 *Weinstein, Fred and Gerald Platt. "The Coming Crisis in
    Psychohistory," J Mod Hist, 47, no. 2 (1975), 202-28.
    In part, an assessment of Wolfenstein's psychoanalysis
    of Lenin.

226 Weisbrod, B. S. "Constant Consideration for Others," in
    LCAM (anthology), 131-33.
    Lenin's physician discusses the compassion shown by
    Lenin for his comrades and for children.

227 "Where Lenin Lived and Worked," Sov Mil R, no. 4 (Apr.
    1970), 38-39.
    A description of Lenin's Kremlin study.

228 White, William C. "Lenin the Individual," Scrib M, 95
    (Mar. 1934), 183-88.
    A general introduction to Lenin's life and work.

229 "Who and What is Lenine?" Outlook, 117 (19 Dec. 1917),
    630.
    Early speculation both on Lenin as a leader and on the
    longevity of his regime.

230 Williams, Albert Rhys. "Biographical Sketch," in LMAHW
    (anthology), 23-39.
    A general, non-interpretive survey of the leading events
    in Lenin's life up to his April 1917 return to Russia
    from Swiss exile. Williams presents most information
    on Lenin's life before 1905. This section was designed
    to serve as an introduction to precede recollections of
    the author's personal contacts with him in 1917.

231 Williams, S. "DeFilippi and Lenin," Art A, 8, no. 6 (Sept.
    1973), 18-21.
    A description of DeFilippi's (1908-1922) paintings of
    Lenin.

232 *Wolfenstein, E. Victor. "Lenin: Revolution Equals Death,"
    in Violence or Nonviolence: A Psychoanalytic Explora-

tion of the Choice of Political Means in Social Change. Princeton: Center of International Studies, 1965; 31-40. An analysis of Lenin's personality as a source of his commitment to violence as a means of social change. Wolfenstein examines the psychological impact of the death of Lenin's father and older brother and argues that Lenin's close identity with these two individuals and his feelings of guilt over their deaths led him to the revolutionary movement, Marxism, and the acceptance of violence as a legitimate means of change. Wolfenstein states that the fact that "Lenin found it necessary to justify the use of force in terms of the Marxist goal of a classless society" indicated that he never fully resolved his feelings of guilt. [HM281.W65]

233   "Workers on Lenin," in AL (anthology), 181-91.
       A series of five short recollections by common workers who met Lenin. Collectively they provide some insight into the impression Lenin frequently made on people.

234   *Woytinsky, W. S. "Lenin," in Stormy Passage. A Personal History through Two Russian Revolutions to Democracy and Freedom: 1905-1960. New York: Vanguard Press, 1961; 118-23.
       A recollection of a series of evening meetings with Lenin and Krupskaya in the 1906-1907 period. Woytinsky describes Lenin as a "complex personality, given to sudden changes in mood, manners, and relations with persons around him," and as a cold fanatic, ruthless in polemics, and thoroughly convinced that his ideas represented absolute truth. Although Woytinsky disagreed with Lenin's Marxism, he respected his "revolutionary temperament, strong will, and resourcefulness." [DK246.W63]

235   Wyzlemblo, Marcin. "Was Lenin's Mother Jewish?" Dissent, 28 (Apr. 1971), 141-44.

236   Yeryomin, Mikhail. "The Story behind Three Lenin Photographs," Sov Life, 1, no. 160 (Jan. 1970), 20-22.
       An account of the circumstances surrounding three previously unidentified photos of Lenin.

237   Zaichikov, Vasili. "Lenin as Others Saw Him," Sov Life, 3, no. 162 (Mar. 1970), 9-11.
       A review of comments on Lenin's personality and character by various people.

238   Zetkin, Clara. "Lenin and the Masses," P Star, 4, no. 33 (Apr. 1970), 9-10.
       Reminiscences of Lenin's sincere concern for the interests of the common man.

239   Zholtovsky, I. V. "In 1918," in LCAM (anthology), 133-36.

An architect's recollection of Lenin's concern for the welfare of others and ideas on the reconstruction of Moscow.

240 Zinoviev, G. "Lenin and the Worker," Labour Mo, 6 (May 1924), 271-75.
A restatement of Lenin's hope to incorporate more workers into the party once they were educated. Zinoviev also discusses Lenin's complete identity with the workers' interests and lifestyle.

241 _____. "Lenin as a Nature Lover," New Rus, 1, no. 7 (16 Dec. 1922), 199-200.

3. Death

242 Arosev, A. "Vladimir Ilich Ulianov (Lenin)," Rus Info R, 4, no. 4 (26 Jan. 1924), 53.
A general review of the affection and admiration expressed for Lenin upon his death.

243 *Averbakh, Mikhail. "Personal Memories of Lenin," Labour Mo, 52, no. 4 (Apr. 1970), 185-89.
An account of how Lenin reacted to the deterioration of his health.

244 Bjerre, P. "Lenin's Illness," Liv Age, 217 (26 May 1923), 457-59.

245 *Crome, L. "Illness and Death," Anglo-Sov J, 30, no. 3 (Apr. 1970), 26-43.
A medical assessment of Lenin's long illness and death.

246 "Doubts about Lenin's Reported Illness," in LHIII (anthology), 72.
An April 12, 1923 report instructing readers to take the news of Lenin's "supposed illness with caution" since so many other reports of his death or illness had been false.

247 *Ede, William R. "Trotsky and Lenin in the 'Skin of Malice,' The Vessel of Stone," Texas Q, 15, no. 2 (1972), 98-120.
Speculation that Lenin's dogmatic and amoralistic qualities may have been due to arteriosclerotic dementia.

248 Foerster, O. "Lenin's Last Illness," Liv Age, 321 (5 Apr. 1924), 647-50.

249 "Funeral Services at Lenin's Burial," in LHIII (anthology), 80.

250 Kamenev, L. "With Lenin in Convalescence," Rus Info R, 3, no. 2 (14 Oct. 1922), 30.

251 *Klemperer, Dr. George. "A Physician's View of Lenin,"
     in LIOUS (anthology), 61-62.
     A description of Lenin's health and personality by a Ber-
     lin physician who was called in as a consultant when
     Lenin became ill in 1922.

252 Koltzov, Michael. "The Last Journey," Rus Info R, 4, no.
     6 (9 Feb. 1924), 85-86.
     An account of Lenin's funeral.

253 "Lenin Is Dead," in LHIII (anthology), 81.

254 "Lenin's Death," Rus Info R, 4, no. 4 (26 Jan. 1924), 50,
     52.

255 "Lenin's Funeral," Rus Info R, 4, no. 5 (2 Feb. 1924), 68-
     69.

256 "Lenin's Grave," Rus Info R, 4, no. 7 (16 Feb. 1924), 110.
     A description of the scene at Lenin's burial.

257 "Lenin's Health," Rus Infor R, 1, no. 19 (1 July 1922), 434.

258 "Lenin's Health," Rus Info R, 1, no. 22 (15 Aug. 1922), 506.

259 "Lenin's Health," Rus Info R, 2, no. 16 (20 Jan. 1923).

260 "Lenin's Health," Rus Info R, 3, no. 11 (15 Sept. 1923), 162-
     163.

261 "Lenin's Health," Rus Info R, 3, no. 15 (13 Oct. 1923), 227.

262 "Lenin's Health; Official Statement," Rus Info R, 2, no. 24
     (17 Mar. 1923), 371.

263 "Lenin's Health; Question of Replacement," Rus Info R, 2,
     no. 25 (24 Mar. 1923), 386.

264 "Lenin's Long Illness," Rus Info R, 4, no. 5 (2 Feb. 1924),
     67.

265 "Nikolai Lenin's Death Reported," in LHIII (anthology), 77.

266 Orloff, Vladimir. "Lenin's Corpse," in The Secret Dossier.
     My Memoirs of Russia's Political Underworld. London:
     George Harrap, 1932; 198-201.
     A charge that Lenin's body decomposed with abnormal
     rapidity and that a professor of anatomy from the Uni-
     versity of Kharkov grafted to Lenin's body fresh parts
     from the body of a recently deceased Red Army soldier
     so that the embalmed Lenin would appear whole.
     [DK254. 07A3]

267   Pollitt, H.   "Lenin's Death," in <u>VILIL</u> (anthology), 82-86.
       Details of Lenin's funeral and the depth of national sorrow.

268   "Report of Lenin's Death Confirmed," in <u>LHIII</u> (anthology),
       78.

269   *Rozanov, Vladimir.   "Reminiscences of Lenin," <u>Sov Lit</u>, no.
       3 (1970), 85-95.
       A description, by Lenin's surgeon, of Lenin's illness
       and frame of mind in the months prior to his death.

C. <u>Assessments</u>

1. Upon Death

270   Artzybasheff, Mikhail P. "The Death of Lenin," <u>Fortn R</u>,
         121 (June 1924), 786-98.
         A negative assessment of Lenin as a destructive and
         criminal thinker who failed to contribute to true progress.

271   Bailey, Herbert. "Passing of Lenin," <u>Fortn R</u>, 121 (Mar.
         1924), 370-80.
         A highly critical appraisal of Lenin's life and work.

272   "Bengali Press on Lenin's Death," in <u>LHIII</u> (anthology), 103-
         06.
         Excerpts from Bengali reactions to Lenin's death.

273   *Bernstein, Herman. "The Passing of Lenin. Cynic and Un-
         scrupulous Opportunist," <u>Cur Hist F</u>, 19, no. 6 (Mar.
         1924), 1017-21.

274   Bukharin, N. "Lenin's Achievement," <u>Rus Info R</u>, 4, no. 6
         (9 Feb. 1924), 83+.
         A eulogy of Lenin presented to the 2nd All Union Soviet
         Congress (26 January 1924).

275   _____. "Our Comrade Lenin," <u>Rus Info R</u>, 4, no. 16
         (19 Apr. 1924), 250.

276   *Chernov, Victor. "Lenin," in <u>Fifty Years of Foreign Affairs</u>,
         Hamilton F. Armstrong, ed. New York: Praeger Press,
         1972; 34-41.
         An assessment, by the Socialist Revolutionary leader, of
         Lenin as a revolutionary and political leader. Chernov
         presents Lenin as a man capable of greatness and ori-
         ginality within the limitations imposed by his narrow-
         minded Marxism. He states that Lenin's power as a
         public speaker, polemicist, and theoretician rested in
         his extraordinary lucidity and logic, and that his power
         as a leader stemmed from his single-mindedness, tacti-
         cal flexibility, and forceful personality. Chernov con-
         cludes that if Lenin made any major contribution to Marx-
         ism, it was in his interpretation of the dictatorship of
         the proletariat. [D443.A72] Originally in <u>For Aff</u>, 2,

no. 3 (15 Mar. 1924), 366-72; reprinted as "Lenin: A Contemporary Portrait," For Aff, 48, no. 3 (1970), 471-77. Also in The Soviet Union, 1922-1962. A Foreign Affairs Reader, Philip E. Mosely, ed. New York: Praeger Press, 1963; 26-33.

277　"Estimate of Lenin," RR, 69 (Apr. 1924), 424-25.
A review of the range of opinions on Lenin expressed in the West upon his death.

278　Evdokimov, T. "The Passing of Lenin. A Soviet Interpretation," Cur Hist F, 19, no. 6 (Mar. 1924), 1030-31.
A praiseful funeral oration.

279　Ewer, W. N. "Post Ducis Mortem," Liv Age, 320 (15 Mar. 1924), 500-02.
An argument that history will someday include Lenin among its list of great leaders.

280　"Extraordinary Personality," in LHIII (anthology), 57.

281　*Fisher, H. A. L. "Lenin," Cornhill, n. s. 56 (Mar. 1924), 257-65.
An appraisal of Lenin as a revolutionary leader emphasizing his great faith in his cause, hatred of capitalism, and tactical flexibility as the sources of his success.

282　"Forces that Made Lenin a Great Revolutionary Leader," Cur Op, 76 (Mar. 1924), 335-36.
An estimate of Lenin as a great leader because "in an extraordinary moment he could bring concentration of thought, power and means to the utmost limits."

283　"From Russia's Standpoint," Rus Info R, 4, no. 6 (9 Feb. 1924), 82-83.
A general tribute to Lenin.

284　*Hibben, Parton. "The Passing of Lenin. The Builder of a New Order," Cur Hist F, 19, no. 6 (Mar. 1924), 1021-24.

285　Hullinger, Ewin W. "Lenin, the Man--Personal Recollections," in The Reforging of Russia. New York: Dutton, 1925; 393-402.
Recollections of Lenin as a speaker, isolating three key characteristics: he spoke as a father to his children; he reduced complex, abstract principles to comprehensible, everyday language; and he always used wit and humor, usually to ridicule. Hullinger also briefly describes Lenin's personal likes and dislikes. Reprint from New York Tribune, 27 Jan. 1924. DK265.H85

286　"Indian Workers Mourn Lenin's Death," in LHIII (anthology), 91-92.

287   Krupskaya, N. K. "Lenin's Widow Speaks," Nation, 118
       (5 Mar. 1924), 268.
       The text of Krupskaya's speech at the opening of the
       2nd All Union Soviet Congress (the day before Lenin's
       funeral) in which she speaks of Lenin's love for the
       people.

288   Lal, Munshi M. "A Friend of Humanity," LHIII (anthology),
       137.

289   "Lenin," Lit D, 80 (2 Feb, 1924), 8-9.
       A review of the contradictory assessments of Lenin upon
       his death.

290   "Lenin," Nation, 118 (6 Feb. 1924), 132.
       A review of those factors on which Lenin's claim to
       greatness is based.

291   "Lenin--Greatest Man of the Age," in LHIII (anthology), 90.

292   "Lenin, Outward Bound," Independent, 112 (2 Feb. 1924), 66.
       A highly critical note on Lenin's personality and accom-
       plishments.

293   "Lenin, Russia's Peculiar New Saint," Lit D, 80 (15 Mar.
       1924), 38-44.
       A critical review of Lenin's theories, tactics, and policies
       and an attack on the eulogies of Lenin presented at his
       funeral.

294   "Lenine," Outlook, 136 (30 Jan. 1924), 170-71.
       An estimate of Lenin and his career contending that "if
       service is a measure of greatness" history will not re-
       cord Lenin among the great of Russia.

295   "Leninism," Labour Mo, 6 (Mar. 1924), 131-39.
       A positive assessment of Lenin, his work, teachings,
       and influence.

296   "Lenin's Legacy," New Sta, 22 (26 Jan. 1924), 442-43.

297   Leuwe, R. "The Machinists' Resolution," in LIOUS (anthol-
       ogy), 152-53.
       A positive assessment of Lenin issued by the International
       Association of Machinists in Seattle.

298   *Lockhart, R. H. Bruce. "Lenin, the Man and His Achieve-
       ment," Edinb R, 239 (Apr. 1924), 295-311.
       A favorable estimate of Lenin's career and policies con-
       cluding that he set Russia on a new, dynamic, and pro-
       gressive path.

299   Maclellan, W. E. "Topics of the Day," Dalhousie R, 4 (Apr.

1924), 121-24.
An estimate of Lenin as a man well-suited to deal with
the anarchy in and economic problems of Russia, but
as a ruthless, tyrannical, and totally unlikable person.

300   No entry.

301   *Martynov, A. "The Great Proletarian Leader," Com Int,
       no. 1 (1924), 29-48.

302   *Myakotin, V. "Lenin, 1870-1924," SEER, 2, no. 6 (Mar.
       1924), 465-86.
       A critical appraisal of Lenin arguing that his thought was
       neither profound nor scholarly but rather was purely
       mechanical, and that his mastery of the technique of re-
       volution and fanatic drive largely account for his success
       and Russia's catastrophe.

303   "On His Death--Press Comments," in IAL (anthology), 48-50.
       Five statements made in the Indian press paying tribute
       to Lenin upon his death.

304   "Passing of a World Figure," in LHIII (anthology), 78-79.

305   Popoff, George. "Rasputin of Radicalism," Liv Age 320 (25
       Mar. 1924), 495-500.
       A presentation of Lenin and Rasputin as clever charlatans
       and Asiatic in spirit whose activities led to the destruc-
       tion of Russia's greatness.

306   *Price, M. P. "Lenin," Labour Mo, 6 (Mar. 1924), 158-65.
       A discussion of Lenin's greatness as being a result of
       his willingness to adapt thought and action to his environ-
       ment rather than trying to force history into a dogmatic mold.

307   *Radek, Karl. "The Passing of Lenin. Master of Realistic
       Thought," Cur Hist F, 19, no. 6 (Mar. 1924), 1026-30.

308   Russell, Bertrand. "To the Memory of Lenin: An Impres-
       sion," New Leader, (25 Jan. 1924), 3+.

309   Rykov, A. I. "Lenin, Leader of the Masses," Rus Info R,
       4, no. 6 (9 Feb. 1924), 86.

310   Snowden, Mrs. Philip. "Lenin as I Knew Him," Liv Age,
       320 (15 Mar. 1924), 493-94.
       Recollections of both Lenin's positive and negative char-
       acteristics and accomplishments.

311   "Socialism of Nikolai Lenin," New Sta, 22 (2 Feb. 1924),
       472-73.

312   Sorokin, P. "The Passing of Lenin. Fanatic and Anti-Social
       Extremist," Cur Hist F, 19, no. 6 (Mar. 1924), 1013-17.

313 *Sorokin, P. and A. L. Strong. "Was Lenin a Failure? A
Debate," Forum, 71 (Apr. 1924), 417-28.
Sorokin presents Lenin as a "destroyer" responsible for
the current ills of Russia and the discrediting of Marxism; while Strong sees him as a great leader of the common man and the creator of a new and progressive Russia.

314 "South Indian Press on Lenin's Death," in LHIII (anthology),
107-10.
A review of the many positive assessments of Lenin upon
his death.

315 *Stalin J. "Lenin," in SOL (anthology), 39-52.
A 28 January 1924 speech, to a memorial meeting of
the Kremlin Military School, identifying Lenin's main
characteristics as a man and statesman as boldness of
thought and action, personal modesty, forcefulness of
logic, unswerving faith in the victory of the cause, fidelity
to principle, and complete dedication to the common
man. Stalin concludes that Lenin was a genius "born
for revolution." Also in Labour Mo, 16 (Jan. 1934), 25-
31.

316 *_____. "On the Death of Lenin," in SOL (anthology), 29-
36.
A 26 January 1924 speech upon Lenin's death, to the 2nd
All Union Congress of Soviets, calling for strict loyalty
to the behests of Lenin, meaning to guard the dictatorship of the proletariat, strengthen the alliance with the
peasantry, consolidate the union of the national republics,
remain faithful to the Communist International, and preserve the purity of the Communist Party. Also published
as The Lenin Heritage. New York: International Publishers, 1934; 13pp.

317 Strong, A. L. "Triumph of Lenin," Nation, 118 (13 Feb.
1924), 159-60.
An account of the love and admiration for Lenin in Russia.

318 Thalheimer, U. "Lenin as a Theoretician," Com Int, no. 1
(1924), 49-53.
A positive estimate of Lenin's contributions to Marxist
political and economic theory. Thalheimer particularly
praises Lenin's application of Marxism to Russian conditions, especially his merging of the peasant and proletarian revolutions and developing a workable dictatorship of the proletariat.

319 "To Laboring Humanity: Address at Funeral Ceremonies,"
Nation, 118 (13 Feb. 1924), 167.

320 *Trotsky, L. "The Passing of Lenin. The Russian in Lenin,"
Cur His F, 19, no. 6 (Mar. 1924), 1024-26.

321 "U. P. Press on Lenin's Death," in LHIII (anthology), 100-02.
Excerpts from some of the many favorable estimates of
Lenin which appeared in the United Provinces Indian
Press in 1924.

322 Vidyarthi, Ganesh S. "There He Sleeps--the Great Destroyer,"
in LHIII (anthology), 146-147.

323 Vrat, Dev. "The Greatness of Lenin," in LHIII (anthology),
123-25.

324 Whibley, C. "Letters of an Englishman: What Is Greatness?"
Eng R, 38 (Mar. 1924), 325-30.

325 *Williams, Ariadna. "Genius of Revolution," Contemp R, 125
(Mar. 1924), 309-18.
An appraisal of Lenin as a master of revolution and mass
psychology unable to use his powers for any creative endeavor.

326 *Zinoviev, G. "Nikolai Lenin," Com Int, no. 1 (1924), 3-28.
A Soviet eulogy of Lenin as a great man, theorist, revolutionary and leader, and an account of Lenin's funeral.

2. Since Death

327 *Abramovitch, Raphael R. "From Socialist Utopia to Totalitarian Empire," Mod R, 1, no. 4 (1947), 249-65.
A discussion of Lenin's philosophy as a utopian one, a
fact which Lenin came to realize when post-1917 Russia
and Europe failed to follow the revolutionary course he
predicted. Rather than relinquish power, Abramovitch
argues, Lenin sought to create, in a totalitarian fashion,
the type of society and world that he had naively believed
would follow the revolution.

328 Acharya, S. K. "Lenin--Architect of the New World Society,"
in LACW (anthology), 67-68.

329 Adel, Daljit Sen. "Contemporary Relevance of Lenin," in
LACW (anthology), 121-24.

330 Albjerg, V. L. "Leader of Soviet Russia," Cur Hist M, 25
(Aug. 1953), 101-06.
A discussion of Lenin's political realism as the key to his
success.

331 Andreyev, Andrei. "Lenin Will Never be Forgotten," W Marxist R, 13, no. 11 (Nov. 1970), 29-32.

332   Andropov, Y. V. "A Report at the Celebration of V. I. Lenin's Birthday," Sov Doc, 2 (11 May 1964), 3-20.

333   Archer, Jules. "Lenin," in Dictators. New York: Hawthorn Books, 1967: 18-26.
       A general assessment of Lenin's life and accomplishments. [D412.7.A7]

334   Arismendi, Rodney. "Lenin, Revolutionary Communist and Revolutionary Leader," W Marxist R, 13, no. 5 (May 1970), 92-102.

335   _____. "Leninism Gives the Key to Understanding the Modern Epoch," W Marxist R, 22, no. 3 (Mar. 1979), 31-33.

336   Avvakum. "Vladimir Ilyich Lenin, 1870-1970," Tablet, 224 (18 Apr. 1970), 373-75; 224 (25 Apr. 1970), 397-99 and 224 (2 May 1970), 421-23.

337   Ayling, S. E. "Vladimir Ilyich Lenin," in Portraits of Power. New York: Barnes and Noble, 1963; 50-71.
       A general assessment of Lenin's qualities as a revolutionary and political leader stressing that from the beginning of his career as a revolutionary, he exhibited remarkable self-confidence and unrelenting hostility to reformist groups and to revolutionaries who held views different from his own. Ayling notes the resentment within the revolutionary movement to Lenin's abrupt behavior and radical tactics and theories, but claims these same qualities gave Lenin his "fiery certainty" which enabled him to win over the Bolshevik Party to the commitment to overthrow the Provisional Government. [D412.6.A9]

338   Baidakov, V. P. "Lenin--A Born Political Leader," in LACW (anthology), 55-58.

339   Barberito, T. "Nikolai Lenin: Dedicated, but Backwards; the Work of the Sodalist," Queens Wk, 56 (Apr. 1964), 8-9.

340   Basavapubnaiah, M. "Lenin--Master Tactician of the Proletarian Class," Peo Dem, (22 Apr. 1970), 51-59.

341   "Battle over the Tomb," Time, 83 (24 Apr. 1964), 26-30.
       A general survey of Lenin's accomplishments and teachings and of rival Sino-Soviet interpretations of Leninism.

342   Berg, Helene and Pierre Hentges. "Lenin Lives On," W Marxist R, 13, no. 6 (June 1970), 3-4.

343   Bharati, Sadand. "Liveliest of the Lively," in LHIII (an-

thology), 134-36.
A positive portrayal of Lenin as a leader able to communicate simply and effectively with the masses and one with a sincere concern for their welfare.

344   Bhargava, M. B. L.   "A Redeemer of Humanity," in LHIII (anthology), 126.

345   *Box, Pelham H.   "Nikolai Lenin," in Three Master Builders and Another.   Studies in Modern Revolutionary and Liberal Leadership.   Freeport, New York: Books for Libraries Press, 1968 (reprint of a 1925 publication); 19-99.
A chronological survey of Lenin's rise to power stressing his inexhaustible energy, masterly elaborations of Marxism, and genius for journalism and polemics.   Box examines Lenin's many disputes with rival socialists in the years before 1917 before turning to an account of how Lenin was able to seize power largely due to his dynamic and aggressive leadership.   In reviewing the policies pursued by Lenin from 1917 to 1922, he asserts that Lenin was a selfless ascetic who was relentless in his assaults upon enemies but not cruel or revengeful, a man who used terror only because he fanatically believed in the righteousness of his cause, and, in the end, one who must be considered as a great revolutionary leader.   [D412.6.B6]

346   Bradford, G.   "Nikolai Lenin," Harper, 161 (July 1930), 232-42.
A positive assessment of Lenin's character and accomplishments.

347   Brezhnev, L. I.   Following Lenin's Course.   Speeches and Articles, 1972-1975.   Moscow: Progress Publishers, 1975; 582pp.
A collection of Brezhnev's articles and speeches on a wide range of subjects, with many references to Lenin, his policies and writings as a source of inspiration and justification for current Soviet policies.   [DK275.B7A513]

348   *_____.   Lenin's Cause Lives on and Triumphs.   Moscow: Novosti Press.   1970; 63pp.
An April 21, 1970 Lenin centennial report to the Central Committee of the CPSU, praising Lenin as a great theoretician and revolutionary, the builder of socialism in the Soviet Union, and a leader of and source of inspiration for the world revolutionary movement.   Brezhnev stresses Lenin's belief in the need for both the fullest development of the Soviet economy and for complete unity within the international socialist camp.   Excerpts in New Times, 17 (1970), 3-20 and Vital S, 36 (1 June 1970), 482-98.

349   Brown, Louise F. and George B. Carson Jr.   "The World of

Nikolai Lenin," in Men and Centuries of European Civilization. Freeport, New York: Books for Libraries Press, 1971 (reprint of a 1948 publication); 528-46.
A brief assessment of Lenin as a revolutionary and political leader precedes a more detailed description of the historical environment within which he functioned. The authors establish the leading characteristics of turn-of-the-century tsarist Russia, trace the growth of revolutionary discontent from 1905 to 1917, and discuss the world reaction to the Bolshevik Revolution. They also provide a brief assessment of Lenin's years in power. [D103.B77 1971]

350 Buck, Tim. "Lenin and the New Problems of Struggle for Peace, Democracy and Socialism," W Marxist R, 13, no. 7 (1970), 7-13.
An assessment of the importance of Lenin's teachings on peaceful coexistence, proletarian hegemony in revolutionary movements and the merging of the socialist and democratic movements.

351 Burles, Jean. "Loyalty to Leninism--Earnest of Victory," W Marxist R, 13, no. 2 (Feb. 1970), 48-51.

352 "Can Lenin's Communism Survive?" US News W Rep, 68 (20 Apr. 1970), 66-70.
An assessment of the problems confronting the Soviet regime which claims to be following Lenin's behests.

353 Ceausescu, Nicolae. Speech Delivered at the Festive Meeting Dedicated to the 100th Anniversary of Vladimir Ilyich Lenin's Birth. Bucharest: Romanian News Agency, 1970; 59pp.
A positive assessment of Lenin's approach to Marxism, his theories on imperialism, national liberation movements, proletarian internationalism and peaceful coexistence, and his policies in constructing socialism in the U.S.S.R. Ceausescu also praises Lenin's teachings on the guiding role of the party throughout every phase of the socialist struggle. [HX312.L43C4513]

354 *Central Committee of the CPSU (B). History of the Communist Party of the Soviet Union (Bolsheviks). Short Course. New York: International Publishers, 1939; 364pp.
A detailed, official history of the birth, evolution and practices of the CPSU in the 1893-1937 period. The editors discuss the basic landmarks in Lenin's career and present an image of him as an insightful, dynamic and dedicated leader without whom Russian Marxism would have strayed down false paths. The many disputes within the Bolshevik Party, especially in 1917, do not receive attention, whereas Lenin's polemics against var-

ious non-Bolshevik Marxist rivals are examined at length. [JN6598.K55E5 1939a]

355   Chernenko, K. "The CPSU's Leninist Tradition: Working for and with the People," W Marxist R, 22, no. 5 (May 1979), 3-15.

356   Chopra, Maya D. Lenin and the Mankind to Self-Determination. Armistar, India: New Age Book Centre, 1972; 56pp.
      A positive account of Lenin's worldwide influence as a revolutionary and a political leader. In spite of what the title suggests, there is little reference to Lenin's views on self-determination. [DK254.L4C518]

357   Churchill, Winston. "Lenin--The Grand Repudiator," in L (anthology), 145-47.
      A portrayal of Lenin as a genius at destroying but a failure as a creator. Churchill praises Lenin for his intellect, energy, and will, but depicts him as a contradictory man in personality and policy who "repudiated everything: God, king, country, morals, treaties, debts ... and the laws and customs of centuries." Excerpt from The World Crisis: The Aftermath. New York: Scribner, 1929; 63-66.

358   Clark, Claire. "Lenin the Revolutionary," Mel Hist J, no. 9 (1970), 25-29.
      A discussion of Lenin's altering of Marxism to fit Russia as the key to his many successes.

359   Coolidge, Olivia. "The Red Revolutionists. Lenin 1870-1924. Trotsky 1879-1940," in Makers of the Red Revolution. Boston: Houghton Mifflin, 1963; 28-102.
      A general survey of the career of Lenin to illustrate "the force that is behind communism, the traditions which made it, the hopes and fears that went into it, and the personalities which shaped it." Coolidge begins with Lenin's youth and traces his career as a Marxist in Russia and abroad with little concern for his theoretical works and polemics. Lenin's activities in 1917 receive more careful attention, while Coolidge only outlines his policies once in power. [DK266.C598]

360   Darby, Douglas. Lenin. Master or Monster? Belmore, Australia: News Digest International, 1970; 16pp.
      An April 17, 1970 address, at Sydney University on the occasion of the centennial of Lenin's birth, discussing Lenin as "the statesman who has had the greatest influence upon mankind." Darby states that Lenin masterminded the revolution, concluded peace with Germany, successfully fought "a dozen internal wars," established centralized control over Russia and started her on the

road to industrialization. Lenin also was a master of
statesmanship, subversion, oratory, and repression.
Darby concludes that in method, goal, and personality
Lenin was, in fact, a master mind of evil: "a self-
trained monster, he had no compunction whatever in the
annihilation of opposition whether it consisted of single
persons, groups or nations." [DK254. L4D3]

361   Davis, J. "Ten Years After; the Leaders Who Span the
Russian Revolution," Survey 57 (1 Feb. 1927), 57-76.

362   Davis, Jerome. "The Lessons to be Learned from Lenin,"
in LIOUS (anthology), 93-95.
An assessment of Lenin as a leader who greatly improved
the conditions of the pre-revolutionary Russian masses
as observed by the author in 1916 Turkestan.

363   *Dazhin, D. "A World Genius," Sov Mil R, no. 3 (Mar.
1970), 2-7.
A collection of quotes from over a score of world leaders
attesting to Lenin's greatness.

364   Deutscher, I. "E. H. Carr as Historian of Soviet Russia,"
Sov St, 6, no. 4 (Apr. 1955), 337-50.
A positive review of Carr's study of the revolution with
the exception of his presentation of Lenin. Deutscher
states that Carr underestimated the strength of Lenin's
Marxism and failed to see the differences between Lenin's
and Stalin's foreign policy and political morality.

365   Dicharov, Zakhar. "A Life Story," in LIOL (anthology),
161-75.
An account of Lenin's influence on the revolutionary life
and accomplishments of labor leader Yelizaveta Vassil-
yeva.

366   *Dobb, Maurice. "A Lecture on Lenin," in On Economic
Theory and Socialism. Collected Papers. New York:
International Publishers, 1955; 155-77.
A sympathetic survey of the standard landmarks in Lenin's career and thought, and a positive assessment of
his personality and character. Dobb stresses that Lenin
was totally lacking in affectation and personal ambition
and that his consequent ability to be a "part of the mass
and lead at the same time" goes far toward uncovering
the secret of his influence. He defends Lenin against
those critics who charge him with being an irascible
schismatic, rigid dogmatist and ruthless leader, and presents a very human image of him as a man who possessed a wealth of positive attributes and whose "negative"
qualities were not due to personal temperament but to the
demands which he made of himself and others in pursuit
of a philosophy which he firmly believed would benefit

mankind. [HB171. D695 1955a] Also in Anglo-Sov J, 30, no. 3 (Apr. 1970), 5-19 and Slav Y, 19 (1940), 34-54.

367 Drabkina, Elizaveta. "In a Thoughtful Hour," Sov Lit, no. 4 (1975), 101-02.
Reflections on Lenin's influence on Russia, the world, and the author's life as a Soviet writer.

368 Eastman, Fred. "Nicolai Lenin," in Men of Power, Volume 5. Freeport, New York: Books for Libraries Press, 1970 (reprint of a 1940 publication); 13-75.
An introduction to the standard highlights of Lenin's career as a revolutionary and a political leader. In assessing Lenin's importance, Eastman raises the question of whether the material improvements brought to Russia by Lenin and his successors are worth the loss of personal freedom which has accompanied them. Whatever the answer, he asserts, Lenin must be recognized as "a supreme example of a man motivated by a single purpose" and as one who possessed numerous admirable personal qualities. Eastman concludes "whether we like him or not, we must recognize him as a man of power." [CT104. E3]

369 *Eastman, Max. "Lenin as an Engineer of Revolution," in Marx, Lenin and the Science of Revolution. Westport, Conneticut: Hyperion, 1973 (reprint of a 1926 publication); 150-68.
An assessment of Lenin's success as a revolutionary as resting in his abandonment of Marxist metaphysics in favor of a pragmatic approach to revolution. Eastman discusses Lenin's party organization, his merging of the proletariat's struggle with that of the peasants and colonial groups, and his sharp turns in policy as being inconsistent with the philosophy of historic determinism but very effective practically. Eastman concludes that Lenin believed that he was acting in a fashion consistent with Marxism and he staged his revolution in the name of Marx, but in fact Russia was, in 1917, uniquely unripe for revolution from a Marxist metaphysical position. [HX56. E3 1973]

370 "Embodiment of Lenin's Ideas," Int Aff, 16, no. 4 (Apr. 1970), 87-97.
Excerpts from speeches at a January 1970 conference in Moscow on "The World Socialist System, The Embodiment of Lenin's Ideas."

371 "Father of Modern Russia," Life, 14 (29 Mar. 1943), 29-32.

372 Fischer, E. "Resurrection of Lenin: Under the Mausoleum, a Revolutionary Democracy," New Sta, 79 (27 Mar. 1970), 438-41.

An evaluation of Lenin as a master revolutionary whose legacy has not been adhered to by the Soviet regime. Fischer also notes Lenin's worry near death over the direction in which Russia was heading.

373 Fischer, Louis. "Lenin's Russia," in Men and Politics. An Autobiography. New York: Duell, Sloan and Pearce, 1941; 46-72.
Lenin is not the focus of this chapter, but it contains several recollections of him as a speaker as well as a discussion of the succession dilemma upon his death. Fischer also provides an assessment of Lenin's importance stating that although he was possessed of selflessness, incredible singlemindedness, and had "an uncanny faculty of seeing and doing the right thing at the right time," he was not the cause of the October Revolution but rather only the manipulator of a revolutionary set of circumstances. [D413. F5A3] Also published as a book Lenin's Russia. Bombay: Padma Publications, 1942; 47pp.

374 *Fueloep-Miller, Rene. "Lenin," in The Mind and Face of Bolshevism. An Examination of Cultural life in Soviet Russia. New York: Harper and Row, 1965 (reprint of a 1926 publication); 27-49.
An analysis of Lenin's personality and character as a leader for insights into the reasons for his political success and the limits of his vision for the future. Fueloep-Miller maintains that the foundation of Lenin's greatness as a leader rested upon his "unvarnished simplicity in manner, thought and action, characteristics which make him at once both a master of the practical side of politics and revolution and intelligible to the workers to whom he appealed." Lenin's greatness, the author asserts, is even more impressive when one considers the magnitude of the problems he faced and the smallness of the party which he commanded: "Bolshevism is entirely the achievement of Lenin, understandable only through him and possible only through him." In spite of Lenin's greatness as a revolutionary, the author states that Lenin's vision of the future was extremely utopian and it betrays an overly simplistic view of the wonder-working powers of technology amidst a nation as backward as Russia. [DK265. F785]

375 "Genius of Lenin Recalled," in LACW (anthology), 11-13.
A summary of the opening remarks at the All India Youth Seminar commemorating the 100th anniversary of Lenin's birth.

376 No entry.

377 Glezerman, G. "V. I. Lenin and the Problems of Scientific

Prevision," <u>Com V</u>, 2, no. 4 (1970), 28-38.
A positive assessment of Lenin as a scientist who saw
solutions to all social problems as a matter of explaining the past, forecasting the future and embarking on
bold practical plans.

378   *Golob, Eugene O.   "Lenin and the Revolutionary Movement,"
in <u>The "Isms": A History and Evaluation</u>.   New York:
Harper and Brothers, 1954; 319-381.
A general survey of Lenin's career as both a revolutionary and political leader.   Golob discusses the standard
highlights of Lenin's creation of the Bolshevik Party,
leadership during the years of reaction after 1905, reaction to World War I, role in the October Revolution, and
leading policies as Soviet leader, and argues that, gradually, theory became to Lenin "no more than rationaliza-
tion for deeds and misdeeds of power," a fact that was
true in 1917, and more so as Lenin accepted the realities of the position in which he found himself from 1918
onwards.   He concludes that Lenin's means undermined
his ends, and only near death did Lenin realize that his
accomplishments were not those he intended, a realization that accounts for his growing dislike of Stalin as the
representative of all that was wrong with Bolshevism.
[HB87. G6 1968]

379   Gorakh.   "Everest among Men," in <u>LHIII</u> (anthology), 97-98.

380   Goul, Roman.   "Lenin and the Gulag Archipelago," <u>Trans
Asso Rus-Am Sch</u>, 8 (1974), 35-58.
Solzhenitsyn's <u>Gulag Archipelago</u> serves as the starting
point for a scathing attack on Lenin as a tyrannical mur-
derer and the Leninites as "gangsters armed with an
ideology."   Goul criticizes Western analysts who have
"swallowed the Soviet line" on Lenin as a great leader.

381   "Great Lenin," <u>New Sta</u>, 32 (16 Mar. 1929), 722-24.

382   Grebennekov, Gennadi.   "Fifty-four Years and Immortality,"
<u>Sov Life</u>, no. 4 (Apr. 1970), 16-19.

383   Gribachov, Nikolai.   "The Loftiest Beginning," <u>P Star</u>, 4,
no. 33 (Apr. 1970), 6-8.

384   Grishin, V. V.   <u>Along the Leninist Road</u>.   Moscow: Novosti
Press, 1968; 37pp.
An April 22, 1968 report, to the Moscow City Party
Committee, commemorating the 98th birthday of Lenin
by discussing the economic and political successes of
the Soviet Union as a continuation of Lenin's policies.
Grishin deals mostly with industrial output, standard of
living, working conditions, housing construction and other
economic gains as examples of the benefits of following

Lenin's guidelines on socialist construction.
[JN6598. K7G69513]

385 *Gurian, Waldemar. "Lenin," in Bolshevism: Theory and
      Practice. New York: AMS Press, 1969 (reprint of a
      1932 publication); 189-96.
      A portrait of Lenin stressing his combination of fanatical
      devotion to "the cause" with the employment of immoral
      and inhuman methods as the source of his success. Gur-
      ian states that Lenin's Marxism was colored by his de-
      sire "to make his ideal a concrete reality" thus he com-
      bined pliant and often un-Marxist strategy with fanatical
      belief in the righteousness of his ultimate goal. Gurian
      suggests that Lenin's hatred of the system, his fanaticism
      and willingness to employ any method in pursuit of his
      goal, may be linked to the very powerful affect upon him
      of his brother's execution for taking part in a conspiracy
      against Alexander III. This study also contains many
      references to Lenin's involvement in the birth, develop-
      ment, theory, strategy, and tactics of Bolshevism both
      as a revolutionary movement and a government.
      [DK265. G846]

386 *Harden, Maximillian. "Lenin," in I Meet My Contemporaries.
      Freeport, New York: Books for Libraries Press, 1968
      (reprint of a 1925 publication); 181-216.
      An appraisal of Lenin as a revolutionary and leader of
      the Bolshevik state. Harden uses Lenin's 1922 speech
      to the 11th Party Congress as a starting point for his
      assessment stating that in it can be seen Lenin's clarity
      of thought, tremendous frankness in recognizing the short-
      comings of his regime, and his complete understanding
      of the Russian peasant. He praises Lenin for his re-
      markable leadership in the revolution: "he was not merely
      the banner, the symbol; no, he was the cause itself,"
      and for the boldness of his transformation of post-revolu-
      tionary Russia. Harden also speculates on who will suc-
      ceed Lenin as party leader. [D412. H3]

387 Harrity, Richard and Ralph G. Martin. "Lenin: The True
      Story of the Evil Genius Who Launched the Global Red
      Threat," Look, 26 (22 May 1962), 31-61.

388 Henry, Ernst. "Lenin: Traits of a Genius," Sov Life, 1,
      no. 208, (Jan. 1974), 4-5.

389 "Heritage of Lenin," Fourth Int, 6 (Jan. 1945), 3-4.

390 Hermann, Jean-Maurice. "Lenin: A Journalist's Viewpoint,"
      Mainstream, 8, no. 7 (18 Oct. 1969), 31-33.

391 *Hook, Sidney. "Lenin," in Marx and the Marxists. New
      York: Van Nostrand, 1955; 75-90.

A portrayal of Lenin as a practical politician who developed a doctrine of revolutionary organization and revolutionary will that constitutes a "far greater deviation
from the traditions of orthodox Marxism than the revisionism he so scathingly excoriated." Hook discusses in
support of this thesis Lenin's views on party organization, the party as the vanguard of the revolution, the
party's role in the dictatorship of the proletariat, and
the general amorality of Lenin's thought. Hook concludes
that "Lenin is one of the most self-deceived fanatics of
history." [HX40.H6]

392   Hunter, W. D. G. "Lenin: A Centenary Review," Can
       Forum, 50 (Apr.-May 1970), 104-07.

393   Jagan, Cheddi. "Lenin and Our Time," W Marxist R, 13,
       no. 4 (Apr. 1970), 53-58.

394   Jain, Vijender. "Lenin--The Crusader," in LACW (anthology),
       34-42.
       An overview of Lenin's life and a synopsis of his ideas
       on democracy, science and technology, youth, and social-
       ist construction.

395   Jamieson, Alan. "Vladimir Ilyich Lenin," in Leaders of the
       Twentieth Century. London: Bell and Sons, 1970; 1-28.
       A discussion of the critical role played by "great men"
       in history, with Lenin's actions in 1917-1918 as a case
       study. Jamieson presents Lenin as an exceptional com-
       bination of "a man of action" who personally took con-
       trol, after April 1917, of the revolutionary movement and
       led it to triumph, inspired victory over counter-revolution
       in the Civil War, and established the NEP and the U.S.S.R.
       as a means of placing the nation on a firm economic and
       political foundation. Jamieson concludes that Lenin dom-
       inated "all aspects of Russian life to an extent previously
       unknown in Russia and the world." [D412.7.J3]

396   Jespersen, Knud. "The Age of Leninism," W Marxist R,
       13, no. 5 (Mar 1970), 30-35.

397   Jones, Brenda. "Lenin," Sun Times M, (12 Apr. 1970),
       28-39.
       A general, centennial assessment of Lenin's life and
       work.

398   Khadilkar, R. K. "Genius of Lenin," in LACW (anthology),
       21-23.
       A portrayal of Lenin as a genius at transforming philosoph-
       ical thought into practical action.

399   Khan, Abdul G. "Great and Noble Revolutionary," in LHIII
       (anthology), 23.

400   King, Beatrice. "Lenin Lives," Anglo-Sov J, 3, no. 1 (Jan.
       1942), 8-16.
       A review of Lenin's accomplishments so the West can
       see why Russians look to Lenin as a source of inspira-
       tion for Soviet military victories over the Nazis.

401   Krukhmalev, Alexander. "Tribunes of the Revolution: Lenin
       and Ideals," Sov Lit, no. 6 (June 1975), 2-3.

402   *"Lenin," Cult Life, 4 (Apr. 1970).
       This issue of Culture and Life is devoted to Lenin and
       pays tribute to him as a great man, philosopher and
       leader.   The articles consist of very brief reminiscences,
       testimonials and reflections on Lenin and his legacy.

403   "Lenin; Communism's Charter Myth," Time, 95 (27 Apr.
       1970), 34-35.
       A discussion of Lenin as a source of legitimacy for Soviet
       rule by terror, terror which Lenin himself used.

404   "Lenin 1870-1924," Peo Dem, (22 Apr. 1970), 69-90.

405   "Lenin, Leninism and the Modern World," Sov Life, 4, no.
       151 (Apr. 1960), 2-5.

406   *"Lenin, Scourge of Prophet? Symposium," Forum, 71 (May
       1924), 692-98.
       Short excerpts from statements by scores of individuals
       with widely ranging views on Lenin's character, thought,
       accomplishments and influence.

407   "Leninism Is Our Guide," W Marxist R, 13, no. 5 (May
       1970), 67-69.

408   "Lenin's Contribution to the Development of Society," Sov
       Life, 11, no. 170 (Nov. 1970), 47.
       Excerpts from answers to a Soviet Life quiz on Lenin's
       greatest contributions.

409   "Lenin's Course," Soc Doc, 2, no. 47 (30 Nov. 1964), 6-10.
       A Pravda editorial pledging eternal pursuit of Lenin's
       behests.

410   Lenin's Ideas and Cause Are Immortal.   Theses of the Cen-
       tral Committee, CPSU, on the Centenary of the Birth of
       Vladimir Ilyich Lenin.   Moscow: Novosti Press, 1970;
       62pp.
       A centennial appreciation of Lenin as the "founder of the
       Proletarian party of a new type, theoretician and leader
       of the Socialist revolution" and of Leninism as "the ban-
       ner of the peoples' struggle against imperialism and for
       the revolutionary renewal of the world."   The author
       traces the standard highpoints in Lenin's career in sup-
       port of this image of Lenin.   [HX40.05]

411   Libedinsky, Yuri. "Lenin Is Always with Us," USSR, 31, no. 4 (1962), 1-5.

412   *Lichtheim, George. "From the Finland Station," in Collected Essays. New York: Viking Press, 1973, 309-15.
      Joel Carmichael's A Short History of the Russian Revolution and Raya Dunayevskaya's Marxism and Freedom serve as a basis for this assessment of the question of whether Lenin personally influenced the historical development of modern Russia. Lichtheim argues that Lenin certainly played a central role in the events of 1917 but that ultimately, Lenin and Leninism have had little impact on the basic direction taken by Russia since conditions were such that without Lenin Russia still would have become an industrial and military power with a nationalized economy and a non-liberal government. Originally in NY R Books, (17 Dec. 1964). [AC8.15 1973]

413   _____. "Happy Birthday," in Collected Essays. New York: Viking Press, 1973, 316-29.
      A review article following the theme that the negative qualities of the Soviet regime which materialized after Lenin's death would have appeared, if in a slightly muted form, even if Lenin had lived to a ripe old age. In the process, Lichtheim discusses Getzler's Martov, Deutscher's The Unfinished Revolution, and The Royal Institute of International Affairs' The Impact of the Russian Revolution, 1917-1967. Originally in NY R Books, (9 Nov. 1967).

414   "Life of Lenin," Illus Wk India, 91, no. 17 (26 Apr. 1970), 8-13.

415   *Lockhart, R. H. Bruce. "Lenin," in The Man and the Hour. Studies of Six Great Men of Our Time, Arthur Bryant, ed. Port Washington: Kennikat, 1972 (reprint of a 1934 publication); 27-56.
      A survey of Lenin's pre-1917 development as a revolutionary, his return to Russia in 1917, leadership in the October Revolution and immediate post-revolutionary policies, and an assessment of Lenin's place in history. Defining great men of history as "those who have had the strength of will to seize one of those main chances which at rare chances history offers to individuals," Lockhart asserts that Lenin certainly was such a man. He praises Lenin for his fanatical will power, sincerity, capacity for work and oratorial ability, and as a great philosopher and creator of a viable economic system. Lockhart claims it is too early to pass judgment on Lenin. [D412.6.G7]

416   Lowry, Charles W. "Lenin As Messiah and As a Realist," in Communism and Christ. New York: Morehouse-Gorham company, 1953; 24-29.

A brief discussion of Lenin's "artful deviation" from Marxism as being a result of the concrete political opportunities and responsibilities which he confronted. Lowry maintains that Lenin was forced to alter Marx's teachings because Lenin concluded that the workers, left to their own efforts, would not revolt therefore a revolutionary party had to organize and lead the revolution for them as well as forge an alliance with the peasantry and oppressed nationalities if the revolution were to succeed. Lowry uses religious jargon in describing Lenin's deviations and draws parallels between the nature of Leninism and organized religion. [HX86.L84]

417 *Ludwig, Emil. "Lenin," in Genius and Character. New York: Harcourt, Brace and Company, 1927, 129-50.
A review of Lenin's career and a discussion of the key to his success as resting in his utter realism, tremendous physique which gave him his energy, and his "cold scientific precision." Ludwig concludes that Lenin is an excellent example of how the will of one man can shape history, a fact which refutes Lenin's deterministic philosophy. [CT154.L8 1927c]

418 Lunacharsky, A. "Scientist, Philosopher, Publicist," Sov Mil R, no. 3 (Mar. 1970), 8-9.

419 McLean, R. "Very Great Man," Sat Night, 55 (27 Apr. 1940), 3.

420 *McNeal, Robert H. "Lenin," in The Bolshevik Tradition. Lenin, Stalin, Khrushchev and Brezhnev. Englewood Cliffs: Prentice-Hall, 1975; 1-70, bib. 196-204.
An analysis of the continuing themes that run through the Communist Party as represented by the careers of Lenin, Stalin, Khrushchev, and Brezhnev. McNeal discusses Lenin's early revolutionary activities, creation of the Bolshevik Party, and activities in the years between the 1905 Revolution and World War I, and then details Lenin's views and work leading to the 1917 revolt as well as his policies to his death. McNeal sees Lenin's contribution to the Bolshevik tradition as being the establishment of the party as the self-proclaimed elite vanguard for the proletariat; the need for a "supreme dictator prophet" (Lenin did this in practice not theory); the creation of a party monopoly on truth causing intense dogmatism; and "a superb heroic myth" embodied in countless memorials to Lenin which collectively depict him as all things to all men. [DK268.A1M3]

421 "Man of Destiny," Indo-As C, 19, no. 2 (Apr. 1970), 1-4.

422 Markoff, A. "Lenin: 13 Years After," Communist, 16 (Jan 1937), 74-81.

423   Mikoyan, A. "Lenin--Revolutionary, Scholar, Statesman,"
in LYAWT (anthology), 47-73.
A case for Lenin's greatness as a revolutionary, a scholar
and statesman by way of an outline of his contributions
to the revolution, formation of the Communist Party and
leadership of the Soviet government. Mikoyan makes
numerous references to Lenin's writings and political
decisions to illustrate Lenin's leadership capacity. Excerpt in Sov Life, no. 4 (Apr. 1970), 6-7.

424   Mitchell, R. J. "Neo-Leninism in Soviet Politics," G Pol
Sci As J, 2, no. 1 (Spring 1974), 73-88.
An argument that, unlike Khrushchev's Leninist rhetoric,
the current Soviet leadership represents a real attempt
to return to Lenin's methods of control, not out of Lenin-
worship but because of necessity.

425   Mukerjee, Hiren. "Lenin: Comrade and Man," in LAI (anthology), 1-14.
A positive assessment of Lenin's qualities as both leader
and man. Mukerjee states that while Lenin was a staunch
revolutionary and leader, he possessed rare human qualities such as modesty, simplicity, and compassion. The
author provides examples of vigorous leadership and humane behavior to support this image of Lenin.

426   Nehru, Jawaharlal. "A Consistent Champion of Working
Masses," in LHIII (anthology), 15-16.

427   _____. "Dogmatism Alien to Lenin's Thought," in LHIII
(anthology), 10-11.
A restatement of Lenin's insistence on a flexible and
creative approach to Marxism.

428   _____. "Lenin," in IAL (anthology), 1-9.
A positive description of Lenin's leadership qualities.
Nehru praises Lenin for his calmness in the face of
emergency, as a man of action, and for his resoluteness,
dedication, and selflessness.

429   _____. "Remarkable Adaptability," in LHIII (anthology),
17. A brief discussion of Lenin's ability to apply Marxist theory to existing conditions.

430   Nikitine, B. V. "The Lenin Museum," in The Fatal Years.
Fresh Revelations on a Chapter of Underground History.
Westport, Connecticut: Hyperion, 1977 (reprint of a 1938
publication); 255-84.
An attempt, by an ex-colonel in the Russian army's Counter-
Espionage Bureau, to counter-balance the heroic image
of Lenin presented by the collection at the Lenin Museum
(Moscow). Nikitine paints a scathing portrait of Lenin
as an evil fanatic who bought his way to power by paying

(with illegally gained funds) criminal elements to spread
Bolshevik propaganda which sought to legitimize robbery
and violence. He presents evidence, obtained through
surveillance and use of agent provocateurs, that Lenin's
political successes, from as early as 1907, were due to
his having sufficient money to bribe others to support
him and to spread propaganda among the proletariat. The
author is particularly virulent when discussing money
Lenin allegedly received from German agents during
World War I: "The criminal classes flocked to the support of the despotic leader of an insignificant party, who
freely scattered German money and openly incited them
to commit robbery." [DK265.9S4N5413]

431   "Nikolai Lenin: Anatomy of a Revolutionary," in Makers of
the Western Tradition. Portrait from History, J. Kelley
Sowards, ed. New York: St. Martin's Press, 1975;
181-94. A brief biographical sketch presenting Lenin
as a complex person who few felt they really knew precedes excerpts from studies of Lenin by Trotsky, Valentinov, and Daniels. [CT104.M29]

432   "Notes of the Month: Leninism Lives," Labour Mo, 52, no.
4 (Apr. 1970), 145-57.

433   "100 Years of Lenin," Humanist, 85 (Mar. 1970), 70-72.

434   Parsons, Howard L. "Lenin, the Creative Marxist," Sov
Un R, 11, no. 236 (1960), 5.

435   Podgorny, Nikolai V. Lenin's Ideas Realized. 1917-1961.
Moscow: Novosti Press, 1969; 39pp.

436   *Pokrovskii, M. N. "Lenin as a Revolutionary Leader," in
Russia in World History. Selected Essays. Ann Arbor:
University of Michigan Press, 1970; 188-202.
An examination, by a Soviet historian, of Lenin's basic
qualities as a leader stressing that his greatest asset
was his political courage: "he was not afraid to assume
the responsibility for political decisions of any size."
Pokrovsky provides three examples of Lenin's political
courage in action and then compares Lenin as a leader
to other revolutionary leaders in Russia, especially Chernov, as well as to Robespierre and Cromwell. [DK5.P653]

437   Ponomaryov, Boris. "The Great Leader of the Revolutionary
Epoch," W Marxist R, 13, no. 2 (Feb. 1970), 4-13.
Also in Int Aff, 16, no. 4 (Apr. 1970), 3-12.

438   "Proudest Monument of Noble Human Endeavor," in LHIII
(anthology), 72.

439   "Pure-Minded Lover of Mankind," in LHIII (anthology), 58-59.

440   Rao, C. Rajeswara. "New Path for Happiness of Man," in
       LAI (anthology), 15-35.
       A positive assessment of Lenin's character, thought, and
       policies. Rao praises Lenin's modesty, simplicity, and
       selflessness, his development of Marxist theory amidst
       20th-century challenges, and his political genius as demon-
       strated as a revolutionary and leader of the Soviet state.
       To support this image of Lenin, Rao provides quotes
       from those who knew Lenin well.

441   "Reedemer of the Poor," in LHIII (anthology), 111-12.

442   "Rishi of the Sudra Age," in LHIII (anthology), 74-75.

443   Rokotov, Timofei. "Leninism Gains World-Wide Recognition,"
       Int Lit, no. 1 (Jan. 1941), 67-76.
       A survey of international praise for Lenin.

444   Roodkowsky, Nikita D. "Lenin (1870-1970)," New Cath W,
       211, no. 1263 (June 1970), 107-11.
       A negative assessment of Lenin's thought and accomplish-
       ments.

445   Rumyantsev, A. M. "Lenin: A Scientist, Revolutionary and
       Statesman," Mainstream, 8, no. 10 (8 Nov. 1969), 21-25;
       8, no. 11 (15 Nov. 1969), 21-24; and 8, no. 12 (17 Nov.
       1969), 17-20.

446   *Salisbury, Harrison. "Lenin," in The History Makers.
       Leaders and Statesmen of the 20th Century, Lord Long-
       ford and Sir John Wheeler-Bennett, eds. New York:
       St. Martin's Press, 1973; 122-37.
       A short survey of Lenin's revolutionary career followed
       by an evaluation of his legacy. Salisbury states that
       Lenin erred frequently in his assessment of both the Rus-
       sian and world revolutionary movements, but nonetheless
       was a genius in the realm of practical politics as both
       his seizure and exercise of power demonstrate. He as-
       serts that much less can be said of Lenin for creating
       a society or a political party consistent with his philosophy
       since both the condition of the Soviet Union and the CPSU
       were far from a comfort to the dying Lenin. Salisbury
       cites the writings of Lenin in his last months to illustrate
       Lenin's frustration and bitterness over the conditions of
       Russia and to indicate the direction Lenin's policies might
       have gone had he lived longer. He concludes that Russia
       would have been significantly different under a long-lived
       Lenin, but that Lenin did, in fact, bequeath the means
       of the distortion if not the destruction of the very society
       he had hoped to create. [D412.7.H57]

447   Samuelson, P. A. "Lenin," Newsweek, 76 (7 Dec. 1970),
       86.

A centenary assessment of Lenin and his impact on history.

448   Sanyal, Bhupendra N.   "Creator of Present Russia," in LHIII (anthology), 143.

449   Schapiro, Leonard.   "Lenin's Heritage," Encounter, 35 (July 1970), 57-59.
An examination of the question "to what extent is Lenin to be blamed for the modern tyranny and brutality of communism."

450   _____.   "Thoughts on the Centenary of Lenin's Birth," Listener, 83 (16 Apr. 1970), 504-05.
A brief discussion of Leninism as a revision of Marxism, Lenin's disappointment with the party's accomplishments as of 1924, and the differences between Leninism and Stalinism.

451 *   _____.   "Was Lenin Necessary?" Commentary, 38, no. 6 (1964), 57-60.
An appraisal of Lenin's affect on Russian history arguing that without Lenin there would not have been a Bolshevik Revolution. Schapiro sees Lenin as a genius at revolution but also as a man who paved the way for Stalin's brutality and the ruination of Russia.

452   Schnittkind, H. T. and D. A. Schnittkind.   "Nikolai Lenin," in Living Biographies of Famous Men.   Garden City: Garden City Publishing Company, 1944; 199-211.
A general review of Lenin's accomplishments and qualities as a leader.

453   Scudder, Vida D.   "A Little Tour in the Mind of Lenin," in The Privilege of Age. Essays Secular and Spiritual. New York: Dutton, 1939; 67-78.
A short, positive assessment of Lenin as a man who possessed a powerful, creative and flexible intellect. Scudder records her surprise, upon reading Lenin, in realizing the depth and power of his thought as expressed in Materialism and Empirio-Criticism and What Is to Be Done?. [PS3537.C975A16 1939]

454   Sekhar, K. Kumara.   "Lenin: A Cold-Blooded Strategist," Swarajya, 14 (9 May 1970), 9-10.

455   Seton-Watson, Hugh.   "Lenin's Revolution," in From Lenin to Khrushchev. The History of World Communism.   New York: Praeger, 1960; 22-49.
A general review of Lenin's establishment of the Bolshevik Party and his leadership of it both in the 1917 revolution and the civil war period. [HX40.S39]

456   Sforza, Count Carlo. "Lenin," in Makers of Modern Europe.
        Portraits and Personal Impressions and Recollections.
        Freeport, New York: Books for Libraries Press, 1969
        (reprint of a 1930 publication); 347-53.
        A short, negative assessment of Lenin stressing the shal-
        lowness of his written works and the narrow-mindedness
        of his politics. Sforza cites discussions he had with two
        men (Krassin and Vorovski) who had known Lenin and
        would not refute Sforza's assessment of Lenin's writings
        as "intellectually miserable."

457   Shcherbakov, A. S. Under the Banner of Lenin and Stalin
        Victory Will be Ours! Moscow: Foreign Languages
        Publishing House, 1943, 16pp.
        A Moscow address (in commemoration of the 19th anni-
        versary of Lenin's death) predicting Russian victory over
        Germany because of the heroic efforts of the Russian
        people and the inspiration provided by both Lenin's memory
        and the leadership of Stalin. [D764. S46413]

458   Shields, Art. "A Visit to the Kremlin," in OL (anthology),
        191-93.
        A recollection of the inspirational effect of a guided visit
        to Lenin's Kremlin apartment.

459   Sirianni, Carmen. "Rereading Lenin," Socialist Rev, 5, no.
        1 (Apr. 1975), 77-88.
        An examination of Lenin's overall revolutionary philosophy
        and the historical context within which it evolved.

460   Soward, F. H. "Nikolai Lenin and a Communist World
        State," in Moulders of National Destinies. London: Ox-
        ford University Press, 1938; 116-25.
        A general, non-interpretive account of the highlights in
        Lenin's career as a revolutionary and political leader up
        to 1921. [D108. S65]

461   *Srivastava, N. N. "Lenin--a Critical Study," Kurukshetra
        U Res J, 4, nos. 1-2 (Apr.-Sept. 1970), 156-64.
        An evaluation of Lenin as a man with many humane quali-
        ties who, ironically, created the "most inhuman state
        machine ever conceived." Srivastava sees Lenin's role
        in the revolution as being the crucial ingredient, and
        asserts that even more important is his ridding Marxism
        of its "Euro-centric" nature. Also in Janata, 25, no.
        14 (26 Apr. 1970), 8-11.

462   Stalin, J. "Lenin as Organizer and Leader of the Russian
        Communist Party," Int Lit, no. 1 (Jan. 1939), 46-51.

463   _____. "Speech Delivered at a Meeting of Voters of the
        Stalin Electoral Area, Moscow" in SOL (anthology), 75-
        83.

A Dec. 11, 1937 speech calling for elected deputies "to emulate Lenin in all things" and in particular to "remain political figures of the Lenin type": fearless in battle, merciless towards enemies, wise in dealing with complex problems, and possessed of love for the people.

464   Steffens, Lincoln. "A Man Named Lenin," in LIOUS (anthology), 65-67.
A brief note on Lenin as a leader deeply concerned with eradicating the social and economic evils faced by the common man.

465   Steinberg, Julien. "Man of the Half Century," Freeman, 1, no. 23 (13 Aug. 1951), 721-23 and 1, no. 24 (27 Aug. 1951), 757-60.
A negative assessment of Lenin and his regime which nonetheless presents Lenin as the most important man in the first half of the 20th century.

466   Strong, Anna L. "Was Lenin a Great Man?" Gal-Jul Q, 2 (1928), 86-99.

467   Suslov, M. A. Following Lenin's Behests. Moscow: Novosti Press, 1975; 29pp.
A report (at the celebration meeting in Moscow dedicated to Lenin's 105th birthday anniversary) on Soviet history as "the continuation, consolidation and development of the great cause of communist construction begun in Lenin's time and carried out according to his behests." Suslov discusses, as Leninist policies, Soviet socialist construction, cooperation with fellow socialist states, support of peaceful coexistence and the waging of ideological warfare against capitalism and imperialism.
[HX313.S8713]

468   Szamuely, Tibor. "The Greatest Revolutionary," Spectator, (18 Apr. 1970), 506-08.

469   Tandon, Shiv N. "Beloved Leader Lenin," in LHIII (anthology), 127-28.

470   *"Thoughts about Lenin," Cult Life, (Sept.-Dec. 1970). A
A series of centennial eulogies on Lenin and his influence.

471   *"Through the Eyes of the World," Sov Lit, no. 3 (1970), 180-91.
A collection of brief excerpts from foreign, positive estimates of Lenin and his career.

472   Tikhonov, Nikolai. "The Sparks of Remembrance," Sov Lit, no. 3 (1970), 151-54.
An account of the inspirational effect of the memory of Lenin.

473   Tito, Josip B.   "Lenin: Thinker and Strategist of the Socialist Revolution," LITW-2 (anthology), 45-57.
A positive presentation of Lenin's creative application of
Marxism to 20th-century conditions as the crux of his
success as a revolutionary and political leader.   Tito
also discusses Lenin's influence on the working class and
national liberation movements.

474   *Toynbee, Arnold.   "A Centenary View of Lenin," Int Aff, 46,
no. 3 (1970), 490-500.
A consideration of Lenin as one of the most influential
men of all times.   Toynbee portrays Lenin as the anti-
thesis of bourgeois life and an intolerant and dictatorial
revolutionary leader.

475   Triumphant March of Lenin's Ideas.   London: Soviet Embassy
Press Department, 1960.
Not available for annotation.

476   Tyazhelnikov, E.   "Soviet Youth Works to Carry Out Lenin's
Behests," in LYAWT (anthology), 8-46.
An address, to the International Youth Seminar, reviewing
Lenin's influence on the development of the Young Communist League and the youth of the Soviet Union, and
discussing the various activities of Soviet youth in following Lenin's behests.

477   *Ulam. Adam B.   The Bolsheviks.   The Intellectual, Personal
and Political History of the Triumph of Communism in
Russia.   New York: Collier, 1968; 598pp.
Although the focus of this scholarly study is the Bolshevik Party and not Lenin, it contains much valuable information on his personality, ideology and role in the
revolutionary movement.   Using a wide range of primary
sources, Ulam examines in detail the evolution of the
party, its convulsions and splits, years of frustration
and seizure and exercise of power, while discussing Lenin as a man "who imparted to Bolshevism and communism
not only its ideology and tactics but also many of his
personal characteristics."   [DK246. U4]

478   *_____.   "Lenin: His Legacy," For Aff, 48, no. 3 (Apr.
1970), 460-70.
A critique of the Soviet celebration of Lenin's 100th anniversary, and an argument that Lenin would not be happy
with the work of his successors, especially in regard to
the bureaucratic nature of the powerful Soviet state and
the growth of Russian nationalism.

479   Vahter, Leonhard.   "The Legacy of Lenin," ACEN News,
145 (Mar. -Apr. 1970), 10-17.
An account of the negative impact of Lenin's legacy on
contemporary Soviet Russia.

480   Vasilyev, Arkadi. "Lenin Lives in Our Hearts and Minds,"
       USSR, 43, no. 4 (Apr. 1960), 1-2.

481   Vieira, Gilberto. "Lenin, Greatest Revolutionary Strategist,"
       W Marxist R, 13, no. 5 (May 1970), 17-22.

482   "Vladimir Ilyich Lenin," Civ Aff, 17, no. 10 (May 1970),
       28-29.

483   *Von Laue, Theodore H. Why Lenin? Why Stalin? A Re-
       appraisal of the Russian Revolution, 1900-1930. Phila-
       delphia: Lippincott, 1964; 242pp., bib. 231-33.
       Although this study does not have a separate chapter on
       Lenin, it contains significant discussion of his life, writ-
       ings, and work. Von Laue examines Lenin's political
       activities, theoretical writings and especially his rise to
       power as part of a thesis which argues that the Russian
       Revolution fits within a broader, world wide historical
       process of economic modernization, a process which the
       Bolsheviks accelerated by imposing "from above" a totali
       tarian revolution in Russia. [DK246.V58]

484   *Wesson, Robert G. Lenin's Legacy. The Story of the CPSU
       Stanford: Hoover Institution Press, 1978; 1-118, bib.
       307-12.
       Although the majority of this study deals with a history
       of the Communist Party after Lenin's death, the first
       four chapters provide an excellent survey of the formatio
       and development of the Bolshevik Party and its conquest
       and consolidation of power. Wesson discusses the land-
       marks in Lenin's establishment of a revolutionary party
       and a theory of revolution consistent with Russian circum
       stances, as well as his leadership of the party in the
       events of 1917 and, especially, the years immediately
       following the revolution. The author states that Russian
       traditions and conditions heavily influenced Lenin at near
       every turn in his revolutionary career, even near death
       when he became "increasingly weighed down by the feelin
       that the old Russia lived on" as he observed bureaucratic
       degeneration replace revolutionary dreams. In assessing
       Lenin as a leader, Wesson states that Lenin was not a
       theorist of any stature and was inconsistent as a Marxist
       but certainly exhibited an incredible drive to power and
       remarkable flexibility in pursuit of his goal. Wesson
       concludes that although Lenin was no despot, the Stalin
       regime did not constitute a break with Leninism but rath
       completed transformations implicit in Lenin's revolution:
       "Stalinism was only Leninism written large."
       [JN6598.K7W46]

485   Zinchenko, O. and A. Garanzha. "Following the Behest of
       Lenin," Sov Mil R, no. 10 (Oct. 1968), 18-20.
       An account of Lenin's influence on the Komsomol and
       Young Communist League.

486   Zinoviev, G.   "V. I. Lenin," Fourth Int, 6 (Jan. 1945), 5-
       17.
       A reprint of a speech given in September 1918, after
       Lenin had been shot, surveying Lenin's life and accom-
       plishments.

2. RUSSIAN REVOLUTIONARY MOVEMENT

A. Precursors

487 *Bailey, Sydney D. "Bolshevism and Nihilism," Fortn R, 179 (Mar. 1953), 188-93.
An assessment of the influence of Russian nihilism (especially Bakunin's Revolutionary Catechism) upon Lenin's concept of party organization.

488 *Billington, James H. "The Bolshevik Debt to Russian Populism," Occidente, 12 (1956), 319-28.

489 *   . "The Leninist Legacy," in The Icon and the Axe. An Interpretive History of Russian Culture. New York: Random House, 1970; 524-32, bib. 599-626.
A comparison of Lenin to his intellectual predecessors in 19th-century Russia. Billington states that Lenin borrowed from the radical traditions of the Russian intelligentsia the conviction that the new order in Russia had to be based upon an all-embracing ideology; the belief that Russia would take the lead in the regeneration of the West; the image of "the people" as a new and ultimate source of moral sanction; and the concept of the party as a dedicated community which would transcend all personal distinction. Lenin differed from his predecessors, Billington maintains, in that he was single-minded; icily logical and acerbic in his assaults on rivals; subjugated morality to party expedience; and championed the cause of centralized and disciplined organization as no revolutionary had before him. [DK32.7.B5]

490 *Boyko, Yuriy. "The Russian Historical Roots of Bolshevism," Ukr R, 2, no. 4 (1955), 46-64.
An examination of the influence of Belinsky, Herzen, Dostoevsky, and Russia's historical traditions upon Lenin and other Marxists.

491 Bullard, Arthur. "Lenin," in The Russian Pendulum. Autocracy-Democracy-Bolshevism. New York: Macmillan, 1919; 1-7.
An investigation of the basic sources of Lenin's doctrine of revolution. Bullard, a journalist who met Lenin in Switzerland in 1905, states that although Lenin took his

basic philosophy from Marx, his organizational precepts came from Blanqui, and his moral principles from Nietzsche. [DK265.B9]

492 Burnham, James. "Lenin's Secret," National R, 22 (13 June 1970), 21.
A note on Lenin's ideological affinities with Nechaev and Blanqui.

493 *Costello, D. P. "Voluntarism and Determinism in Bolshevist Doctrine," Sov St, 12, no. 4 (1960), 394-403.
An appraisal of the influence of Tkachev and Russian historical circumstances upon Lenin's conclusion that Russia was ripe for socialist revolution.

494 *Daniels, Robert V. "Lenin and the Russian Revolutionary Tradition," Harv Sl St, 4 (1957), 339-53.
An argument that "Lenin radically transformed Marxism by blending with it ideas put forth by 19th-century Russian radicals."

495 *Fedenko, Panas. "The Historical Roots of Bolshevism," St Sov Un, 9, no. 1 (1969), 1-25.
A consideration of the influence of Chernyshevsky, Nechaev, Bakunin and Tkachev upon Lenin's theory of revolution.

496 *Halbrook, Stephan P. "Lenin's Bakuninism," Int R Hist Pol Sci, 8, no. 1 (Feb. 1971), 89-111.
An argument that Lenin had more in common with Bakunin than with Marx.

497 *Hammer, Darrell P. "The Dictatorship of the Proletariat," in LAL (anthology), 25-42.
An examination of Lenin's concept of the dictatorship of the proletariat in comparison to the concepts held by Marx, Plekhanov, and 19th-century Russian Populists. Hammer emphasizes the similarity between Lenin's writings on the dictatorship of the proletariat and those of P. Lavrov who contended that the workers' revolution could only be successful if led by a revolutionary dictatorship of a minority operating through a centralized party, and that the revolution (which would occur first in Russia) would be followed by a long period of reeducation and rehabilitation of the masses by the dictatorship of the proletariat.

498 *Karpovich, Michael. "Forerunner of Lenin: P. N. Tkachev," R Pol, 6 (Oct. 1944), 336-50.

499 Kheraskov, Ivan. "A Leninist before Lenin: Ernest Coeurderoy (1825-1862)," R Pol, 11 (Jan. 1949), 17-25.

500 *Krupskaya, Nadezhda. "Lenin and Chernyshevsky," in LAB (anthology), 132-37.

A discussion of Chernyshevsky's influence on Lenin's personality, attitude towards liberalism, and his writings, especially What Is to Be Done? and What the "Friends of the People" Are: How They Fight the Social Democrats.

501   Lichtheim, George. "Precursors of Lenin," Encounter, 16 (Apr. 1961), 78-81.
An assessment of the 19th-century Russian roots of Leninism, with emphasis on the influence of Tkachev and Bakunin. (review article)

502   Malaniuk, Evhen. "To the Problem of Bolshevism," Ukr R, 13, no. 1, 17-32; no. 2, 32-46; no. 3 (1966), 40-54.
In part, a discussion of the Russian roots of Lenin's Marxism.

503   *Menashe, Louis. "Vladimir Ilyich Bakunin: An Essay on Lenin," Socialist Rev, 3, no. 18 (Nov.-Dec. 1973), 9-54.
An argument that much of what Lenin wrote and thought is consistent with Russian anarchism, but once in power he realized that such utopian ideals were unworkable.

504   *Pipes, Richard. "Russian Marxism and Its Populist Background," Rus R, 19, no. 4 (Oct. 1960), 316-37.
A discussion of Populist influence on Lenin's concept of party organization and his theory of revolution.

505   *Pokrovskii, M. N. "Lenin's Role in the Russian Revolution," in Russia in World History. Selected Essays. Ann Arbor: University of Michigan Press, 1970; 173-87.
A discussion, by a Soviet historian, of Lenin's place in the revolutionary movement stressing the importance of various 19th-century Russian influences (especially Tkachev and Bakunin) on his thought and tactics. Pokrovskii states that although Lenin's leadership was certainly an important factor in the success of the revolution, Lenin was not the fountainhead of the revolutionary movement: "Lenin was not a man who fell out of the sky into a spontaneous workers' movement." [DK5. P653]

506   *Pomper, Philip. "Nečaev, Lenin and Stalin: The Psychology of Leadership," Jahr Ges Ost, 26, no. 1 (11-30), 1978.
A critique of those interpretations which argue that Nechaev was a forerunner of Lenin and Stalin.

507   *Posin, Jack A. "Chernyshevsky, Dobrolyubov, and Pisarev. The Forerunners of Bolshevism," University of California at Berkeley, 1939 (dissertation).

508   *Prawdin, Michael. "Lenin," in The Unmentionable Nechaev. A Key to Bolshevism. New York: Roy Publishers, 1961; 117-92, bib. 193-96.

An investigation into the affinities between the thought
and methodology of Nechaev and Lenin. Prawdin isolates
as Lenin's Nechaev-like principles and practices: his
belief that the workers must be led by a professional,
secretive, and disciplined elite; complete identification
of the fate of the revolutionary movement with that of
himself; pursuit of highly manipulative tactics in intra-
party affairs; use of terror, theft, or any other unscu-
pulous tactic to advance the cause; and his creation of
an undemocratic state apparatus to rule the workers after
the revolution. Prawdin states that these similarities,
once recognized by Bolshevik historians, have been ob-
scured or denied more recently by the Soviets because
"it was generally known that Nechaev ... had tried to
to lay his hands on the Marxist organization only in order
to use it for his own purposes. If Nechaev could be
describes as the father of Bolshevism, then the danger
of a comparison between his and Lenin's relation to Marxism could not be overlooked." [DK219.6.N4C47]

509   *Scanlan, James P. "Nicholas Chernyshevsky and Philosophical Materialism in Russia," J Hist Phil, 8, no. 1 (1970),
65-86.
In part, a discussion of Chernyshevsky as the first philosopher to influence Plekhanov and Lenin.

510   Schapiro, Leonard B. "The Influence of P. N. Tkachev on
Lenin," in Rationalism and Nationalism in 19th Century
Russian Thought. New Haven: Yale University Press,
1967; 139-42.
A brief comparison of the thought of Lenin and Tkachev
on the "question of revolutionary organization and the respective roles of organization and mass in the revolution.'
Schapiro states that both men drew upon "the same national instincts and traditions," but there is no direct
evidence of Tkachev's influence on Lenin. [JA84.R9S353]

511   *Stepun, Fedor. "The Russian Intelligentsia and Bolshevism,
Rus R, 17, no. 4 (1958), 263-77.
A presentation of Tkachev, Bakunin, and Nechaev as ideo-
logical ancestors of Lenin.

512   *Theen, Rolf H. W. "The Idea of the Revolutionary State:
Tkachev, Trotsky, Lenin," Rus R, 31 (1972), 383-97.

513   *Tompkins, Stuart R. "The Essence of Bolshevism," in The
Triumph of Bolshevism. Revolution or Reaction? Norman: University of Oklahoma Press, 1967; 276-98, bib.
299-319.
An examination of Lenin's establishment of the Bolshevik
Party and its principles and practices in view of the influence of Russian political traditions. Tompkins argues
that Lenin's centralist thought represented a break with

classical Marxism but certainly not with the political
realities of Russia's past. Lenin's views on party organization, the dictatorship of the proletariat, and revolutionary tactics, Tompkins contends, all bear more
similarity to 19th-century Russian radical thought than
to Marxism, and that the state which he eventually created
seems closer to the old tsarist state than to any ideal
state pursued by Russian revolutionaries. [DK32.7.T58]

514 *Utechin, S. V. "The 'Prepatory Trend' in the Russian Revolutionary Movement in the 1880's," St Anth P, 12
(1962), 7-22.
In part, a discussion of Lenin's relation to the main developments in the revolutionary movement in the 1880's,
namely the merging of "Marxist ideas on economics and
the philosophy of history" with "the views on organization, strategy and tactics which had been current among
Russian revolutionaries of the 1860's."

515 *_____. "Who Taught Lenin?," Twent Cent, 168 (July
1960), 8-16.
An assessment of the Russian foundations of Lenin's
thought on party organization and revolution, with most
attention given to the influence of N. Ogarev.

516 Varlamov, Volodymyr. "Bakunin and the Russian Jacobins
and Blanquists," in Rewriting Russian History, Cyril E.
Black, ed. New York: Random House, 1962; 289-318.
In part, a review of Soviet historians' writings on the influence of Bakunin and Nechaev upon Lenin. [DK38.B5]

517 *Vishniak, Mark. "The Real Lenin," Mod R, 2, no. 2 (Feb.
1948), 99-112.
A sketch of Lenin's ideology as a blend of anarchism,
Populism, Jacobinism, and Marxism--much influenced
by Lenin's own personality.

518 Walker, Franklin A. "P. L. Lavrov's Concept of the Party,"
West Pol Q, 19, no. 2 (June 1966), 235-50.
In part, an appraisal of the similarities and differences
between Lavrov and Lenin on party doctrine.

519 *Weeks, Albert L. "Peter Tkachev: The Forerunner of
Lenin," in LAL (anthology), 3-24.
An examination both of the links between the thought of
Tkachev and Lenin and of the interpretation of this connection by Soviet historians. Weeks states that the many
similarities between Tkachev and Lenin were initially
recognized by some Soviet historians (S. Mitskevich),
but that by the 1930's these affinities were no longer
being acknowledged and now the Soviets not only dismiss
the question of Tkachev's influence upon Lenin but relegate this important theorist to an obscure corner of the
revolutionary movement.

520   *   . "Tkachevism, Leninism and Soviet Historians,"
in The First Bolshevik. A Political Biography of Peter
Tkachev. New York: New York University Press, 1968;
176-87.
A historiographical review of Soviet interpretations of
Tkachev's influence upon Lenin. Weeks devotes most
attention to the 1920's debate between S. Mitskevich and
N. Baturin over the Lenin-Tkachev kinship, mostly in
regard to the similarities between the two revolutionaries'
assessments of the weaknesses of Russian capitalism,
which led them to be optimistic over the chances for
revolution in a backward country such as Russia.
[HX312. T55W4]

B. Theory and Activity: Pre-1917

521   Abramowitz, Isidore, ed. "The Political Man: Vladimir
       Lenin," in The Great Prisoners. The First Anthology
       of Literature Written in Prison. New York: Dutton,
       1946; 718-25.
       A brief introduction to a series of letters written by
       Lenin while awaiting exile to Siberia in 1896.
       [PN6014.A2]

522   Afanasyev, V. et al. "The Development of Scientific Social-
       ism by Lenin," in Fundamentals of Scientific Socialism.
       Moscow: Progress Publishers, 1969; 37-49.
       A favorable summary of Lenin's theory of revolution.
       [HX44.A3613]

523   Afanasyev, V. G. "Lenin on Peaceful and Non-Peaceful
       Paths of Socialist Revolution," St Sov Phil, 17 (Spring
       1979), 21-43.

524   Amort, Cestmir. "Lenin in Prague," W Marxist R, 13, no.
       6 (June 1970), 38-42.
       An account of Lenin's activities at the 1912 Bolshevik
       Party Conference in Prague.

525   *Anderson, Thornton. "The Marxist," in Russian Political
       Thought. Ithaca: Cornell University Press, 1967; 293-
       312, bib. 400-37.
       Lenin is not the sole focus of this chapter, but as an
       overview of Russian Marxism in the 1883-1916 period,
       it contains significant discussion of his development of
       a theory of revolution. Anderson emphasizes that Lenin,
       by 1916 had "come almost full circle" in his thought in
       that he had returned to the positions which he had initially
       rejected, namely that socialist revolution could take place
       without the full development of capitalism and that this
       revolution could be led by a professional elite represent-
       ing the proletarian minority of the population.
       [JA84.R9A47]

526   *Ascher, Abraham, ed. The Mensheviks in the Russian Re-
       volution. Ithaca: Cornell University Press, 1976; 147pp.,
       bib. 140-41.
       Lenin is not the focus of this study, but as a collection

of documents on Menshevism, it includes much information on his split with the Menshevik faction of the RSDLP
and relations with it throughout the revolutionary period.
[JN6598. S6M36]

527   *Avtorkhanov, A.   "Lenin and the Bolshevik Rise to Power,"
St Sov Un, 10, no. 2 (1970), 1-79.
A survey of Lenin's revolutionary thought and activity
up to his April 1917 return to Russia.

528   *Badayev, A. E.   The Bolsheviks in the Tsarist Duma.   New
York: Howard Fertig, 1973 (reprint of a 1932 publication); 250pp.
Reminiscences, by a Bolshevik member of the Fourth
Duma, which, though not centered upon Lenin, provide
valuable insights into his policies (1912-1914) towards
the Duma and into his differences with rival political
parties.   [DK260. B3 1973]

529   Balshy, Prabin.   "Lenin and Revolution: A Comment," Ec
Pol W, 4 (20 Dec. 1969), 1959-1962.

530   *Becker, Frances B.   "Lenin's Application of Marx's Theory
of Revolutionary Tactics," Am Sociol R, 2 (June 1937),
353-64.

531   Bikhenin, N.   "Lenin on the Historic Mission of the Working
Class and the Communist Party," in LTCOA (anthology),
168-77.
A discussion of Lenin's contribution, in theory and practice, to the emergence of the proletariat as the leader
of all the working masses in the revolutionary movement.
Translated from Pravda (14 Feb. 1969).

532   Bobrovskaya, T. S.   "In Geneva," in NBPA (anthology), 58-
59.
A recollection of a conversation with Lenin on the peasant
movement in Russia.

533   Borques, Marta.   "Lenin's Theory of Revolution," W Marxist
R, 13, no. 3 (Mar. 1970), 50-53.

534   *Byrner, Cyril.   "Lenin and the Search for an Elite," Can
S P, 2 (1957), 47-56.

535   Carter, Edward H.   "Lenin, Creator of the New Russia,"
in Russian Cavalcade.   London: Nelson and Sons, 1944:
65-71.
A non-interpretive survey of Lenin's activities up to the
1917 revolution.   [DK41. C28]

536   *Cliff, Tony.   Lenin.   Vol. I.   Building the Party.   London:
Pluto Press, 1975; 398pp.

A detailed examination of Lenin's career up to the outbreak of World War I. Cliff discusses all of the landmarks in Lenin's thought and activity during this time
period, and stresses the point that Lenin was extremely
effective in creating a party and formulating a program
uniquely suited for shaping the Russian workers' movement largely because of his ability to interpret properly
and adapt to the realities of turn-of-the-century Russia.
[DK254. L4C6]

537   *Cohan, A. S. "The Leninist Theory of Revolution," in Theo-
       ries of Revolution. An Introduction. London: Nelson
       and Sons, 1975; 77-93.
       An analysis of Lenin's theory of revolution in terms of
       what it accepts and avoids in Marxist theory. Cohan
       contends that Lenin accepted the philosophical correctness
       of "the Marxian model of society and revolutionary change,"
       but in applying this model to the real situation in Russia
       he was forced to reject Marxian propositions on "the
       stages of revolution, degree of proletarian participation
       at the early stages, and the role of the vanguard party."
       The effect upon the world of Lenin's broadening of Marx-
       ian revolutionary theory from one applicable only to ad-
       vanced capitalist nations to one usable by backward so-
       cieties, Cohan states, can hardly be over-emphasized.
       [JC491. C65 1975]

538   Dabčević-Kučar, Savka. "Lenin, Revolutionary Theory and
       Practice," in LIPOY (anthology), 25-30.
       A centennial appreciation of the interaction of theory and
       practice in Lenin's leadership of the Russian revolution-
       ary movement. The author maintains that Lenin's theore-
       tical works were always rooted in an assessment of real
       historical conditions, while his practical policies were
       always based upon carefully formulated theoretical founda-
       tions.

539   *Dan, Theodore. "Bolshevism and Menshevism," in The Ori-
       gins of Bolshevism. New York: Shocken, 1970; 236-407.
       Lenin is not the focus of this chapter, but as a study
       of the ideological and organizational issues that divided
       the RSDLP, it contains numerous and valuable references
       to Lenin. More importantly, this work is written by a
       major Menshevik leader and writer who had much con-
       tact with Lenin. Other chapters in this study also pro-
       vide useful information on the evolution of Bolshevism
       in the pre-revolutionary era. [HX312. D333]

540   Daniels, Robert. "Leninism and the Russian Revolution,"
       in The Nature of Communism. New York: Random
       House, 1962; 18-29.
       A discussion of Lenin's organizational and tactical pre-
       cepts as a deviation from classical Marxism. Daniels

asserts that at the root of Lenin's elitist and centralist organizational principles was the belief that "class political consciousness can be brought to the workers only from without," a belief wholly contradictory to Marxism. Lenin's creation of the party as the guardian of truth, and his belief that revolution could be made through sheer organizational force, Daniels concludes, largely account for the totalitarian turn taken by Russian Marxism. [HX56.D3]

541 *Deutscher, Isaac. "Lenin: The Making of a Revolutionary," Ramparts M, 9 (Aug. 1970), 40-47.

542 *Dunayevskaya, Raya. "Forms of Organization: The Relationship of the Spontaneous Self-Organization of the Proletariat to the 'Vanguard Party,' " in Marxism and Freedom from 1776 until Today. New York: Twayne, 1964, 177-93.
An analysis of Lenin's thought on party membership and the party's relation to the proletariat, and a review of his polemics with rival Russian Marxists over the party question. In particular, Dunayevskaya examines the impact of the 1905 Revolution on Russian Marxists, stating that while many became discouraged because of the "reaction" which set in after the revolution, Lenin never despaired and, in fact, treated this episode as a valuable lesson in that he "took the highest point reached by the Revolution and built from there." The revolution's failure, Dunayevskaya states, led Lenin to believe all the more in the need for party guidance of the revolutionary movement, and to reject the general strike as a method of revolution in favor of concerted action by the soviets. [HX36.D8]

543 Dunn, John. "Russia," in Modern Revolutions: An Introduction to and an Analysis of the Political Phenomenon. Cambridge: Cambridge University Press, 1972; 24-47. An overview of Lenin's theory of revolution and the roots of the October Revolution. [JC491.D85]

544 *Eastman, Max. "Bolshevism," in Marx, Lenin and the Science of Revolution. Westport, Conn.: Hyperion, 1973 (reprint of a 1926 publication); 141-49. An analysis of What Is to Be Done? as Lenin's attempt to deal with "the large and altogether peculiar set of engineering problems" confronting those who seek to apply Marxism to real society. Eastman discusses in this context Lenin's 1903 stance on party organization, and concludes that Lenin, in his concern for the many practical aspects of revolution, contradicted Marx by denying that the proletariat would naturally come to revolution: "from the first page to the last, it (What Is to Be Done?) is the practical science of Marxism, with the

metaphysics stamped under foot and ignored." [HX56.E3]
Excerpt in New Masses, 3 (Nov. 1927), 14-6.

545 *Ehrenberg, John R. "Lenin and the Politics of Organization."
Sci Soc, 43, no. 1 (Spring 1979), 70-86.
An examination of Lenin's views on party organization
as an extension of his general analysis of the nature of
Russian society.

546 *Elwood, Ralph C. "The Congress that Never Was. Lenin's
Attempt to Call a '6th' Party Congress in 1914," Sov St,
31 (July 1979), 343-63.

547 *_____. "Lenin and Pravda, 1912-1914," Slav R, 31 (1972),
355-80.
An attack on those who claim that Lenin was the founder
and director of Pravda.

548 *_____. "Lenin and the Social Democratic Schools for
Underground Party Workers," Pol Sci Q, 81, no. 3
(1966), 370-91.
An assessment of Lenin's work, in 1911, in Longjumeau,
France training underground party workers. Elwood
states that although no new leaders emerged from the
school, Lenin believed the program to be a success because it helped him to gain control of the party machine.

549 Ewart, Andrew. "Lenin," in 100 Great Modern Lives. London: Century Books, 1972; 349-55.
An introduction to Lenin's career as a revolutionary
through the October Revolution. [CT119.C35]

550 Fedoseyev, P. N. "Lenin on the Motive Forces of Revolution," New Times, no. 10 (10 Mar. 1970), 18-21.

551 *Filatov, V. P. "Creating a Revolutionary Party," in LR
(anthology), 60-85.
A Soviet account of Lenin's "growing conviction that Russia needed a new type of revolutionary party, his efforts
to found and sustain it, and his views on the revolutionary movement and the forms and methods applicable to
the coming revolutionary conflict."

552 *Frank, Victor S. "Lenin and the Russian Intelligentsia," in
LMTL (anthology), 23-36.
A discussion of the question "was Lenin a member of
the intelligentsia." Frank sees Lenin's social roots as
an amalgam of the aristocratic and plebeian traditions
of the intelligentsia, and his non-acquisitive mode of
life as being that of the typical Russian intelligent. However, Lenin was contemptuous of the sentimentality, political flabbiness, and sense of martyrdom which characterized so many members of the intelligentsia, charac-

teristics, Frank states, which were seen by Lenin as part of the "old order" in Russian that had to be eliminated.

553 *Frankel, Jonathan. "Economism: A Heresy Exploited," Slav R, 22, no. 2 (1963), 263-84.
An analysis of Lenin's struggle against Economism as one which gave him a chance to develop freely his own organizational theories and leadership and which marks the beginning of his lifelong war against "subversion" within Russian Marxism.

554 *Futrell, Michael. "Lenin's Friend," in Northern Underground. Episodes of Russian Revolutionary Transport and Communications through Scandinavia and Finland, 1863-1917. New York; Praeger, 1963; 85-116.
Alexander Shlyapnikov, not Lenin, is the focus of this chapter, but it contains interesting insights into the Scandinavian underground network (created by Shlyapnikov) employed, during World War I, by Lenin for transport and communications into and out of Russia.
[DK262. F96]

555 Gadre, D. T. "Lenin--The Architect of the Russian Revolution," in LHIII (anthology); 86-89.

556 Gopner, S. I. "Lenin in Paris," in ROL (anthology); 65-72.
Reminiscences of Lenin's activity in Paris as an exile. Gopner notes Lenin's work habits, concern for organizational matters, and eagerness to seek out any new Russian emigrés in Paris as a means of learning all that he could about events in Russia.

557 Gorakh. "Lenin's Astute Comprehension of Problems," in LHIII (anthology), 95.
A positive note on Lenin's careful study of all problems related to the revolution prior to deciding on any course of action.

558 *Gorky, Maxim. "V. I. Lenin," in AL (anthology); 23-47.
A recollection of Lenin and his activities at the 1907 London Congress of the RSDLP. Excerpt from Days with Lenin. New York: International Publishers, 1932.

559 *Gray, Alexander. "Lenin," in The Socialist Tradition. Moses to Lenin. London: Longmans, Green and Company, 1946; 459-86.
An examination of Lenin's revolutionary thought and tactics in terms of their place within the Marxist tradition. Gray stresses the point that it was in the area of practical application of Marx's teachings that Lenin excelled, especially in regard to the art of insurrection. He concludes that Lenin managed "to get things done," a unique

epitaph for those most prominent in the socialist tradition. [HX21. G7]

560   Gruppi, Luciano. "Leninism as a Method of Revolutionary
       Action," W Marxist R, 13, no. 2 (Feb. 1970), 41-44.

561   Guedalla, Philip. "Lenin," in The Liberators. London:
       Hodder and Stoughton, 1942; 86-93.
       A discussion of Lenin as a man who changed "the whole
       course of history in Russia." Guedalla surveys Lenin's
       career as a revolutionary up to April of 1917, but offers
       no specifics in support of his thesis. [D108. G8]

562   Gurley, John G. "Lenin and the Revolution against Capital-
       ism," in Challengers to Capitalism. Marx, Lenin and
       Mao. San Francisco: San Francisco Book Company,
       1976; 63-95.
       A review of Lenin's revolutionary thought and activity
       as part of an argument that Lenin was the most effective
       challenger to capitalism that history has ever seen.
       Gurley stresses the importance of Lenin's assertion that
       Russia did not have to go through a bourgeois-led revolu-
       tion to remove feudal remnants and fully develop capital-
       ism, but rather the proletariat could take the lead in
       both of these undertakings. He concludes that if Marx
       was the supreme critic of capitalism and Mao the archi-
       tect of a new society, then Lenin was the master revolu-
       tionary against capitalism. [HX56. G87]

563   *Haimson, Leopold. "Consciousness and Spontaneity: Explora-
       tions into the Origins of Bolshevism and Menshevism,"
       Harvard University, 1952 (dissertation).

564   *_____. The Russian Marxists and the Origins of Bolshe-
       vism. Boston: Beacon, 1966; 246pp., bib. 235-40.
       This scholarly study of the early years of Russian Social
       Democracy has only one chapter devoted to Lenin (an-
       notated separately) but it contains throughout much infor-
       mation on Lenin's personality, beliefs, and early activi-
       ties as a Marxist. Haimson develops the thesis that the
       differences which divided the RSDLP were a result of
       rival interpretations of the role of spontaneity and con-
       sciousness in the revolutionary process. In discussing
       Lenin's thoughts on this issue, Haimson contends that
       since Lenin lacked Plekhanov's belief in the inevitability
       of the laws of history and Akselrod's confidence in the
       proletariat, he chose to place faith in a centralized party
       organization as a means of gaining control over the spon-
       taneous forces of revolution so as to direct them along
       the proper path. [HX313. H3]

565   Hall, Gus. "Use of Objective Factors in Hastening Revolu-
       tionary Crisis," Pol Aff, 49 (Apr. 1970), 2-13.

A restatement of Lenin's teachings on the place of spontaneity and consciousness in the revolutionary movement.

566 *Hammond, Thomas T. "Leninist Authoritarianism before the Revolution," in Continuity and Change in Russian and and Soviet Thought, E. J. Simmons, ed. Cambridge: Harvard University Press, 1955; 144-56.
An analysis of Lenin's thought about trade unions in the 1898-1908 period as "a good preview of the authoritarianism which was to carry over into the post-revolutionary period and impose its mark on so many areas of Soviet society." Hammond sees four characteristics of Lenin's thought in this period which support this contention: his vanguardism, elitism, fear of spontaneity, and support for a party monopoly of power. [DK263.3J6]

567 *Harding, Neil. "Lenin's Early Writings. The Problem of Context," Pol St, 23, no. 4 (Dec. 1975), 442-58.

568 * _____. Lenin's Political Thought. Vol. I. Theory and Practice in the Democratic Revolution. London: Macmillan, 1977; 360pp. bib. 333-39.
An interpretation of Lenin's political thought (up to 1914) as the logical and consistent expression of his economic and social analyses. Harding criticizes those who assert that Lenin was inconsistent and unorthodox in his Marxism, and postulates instead that Lenin's The Development of Capitalism in Russia provided a firm Marxist socio-economic foundation for Lenin's politics. This economic analysis led Lenin to see the proletariat, allied with other exploited groups in Russia, as the only force that could bring the bourgeois-democratic phase of revolution to the point of consummation. This same analysis, Harding argues, also led Lenin to the conclusion that the level of Russia's productive forces could not support a socialist revolution. Only after 1914, when he developed a new interpretation of capitalism, in his study Imperialism, did he alter his political goals and strategies toward a more immediate socialist revolution, a development which is the focus of volume two of Harding's study. [JC267.L46H37]
568a Reviewed in:
Am Pol Sci R, 73 (Dec. 1979), 675.
Choice, 16 (June 1979), 582.
Sociol R, 26 (Aug. 1978), 675.

569 Hollis, Christopher. "Three Figures in Soviet Russia," Ave Maria, 46 (6 Nov. 1937), 577-81.
In part, a discussion of Lenin's use of manipulative tactic in his rise to power.

570 *Hook, Sidney. "Myth and Fact in the Marxist Theory of Revolution and Violence," J Hist Ideas, 34, no. 2 (Apr.-June 1973), 263-80.

A discussion of Lenin's interpretation of the dictatorship of the proletariat and his use of violence as major revisions of the views of Marx and Engels.

571   Horowitz, D. "Lenin, the Making of a Revolutionary," Ramparts M, 9, no. 2 (Aug. 1970), 38-40.

572   Hudson, G. F. "Lenin," in Fifty Years of Communism. Theory and Practice, 1917-1967. New York: Basic Books, 1968; 38-49.
An examination of the circumstances in Russia (1898-1907) which led Lenin to his centralist organizational views and to his seeing the peasantry as a necessary ally for the proletariat. Hudson isolates the oppressive Russian political system and the disunified character of the workers' movement with its tendency towards "Economism" as the root of Lenin's insistence on the need for a centralized vanguard party to lead the proletariat. After the collapse of the revolutionary movement following the 1905 Revolution, Hudson states, Lenin came to believe that even the vanguard party would not be able to lead the workers in a successful socialist revolution without the assistance of the peasantry. [HX40.H74]

573   *Inkeles, Alex. "Leninist Theory and Public Opinion," in Public Opinion in Soviet Russia. A Study in Mass Persuasion. Cambridge: Harvard University Press, 1950; 11-25.
An examination of Lenin's manipulation of public opinion as a consequence of his lack of confidence in the ability of the workers to develop proper revolutionary consciousness. Inkeles contends that the uncritical extension of the idea that the masses are helpless without the party has "shaped the whole course of development of Soviet society as we see it today." [HM263.I52]

574   *Jenness, D. "Lenin as Election Campaign Manager," Int Soc R, 32, no. 2 (Feb. 1971), 9-15, 28-31.
A study of Lenin's tactics in a promoting the election of Bolshevik candidates to the Duma.

575   Kahan, Arcadius. "The Peasant, the Party and the System," Prob Com, 9, no. 4 (1960), 27-36.
In part, a discussion of Lenin's belief that it was essential to control or neutralize the peasants by forming a temporary alliance with them.

576   *Kariel, Henry S. "The Apotheosis of Strategy: V. I. Lenin," in In Search of Authority. Twentieth-Century Political Thought. New York: Glencoe Press, 1964; 130-44.
An analysis of how Lenin arrived at the organizational principles, strategies, and tactics of the Bolshevik Party. Kariel argues that Lenin was "pre-eminently a man of action" who consequently chose not to dwell on debating

the philosophical truth of Marxism but rather sought a pragmatic verification of its truthfulness by using the theory successfully "as an intellectual weapon in the quest for power." He therefore created a political organization based more on practical than Marxist concerns, and then rationalized it as being Marxist simply because it was successful in leading a socialist revolution. [JA83. K27]

577   *Katkov, George and Harold Shukman.   Lenin's Path to Power. London: Macmillan, 1971; 128pp.
A general, illustrated review of Lenin's rise to and conquest of power. The authors stress that Lenin was not the master director of events that some interpretations (Soviet) assert, but was the leader (often disillusioned) of a tiny, disorganized, and fragmented band of radicals who spent the bulk of his pre-1917 adult life in exile completely out of touch with Russian realities. It was not Lenin's ability as a leader nor his mastery of the dialectics of history that brought him to power in 1917, the authors assert, but rather German financial assistance and his manipulation of a chaotic situation caused by the war and the ineptness of the Provisional Government. [DK254. L4K29]

578   *Kautsky, Karl. "The Beginning of Bolshevism," in Social Democracy versus Communism. New York: Rand School Press, 1946; 48-55.
A critical account, by a rival Marxist, of Lenin's creation of a party organization inconsistent with the teachings of Marx. Quoting Rosa Luxemburg's 1904 critique of Lenin's party doctrine, Kautsky states that Lenin's organizational thought is laden with dangers for the workers' movement because of its centrist and dictatorial qualities. Kautsky also charges that Lenin's authoritarianism was the source of the many factional disputes which split and intellectually impoverished Russian Social Democracy.

579   Keep, John. The Bolshevik Revolution: Prototype or Myth?," St Sov Un, 11, no. 4 (1971), 46-60.
In part, a consideration of Lenin's theory of revolution as a model for other revolutions.

580   *_____. "Lenin as Tactician," in LMTL (anthology), 135-58.
An argument that "whatever Lenin's merits are as a philosopher, historian, or literary critic, he was preeminently a politician, and it was as master of political tactics ... that he won his greatest success." Keep states that Lenin's tactics were based upon such beliefs as: the most effective catalyst for change is a strictly disciplined body of professional revolutionaries bound by

loyalty to their leader; moral scruples should not apply
to relations with opponents; struggle is inherent in all
existence; and minute preparation for all eventualities
is essential to success. At the very heart of his tactics
was his belief that extreme flexibility must be maintained
at all times so as to be bold in the face of opportunity,
retreat when confronted by superior forces, and to make
compromises whenever necessary. Keep provides two
examples of Lenin's application of these tactics: the
1903 Bolshevik-Menshevik schism and the October Revolution.

581 *_____. The Rise of Social Democracy in Russia. Oxford:
Clarendon Press, 1963; 334pp., bib. 304-22.
Lenin is not the focus of any one chapter in this scholarly
study of Russian Social Democracy, but it contains a
vast amount of information on nearly every aspect of
his involvement with this movement up to 1907.
[JN6598. S6K4]

582 *Kilroy-Silk, Robert. "Lenin--The Revolutionary Challenge
to Socialist Orthodoxy," in Socialism since Marx. New
York: Taplinger, 1972; 112-44.
An examination of the foundations of Lenin's break with
Social Democracy due to its "lack of revolutionary ar-
dour" and of his return to the revolutionary Marx.
Kilroy-Silk sees Lenin's return to the "voluntarist, in-
surrectionist Marx of before 1850" as being a result of
Lenin's living in circumstances similar to those which
confronted Marx in mid-19th century Europe. Lenin's
writings and actions, therefore, show disregard for the
thought of the "mature Marx," and instead focus upon
issues which occupied the mind of the young Marx, especially those which concerned the techniques of revolution. [HX40. K49 1973]

583 *Kindersley, Richard. The First Russian Revisionists. A
Study of "Legal Marxism" in Russia. Oxford: Clarendon, 1962; 260pp., bib. 244-52.
This scholarly study of "Legal Marxism" does not focus
upon Lenin, but it contains significant and interpretive
information on his polemics against P. Struve and S.
Bulgakov. [HX312. K5]

584 *Kingston-Mann, Esther. "Lenin: The Beginnings of Marxist
Peasant Revolution, 1893-1917," Johns Hopkins University,
1970 (dissertation).

585 *_____. "Lenin and the Beginnings of Marxist Peasant
Revolution: The Burden of Political Opportunity, July-
October 1917," SEER, 50 (Oct. 1972), 570-38.

586 *_____. "Lenin and the Challenge of Peasant Militance:

From Bloody Sunday, 1905, to the Dissolution of the First Duma," Rus R, 38, no. 4 (1979), 434-55.

587 *_____. "Proletarian Theory and Peasant Practice: Lenin. 1901-1904," Sov St, 26, no. 4 (Oct. 1974), 522-39.

588 Kochan, Lionel. "Lenin in London." Hist Today, 20, no. 4 (1970), 229-35.
An account of Lenin's exile in London, with most attention given to his activities at the 1903 and 1907 RSDLP Congresses.

589 *Kolakowski, Leszek. "Marxism in Russia before the Rise of Bolshevism," in Main Currents of Marxism. Its Rise, Growth and Dissolution. Vol. 2. The Golden Age. Oxford: Clarendon, 1978; 356-80, bib. 529-36.
A discussion of Lenin's writings of the 1890's against Populism, Legal Marxism, and Economism. Kolakowski reviews the content of Lenin's journalistic and more substantive works while stressing that Lenin stood out from other Russian Marxists of the time because of his overriding concern for the practical applications of Marxist theory. [HX36. K61813]

590 *_____. "The Rise of Leninism," in Main Currents of Marxism. Its Rise, Growth and Dissolution. Vol. 2. The Golden Age. Oxford: Clarendon, 1978; 381-412.
An analysis of the basic principles of Lenin's doctrine of revolution, as formulated in the 1901-1903 period, in terms of their consistency with the principles of Marx and relation to the thought of other Russian Marxists. Kolakowski states that because of Marxism's ambiguous qualities, it is difficult to label Lenin as being "unorthodox." However, he did stray from classical Marxism in his doctrine on the party, support for an alliance between the peasantry and proletariat, and his assessment of the national movement as a progressive one to be allied with that of socialism. The most significant aspect of Lenin's thought in this period, Kolakowski asserts, was his belief that "the party with its 'correct' theoretical consciousness embodies the proletarian consciousness irrespective of what the real, empirical proletariat may think about itself or about the party." [HX36. K61813]

591 Konovalov, V. "The Difficult Years--Pages from Lenin's Life," Sov Mil R, no. 7 (July 1969), 10-13.
A review of Lenin's activities during the "years of reaction" (1907-1910).

592 *Konyukhovsky, V. N. "Lenin, the Years of Reaction" in LR (anthology), 108-17.
A discussion of Lenin's difficulties in the 1907-1910

period when "the revolution was in abeyance, police terror
raged unchecked, and the internal Party crisis has taken
a grave turn." Konyukhovsky presents Lenin as a guiding light in these years of disillusionment who showed
others the wisdom of organized retreat to regroup forces,
adapt tactics, and develop theory for practical application
once the revolutionary movement resumed its inevitable
march forward.

593   _____. "The Revolutionary Upsurge," in LR (anthology),
        188-21.
        A brief review of Lenin's actions in 1910 when the re-
        volutionary movement showed signs of reviving after
        several years of inactivity. Konyukhovsky devotes most
        of his attention to discussing the origins and significance
        of Lenin's decision to eject all deviationists from the
        party and to establish the Bolshevik line as the party's
        only program.

594   *_____. "The Russian Autocracy under Fire," in LR (an-
        thology), 86-107.
        A favorable review of Lenin's assessment of and tactics
        during the 1905 Revolution, with most concern shown for
        his Two Tactics of Social-Democracy in the Democratic
        Revolution. Konyukhovsky stresses the importance of
        both Lenin's conclusion that "in the imperialist stage,
        when the bourgeoisie's progressive potential is exhausted,
        the proletariat becomes the dominant revolutionary force"
        and his practical activities in designing tactics and a
        party program consistent with this conclusion.

595   Korostovetz, V. de. "Memories of Lenin," Contemp R, 169
        (Feb. 1946), 88-92.
        Critical recollections of talks with Lenin in Zurich (1907)
        about the failure of the 1905 Revolution, prospects for
        another revolution in Russia, and Bolshevik policy towards
        the peasants, religion, and the international communist
        movement.

596   Krasin, Y. A. "Lenin's Contribution to the Marxist Theory
        of Socialist Revolution," in LGT (anthology), 136-62.
        A Soviet review of Lenin's adaptation of the Marxist
        theory of revolution to 20th-century conditions, and a de-
        fense of Lenin against Western critics (especially Meyer,
        Marcuse, and Carew Hunt) who accuse him of perverting
        the ideas of Marx.

597   *Krzhyzhanovsky, G. M. "Vladimir Ilyich," in ROL (anthol-
        ogy), 7-38.
        Recollections of Lenin's early revolutionary activities,
        including his initial involvement with Marxism, his arrest,
        detention, and exile to Siberia, and his participation in
        various party meetings.

598 *Kudryavtsev, A., et al. <u>Lenin's Geneva Addresses.</u> Moscow: Progress Publishers, 1969; 143pp.
A detailed, chronological account of Lenin's activities, writings, and contacts with various revolutionary personalities during his four stays in Geneva (1895, 1900, 1903-1905, and 1908). [DK254. L446K813]

599 *Lane, David. <u>The Roots of Russian Communism: A Social and Historical Study of Russian Social Democracy, 1898-1907.</u> University Park: Pennsylvania State University, 1975; 240pp., bib. 219-30.
Lenin is not the focus of any one chapter in this work, but as a scholarly study of the social composition, structure, and political activity of the RSDLP up to 1905, it is a valuable source of information on his early revolutionary career. [HX312. L22]

600 "Lenine and Trotzky, the Men Who Want More," <u>Lit D</u>, 55 (24 Nov. 1917), 41.
A brief survey of the careers of Lenin and Trotsky from 1905 to 1917.

601 <u>Leninist Strategy and Tactics.</u> Moscow: Novosti Press, 1970; 79pp.
A restatement of Lenin's views on strategy and tactics, with equal attention to his teachings on the hegemony of the proletariat, telescoping phases of the revolution, alliance with the peasant and national liberation movements, and maintenance of complete tactical flexibility in face of changing circumstances and opportunities. [HX518. S8S7313]

602 "Lenin's Geneva Days," <u>Liv Age</u>, 347 (Nov. 1934), 205-09.
An account of Lenin's activities in Geneva in 1908.

603 "Lenin's Theory of Socialist Revolution," <u>Sov Mil R</u>, no. 10 (Oct. 1979), 2-4.

604 *Levin, Alfred. "Lenin and Parliament," <u>LAL</u> (anthology), 111-35.
A scholarly account of Lenin's attitude towards the Imperial Duma in the years 1905-1907. Levin establishes Lenin's initial hostile attitude towards the Duma as a "sham institution" to be avoided by the Social Democrats, and then discusses in detail Lenin's about-face, in 1906, to a position of support for participation in the Duma because of the need for a platform to rekindle the sagging revolutionary fervor of the workers. However, Levin states, Lenin did not alter his initial hostility towards parliamentarians or parliament as an institution, but only accepted working with the Duma as a necessary and temporary expedient.

605 *Lichtheim, George. "The Transmutation of a Doctrine,"
Prob Com, 15, no. 4 (1966), 14-25.
A discussion of Lenin's doctrine of revolution as one
at odds with the teachings of Marx in that Lenin elevated
conscious action and party control over the spontaneous
action and leadership of the proletariat.

606 *Liebman, Marcel. "Lenin in 1905: A Revolution that Shook
a Doctrine," in LT (anthology); 57-75.
An investigation into the impact of the 1905 Revolution on
Lenin's previous views on party organization, the role
of the masses in revolution, and revolutionary strategy.
Liebman argues that Lenin's support of an elitist, centralized party of professional revolutionaries as the leader
of the workers' movement was democratized by the events
of 1905. Lenin was so impressed by the spontaneous
revolutionary fervor of the proletariat that he called for
a broadening of party membership, proletarianization of
cadres, and a more liberal type of democratic centralism. However, Liebman states, with the 1907 disintegration of the revolutionary movement, Lenin returned to
his earlier authoritarian and centrist views on the party
and it relation to the workers.

607 Limberg, Wayne P. "Permanent Revolution: Materials on
the Origins and Meaning of the Theory and Its Influence
on Marxist-Leninist Thought," Georgetown University,
1974 (dissertation).

608 Lunacharsky, Anatole. "Leader of the Proletarian Revolution,"
in AL (anthology); 5-8.
A brief outline of Lenin's qualities as a revolutionary
leader stressing that although his leadership was extremely
important in shaping the Russian revolutionary movement,
it does not represent a refutation of Marx's teachings on
the role of the individual in history.

609 *Luxemburg, Rosa. "Organizational Question and Social Democracy," in Rosa Luxemburg Speaks, Mary-Alice Waters, ed. New York: Pathfinder Press, 1970; 112-30.
A 1904 attack on Lenin's views on party organization
and leadership as expressed in What Is to Be Done?
and One Step Forward, Two Steps Back. Luxemburg re-
jects Lenin's argument for a party consisting of professional revolutionaries separate from the working class,
and, instead, calls for a revolutionary party which would
encompass the organized proletariat. She also criticizes
Lenin for lack of faith in the revolutionary ardor of the
workers and for his consequent over-emphasis of the
need for conscious direction of the revolutionary movement. [HX276. L8433] Also published as "Leninism or
Marxism?" in The Russian Revolution and Leninism or

Marxism? Ann Arbor: University of Michigan Press, 1967; 81-108.

610 McClosky, Herbert and John E. Turner. "Bolshevism and the Revolutionary Heritage," in The Soviet Dictatorship. New York: McGraw-Hill, 1960; 39-72.
A general review of the origins, development and triumph of Bolshevism. [DK266.M18]

611 *McKenzie, Kermit E. "Lenin's 'Revolutionary Democratic Dictatorship of the Proletariat and Peasantry,'" in Essays in Russian and Soviet History in Honor of Geroid Tanquary Robinson. New York: Columbia University, 1963; 149-63.
An analysis of Lenin's concept of the dictatorship of the proletariat as a leading example of his transformation of the deterministic philosophy of Marx into a voluntaristic one which maximized "the freedom of action of the party-led proletariat." McKenzie argues that Lenin's call both for proletarian leadership in the bourgeois stage of the revolution and for an alliance between the proletariat and peasantry were radical departures from Marxism and were an attempt by Lenin to "crowd out" the bourgeoisie from any creative role in the revolutionary process. [DK4.C8]

612 Maitan, Livio. "The Theory of Permanent Revolution," in Fifty Years of World Revolution (1917-1967). An International Symposium, Ernest Mandel, ed. New York: Merit Publishers, 1968; 50-69.
Lenin is not the focus of this essay, but it contains significant discussion of his concept and use of the theory of permanent revolution. [HX40.M256]

613 *Mandel, Ernest. The Leninist Theory of Organization: Its Relevance for Today. London: International Marxist Group, 1971; 24pp.
A positive assessment of Lenin's criticism of the "spontaneous approach" to revolution, and a review of the basic points advanced by him in support of a disciplined, centralized body of professional revolutionaries acting as the revolutionary conscience of the proletariat. [HX312.L43M3413]

614 Marcu, Valeriu. "Lenin in Zurich," For Aff, 21 (Apr. 1943), 548-59.
A recollection of a conversation with Lenin, most of which was on the question of World War I's impact on the revolutionary movement.

615 Masyagin, A. "At the Sources of the Bolshevik Party," W Marxist R, 13, no. 12 (Dec. 1970), 104-06.
A discussion of Lenin's role in the St. Petersburg League for the Emancipation of the Working Class.

616   *Medish, Vadim. "Lenin and Japanese Money," Rus R, 24,
      no. 2 (1965), 165-76.
      A discussion of Lenin's contacts, during the Russo-
      Japanese War, with Colonel Akashi over the possibility
      of Japanese financial support for the Bolsheviks.

617   Mendel, Arthur P. Dilemmas of Progress in Tsarist Russia:
      Legal Marxism and Legal Populism. Cambridge: Har-
      vard University Press, 1961; 310pp. , bib. 255-64.
      Lenin is not the focus of any one chapter in this study,
      but it includes a discussion of his opposition to "Legal
      Marxism." [HX312. M44]

618   *_____. "Lenin and the Premature Socialist Revolution,"
      in Essential Works of Marxism. New York: Bantam
      Books, 1961; 83-100.
      A discussion of Lenin's adaptation of Marxism to Russian
      circumstances. Mendel stresses the point that the under-
      developed nature of the Russian economy was the root
      of Lenin's belief that Russia should shorten or skip the
      capitalist phase of development; that the proletariat was
      too immature to carry out a revolution without an elite
      to lead it; and that the proletariat's alliance with the
      peasantry was essential if the revolution were to be suc-
      cessful. [HX15. M4]

619   *Meyer, Alfred G. "Lenin's Theory of Revolution," Harvard
      University, 1950 (dissertation).

620   *Molyneux, John. "Lenin and the Birth of Bolshevism" in
      Marxism and the Party. London: Pluto Press, 1978;
      36-55.
      A study of Lenin's activities in the 1897-1903 period
      stressing that his ideas marked a break with fatalism
      and constituted a tremendous step forward for Marxist
      theory. [HX36. M646]

621   _____. "Lenin: From Russian Bolshevism to the Com-
      munist International," in Marxism and the Party. Lon-
      don: Pluto Press, 1978; 56-95.
      A Marxist overview of the leading events in Lenin's re-
      volutionary career in the 1905-1919 period.

622   Nadejena, Lydia. "Nikolay Lenin," in The Torch of Free-
      dom, Emil Ludwig and Henry B. Dranz, eds. Port Wash-
      ington: Kennikat, 1972 (reprint of a 1943 publication);
      381-406.
      A survey of the leading developments in Lenin's career
      up to 1917 stressing the point that while his fierce polem-
      ics and rapid shifts in tactics repelled many, he must
      be considered the "moving force" of the Russian revolu-
      tionary movement. [CT105L8]

623   Nakoryakov, N. N. "At the Fifth Party Congress," in LAG

(anthology), 340-46.
A review of Gorky's reminiscences of Lenin's activities at the 5th Party Congress in London.

624   Narayan, J. "Lenin against 'Economism,'" in LHIII (anthology), 37.
A note on What Is to Be Done? as a critical commentary on "Economism."

625   Nehru, Jawaharlal. "Uncompromising Strategist of Revolution," in LHII (anthology), 11-12.
A review of Lenin's pre-1917 ideas on revolutionary strategy.

626   Neuberg, A. "Bolshevism and Insurrection," in Armed Insurrection. New York: St. Martin's, 1970 (reprint of a 1928 publication); 41-60.
A Marxist restatement of Lenin's basic teachings on revolution, and an attack on those socialists who either criticized or failed to follow them.   [JC491.N476]

627   Nohara, W. K. "When Japan Backed Lenin," Liv Age, 341 (Feb. 1932), 497-99.
A charge that, during the Russo-Japanese War, Lenin met in Finland with an agent of the Japanese government to receive financial backing for the revolutionary movement.

628   *Norman, Nelson F. "Lenin and the Organization of the Bolshevik Party, 1897-1903," University of Illinois, 1949 (dissertation).

629   *Novy, Vilem et al. "Organized and Organizing Force," W Marxist R, 15, no. 9 (Sept. 1972), 31-46.
A review of Lenin's One Step Forward, Two Steps Back as part of a series of articles on the contemporary relevance of his major works.

630   Numata, Hidesato. "Leninism and the Question of Parliament in Modern Revolution," W Marxist R, 13, no. 3 (Mar. 1970), 3-6.

631   *Page, Stanley W. "Lenin and Peasant 'Bolshevism' in Latvia, 1903-1915," J Baltic St, 3, no. 2 (1972), 95-112.
An examination of the influence of the revolutionary actions of the Latvian rural proletariat on Lenin's Two Tactics of Social Democracy in the Democratic Revolution. Page also discusses the failure of Lenin's efforts to win the support of the Menshevik-oriented Latvian Social Democrats.

632   Petrovsky, G. I. "Our Wise Leader," in ROL (anthology), 81-88.

Recollections, by a fellow Bolshevik, of Lenin's concern for and knowledge of the mood of the masses during the 1914-1917 period.

633 *Pipes, Richard. "The Origins of Bolshevism: The Intellectual Evolution of Young Lenin," in Revolutionary Russia: A Symposium, Richard Pipes, ed. Garden City: Double-day, 1969; 33-79.
A study of Lenin's political thought as it developed in the 1887-1900 period. Pipes states that Lenin's thought went through four phases as he attempted to determine the relationship between socialism, democracy and the three main social classes of Russia: 1887-1892, when he "believed that the revolution would derive its force from the peasant masses and its leadership from a con-spiratorial group...."; 1892-1893, when he "lost faith in the peasantry's revolutionary capacity and turned to the proletariat while clinging to his previous methodologi-cal principles"; 1895-1899, when, as a Social Democrat, he believed that "socialism could triumph only as a re-sult of a broad oppositional movement of all social classes...."; and, lastly, 1899, when "under the shock of various disappointments ... he lost faith in both the working class and the liberal bourgeoisie and evolved an undemocratic philosophy of socialism, which fused Jacobin and Marxist elements to produce ... bolshevism." [DK265. A135]

634 Pomper, Philip. "The Revolutionary Era," in The Russian Revolutionary Intelligentsia. New York: Crowell, 1971; 148-96; bib. 197-208.
Lenin is not central to this chapter, but it contains use-ful information on his revolutionary activities in the 1890's, split with the Mensheviks, and assessment of the 1905 Revolution. [HN523. P674]

635 *Popov, Nikolai N. Outline History of the Communist Party of the Soviet Union. New York: International Publishers, 1934; 414pp.
A comprehensive Soviet review, written in the Stalin era, of the development of the Bolshevik Party up to the Oc-tober Revolution. Although the party and not Lenin is the focus of this study (in its 16th edition in 1934), it contains a vast amount of material on him as a revolu-tionary genius who shaped the party throughout its his-tory. [DK63. P62]

636 *Porshnev, B. F. "Lenin's Science of Revolution and Social Psychology," in Social Psychology and History. Moscow: Progress Publishers, 1970; 11-64.
A discussion of Lenin as a psychologist in that he made "many observations bearing on the frame of mind, psy-chical change and state of various strata of society...."

Porshnev praises Lenin for his "psychical vigilance" and acute perception in assessing the slightest symptoms of revolutionary sentiment among the masses and for insisting that the Bolshevik Party understand the mind of each stratum of society before considering any policy. Lenin's views on the relation between spontaneity and consciousness in the revolutionary movement and on the psychological relationship between the party and the workers also receive considerable attention, with the revolutions of 1905 and 1917 serving as case studies.
[HM251. P713]

637 *Rees, J. C. "Lenin and Marxism," in LMTL (anthology), 87-106.
An exploration of the question of how Lenin, as a Marxist, could call for a proletarian revolution in a country as backward as Russia. Rees dismisses the facile interpretation that "Lenin was after power and that his excursions into Marxist theory were just window dressing," arguing that the ambiguous legacy of Marx and the difficulties which accompany strict practical adherence to any theory make it difficult to present Lenin as a mere political opportunist. He presents Two Tactics of Social Democracy in the Democratic Revolution as an illustration of Lenin's Marxist logic in combining "a peasant war with the working class movement."

638 "Reminiscences of the Second Party Congress," Sov Life, 8, no. 203 (Aug. 1973), 10-11.

639 Rubin, Daniel. "The Leninist Party: Vehicle for Revolution," Pol Aff, 49 (Apr. 1970), 36-47.

640 *Salisbury, Harrison E. Black Night, White Snow: Russia's Revolutions, 1905-1917. Garden City: Doubleday, 1978; 656pp. , bib. 613-32.
A comprehensive survey of the leading revolutionary events and personalities of the 1905-1917 period. In referring to Lenin, Salisbury develops the thesis that, far from being the master planner that some biographers depict him as, he was, in fact, "badly out of touch with Russia, and no one was more surprised than he when revolution came to it." Lenin's astuteness, however, Salisbury claims, enabled him to read well the opportunity for revolution and "to ride the tidal wave to power."
[DK265. S2926]

641 Salvadori, Massimo. "Lenin and the Bolsheviks," in The Rise of Modern Communism. A Brief History of the Communist Movement in the 20th Century. New York: Holt, 1953; 9-16.
A brief and general introduction to Lenin's development of the Bolshevik Party up to 1917. [HX40. S28]

642   Schiebel, Joseph. "Aziatchina: The Controversy Concerning the Nature of Russian Society and the Organization of the Bolshevik Party," University of Washington, 1972 (dissertation).

643   Schwarz, Solomon M. "The Genesis of the Bureau of the Committees of the Majority (BCM)," in The Russian Revolution of 1905. The Workers' Movement and the Formation of Bolshevism and Menshevism. Chicago: University of Chicago Press, 1967; 257-66.
       An attack, by a Marxist contemporary of Lenin, on the party's official version of the formation of the BCM. Schwarz contends that the BCM did not emanate from any popular initiative by party workers in Russia, but rather was conceived by Lenin alone while in Switzerland. [JN6598. S6S37]

644   *   . "Lenin's Theory of Trade Unions, 'Spontaneity,' and 'Consciousness,'" in The Russian Revolution of 1905. The Workers' Movement and the Formation of Bolshevism and Menshevism. Chicago: University of Chicago Press, 1967; 325-30.
       A brief argument that although the main theme of Lenin's What Is to Be Done? is that trade unions, without party guidance, tend to gravitate towards bourgeois ideology, there are nonetheless signs in the pamphlet that Lenin reluctantly came to such a conclusion. Schwarz deplores the fact that the Bolshevik Party seized upon the most radical and undemocratic implications of What Is to Be Done?, and converted the party into a dictatorial one. [JN6598. S6S37]

645   *   . The Russian Revolution of 1905. The Workers' Movement and the Formation of Bolshevism and Menshevism. Chicago: University of Chicago Press, 1967; 361pp.
       A detailed account of "the actual process by which Bolshevism and Menshevism assumed their separate identities ... amidst the crucible of the 1905 Revolution." Schwarz does not present a separate chapter on Lenin, but provides much information on and insight into Lenin's thought on the trade unions, strike movement, soviets, and the general tactics and policies to be followed by the party during the 1905 Revolution. The two articles by Schwarz appended to this study have been annotated individually (see preceding two entries). [JN6598. S6S37]

646   *Seliger, Martin. "Unacknowledged and Acknowledged Breakaway/An Interim Balance," in The Marxist Conception of Ideology. A Critical Essay. London: Cambridge University Press, 1977; 81-117.
       A scholarly assessment of the change in Lenin's attitude towards ideology as he left, early in his career, the realm of theory for that of political action. Seliger states

that Lenin's shift from the negative view of ideology expressed by Marx and Engels to a far more positive one was due largely to his turn to "political voluntarism" and away from the deterministic fundamentals of Marxism, a point which the author substantiates through a careful examination of Lenin's debates (especially with Bernstein and Kautsky) over the concept of ideology. [HX44. S394]

647   *Sen, Mohit.   "Lenin and Revolution," in LAI (anthology), 102-34.
A positive assessment of What Is to Be Done?, Two Tactics of Social Democracy in the Democratic Revolution, and State and Revolution in support of the contention that Lenin's genius in revolutionary tactics and strategy was rooted in theory.   Excerpt in Ec Pol W, 4, no. 31 (1 Aug. 1969), 1271-76.

648   Senn, Alfred E.   "The Bolshevik Conference in Bern, 1915," Slav R, 25, no. 4 (1966), 676-78.

649   *_____.   "The Leninist Offensive," in The Russian Revolution in Switzerland. 1914-1917.   Madison: University of Wisconsin Press, 1971; 30-45.
An examination of Lenin's radical position on World War I, which called for the transformation of the imperialist war into a civil one, and the heated polemics which it triggered within the Russian emigré community in Switzerland as well as within the Second International.   This study contains much additional information on Lenin's thought, activity, and relations with fellow emigrés in the 1914-1917 period.   [DK262. S444]

650   Sherkovin, Yu. A.   "Lenin and Marxist Social Psychology," in LR (anthology), 34-42.
A presentation of Lenin as a pioneer in the field of revolutionary psychology because he recognized that "the course and outcome of the revolution would largely depend on the proletarian consciousness" and that the Bolshevik Party had to understand fully the psychological preconditions of revolution if it were to guide successfully the workers' movement.

651   Simoniya, N.   "Lenin's Concept of Revolutionary-Democratic Dictatorship and Non-Capitalist Development," in LARIE (anthology), 34-56.
A positive restatement of Lenin's views on the possibility of the peaceful development of the bourgeois-democratic revolution and on why such development was not possible in a backward capitalist nation such as Russia.

652   Skousen, W. Cleon.   "The Early Life of Nikolai (V. I.) Lenin," in The Naked Communist.   Salt Lake City:

Ensign Publishing Company, 1962; 93-97.
A survey of Lenin's activities in the 1886-1903 period.
[HX56. S5]

653   *Solzhenitsyn, Alexander. <u>Lenin in Zurich.</u> New York: Farrar, Straus and Giroux, 1976; 309pp.
An examination of Lenin's stay in Switzerland, 1914-1917,
with most attention given to the personal side of his life.
Solzhenitsyn discusses Lenin's frustration at being isolated
from events in Russia, despair over the future of the
Bolshevik Party, and his polemics with rival socialists,
while providing many details on the non-political Lenin,
including his relationship with Inessa Armand.   Solzhenitsyn often projects what Lenin might have said or felt in
a particular situation, and presents in the process an
image of Lenin as a fallible human being who was often
confused, emotional, and embittered, and was possessed
with the idea of seizing power in Russia.   Lenin's connection with Alexander Helphand (Parvus) and the German government as a means of returning to Russia also
receives considerable attention.   [PZ4. S69Le]

653a   Reviewed in:
*<u>America</u>, 135 (10 July 1976), 11-13, by C. Hughes.
<u>Can Forum</u>, (Oct. 1976), 35, by G. Ignatieff.
*<u>Can S P</u>, 19 (June 1977), 123-37, by M. Friedberg.
*<u>Can S P</u>, 19 (June 1977), 138-52, by A. G. Meyer.
*<u>Can S P</u>, 19 (June 1977), 153-60, by A. E. Senn.
*<u>Dissent</u>, 24 (Summer 1977), 324-36, by B. Souvarine.
*<u>Encounter</u>, 47 (July 1976), 25-27.
<u>Listener</u>, (22 Apr. 1976), 514, by J. Bayley.
<u>Lon M</u>, (Aug. -Sept. 1976), 97, by K. Fitzlyon.
<u>Mod Age</u>, (Fall 1978), 426, by A. Kerrigan.
<u>N Y Times Bk R</u>, (25 Apr. 1976), 6-7, by S. Kar-
linsky.
<u>New Yorker</u>, (11 Oct. 1976), 159, by G. Steiner.
<u>Newsweek</u>, 86 (10 Nov. 1975), 48, by A. Deming and
S. Shabad.
*<u>Newsweek</u>, 87 (12 Apr. 1976), 98-99, by P. Zimmer-
man.
<u>Partisan R</u>, (Feb. 1978), 311, by L. Schapiro.
<u>Rus Lang J</u>, (Fall 1977), 214, by R. M. Slusser.
<u>Rus R</u>, (Apr. 1977), 224, by J. W. Hulse.
*<u>Sov St</u>, 28 (Apr. 1976), 276-79, by G. Hosking.
*<u>Survey</u>, 24 (Winter 1979), 204-12, by D. S. Anin.
<u>TLS</u>, (23 Apr. 1976), 489, by M. Scammel.

654   Spiro, George. "The Plekhanov-Lenin Betrayal of the 1905
Revolution on Anti-Semitic Grounds," in <u>Marxism and
the Bolshevik State.</u> New York: Red Star Press, 1951;
681-704.
A charge that Plekhanov and Lenin, "despite the clear
understanding of the purpose behind the tsar's anti-
Semitic policy, and in violation of the pledge to fulfill

their duty to the proletariat ... shirked that duty" and succumbed to their own anti-Semitic feelings by failing to take a stand against the pogroms carried out by the government after the 1905 Revolution. [JN6511. S6]

655   Stalin, Joseph. "Interview Given to the German Writer Emil Ludwig," in SOL; (anthology) 67-71.
A 13 December 1931 interview in which Stalin stated that although Lenin was in exile for years, "very few of those who remained in Russia were as closely associated with Russian affairs and with the working class movement ... as Lenin was."

656 *_____. "Lenin As the Organizer and Leader of the Russian Communist Party," in SOL (anthology); 7-20.
A speech, on the occasion of Lenin's 50th birthday, praising Lenin for his role in founding the Bolshevik Party, countering Menshevism, and developing tactics and a revolutionary program consistent with Russian realities. Stalin discusses What Is to Be Done? and One Step Forward, Two Steps Back as examples of Lenin's ability to apply Marxism as a practical guide for Russian revolutionary policy.

657   _____. "Speech Delivered at a Reception in the Kremlin to Higher Educational Workers," in SOL (anthology); 87-90.
A discussion of Lenin's penetrating analysis of "social development in Russia and of the international situation" as the source of his conclusion that Russia was ready for a socialist revolution.

658 *Stewart, James D. "Reading Lenin's What Is to Be Done?" in Friends, Enemies, and Strangers. Theorizing in Art, Science, and Everyday Life, Alan Blum and Peter McHugh, eds. Norwood, N. J.: Ablex Publishing Company, 1979; 95-107.
An analysis of What Is to Be Done? for insight into Lenin's thought on the relation between speech and action, or, more generally, the relation of theory to action. Stewart states that in What Is to Be Done?, Lenin essentially tried to stress the importance of steering a path between the extremes of reformism and terrorism as eternal tendencies within the workers' movement. In relating this to his speech-action conceptual scheme, Stewart asserts that Lenin therefore believed that speech had to be purposeful, responsible and principled, as opposed to either spontaneous, vascillating or opportunistic. Lenin saw reformism as bowing "to spontaneity by failing to struggle with the workers," while terrorism simply allowed spontaneous and selfish interests to dictate action. [HM26. F74]

659   *Swabey, Marie C. "Predictions and Might Have Beens," in
       Judgment of History. New York: Philosophical Library,
       1954; 152-62.
       An attack on Lenin's interpretation of the Russian revolu-
       tionary movement asserting that it is far from the scientif-
       ic assessment of historical laws which it claims to be.
       Swabey states that Lenin's success in predicting the
       course that the revolutionary movement would take was
       due more to his "ruthless pressure and propaganda in
       forcing a fluid political situation into channels open to
       capture by a trained fanatical minority than to any scien-
       tific knowledge of the laws of history." Lenin's success
       in 1917, Swabey contends, largely accounts for the aura
       of infallibility which surrounds his thought and obscures
       his numerous failures in prediction. [D16.8.S95]

660   Titarenko, Stepan. "Confirmed by History: The 70th An-
       niversary of the 2nd RSDLP Congress," Sov Life, 8, no.
       203 6-7.
       A brief review of Lenin's conflict with the Mensheviks.

661   Tompkins, Stuart R. "The Beginnings of Marxism in Russia,"
       in The Russian Intelligentsia: Makers of the Revolution-
       ary State. Norman: Oklahoma University Press, 1957;
       148-60.
       Lenin is not the focus of this chapter, but it contains a
       discussion of his involvement in the revolutionary move-
       ment in the 1893-1903 period. [DK32.7T58]

662   *Treadgold, Donald W. Lenin and His Rivals. The Struggle
       for Russia's Future, 1898-1906. Westport, Conn. :
       Greenwood Press, 1976 (reprint of a 1955 publication);
       291pp.
       A scholarly study of the groups and individuals that played
       a major role in shaping the political parties which emerged
       in Russia in the 1898-1906 period. Treadgold examines
       Lenin's thought and activity as a response to Russian de-
       velopments of the time and to the positions advanced by
       rival political groups. He demonstrates how Lenin, like
       his rivals, sought to construct "almost mathematically
       formal patterns of the course of future events" and then
       to "translate these patterns into reality with the utmost
       vigor and unlimited confidence," but that the rivalry
       among and disunity within the various parties (especially
       fomented by Lenin) prevented positive and effective action
       even amidst the opportunities offered by the 1905 Revolu-
       tion. [DK263.T74]

662a   Reviewed in:
        Am Hist R, 61 (Oct. 1955), 134, by G. Lantzeff.
        Annals AAPSS, 301 (Sept. 1955), 242, by E. Helm-
           reich.
        Lib J, 80 (1 May 1955), 1145, by H. Bernt.

New Sta Nat, 50 (5 Nov. 1955), 585, by A. J. P.
Taylor.
Slav R, 15, no. 1 (1956), 129, by L. Haimson.

663   Treviranus, G. R.   "Lenin's Vision," in Revolutions in Russia.   Their Lessons for the Western World.   New York:
Harper and Brothers, 1944; 44-53.
A survey of Lenin's 1907-1912 attempts to regroup and
rekindle the revolutionary movement following the reaction which set in after the 1905 Revolution.   Treviranus
stresses that more than ever Lenin was convinced of the
need to maintain ideological purity in the Marxist party,
a belief responsible for his "wrecking activities" within
the party.   [DK265. T67]

664   Tropkin, N. V.   "The Strategy and Tactics of Leninism,"
in LGT (anthology); 163-96.
A restatement of Lenin's dictates on strategy, and a
characterization of them as a scientifically devised, har-
monious system of guidelines which allowed the Bolsheviks to be aggressive, passive, or compromising depend-
ing upon the immediate circumstances, and which largely
account for the effective actions of the party in comparison to all other political groups of the times.

665   *Valentinov, Nikolay.   Encounters with Lenin.   London: Oxford University Press, 1968; 273pp.
Reminiscences, by a colleague, of Lenin's personality,
character, and revolutionary activity in the 1904-1905
period.   Valentinov recollects details of disputes, developments, and decisions within the party; describes
Lenin's work habits and methods, and recreates (in a
dialogue form) his many conversations with him on both
political and non-political matters.   Although he was a
disciple of Lenin, Valentinov does not present a hagiographic account of Lenin's life, a point well-noted in a
preface by Michael Karpovich: "Valentinov did not lose
his intellectual independence, or become a blind admirer,'
but rather "maintained his capacity for detached, shrewd
observation."   [DK254. L42V313]   Excerpt in Rus R, 13
(July 1954), 176-85.
665a   Reviewed in:
Am Hist R, 74 (June 1969), 1668, by S. W. Page.
Antioch R, (Summer 1969), 263.
Can S P, 11 (1960), 289-90, by R. C. Elwood.
*Can S P, 18 (1976), 442-56, by S. W. Page.
Contemp R, (Feb. 1969), 105, by P. Wilkenson.
Hist Today, (Feb. 1969), 135, by W. J. Fishman.
Listener, (14 Nov. 1968), 648, by R. Conquest.
*Nation, 208 (9 June 1969), 733-35, by J. M. Cammett.
National R, (23 Jan. 1969), 78, by G. Davenport.
N Y Times Bk R, (23 Mar. 1969), 10, by J. H. Bil-
lington.

New Yorker, (7 Dec. 1968), 246.
Newsweek, 72 (2 Dec. 1968), 106, by F. Y. Blumen-
feld.
Prob Com, 18, no. 4 (1969), 98-99, by A. Dallin.
R Meta, (Sept. 1969), 141.
*Rus R, 29 (Oct. 1969), 457-63, by A. Parry.
Slav R, 28 (June 1969), 332, by S. Baron.
Sov St, (Jan. 1969), 400, by J. Miller.
Va Q R, (Winter 1969), 30.

666   Vidyalankar, P. N. "The Bolsheviks Were True to the Mass-
       es and Lenin Was a Great Soul," in LHIII (anthology),
       68-70.
       A positive account Lenin's leadership of the revolutionary
       movement, with most attention given to his role in the
       formation of soviets in the countryside.

667   *Walicki, A. The Controversy over Capitalism. Studies in
       the Social Philosophy of the Russian Populists. Oxford:
       Clarendon, 1969; 197pp.
       Lenin is not the center of any one chapter in this study
       of Populism and its clash with Marxism, but it contains
       many references to and some discussion of his interpre-
       tation of Populism and its role in the social Democrats'
       polemics against the Populists in the 1890's. [HX312.W28]

668   *Weber, Nicholas S. "The Search for a Theory of Marxist
       Revolution in Russia of 1905: The Mensheviks and Le-
       nin," Indian Pol Sci R, 12, no. 2 (1978), 129-52.

669   Weisbord, Albert. "Bolshevism," in The Conquest of Power,
       Vol. 2. New York: Covici-Friede Publishers, 1937;
       776-802.
       A discussion of the pre-1903 principles of Lenin's thought
       stressing his belief that it was essential to establish a
       union of all oppressed peoples under the leadership of
       a tightly disciplined and centralized party of professional
       revolutionaries. [JA83.W4]

670   Wesson, Robert G. "The Revolution," in The Soviet Russian
       State. New York: Wiley and Sons, 1972; 35-62.
       An introduction to Lenin's rise to power emphasizing the
       role played by his creation of a formidable political ma-
       chine, willingness to seek assistance from any quarter
       that would advance the cause of revolution, and his mas-
       terful propaganda capitalizing on the immediate desires
       of the majority of the Russian people. [JN6515 1972.W47]

671   *Wilcox, E. H. "Lenin as a Protégé of the Old Regime,"
       Fortn R, 109 (Apr. 1918), 500-10.
       An argument that the Okhrana (tsarist secret police)
       tolerated Lenin and the Bolsheviks so as to justify its
       own existence by having a threat at which to point.   Wil-

cox examines the activities of Malinovsky, a police agent who infiltrated the Bolshevik Party, as an illustration of his argument.

672 *Wildman, Allan K. "Lenin's Battle with Kustarnichestvo: The Iskra Organization in Russia," Slav R, 23, no. 3 (Sept. 1964), 479-503.
An appraisal of Lenin's role in the ascendancy of the Iskra group at the 2nd Congress of the RSDLP for insights into his motives for divorcing Social Democracy from the workers' movement.

673 *_____. The Making of a Workers' Revolution. Russian Social Democracy, 1891-1903. Chicago: University of Chicago Press, 1967; 271pp.
This scholarly study is not focused upon Lenin, but it provides much information on and many insights into his early revolutionary activity and thought. [JN6598.S6W5]

674 *Wilson, Edmund. "Lenin: The Great Headmaster," in To the Finland Station. A Study in the Writing and Acting of History. Garden City: Doubleday, 1953; 372-402.
An examination of the influence of historical conditions and Lenin's personality in shaping his political philosophy of the 1893-1903 period. Wilson isolates as Lenin's principal characteristics his practicality and single-mindedness, and argues that his "headmaster mentality" was more influential than historical circumstances in determining his attitude towards associates and the workers' movement. [HX36.W5]

675 Wittfogel, Karl A. "The Marxist View of Russian Society and Revolution," W Pol, 12, no. 4 (July 1960), 487-508.
In part, a discussion of the influence of Marx's view of Russia as a "semi-Asiatic" despotic state on Lenin's development of a theory of revolution for backward societies.

676 _____. "The Operational Ideas of Communist Doctrine," Prob Com, 10, no. 5 (1961), 30-36.
In part, an examination of Lenin's "operational code" as a revision of Marxism in a totalitarian direction.

677 *Wolfe, Bertram D. "Dictatorship of Class, Party, or Doctrine?" in Marxism: 100 Years in the Life of a Doctrine. New York: Dell, 1967; 183-210.
A critique of Lenin's views on the relation of party to class in light of the writings of Marx and Engels. Wolfe states that Marx and Engels "make it clear that they oppose 'sects,' small minority organizations, or parties made up of a revolutionary elite, that seek to ... substitute themselves for the working class...." Lenin's What Is to Be Done? as well as his other writings on

the organizational question, Wolfe maintains, are flagrantly at odds with those of Marx and Engels since Lenin "from the outset favored not a party of the class but a party for the class." [HX40. W52]

678 *_____. "What Lenin Made of the Testament of Engels," Marxism: 100 Years in the Life of a Doctrine. New York: Dell, 1967; 83-101.
A critical appraisal of Lenin's assessment of World War I and its relation to the revolution. Wolfe argues that Lenin's 1914 position on the war differs significantly from Engels' interpretation of war and contradicts Lenin's own interpretation stated as late as 1913, a contradiction which Lenin attempted to conceal by projecting backwards in time his 1914 views. [HX40. W52]

679 *_____. "War Comes to Russia in Exile," Rus R, 20, no. 4 (1961), 294-311.
In part, a review of Lenin's radical anti-war position and its impact on the Russian emigré community in Switzerland.

680 *Wrebiak, T. , et al. "Consistent Democracy in the Passage to Socialism," W Marxist R, 16, no. 1 (Jan. 1973), 42-59.
A review of Lenin's Two Tactics of Social Democracy in the Democratic Revolution as part of a series of articles on the contemporary relevance of his major writings.

681 Yermolenko, Dmitri. "Revolution and Philosophy," Sov Life, 12, no. 159 (Dec. 1969), 38-39, 44.
A brief survey of Lenin's application of philosophy to revolutionary theory and practice.

682 *Zarodov, K. , et al. "Uniting Scientific Socialism with Social Activity of Working Class," W Marxist R, 15, no. 5 (May 1972), 5-21.
A review of What Is to Be Done? as part of a series of articles on the contemporary relevance of Lenin's major writings.

683 Zelikson-Bobrovskaya, C. S. "Unforgettable Meetings," in ROL (anthology), 39-64.
A recollection of meetings with Lenin in Geneva concerning a wide range of matters associated with the party, especially the publication of Iskra.

C. 1917 Revolutions

684   Ambartsumov, Yevgeni. "Lenin as a Political Leader,"
       Sov Life, 1, no. 160 (Jan. 1970), 16-17.
       An account of Lenin's leadership in the October Revolu-
       tion.

685   *Anweiler, Oskar. "Bolshevism and Councils, 1917," in The
       Soviets: The Russian Workers, Peasants and Soldiers
       Councils, 1905-1921. New York: Pantheon Books, 1974;
       144-207, bib. 309-24.
       A detailed examination of the relationship between Lenin
       and the soviets in the months before and during the Oc-
       tober Revolution. Anweiler writes that Lenin, prior to
       1917, viewed the soviets as "instruments of strikes and
       insurrection," and believed that the revolution would be
       led by Bolshevik organizations in the factories, army,
       and elsewhere. However, in the winter of 1916-1917, he
       reversed his position by developing the idea that the
       soviets would not only seize power but would be the in-
       stitution which would replace the old state machinery
       after the revolution. Anweiler asserts that Lenin's pub-
       lic idealization of the soviets was very different from
       his real intention which was to use them only as a means
       to gain power, an intention which he cloaked well through
       the slogan "all power to the soviets." [HX313.A713]

686   *Avtorkhanov, A. "Lenin and the Bolshevik Rise to Power,"
       St Sov Un, 10, no. 3 (1970), 1-73.
       An assessment of Lenin's activities from April to Oc-
       tober of 1917 arguing that, contrary to the official Soviet
       line, Lenin was faced with considerable fragmentation
       and disorganization within the Bolshevik Party.

687   Bonch-Bruyevich, Vladimir D. "The First Day," Sov Mil R,
       no. 10 (Oct. 1977), 9-11.
       Reminiscences of Lenin's actions on day one of the Oc-
       tober Revolution.

688   *_____. "Lenin in Petrograd and Moscow," Sov Lit, no.
       3 (1970), 20-38.
       A series of reminiscences of Lenin's activities during
       and immediately after the revolution.

689 _____. "No Rhetoric, Please," in NBPA (anthology), 86-87.
A brief recollection of Lenin's unfavorable reaction to the pomp which he encountered upon arriving at the Finland Station in April of 1917.

690 *Bubnov, A. "Lenin during the October Days," in LIOR (anthology), 25-29.
Recollections of opposition within the Bolshevik Party's Central Committee to Lenin's call for an insurrection in October of 1917.

691 *Bullard, Arthur. "German Gold," in The Russian Pendulum. Autocracy-Democracy-Bolshevism. New York: Macmillan, 1919; 95-110.
An investigation of the question of Lenin's relationship with the German government arguing that Germany's subsidization of revolutionary discontent elsewhere (India, Ireland, Egypt) and the vast amounts of money the Bolsheviks spent on propaganda both point towards Lenin having received very large sums of money from the Germans. Bullard notes that even if Lenin did receive such funds, it is absurd to conclude that he was a German agent, especially since he firmly believed that revolution would occur in Germany soon after it succeeded in Russia. [DK265.B9]

692 *Carmichael, Joel. "April--Lenin Arrives," in A Short History of the Russian Revolution. New York: Basic Books, 1964; 64-78.
An account of Lenin's April return to Russia, and an argument that his April Theses is consistent with his long-standing voluntarism. Carmichael also states that although Lenin looked at the question of the revolution from a purely practical perspective, he felt compelled to seek an ideological justification for his radical position by adapting Trotsky's theory of permanent revolution. This study contains much additional information on Lenin's leadership of the party in 1917. [DK265.C383]

693 *_____. "German Money and Bolshevik Honour. The 'Scandal' of 1917," Encounter, 42, no. 3 (Mar. 1974), 81-90.

694 *_____. "Lenin + ? Equals Trotsky--Behind the Bolshevik Putsch," Midstream, 21, no. 10 (1975), 20-34.
An appraisal of the role played by Alexander Helphand (Parvus) in procuring German assistance for Lenin.

695 *Carr, Albert. "Lenin: The Science of Revolution," in Juggernaut. The Path of Dictatorship. New York: Viking, 1939; 231-62.
A presentation of Lenin as the crucial ingredient in the

October Revolution arguing that, although many of the preconditions for revolution were in existence in 1917, "these factors alone might have meant nothing had it not been for the astonishing ability and foresight of Lenin. In support of this statement, Carr discusses Lenin's revolutionary program, propaganda, and step-by-step guidance of the party in 1917, and concludes that "Lenin was, in truth, an original kind of scientist, the world's first technical specialist in revolution." [D108. C3]

696　*Carsten, F. L. "Was Lenin a German Agent?," Prob Com, 8, no. 1 (1959), 44-48.
An analysis of the conflicting accounts of Lenin's German connections as advanced by Zeman (Germany and the Russian Revolution) and Moorehead (The Russian Revolution).

697　*"The Charges against the Bolsheviks," in The Russian Provisional Government 1917. Documents, Vol. 3, Robert P. Browder and Alexander F. Kerensky, eds. Stanford: Stanford University Press, 1961; 1364-82.
A collection of documents upon which was based the July 1917 charge that Lenin was a German agent. The editors include the communiqué, released by Minister of Justice Perevezev, which listed the charges; the Bolshevik Party's official denial; a statement by the Central Executive Committee of the Soviet calling for an investigation of the charges, and a series of comments on the whole affair by N. Nekrasov, M. Tereshchenko, and A. Kerensky. [DK265. 19. B7]

698　"Chernov on Lenin," in The Russian Provisional Government 1917. Documents, Vol. 3, Robert P. Browder and Alexander F. Kerensky, eds. Stanford: Stanford University Press, 1961; 1208-10.
An attack on Lenin's April Theses as the product of a narrow-minded and totally irresponsible fanatic, and a plea for socialists to counter Lenin's 'madness' before it provoked hysteria. [DK265. 19. B7]

699　*Chernov, V. "Descent into Bolshevism," in The Great Russian Revolution. New York: Russell and Russell, 1966 (reprint of a 1936 publication); 403-34.
A charge that Lenin came to power not because his leadership qualities won for him the support of the majority of Russians, but because he used well the destructive force of the "declassed mob" (a minority of the proletariat). This lack of true popular support, Chernov argues, predetermined that Lenin's government would be a dictatorial one. [DK265. C48]

700　*Cliff, Tony. Lenin. Vol. II. All Power to the Soviets. London: Pluto Press, 1976; 412pp.
A detailed examination of Lenin's revolutionary thought

and activity from the outbreak of World War I to the October Revolution. Cliff devotes the vast majority of his attention to Lenin's activities in the summer of 1917, where he argues that the Bolshevik Party was far from being a monolith under Lenin's control. Lenin, in fact, was constantly struggling with the conservatism of the party leadership and with the revolutionary impatience of the party's lower ranks and the Petrograd workers as he sought to select the correct moment for revolution. Cliff also devotes considerable attention to Lenin's various writings during this three year period. [DK254. L4C6]

701 Crankshaw, Edward. "When Lenin Returned," Atlan Mo, 194, no. 4, (1954), 63-68.

702 Daniels, Robert V. "The Bolshevik Gamble," Rus R, 26, no. 4 (Oct. 1967), 331-46.
An argument that the October Revolution was neither inevitable nor the result of Lenin's masterly leadership.

703 * _____. Red October. The Bolshevik Revolution of 1917. New York: Scribner's Sons, 1967; 269pp. , bib. 247-60.
A comprehensive analysis of the events of October 1917 which led to the Bolshevik seizure of power stressing the inadequacy of those interpretations which emphasize the planned and organized character of the insurrection. Daniels studies carefully Lenin's efforts to persuade the party's leadership that the time for revolution had arrived and asserts that Lenin, by October 19th, had "lost hope that an insurrection could still be launched before the Congress of Soviets.... He was not to be heard from again until the revolution was actually underway." The revolution actually began, Daniels argues, as an unplanned, fitful and defensive response, by lower level agencies and the workers themselves, to Kerensky's "ill-conceived countermove" against the Bolshevik threat to the Provisional Government. Lenin only brought guidance to the revolution once it was already underway. [DK265. D27]

704 _____, ed. The Russian Revolution. Englewood Cliffs: Prentice-Hall, 1972; 184pp. , bib. 183-84.
A collection of excerpts from primary documents on the events of 1917, with short introductions and transitions provided by the editor. Daniels includes materials dealing with Lenin's opposition to the Provisional Government, his plans for revolution, and his actual leadership of the revolt itself. [DK265. A5167]

705 Dewey, H. W. "Lenin's Journey in the Sealed Train," NY Times M, (26 Mar. 1967), 26-27+.

706 Dosch-Fleurot, Arno. "Lenin," in Through War to Revolution.

Being the Experiences of a Newspaper Correspondent in War and Revolution. 1914-1920. London: John Lane and Bodley Head, 1931; 148-65.
An account of the effectiveness of Lenin's propaganda campaign launched against the Provisional Government after his April return to Russia. [D521.D6]

707 Fischer, Fritz. "Lenin and the Germans," in L (anthology), 150-52.
A discussion of the circumstances which led to German support for Lenin's return to Russia. Fischer discounts the charge that Lenin was a German agent, but rather sees a policy of reciprocal aid as the cause of their temporary cooperation. Excerpt from Germany's Aims in the First World War. New York: Norton, 1967; 367-68.

708 *Frankel, Jonathan. "Lenin's Doctrinal Revolution of April 1917," J Contemp Hist, 4, no. 2 (Apr. 1969), 117-42.
An argument that Lenin's April Theses, contrary to most interpretations, added nothing positive or new to the "old Lenin."

709 *Futrell, Michael. "Thermometers, Contraceptives, Bolsheviks, etc.," in Northern Underground. Episodes of Russian Revolutionary Transport and Communications through Scandinavia and Finland, 1863-1917. New York: Praeger, 1963; 152-96.
An examination of the activities of Jacob Fürstenberg, a vital link in Lenin's wartime Scandinavian underground network, for insights into the question of whether or not Lenin received German financial assistance in 1917. Futrell states that Lenin's communications with Fürstenberg do not reveal any "hard evidence" that Lenin was receiving such assistance. He speculates that the money which reached the Bolshevik Party from Stockholm was gathered by Fürstenberg through illegal dealings with German-backed smugglers, and that it is unlikely that Lenin was aware of Fürstenberg's sources but merely accepted without question the money which Fürstenberg, a devout Bolshevik, raised in support of the revolution. [DK262.F96]

710 Galbraith, John K. "Lenin and the Great Ungluing," Listener, 97 (10 Feb. 1977), 167-70.

711 "German Gold Paid to Lenin," Cur Hist M, 14 (Apr. 1921), 56.

712 "German Money for Lenin (1917)," Tablet, 207 (21 Apr. 1956), 362.

713 *Geyer, Dietrich. "The Bolshevik Insurrection in Petrograd,"

in Revolutionary Russia: A Symposium, Richard Pipes, ed. Garden City: Doubleday, 1969; 209-28. An inquiry into the circumstances and steps which brought success to the Bolshevik revolt. Geyer contends that although Lenin studied carefully the art of insurrection and was astonishingly confident in the accuracy of his assessment of the revolutionary scene, it was, in fact, Trotsky's speeches highlighting the imminent danger to Petrograd posed by counter-revolutionary treachery that led the soviets to support the Bolshevik seizure of power as a defensive measure. [DK265.A135]

714   Glezerman, G. E. "On the Interrelationship between Objective Conditions and the Subjective Factor in the October Revolution," St Sov Phil, 7, no. 1 (1968), 14-25. In part, a discussion of Lenin's assessment of the revolutionary conditions in 1917 in Russia.

715   *Goodspeed, D. J. "Petrograd 1917," in The Conspirators. A Study of the Coup d'Etat. New York: Viking, 1962; 70-107. An analysis of Lenin's actions in October of 1917 arguing that Lenin staged a coup d'etat as opposed to having led a popular, mass revolution. Goodspeed contends that Lenin's careful planning and narrow focus of attack fit perfectly the definition of a coup as "the capture of the state by conspiracy and sudden, focused violence." In spite of Lenin's brilliant organization of the coup, Goodspeed concludes, it was quite poorly executed and succeeded largely because of the ineptness and unpopularity of the Provisional Government. [JC494.C6]

716   Higgins, Jim. "1917: Lenin and the Working Class," Call, 19, no. 8 (Jan. 1968), 5-10.

717   *Hook, Sidney. "The Russian Revolution: A Test Case," in The Hero in History. A Study in Limitation and Possibility. New York: John Day, 1943; 184-228. An argument that the October Revolution could not have succeeded without Lenin. Hook states that Lenin singlehandedly reversed the position of the Bolshevik Party from one of compromise to one of commitment to revolution; selected the proper moment to stage the revolution; led the party through the revolt itself; and followed policies immediately after October that enabled the Bolsheviks to remain in power. In each of these instances, Hook asserts, "if Lenin had not been on the scene, not a single revolutionary leader could have substituted for him." [D16.9H67 1950]

718   No Entry.

719   Iman, Zafar. "Lenin and the Russian Revolution," Mainstream, 16, no. 34 (22 Apr. 1978), 29-31+.

720   Ivanov, O. "Strategist of the Revolution," Sov Mil R, no.
       3 (Mar. 1970), 7-9.

721   *Katkov, George. "German Foreign Office Documents on Fi-
       nancial Support to the Bolsheviks in 1917," Int Aff, 32,
       no. 2 (Apr. 1956), 181-98.

722   *_____. "German Political Intervention," in Russia 1917.
       The February Revolution. New York: Harper and Row,
       1967; 63-118, bib. 447-52.
       An interpretive discussion of the growth of the German
       government's interest in Lenin as a possible means of
       disrupting Russia's war effort. Katkov states that Ger-
       many's concern for promoting revolution in Russia began
       as soon as the war started, but only later (through the
       efforts of Helphand and others) was Lenin seen as the
       best prospect for provoking such a revolt. Once Lenin
       was selected as the German catalyst for revolt, Katkov
       argues, the Bolsheviks were the recipients of massive
       financial support from Germany, a claim which he sup-
       ports by reviewing Allied information on this issue and
       by refuting the defensive argument which Lenin put forth
       against the charge that he was a German agent.
       [DK265.19.K3 1967] For a similar argument see Katkov's
       "German Political Intervention in Russia during World
       War I" in Revolutionary Russia: A Symposium, Richard
       Pipes, ed. Garden City: Doubleday, 1968; 80-122.

723   Keep, John. "1917: The Tyranny of Paris over Petrograd,"
       Sov St, 20, no. 1 (1968), 22-35.
       A discussion of how the legacy of the French Revolution
       may have influenced the vision and judgment of Lenin
       and Trotsky in 1917.

724   Keller, Werner. "Germany Finances Lenin," in East Minus
       West=Zero. Russia's Debt to the Western World, 862-
       1962. New York: Putnam's Sons, 1961; 189-94.
       An argument that financial support from the German
       government was instrumental in Lenin's seizure and main-
       tenance of power. [DK67.K413]

725   *Kennan, George. "The Sisson Documents," J Mod Hist, 28,
       no. 2 (June 1956), 130-54.
       A detailed investigation of the Sisson Documents arguing
       that they have so many inaccuracies and improbabilities
       in them that they must be dismissed as forgeries, prob-
       ably at the hand of A. Ossendowski.

726   *Kerensky, Alexander F. "The Lenin-Ludendorff Alliance,"
       in The Crucifixion of Liberty. New York: Kraus, 1972
       (reprint of a 1934 publication); 313-32.
       An emotional attack, by the last leader of the Provisional
       Government, on Lenin as a German agent. Kerensky

states that Lenin not only arrived in Petrograd with the aid of the German government, but that his revolutionary activities were financed by Germany and were coordinated with military plans for a counter-offensive. He concludes that even if Lenin's motives were based only on his desire to seize power rather than serve Germany, he is still a disgusting traitor who "deliberately sacrificed Russia to his beliefs." [DK265.K395]

727 * _____. "Lenin's Way to Power," in The Crucifixion of Liberty. New York: Kraus, 1972 (reprint of a 1934 publication); 361-94.
An argument that Lenin came to power by spreading panic over the insane attempt by General Kornilov to replace the Provisional Government with a right-wing dictatorship. Kerensky asserts that prior to the Kornilov affair, Russia was moving towards democracy while Lenin was hiding in disgrace over the abortive July uprising, and that without the counter-revolutionary threat posed by Kornilov, Lenin never would have been able to deceive the workers into a revolt that has been Russia's ruination. [DK265.K395]

728 *Kingston-Mann, Esther. "Problems of Order and Revolution: The Peasant Question in March and April, 1917," Rus Hist, 6 (1979), 39-56.

729 Kirby, Louis P. "Lenin Returns," in The Russian Revolution. Boston: Meador Publishing Company, 1940; 175-204, bib. 677-78.
An account of Lenin's April 1917 return to Russia and his activities in the few days thereafter stressing that German financial support of the Bolsheviks enabled him to launch his ambitious plan to overthrow the Provisional Government. [DK266.K53]

730 _____. "Lenin Strikes Again," in The Russian Revolution. Boston: Meador Publishing Company, 1940; 246-93.
An analysis of Lenin's preparation for and leadership of the October Revolution. Kirby presents a highly negative image of Lenin and the Bolshevik leadership as shabby, lawless, jail-embittered adventurers. [DK266.K53]

731 Kochan, Lionel. "Lenin Arrives," in Russia in Revolution, 1890-1918. New York: New American Library, 1966; 205-11, bib. 327-42.
A general review of Lenin's return from Swiss exile, his proclamation of the April Theses, and the campaign to win both party and popular support for his radical program. [DK262.K6]

732 Krastyn, J. "The Struggles of the Bolsheviki for the Peasantry in the October Revolution," Agr Prob, 10-11 (1932), 56-70.

733 Krupskaya, N. K. "Lenin as a Propagandist and Agitator,"
     Sov Ed, 12, nos. 3-5 (Jan.-Mar. 1970), 63-64.

734 "Lenin and October," Sov Mil R, no. 10 (Oct. 1977), 18-20.

735 "Lenin: The Man and His Aims," in LHIII (anthology), 50-
     51.
     An attack on those who claim that Lenin was a German
     agent.

736 *"Lenine and Trotzky German Agents," Cur Hist M, 9, part
     I (Nov.-Dec. 1918), 291-306; 512-28.
     Copies of the Sisson documents and the report of the
     commission which studied their authenticity.

737 *Liebman, Marcel. The Russian Revolution. New York:
     Random House, 1970; 391pp., bib. 371-76.
     Lenin is not focus of this study, but it contains a com-
     prehensive account of the historical and ideological cli-
     mate of revolutionary Russia as well as a great deal of
     information on Lenin as the chief protagonist of the
     events of 1917. An excellent subject index makes for
     easy location of material on Lenin. [DK265. L41913]

738 Lippmann, W. and C. Merz. "Test of the News; an Examin-
     ation of the News Reports in the New York Times on
     Aspects of the Russian Revolution of Special Importance
     to Americans, March 1917-March 1920," New Rep, 23,
     supp. (4 Aug. 1920), 1-42; (11 Aug. 1920), 299-301.

739 *Longley, D. A. "The Divisions in the Bolshevik Party in
     March 1917," Sov St, 24, no. 1 (1972), 61-76.
     A critique of the accepted interpretation of a three-part
     division (right-center-left) within the party upon Lenin's
     April return to Russia.

740 *Lunacharsky, Anatole. "Smolny on the Great Night," Sov
     Lit, no. 3 (1970), 11-15.

741 Mailloux, Kenneth F. and Heloise P. Mailloux. Lenin. The
     Exile Returns. Princeton: Auerbach, 1971; 150pp., bib.
     144-46.
     A popularly oriented account of Lenin's leadership in the
     April-October period presenting him as the crucial in-
     gredient in the October Revolution and as a man who
     "changed the course of history."

742 Markoff, A. "Lenin on Agitation and Propaganda and the
     Tasks of the Communist Party," Communist, 13 (Jan.
     1934), 107-12.
     In part, a review of Lenin's use of propaganda in 1917.

743 Mavor, James. The Russian Revolution. New York: Mac-
     millan, 1928; 470pp., bib. 441-45.

Although Lenin is not the sole focus of any one chapter in this study, it contains significant information on his thought, policies, and leadership before, during and immediately after the October Revolution. [DK265.M37]

744 *Medvedev, Roy A. The October Revolution. New York: Columbia University Press, 1979; 240pp.
A general study, by a Soviet historian and dissident, of the Bolsheviks' seizure of power and consolidation of their position up to spring, 1918. In examining Lenin's leadership in 1917, Medvedev stresses the negative response within the Bolshevik Party to Lenin's argument that Russia was ripe for a socialist revolution, and that without Lenin's aggressive tactics and tireless labor the revolt may not have taken place. Lenin's early policies as Soviet leader do not receive the same type of praise, however, as Medvedev contends that they led directly to the bloodshed of the Civil War. [DK265.M375]

745 *Melgunov, S. P. The Bolshevik Seizure of Power. Santa Barbara: ABC-Clio Press, 1972; 260pp.
A general study, written by a Russian historian and contemporary of the October Revolution. Melgunov examines the landmark events and developments of 1917, and questions those analysts who assert that Lenin was a brilliant revolutionary tactician who led a carefully planned and widely popular revolt. [DK265.M39613 1972]

746 Merindol, Gaston de. "Lenin and Trotzky," Liv Age, 299 (12 Oct. 1918), 89-92.
Two separate sketches on the Bolshevik leaders, with that of Lenin noting his qualities as a revolutionary and his ties with the German government.

747 Mieli, Renato. "Lenin and the Revolution," Prob Com, 16, no. 6 (Nov.-Dec. 1967), 71-75.

748 *Miliukov, Paul N. The Russian Revolution, Vol. I. Gulf Breeze, Florida: Academic International Press, 1978; 227pp.
Lenin is not the sole focus of any one chapter in this work, but as a major study of the revolution written by a Russian liberal leader and intellectual of the times, it is an exceptionally valuable source of information on the major events and personalities of 1917 Russia. [DK265.M49313]

749 *Moorehead, Alan. "The German Revolutionary Net," in The Russian Revolution. New York: Bantam Books, 1959; 112-32.
A discussion of the German government's involvement in the promotion of revolution in Russia in the pre-1917 period, with some reference to Lenin's connections with Helphand and Kesuela. [DK265.M79]

750   *   _____. "Lenin's Return," in The Russian Revolution.
New York: Bantam Books, 1959; 174-89.
An account of Lenin's reaction to news of the February
Revolution, his efforts to return to Russia from Switzer-
land, and the impact of his radical program announced
upon arrival in Petrograd. [DK265.M79]

751   *Mushtukov, Viktor and Vadim Kruchina-Bogdanov. Lenin and
the Revolution. Moscow: Novosti Press, 1970; 292pp.
A positive account of Lenin's thought and activity in the
February-October 1917 period, with much reliance upon
Lenin's own words. Although hagiographic and attributing to Lenin foresight and control of events questioned
by Western analysts, this work presents excellent detail
on some of the events of 1917, especially the abortive
revolt of July. [DK254.L46M87]

752   *Nikitine, B. V. "German Money," in The Fatal Years.
Fresh Revelations on a Chapter of Underground History.
Westport, Conn.: Hyperion, 1977 (reprint of a 1938 pub-
lication); 108-32.
A presentation, by a colonel in the tsarist counter-
espionage office, of evidence (letters, telegrams, inter-
rogation transcripts, surveillance reports) detailing
Lenin's alleged financial involvement with German agents.
[DK265.9S4N5413]

753   *Page, Stanley W. "Lenin in 1917: From April to July,"
Harv Sl St, 4 (1957), 435-55.

754   *   _____. "Lenin's April Theses and the Latvian Peasant-
Soldiery," in Reconsiderations on the Russian Revolution,
Ralph C. Elwood, ed. Cambridge, Mass.: Slavica,
1976; 154-72. [DK265.A138]

755   *Page, Stanley W. and Andrew Ezergailis. "The Lenin-Lat-
vian Axis in the November Seizure of Power," Can S P,
19, no. 1 (1977), 32-49.

756   Parry, Albert. "Power Was Lying in the Streets; We Picked
It Up," NY Times M, (28 Sept. 1969), 30-31+.

757   *Payne, Robert. "The Coming of Lenin," in The Rise and
Fall of Stalin. New York: Simon and Schuster, 1965;
163-75, bib. 725-29.
A review of the stark contrast between Lenin's radical
"Letters from Afar" and the moderate position taken
by Stalin and other Bolshevik leaders prior to Lenin's
return from Swiss exile. Payne also discusses, in subsequent sections, Stalin's shift to a position supportive
of Lenin's and his work, as a "shadow behind the scenes,"
in the summer of 1917 to advance the program of revolution set by Lenin. [DK268.S8P37]

758 *Pearson, Michael. The Sealed Train. New York: Putnam's
Sons, 1975; 320pp. , bib. 308-13.
An investigation of the controversial circumstances surrounding Lenin's connection with the German government
in 1917. Pearson discusses how and why the German
government came to an agreement with Lenin on the matter of his return to Russia, and provides details on the
departure and the journey itself as well as on Lenin's
arrival in Petrograd. Lenin's delay in Berlin while in
transit, Pearson speculates, may have been due to a
secret meeting between Lenin and members of the German government at which the latter pledged massive financial assistance to the Bolsheviks and thereby emboldened
Lenin to adopt an ambitious and radical position against
the Provisional Government. [DK254. L443P4] Excerpt
in Horizon, 16 (Spring 1974), 49-55.

759 Pethybridge, Roger. "Propaganda and Political Rumors,"
in The Spread of the Russian Revolution: Essays on
1917. New York: St. Martin's Press, 1972; 140-75.
Lenin is not the focus of this chapter, but it contains
some discussion of his use of propaganda in 1917.
[DK265. P393]

760 Podvoisky, Nikolai. Petrograd, October, 1917: Reminiscences. Moscow: Foreign Languages Publishing House,
1957.
Not available for annotation. Excerpts in Sov Mil R,
no. 10, supp. Oct. 1977), 1-16; L (anthology), 155-57.

761 *Rabinowitch, Alexander. "Lenin's campaign for an Insurrection," in The Bolsheviks Come to Power. The Revolution of 1917 in Petrograd. New York: Norton, 1976;
191-208.
A scholarly analysis of Lenin's difficult struggle to win
Bolshevik Party and popular support for armed revolt.
Rabinowitch examines the intra-party dispute triggered
by Lenin's April Theses (especially between the conservative Central Committee and the radical Bolshevik Petersburg Committee) and develops the thesis that the party
was badly disorganized and sharply divided throughout
the months which preceded the revolt. In subsequent
chapters (not focused upon Lenin alone) Rabinowitch provides much additional valuable information on Lenin's
role in the insurrection. [DK265. 8. L4R27]

762 *_____. "The Petrograd Garrison and the Bolshevik Seizure
of Power," in Revolution and Politics in Russia. Essays in Memory of B. I. Nicolaevsky, Alexander and
Janet Rabinowitch, eds. Bloomington: Indiana University
Press, 1972; 172-91.
Although not specifically on Lenin, this essay provides
useful information on and insights into Lenin's struggle

with the Provisional Government, Petrograd Soviet, and other socialist parties to win the support of the crucially important garrison forces of Petrograd. [DK246. R47]

763   *_____. Prelude to Revolution. The Petrograd Bolsheviks and the July 1917 Uprising. Bloomington: Indiana University Press, 1968; 299pp. , 236-52.
A comprehensive examination of Bolshevik involvement in the July revolt of 1917 contending that this event can be best understood through a consideration of the beliefs, character, and action of the three main Bolshevik organizations in Petrograd rather than by studying the thought and policies of Lenin. To this end, Rabinowitch analyzes the role played in July by the radical Petersburg Committee, the somewhat less radical Bolshevik Military Organization, and the conservative, fragmented Central Committee. There emerges from this analysis a picture of the chaotic, divisive, and polycentric nature of Lenin's party organization, a picture which casts considerable doubt on those interpretations which present Lenin as the commander of a cohesive revolutionary party.
[DK265. 8. L4R3]

764   "Rabochaia Gazeta on Lenin's Program," in The Russian Provisional Government 1917. Documents, Vol. 3, Robert P. Browder and Alexander F. Kerensky, eds. Stanford: Stanford University Press, 1961; 1208.
A brief excerpt from an April 1917 article which attacked Lenin's April Theses as a program that disregarded the objective conditions in Russia and could only do harm to the revolution by arousing popular hostility against it.
[DK265. 19. B7]

765   Radkey, Oliver H. The Agrarian Foes of Bolshevism. Promise and Default of the Russian Socialist Revolutionaries, February to October 1917. New York: Columbia University Press, 1962; 521pp. , bib. 486-500.
Lenin is not the focus of any one chapter in this scholarly study of the 1917 activities of the Socialist Revolutionary Party, but it contains a discussion of his criticism of the SR's and his adaptation of their land program.
[JN6598. S65R2]

766   Rakhya, E. "On the Eve of the October Revolution," in LIOR (anthology), 11-18.
A recollection, by Lenin's bodyguard, of both the mood of the capital and Lenin's activities on the eve of the October Revolution.

767   *Raskolnikov, F. "The October Revolution," in LIOR (anthology), 30-43.
A reminiscence of the actions of Lenin immediately following the revolution, with most attention given to his

work in planning the defense of Petrograd against an anticipated Kerensky counter-offensive.

768 *Reed, John. Ten Days that Shook the World. New York: Modern Library, 1960; 439pp. (first published in 1919). Lenin is not the focus of this recollection of the October Revolution, but it is a valuable and much quoted source of information on his activities during the revolt. Reed, an American journalist, radical, and friend of Lenin, provides a detailed, eye-witness, and sympathetic account of the days surrounding the revolution. To quote Bertram Wolfe's introduction: "as a record of significant detail, as a repository of facts for the historian, his book is crammed with precious material: interviews, speeches, resolutions, press accounts." [DK265.R38] Excerpt in L (anthology), 143.

769 *Roberts, Henry L. "Causality and Contingency in March and November 1917," in Eastern Europe: Politics, Revolution, and Diplomacy. New York: Knopf, 1970; 221-40. An argument that, unlike the February Revolution which was "the consequence of substantial and necessary causes," the advent of the Bolsheviks "was not geared to any real political or historical necessity." Roberts contends that Lenin was successful in October because of a combination of luck and his ability to manipulate to Bolshevik advantage a chaotic situation, and not because of any carefully designed blueprint of revolution. [DR48.R56]

770 Rogger, Hans. "October 1917 and the Tradition of Revolution," Rus R, 27, no. 4 (1968), 395-413. An appraisal of Lenin's role in the revolution, with much reference to R. Daniels' Russian Review article of October, 1967.

771 Ross, Edward Alsworth. "German Agents," in The Russian Bolshevik Revolution. New York: Century, 1921; 174-81. A discussion of the July 1917 campaign to discredit Lenin and the Bolsheviks by branding them as German agents. Ross summarizes the charges leveled against Lenin by Burtsev and Pereverzev (Minister of Justice), and reviews why the campaign failed to discredit Lenin in the eyes of the workers. [DK265.R72]

772 _____. "Lenin and His Slogan," in The Russian Bolshevik Revolution. New York: Century, 1921; 102-12. A general survey of the contents and impact of Lenin's April Theses. [DK265.R72]

773 *Saul, Norman E. "Lenin's Decision to Seize Power: The Influence of Events in Finland," Sov St, 24, no. 4 (Apr. 1973), 491-505.

An argument that Lenin's isolated position in Finland (August-October of 1917) gave him a perspective on events in Russia which enabled him to see revolution as an immediate possibility and necessity.

774   Scharlau, W. "Parvus-Helphand and the First World War," St. Anthony's College, Oxford, 1963 (dissertation).

775   Schillinger, Elisabeth H. "British and U. S. Newspaper Coverage of the Bolshevik Revolution," Journalism Q, 43, no. 1 (1966), 10-16, 24.
An account of the poor Western coverage of the revolution, and a contention that the press gave Lenin far less credit for ability than history has shown he is due.

776   *Schurer, H. "Karl Moor: German Agent and Friend of Lenin," J Contemp Hist, 5, no. 2 (1970), 131-52.
A discussion of Moor's acceptance by Lenin as a great internationalist, while, in fact, he was an agent (1917-1919) of the German, Swiss, and Austrian governments, a fact much later discovered and the cause of his being written out of official documents on Lenin.

777   *Senn, Alfred. "The Myth of German Money during the First World War," Sov St, 28, no. 1 (Jan. 1976), 83-90.

778   *_____. "New Documents on Lenin's Departure from Switzerland, 1917," Int R Soc Hist, 19, no. 2 (1974), 245-76.
A series of documents issued in October of 1917 by the Russian Emigré Commission which investigated Lenin's German connections.

779   *Sherkovin, Yu. A. "Lenin's Leading Role in the October Revolution," in LR (anthology), 133-56.
A favorable review of Lenin's actions in the February-October 1917 period, attributing to Lenin much insight into and control over the course of events.

780   *Shukman, Harold. Lenin and the Russian Revolution. New York: Putnam's Sons, 1967; 224pp., bib. 210-12.
An analysis of the conditions and policies which led to the collapse of both the tsarist and Provisional Governments, and an assessment of the role played by Lenin in the revolutionary process. Shukman stresses the importance of Lenin's forging of a revolutionary party, in the years prior to 1917, which could respond effectively to the opportunities presented by wartime difficulties and the Provisional Government's failure to cope with them. The author also contends that Lenin's claim to greatness as a leader rests more with his ability to retain rather than seize power, a feat which he accomplished by compromising his Marxist principles, dumping the utopianism

of State and Revolution, using of violence and terror,
and establishing a monopoly of power for the Bolshevik
Party. [DK262. S48]

780a   Reviewed in:
Am Hist R, (Dec. 1969), 546, by S. W. Page.
History (L), (Oct. 1968), 471, by J. Keep.
Hist Today, (July 1967), 491, by W. J. Fishman.
Int Aff (L), (Jan. 1968), 756, by M. Hookham.
New Sta, (42 Mar. 1967), 411, by J. P. Nettl.
Rus R, (Oct. 1967), 391, by A. E. Adams.
SEER, (Jan. 1968), 251, by B. Hollingsworth.
Spectator, (3 Mar. 1967), 251, by R. Hingley.
TLS, (16 Mar. 1967), 225.

781   *Sisson, Edgar. "The German-Bolshevik Conspiracy," in
One Hundred Red Days. A Personal Recollection of the
Bolshevik Revolution. New Haven: Yale University
Press, 1931, appendix; 1-30.
A collection of documents which allegedly illustrate that
Lenin was a paid agent of the German government. Sisson, a special envoy of President Wilson, presents letters, telegrams, copies of secret transactions and other
documents which he contends illustrate that Lenin's
government was "not a Russian government at all, but
a German government acting solely in the interests of
Germany." He includes a copy of the Report of the
Special Committee on the Genuineness of the Documents
to counter charges, made in 1918, that the documents
were not authentic. Although the documents were important at the time for casting doubt on Lenin's integrity,
more contemporary scholarship (G. Kennan) has revealed
that they are forgeries. Also published as The German-
Bolshevik Conspiracy. Washington: Committee on Public
Information, 1918. [DK265. S515]

782   . One Hundred Red Days. A Personal Recollection
of the Bolshevik Revolution. New Haven: Yale University Press, 1931, appendix; 1-30.
A bitter assault on Lenin, the Bolshevik Revolution, and
the policies pursued by the Bolsheviks in the months
following the revolution. Sisson presents Lenin as an
evil genius who seized any and all opportunities to advance his destructive philosophy. In support of this
image of Lenin, he discusses Lenin's policies as being
unscrupulous, dictatorial, and the cause of the "brigand-
age and murderous civil war in Russia," and develops
the thesis that Lenin was "a working ally of Germany" as illustrated by the documents which he appends to his study
(see annotation in item 781). [DK265. S515]

783   *Smirnitsky, Nikolai et al. "The Russian Revolution," Sov
Life, 9-12, nos. 120-135 (Sept. 1966-Dec. 1967).
A sixteen-part series of articles on the revolution and
Lenin's role in it.

784   Smith, Adolphe. "Lenin: A Russian Traitor," National R,
       (Apr. 1921), 183-94.

785   *Sobolev, P. N. et al. The Great October Socialist Revolu-
           tion. Moscow: Progress Publishers, 1977; 560pp.
           Lenin is not the sole focus of any one chapter in this
           Soviet history of the October Revolution, but it contains
           hundreds of sections on and references to his thought
           and leadership which collectively present him as the
           master planner-theoretician-revolutionary who led the
           Bolshevik Party and the workers at every turn of events
           in 1917. [DK265.I74513]

786   Sokolnikov, G. "Lenin in October," in LIOR (anthology),
       19-24.
           A recollection of Lenin's work in planning the fine de-
           tails of the revolt itself.

787   Stacey, F. W. Lenin and the Russian Revolutions. London:
       Edward Arnold Publishers, 1968; 63pp.
           As part of the "Archives Series" designed for young
           readers, this booklet presents primary materials to il-
           lustrate the causes of the revolution and the role played
           in it by Lenin. Stacey selects excerpts from such pri-
           mary sources as Reed, Sukhanov, Kerensky, Stalin,
           Krupskaya, and others, and provides a historical intro-
           duction for each group of sources. [DK265.A5427]

788   Stalin, Joseph. "The Genius of Revolution," in LIOR (anthol-
       ogy), 7-10.
           A brief description of Lenin's positive qualities as a rev-
           olutionary leader, with the October Revolution serving
           as a case study.

789   *   . The October Revolution. New York: International
       Publishers, 1978 (reprint of a 1934 publication); 168pp.
           A collection of articles and speeches (1920-1927) on the
           planning and execution of the revolution. Stalin estab-
           lishes the guiding role of Lenin in 1917, underplays the
           divisions within the party, and attempts to discredit the
           role played by Trotsky in the revolt as well as to refute
           the interpretation of the revolution advanced by Trotsky.
           [DK265.S667713 1978]

790   *Stalin, Joseph et al. Lenin in Action. The Early Days of
       Soviet Power. Personal Reminisences of Lenin in the
       Revolution of 1917. London: Martin Laurence, 1934.
           Not available for annotation.

791   *Sukhanov, N. N. "Lenin's Arrival," in The Russian Revolu-
           tion: An Eyewitness Account, Vol. I. New York: Har-
           per, 1962; 269-92.
           An eyewitness, widely quoted account of the atmosphere

surrounding Lenin's arrival at the Finland Station in April of
1917. Sukhanov describes the anticipation of the crowd, Lenin's welcome, his speeches, and the crowd's reaction. In
particular, he notes the shock caused by the radicalness of
Lenin's position that the socialist leadership in Russia was
betraying the workers by supporting the Provisional Government and the war, a position for which Lenin was later able
to win considerable support, Sukhanov claims, because of his
fanaticism and demogoguery. [DK265. S8475] Excerpts in
The Russian Revolution: An Anthology, M. Dziewanowski,
ed. New York: Crowell, 1970; 67-100; Liv Age, 314 (23
Sept. 1922), 759-64; L (anthology), 143-45, 152-55; The Russian Revolution of 1917. Contemporary Accounts, D. von
Mohrenschildt, ed. New York: Oxford University Press,
1971; 129-34.

792   *Tompkins, Stuart R. "Lenin's Tortuous and Devious Road to Vic-
       tory," in The Triumph of Bolshevism. Revolution or Reac-
       tion? Norman: University of Oklahoma Press, 1967; 239-75,
       bib. 299-319.
       An examination of Lenin's involvement with the German gov-
       ernment in 1917. Tompkins reviews the various sources of
       information on Lenin's German ties from when he left Swit-
       zerland through the period of the revolution, and maintains
       that only the more recent discovery (by Allied officers after
       World War II) of German Foreign Ministry documents on sup-
       port for Lenin can be accepted as "incontestable proof that
       the Bolsheviks had received money from the German govern-
       ment [to the sum of] approximately 18 million dollars."
       [HX312. T6]

793   Treviranus, G. R. "Lenin Wins," in Revolutions in Russia.
       Their Lessons for the Western World. New York: Harper
       and Brothers, 1944; 177-27.
       A discussion of Lenin's leadership in the October Revolution
       contending that his attention to even the smallest of details
       largely accounts for the superiority which the Bolsheviks had
       over other political parties and the Provisional Government.
       [DK265. T67]

794   *Trotsky, Leon. "Lenin Summons to Insurrection," in The Rus-
       sian Revolution. The Overthrow of Tzarism and the Triumph
       of the Soviets. Garden City: Doubleday, 1959; 261-303.
       Recollections of Lenin's struggle with the Central Committee
       of the Bolshevik Party over the question of staging an armed
       insurrection in October. Trotsky states that Lenin's call for
       revolution met much opposition from within the party and that
       without Lenin's tireless efforts, the opportunity for revolt
       would have been missed. This fact, Trotsky asserts, has
       been much obscured by Stalinist attempts to "wipe out of his-
       toric memory every recollection of how the October Revolu-
       tion was in reality prepared and achieved." [DK265. T7613]

795   *_____. "The Bolsheviks and Lenin," in The Russian Revolu-

tion. The Overthrow of Tzarism and the Triumph
of the Soviets. Garden City: Doubleday, 1959; 212-39.
A discussion of the April crisis in the Bolshevik Party
triggered by Lenin's call for non-support of the Provisional Government and for the seizure of power by the
soviets. Trotsky records the shock and bewilderment
among party leaders who, led by Stalin and Kamenev,
had been supporting the Provisional Government while
Lenin was in exile. [DK165.T7613]

796   Tyrkova-Williams, Ariadna. "The Bolsheviks and the Ger-
       mans," in From Liberty to Brest-Litovsk. The First
       Year of the Russian Revolution. London: Macmillan,
       1919; 287-95.
       An argument that, in addition to transporting Lenin from
       Switzerland to Russia, the German government was the
       source of the enormous sums of money spent by Lenin
       on propaganda and agitation and that Germany printed
       Bolshevik propaganda pamphlets and leaflets as well as
       provided military assistance to the Red Guard.
       [DK265.W47]

797   _____. "Lenin and His Watchword," in From Liberty to
       Brest-Litovsk. The First Year of the Russian Revolu-
       tion. London: Macmillan, 1919; 62-82.
       A critical review of Lenin's April Theses and the policies
       which he followed in subverting the authority of the Pro-
       visional Government and demoralizing the army. The
       author sees Lenin as being a ruthless fanatic who, with
       German backing, was able to launch a propaganda cam-
       paign that so deceived the workers that he was able to
       seize power and establish a dictatorship over all social
       classes in Russia. [DK265.W47]

798   Vakhromeyev, V. I. "Lenin in the October Days," in LIOR
       (anthology), 57-61.
       A recollection, by the Chairman of the Petrograd Military
       and Naval Committee, of meetings with Lenin over plan-
       ning the military details of the October Revolution.

799   *Vasilyev, Vasili. "Meetings with Lenin," Sov Lit, no. 4
       (1978), 3-19.
       A series of recollections of Lenin's leadership during
       the revolutionary period. Vasilyev records the reaction
       to Lenin's April arrival at the Finland Station, the im-
       pact of his April Theses, and his argument for peace
       with Germany, and provides examples of his leadership
       from the post-1917 period.

800   Walsh, Edmund A. "Lenin and a Sealed Car from Germany,"
       in The Fall of the Russian Empire. New York: Blue
       Ribbon Books, 1928; 216-31.
       A discussion of the German government's program to
       subvert the Provisional Government by financing and as-
       sisting the return of Russian revolutionaries living in

exile in Europe. Walsh states that the German government acted with full awareness that Lenin believed he
was using Germany and that once revolution began in
Russia it would spread to Germany, but it believed that
the risk was worth taking because of the immense benefits to be had by Russia's withdrawal from the war.
[DK265.W335]

801   Watt, D. C. "From the Finland Station," Spectator, 200
       (16 May 1958), 617+.
       A review of newly released documents from the German
       archives concerning the transport of Lenin from Switzer-
       land to Russia.

802   Weisbord, Albert. "The Russian Revolution," in The Con-
       quest of Power, Vol. 2. New York: Covici-Friede,
       1937; 859-900.
       A general review of Lenin's leadership of the Bolshevik
       Party in 1917. [JA83.W4]

803   *Wheeler-Bennett, John W. "Kerensky, Lenin and Peace,"
       in Brest-Litovsk. The Forgotten Peace. March 1918.
       New York: Norton, 1971 (reprint of a 1938 publication);
       21-62.
       A useful overview of the policies pursued by the Provi-
       sional Government and Lenin in the months between the
       two revolutions of 1917. Wheeler-Bennett discusses the
       circumstances surrounding Lenin's return from Switzer-
       land to Russia, the deterioration of the prestige and au-
       thority of the Provisional Government, and Lenin's mili-
       tant efforts to harness the growing discontent in support
       of a Bolshevik led socialist revolution. In subsequent
       sections, the author provides considerable detail on Le-
       nin's involvement in the Brest-Litovsk negotiations.
       [DK614.B6W45]

804   Williams, William A. American-Russian Relations, 1781-
       1947. New York: Rinehart, 1952; 357pp, bib. 285-87.
       Lenin is not the focus of any one chapter in this study,
       but it contains significant information on American reac-
       tions to the Russian Revolution and to the charge that
       Lenin was a German agent. [E183.8.R9W63]

805   *Wilson, Edmund. "Lenin at the Finland Station," in To the
       Finland Station. A Study in the Writing and Acting of
       History. Garden City: Doubleday, 1953; 456-74.
       A discussion of Lenin's reaction to the outbreak of the
       February Revolution, his return to Petrograd, and the
       reaction of those who greeted Lenin upon his arrival at
       the Finland Station. Wilson devotes most of his attention
       to a restatement of the contents of the April Theses and
       an account of the shock which it caused even among Le-
       nin's most ardent supporters. [HX36.W5]

806 *Woodward, David. "Lenin's Journey," Hist Today, 8, no.
        5 (May 1958), 306-12. Reply, Otto Heibrunn, 8, no. 8
        (Aug. 1958), 585.

807 *Zeman, Z. A. B., ed. Germany and the Revolution in Rus-
        sia, 1915-1918. London: Oxford University Press, 1958;
        157pp.
        A collection of 136 documents (written in the 1915-1918
        period) from the archives of the German Foreign Minis-
        try dealing with the German government's attitude towards
        and involvement with the Russian revolutionary movement,
        the revolution, and the Bolshevik regime. Most of the
        documents related to Lenin deal with German assistance
        in his return to Russia in 1917, though even here there
        is no evidence that he was in direct contact with the
        German government. A subject index makes for conven-
        ient location of the 44 documents that pertain to Lenin.
        [DK265.A522]

808 *Zeman, Z. A. B. and W. B. Scharlau. The Merchant of
        Revolution. The Life of Alexander Israel Helphand (Par-
        vus), 1867-1924. London: Oxford University Press,
        1965; 306pp., bib. 282-90.
        In part, a discussion of Helphand's involvement as an
        intermediary between Lenin and the German government
        prior to Lenin's return to Russia in 1917. [HX40.H3653]

809 Zweig, Stefan. "The Sealed Train: Lenin Leaves Zurich,"
        in The Tide of Fortune. Twelve Historical Miniatures.
        New York: Viking, 1940; 247-62.
        An account of Lenin's reaction to the February Revolu-
        tion and his negotiations with the German government for
        return to Russia by way of Germany.
        [PT2653.W42T52 1940]

POLITICAL THEORY AND PRACTICE, 1917-1924

A. Theory

810   *Abbo, John A. "Modern Times: Lenin," in Political Thought.
          Men and Ideas. Westminster, Maryland: Newman Press,
          1960; 349-68.
          An argument that Lenin must be considered as a major
          political philosopher. Abbo rejects those interpretations
          which claim that Lenin is impressive as a man of action
          but not as a theoretician, and maintains instead that
          since Lenin's actions were always based upon his theory
          of revolution, it is not possible to accept his greatness
          in one sphere but not the other. Adding to Lenin's claim
          to greatness as an ideologist, Abbo states, is the tre-
          mendous posthumous impact of his works, especially Im-
          perialism and State and Revolution. [JA81.A3]

811   Acton, H. B. "Lenin's The State and Revolution," Listener,
          70 (24 Oct. 1963), 649-50.

812   Ahluwania, A. S. "Lenin on the Role of Youth," in LACW
          (anthology), 61-63.
          A discussion of Lenin's awareness of the importance of
          involving youth in both the socialist movement and the
          building of a socialist society.

813   Amelchenko, V. "Force of Lenin's Ideas," Sov Mil R, no.
          3 (Mar. 1976), 2-4.
          A review of Lenin's thought on the ideological struggle
          against capitalism.

814   *Anderson, Thornton. "Lenin: The Primacy of the Political,"
          in Masters of Russian Marxism. New York: Appleton-
          Century-Crofts, 1963; 44-61, bib. 87-89.
          An examination of Lenin's deviation from Marxism through
          his elevation of political over economic forces in deter-
          mining the strategy, tactics, organization and timing of
          the Russian Revolution. Anderson asserts that Lenin's
          emphasis of the political factor led him to organize a
          party that could function independently of the proletariat
          and therefore seize and maintain power on its own, an
          assertion which he supports through an analysis of Le-
          nin's political thought and policies from What Is to Be
          Done? through 1921. [HX40.A73]

131

815   Asharin, V. Leninist Party Principles and Norms of Party
       Life. Moscow: Novosti Press, 1974; 47pp.
       A restatement of the rules and principles governing the
       party as established by Lenin. Asharin provides most
       information on Lenin's principles of democratic central-
       ism; his insistence on ideological purity; views on mem-
       bership and self-criticism; and his teachings on the guid-
       ing role to be played by the party both in the revolution-
       ary movement and in the building of socialism.
       [JN6598. K7A7277]

816   Ashley, William J. "Bolshevism and Democracy," in Quar
       R, 235 (Jan. 1921), 157-74.
       In part, a review of State and Revolution and Proletarian
       Revolution and the Renegade Kautsky.

817   *Avramova, Bistra et al. "Contours of a Great Plan," W
       Marxist R, 16, no. 12 (Dec. 1973), 8-22.
       A review of Lenin's leading writings of the December
       1922-March 1923 period.

818   *Avtorkhanov, A. "Lenin's Doctrine of Dictatorship," St Sov
       Un, 3, no. 3 (1969), 5-19.
       An evaluation of Lenin's concept of the dictatorship of
       the proletariat, with most attention given to the role as-
       signed by him to the party and coercion in its implemen-
       tation and operation.

819   *Banchero, Gabriel et al. "The Bourgeois State and the Work-
       ing Class," W Marxist R, 16, no. 8 (Aug. 1973), 15-29.
       A review of State and Revolution as part of a series of
       articles on the contemporary relevance of Lenin's major
       works.

820   *Barfield, Rodney. "Lenin's Utopianism: State and Revolu-
       tion," Slav R, 30, no. 1 (1971), 45-56.
       A positive assessment of State and Revolution as a the-
       oretical work written for the future and as one which
       is not inconsistent with Lenin's overall philosophy of re-
       volution.

821   Barghoorn, Frederick C. "Medvedev's Democratic Leninism,"
       Slav R, 32, no. 3 (1973), 590-94.
       A review article on Medvedev's Kniga o Sotsialisticheskoi
       Demokratii (1972), in which Medvedev develops an argu-
       ment that democracy is inherent in Leninism.

822   Beeching, Elsie. "Lenin and the Role of Women," Com V,
       2, no. 2 (Mar.-Apr. 1970), 35-39.
       A discussion of Lenin's interest in the emancipation of
       women as part of the socialist revolution.

823   *Bellis, Paul. "Lenin and the Bolshevik Experience," in

Marxism and the USSR. The Theory of Proletarian Dictatorship and the Marxist Analysis of Soviet Society. Atlantic Highlands, N.J.: Humanities Press, 1979; 30-55. A critique of Lenin's views on the role of the state, party and the dictatorship of the proletariat in the period of socialist construction. Bellis examines State and Revolution as Lenin's most definitive statement on this subject stressing that in it Lenin called for the complete and immediate destruction of the bourgeois state apparatus and its replacement by "institutions of a fundamentally different type" which would have "a democratic and mass participatory character." Such characteristics, Bellis states, bear little resemblance to those of the centralized, bureaucratic, party-dominated state which Lenin created. [JC474.B365 1979b]

824   Bettelheim, Charles. "The Dictatorship of the Proletariat," Monthly R, 23, no. 6 (1971), 55-76.
In part, a discussion of Lenin's teachings on the dictatorship of the proletariat.

825   Bhushan, M. G. S. "Lenin and Youth," in LACW (anthology), 59-60.
An account of Lenin's support for the involvement of young people in the party and the implementation of its policies.

826   Blit, L. "The Party of Lenin and Stalin," Socialist Com, 16 (Oct. 1952), 233-35+.

827   Bobroff, Anne. "The Bolsheviks and Working Women," Rad Amer, 10, no. 3 (1976), 51-73.
In part, a favorable restatement of Lenin's opposition to a women's organization separate from the working class movement.

828   Bochenski, I. M. and G. Niemeyer, G., eds. Handbook on Communism. New York: Praeger, 1962; 686pp., bib. 649-74.
Intended as "a reference book furnishing information on specific aspects of communism," this work does not contain a separate chapter on Lenin, but presents much information on his political thought and practice. A detailed index makes it convenient to locate the many references to Lenin. [HX276.B723]

829   Boggs, J. "The Role of the Vanguard Party," Monthly R, 21, no. 11 (Apr. 1970), 9-24.

830   Bonch-Bruyevich, V. "Against Bureaucratic Style," in NBPA (anthology), 199.
A statement on Lenin's belief that decrees, announcements, and newspaper articles should be written in a clear, precise style understandable to the masses.

831   *Buber, Martin. "Lenin and the Renewal of Society," in Paths
        to Utopia. Boston: Beacon, 1958; 99-128.
        An analysis of the centrist tendencies of Lenin's social-
        ism. Buber states that Lenin's belief in centrist action
        as the best means of staging a successful revolution car-
        ried over, quite naturally, to his approach to reconstruct-
        ing society once in power. He points out that Marx pro-
        vided little practical guidance on how the new socialist
        society would be created, and therefore when Lenin opted
        for rigidly centralized control of socialist construction,
        he was responding more to Russian reality and political
        habit than to the dictates of Marxism. Buber traces the
        steps followed by Lenin as he established party control
        over the soviets, trade unions, cooperatives, and other
        independent organizations which might question Bolshevik
        policy. [HX36. B8]

832   *Carlo, Antonio. "Lenin on the Party," Telos, no. 17 (Fall
        1973), 2-40.
        An examination of the complex evolution of Lenin's views
        on the state from his writing of What Is to Be Done?
        until the time of his death.

833   Ceterchi, Ivan and Maria Colceriu-Leiss. "State, Democracy
        and Nation in Lenin's Conception," in CFOLI (anthology),
        102-21.
        A review of Lenin's thought and policies on the state,
        its establishment and operation.

834   *Chambre, Henri. "The Revolutionary State," in From Karl
        Marx to Mao Tse-tung. A Systematic Survey of Marxism
        Leninism. New York: Kennedy and Sons, 1963; 181-
        200.
        A critical assessment of State and Revolution and the
        policies pursued by Lenin as he deviated from its cen-
        tral principles. Chambre argues that Lenin's thought on
        the nature of the socialist state is riddled with utopian-
        ism, especially in regard to the withering away of the
        state, an institution which cannot disappear as it is neede
        to educate the masses, manage socialist property and
        defend socialism against its enemies. [HX39. C483]

835   Chaudhuri, Tridib. "Lenin and Democratic Centralism,"
        Call, 24, no. 1 (Spet. 1972), 5-14.

836   Chesnokov, D. I. "Contemporaneity and the Leninist Teach-
        ing of the Creative Role of the Socialist State," in DORT
        (anthology), 204-36.
        A positive presentation of Lenin's views on the distinc-
        tions between the bourgeois and socialist states and on
        the destructive and constructive tasks of the socialist
        state. Chesnokov also defends Lenin against various crit-
        ics, and demonstrates how the CPSU has followed Le-
        nin's teachings on the state.

837   Childs, David. "The State and Revolution," in Marx and the
      Marxists. New York: Barnes and Noble, 1973; 95-104.
      A restatement of the main principles of State and Revolu-
      tion, and a discussion of why Lenin was unable to follow
      them in practice. [HX36. C52]

838   *Chkhikvadze, Victor M. The State, Democracy and Legality
      in the USSR. Lenin's Ideas Today. Moscow: Progress
      Publishers, 1972; 371pp.
      A comprehensive Soviet summary of Lenin's theory of the
      state and law; his concept of the dictatorship of the pro-
      letariat and its relation to democracy; his guidelines for
      the construction of a socialist system; and his contribu-
      tions to Soviet nationality policy. In addition, Chkhikvadze
      defends Lenin against critics of all types, and shows the
      relevancy of his ideas to the contemporary socialist world.
      [JC474. C5213]

839   Cole, G. D. H. A History of Socialist Thought. Vol. IV,
      Part I. Communism and Social Democracy, 1914-1931.
      London: Macmillan, 1958; 455pp.
      Although Lenin is not the focus of any one chapter in
      this study, it contains considerable information on his
      political leadership, thought, and practices. [HX36. C57]

840   *Colletti, Lucio. "Lenin's State and Revolution," in From
      Rousseau. Studies in Ideology and Society. New York:
      Monthly Review, 1972; 219-28.
      An examination of the main themes of State and Revolu-
      tion within the context of Lenin's anti-Kautsky polemics.
      Colletti asserts that Lenin's central thesis is that "the
      revolution cannot be restricted to the seizure of power,
      it must also be the destruction of the old State," and
      that Lenin devised this argument to refute Kautsky's as-
      sertion that the old state machine had to be seized but
      not destroyed. Lenin believed that the destruction of the
      old state apparatus was essential if the restrictive forms
      and limits of bourgeois democracy were to be replaced
      by a direct, proletarian democracy; whereas Kautsky felt
      that the state could not be eliminated since bureaucracy
      was a permanent feature of government. In the end,
      Colletti states, Lenin's ideal of the soviets functioning
      as the institution of proletarian democracy has not served
      as the foundation on which the Bolshevik state has been built.
      [HX541. C6213] Also in Revolution and Class Struggle.
      A Reader in Marxist Politics, Robin Blackburn, ed.
      Atlantic Highlands, N. J.: Humanities Press, 1978; 69-
      77.

841   "A Continuing State after Sixty Years," Yojana, 21, no. 19
      (1 Nov. 1977), 3-4.
      An investigation of the reasons that the Soviet state has
      failed to wither away in accord with Lenin's predictions
      in State and Revolution.

842 *Crichton, G. H. "Bolshevism in Theory and Practice,"
Edinb R, 232 (Oct. 1920), 290-306.
A critical review of Lenin's writings on the destruction
of the bourgeois state and morality and on the withering
away of the socialist state, with most attention given to
his State and Revolution and The Soviets at Work (1918).

843 Currie, Don. "Lenin and the Role of Scientific Socialism,"
Com V, 2, no. 2 (Mar.-Apr. 1970), 21-24.

844 *Daniels, Robert. "The Communist Party," in The Nature of
Communism. New York: Random House, 1962; 85-121.
A discussion of Lenin's impact on the communist movement as stemming primarily from his "development and
use of a singular political institution--the intricate, militarily organized machine of control known as the Communist Party." Daniels examines the creation of the
Bolshevik Party, its leading characteristics, and its
functioning before, during, and after the October Revolution, and emphasizes the point that leadership and organization both brought Lenin to power and kept him there
after the revolution. The authoritarian qualities of the
Soviet state, Daniels maintains, are but logical extension
of the original principles on which the Bolshevik Party
was based. [HX56. D3]

845 *_____. "The State and Revolution: A Case Study in the
Genesis and Transformation of Communist Ideology,"
ASEER, 12 (Feb. 1953), 22-43.
An examination of the disparity between What Is to Be
Done? and State and Revolution in regard to the role to
be played by the party. Daniels argues that the former
work is far more consistent with Lenin's overall philoso-
phy than is State and Revolution.

846 Deal, Roy Linney. Lenin's Master Plan. Miracle or Mirage?
New York: Vantage Press, 1972; 188pp.
Lenin is not the focus of any one chapter in this work,
but it contains many references to him, mostly as the
creator of a totalitarian organization which has used a
combination of deceit and violence to win power, rule
Russia, and influence the world. Deal devotes considerable effort to showing how the Communist Party is por-
trayed by the Soviets as a democratic organization but
in fact is a totalitarian one. [HX312. D39]

847 *DeGeorge, Richard T. "Lenin and the Party," in Patterns
of Soviet Thought. Ann Arbor: University of Michigan
Press, 1966; 128-45.
A critical investigation of Lenin's thought on the nature
and role of the party both in the revolutionary movement
and the building of socialism. DeGeorge reviews Lenin's
principal writings on the party, and concludes that they

represent a major revision of Marxism in that they deny
the inevitability of the revolution while asserting the importance of voluntarism and centralism. The importance
of Lenin's party doctrine, however, cannot be denied,
DeGeorge asserts, since it is the key to Lenin's success
as a leader. [B809. 8. D4]

848   Denisov, V. "Lenin on the Crisis in Bourgeois Democracy,"
       Int Aff, 16, no. 4 (Apr. 1970), 24-29.

849   Diz, Juan. "Leninism and Some Aspects of the Ideological
       Struggle," W Marxist R, 13, no. 3 (Mar. 1970), 22-25.
       A favorable review of Lenin's teachings on the democratic
       nature of socialism and the undemocratic qualities of
       bourgeois democracy.

850   *Dobrin, S. "Lenin on Equality and the Webbs on Lenin,"
       Sov St, 8, no. 4 (1957), 337-57.
       An examination of the Webbs' argument that Lenin was
       an enemy of equality.

851   Dominitz, S. "The Undialectical State: A Study in Marxist
       Political Theory," Australasian J Phil, 26 (May 1948),
       33-41.
       In part, an appraisal of Lenin's theory of the state as
       one much to be rejected for its unscientific assumptions,
       unwarranted optimism, and oversimplification of the gov-
       erning process.

852   Downs, Robert B. "Dictatorship of the Proletariat. Nikolai
       Lenin's The State and Revolution," in Moulders of the
       Modern Mind. 111 Books that Shaped Western Civiliza-
       tion. New York: Barnes and Noble, 1961; 356-68.
       A consideration of State and Revolution as a major con-
       tribution to Marxist theory, but one which must be quali-
       fied because of those features of current Soviet society
       that are contrary to its leading principles.
       [Z1035. 9. D63]

853   Ebenstein, William. "Totalitarian Communism," in Introduc-
       tion to Political Philosophy. New York: Rinehart and
       Company, 1952; 230-37.
       A review of What Is to Be Done? and State and Revolu-
       tion as, respectively, Lenin's most important theoretical
       contribution to Marxism and his most influential work.
       Ebenstein sees the fundamental assumption behind these
       two works as being that "the majority of the people is
       incapable of understanding and acting 'correctly'", an
       assumption which led Lenin to believe that he had the
       right and the duty to lead the masses and to employ any
       means necessary to establish and secure his leadership.
       [JA81. E2]

854 *Emmanuel, A. "The State in the Transition Period," New
        Left R, no. 113-114 (Jan. Apr. 1979), 111-31.
        An appraisal of the thought of Marx, Kautsky, and Lenin
        on the state, the dictatorship of the proletariat, and the
        withering away of the state.

855 Fedorov, Boris V. Theory of Politics and Lenin's Legacy.
        Some Theoretical Aspects of Politics. Moscow: Novosti
        Press, 1969; 71pp.
        A Soviet portrayal of Lenin as a genius who possessed
        extraordinary political insight and intelligence. Fedorov
        provides numerous examples of Lenin's "scientific pre-
        vision" before, during, and after the revolution, and
        praises Lenin for his administrative skills and ability to
        select the right man for any task. [HX313.F36]

856 Fedoseyev, Pyotr. "Lenin's Critique of Subjectivism and
        Objectivism," Rev W, 10 (1974), 23-42.
        A positive assessment of Lenin's struggle against volun-
        tarism based on subjectivism, and fatalism based on a
        mechanistic understanding of the objective laws of develop-
        ment.

857 Fellman, David. "The Emergence of Leninist Bolshevism,"
        in The Soviet Polity. Government and Politics in the
        USSR. New York: Dodd, Mead and Company, 1971; 111-
        18.
        A brief, non-interpretive summary of the leading land-
        marks in Lenin's development of the Bolshevik Party up
        to 1922. [HX40.K35]

858 Fischer, Ernst and Franz Marek. The Essential Lenin. New
        York: Herder and Herder, 1972; 191pp.
        A restatement of Lenin's basic political thought and poli-
        cies relying heavily on quotes from Lenin's works. The
        authors limit themselves to providing introductions, short
        elaborations, and transitions between subjects, and state
        that the only value judgment in their book is in the selec-
        tion of subjects and suitable quotations to illustrate Le-
        nin's thought. [DK254.L46F513]

859 *Fleron, Frederic and Lou Fleron. "Administration Theory
        as Repressive Theory," Newsletter Comp St Com, 6,
        no. 1 (Nov. 1972), 4-41.
        A criticism of Lenin for derailing Marxism, particularly
        in regard to the organization and operation of the social-
        ist state.

860 Forster, Henry A. Analysis of Premier Lenin's Address to
        the All-Russian Soviet Congress. New York: New York
        State Bar Association, 1919; 9pp.
        An assertion that total disaster would befall Russia if
        Lenin's dictates (dictatorship, censorship, socialization

of the economy) were followed. Forster states that Russia would become a "Caucasian China" and would be "utterly defenseless, pacifist, fat, spiritless and without any of the rugged virtues of citizenship." [DK265.U43]

861   Frankel, Boris. "On the State of the State: Marxist Theories of the State after Leninism," Theo Soc, 7, nos. 1-2 (Jan.-Mar. 1979), 199-242.
In part, an assessment of State and Revolution.

862   *Garaudy, Roger. "The Soviet Union: Birth of a Model of Socialism," in The Turning Point of Socialism. New York: Grove Press, 1970; 77-139.
An examination, by a French Marxist, of Lenin's doctrine on revolution, the party, and state, and an attack on Stalin and his successors for perverting Lenin's teachings. Garaudy states that Lenin demonstrated political genius in adapting Marxism to Russian conditions and that Lenin was well aware of the fact that his theory of revolution was not suitable as a model for European Marxists. In examining the distinctive qualities of Lenin's thought on the party, state, dictatorship of the proletariat, and socialist construction, Garaudy maintains that Lenin in no way intended the party to replace the proletariat as the ruler of the Soviet state, that he was a devout enemy of bureaucracy, and firmly believed that the cultural revolution would lead to the end of the political centralism which was essential after the revolution. It has been Lenin's successors, Garaudy argues, who have made the party dictatorship an end instead of a means to an end as intended by Lenin. [HX44.G3513]

863   Gerson, Lennard. "Lenin's Theory of Terror," in The Secret Police in Lenin's Russia. Philadelphia: Temple University Press, 1976; 4-8.
A brief discussion of Lenin's views on terror as a political weapon and his use of terror in the years immediately following the October Revolution. Gerson notes Lenin's willingness to use terror whenever necessary, and criticizes him for naively believing that only a short period of violence would be necessary to eliminate that "insignificant minority of the population" which would oppose Bolshevik policies. [HV8224.G47]

864   Ginsborg, Paul. The Politics of Lenin. London: International Socialists, 1974; 31pp.
A primer-like introduction to the basics of Lenin's political theory and practice. [HX312.L43G55]

865   *Giradin, Jean Claude. "On the Marxist Theory of State," Pol Soc, 4, no. 2 (Winter 1974), 193-223.
In part, an analysis of Lenin's theory of state and its relation to the thought of Marx and Engels.

866   Gorakh. "A Real Democrat," in LHIII (anthology), 95-97.
       A favorable discussion of Lenin's concept of socialist
       democracy.

867   Hallinan, Matthew. "Lenin on the Dictatorship of the Pro-
       letariat," Pol Aff, 49, no. 4 (Apr. 1970), 48-57.

868   Harmon, M. Judd. "Lenin," in Political Thought from Plato
       to the Present. New York: McGraw-Hill, 1964; 409-35,
       bib. 435-36.
       A general introduction to Lenin's thought on imperialism,
       party organization, and the socialist state stressing the
       point that it was rooted more in Russian reality than in
       Marxism. [JA81. H3]

869   Hearn, Francis. "Rationality and Bureaucracy: Maoist Con-
       tributions to a Marxist Theory of Bureaucracy," Sociol
       Q, 19 (Winter 1978), 37-54.
       In part, an appraisal of Lenin's views on bureaucracy
       and the state.

870   Husak, Gustav. "Lenin's Ideas on the State and Democracy
       Are Meaningful Today," in LITW-2 (anthology), 90-107.
       A review of Lenin's teachings and policies on the social-
       ist state and democracy, and an argument for their com-
       plete and systematic application by the socialist states
       of the world.

871   Igritsky, Yuri. "Freedom of Discussion--Unity of Action,"
       Sov Lit, no. 11 (Nov. 1979), 16-17.
       A review of Lenin's support for freedom of discussion
       within the Bolshevik Party while insisting at the same
       time that the Party maintain strict discipline and central-
       ization.

872   *Ionescu, Ghita. "Lenin, the Commune and the State--
       Thoughts for a Centenary," Gov Opp, 5, no. 2 (1970),
       131-65.
       A discussion of Lenin as a great and dedicated revolu-
       tionary who, nonetheless, erred by failing to see that
       the concept of the commune is incompatible with that of
       the organized state.

873   James, Cyril. Lenin, Trotsky and the Vanguard Party.
       Detroit: Facing Reality Publishing Committee, 1963;
       7pp.
       Unavailable for annotation.

874   *Janos, Andrew C. "The Communist Theory of the State and
       Revolution," in Communism and Revolution. The Strate-
       gic Uses of Political Violence, Cyril E. Black and Thomas
       P. Thornton, eds. Princeton: Princeton University
       Press, 1967; 27-42.

Lenin is not the focus of this essay, but it contains significant discussion of his thought on the destruction of the bourgeois state and the establishment of a state serving proletarian interests. [HX44.B55]

875 Karavaev, A. "The Soviet State: Theory and Practice: The Withering Away of the State," B Inst St USSR, 8, no. 4 (1961), 3-13.
In part, an analysis of Lenin's views on the longevity of the socialist state.

876 *Kautsky, Karl. The Dictatorship of the Proletariat. Ann Arbor: University of Michigan Press, 1964 (reprint of a 1919 publication); 149pp.
An attack, by a rival Marxist, on Lenin's concept of party organization and the dictatorship of the proletariat as well as on his oppressive policies as Soviet leader. In particular, Kautsky criticizes Lenin for dissolving the Constituent Assembly and for persecuting any group opposed to the Bolsheviks, and argues that Lenin's undemocratic regime is a product of a revolution staged prior to the development of proper conditions and thus reliant upon a small and intellectually immature proletariat unable to rule democratically as a majority of the population. [DK265.K33]

877 *_____. "Lenin and the Russian Revolution of 1917," in Social Democracy versus Communism. New York: Rand School Press, 1946; 56-66.
An attack on Lenin as a dictator whose "aim in the Russian Revolution was to destroy not only all organs of self-administration, but also all other parties and socialist organizations except his own." Kautsky deplores Lenin's rejection of a popular front of socialist parties to build a new order in Russia, a rejection which not only thwarted democracy but caused three years of brutal civil war and the establishment of a distinctly un-Marxist political system in Russia. [HX40.K35] Excerpt in Verdict of Three Decades. From the Literature of Individual Revolt against Soviet Communism, 1917-1950, ed. Julien Steinberg. Freeport: Books for Libraries Press, 1971 (reprint of a 1950 publication); 21-46.

878 Kazakevich, Emmanuil. The Blue Notebook. Moscow: Progress Publishers, 1969; 105pp.
A fanciful recreation of Lenin's days of exile in 1917 during which he wrote State and Revolution from notes jotted down in a blue notebook. [FZ3.K188B5] Excerpt in Sov Life, 10, no. 157 (Oct. 1969), 26-31.

879 *Keep, John L. H., ed. The Debate on Soviet Power. Minutes of the All-Russian Central Executive Committee of Soviets. Second Convocation. October 1917-January 1918. Oxford: Clarendon, 1979; 465pp.

A useful document indicating the feelings of Lenin, his supporters, and rivals on the question of the nature of the post-revolution government. An extensive index makes for convenient location of information pertinent to Lenin. [JN6526 1917. R87]

880 *Kelsen, Hans. "Lenin's Theory of State and Law," in The Communist Theory of Law. New York: Praeger, 1955; 51-61.
A restatement of and critical commentary on Lenin's concept of the state and justice within it. Kelsen contends that by 1919 Lenin began to realize that the state could not begin to wither away in Russia before socialism had triumphed on a global basis. This meant that injustice and the coercive qualities of the state would have to continue long past the time when Lenin initially believed (as stated in State and Revolution) they would disappear. Kelsen also criticizes Lenin's definition of the state for having the same "unscientific" and "subjective" qualities that Lenin attributed to bourgeois doctrine. [JN6569. L415]

881 *_____. The Political Theory of Bolshevism. Berkeley: University of California Press, 1948; 59pp.
Lenin is not the focus of this critical examination of the dictatorial elements of Bolshevism in theory and practice, but it contains a discussion of his concept of the dictatorship of the proletariat and his critique of bourgeois democracy. [JA37. C3]

882 Kin, David. V. I. Lenin on the Soviets. Moscow: Centrizdat, 1931; 38pp.
A collection of quotes from Lenin on the various roles played by the soviets before, during, and after the revolution. Kin supplies short introductions to and elaborations on Lenin's words as well as transitions from point to point. [HX56. L455K54]

883 *Kleubort, Daniel. "Lenin on the State: Theory and Practice after October," University of Chicago, 1977 (dissertation).

884 *Kolakowski, Leszek. "The Fortunes of Leninism: From a Theory of the State to a State Ideology," in Main Currents of Marxism. Its Rise, Growth and Dissolution. Vol II. The Golden Age. Oxford: Clarendon, 1978; 467-528, bib. 529-36.
A critical analysis of Lenin's political thought and practice, with most attention given to the 1917-1921 period. Kolakowski isolates those principles in Lenin's thought which determined the totalitarian character of the Soviet state, most importantly, Lenin's belief (since 1903) that "categories such as freedom and political equality were

not intrinsic values but only instruments of the class struggle" and that the Bolshevik Party, throught its scientific understanding of society, was the "true keeper of the proletariat's consciousness." These beliefs led to his post-1917 abolition of the traditional forms of democracy (parliament, civil liberties, political parties) and his emasculation of all organizations that rivaled the Bolsheviks' monopoly of power. By the time of Lenin's death, Kolakowski concludes, the revolutionary dreams of Russian Marxism "survived only in the form of phraseological remnants decorating the regime's totalitarian imperialism." [HX36. K61813]

885 Kositsyn, Alexander. "Democracy, for Whom Is It Meant?," Sov Life, 10, no. 157 (Oct. 1969), 24-25.
A restatement of Lenin's concept of socialist democracy.

886 Krasin, Yu. "The International Significance of Lenin's Theory of the Party," Soc Theo Prac, 2, no. 67 (Feb. 1979), 39-47.

887 Krishnan, N. K. "Lenin and the State," in LAI (anthology), 86-101.
A defense of State and Revolution and Lenin's policies toward the state, and an attack on reformist, opportunist and bourgeois critics of Lenin.

888 Laborde, Julio. "Lenin and the Party of a New Type," W Marxist R, 13, no. 2 (Feb. 1970), 31-33.

889 *Lapenna, Ivo. "Lenin, Law and Legality," in LMTL (anthology).
An analysis of Lenin's concept of legality in comparison to the standard definition of legality as "a system of law, a system of guarantees for the correct implementation of law, and minimum legal standards." Lapenna states that Lenin saw law in a subservient relationship to the dictatorship of the proletariat, a fact illustrated by early Soviet decrees which were issued either for propaganda purposes or for legalizing "arbitrariness and all kinds of illegality and terror." Only with the NEP period did Lenin begin to supervise the establishment of legislation to secure the normal functions of a state, but even then legality did not rest in "a system of law with a socialist character" but in "'legality' as arbitrarily defined by the top rulers of the party."

890 Laski, Harold J. "The Communist Theory of State," in Communism. New York: A. M. Kelley Publishers, 1968; 123-82, bib. 252-54.
Lenin is not the focus of this chapter, but it includes a discussion his theory on and policies toward the Soviet state. [HX40. L29 1968]

891   Lefort, Claude. "What Is Bureaucracy?," Telos, 22 (Winter
       1974-1975), 31-65.
       In part, an assessment of State and Revolution as a rep-
       resentative of the Marxist concept of bureaucracy and
       the state.

892   "Lenin on the Party," Sov Life," 3 no. 174 (Mar. 1971), 7.

893   Lenin's Party Doctrine and the Present Day.   Moscow:
       Novosti Press, 1969; 51pp.
       A positive restatement of Lenin's dictates on the role of
       the party in the revolutionary movement and the Soviet
       state.   The author also reviews Lenin's teachings on the
       inner mechanics of the party's operation.
       [JN6598. K7L44216]

894   *Lerner, Max.   "Lenin's The State and Revolution," in Books
       that Changed Our Minds, Malcolm Cowley and Bernard
       Smith, eds.   New York: Kelmscott, 1939; 195-216.
       An examination of the writing, contents and significance
       of State and Revolution.   Lerner discusses Lenin's ac-
       cumulation of information on the nature and duties of the
       socialist state which would be formed immediately after
       a revolution, a task which he clearly felt to be crucial
       since, in the event of his death, this work was to be
       "his legacy to the revolutionary movement." Lerner
       notes the intellectual strengths of State and Revolution
       (in spite of its Marxist clichés and bitter polemics), but
       questions Lenin's concept of the state, and sees a con-
       tradiction between the assertion that the violent destruc-
       tion of the state is inevitable and the belief that each
       national experience is unique.   In spite of these deficien-
       cies and the fact that Lenin erred in claiming that Marx
       supported "a clean sweep of the political machinery of
       the past," Lerner concludes, Lenin is one of the few
       towering political theorists since Machiavelli.
       [Z1003. C87]   Also in Ideas are Weapons.   The History
       and Uses of Ideas.   New York: Viking, 1939; 326-37;
       excerpt in New Rep, 100 (30 Aug. 1939), 92-96.

895   Loktev, I.   "Lenin's Theory of the Socialist State," in LOSS
       (anthology), 5-18.
       A positive presentation of Lenin's views on the state,
       trade unions, the dictatorship of the proletariat, and
       bourgeois democracy.

896   *Lowenthal, Richard.   "The Model of the Totalitarian State,"
       in The Impact of the Russian Revolution, Royal Institute
       of International Affairs.   London: Oxford University
       Press, 1967; 274-352.
       Lenin is not the focus of this essay, but it contains sig-
       nificant discussion of his contribution to the creation of
       the single-party totalitarian state which has so influenced

the modern world. Lowenthal sees Lenin's concept of
party organization and his belief that only the Bolshevik
Party could win and maintain power for the workers as
being instrumental in shaping the totalitarian character
of the Soviet state. [DK265.9.I515] Excerpts in L (anthology), 189-95; Encounter, 29, no. 4 (Oct. 1967), 21-
31.

897 Lustig, J. "On Organization: The Leninist Party," Pol Soc,
     7, no. 1 (1977), 27-34.

898 Malhorta, Autar S. "Lenin and the Party," in LAI (anthol-
     ogy), 192-236.
     A presentation of Lenin as the man who "elaborated the
     ideological, theoretical and organizational principles for
     the party which has become the model for communist
     parties the world over." Quoting heavily from Lenin's
     writings, Malhorta traces Lenin's efforts to establish a
     "party of a new type" to lead the revolutionary movement,
     create the new socialist society, and encourage the suc-
     cess of revolutions elsewhere.

899 *Mandel, Ernest. "The Leninist Theory of Organization: Its
     Relevance for Today," Int Soc R, 31, no. 9 (Dec. 1970),
     27-50.
     An assessment of the interrelationship, in Lenin's thought,
     between the party, the state, and the various social class-
     es of Russia.

900 *Mayer, Jacob P. "Bolshevism: State and Proletarian Dicta-
     torship," in Political Thought. The European Tradition.
     Freeport: Books for Libraries Press, 1970 (reprint of
     a 1930 publication); 437-45.
     A restatement of the leading principles of State and Re-
     volution, and a criticism of Lenin for neglecting the
     "evolutionary tendencies of the Marxist doctrine of the
     state" and for oversimplifying the complexity of and need
     for a state bureaucracy.

901 *Medalie, Richard J. "The Communist Theory of State,"
     ASEER, 18, no. 4 (Dec. 1959), 510-25.
     A critique of Robert Daniels' interpretation (in a Dec.
     1953 ASEER article) of State and Revolution, and an argu-
     ment that Lenin, as well as Stalin and Khrushchev, de-
     veloped a theory of the state at odds with that of Marx
     and Engels.

902 Mikheyev, V. I. and N. I. Osmova. "Political Doctrines in
     the 20th Century," Cahiers H M, 12, nos. 1-2 (1970),
     189-210.
     A discussion of Lenin's theories on the dictatorship of
     the proletariat, socialist revolution, and the progressive
     role of the working class as being the most important
     twentieth-century contribution to political theory.

903 *Miliband, Ralph. "The State and Revolution," in LT (anthol-
        ogy), An examination of State and Revolution stressing
        Lenin's failure to establish clearly the type of state con-
        sistent with the exercise of socialist power. Miliband
        argues that Lenin's concept of a socialist state as one
        without a standing army, large bureaucracy, or a parli-
        amentary body, but rather one based upon a voluntary
        association of armed workers, fails to consider how such
        a state would actually function. For lack of such guide-
        lines, the dictatorship of the party emerged as the direct-
        ing force behind Lenin's loosely described socialist state.
        Miliband praises State and Revolution for its assertion
        that the socialist state must be an anti-bureaucratic,
        directly democratic one. Also in Socialist Reg (1970),
        309-19.

904 Mohan, T. Chandra. "Lenin on the Historic Role of Youth,"
        in LAW (anthology), 77-80.
        A restatement of Lenin's belief that youth should be an
        integral part of the socialist system.

905 *Moore, Stanley W. The Critique of Capitalist Democracy.
        An Introduction to the Theory of State in Marx, Engels,
        and Lenin. New York: Paine-Whitman Publishers, 1957;
        180pp. , bib. 137-76.
        The stated aim of this study is "to define the central
        ideas and to formulate the main propositions in the criti-
        que of capitalist democracy developed by Marx, Engels,
        and Lenin. It presents no evidence for or against their
        theory. It presents no alternative theories. It can help
        only those who take seriously their responsibility to find
        out what these thinkers actually say, before deciding in
        the light of evidence to what extent their statements are
        true." To this end, Moore collects and organizes, and
        provides introductions, summaries, and transitions for
        a wide range of Lenin's writings on the state.
        [JC423.M68]

906 Mukhamedzhanov, Mansur. "Lenin and the Younger Genera-
        tion," Cult Life, 8 (Aug. 1969), 23+.
        A discussion of Lenin's views on the place of youth or-
        ganizations in the socialist state.

907 *Obichkin, G. D. "Lenin's Theory of the New Type of Pro-
        letarian Party," in LGT (anthology), 197-219.
        An account of the evolution of Lenin's thought on the role,
        organization, strategy, and tactics of the party. Obich-
        kin restates Lenin's basic party doctrine while demon-
        strating that it was "conceived, enriched, and formulated
        as the Party itself grew" in response to changing his-
        torical circumstances. He also defends Lenin against
        those who charge that his theory of the party is wholly
        opportunistic, and demonstrates that the roots of Lenin's

party doctrine rest firmly in the teachings of Marx. Excerpt in W Marxist R, 3, no. 5 (May 1960), 23-30.

908   *Olgin, Constantine. "Convergence Theory and the 'Leninist Theory of the Socialist Revolution,'" B Inst St USSR, 17, no. 8 (Aug. 1970), 23-48.
A discussion of Lenin's views on the ideological struggle against capitalism as proof that the West can expect no softening of the Soviet position on convergence theory.

909   Olgin, M. J. "Lenine and the Bolsheviks: Record and Theories of the Petrograd Leader of the 'Reds,'" Asia, 17 (Dec. 1917), 779-83.

910   Ossendowski, Ferdynand. "The Dictatorship of the Proletariat," in Dictatorship on Its Trial. Freeport: Books for Libraries Press, 1970 (reprint of a 1930 publication); 169-207.
An assessment of the role played by Lenin and historical circumstances in bringing about a dictatorship of the proletariat in Russia. Ossendowski states that the history of Russia and the nature of the Russian people were conducive to the development of a dictatorial government, but that Lenin's political philosophy and leadership as well as his intuitive understanding of the masses were the crucial ingredients in setting the dictatorship of the proletariat's totalitarian character. [D107. F65]

911   Owen, A. L. R. "A Critique of Lenin's Theory of State," in Selig Perlman's Lectures on Capitalism and Socialism. Madison: University of Milwaukee Press, 1976; 30-34. A brief criticism of State and Revolution for postulating a purely class-based concept of the state and thereby overlooking the vital force of nationalism. [HX56. P38]

912   Pankin, Boris. "Words Across the Years," W Marxist R, 13, no. 11 (Nov. 1970), 32-38.
A review of Lenin's speech "The Tasks of Youth Leagues" as the basis of the principles governing contemporary proletarian youth organizations.

913   Papandreou, Andreas G. "Marx, Lenin, and 'the Dictatorship of the Proletariat,'" J Hel D, 2, no. 4 (1975), 9-15.

914   Pastukhov, B. "Leninist Principles of Organization and Activity of the Leninist Young Communist League," in LYAWT (anthology), 140-82.
A restatement of Lenin's teachings on the paramount importance of winning for communism the support of the nation's youth through organizing youth agencies to enlist the young in service of the cause.

915 *Platkovsky, V. V. "Lenin's Theory of the Dictatorship of the Proletariat and the Socialist State," in LGT (anthology), 220-48.
A sympathetic review of Lenin's doctrine on the state and a defense of it against critics who assert that it is inconsistent with the teachings of Marx.

916 Polyakov, V. "Lenin on the Role of the Masses in Governing the State," in LOSS (anthology), 19-37.
A summary of Lenin's critique of bourgeois democracy and his views on the democratic qualities of the dictatorship of the proletariat. Polyakov emphasizes Lenin's belief that with proper education the masses could be broadly involved, through a variety of organizations, in the governing of the state.

917 Pronin, I. and M. Stepichev. Leninist Standards of Party Life. Moscow: Progress Publishers, 1978; 148pp.
A discussion of the principles and norms of party life worked out by Lenin, and how they "determine the forms of Party organization, its internal activity and methods of work."

918 *Ramundo, Bernard A. "Leninism: Rationale of Party Dictatorship," in LAL (anthology), 101-10.
A critical appraisal of Lenin's party doctrine arguing that "Lenin drew upon the theories of Marx and Engels for legitimacy in fashioning a Party dictatorship uninhibited by law, morality and ideology in directing the 'build- of communism.'" The Leninist system of power which emerged from this party doctrine, Ramundo states, "had the trappings of orthodoxy and ... the practical flexibility of revolutionary legality." The current Soviet regime, the author asserts, uses the same flexible legality employed by Lenin, and draws not only from Marx and Engels for orthodoxy, but also from "Lenin's creative application of Marxism, and the charisma of Lenin and his wisdom."

919 *Roberts, Henry L. "Lenin and Power," in Eastern Europe: Politics, Revolution, and Diplomacy. New York: Knopf, 1970; 241-63.
The author's stated purpose is to discuss "the contradictions and dilemmas confronting the revolutionary before and after he has come to power; the nature of his sense of responsibility, to whom or to what; and the criteria of 'responsible' behavior of an explicitly ... revolutionary regime." Roberts states that in the years before 1917 Lenin had thoroughly committed himself to one goal: the seizure of power, and had managed to reconcile (in his own mind) Marxist ideology with his belief in the urgency of revolution. Once in power, he felt no responsibility to any "democratically arrived constitutional body" but only

to a vague " 'objective' identity of interests" between his party and the masses. Roberts concludes that, in reality, this meant that Lenin recognized "no responsibility to an entity, be it party or a person, outside the frame of his own will and thought," hence, though he believed he acted responsibly, his behavior was irresponsible by any objective standards. [DR48.R56] Also in The Responsibility of Power. Historical Essays in Honor of Hajo Holborn. Garden City: Doubleday, 1967; 335-52.

920 Rothstein, Andrew. "Lenin on Bourgeois Democracy," in VILIL (anthology), 99-101.

921 Runkle, Gerald. "Lenin," in A History of Western Political Theory. New York: Ronald Press Company, 1968; 516-26.
A general survey of Lenin's political thought, and an argument that although his concept of revolution is more opportunistic than it is Marxist, his theory of state is consistent with the thought of Marx. Runkle maintains, though, that neither Lenin nor his successors have used State and Revolution as a guide to Soviet policy towards the state. [JA81.R84]

922 Russell, Bertrand. "Bolshevik Theory," in Bolshevism: Theory and Practice. New York: Arno, 1972 (reprint of a 1920 publication); 123-92.
Lenin is not the focus of this chapter, but it contains references to his thought and policies and is important as an early and influential English reaction to his regime. Russell states that he is "compelled to reject Bolshevism for two reasons: ... because the price mankind must pay to achieve Communism by Bolshevik methods is too terrible," and because the results of Bolshevism would not be "what the Bolsheviks profess to desire." [DK265.R82] Excerpt in Verdict of Three Decades, ed. Julius Steinberg. Freeport: Books for Libraries Press, 1971 (reprint of a 1950 publication); 74-83.

923 *Santamaria, Ulysses and Alain Manville. "Lenin and the Problem of Transition," Telos, no. 27 (Spring 1976), 79-96.
A critique of Lenin's thought on the transition from capitalism to socialism arguing that it is similar to the theoretical foundations of the evolutionary materialism (Economism) which he had previously attacked.

924 *Sawer, Marian. "The Genesis of The State and Revolution," Socialist Reg (1977), 208-27.

925 *Schapiro, Leonard B. "Lenin's Contribution to Politics," Pol Q, 35, no. 1 (Jan.-Mar. 1964), 9-22.
A discussion of Lenin's political thought as a dangerous

combination of utopian and revolutionary ideals which led directly to the first modern totalitarian state.

926 *Selznick, Philip. "The Relevance of Leninism," in The Organizational Weapon. A Study of Bolshevik Strategy and Tactics. New York: McGraw-Hill, 1952; 4-8.
An assessment of Lenin's views on the nature of power and politics. Selznick states that Lenin viewed power not in a narrow political sense but as being inherent in all institutions and groups, and consequently believed it to be essential to gain control over traditionally non-political groups and organizations and then politicize them in support of Bolshevism. This study contains many additional references to Lenin's political thought, strategies, and practices. [HX56. S4]

927 Sen, Lalit. "Youth--The Instrument of Change," in LACW (anthology), 81-84.
A restatement of Lenin's belief that socialism could only be successful ultimately if the youth of the nation actively supported it.

928 Sen, Mohit. "Lenin on the Socialist State," India Q, 27, no. 1 (Jan.-Mar. 1971), 6-15.

929 Shadwell, A. "Bolshevism--According to Lenine and Trotzky," N Cent, 85 (Feb. 1919), 232-48.
A critical review of Lenin's The Immediate Tasks of Soviet Government.

930 Shankar, Kripa. "Lenin on the Proletarian State," Mainstream, 8, no. 33 (18 Apr. 1970), 32-33.

931 *Smith, David G. "The Political Theory of V. I. Lenin: Some Fundamental Concepts as the Basis for a Systematic Critique," Johns Hopkins University, 1953 (dissertation).

932 *Somerville, John. "Lenin on Democracy," in Soviet Philosophy. A Study of Theory and Practice. New York: Philosophical Library, 1946; 42-47.
A clarification of Lenin's use of the terms "democracy" and "dictatorship." Somerville restates Lenin's thought on these two concepts, and discusses why it is as erroneous to compare the dictatorship of the proletariat to other dictatorships (especially fascist) as it is to accept the Soviet system as a democracy simply because it calls itself one. [B4231. S6]

933 Spargo, J. "Bolshevism, a Caricature of Marxist Theories," W's Work, 39 (Nov. 1919), 28-32.
A presentation of Lenin's philosophy and actions as being directly opposed to Marxism.

934 Spirikin, Aleksandr G. Lenin on State and Democracy.
Moscow: Novosti Press, 1968; 64pp. Unavailable for
annotation.

935 No entry.

936 Szymanski, A. et al. "Leninism and the Culture of Resis-
tance," Socialist Rev, 4, no. 2 (Apr. 1974), 109-27.
A defense of Lenin's party doctrine against those who
charge that it is not applicable to all societies.

937 *Thompson, Ronald B. "Lenin's Notebook on the State, 1916-
1917," University of Chicago, 1954 (dissertation).

938 Timasheff, N. S. "The Soviet Concept of Democracy," R
Pol, 12, no. 4 (Dec. 1950), 506-18.
In part, a discussion of Lenin's concept of bourgeois
democracy and the dictatorship of the proletariat.

939 Titarenko, S. "Lenin--Organizer and Leader of the Communist Party," in LYAWT (anthology), 74-96.
A survey of Lenin's organization, development, and
leadership of the Bolshevik Party stressing his faithfulness to the principles of Marx. Titarenko also reviews
various Western writings on Lenin's party doctrine and
leadership.

940 _____. "Modern Times and Lenin's Teaching of the
Party," in DORT (anthology), 168-203.
A restatement of Lenin's party doctrine and an account
of the role played by the party, under Lenin's leadership, before, during, and after the revolution.

941 Tomashne, L. T. "Political Pluralism or Democratic Centralism?," Sov St Phil, 18 (Summer 1979), 75-86.
In part, a review of Lenin's teachings on the mechanics
of democratic centralism.

942 Trushchenko, N. "Lenin on the Role and Tasks of the Youth,"
in LYAWT (anthology), 97-119.
A survey of Lenin's thought on the role of youth in both
the revolution and the building of socialism stressing his
belief that youthful militants were a powerful force in
every society of the world and consequently should be
drawn into the socialist movement at as early an age as
possible.

943 Tucker, Robert C. "Radicalism and De-Radicalization under
Lenin and Stalin," in The Marxian Revolutionary Idea.
New York: Norton, 1969; 198-203.
A brief discussion of the cyclical fortunes of the radical
Marx in Lenin's ideology and practice. [HX39.5.T8]

944   "The Victorious Working Class and the Building of the New
          Society," in LAWRWM (anthology), 268-302.
          A favorable account of Lenin's contributions to the theory
          and practice of socialist construction contending that "the
          significance of the Leninist experience of building the
          new society has reached beyond national boundaries, ac-
          quiring a genuinely global character."

945   Vukasovic, Milan. "Lenin and Socialist Democracy," in
          LIPOY (anthology), 31-34.
          A positive assessment of Lenin's concept of the dictator-
          ship of the proletariat emphasizing the importance of his
          belief that the workers must be drawn into the actual
          management of the state if socialist democracy was to
          avoid the pitfalls of bureaucracy. Vukasovic contends
          that Lenin was "the architect of a new democracy ...
          direct, self-managing, and socialistic."

946   Vyas, H. K. "Lenin: Against Revisionism, Dogmatism and
          Sectarianism," in LAI (anthology), 160-78.
          A sympathetic survey of Lenin's polemics against Martov,
          Kautsky, and others over questions involving the party,
          revolution, the state and the dictatorship of the proletar-
          iat.

947   *Wesson, Robert. "Lenin's State," in The Soviet Russian
          State. New York: Wiley and Sons, 1972; 63-73.
          An examination of the political metamorphosis which took
          place in Russia under Lenin's leadership, 1917-1921.
          Wesson traces the steps followed by Lenin in the crea-
          tion of an all-powerful political entity, beginning with
          the decision to overthrow the Provisional Government
          without waiting for the approval of the Congress of So-
          viets, and ending with the Tenth Party Congress which
          extended dictatorial control over the Communist Party
          itself. Wesson stresses Lenin's leading role in this
          process, and concludes that although Lenin never fully
          realized or utilized the potentialities of the new despotic
          state, such a regime stood fully created when Stalin as-
          sumed power. [JN6515 1972.W47]

948   *_____. "The Leninist Resynthesis," in The Russian Di-
          lemma. A Political and Geopolitical View. New Bruns-
          wick: Rutgers University Press, 1974; 68-93.
          An analysis of the sources of the autocratic regime
          created by Lenin to deal with the massive problems which
          backward Russia presented to the Bolsheviks. Wesson
          states that Lenin turned his back on Marxism, Western
          traditions, and the Bolsheviks' own program as formulated
          before 1917, and instead recreated many of the features
          of the old imperial Russian state as an effective means
          of maintaining Bolshevik power. Lenin couched his poli-
          cies in Marxist jargon, and borrowed liberally from the

West, Wesson maintains, but for very un-Marxist and non-Western purposes. [DK43.W4]

949 * _____. "The Viability of the Leninist Synthesis," Orbis, 17, no. 4 (Winter 1974), 1215-1250.
A critique of the ability of the Leninist state to establish a permanent and stable political apparatus for itself.

950 *Wolfe, Bertram D. "The Influence of Lenin on the History of Our Times: The Question of Totalitarianism," in LAL (anthology), 293-312.
An analysis of the evolution and nature of Lenin's totalitarianism within the context of the 20th-century as "an age of force and violence." Wolfe sees Lenin's totalitarianism as stemming from his dogmatic and domineering attitude, his amorality, the extremely centralized nature of his party organization, his concept of proletarian dictatorship as unlimited power resting directly on force, and his complete distrust of all spontaneity, even within his own party. Wolfe concludes that Lenin's political doctrine and practices have only added to the brutal qualities which characterize the modern age.

951 * _____. "Lenin, the Architect of 20th Century Totalitarianism," An Ideology in Power. Reflections on the Russian Revolution. New York: Stein and Day, 1969; 164-80.
An analysis of the personal qualities and theoretical views possessed by Lenin which led him to create a totalitarian party and regime. Wolfe states that Lenin's definition of dictatorship and his "total rejection of the existing world and his conviction that he was the infallible interpreter of an infallible doctrine" combined to produce a powerful brand of totalitarianism. Lenin rationalized his authoritarian regime, Wolfe asserts, "by four feats of semantic juggling: confounding the proletariat with the people ... the party with the proletariat ... the party machine with the party ... and the Vozhd or Leader with the party machine." [DK265.W58] Excerpt in LDMORP (anthology), 75-78.

952 _____. "Reflections on the Future of the Soviet System," Rus R, 26 (Apr. 1967), 107-28.
In part, an examination of the sources of Lenin's revolutionary thought and his contributions to the dictatorial nature of the Soviet regime.

953 Yakolev, M. "Democracy of the Soviet State," Cult Life, 2 (Feb. 1970), 4-5.
A note on Soviet democracy being rooted in Lenin's teachings on the state and the dictatorship of the proletariat.

954 *Yermolovich, N. Lenin on the Party and the People. Mos-

cow: Foreign Languages Publishing House, 1964; 53pp.
A positive account of Lenin's writings on the common
man's role in history. Yermolovich restates Lenin's
criticism of bourgeois historians who stress the role
played by key individuals, as opposed to the masses, in
shaping history, and presents Lenin as an example of
an individual who was great because he guided the people
and created a party that could maximize the power of the
people. The author also discusses Lenin's insistence
that the party maintain the closest possible personal
contact with the people as a means of divining their mood
and needs. [HX313. E713]

955   Zarodov, Konstantin. "Leninism on Consolidating the Victory
of the Revolution," W Marxist R, 18, no. 4 (Apr. 1975),
65-77.
A review of Lenin's thought on the problems that the
socialist revolution confronts on its "second day" as it
seeks to consolidate its position.

956   *Zetkin, Clara. Lenin on the Woman Question. New York:
International Publishers, 1934; 31pp.
An account of Lenin's views on women's equality and
the place of the women's movement within the broader
struggle against the bourgeoisie. Zetkin recreates her
many conversations with Lenin on such issues as bourgeois morality, sex, and the special demands of the Russian women's movement, and notes in particular Lenin's
disgust with communist women who gave more attention
to the 'woman question' than to the larger concern of
advancing the cause of socialism. [HQ1233. Z4] Excerpts
in LDMORP (anthology), 19-24; NBPA (anthology), 221-24.

Cross-Reference: For pre-1917 political theory, see Russian Revolutionary Movement (II-A, II-B).

B. Practice

957 *Aaron, Daniel. "The Three Faces of Lenin," Survey, 41
(Apr. 1962), 43-57.
An account of the waning of the initial enthusiasm in
Western radical circles for Lenin and his regime as a
result of the increasingly undemocratic policies which
he pursued.

958 Abbott, E. H. "Black Wave: Bolshevism as Interpreted in
Interviews with Four Russian Leaders," Outlook, 121
(30 Apr. 1919), 734-38.
Interviews with S. Sazonov, N. Tchaikovsky, Prince Lvov,
and Baron Korff on Lenin, his goals and policies, and
the stability of his regime.

959 *Abramovitch, Raphael R. The Soviet Revolution, 1917-1939.
London: Allen and Unwin, 1962; 7-296.
Although a general study and covering years well after
Lenin's death, this work, written by a Menshevik leader
who actively opposed Lenin, provides many insights into
Lenin's seizure of power and, especially, his post-1917
policies. Abramovitch contends that the premature (in
a Marxist sense) nature of the October Revolution largely
determined the brutal and dictatorial qualities of Lenin's
regime, a contention in whose light he examines Lenin's
principal policies as Soviet leader. [DK266.A45]

960 Ambartsumov, Y. How Socialism Began. Russia under
Lenin's Leadership, 1917-1923. Moscow: Progress
Publishers, 1977; 354pp.
A review of the Soviet path to socialism, with much reference to the role played by Lenin's astuteness, audacity,
and concern for the masses as factors in determining
the Bolsheviks' success. [HX313.A65513]

961 Amrita, Patricia B. "An Intellectual Giant," in LHIII (anthology), 55-57.
An account of Bertrand Russell's interview with Lenin,
and a critical review of Lloyd George's comment that
"the Soviet working classes were in a condition approxi-
mate in many respects to slavery."

962 *Anderson, Thornton. "The First Decade: Left Then Right,"

in Russian Political Thought. Ithaca: Cornell University Press, 1967; 315-36, bib. 400-37.

An examination of the Thermidorean direction of Lenin's policies once he seized power. Anderson discusses as rightist policies Lenin's establishment of a minority government with severe restrictions on democracy; restoration of capitalism through the NEP; opposition to workers' control and independent trade unions; and substitution of national concerns for the international struggle to advance socialism. Although viewed by Lenin as temporary measures, Anderson states that these policies and the very precedent of such radical adaptations of Marxism had an immense affect on the character of contemporary Soviet communism. [JA84. R9A47]

963 *Andics, Hellmut. Rule of Terror. Russia under Lenin and Stalin. New York: Holt, Rinehart and Winston, 1969; 9-83.

A study of Soviet violence as an instrument of terror rooted in Lenin's thought and policies and reaching its maturity in the practice of Stalinism. Andics argues against those who contend that the mass terror employed by Stalin was an aberration of Leninism, stating that such policies "are as old as the Bolshevik Party itself." To support this statement, Andics systematically traces Lenin's development of an ideology of violence, while stressing the point that a socialist revolution in a backward country such as Russia was bound to meet massive opposition and therein be encouraged to use terror and violence as a means of maintaining power. [DK266. A6313]

964 Avrich, Paul. Kronstadt 1921. Princeton: Princeton University Press, 1970.

Lenin is not the focus of any one chapter in this study, but it includes significant information on his involvement with the Kronstadt crisis. [DK265. 8K7A88]

965 _____. The Russian Anarchists. Princeton: Princeton University Press, 1967; 303pp., bib. 259-89.

Lenin is not the focus of any one chapter in this scholarly study of Russian anarchism in the 1905-1921 period, but it contains significant information on Lenin's policies toward anarchism. [HX914. A9]

966 Babayants, A. A. "Creating a New State System," in LR (anthology), 157-74.

A sympathetic review of the principal policies and accomplishments of Lenin in the 1917-1921 period, and a defense of Lenin against those who charge that he created an undemocratic state.

967 Bainville, Jacques. "Lenin, Dictator," in Dictators. London: Jonathan Cape, 1937; 180-88.

A discussion of Lenin's creation of a dictatorial state as a consequence of the failure of his pre-1917 political program to be a workable one. As dictatorial policies, Bainville examines Lenin's dismissal of the Constituent Assembly, censorship of the press, establishment of "War Communism," creation of the Cheka, and suppression of the national liberation movement. [JC495.B32]

968 Bandini, Albert R. "From Lycurgus to Lenine; Experiments in Communism," Cath W, 117 (Auf. 1923), 636-46.
In part, a critical survey of Lenin's political practices, and an argument that the Bolshevik state is doomed to failure.

969 Berkman, Alexander. "Lenin," The Bolshevik Myth (Diary, 1920-1922). New York: Boni and Liveright, 1925; 89-92.
A recollection of a 1920 conversation with Lenin on the dictatorship of the proletariat, peasant hostility to Bolshevism, and Lenin's curtailment of freedom of speech. Berkman also comments on Lenin's character, noting single-mindedness as his principal trait. [DK265.B45]

970 *Bettelheim, Charles. "The Balance Sheet of Five Years of Revolution and the Prospects on the Eve of Lenin's Death," in Class Struggles in the USSR, Vol. I. New York: Monthly Review Press, 1976; 437-530.
An examination of Lenin's efforts (1921-1923) to compose a balance sheet of the revolution to determine clearly the successes of and deficiencies in past Bolshevik policies and to establish a list of priorities for future implementation. Bettelheim discusses Lenin's assessment of War Communism as an error-laden policy which nonetheless was necessary to gauge the depth of the obstacles which capitalism presented, and criticizes Lenin because, as a Marxist, he should have realized that production relations could not be transformed by political measures. Bettelheim states that as Lenin assessed the NEP, he came to realize that the construction of socialism's preconditions was a far more complex process than he had believed it to be, a realization which led him to prepare a major reinterpretation of the NEP, the completion of which his death prevented. [DK266.B4413]

971 Bonch-Bruyevich, V. "The Arms of the Soviet State," in AL (anthology), 56-58.
A recollection of Lenin's insistence that the sword which was on the artist's draft of the "arms of the Soviet state" must be removed while the hammer, sickle, and red star were to be retained. Excerpt in New Age, 11, no. 16 (21 Apr. 1963), 17.

972 *Bryant, Louise. "Lenine and Trotsky," in Six Red Months in

Russia. New York: George Doran Company, 1918; 135-47.
A favorable account, by an American observer, of Lenin in his first months in power as Soviet leader. Bryant attacks the then (1918) current misconceptions about Lenin as a power hungry and irrational tyrant, and presents instead an image of him as a skilled, dedicated and popular leader pursuing policies to benefit the common man in Russia. [DK265.B77]

973 *Carr, Edward H. A History of Soviet Russia. The Bolshevik Revolution 1917-1923, Vol. I. New York: Macmillan, 1951; 430pp.
Lenin is not the focus of this widely acclaimed study of the first years of the Soviet state, but it contains a vast amount of information on and many assessments of his policies and thought as Soviet leader. Carr's chapter on State and Revolution has been annotated and listed separately. [DK266.C263]

974 *_____. "Lenin: The Master Builder," in Studies in Revolution. New York: Barnes and Noble, 1962 (reprint of a 1950 publication); 134-51.
A discussion of Lenin's constructive qualities as a political leader. Carr states that "Lenin, for all his fame as a revolutionary leader, was a creator rather than a destroyer" who rose to his full stature "as administrator, head of government, organizer and supreme political tactician." In line with this thesis, Carr examines Lenin's leading policies while praising him in general for placing the reconstruction of Russia ahead of international revolution and radical socialist policies at home. [HX36.C35]

975 *Carroll, E. Malcolm. Soviet Communism and Western Opinion, 1919-1921. Chapel Hill: University of North Carolina Press, 1965; 302pp.
Lenin is not the center of any one chapter in this study, but it contains many references to and short sections on Western assessments of his policies, philosophy and leadership. [DK265.C384]

976 Ciliga, Anton. "Lenin, too ...," in The Russian Enigma. London: Labour Book Service, 1940; 274-77.
A brief discussion of the "ugliness" of the Stalin era as being rooted in Lenin's failure to see that his own bureaucracy constituted a far greater threat to revolutionary socialism than did the political opposition to Bolshevism which so worried him. [DK267.C5543]

977 *Cliff, Tony. Lenin. Vol. III. Revolution Besieged. London: Pluto Press, 1978; 230pp.
A detailed examination of Lenin's leadership in the 1917-

1921 period. Cliff discusses each of the major landmarks in Lenin's policy-making during these years while
stressing that this was a time of great frustration for
Lenin in that "the grim reality of Russian backwardness
and peasant conservatism, combined with the tardiness
of the international revolution, led to an increasing im-
potence and inability of the Bolsheviks to shape reality."
This contrasts sharply, Cliff states, with the previous
success of Lenin in adapting to and shaping history.
[DK254. L4C6]

978   Committee of the Youth Organizations of the USSR. Taking
       Counsel with Lenin. Moscow: Progress Publishers.
       1967; 95pp.
       In part, a review of Lenin's autumn 1920 speech to the
       Third Congress of the All-Union Young Communist Lea-
       gue. [HQ799.R9K5824]

979   "Communism under Lenin and Stalin," Senior S, 80 (7 Feb.
       1962), 22-24.

980   "Conservative Opinions on Lenin," LMAHW (anthology), 191-
       95.
       A series of four Western appraisals of Lenin's leader-
       ship qualities.

981   Crane, Paul S. "Soviet Communism: The Facts: Lenin's
       Terror," Chris Order, 2 (June 1961), 345-50.

982   *Daniels, Robert V. The Conscience of the Revolution. Com-
       munist Opposition in Soviet Russia. Cambridge: Har-
       vard University Press, 1960; 526pp. , bib. 439-48.
       Lenin is not the focus of this study, but as a scholarly
       examination of the differences within the communist move-
       ment in Russia (1917-1929), it contains many references
       to and considerable discussion of Lenin and his policies
       toward the opposition to Bolshevism. Daniels identifies
       the sources of the communist opposition's failure as being
       its lack of leadership, its disunity, failure to develop a
       distinct alternative to Leninism, and its being transfixed
       by Lenin's teachings on the mortal threat posed by fac-
       tionalism within the Communist Party. Daniels also ex-
       amines the influence of post-1917 historical circumstances
       in shaping the Communist Party into an organization
       totally intolerant of political opposition. [HX312. D34]

983   Domenach, J. M. "Leninist Propaganda," Pub Op Q, 15
       (Summer 1951), 265-73.

984   Dreiser, Theodore. "Lenin," Int Lit, nos. 4-5 (Apr.-May
       1940), 82.
       A statement on Lenin as a leader who advanced the cause
       of justice in Russia.

985 *Drobizhev, V. <u>Lenin As Head of Government</u>. Moscow:
Novosti Press, 1970; 181pp.
A positive appraisal of Lenin's policies in the 1917-1923
period. Drobizhev discusses each of Lenin's major political and economic decisions of the era, while presenting
an image of him as a friend of the common man and an
enemy of bureaucracy. [JN6515. 1917 D7613]

986 *Fainsod, Merle. <u>How Russia Is Ruled</u>. Cambridge: Harvard University Press, 1963; 684pp., bib. 605-13.
Lenin is not the focus of any one chapter in this scholarly
study of the means by which the Bolsheviks and their
successors have ruled Russia, but it contains significant
information on and discussion of his thought and policies
as Soviet leader. [JN6531. F3]

987 *Farbman, Michael S. <u>Bolshevism in Retreat</u>. London: W.
Collins and Sons, 1923; 312pp.
A detailed account of the ebbing of Lenin's revolutionary
fervor and its replacement by more sober and realistic
policies in the 1918-1922 period. Farbman discusses the
failure of War Communism and of European socialist revolutions as the main causes of Lenin's realization that
it was essential to consolidate the party's position both
at home and abroad. He examines the process of consolidation as represented by Lenin's industrial, national,
agricultural and foreign policies as well as by the replacement of the utopian ideals of <u>State and Revolution</u>
with more traditional concepts on bureaucracy and the
state apparatus. In spite of the various reversals in
policy which Lenin was forced to implement, Farbman
presents a very favorable image of Lenin's leadership
qualities. [DK265. F33]

988 *Fedyukin, S. A. "V. I. Lenin on the Use of Bourgeois
Specialists as a Form of Class Struggle," in <u>The Great
October Revolution and the Intelligentsia</u>. Moscow: Progress, 1975; 43-67.
A Soviet discussion of how "the almost complete lack of
qualified cadres necessary for the running of the state,
the national economy, and the army" brought Lenin to
the policy of using the old intelligentsia to build and defend socialism. Fedyukin examines this policy in view
of Lenin's concern for the broader question of the party's
attitude towards Russia's cultural heritage and for countering those within the party who desired a total break
with the past. [HT690. R9F4313]

989 *Francis, David R. <u>Russia from the American Embassy:
April, 1916-November, 1918</u>. New York: Arno, 1970.
Although Lenin is not central to any one chapter in this
work, it contains many references to his policies, philosophy, and leadership qualities. [DK265. F65]

990   Fuller, J. F. C. "Lenin and the Russian Revolution," in
       The Conduct of War, 1789-1961. London: Minerva
       Press, 1968; 183-201.
       A general review of Lenin's seizure and exercise of
       power in the 1917-1921 period. Fuller maintains that
       Lenin was an excellent political opportunist, but showed
       inexplicable naiveté and utopianism in his vision of the
       post-revolutionary political order, a vision which he was
       forced to abandon due to the political realities of Civil
       War Russia. [U39. F8]

991   Gellner, J. "My Russian Revolution and Lenin's," Sat Night,
       82 (Nov. 1967), 44-46.
       A recollection of the negative reaction in Czechoslovakia
       to Lenin's anti-democratic policies of the 1917-1922
       period.

992   *Gorbunov, N. P. Lenin. Chairman of the Council of People's
       Commissars. Moscow: Cooperative Publishing Society,
       1934; 39pp.
       Reminiscences (1917-1918), by a secretary to the Coun-
       cil of People's Commissars, of Lenin's conflict with the
       State Bank over the transfer of 25,000,000 roubles to
       the Bolsheviks; his reception of many visitors (mostly
       common workers); interest in and influence on science
       and technology; concern for establishing a telegraph net-
       work throughout the country; ability to appoint the right
       person for any task; and his reprimand of the author for
       raising Lenin's salary without authorization.
       [DK254. L4G6313]

993   *Gorky, Maxim. "Napoleon of Socialism," in LDMORP (an-
       thology), 79-81.
       A November 1917 attack on the undemocratic policies
       and methods of Lenin as a betrayal of the Bolshevik
       program and a step towards bloody anarchy and the ruin-
       ation of the proletariat. Excerpt from Untimely Thoughts.
       Essays on Revolution, Culture and the Bolsheviks, 1917-
       1918. New York: Eriksson, 1968; 85-89.

994   Hanson, Ole. "How the World War Saved, the Revolution
       Destroyed, and Lenin Reestablished Czarism," in Ameri-
       canism versus Bolshevism. Garden City: Doubleday,
       1920; 169-93.
       Criticism of Lenin for the means by which he seized
       power (reliance on German financial aid) and for the
       policies which he implemented as Soviet leader. Hanson
       claims that Lenin's dictatorial measures reestablished
       the same type of political system that existed prior to
       the February Revolution: "Russia did not benefit by trad-
       ing Nicholas II for Nikolai I." [HX61. H3]

995   *Heller, Michael. "Lenin and the Cheka," Survey, 24, no. 2
       (Spring 1979), 175-92.

996   Heroys, V. Lenin's Fighting Force. Why Soviet Russia Is
        Bound to Collapse. London: Russian Liberation Com-
        mittee, 1919; 18pp.
        A sharp attack, by a former tsarist general, on Lenin's
        regime asserting that it is doomed to failure because
        of the narrowness of its popular base. Heroys predicts
        that even Lenin's dictatorial policies and liberal use of
        terror would not be able stem the rising tide of opposi-
        tion (especially in the countryside) to Bolshevism.
        [DK265. H35]

997   *Holman, Glenn P. , Jr. " 'War Communism,' or the Be-
        sieger Besieged: A Study of Lenin's Social and Political
        Objectives from 1918-1921," Georgetown University,
        1973 (dissertation).

998   Iroshnikov, Mikhail. "At the Helm of State: One Day in
        Lenin's Life," Sov Life, no. 4 (Apr. 1970), 22-25.
        A description of Lenin's activities on 18 November 1917
        as an example of his typical day while working at Smolny
        in the 25 October 1917-10 March 1918 period.

999   Kidwai, S. M. H. "Marvellous Political Genius," in LHIII
        (anthology), 140-41.

1000   Klieforth, A. W. Bolshevism. By an Eye-Witness from
        Wisconsin. Milwaukee: American Constitution League,
        1920.
        An attack on Lenin's policies for their extremist and
        undemocratic qualities. [DK265. K5]

1001   Kuritsyn, V. "Left-Opportunist Distortions of Lenin's Teach-
        ing on the Socialist State: A Critical Survey," in LTCOA
        (anthology), 240-63.
        A defense of Lenin's policies, especially in the construc-
        tion of socialism, against critics on the left, most not-
        ably Trotsky. From Voprosy istorii KPSS, no. 8
        (1969).

1002   *Leggett, G. H. "Lenin, Terror and the Political Police,"
        Survey, 21 (Autumn 1975), 157-87.

1003   *_____. "Lenin's Reported Destruction of the Cheka Ar-
        chive," Survey, 24 (Spring 1979), 193-99.

1004   *Leites, Nathan. The Operational Code of the Politburo.
        New York: McGraw-Hill, 1951, 100pp.
        An analysis, through the writings of Lenin and Stalin,
        of "the rules Bolsheviks believe to be necessary for
        effective political conduct" in regard to the outside
        world. Leites presents his findings in regard to the
        outside world. Leites presents his findings under twenty
        headings, with most detail on the party's formulation of

the general line, determination of effective action, use of flexible tactics, and its belief in the danger of annihilation at the hands of capitalists.
[JN6598. K7L37 1951]

1005   "Lenine under Socialist Fire," Lit D, 74 (12 Aug. 1922), 9.
A review of European socialist criticism of Lenin due to the trial of Socialist Revolutionary leaders.

1006   "Lenin's First Interview with an American Correspondent," USSR, 88, no. 11 (Dec. 1923), 21.
A summary of Lenin's interview with Gregory Jarros (Associated Press), on 12 November 1917, on the upcoming Constituent Assembly's meeting.

1007   *Liberman, Simon. Building Lenin's Russia. Westport, Conn.: Hyperion Press, 1945 (reprint of a 1925 publication); 392pp.
An account of the author's work for Lenin's government as a specialist in the timber industry. During this time, Liberman, a Menshevik, had many contacts and meetings with Lenin, and from these and general observations on the history of the times, he presents a picture of Lenin as a man and a political leader. He stresses the point that Lenin had an unshakeable faith in the rightness of his cause and, consequently, had no moral misgivings about eliminating any obstacles in his path. Liberman provides numerous examples of the violent methods employed by Lenin and other Bolsheviks in implementing Soviet policies, but notes that Lenin's dictatorial methods must be assessed in the light of the remarkable material gains made in Russia under his leadership. [DK265. 7L57 1978]

1008   Ludwig, Emil. "Lenin, Revolutionary Engineer," Liv Age, 319 (20 Oct. 1923), 116-22.
A sympathetic appraisal of Lenin's leadership and accomplishments.

1009   Lunacharsky, A. "Lenin in the Council of People's Commissars," Sov Mil R, no. 1 (Jan. 1970), 15-16.

1010   *Luxemburg, Rosa. "The Russian Revolution," in Rosa Luxemburg Speaks, ed. Mary-Alice Waters. New York: Pathfinder Press, 1970; 365-95.
An assessment, written in 1918, of the October Revolution and the policies followed by Lenin immediately thereafter. Luxemburg, a German Marxist leader, praises Lenin and the Bolsheviks for having the wisdom and courage to advance the revolutionary tide in Russia before counter-revolution could destroy the gains won in the February Revolution. The policies pursued by

Lenin after the revolution, however, do not receive the same support. Luxemburg criticizes Lenin's land decree and nationality program as being "bourgeois," and attacks his basic conception of the dictatorship of the proletariat as an undemocratic one. In particular, she argues that any regime founded on the rule by a party in the name of the proletariat but which denies that class the right to control its own destiny, must inevitably degenerate into a totalitarian system run by a self-perpetuating central committee. [HX276.L8433] Excerpt in L (anthology), 140-41.

1011   McBride, Isaac. "In the Name of Emancipating Mankind," in LIOUS (anthology), 55-57.
An excerpt from a September 1919 interview with Lenin on the question of the Soviet system being a dictatorship of the majority over a minority and on American economic sanctions against the Bolshevik state.

1012   McClosky, Herbert and John E. Turner. "The Lenin Era," in The Soviet Dictatorship. New York: McGraw-Hill, 1960; 73-99.
An examination of the steps taken by Lenin as he established complete control over the press, labor unions, the soviets, and political opposition. The authors also discuss Lenin's extension of dictatorial control over the Bolshevik Party itself as power passed into the hands of an ever-shrinking number of people within the party. [DK266.M18]

1013   McKenna, Lambert. "Nikolai Lenin," Studies, 10, no. 40 (Dec. 1921), 553-72.
A general evaluation of Lenin's accomplishments, and an assessment of the NEP as a negation of Bolshevism.

1014   Mangold, K. P. "Lenin's Cardinal Rules of Poverty and Recall," Orbis, 8, no. 4 (Winter 1965), 955-71.

1015   Marcus, J. A. "What Became of Lenin's Dream?," Nations Bus, 36 (Apr. 1948), 47-49, 91-93.
An attack on the policies of the Soviet state as a betrayal of Lenin's wishes.

1016   *Martov, Julius. The State and the Socialist Revolution. New York: International Review, 1938; 62pp.
A collection of three essays, written in 1918-1919 by a Menshevik leader, which attack the policies pursued by Lenin. Martov criticizes Lenin's assertion that the Soviet state was a democratic one, and argues that the actions of the courts, police, military, bureaucracy and the Bolshevik Party are all clearly undemocratic. In fact, Martov charges, Lenin created not a dictatorship of the proletariat but a party dictatorship over the pro-

letariat. [HX314.M38] Excerpt in Verdict of Three Decades, ed. Julius Steinberg. Freeport: Books for Libraries Press, 1971 (reprint of a 1950 publication); 58-73.

1017   Martynov, A. "The Leninist Struggle for the Slogan of Soviet Power in the Present Situation," Communist, 13 (Sept. 1934), 903-12.

1018   Maximoff, G. P. "Lenin's Road to Power," in The Guillotine at Work. Twenty Years of Terror in Russia. Chicago: Globus Printing Corporation, 1940; 19-34. A survey of Lenin's seizure and consolidation of power stressing the role played by deceit and terror in determining his success. Maximoff contends that Lenin deliberately lied to the national minorities, peasants and even the proletariat as he schemed his way to power, and, once in power, he turned to terror and dictatorial rule because the Russian masses became aware of the fact that he had deceived them from the very beginning of his campaign to overthrow the government. [DK266.M26]

1019   Medem, Vladimir. "On Terror," Dissent, 22, no. 2 (Spring 1975), 189-90. A reprint of a 1918 article criticizing Lenin's use of terror.

1020   Menon, V. K. Krishna. "Lenin--Harbinger of a New Social Order," in LACW (anthology), 18-20. A tribute to Lenin as the creator of the first workers' state in the world.

1021   Mohrenschildt, Dimitri von. "Reporting the Bolshevik Revolution," B Inst St USSR, 14, no. 5 (1967), 3-10. A review of American press interpretations of Lenin and the Bolsheviks in the 1917-1921 period.

1022   Morgan, Glenn G. "Lenin's Letter on the Soviet Procuracy," ASEER, 19, no. 1 (1960), 10-28. A dispute of the Soviet claim that Lenin's letter of 20 May 1922 was the basis of the Procuracy's (attorney general's office) revival and restructure.

1023   Nehru, Jawaharlal. "Greatest Man of Action," in LHIII (anthology), 6-9. A general review of Lenin's leadership of the Soviet state as a means of illustrating that he was both a theorist and man of action.

1024   Palij, Michael. "Makhno's Visits with Kropotkin and Lenin," in The Anarchism of Nestor Makhno, 1918-1921. Seattle: University of Washington Press, 1976; 90-95.

An account of Makhno's June 1918 conversation with
Lenin on the Ukrainian peasants' attitude towards Bol-
shevism and the slogan "all power to the soviets."
Palij notes Makhno's respect for Lenin but resentment
over Lenin's negative attitude towards anarchism.
[DK265. 8. D4P23]

1025   *Parry, Albert. "Lenin: High Priest of Terror," and suc-
        ceeding sections) in Terrorism from Robespierre to
        Arafat. New York: Vanguard Press, 1976; 131-70,
        bib. 577-79.
        An analysis of Lenin's thought on and practice of terror
        both as a revolutionary and political leader. Parry
        states that although Lenin was opposed, as a revolution-
        ary, to terror as a regular policy, this was not due to
        any moral scruples about its use, but rather to his
        belief that it was ineffective as a weapon against tsar-
        ism. Once in power, however, he turned to wholesale
        use of terror not only against counter-revolutionaries
        but also against any group or person that challenged
        his monopoly of power. Lenin felt quite righteous in
        his use of terror since exploiters and those opposed
        to progress were the ones being eliminated. Parry
        criticizes Lenin for murdering many innocent people
        through his belief that "it is better to destroy one-
        hundred innocent people than to let one guilty one es-
        cape," and for setting the tone for the contemporary
        terrorism of Arafat, Hawatmeh, and others.
        [HV6431. P37]

1026   Pospelov, P. N. "Along the Leninist Road," New Times,
        16 (21 Apr. 1970), 1-3.
        An appreciation of Lenin's policies of 1917-1921 for
        establishing and defending socialism.

1027   *Possony, Stefan T. "Lenin and Meta-Strategy," in LAL (an-
        thology), 269-92.
        An appraisal of the effectiveness of Lenin's strategy
        in accumulating, conquering, and controlling power.
        Possony divides the concept of strategy into three parts:
        operational, resource and "meta-strategy." As an
        operational and resource strategist, he does not see
        Lenin's performance as being outstanding, but as a
        meta-strategist Lenin was a master. Defining meta-
        strategy as interdependent command and use of political
        and military forces, Possony discusses Lenin as a
        genius at psychological warfare, propaganda, and sub-
        version on a permanent and global basis.

1028   _____. "So Are They All Honorable Men?," Ukr Q, 21,
        no. 1 (1965), 28-35.
        In part, a criticism of Lenin for having a hypocritical
        attitude towards the use of terror.

1029   *Reshetar, John Jr. "Leninism in Practice," in A Concise
        History of the Communist Party of the Soviet Union.
        New York: Praeger, 1964; 140-76, bib. 341-54.
        An examination of Lenin's major policies as Soviet
        leader. Reshetar discusses Lenin's dissolution of the
        Constituent Assembly; conclusion of peace with Germany;
        leadership of the army during the Civil War; struggle
        against opposition within the party as well as from ri-
        val socialist groups; and his response to various eco-
        nomic problems. He states that Lenin was forced to
        adjust many of his pre-revolution assumptions on the
        nature of the state, exhibited remarkable flexibility in
        his policies, and contributed greatly to the growth of
        centralism within the party and state machinery.
        [JN6598. K7R45]

1030   Rigby, Thomas H. "The Birth of the Council of People's
        Commissars," Aust J Pol Hist, 20, no. 1 (1974), 70-
        75.
        In part, a review of Lenin's notes of 24-25 October
        1917 on the establishment of the Council of People's
        Commissars.

1031   *_____. Lenin's Government: Sovnarkom 1917-1922.
        Cambridge: Cambridge University Press, 1979; 320pp.,
        bib. 297-307.
        A scholarly analysis of the operation of the Sovnarkom
        (Council of People's Commissars) under Lenin and of
        its gradual eclipse by the Politburo as Russia's leading
        governing body. Rigby examines the Sovnarkom's ori-
        gins and the creation of its bureaucracy, and discusses
        Lenin's use of this body as the government of the re-
        public in the years immediately following the revolution.
        In tracing the demise of the Sovnarkom, Rigby empha-
        sizes both Lenin's excessive preoccupation with minute and
        minor details as a cause of its inability to cope with
        larger problems and, more importantly, Lenin's failure
        to make adequate arrangements, as his health deter-
        iorated, for permanent and stable leadership for the
        Sovnarkom. The author concludes that had Lenin en-
        trusted the leadership of the Sovnarkom to an able re-
        placement, he could have checked the shift in power
        within the government to the bureaucratic apparatus of
        the Politburo. [JN6515 1979. R54]

1032   *Robins, Raymond. "Impressions, As Told to William Hard,"
        in LMAHW (anthology), 125-63.
        Recollections, by the head of the American Red Cross
        Mission in Russia, of various conversations with Lenin
        dealing with such issues as workers' control of the
        factories, the Bolshevik state, labor discipline, and
        the Treaty of Brest-Litovsk. Robins stresses the ef-
        fectiveness of Lenin as a leader and the strength in

Russia of the ideals which he represents. Also published as "The Personality and Power of Nikolai Lenin" in Raymond Robins' Own Story, ed. William Hard. New York: Harper and Brothers, 1920; 154-86; excerpt in LIOUS (anthology), 41-51.

1033 *Rosenberg, Arthur. A History of Bolshevism. From Marx to the First Five Year Plan. New York: Russell and Russell, 1965 (reprint of a 1934 publication); 250pp., bib. 241-46.
A critical study of the evolution of Bolshevism stressing that its rigid party dictatorship and national brand of socialism represent major deviations from Marxism, and that, consequently, Bolshevik Russia is disqualified as both a model for and leader of the world's communist movement. [DK265.R69]

1034 *Rosmer, Alfred. Moscow under Lenin. New York: Monthly Review Press, 1972 (reprint of a 1953 publication); 253pp., bib. 229-248.
An account of Lenin's leadership in the 1920-1923 period. Rosmer, a French Trotskyite who witnessed many of the events of the period which he describes, sets as his purpose to determine if the Stalinist totalitarian regime was "a logical and inevitable development of Leninism." He reviews each of the major events, decisions, and developments of the early 1920's, and concludes that although Lenin's policies certainly are not above reproach, they bear little resemblance to the practices of the totalitarian and bureaucratic Stalin regime. [DK265.R69913]

1035 *Rostow, W. W. et al. "The Evolution of Soviet Rule," in The Dynamics of Soviet Society. New York: Norton, 1967; 17-166.
Lenin is not the focus of this chapter, but it contains significant discussion of his role in determining the nature of and the policies pursued by the Soviet state. Rostow stresses as Lenin's contributions to Soviet rule the establishment of the party "as the disciplined instrument of Marxist history, responsible only to its own correct analysis and for the application of correct laws to historical change"; his removal from Marxist pre-revolutionary thought, "of the ideological baggage of parliamentary democracy"; and his setting of the precedent that actions enhancing the power of the party have priority over those which, though consistent with Marxism and/or the majority's will, would erode the party's power. [HN523.R6]

1036 Russell, Bertrand. "A Visit to Lenin 1920," in L (anthology), 166-68.
A recollection of a 1920 conversation with Lenin on

such topics as parliamentary democracy, the likelihood
of a socialist revolution in England, the problems confronting communism in a peasant nation such as Russia,
and the ability of the Soviet state to survive in a hostile
capitalist world. Russell notes Lenin's narrow-minded-
ness and fanaticism, but praises him for his courage
and resolve. Excerpt from The Practice and Theory
of Bolshevism. New York: Simon and Schuster, 1964;
32-36.

1037   Salvadori, Massimo. "Lenin: Architect of the Soviet State,"
        in Modern Socialism. New York: Walker and Company,
        1968; 179-98.
        A sketch of Lenin's accomplishments as a revolutionary
        and political leader precedes excerpts from What Is to
        Be Done? and State and Revolution. [HX36. S37]

1038   *Schapiro, Leonard. The Communist Party of the Soviet
        Union. New York: Vintage Books, 1964; 631pp., bib.
        590-601.
        Although Lenin is not the focus of any one chapter in
        this scholarly study of the Communist Party, it is a
        valuable source of information on his guiding role in
        the party's creation, philosophy, organization, tactics,
        policies, internal disputes, and struggles against politi-
        cal rivals. An extensive index makes for convenient
        location of material on Lenin. [JN6598. K7S35]

1039   *_____. "Leninism Triumphant," in The Origin of the
        Communist Autocracy. Political Opposition in the
        Soviet State, 1917-1922. New York: Praeger, 1965;
        343-62, bib. 369-88.
        An assessment of the role played by historical circum-
        stances, the weaknesses of the opposition, and the
        leadership of Lenin in the establishment of a one-party
        state in Russia. Schapiro states that the threat to the
        revolution during the Civil War justified, in the eyes
        of the Bolsheviks and many other socialists, the use of
        force and dictatorial methods of ruling. Those social-
        ists who were opposed to these methods were either
        too scrupulous or disorganized to consider an armed
        response to them. Once the Civil War ended, however,
        political opposition to Lenin's regime increased drasti-
        cally since the rationale for the monopoly of power had
        been removed. It was at this point, Schapiro asserts,
        that Lenin made the fateful decision to maintain the
        party's dictatorship while reducing only the economic
        causes of discontent. By treating all non-Bolshevik
        communists as counter-revolutionaries, Schapiro con-
        cludes, Lenin set the precedent for the Stalinist prac-
        tice of purging those within the party who opposed the
        party's 'majority. ' [DK266. 5. S3]

1040   *_____. "Putting the Lid on Leninism," in Political Opposition in One-Party States. New York: Wiley and
Sons, 1972; 33-57.
An investigation of the reasons which led Lenin to his
March 1921 decision to "put the lid on opposition"
within the Bolshevik Party. Schapiro states that the
historical circumstances of the times (especially economic calamity and the Kronstadt Revolt) caused Lenin
to believe that both opposition to and debate within the
party had to be checked or else counter-revolution
might triumph. Whether or not Lenin intended this policy
to be permanent, Schapiro states, it is not possible to determine, but its results are perfectly clear: emasculation
of party vitality, encouragement of intrigue and manipulation as opposed to open discussion, and the establishment
of arbitrary, one-man rule over the party. [JC474. S32]
Also in The Origin of the Communist Autocracy. Political
Opposition in the Soviet State, 1917-1922. New York:
Praeger, 1965; 314-42; Gov Opp, 2, no. 2 (Jan.-Apr.
1967), 181-203.

1041   Scott, E. J. "The Cheka," St Anth P, 1 (1956), 1-23.
In part, a discussion of Lenin's involvement in the
Cheka's founding and the policies which it pursued in
the 1918-1922 period.

1042   *Serge, Victor. Memoirs of a Revolutionary, 1901-1941.
London: Oxford University Press, 1963; 401pp.
Although Lenin is only mentioned in scattered sections,
this set of memoirs, written by a Russian Marxist who
knew Lenin, contains much information on the inner
workings of the Bolshevik Party and Lenin's leadership
of it, especially in the months immediately after the
October Revolution. [DK254. S39A313]

1043   *_____. Year One of the Russian Revolution. New York:
Holt, Rinehart and Winston, 1972 (reprint of a 1930
publication); 436pp.
This work does not have a separate chapter on Lenin,
but it contains useful information and valuable insights
into his role in the October Revolution and the policies that he implemented in the first year of his leadership. Serge emphasizes the point that Lenin came to
power amidst a genuine mass revolution, not a Bolshevik coup d'etat, but mass support dissipated in the few
months after the revolution, a development which caused
Lenin to resort to dictatorial policies and methods in
governing the country. [DK265. S43638]

1044   *Service, Robert. The Bolshevik Party in Revolution. A
Study in Organisational Changes 1917-1923. New York:
Barnes and Noble, 1979; 246.
Lenin is not the focus of this study, but it includes
considerable discussion of his leadership of the Bolshe-

vik Party after the revolution. The thesis advanced by Service is that the party underwent, by 1923, an "internal metamorphosis" as it became less proletarian in its composition, less urban in its geographic distribution, and more disciplined and less democratic in its character. Service sees the source of this last change as being due to a combination of Lenin's leadership, historical circumstances, and pressure exerted on the Central Committee by local Bolshevik leaders who called for more central control and assistance in governing the countryside. [JN6598. K7S4533 1979]

1045   Shotman, A. V. "I. D. Putintsev Visits Lenin," in LCAM (anthology), 174-75.
An account of a visit with Lenin by an old cossack who spoke candidly about the strengths and weaknesses of Lenin's policies and the Soviet system.

1046   "Socialist View of Lenin," RR, 66 (Sept. 1922), 319-320.
An attack on Lenin for pursuit of thoroughly undemocratic policies. Excerpt from an article by M. Charasch in Revue Suisse (Aug. 1922).

1047   Spargo, John. "Bolshevist Theory and Practice," in Bolshevism: The Enemy of Political and Industrial Democracy. New York: Harper and Brother, 1919; 262-323.
Lenin is not the focus of this chapter, but it contains numerous critical references to his early policies, especially his decree on land and support of workers' control, as only tactics to win popular support. Spargo also criticizes the "indecent peace" which Lenin concluded with Germany. [DK265. S6]

1048   Spiro, George. "Lenin's Burocratism and Russian Nationalism," in Marxism and the Bolshevik State. New York: Red Star Press, 1951; 259-558.
A critical examination of Lenin's policies as Soviet leader arguing that they are responsible for the bureaucratic totalitarianism and Russian nationalism which later blossomed under Stalin. Spiro asserts that Lenin was by nature opposed to democracy, and that he used slogans on workers' control, power to the soviets, and democratic elections as "just so much demagogy to catch the workers." [JN6511. S6]

1049   Steffens, Lincoln. "I Saw the Future," in LIOUS (anthology), 67-69.
An account of a 1919 conversation with Lenin on Bolshevik use of propaganda and terror.

1050   Steinberg, I. In the Workshop of the Revolution. New York: Rinehart and Company, 1953; 306pp.

Lenin is not the focus of any one chapter in this study, but it contains significant discussion and criticism of his policies in the 1917-1921 period, especially his use of force and terror against political rivals (such as the author) and the peasantry. [DK265.S7373] Excerpt in L (anthology), 164-65.

1051   Titarenko, S. "Lenin's Struggle against Anarcho-Syndicalism," in LTCOA (anthology), 219-30.
A defense of Lenin's position in the party's struggle against "the anarcho-syndicalist deviation" of 1920-1921, and a restatement of his views and policies on the role of trade unions in Soviet society. Also in Mainstream, 7, no. 3 (5 Apr. 1969), 24-27.

1052   Towster, John. Political Power in the USSR, 1917-1947. New York: Oxford University Press, 1948; 443pp., 419-430.
Lenin is not the focus of any one chapter in this study, but it contains many references to and short sections on his policies regarding the state, party, soviets, law and the nationalities. [JN6518.T6]

1053   Utechin, S. V. "Bolsheviks and Their Allies after 1917: the Ideological Pattern," Sov St, 10, no. 2 (1958/1959), 113-35.
In part, a review of Lenin's reactions to the ideological disunity within and political opposition outside of the Bolshevik Party.

1054   Walsh, Warren B. "The Soviet Way: Early Developments," in Great Issues: The Making of Current American Policy, Stuart G. Brown, ed. New York: Harper and Brothers, 1951; 181-201.
An examination of the policies pursued by Lenin as Soviet leader stressing that they represent a radically different approach to problem solving than that which is employed by Western governments. Walsh discusses the monumental nature of the problems which confronted Lenin as the source of his having to employ dictatorial methods increasingly at variance with previously stated political philosophy. [D840.B7]

1055   Wigderon, S. "Moscow under Lenin," Int Soc R, 36, no. 2 (Feb. 1975), 46-58.

1056   Wilcox, E. H. "Lenin and Bolshevism," Fortn R, 109 (Mar. 1918), 371-83.
A review of Lenin's development of Bolshevism, with much attention given to the prospect of the soviets serving as a basis of government as described by Lenin.

1057   *Williams, Albert Rhys. "Ten Months with Lenin," in

LMAHW (anthology), 43-121.
Recollections and observations, by an American socialist, of Lenin and his accomplishments. Williams states
that his work is intended to be a counter-weight to the
fanciful, inaccurate and negative descriptions of Lenin
prevalent in the Western press. He presents an image
of Lenin as a dynamic, dedicated and humble leader
following realistic policies in implementing socialism in
Russia. Williams also provides many anecdotal accounts of Lenin's views on such diverse topics as intellectuals, American capitalism, the proletariat, political
tactics and Russia's future. Also in Through the Russian Revolution. Moscow: Progress Publishers, 1973;
22-58. Excerpts in Asia, 19 (1919), 764-70; L (anthology), 165-66; LIOUS (anthology), 27-41; Sov Life, 11,
no. 158 (Nov. 1969), 30-32.

1058   *Zetkin, Klara.   My Recollections of Lenin.   Moscow:
Foreign Languages Publishing House, 1956; 94pp.
This work combines Zetkin's My Recollections of Lenin
(1924); From My Memorandum Book (1925); and Lenin
and the Masses (1929).   To quote the editors, "Zetkin's
recollections tell the story of her meetings with Lenin
in 1920, 1921, and 1922.   She sets forth his views on
art, culture, the international women's movement, the
German revolutionary movement, and other problems."
In a forward, N. Krupskaya states that Lenin "was
very fond of Klara Zetkin and held her in high esteem
as a stalwart revolutionary, a thorough Marxist, and
an implacable foe of opportunism ... and enjoyed heart-
to-heart talks with her on subjects in which he was en-
grossed.   He liked to discuss aspects of problems which
he did not moot officially."   Throughout, Zetkin presents Lenin as a thoughtful and dedicated revolutionary
deeply interested in the common man's welfare.
[DK254. L4Z4 1956]

1059   *_____.   Reminiscences of Lenin.   New York: International Publishers, 1934; 64pp.
A series of recollections of Lenin grouped under the
headings: A Party Meeting (1920); Lenin on Culture;
The Polish War; The German Question; The Fourth
World Congress (Comintern); and Women, Sex and Mar-
riage.   Zetkin provides a wide range of useful insights
into Lenin's thought, policies, personality, character,
tastes and values.   [DK254. L4Z4]

C. Political Succession

1060   *Basseches, Nikolaus. "Lenin and Stalin," in Stalin. London: Staples Press, 1952; 101-10.
         An assessment of Stalin's personal relationship with Lenin, with most attention given to the years immediately preceding Lenin's death. Basseches states that Lenin had never admitted Stalin into his inner circle of friends and, in fact, "remained to the last decidedly distant from Stalin" who was jealous of all those who were close to Lenin, including Krupskaya. The collapse of relations between Lenin and Stalin in 1922 and 1923, the author maintains, was prompted as much by Stalin's rudeness towards Krupskaya as by his crude policies, and therefore most of the top Bolshevik leadership tended to view Lenin's negative opinion of Stalin as being more personal than political. [DK268.S8B]

1061   Benson, S. E. "Trotsky and the Legend of Lenin's Mantle," Bulletin, 5, no. 3 (May 1942), sup. 1-3.
         An attack on Trotsky's claim that Lenin sought him out as an ally against Stalin and that Lenin intended for Trotsky to be his successor.

1062   "Bolshevik Clerk Who May Succeed Lenin," Lit D, 77 (14 Apr. 1923), 64-67.
         A discussion of Lenin's illness and speculation that Stalin may be Lenin's successor.

1063   *Bornstein, Joseph. "The Death of Lenin," in The Politics of Murder. New York: Sloane, 1950; 238-95.
         An investigation of the circumstances surrounding Lenin' death and of the possibility that Stalin had Lenin murdered. Bornstein states that if the case against Stalin were brought to court, it would probably be dismissed a being a circumstantial one, but nonetheless there is sufficient mystery associated with Lenin's death to warrant suspicion of Stalin as his murderer. In support of this contention, Bornstein presents as evidence: Lenin's concern for the direction in which the party was heading was a direct threat to Stalin's security; Stalin's access to the means to eliminate Lenin through loyal Vice-Chief of the GPU (secret police) Yagoda, who was an expert on poisons and was later charged

174

with heading a group of Kremlin doctors who "murdered by medicine"; the incomplete nature of Lenin's autopsy which failed to test for poison; and, most importantly, Stalin's record of brutality after Lenin's death which indicates that he had the disposition to murder Lenin. [HV6278.B6 1950]. Excerpt in Cath D, 15 (May 1951), 58-62.

1064   Brophy, L. "Lenin's Too-Late Remorse," Soc Justice R, 63 (Sept. 1970), 148-51.
A discussion of Lenin's misgivings near death over the party and state which he had created.

1065   *Daniels, Robert V. "Soviet Succession: Lenin and Stalin," Rus R, 12 (July 1953), 153-72.
An examination of Lenin's 1922-1924 criticism of Stalin, worry over party leadership after his death, and hope for collective rule by the party's top figures.

1066   Delbars, Yves. "Lenin's Testament and the Conquest of Power," in The Real Stalin. London: Allen and Unwin, 1953; 122-30, bib. 419-22.
A review of the contents of Lenin's testament, and a sympathetic account of Stalin's efforts, in 1923-1924, to advance his own position within the party.
[DK268.S8D454]

1067   *Deutscher, Isaac. "The Moral Dilemmas of Lenin," in Ironies of History. Essays on Contemporary Communism. London: Oxford University Press, 1966; 167-73.
An argument that Lenin suffered only one true moral crisis in his life, that which plagued him as he realized, in his declining years, that the state which he had created was neither operating as designed nor following the course intended. Deutscher establishes that Lenin, throughout his life, had only one standard for the morality of any action--did it hasten "the end of the bourgeois order and the establishment of the proletarian dictatorship"; thus when the Soviet government ceased to advance the cause of the proletariat, Lenin found himself in a moral dilemma, escape from which could be had only by denouncing his own party. Deutscher concludes that Lenin's moral greatness rests in his admission, in December 1922 policy notes, that he was "strongly guilty before the workers of Russia" for not preventing the perversion of Bolshevik goals that was occurring as the party developed along increasingly dictatorial, bureaucratic, and oppressive lines.
[HX40.D423] Originally in Listener (5 Feb. 1959), 245-49; excerpt in L (anthology), 196-99.

1068   *_____. The Prophet Armed. Trotsky: 1921-1929, Vol. II. New York: Random House, 1965; 490pp., bib. 473-80.

Lenin is not the focus of any one chapter in this widely acclaimed biography of Trotsky, but it contains much information on and discussion of his relationship with Trotsky and Stalin in the two years preceding his death. [DK254. T6D42]

1069   *Duranty, Walter. "Lenin and Stalin," in I Write As I Please. New York: Simon and Schuster, 1935; 175-88.
A 1923 account of Stalin's emergence, amidst Lenin's months of failing health, as the likely heir to Lenin's position as party leader. Duranty examines Stalin's relations with Lenin, compares his strengths to those of Trotsky, and speculates on inner-party developments once Lenin dies. [DK266. D83]

1070   * _____ . "Lenin's Funeral and Trotzky's," in I Write As I Please. New York: Simon and Schuster, 1935; 217-30.
A discussion (1924) of Trotsky's absence from Lenin's funeral as an inexcusable political blunder which Stalin would use as an effective tool in his struggle to become Lenin's successor. [DK266. D83]

1071   *Eastman, Max. Since Lenin Died. London: Labour Publishing Company, 1925; 158pp.
An examination of the issues, personalities, and factions involved in the struggle for party leadership after Lenin's death. Eastman cites Lenin's testament as direct proof of the dead leader's low opinion of Stalin and high regard for Trotsky, and discusses Lenin's worry, in his last months, over the emergence of an extensive and potentially tyrannical bureaucracy under Stalin's control. The twisted image of Leninism presented by Stalin and his colleagues as a means of discrediting Trotsky, Eastman states, along with the suppression of Lenin's testament, were a flagrant insult to Lenin's greatness: "If you danced on the corpse of Vladimir Ilyich, you would insult his spirit less than by clapping the censorship on his last words to his party...." [D267. E3] Excerpt in Verdict of Three Decades, ed. Julius Steinberg; 193-202.

1072   Evans, Ernestine. "And after Lenine?," Cent M, 105 (Dec. 1922), 256-70.
Speculation on the state of Lenin's health and the identity of his successor.

1073   *Farbman, Michael. "Leninism without Lenin," in After Lenin. The New Phase in Russia. London: Leonard Parsons, 1924; 3-85.
An analysis of the dissension within the CPSU just before and after Lenin's death. Farbman states that

"despite its apparent and phenomenal unity, the party led by Lenin since 1917 has never really been homogenous." From its beginning, "Every big ... crisis in Russia ... has always been followed by a heated controversy and a threatened split in the Communist Party," but these crises were always resolved by surrender to the will of Lenin. Lenin's death, Farbman maintains, removed the traditional means of settling party disputes, and the lack of any able successor to Lenin meant that the party had to find some other way to resolve its differences. [DK267. F3]

1074   Grey, Ian. "Lenin Dies," in The First Fifty Years. Soviet Russia 1917-1967. New York: Coward-McCann, 1967; 196-206.
An account of Lenin's death and of the struggle within the party to replace his leadership. Grey provides most information on Lenin's growing suspicion of Stalin, the disputes between Stalin and Trotsky in 1923, and the testament which Lenin left to the party.
[DK266. G717]

1075   Grinko, V. A. et al. The Bolshevik Party's Struggle against Trotskyism. Moscow: Progress, 1969; 239pp.
A Soviet account of Lenin's differences with Trotsky in the years preceding the revolutions of 1917, and a charge that even though Trotsky joined the Bolshevik Party in 1917 (out of the "utter bankruptcy" of his position), he continued to be a rabid enemy of Leninism, as his 1917-1927 activities demonstrate.
[JN6598. S6B59513]

1076   *Hingley, Ronald. "Shadow over Lenin," Joseph Stalin: Man and Legend. New York: McGraw-Hill, 1974; 133-56, bib. 454-68.
A discussion of Stalin's accumulation of power in the 1920-1924 period and the consequent crisis within the party as Lenin emerged as a severe critic of Stalin. Hingley traces, in a step-by-step fashion, the actions of Stalin and the reactions of Lenin in 1922-1923 stressing those developments which angered Lenin to the point where he felt compelled to remove Stalin from any position of authority within the party.
[DK268. S8H56]

1077   Hunter, J. C. Trotsky and the Suppression of Lenin's Testament. New York: Leninist League, 1940; 8pp.
An attack on Trotsky for complicity in the Stalinist cover-up involving Lenin's testament. Hunter states that Trotsky's criticism of Max Eastman for exposing the Stalinist plot to suppress the testament is proof that Trotsky betrayed the workers: "blinding the workers to the truth about the renegacy of the Bolshevik leadership, Trotsky paralyzed them."

1078   *Jenkins, David. "The Power Struggle after the Tenth Party
        Congress," St Sov Un, 9, no. 1 (1969), 96-104.
        A discussion of the failure of Lenin's 1921 ban on fac-
        tionalism to prevent disunity from plaguing the party,
        and an account of Lenin's growing hostility towards
        Stalin in 1922 and 1923.

1079   Kamenev, L. "Leninism or Trotskyism," in The Errors
        of Trotskyism. London: Communist Party of Great
        Britain, 1925; 245-316.
        An attack on Trotsky's article "The Lessons of Octo-
        ber" as being representative of the general anti-Leninist
        line of thought long pursued by him. In support of this
        charge, Kamenev surveys the various disputes between
        Lenin and Trotsky in the pre-1917 period as well as
        their differences over concluding peace with Germany,
        the dictatorship of the proletariat, and other post-1917
        issues. [DK265. E85]

1080   "Lenin and after," Nation, 116 (28 Mar. 1923), 354.
        Speculation on whether the Bolsheviks can survive with-
        out Lenin's leadership.

1081   "Lenin Warned: Get Rid of Stalin," Newsweek, (2 Apr.
        1956), 44.

1082   "Lenin's Nightmare," Ave Maria, 73 (17 Mar. 1951), 322-
        23.
        A statement that Lenin suffered great remorse, in early
        1924, for having been the cause of so much misery
        in Russia.

1083   "Lenin's Testament," New Sta, 52 (9 June 1956), 646; (30
        June 1956), 755. Discussion, 52 (21 July-18 Aug. 1956),
        136, 162, 187.

1084   *Lermolo, Elizabeth. "Chapter XI," Face of a Victim. New
        York: Harper and Brothers, 1955; 132-37.
        An account of a prison conversation between the author
        and Gavril Volkov (Lenin's personal chef) during which
        Volkov told her that on 21 January 1924 he found Lenin
        gasping in his bed that he had been poisoned. Volkov
        stated that he had never told anyone about this because
        he feared that Stalin would have him killed, but now
        he felt that his execution was imminent so he had to
        confide in someone. [DK6295. R9L48]

1085   *Levine, Isaac Don. "Did Stalin Poison Lenin?," in Stalin's
        Great Secret. New York: Coward-McCann, 1956; 58-
        72.
        A review of the cases advanced by Trotsky and Lermolo
        that Stalin poisoned Lenin, and a circumstantial argu-
        ment in support of their claims. Levine presents as

evidence against Stalin his later involvement in the
murder of several individuals, including Frunze, Pilnyak,
and Trotsky. [DK268. S8L43]

1086 _____. "Disowned by Lenin," in Stalin. New York:
Cosmopolitan Book Corporation, 1931; 195-218.
A survey of the deterioration in relations between Lenin
and Stalin from 1920 until Lenin's death. Levine states
that Lenin began to become irritated with Stalin when
the latter failed to execute Lenin's order for the creation of an effective control commission to combat bureaucratic arbitrariness within the party and state apparatus.
Lenin's criticism led Stalin to feel insecure about his
position in the party and to consequent measures to
protect himself through the creation of a political machine which he could dominate. This, in turn, Levine
maintains, further angered Lenin who then sought out
Trotsky as an ally for a campaign to remove Stalin
from his position within the party. [DK268. S8L4]

1087 *Lewin, Moshe. Lenin's Last Struggle. New York: Random
House, 1968; 193pp.
An assessment, based on primary documents, of Lenin's
last years stressing his disillusionment over the bur-
geoning bureaucracy within the party. Lewin states
that, in spite of poor health, Lenin worked vigorously
on a program of reform to counter bureaucratic abuse
of power by creating a series of "checks and balances,"
a reform which would also curb Stalin's power and such
undesirable developments as the growth of Russian
chauvinism. [DK266. 5. L4513]

1087a Reviewed in:
Economist, (18 Oct. 1969), 60.
Eng Hist R, (Apr. 1970), 442, by E. H. Carr.
Historian, (Nov. 1970), 287, by D. Treadgold.
History, (Feb. 1971), 140, by J. Barber.
Int Aff, (Apr. 1971), 359, by V. Conolly.
Listener, (27 Nov. 1969), 754, by S. Hood.
*Monthly R, 21 (June 1969), 45-55, by H. Brauerman.
Nation, 208 (9 June 1969), 773-75, by J. Cammett.
N Y Times Bk R, (23 Mar. 1969), 12, by J. Billing-
ton.
New Yorker, (15 Feb. 1969), 124.
*Rus R, 29 (Oct. 1970), 457-63, by A. Parry.
Soc St, (Nov. 1970), 287, by D. Treadgold.
Sov St, (Jan. 1971), 448, by S. Monas.

1088 Lyons, Eugene. "Disowned by Lenin," in Stalin. Czar of
All the Russias. Philadelphia: Lippincott, 1940; 140-
48.
A review of Stalin's relations with Lenin during Lenin's
last twenty months. Lyons states that Lenin was so
upset over Stalin's abuse of power that he was about to

take drastic steps against him, but that his poor health
limited him to producing only his last testament as a
written indication of his displeasure with Stalin.
[DK268. S8L9]

1089   *McNeal, Robert H.   "Lenin's Attack on Stalin: Review and
Reappraisal," ASEER, 18, no. 3 (Oct. 1959), 295-314.
An investigation of why Lenin was unable to decide on
a decisive anti-Stalin position until the eve of his fatal
stroke.

1090   Marlen, George (George Spiro). Earl Browder. Communist
or Tool of Wall Street. Stalin, Trotsky or Lenin?
New York: Van Rees Press, 1937, 493pp.
Lenin is not the focus of this polemic against Earl
Browder, but he is frequently cited in the author's at-
tempt "to demarcate sharply the teachings of Marx and
Lenin from the opportunism of the Stalin and Trotsky
schools." [HX86. S755]

1091   *Medvedev, Roy A.   "In the Shadow of Lenin," in On Stalin
and Stalinism. Oxford: Oxford University Press, 1979;
19-36.
An assessment, by a Soviet historian and dissident, of
Lenin's relations with Stalin in the few years prior to
Lenin's death. Medvedev contends that although Lenin
criticized Stalin for policy failures and personal shortcomings, he did not single him out for particular abuse
but rather was more concerned with the danger of a
split within the party and the growth of the party's
bureaucracy. Lenin's last testament was designed to
prevent any one person from gaining control of the
party, and not as an attack on Stalin or an indication
that he favored Trotsky as his successor. Additionally,
Medvedev dismisses totally charges that Stalin poisoned
Lenin out of fear that Lenin was about to remove him
from the party. [DK267. M416]

1092   *Meijer, Jan, ed.   The Trotsky Papers. 1917-1922. 2
vols. Hague: Mouton, 1964, 1971; 858pp, 894pp, bib.
869-75 (vol. 2).
A compilation of Trotsky documents from the 1917-
1922 period, many of which are addressed to, written
by, or refer to Lenin. Collectively these documents
are a valuable source of information on the relations
between Lenin and Trotsky and on their views toward
a wide range of events and policies. The editor's extensive subject index makes for easy location of material related to Lenin. [DK254. T6A28 1964]

1093   *Payne, Robert. "The Battle with Lenin," in The Rise and
Fall of Stalin. New York: Simon and Schuster, 1965;
281-338, bib. 725-29.

An account of Lenin's growing suspicion of and animosity towards Stalin, beginning with the 1922 party debate on nationality policy. Payne pays particularly close attention to the case which Lenin and his secretary (L. Fotiyeva) prepared against Stalin to deflate his power within the party, and develops an argument that Stalin, out of fear of an impending attack by Lenin, arranged to have Lenin poisoned. [DK254. T6P35]

1094 *_____. "The Long Death of Lenin," in The Life and Death of Trotsky. New York: McGraw-Hill, 1977; 248-63.
An examination of Lenin's progressively deteriorating health and his growing dislike of Stalin. Payne discusses the nature of Lenin's illness and the crippling effect it had both on his performance of any party duties and his ability to deal energetically with Stalin's crude policies and behavior. Stalin's attempts to offset any decisions by Lenin that might jeopardize his own future in the party also receive careful attention. [PR6031. A93L56]

1095 Reswick, William. "Lenin's Death--Stalin's Intrigue," in I Dreamt Revolution. Chicago: Regnery, 1952; 52-73.
A general survey of the events surrounding Lenin's illness and death, with most attention given to the struggle between Trotsky and Stalin to replace Lenin as party leader. [DK267. R43]

1096 *Rush, Myron. "The Lenin Succession," in Political Succession in the USSR. New York: Columbia University Press, 1965; 10-41.
Although the majority of this chapter is centered on the emergence, after Lenin's death, of the Trotsky-Stalin battle for party leadership, it includes significant information on Lenin's last months and the fate of his testament. [JN6541. R78]

1097 *Schapiro, Leonard. "Lenin and the Russian Revolution," Hist Today, 20, no. 5 (1970), 324-30.
An examination of whether or not Lenin was disappointed and frustrated, during his last days, with the path taken by the Russian Revolution.

1098 Schuman, Frederick L. "From Lenin to Stalin," in Russia since 1917. Four Decades of Soviet Politics. New York: Knopf, 1962; 130-37.
A review of Lenin's thoughts on the question of how the party would function without him, his disenchantment with Stalin, and the fate of his political testament. [DK266. S428]

1099 *Serge, Victor. From Lenin to Stalin. New York: Monad, 1973; 9-62.

A positive account, by a CPSU member exiled by Stalin, of Lenin's accomplishments and Trotsky's assistance to Lenin, and an attack on the Stalin regime as a complete perversion of Lenin's most basic principles and policies. [DK266. S48 1973]

1100 Spiro, George. "Lenin's Break with Stalin," in Marxism and the Bolshevik State. New York: Red Star Press, 1951; 17-26.
A discussion of Lenin's irritation with Stalin and his nationality policies, and an argument that Trotsky actively opposed Lenin's plan to remove Stalin from power and, in fact, worked out a compromise with Stalin which would enable the latter to retain his position in return for changing the policies and methods criticized by Lenin. [JN6511. S6]

1101 *Stalin, Joseph. "Trotskyism or Leninism?," in The October Revolution. A Collection of Articles and Speeches by Joseph Stalin. New York: International Publishers, 1978; 68-94.
A 19 November 1924 speech attacking Trotsky's interpretation of the October Revolution and characterizing his thought as an "ideology incompatible with Leninism." Stalin criticizes Trotsky for asserting that the party was plagued by divisions just prior to the revolution, and then reviews the differences between Lenin and Trotsky which existed before 1917. [DK265. S667713] Also in The Errors of Trotskyism. London: Communist Party of Great Britain, 1925; 206-44.

1102 *Trotsky, Leon. "Did Stalin Poison Lenin?," Lib M (10 Aug. 1940).

1103 * _____. "On Lenin's Testament," in Lenin's Fight against Stalinism, R. Bloch, ed. New York: Pathfinder, 1975; 30-59.
A discussion of Lenin's testament as a document rooted both in Lenin's concern, in the months before his death, with "the monstrous growth of bureaucratic power" centered in the office held by Stalin, and in disputes with Stalin over foreign trade and nationality policy. Trotsky also criticizes the interpretation of the testament advanced by Emil Ludwig who accepted as fact Radek's erroneous account of the testament and Trotsky's response to it. [HX313. L4135] Also published as The Suppressed Testament of Lenin. New York: Pioneer Publishers, 1935; 41pp.

1104 * _____. The Real Situation in Russia. New York: Harcourt, Brace and Company, 1928.
A 1927 critique of the policies pursued by the CPSU since Lenin's death, and an attack on Stalin's "falsifica-

tion of history" through complete perversion of Trotsky's relations with Lenin in 1917 and afterwards. Trotsky also recounts Lenin's criticism of Stalin as the personal embodiment of all that was wrong with the party. [DK267. T7]

1105 *Ulam, Adam B. "In Lenin's Shadow," in Stalin. The Man and His Era. New York: Viking Press, 1973; 192-233. An examination of Stalin's diligent work behind the main political arena as he quietly took charge of the party apparatus. Ulam states that Lenin initially supported Stalin as the party's administrative specialist and only came to be suspicious of him when Stalin began to abuse power once the only check, Lenin, was removed from an active role in party affairs. Lenin's plans to limit Stalin's power, and Stalin's measured responses to the threat which Lenin posed to his position also receive considerable attention. [DK268. S8U4]

1106 *_____. "Lenin's Last Phase," Survey, 21, nos. 1-2 (Winter-Spring 1975), 148-59. An inquiry into Lenin's critical state of mind, as he neared death, on party bureaucracy and leadership as well as on the cultural revolution.

1107 Vlasov, B. S. and I. P. Ganenko, comps. Against Trotskyism. The Struggle of Lenin and the CPSU against Trotskyism. A Collection of Documents. Moscow: Progress Publishers, 1972; 406pp. A collection of speeches, letters, resolutions, telegrams, and other primary materials dealing with the struggle against Trotskyism. Although the title suggests that the struggle was conducted by Lenin, the vast majority of the documents are not in his name and, in fact, were composed after his death. The compilers state that the battle began in 1903 and was continued in Lenin's name by the party following his 1924 death. [JN6598. S6B59713]

1108 Warth, Robert D. "NEP and the Close of the Lenin Era," in Leon Trotsky. Boston: Twayne, 1977; 113-34. Lenin is not the focus of this chapter, but it contains significant information on the last two years of his life, especially in regard to his relations with Trotsky and Stalin. [DK254. T6W37]

1109 *Woods, Alan and Ted Grant. Lenin and Trotsky. What They Really Stood for. A Reply to Monte Johnson. London: Militant, 1976; 151pp. , bib. 149-51. A positive account of Lenin's relationship with Trotsky, and a critique of the anti-Trotsky views of Monte Johnson as advanced in an article published in the Young Communist League's journal Cognito. The authors criticize Johnson for over-emphasizing the 1903-1917 era in which Lenin and Trotsky were political rivals, while neglecting the 1917-1923 period during which Lenin had complete trust in Trotsky and sought him out as an ally against Stalin. [HX313.W66 1976]

4. MILITARY THEORY AND LEADERSHIP

1110   Adams, Arthur E. "The Bolsheviks and the Ukrainian
        Front in 1918-1919," SEER, 36, no. 87 (1958), 396-
        417.
        In part, on Lenin's involvement in the military opera-
        tions in the Ukraine.

1111   *Aralov, S. "Lenin Was Beside Us," Sov Mil R, no. 1
        (Jan. 1978), 14-17.
        A recollection, by the chief of operations for military
        and naval affairs during the Civil War, of Lenin's close,
        detailed and effective work on a variety of military mat-
        ters.

1112   "At the Head of the Defence Council," Sov Mil R, no. 10
        (Oct. 1979), 5-7.
        A discussion of Lenin's 1918-1920 activities as head of
        the Defense Council during the Civil War.

1113   Azovtsev, N. and S. Gusarevich. "Lenin's Exposure of
        Militarism," Int Aff, 16, no. 4 (Apr. 1970), 19-20.

1114   Babenko, I. "Lenin's Ideas," in Soviet Officers. Moscow:
        Progress Publishers, 1976; 17-22.
        A brief discussion of Lenin's views on the crucial im-
        portance of adequately trained military personnel. Ba-
        benko states that Lenin was particularly concerned with
        the need to train, educate, and appoint command person-
        nel who in turn would play a leading role in the military-
        political education of the lower ranks of the armed
        forces. [UB415.R982713]

1115   Basov, N. I. "Sociopolitical Substance of Civil Defense,"
        in PHVIL (anthology), 240-252.
        A Leninist analysis of the class-political nature of civil
        defense. Citing Lenin, Basov asserts that "the civil
        defense of any country constitutes a unity of two organ-
        ically interlinked aspects: sociopolitical and material-
        technical," and that civil defense in capitalist countries
        is designed to enable foreign policy to be more im-
        perialistic and anti-communist, while in the Soviet Union
        socialist humanitarianism permeates all civil defense
        activities. Basov relates this discussion to Lenin's
        concept of just and unjust wars.

1116   Bochkaryov, K. "Lenin on Just and Unjust Wars," Sov Mil
        R, no. 4 (Apr. 1971), 13-15.

1117   *Bonch-Bruyevich, Mikhail. "To Meet Lenin....," Sov Lit,
        no. 3 (1970), 55-59.
        A recollection of 1917-1918 meetings with Lenin on the
        creation of a workers' army to defend the Soviet state
        against German aggression.

1118   Bondarenko, V. M. "Science as a Factor in Strengthening
        the National Defense Capability," in PHVIL (anthology),
        173-86.
        A positive discussion of Lenin's views on the role of
        science in a socialist state and the relationship between
        science and an effective military force. Bondarenko
        restates Lenin's teachings on the need for maximum de-
        velopment of science through centralized planning and
        and a firm financial-physical support base, and for a
        full application of science to the economic development
        of the nation. Bondarenko asserts that Lenin saw a
        crucial connection between a thriving socialist science
        community and equally healthy defense capability, a
        connection whose validity is demonstrated by the highly
        scientific and technical foundations of the modern Soviet
        army.

1119   *Collins, D. N. "The Russian Red Guard of 1917 and Lenin's
        Utopia," J Rus St, no. 32 (1976), 3-12.
        A discussion of Lenin's concept of the Red Guard and
        the role of the Guard in 1917.

1120   *Davis, Donald E. "Lenin's Theory of War," Indiana Univer-
        sity, 1970 (dissertation).

1121   *Davis, Donald E. and Walter S. Kohn. "Lenin as a Dis-
        ciple of Clausewitz," Mil R, 51, no. 9 (Sept. 1971),
        49-55.

1122   *   . "Lenin's Notebook on Clausewitz," Sov Armed
        Fo R An, 1 (1977), 188-221.

1123   Dmitriev, A. P. "Significance of Lenin's Ideas for Improv-
        ing Troop Control," in PHVIL (anthology), 231-39.
        A positive, general discussion of Lenin's insistence on
        a thoroughly scientific approach to management and con-
        trol of troops. Dmitriev presents Lenin's main views
        on this subject as being: rigorous training in scientific
        management principles of all persons employed in the
        area of management (including a formal exam); a full
        utilization of mathematical calculations in determing and
        implementing troop strategy; strict division of labor with
        clear-cut determination of duties of control; close coor-
        dination of all activities and information; and the com-

plete equipping of all operations stations with modern communications gear and apparatus.

1124   *Earle, Edward, M. "Lenin, Trotsky, Stalin: Soviet Concepts of War," in Makers of Modern Strategy. Princeton: Princeton University Press, 1943; 322-64.
A general discussion of both Lenin's theoretical views on warfare and the military policies he pursued as Soviet leader. Earle isolates Clausewitz's dictum "war is politics continued by other means" as the guiding principle behind Lenin's approach to war and diplomacy, and discusses in its light Lenin's views and actions in regard to concluding peace with Germany and conducting the Civil War. The author also examines the influence on Lenin of the practical realities of warfare and how though the Red Army was billed by Lenin as "an army of a new type" its excellence rested upon adherence to traditional emphasis on military technique, "discipline and tactical excellence of troops, high standards of professional competence among field and staff officers, and adherence to sound strategic principles." Earle concludes that Lenin emerged from the Civil War with a comprehensive image of the Soviet military force as a revolutionary people's army utilizing from bourgeois military science all that was of assistance in the defense and advancement of socialism. [U39.E2]

1125   *Erickson, John. "Lenin as Civil War Leader," in LMTL (anthology), 159-86.
A presentation of Lenin's role in the Civil War as being that of the master coordinator, "a man and a machine, ideas and action, strategic insight and political outlook, administrative supervision, and political control all rolled into one." Erickson discusses Lenin's juggling of priorities on the various fronts of the war, his clash at the Eighth Party Congress with those who criticized the recreation of the old army, and his attempts to export revolution by having Soviet armies advance through Poland to Germany. Erickson sees Lenin's military policies as being remarkably flexible and successful during the Civil War, but failing in Poland due to misassessment of the relation between war and revolution.

1126   *Fedenko, P. "Lenin's Views on War and Peaceful Coexistence," B Inst St USSR, 10, no. 3 (Mar. 1963), 27-36.
An argument that Lenin believed in the inevitability of war as long as capitalism existed and thus it is difficult to see him as a friend of the 1961 C.P.S.U. program even though he is cited by the party for support for its peaceful coexistence policies.

1127   Frantsov, G. P. "Lenin's Ideas of Struggle for Peace," in Philosophy and Sociology. Moscow: Progress Publishers, 1975; 232-42.

An attack on those critics who assert that Lenin believed that "communism had to be ushered in by military disaster" and that revolution should be spread by
wars of conquest. Frantsov counters these charges by
stating that Lenin supported war only as a means of
protecting socialist revolutionary regimes against imperialist backed counter-revolutions, and that Lenin,
as Soviet leader, pursued a foreign policy aimed at
maintaining and consolidating peaceful relations with
capitalist states. [HX542. F6613]

1128 _____. "What Lenin Actually Said About Revolution and
War," in Philosophy and Sociology. Moscow: Progress
Publishers, 1975; 229-31.
A defense of Lenin against critics who claim he was
an advocate of war as a means of advancing revolution.
Frantsov states that Lenin believed that modern war
threatened "the very existence of human society," and
that he worked vigorously to expose the true (imperialist)
roots of war and to advance the cause of socialism as
the best means of preventing future wars.
[HX542. F6613]

1129 Fuller, J. F. C. "Soviet Revolutionary Warfare," in The
Conduct of War, 1917-1961. New York: Minerva
Press, 1968; 205-208.
A brief discussion of Lenin's military policies in the
1918-1922 period. Fuller asserts that Lenin's Civil
War policies reflected a close reading of Clausewitz,
especially in regard to the theory of unified war, war
as a continuation of politics, and the theory of defensive
and counter-offensive warfare. Fuller argues that unlike Clausewitz, Lenin failed to recognize that morality
and ethics have a place in warfare. [U39. F38]

1130 Golikov, G. "Heading the Insurgent People," Sov Mil R,
no. 11 (Nov. 1969), 11-15.
A review of Lenin's military decisions on October 26,
1917, as an example of his leadership during the Bolshevik Revolution.

1131 *Golub, P. "Lenin's Military Programme for the Party
During the First Russian Revolution," in The Bolsheviks
and the Armed Forces in Three Revolutions. Moscow:
Progress Publishers, 1979; 48-65.
A Soviet account of how Lenin, during the 1905-1907
period, worked out the general principles upon which
Bolshevik military strategy was to be based in the revolution of 1917. Golub isolates Lenin's main principle
as being that the proletariat must have its own armed
forces, work vigorously to win over to the proletariat's
cause regular army members, and draw into the workers' army all oppressed groups in Russia.
[UA770. G6513]

1132 *_____. "The Revolutionary Forces of the Army and
Navy in Lenin's Plan for the Armed Uprising," in The
Bolsheviks and the Armed Forces in Three Revolutions.
Moscow: Progress Publishers, 1979; 257-84.
A Soviet summary of Lenin's campaign to win garrison
support for the revolution and of his use of this support
in the October Revolution. [UA770. G6513]

1133 *Hahlweg, Werner. "Clausewitz, Lenin and Communist Military Attitudes Today," J Roy U Serv Inst, 105, no. 618
(1970), 221-25.

1134 *Horowitz, Irving. "Vladimir Lenin: The Historical Vision,"
in The Idea of War and Peace in Contemporary Philosophy. New York: Paine-Whitman Publishers, 1957;
124-41.
An analysis of Lenin's concept of just and unjust warfare. Horowitz first summarizes Lenin's view of just
wars as being those which advanced the interests of
exploited people while unjust conflicts advanced the interests of the exploiters, and then applies this interpretation of war to the case of World War II. Horowitz
concludes that "Lenin's concept of just and unjust war
is by itself internally consistent and yet inadequate for
the empirical determination of a given conflict" because
once a theory "becomes a substitute for the further
probing of the human situation, it loses contact with
reality altogether." [JX1952. H72]

1135 Hudson, George E. "Soviet Naval Doctrine under Lenin
and Stalin," Sov St, 28 (Jan. 1976), 42-65.

1136 Ivanov, V. N. "Lenin's Ideas on Scientific Guidance of
Military Organizational Development," in PHVIL (anthology), 223-31.
A favorable assessment of Lenin's role in establishing
the organizational foundations of Soviet military forces.
Ivanov isolates as Lenin's principal contributions his
insistence on a scientific approach to military management, on borrowing selectively from the bourgeois military heritage, on full utilization of trained specialists,
strict centralization in allocation and use of manpower
and resources, and on the guiding role of the party at
every phase of military organization and operation.
Ivanov also traces Lenin's struggle to establish these
principles in the face of opposition by various "opportunist" groups and individuals, and demonstrates the
truthfulness of his teachings by illustrations from successful Soviet military operations in the Civil War and
World War II.

1137 Kalinin, M. "Lenin in Defence of the Socialist Fatherland,"
in OL (anthology), 110-29.

A review of Lenin's military teachings and policies for insights into the proper strategies and tactics to be followed by Soviet leadership in World War II. Excerpt from On Communist Education and the Soldier's Duty. Moscow: Military Publishing House, 1967; 566-76.

1138   Kamenev, S. "Lenin's School of Military Leadership," Sov Mil R, no. 3 (Mar. 1970), 14-15.
A brief note, by a Soviet commander on the Eastern Front, on Lenin's leadership during the Civil War.

1139   _____. "Reminiscences of Lenin," in OL (anthology), 137-43.
A recollection, by a Soviet commander, of Lenin's daily and direct supervision of the Red Army during the Civil War. From Sov Mil R, no. 4 (1967), 3-7.

1140   Karabanov, N. B. "Lenin on the Nature of the Era and the Content of Wars," in PHVIL (anthology), 7-13.
A Soviet elaboration on Lenin's principle that a given war cannot be comprehended separate from an analysis of the historical era which produces it. Karabanov reviews Lenin's rationale for identifying most nineteenth-century wars as bourgeois-progressive struggles against feudal remnants and political absolutism, and twentieth century wars as predatory imperialist struggles launched by monopoly capitalism. Karabanov also discusses Lenin's assessment of World War I as a case study of scientific analysis of warfare.

1141   Karpinsky, V. "Lenin-Leader," in OL (anthology), 172-75.
A description of Lenin's calm and courage in making important decisions. Karpinsky provides as examples of these leadership qualities Lenin's November 20, 1917 replacement of Dukhonin with Krylenko for refusal to negotiate peace with Germany, and his rejection of the German government's demand, after the assassination of Ambassador Mirbach, that German troops be stationed in the capital. Originally in Sov Mil R, no. 10 (1967), 9-11.

1142   Khalipov, V. F. "The Problem of War and Peace in the Present Era," in PHVIL (anthology), 13-22.
A positive review of Lenin's scientific approach to determining the nature of a war by assessing the features of the era within which it occurs. Khalipov identifies, as did Lenin, the contemporary age as a "protracted period during which socialist and capitalist states will exist side by side," and then discusses Lenin's warning that throughout this period the exploiters would inevitably attempt to subvert and overthrow socialist states through reactionary wars. Khalipov stresses that even though such a reactionary war would be a thermonuclear one,

the imperialists, in their fanatic desire to preserve
their crumbling state, may resort to such weaponry.

1143   Kolobyakov, A. F. "On Guard Duty in the Kremlin," in
OL (anthology), 187-89.
A recollection of Lenin's friendly concern for Red Army
men as observed by Kolobyakov while on duty at the
Kremlin. Also in LCAM (anthology), 169-71.

1144   Kondratkov, T. R. "Critique of the Bourgeois Concepts of
the Sources of Leninist Doctrine on War," in PHVIL
(anthology), 39-45.
A Soviet refutation of the various Western criticism of
Lenin's doctrine of war. Kondratkov concentrates his
attack on those who use the German military theorist,
Clausewitz, as their prime source, stating that while
Lenin accepted Clausewitz's connection between war and
politics, he critically reworked the great bulk of Clausewitz's idealistic teachings thus creating a "totally new
doctrine of war" based on a dialectical materialist interpretation of war's class content and character.

1145   _____. "Principal Methods of Distortion of Lenin's Views
on the Essence and Nature of War," in PHVIL (anthology), 45-51.
A continuation of the author's critique of bourgeois concepts of warfare, focusing on the Western claim that
the advent of thermonuclear weapons has made obsolete
Lenin's concept of war as a violent extension of politics.
Kondratkov contends that the relation between war and
politics is just as direct and powerful as in Lenin's
era since the imperialist nations consistently use thermonuclear blackmail as a political tool in pursuit of
class goals, and since if nuclear war is fought it will
certainly possess a class essence and character. Kondratkov also defends Lenin's definition of a "small" war
as well as his division of wars into just and unjust types.

1146   _____. "War as a Continuation of Policy," Sov Mil R,
no. 2 (1974), 7-9.
A Leninist discussion of the relation between detente,
class struggle, and warfare.

1147   Konoplev, V. K. "Methodology of Leninist Scientific Foresight," in PHVIL (anthology), 253-67.
A sympathetic discussion of Lenin's ability to predict,
on a scientific basis, both the general course of military
development as well as the direction that specific military events and strategies would or should go. Konoplev
outlines the basis of the Leninist methodology of obtaining scientific foresight into military developments and
then gives several examples of its practical application
by Lenin during the Russian Civil War. The author
states that while Lenin's scientific approach to military

problems has yielded many practical advantages for
Soviet military leaders, this approach must not be expected to produce exact and accurate conclusions in
every instance because of warfare's random occurrences
and the lack of complete situational data due to conscious
concealment by the enemy.

1148   *Korablev, Y.   Lenin--the Founder of the Soviet Armed
       Forces.   Moscow: Progress Publishers, 1977; 207pp.
       A summary of Lenin's role in creating Soviet military
       forces and establishing their general tactics and strategy.
       Korablev begins with a survey of Lenin's pre-revolution-
       ary thought on the need for the party and workers to be
       fully prepared for military struggle against tsarism and
       capitalism alike, a struggle for which Lenin prepared
       himself by reading Clausewitz carefully.   Korablev dis-
       cusses Lenin's military leadership during the October
       Revolution and Civil War, stressing his involvement in
       everything from grand strategy to the smallest details.
       Korablev concludes that Lenin left "an invaluable legacy
       of military theory in which he gave brilliant examples
       of the theoretical and practical solutions to key problems
       in strategy, operational art, and tactics.   Lenin's con-
       tribution to the art of war is so great that he is justly
       recognized as the founder of Soviet military science."
       [UA772. K58513]

1149   Korotkov, I.   "The Military-Theoretical Legacy of Lenin,"
       Sov Mil R, no. 4 (April 1968), 2-6.
       A Soviet discussion of Lenin's study of warfare, just
       and unjust wars, tactics and organization, and the re-
       lation between war and revolution.   Korotkov also re-
       views Lenin's role in the military preparations for the
       October Revolution and in defending the Bolshevik state.
       Also in OL (antholggy), 197-209 and LDMORP (anthol-
       ogy), 25-29.

1150   Kozlov, V. G.   "V. I. Lenin on the Material Prerequisites
       for the Military Power of the Socialist State," in PHVIL
       (anthology), 137-53.
       A Soviet elaboration of Lenin's belief that a well-de-
       veloped economic system is "the principal material
       prerequisite for the military strength of the state and
       its success in the conduct of war."   Kozlov discusses
       Lenin's views on the advantages of a centralized scienti-
       fically planned defense industry over the wasteful, un-
       coordinated character of the capitalist defense industry,
       and his support for international socialist military-
       economic cooperation as the bases for contemporary
       Soviet defense policy.

1151   *Krushin, Peter.   "Lenin and the Soviet Armed Forces,"
       St. Sov Un, 10, no. 1 (1970), 19-36.

An attack on the Soviet image of Lenin as a military genius, creator of Soviet military science, and the source of the Bolshevik victory in the Civil War.

1152　Kuzmin, D.　"Heading the Defence of the Soviet Republic," Sov Mil R no. 3 (Mar. 1970), 30-35.

1153　_____.　"Lenin and Soviet Military Cadres," Sov Mil R, no. 1 (Jan. 1970), 8-12.

1154　"Lenin and Soviet Officers," in OL (anthology), 176-77.
　　　　A brief note on Lenin's views on the training and appointment of military officers, party leadership of military education, and Soviet use of former tsarist officers. Excerpt from V. I. Lenin. A Biography. Moscow: Progress Publishers, 1966; 397-98.

1155　*Lenin and the Build-up of the Soviet Armed Forces.　Moscow: Novosti Press, 1969; 70pp.
　　　　A positive presentation of Lenin as the source of both the philosophical principles and practical guidelines upon which Soviet armed forces are based. The author summarizes Lenin's views on the sources and class characteristics of wars; the major conditions for achieving victory in defense of socialism; the key components of an effective fighting force; the economic and psychological importance of the "role of the rear"; and his general principles on military science. Also reviewed is Lenin's leadership in the October Revolution and Civil War as proof of the contention that Lenin not only is the father of the Red Army but was also a military genius. [UA770. L4313]

1156　"Lenin's Talk with Kronstadt," Rus Info R, 4, no. 6 (9 Feb. 1924), 94.
　　　　A record of a telegraph conversation between Lenin and the Kronstadt fortress on the request for military support during the October Revolution.

1157　*Lisenkov, M. M.　"V. I. Lenin on the Cultural Revolution and Its Significance in Strengthening the Armed Forces," in PHVIL (anthology), 154-172.
　　　　A favorable assessment of Lenin's belief that the development of socialist culture was a fundamental prerequisite to the establishment of an effective fighting force. Lisenkov emphasizes Lenin's argument that literacy, indoctrination in socialist ideals, and comprehensive technical training were all essential to the army's combat strength.

1158　Lukava, G.　"The Art of Victory," Sov Mil R, no. 3 (Mar. 1970), 42-44.

1158a _____ . "Leninist Methodology of Solving Problems of
Military Science," in PHVIL (anthology), 103-10.
A summary of Lenin's contributions to Soviet military
strategy and tactics. Lukava supports his contention
that Lenin's contributions were both many and brilliant
by discussing Lenin's teachings on the concentration of
men and weapons on a decisive axis; application of the
correct forms of combat; interrelation between offensive
and defensive operations; seizure and maintenance of
strategic initiative; and on the coordination of troop
action. Lukava concludes that Lenin's philosophical
heritage in military science is "an inexhaustible source
of innovative development of" Soviet Strategy and tactics.

1159 Mal'tsev, Y. Y. "Leninist Concepts of the Defense of Socialism," USAF Translations, (Oct. 1974). Translated
from Krasnaia Zvezda, (14 Feb. 1974).

1160 Marxism-Leninism on War and Army. Moscow: Progress
Publishers, 1972, 335pp.
This study does not contain a separate section on Lenin
but includes considerable information on his thought on
military tactics and strategy, the relation between war
and politics, just and unjust wars, socialist defense,
and his contributions to the general laws of military
science. [U21.2M3613]

1161 *Mladenovic, M. "Lenin and Clausewitz," New R, 7, no.
3 (Sept. 1967), 8-35.

1162 Morozov, V. I. "Lenin and the Creation of Soviet Military
Science," in PHVIL (anthology), 95-103.
A Soviet discussion of Lenin's application of materialist
dialectics to military science. Morozov states that
when Russia emerged as the world's first socialist state,
the need arose for a socialist approach to military
science as a means of defense against imperialist aggression, a need which Lenin fully satisfied. Morozov
credits Lenin with establishing the "military program
of the proletarian revolution, the doctrine of defense
of the socialist homeland, the significance of scientific
military theory for the socialist state, for creating its
foundations and revealing its characteristic traits and
features." Morozov praises Lenin most for his placing
military science on a purely empirical level.

1163 Moskalenko, K. "True to Lenin's Behests," Sov Mil R,
no. 3 (Mar. 1970), 36-40.
A discussion of how Soviet military forces have been
shaped by Lenin's military principles.

1164 Nemirov, N. "V. I. Lenin-Honorary Red Army Man," in
OL (anthology), 145-52.

A recollection of how Lenin's messages and speeches often conveyed his concern for the soldier and led directly to his being given honorary status in the Red Army. Originally in Sov Mil R, no. 2 (1968), 6-8.

1165   O'Ballance, Edgar. The Red Army. A Short History. New York: Praeger Press, 1964; 237pp. Lenin is not the focus of any individual chapter in this study, but it contains information on his involvement in and thinking on military affairs. [UA772.O26]

1166   Pankratov, N. "The Assault in October," Sov Mil R, no. 10 (Oct. 1977), 13-15. An account of Lenin's military preparations for the October Revolution.

1167   _____. "At the Head of the Defence Council," Sov Mil R, no. 10 (Oct. 1979), 5+. A positive assessment of Lenin's Civil War leadership as Chairman of the Council of Workers' and Peasants' Defence.

1168   _____. "V. I. Lenin-Leader in the Defence of the Socialist Motherland," Sov Mil R, no. 10 (Oct. 1978), 2-5.

1169   Pelliccia, Antonio. "Clausewitz and Soviet Politico-Military Strategy," Mil R, 56, no. 8 (1976), 23-33. In part, a discussion of Lenin's interpretation of Clausewitz.

1170   *Pethybridge, Roger W. "The Bolsheviks and Technical Disorder," SEER, 49 no. 116 (1971), 410-24. An argument that Lenin's sowing of anarchy in the Russian army prior to October 1917 was so successful that it threatened his own regime after 1917 and was in part responsible for the extreme measures of War Communism.

1171   Podvoisky, N. I. "Lenin Was in Our Ranks," in OL (anthology), 84-89. An account, by the Chairman of the Military Organization of the Bolshevik Party, of an October 17, 1917 meeting with Lenin on military preparations for the October Revolution. Originally in Sov Mil R, no. 4 (1966), 3-5.

1172   Ponomarev, N. A. "Critique of an Opportunistic and Revisionist Interpretation of the Essence of War," in PHVIL (anthology), 51-57. A Soviet defense of Lenin's definition of the class essence of war against the interpretations advanced by right and left-wing socialists. As in Lenin's time, Ponomarev states, today's right-wing socialists especially Great Britain's Labour Party) support the aggressive imperialist policies of the bourgeoisie and attempt to obscure this support by presenting the socialist nations as aggressors thereby forgetting totally the class character of all warfare. Ponomarev criticizes the left socialists for failure to follow Lenin's dictate on determining the nature of a given historical era before developing any position on a specific war. Ponomarev points out that Lenin identified the modern era as one in which capitalist and socialist states must coexist peacefully while waiting for the natural contradictions in the capitalist states to produce socialist revolutions.

1173 _____. "Leninist Critique of Bourgeois Militarism and the Contemporary World," in <u>PHVIL</u> (anthology), 58-77. A Soviet summary of Lenin's teachings on the origins, features, and functions of militarism. Ponomarev discusses militarism as a by-product of the imperialist policies of monopoly capitalism and as serving to expand capitalist holdings abroad and to crush proletarian movements which oppose capitalism. Ponomarev also reviews Lenin's critique of the "ideologica apologia of militarism" stressing the validity of Lenin's attack on bourgeois interpretations of war as a phenomenon inherent in mankind.

1174 Pozmorgov. "Lenin on the New Type of Army," <u>Sov Mil R</u>, no. 4 (Apr. 1972), 11-13.

1175 *Rybkin, Ye. I. "Leninist Principles of Sociological Analysis of Wars and Contemporary Problems," in <u>PHVIL</u> (anthology), 23-38. A Soviet review of Lenin's teachings on the "causes of wars, their social character and substance, and a study of their effect on society and on various social processes." Rybkin discusses Lenin's and Clausewitz's view that "war is a continuation of politics by violent means" and how Lenin identified the particular political content of each war by analyzing the conditions of a given historical era and the specific policies of given social classes. More particularly, Rybkin states, Lenin insisted that to determine the social character of war, one must first examine "the causes of the war, the aims of the war, and the classes which are waging it." Rybkin then reviews Lenin's classification of wars into oppressor versus oppressed; oppressor versus oppressor, and capitalist versus socialist.

1176 *Seleznev, I. A. "The Role and Place of Ideological Struggle in Modern Warfare," in <u>PHVIL</u> (anthology), 206-22. A favorable presentation, by a Soviet specialist, of Lenin's views on the use of propaganda in undermining the enemy while solidifying and channeling popular support for warfare. Seleznev discusses Lenin's personal involvement, during World War I and the Civil War, in propaganda and agitation, stressing that though Lenin believed ideological warfare to be important, he always asserted that it must play a secondary role to armed warfare as the principal means of achieving victory. Seleznev provides examples of Lenin's utilization of both tactical and strategic ideological warfare, and reviews his wartime propaganda.

1177 Semyonov, A. S. "In a Military Hospital," in LCAM (anthology), 163-67.
A recollection of Lenin's concern for Red Army soldiers as exhibited by his visit to and speech at a military hospital.

1178 Shevchenko, A. "Lenin's Ideas on the Defence of Socialism in Action," Sov Mil R, no. 5 (May 1977), 2-5.

1179 Shirman, A. A. "Social Activity of the Masses and the Defense of Socialism," in PHVIL (anthology), 119-36.
A Soviet discussion of Lenin's belief that the "revolutionary creativity" and enthusiasm of the workers constituted an immense asset in the defense of the socialist state. Shirman re-states Lenin's belief that effective defense must utilize the energies of the masses by first contrasting the just goals of socialist defense with the unjust goals of bourgeois imperialism and then developing means to organize and channel these energies, whether in the army itself or through partisan units, civilian support groups, and home guard detachments. Shirman also discusses Lenin's dictum that the maximum use of mass support cannot be achieved spontaneously but only under the guidance of the party.

1180 Shmelyov, M. "The Leninist Style of Work," Sov Mil R, no. 4 (Apr. 1974), 12-14.
A review of Lenin's political and military tactics as a combination of audacity and flexibility.

1181 Shumikhin, N. "Leninist Doctrine on the Defense of Socialism and the Present," USAF Translations, (Aug. 1974). Translated from Kryl'ia Rodiny, (Apr. 1974).

1182 Sidelnikov, I. "V. I. Lenin on the Defence of the Socialist Motherland," Sov Mil R, no. 3 (Mar. 1974), 2-4.

1183 Sofronov, G. "A Talk with V. I. Lenin," in OL (anthology), 178-86.
A recollection of Lenin's Civil War address to military cadets in which he announced that twenty cadets would graduate early to go to the front because trained military officers were badly needed there. Translated from Voenno-Istorichesky Zhurnal, no. 4 (1963), 52.

1184   Somerville, John. "Marxism and the 'Just War' Today,"
        in Howard L. Parsons and John Somerville, eds.
        Marxism, Revolution and Peace. Amsterdam: B. R.
        Gruner, 1977; 75-83.
        In part, a discussion of Lenin's theory of "just and un-
        just wars" and its applicability to contemporary wars
        of national liberation. [B809.8S557]

1185   Spirov, K. V. "Critique of the Methodological Foundations
        of Bourgeois Military Theory," in PHVIL (anthology),
        110-18.
        A Soviet discussion of Lenin's "unmasking of the aggres-
        sive, reactionary substance of the military ideology of
        imperialism." Spirov states that Lenin demonstrated
        the bankruptcy of bourgeois military theory by exposing
        its metaphysical methodology in its assessment of war
        between bourgeois and socialist states. Western ideolo-
        gists, Spirov asserts, fail to recognize the peculiar
        strengths, pointed out by Lenin, which socialist military
        forces contain, largely because these ideologists are
        blinded by "class narrowness and an anti-scientific"
        approach to military theory.

1186   Sredin, G. "Marxist-Leninist Doctrine on War and the
        Army," Sov Mil R, no. 1 (Jan. 1978), 18-21, 42.

1187   *Thompson, John M. "Lenin's Analysis of Intervention,"
        ASEER, 17, no. 2 (Apr. 1958), 151-60.
        An examination of Lenin's assessment of the motives
        for Allied intervention in Russia's Civil War.

1188   *Timorin, A. A. "V. I. Lenin on the Socialist Army and
        the Laws Governing Its Development," in PHVIL (an-
        thology), 78-94.
        A positive assessment of Lenin's role in developing the
        concept of a socialist army. Timorin discusses Lenin's
        alteration, due to historical circumstances, of the tra-
        ditional Marxist view that a socialist state would not
        need a permanent military force, and then elaborates
        on the characteristics, outlined by Lenin, uniquely pos-
        sessed by the socialist army as well as those which it
        must share with bourgeois armies. Timorin also re-
        states Lenin's views on the various internal functions
        of the socialist army and its role in defending Soviet
        and international socialism through military alliances
        with other socialist states.

1189   Tybkin, Ye. S. "The Leninist Concept of War and the
        Present," USAF Translations, (Jan. 1974). Translated
        from Kommunist Vooruzhennykh Sil, (Oct. 1973).

1190   *Volkogonov, D. A. "Lenin's Ideas on Moral-Political and
        Psychological Training of Troops," in PHVIL (anthology),
        187-205.

A positive account of Lenin's thought on "the importance of the moral-political factor in war and on the principal means and methods of strengthening it." Volkogonov reviews Lenin's teaching on the necessity of indoctrinating all combat personnel with the proper ideological orientation, meaning "a well-balanced system of socialist views on war, its political goals, and consequences, as well as ideas of patriotism and internationalism...." Such indoctrination, Lenin believed, would result in the creation of a communist fighting force with sufficient dedication and confidence to cope on moral, political, and psychological levels with the many demands of modern warfare. Volkogonov also supports with examples Lenin's contention that no political force can effectively possess these positive moral qualities without the proper material-historical conditions, a fact which the author believes is the secret source of Soviet military superiority (in Lenin's time and now) over bourgeois military forces.

1191   Vorobyov, I. "Choice of Direction of Main Blow," Sov Mil R, no. 3 (Mar. 1970), 45-47.

1192   White, D. Fedotoff. The Growth of the Red Army. Princeton: Princeton University Press, 1944, 486pp.
        This study does not contain a chapter on Lenin, but includes a discussion of his military thought and policies. [UA772.W4]

1193   *Wolfe, Bertram D. "Lenin and Class War," Orbis, 3 (1960), 443-57.
        An attack on the Soviet writings which cloud the aggressive nature of Lenin's thought on class war.

1194   *_____. War is the Womb of Revolution: Lenin 'Consults' Hegel," Antioch R, 16, no. 2 (June 1956), 190-97.
        A discussion of Lenin's concept of war as being rooted more in the thought of Hegel than in Marx.

1195   Zhilin, P. "The Wealth of Lenin's Legacy in Military History," Sov Mil R, no. 2 (Feb. 1970), 4-7.

1196   Zvenzlovsky, A. "Lenin and the Formation of the Red Army," Sov Mil R, no. 5 (May 1971), 58-60.

5. ECONOMIC THEORY AND PRACTICE

A. Theory

1197   *Aden, U.   "The Graveworms of the Revolution: the Communist View of the Petty Bourgeoisie," B Inst St USSR,
18, no. 1 (1971), 5-21.
A discussion of Lenin's The Development of Capitalism
in Russia as a source of insight into his views on and
the policies toward the petty bourgeoisie.

1198   Alavi, Hamza.   "Imperialism Old and New," Socialist Reg,
(1964), 104-26.

1199   *Aron, Raymond.   "The Leninist Myth of Imperialism," in
The Century of Total War.   Boston: Beacon, 1968;
56-73.
A sharp critique of Lenin's theory of imperialism as a
superficial one which erred in asserting that twentieth-
century wars "have as their stake and their meaning
the division of the planet."   Aron argues that the European nations' African colonial empires were not founded
because of the alleged economic contradictions inherent
in capitalism, and that no statesman believed, in 1914,
that "the acquisition of distant possessions justified a
European war."   He contends that if economic-colonial
rivalry were the chief causes of World War I, then
Russia would have been an enemy of Britain and an ally
of Austria while Britain and the United States would
surely have been foes.   Originally in Partisan R, 18,
no. 6 (Nov.-Dec. 1951), 646-62.   [JX1395.D78]

1200   *_____.   "The Leninist Myth of Imperialism and Nazi
Imperialism," in The Imperialist Reader, Louis L.
Snyder.   Port Washington: Kennikat, 1973 (reprint of
a 1962 publication); 469-77.
An attack on Lenin's claim that economic interests
were the main motive behind imperialism.   Aron assesses Nazi imperialism as a means of demonstrating
that considerations of race, culture, power, and passion
were more instrumental in fostering Nazi aggression
than were the economic motives stressed by Lenin.
[JC359.S65]

1201   *Arrighi, Giovanni. The Geometry of Imperialism. The
       Limits of Hobson's Paradigm. London: NLB, 1978;
       160pp., 156-58.
       Lenin is not the focus of any one chapter in this study,
       but it contains significant discussion of his paradigm
       of imperialism. [JC359.A6813]

1202   Bachmann, Kurt. "Leninism and the Anti-Monopoly Strug-
       gle," in LITW-2 (anthology), 212-22.
       A review, by German communist Kurt Bachmann, of
       Lenin's teachings on imperialism and monopoly capital-
       ism, and a Leninist assessment of the proper tactics to
       be employed by contemporary communists struggling
       against these evils.

1203   *Bart, Philip et al. "The Theoretical Basis of the Anti-
       Imperialist Struggle," W Marxist R, 16, no. 5 (May
       1973), 17-29.
       A review of Lenin's Imperialism as part of a series of
       articles on the contemporary relevance of his major
       works.

1204   Bjarnason, Emil. "Lenin and State-Monopoly Capitalism,"
       Communist V, 2, no. 2 (Mar.-Apr. 1970), 16-20.

1205   *Bose, Arun. "Lenin on Socialist Economy," India Q, 27,
       no. 1 (Jan.-Mar. 1971), 16-27.
       An argument that Lenin's contributions to Marxist eco-
       nomics are original and significant and have been ne-
       glected by most Western analysts.

1206   Bowman, William T. "Lenin in London," Contemp R, 191
       (June 1957), 336-68.
       A recollection of a 1902 debate with Lenin, who posed
       as a man named Richter, at a London public meeting
       over British colonial policy in Africa.

1207   Braginsky, M. I. "Leninist Analysis of the Process of
       Formation of the Proletariat in Russia and Its Relevance
       to Africa," in HDASPIA (anthology), 85-98.
       A discussion of Lenin's The Development of Capitalism
       in Russia for insights into the nature of the African
       proletariat and migrant peasantry and their ability to
       lead the revolutionary movement in Africa.

1208   *Bregel, E. "Lenin on Theories of Imperialism," Main-
       stream, 7, no. 42 (21 June 1969), 25-29 and 7, 43
       (28 June 1969), 25-26.

1209   *Buchmann, Albert. "Lenin's Theory of Imperialism Con-
       firmed," W Marxist R, 13, no. 2 (Feb. 1970), 34-37.

1210   *Carleton, W. G. "Leninism and the Legacy of Western
       Imperialism," Yale R, 15, no. 4 (June 1962), 505-18.

1211   *Carlo, Antonio. "Towards a Redefinition of Imperialism,"
          Telos, no. 20 (Summer 1974), 108-19.
          A critical assessment of Lenin's theory as one needing
          revision in light of modern economic developments.

1212   Chambre, Henri. "Imperialism According to Lenin," in
          From Karl Marx to Mao Tse-tung. A Systematic Sur-
          vey of Marxism-Leninism. New York: Kennedy and
          Sons, 1963; 169-180.
          A critical review of the basic points of Lenin's theory
          of imperialism. Chambre first compares Lenin's ideas
          to those of Luxemburg and R. Hilferding before attack-
          ing them for their superficiality. He argues that Lenin
          failed to explain the general phenomenon of capitalist
          expansion but instead "described one period of it, the
          early twentieth century, and he described it badly."
          In support of this contention, Chambre states that Lenin
          failed to see that capitalist expansion has added to the
          general living standard, and erred both in his estimate
          of growing antagonisms between workers and leaders
          in capitalist-imperialist countries and his branding
          European Social Democrats as corrupt because they
          were loyal to their capitalist states during World War
          I. [HX39. C483]

1213   Cheprakov, V. "Imperialism: Its Essence and National
          Types," in LVI (anthology), 66-88.
          A Soviet assessment of contemporary imperialism in
          the light of Lenin's teachings. Cheprakov states that
          Lenin's basic principles as well as his methodological
          approach constitute an accurate guide for current as-
          sessments of imperialism. The fact that imperialism
          has changed since Lenin's time in no way invalidates
          his theory since it stresses that national variations and
          the mutability of specific features of imperialism would
          naturally lead to changes requiring adjustments in
          Leninist terms.

1214   *Childs, David. "Lenin on War and Imperialism," in Marx
          and the Marxists. New York: Barnes and Noble,
          1973; 81-86.
          A review of the criticism of Lenin's argument that
          capitalism's need to export capital was at the root of
          both modern imperialism and war. [HX36. C52]

1215   *Churchward, L. G. "Soviet Revision of Lenin's Imperial-
          ism," Aust J Pol Hist, 8, no. 1 (May 1962), 57-65.

1216   *_____. "Towards the Understanding of Lenin's Imperial-
          ism," Aust J Pol Hist, 5, no. 1 (1959), 76-83.
          A statement on the lack of scholarly attention given by
          critics to Lenin's theory of imperialism, and a positive
          assessment of Lenin's research into the economic foun-
          dations of imperialism.

1217   Clarkson, Stephen. "Marxism-Leninism as a System for
        Comparative Analysis of Underdevelopment," Pol Sci R,
        11, nos. 2-3 (Apr.-Sept. 1972), 124-37.
        Includes a section on Lenin's concept of non-capitalist
        development.

1218   Coates, Z. K. "Lenin, the Economist and Statesman,"
        Sov Un R, 6, no. 4 (24 Jan. 1925), 71-72.

1219   Constantinescu, Miron. "Lenin and Social Research," in
        CFOLI (anthology), 181-96.
        A centennial appreciation of Lenin as a social scientist
        of profound depth and influence. Constantinescu praises
        Lenin's method of social, economic, and historical re-
        search, especially his attention to detail and statistics,
        citing The Development of Capitalism in Russia as a
        monumental, scientific piece of analysis.

1220   *"Contemporary Imperialism in the Light of Lenin's Doctrine,"
        W Marxist R, 19 (Mar. 1976), 40-74.

1221   *Desai, Meghnad. "The Role of Exchange and Market Re-
        lationship in the Economics of the Transition Period:
        Lenin on Tax in Kind," Indian Eco R, 11, no. 1 (Apr.
        1976), 61-68.

1222   Dev, Narendra. "Lenin's Book Complementary to Marx's
        Capital," in LHIII (anthology), 31-32.

1223   Evans, P. "Industrialization and Imperialism: Growth and
        Stagnation on Periphery," Berkeley J Sociol, 20 (1975-
        1976), 113-47.
        Includes a section on Lenin's assessment of imperial-
        ism.

1224   Evanshon, J. "Workers and Imperialism: Where Is the
        Aristocracy of Labor?" Insurg Soc, 7, no. 2 (Spring
        1977), 54-63.
        In part, a discussion of contemporary misapplications
        of Lenin's views on the aristocracy of labor.

1225   Ferguson, D. Francis. "Rural-Urban Relations and Peasant
        Radicalism: A Preliminary Statement," Comp Stud S,
        18, no. 1 (Jan. 1976), 106-18.
        Includes a section on Lenin's The Development of Capi-
        talism in Russia.

1226   Freed, Norman. "Lenin and the Scientific Revolution,"
        Communist V, 2, no. 2 (Mar.-Apr. 1970), 1-4.
        A portrayal of Lenin as one of the first to forecast the
        influence of the revolution in science on capitalism's
        decline.

1227   Galeano, Edvardo. "Latin America and the Theory of

Imperialism," in <u>LT</u> (anthology), 25-45.
A discussion of contemporary imperialism with much
reference to Lenin. Galeano accepts Lenin's basic conclusions on imperialism, and attempts to up-date them
by examining the "new imperialism" which has emerged
in Latin America since Lenin's death.

1228   *Gann, L. H. "Neo-Colonialism, Imperialism and the 'new
class,'" <u>Survey</u>, 19, no. 1 (1973), 165-83.
In part, a critique of Lenin's theory on imperialism as
an alibi for the failure of Marx's prophecies.

1229   Germain, E. "The Theory of State Capitalism," <u>Fourth
Int</u>, 12 (Sept. 1951), 145-56.

1230   *Glezerman, G. "The Leninist Principle of Correlation of
Politics and Economics," in <u>LT</u> (anthology), 156-67.
A Soviet discussion of Lenin's adherence to and development of the Marxist precept that economics plays the
determining role in historical and political development,
while still recognizing and utilizing the power of politics
to influence economic development. Besides giving examples of how Lenin used political force to bring about
revolution and build socialism in Russia, Glezerman
defends Lenin against bourgeois critics who contend
that Lenin's actions are contradictory to Marxism and
"left-wing" revisionists who believe politics can be independent of economics.

1231   Gollan, John. "Leninism and Present-Day Problems of
Anti-Imperialist Struggle," in <u>LITW-2</u> (anthology), 116-
30.
A positive assessment, by a British communist, of
Lenin's theory of imperialism, and a dicussion, in
Leninist terms, of the decline of British imperialism
and the growing militancy of the British labor move-
ment.

1232   *   . "Lenin's Analysis of Imperialism and Some Developments of Monopoly," <u>W Marxist R</u>, 13, no. 3
(Mar. 1970), 71-78.

1233   Gonzalez, Gilbert G. "The Relationship Between Monopoly
Capitalism and Progressive Education," <u>Insurg Soc</u>,
7, no. 4 (1977), 25-41.
An application of Lenin's theory of monopoly capitalism
to an analysis of U. S. progressive education.

1234   Grundy, Kenneth W. "Marxism-Leninism and African Underdevelopment: The Mali Approach," <u>Int J</u>, 17 (Summer
1962), 300-04.
A discussion of Malian ideas on underdevelopment as
being more consistent with Leninism than Western ideas
on the subject.

1235   Harding, N. "Lenin and His Critics: Some Problems of
        Interpretation," Arch Eur Soc, 17, no. 2 (1976), 366-
        83.
        An argument that Lenin's political practices were based
        on and consistent with his economic theories as expres-
        sed in The Development of Capitalism in Russia and
        Imperialism.

1236   Harris, Lement. "Lenin's Studies on U. S. Agriculture,"
        New World R, 38, no. 2 (1970), 76-79.

1237   *Hobsbawm, Eric. "Lenin and the 'Aristocracy of Labour,'"
        in LT (anthology), 47-56.
        A critical examination of Lenin's concept of an "aris-
        tocracy of labour" as an attempt by Lenin not to under-
        stand this phenomenon but rather to explain the 1914
        collapse of the Second International. Hobsbawn main-
        tains that Lenin understood the size of this sector of
        the labor movement and failed to realize that reforms
        and benefits in England were being extended to the ma-
        jority of workers. He states that Lenin's writings
        during the war (especially Imperialism) were less dis-
        passionate and sound than his earlier work on the "aris-
        tocracy of labour," which Marxists can still consult
        with value for an illuminating critique of social reform-
        ism. Also in Revolutionaries. Contemporary Essays.
        New York: Pantheon Press, 1973, 121-29.

1238   *Holdsworth, Mary. "Lenin's Imperialism in Retrospect,"
        in Essays in Honor of E. H. Carr, C. Abramsky and
        B. J. Williams, eds. London: Macmillan, 1974; 341-
        51.
        A discussion of how Lenin's ideas on imperialism "have
        been internationalized by modern leaders and in what
        situation and in what sense they have been rejected or
        modified." Holdsworth asserts that once the Marxist
        polemics and consequent irrelevant digressions are re-
        moved from Lenin's theory, there emerges a rigidly
        empirical approach to understanding imperialism. She
        states that it is Lenin's methodology, especially his
        quantification of imperialism through use of massive
        socio-economic data, which continues to influence modern
        studies of imperialism, even though several of his
        principles are quite ambivalent and his stress on the
        necessity of class conflict has been superseded by con-
        temporary interpretations. [DK246. E85]

1239   *Hunt, Alan. "Lenin and Sociology," Sociol R, 24, no. 1
        (1976), 5-22.
        An assessment of Lenin's polemics in the 1890's against
        the Populist interpretation of Russian capitalism.

1240   Inozemtsev, N. "Imperialist Strategy Today," in LVI (an-
        thology), 116-36.

A Leninist discussion of the foreign policies of the
leading Western nations as examples of imperialism's
attempt to flourish in a world incredibly hostile to its
existence. Inozemtsev attempts to demonstrate how the
imperialists' attempts at adaptation, especially through
alliances hostile to both the socialist and national liberation movements, are consistent with Lenin's interpretation of imperialism.

1241   Institute of World Economics and International Relations,
       U. S. S. R. Academy of Sciences. "Lenin's Doctrine of
       Imperialism and Our Time," in LVI (anthology), 5-65.
       A favorable review of Lenin's Imperialism, and a dis-
       cussion of its applicability to contemporary capitalism.
       The editors state that the Soviet Union's pursuit of a
       foreign policy consistent with Lenin's scientific teach-
       ings on imperialism has (as Lenin predicted) deterred
       imperialist aggression, caused a leftward shift in in-
       dustrially developed nations, and accelerated national
       liberation for the oppressed colonial and backward areas
       of the world. The editors further assert that the flex-
       ible tactics employed by Soviet leaders in foreign policy
       are a direct application of one of Lenin's most impor-
       tant dictates: always consider changing world circum-
       stances before adopting any particular method of re-
       sponse and treatment.

1242   International Theoretical Conference 1976. "Contemporary
       Imperialism in the Light of Lenin's Doctrine," W Marx-
       ist R, 19, no. 3 (Mar. 1976), 40-74.
       Brief summary statements of reports to the conference
       by its participants.

1243   International Theoretical Conference 1976. Lenin's Doctrine
       of Imperialism and the Contemporary Stage of the Gen-
       eral Crisis of Capitalism. Prague, 1976; 109pp.
       Not available for annotation.

1244   Jijon, Milton. "Lenin's Teaching on Imperialism and Our
       Time," W Marxist R, 13, no. 3 (Mar. 1970), 59-62.

1245   *Jowitt, Kenneth. The Leninist Response to National De-
       pendency. Berkeley: University of California Press,
       1978; 85pp.
       An analysis of the nature of the "Leninist" political
       solution to establishing a modern socialist and indus-
       trialized society in a predominantly peasant and eco-
       nomically backward nation. Jowitt first describes care-
       fully the leading features of peasant "dependent" socie-
       ties, and then reviews "the Leninist" response both to
       the problems of and opportunities presented by such
       societies. He centers on the unique nature of the Le-
       ninist organization, claiming that it took "the fundamental

conflicting notions of individual heroism and organizational impersonalism and recast them in the form of
an organizational hero--the Bolshevik Party." The resulting organization uses charismatic arbitrariness and
"sober empirical examination" in determining the "correct line" to be followed in solving any problem. The
author also examines how and why such an organization
has been intelligible to and influential on peasant societies, stressing in particular the positive impact of
its collectivization strategy. [HN960. J68]

1246   Kashtan, William. "Lenin and Contemporary Imperialism,"
        Com V, 2, no. 2 (Mar.-Apr. 1970), 5-10.

1247   *Kemp, Tom. "The Epigones of Lenin and 'Orthodox Marx-
        ism,'" in Theories of Imperialism. London: Dobson,
        1967; 106-33.
        The author's stated aim is to examine "the expositions
        and interpretations of Lenin ... by those who purport to
        be his disciples, not only in order to show what they
        contain which is erroneous and contrary to his own
        method and teaching but to demonstrate how the vulgar-
        izers and dogmatists have been able to pass off as good
        coin what is, in fact, a lamentable counterfeit." Kemp
        critically reviews the writings of I. Lapidus and K.
        Ostrovityanov (1929), A. Leontief (1935), M. Dobb
        (1937), and P. Sweezy (1946), and argues that these
        works suffer from "the dead hand of orthodoxy" and
        have "permitted the critics and opponents of Marxism
        ... to demolish their simplified and distorted views."
        [HB97. 5. K35]

1248   *_____. "The Epigones of Lenin and the Theory of Im-
        perialism," Review, 4 (1962), 32-44.
        A critique of Lenin's theory of imperialism as handled
        in Soviet textbooks on political economy claiming that
        Soviet writers compromised their intellectual integrity
        and consequently contributed nothing new to the study
        of imperialism.

1249   *_____. "Lenin and the Contradictions of Capitalism,"
        in Theories of Imperialism. London: Dobson, 1967;
        63-85.
        The author's stated aim is to determine "what seems
        to be essentially valid in Imperialism and to sift it out
        from the inadequate or misleading parts." Kemp as-
        serts that Lenin's theory suffers from a number of
        limitations as a guide to contemporary imperialism:
        it is based on insufficient empirical evidence; it fails
        to consider the connection between imperialism, the
        declining rate of profit, and the problem of the realiza-
        tion of surplus value; and it does not develop an ade-
        quate alternative to under-consumption as a motive for

imperialism. He states that the theory has suffered
from the attempts of disciples to adhere dogmatically
to it, even though Lenin "would have been the last person to claim either completeness or finality for his
analysis." Kemp concludes that in spite of its limita-
tions, Lenin's theory of imperialism "comes nearest to
being a full and satisfactory treatment of the subject.
[HB97. 5. K35]

1250   *_____. "Lenin's Imperialism Today," Call, 23, no. 12
(Aug. 1972), 16-20.

1251   Khlynov, V. "Development of State Capitalism in China
and the Maoist Attitude to the National Bourgeoisie,"
in LAMCP (anthology), 139-65.
A Soviet assessment of the Chinese Communist Party's
pre-1956 adherence to Lenin's principles on the development of state capitalism, and a critique of its post-
1956 "radical deviations" from them. Khlynov assaults
in particular the Maoist policy of amalgamation of industrial enterprises as one which favored the big capitalists at the expense of the small and majority of capitalists. He sees this as a direct violation of Lenin's
teaching that state capitalism should be fully developed
as the logical means of eliminating the need for any
bourgeois class. Instead, Khlynov argues, the Maoists
have chosen to ally themselves with the powerful upper
bourgeoisie and thereby perpetuate the latter's privileged position.

1252   *Khromushin, G. B. Lenin on Modern Capitalism. Moscow:
Novosti Press, 1970; 119pp.
A presentation of Lenin's Imperialism as "essential for
understanding the socio-economic shifts taking place in
the capitalist countries." Khromushin summarizes the
main points of Imperialism, defends the work against
Western critics (especially John Galbraith), and illustrates how its main points can be applied, with little
adaptation, to contemporary capitalism. He pays particular attention to Lenin's criticism of the doctrine of
democratization of capital and his examination of
monopoly as the essence of capitalism in the age of
imperialism. [HC54. K485]

1253   *Kiernan, V. G. "The Marxist Theory of Imperialism," in
Marxism and Imperialism. New York: St. Martin's
Press, 1974; 1-68.
A survey of the views on imperialism of various Marx-
ists with most attention being given to those of Lenin.
After reviewing the thought of Kautsky (1909), Luxem-
burg (1913), and Bukharin (1915), Kiernan discusses
Lenin's Imperialism (1916) as a great piece of synthesis
rather than as an innovation study. He critically sum-

marizes its main points, but states that its "belittlers have found no better interpretation" and that the final interpretation of imperialism must rely in part on the valid points of Lenin's theory. [HX36. K5]

1254   Kozlov, G. A. "Lenin's Development of the Political Economy of Socialism," in LGT (anthology), 104-35.
A Soviet discussion of how although Marx and Engels stated the general principles of the political economy of socialism, when proletarian revolution and building socialism became the order of the day it was Lenin who worked out the scientific application of these principles to Russian reality. Kozlov praises Lenin for his assessment of imperialism and for developing the theory that uneven capitalist development necessitated the emergence of socialism first in only one or a few countries. He isolates Lenin's main dictates in the building of a socialist economy as being to introduce, first and foremost, the socialist mode of production, to plan centrally the development of the socialist economy, to establish a new socialist labor discipline, to combine moral and material incentives for labor, and to increase the means of production before increasing the production of consumer goods.

1255   Kumaramangalam, Mohan. "Lenin: The Architect of Planning," Yojana, 14, no. 7 (19 Apr. 1970), 3-5.

1256   Kursky, A. "Leninist Principles of Planning," Commerce, 120, no. 3075 (11 April 1970), 2-5.

1257   Kuzminov, I. "Lenin's Theory of Imperialism and the Modern World," Int Aff, 6 (June 1977), 94-103.

1258   Labina, S. N. "Lenin on Socialism in Less Developed Countries through the Non-Capitalist Path," Mainstream, 11, no. 11 (11 Nov. 1972), 26-28.

1259   *Larionov, M. P. "On Methods and Methodology of Social Research in the Works of Lenin," Sov St Phil, 9 (Summer 1970), 81-96.
A study of Lenin's The Development of Capitalism in Russia and Imperialism as examples of his research methodology.

1260   Lawton, Lancelot. "Results of Leninism," Fortn R, 122 (Nov. 1924), 670-78.
An argument that Leninism has failed since it has not been able to replace bourgeois with socialist elements in Russia's economy and culture.

1261   Leontyev, L. A. "Basic Trends of the Development of Modern Imperialism," in DORT (anthology), 101-51.

A Soviet defense of Lenin's interpretation of imperialism, and a discussion of contemporary monopoly capitalism and imperialism in light of Lenin's teachings.

1262 *Lumer, Hyman. "Lenin on the General Crisis in Capitalism," Pol Aff, 48, no. 12 (Dec. 1969), 1-16.
A positive restatement of Lenin's views on monopoly capitalism as stated in Imperialism. Excerpt in W Marxist R, 13, no. 2 (Feb. 1970), 25-28.

1263 *McMichael, Philip. "Concept of Primitive Accumulation: Lenin's Contributions," J Contemp Asia, 7, no. 4 (1977), 497-512.
An assessment of Lenin's views on primitive accumulation as discussed in The Development of Capitalism in Russia.

1264 *Magdoff, Harry. "How to Make a Molehill out of a Mountain," Monthly R, 28, no. 10 (Mar. 1977), 1-18.
A critique of Syzmanski's article on imperialism as one which distorts and oversimplifies Lenin's theory. Revised edition titled "Imperialism and the State: External and Internal Effects," Insurg Soc, (Spring 1977). Also in Imperialism: From the Colonial Age to the Present. New York: Monthly Review Press, 1978.

1265 *_____. "Imperialism: A Historical Survey," Monthly R, 24, no. 1 (May 1972), 1-18.
A discussion of the relation of Lenin's theory to modern theories of imperialism.

1266 Malysh, A. I. "Lenin's Contribution to Marxist Agrarian Theory," in LGT (anthology), 275-304.
A Soviet review of Lenin's thought on the "agrarian problem" in Russia before, during, and after the October Revolution. Malysh first summarizes Lenin's writings (New Economic Developments in Peasant Life and The Development of Capitalism in Russia) on the evolution of agriculture in Russia stressing as Lenin's main point that capitalism had successfully spread throughout the countryside and had resulted in "the disintegration and proletarianization of the peasantry." He then discusses Lenin's development of a program for the Russian socialist movement consistent with capitalism's development in the countryside. Malysh also restates Lenin's thought on the distribution and nationalization of land after the socialist revolution and on the eventual need to socialize, centralize, and industrialize agriculture in Russia.

1267 Marshall, Howard D. "Nikolai Lenin," in The Great Economists. A History of Economic Thought. New York: Pitman, 1967; 178-82, bib. 375-82.
A discussion of Lenin's Imperialism as an attempt to explain why capitalist profits failed to decline and why

the class consciousness of the Western proletariat gave way to patriotism in 1914. [HB75.M36]

1268   "Marx, Engels and Lenin on Non-Capitalist Path and Its Revisionist Distortions in Our Times," Peo Dem, 6, no. 48 (29 Nov. 1970), 2+.

1269   *Mileikovsky, Abram. "Lenin's Theory of Imperialism and New Phenomena in the Capitalist Economy," W Marxist R, 13, no. 6 (June 1970), 28-34.

1270   Morgenbesser, Sidney. "Imperialism: Some Preliminary Distinctions," Phil Pub Aff, 3 (Fall 1973), 3-44.
Includes a section on Lenin's theory of imperialism.

1271   Namsarai, Tsogtyn. "Non-Capitalist Development of Backwards Countries towards Socialism," W Marxist R, 13, no. 3 (Mar. 1970), 19-22.
A discussion of the influence in Mongolia of Lenin's teachings on non-capitalist development.

1272   "National Economy Planning: Development of Leninist Principles in Organizing National Economic Planning," Prob Ec, 6 (Apr. 1964), 3-18.
An editorial on Lenin's teachings on economic planning, and a discussion of their implementation by way of the program announced at the 22nd Congress of the Communist Party of the Soviet Union.

1273   *Nicolaus, Martin. "The Theory of the Labor Aristocracy," in LT (anthology), 91-101.
A summary of Lenin's theory of the aristocracy of labor stressing its relevance to today's world. Nicolaus discusses, in a favorable light, the theory's basics and Lenin's development of them in the 1905-1914 period. He uses the theory to illustrate how certain sectors of the contemporary proletariat have been able to maintain their privileged position by selling out to a bourgeoisie which supports them by exploiting, on an ever-increasing scale, the majority of the proletariat. As imperialism is challenged and declines, Nicolaus argues, the bourgeoisie will be forced to re-proletarianize this aristocracy of labor, and therein, as Lenin believed, rekindle the revolutionary movement of the workers.

1274   *Nove, Alec. "Lenin as Economist," in LMTL (anthology), 187-210.
An analysis of Lenin's economic thought in the pre-1905 period (especially the Development of Capitalism in Russia), his Imperialism: The Highest Stage of Capitalism, and his activities as an "economist" while leader of the Soviet state. Nove states that after 1899, Lenin contributed very little as an economic theorist since his theory of imperialism was only a forceful restatement of current views, and his policy of War Commun-

ism and the New Economic Plan were only adaptations
to temporary circumstances rather than carefully planned economic theories. Nove maintains that although
not a formal economist, Lenin could handle statistics
well, understood Marxian economics, and was "skilled
in argument about the economic structure and policy."

1275   Oleinik, I. "Leninism and the International Significance of
the Experience Gained in Socialist Construction," Int
Aff, 16, nos. 2-3 (Feb.-Mar. 1970), 27-33.

1276   *Olgin, Constantine. "Lenin and the Economics of Socialism,"
St Sov Un, 9, no. 1 (1969), 105-26.
A chronological survey of Lenin's development of a
theory of economics, with most attention to The De-
velopment of Capitalism in Russia, Imperialism, and
New Economic Program.

1277   Owen, A. L. R. "Structural Changes in Capitalism and
Lenin's Idea of Imperialism," in Selig Perlman's Lectures on Capitalism and Socialism. Madison: University of Wisconsin Press, 1976; 35-39.
A survey of the influence on Lenin of the theories of
imperialism advanced by Hilferding and Hobson, followed by a summary of Lenin's theory of imperialism.
[HX56. P38]

1278   *Owen, Lancelot A. "Lenin and the Peasant Movement,"
in The Russian Peasant Movement, 1906-1917. London:
King and Son, 1937; 83-131, bib. 251-57.
An examination of the evolution of Lenin's views on the
agrarian question stressing that his combining the peasant movement with that of the proletariat was moved
by tactical considerations rather than by any concern
for the peasants per se. Owen argues that Lenin's
support of the peasants' demand for general redivision
of the land was designed to promote Bolshevik popularity
among the peasants, and that Lenin never accepted the
peasants' individual right to ownership of property but
only their desire to destroy the "old bondage relation"
in the countryside. Owen examines in detail Lenin's
essay of June 18, 1908 on the agrarian problem to support this contention. [DK260.09]

1279   Owen, Roger and Robert Sutcliffe, eds. Studies in the
Theory of Imperialism. 1972.
Unavailable for annotation.

1280   *Ozinga, James R. "The Relevance of Marx and Lenin to
the Soviet Transition to Communism," Michigan State,
1968 (dissertation).

1281   Pekshev, V. "The Leninist Principles of External Economic
Relations," New Times, 14 (7 Apr. 1970), 18-21.

A restatement of Lenin's principles of economic cooperation with socialist countries, trade with capitalist states, and material aid to national liberation movements.

1282 *Perlo, Victor. "Lenin's Research Methods," Pol Aff, 49, no. 5 (May 1970), 28-39.
An examination of Lenin's work (1914-1916) on Imperialism and study of American capitalism for insights into his research methodology.

1283 *Pierard, Richard V. "Economic Imperialism--Reflections on a Historical Myth," Int R Hist Pol Sci, 10, no. 3 (1973), 89-102.
A critique of the theories of imperialism advanced by Hobson, Lenin and others which argue that imperialism is based upon economic motives alone.

1284 Pilling, Geoffrey. "Imperialism, Trade and 'Unequal Exchange': The Work of Aghiri Emmanuel," Ec Soc, 2 (1973), 164+.
In part, an assessment of Emmanuel's attack on Lenin's Imperialism.

1285 Pletnev, E. and R. Kossopalov. "Lenin and Social Progress," Int Labor R, 101, no. 4 (Apr. 1970), 317-30.
A discussion of Lenin's inability to measure social progress in technical or economic terms but only in terms of the position occupied by the workers in society. The authors also survey social and economic improvements for the workers implemented under Lenin and his successors.

1286 *Pokshishevskii, V. V. "Population Migration and Its Evaluation in Lenin's Works," Sov Ed, 12, nos. 3-5 (Jan.-Mar. 1970), 86-100.
A positive assessment of Lenin's methodology and use of statistics, with most reference to his The Development of Capitalism in Russia and New Data on the Laws of Capitalist Development of Agriculture.

1287 *Pozhidayev, G. P. "Lenin and Economic Theory," in LR (anthology), 43-59.
A Soviet discussion of Lenin's contributions to Marxist economic theory. The author divides these contributions into three main areas: his elaboration and clarification of Marxian economics, development of the theory of imperialism, and his economic program for the construction of a socialist order. In the first category, Pozhidayev reviews Lenin's war against revisionism (especially the economism of Bernstein), his defense of the labor theory of value, and his assessment of the development of capitalism in Russian agriculture. The author then summarizes Lenin's updating, in Imperial-

ism, of Marxian economics to the conditions created by the growth of monopoly capitalism. Lastly, he discusses Lenin's support, during the transition from capitalism to socialism, for heavy industry, the socialization of all production, centralized planning, and full use of advanced capitalist technology.

1288 *Radulescu-Zoner, Serban. "Aspects of International Life at the Beginning of the Twentieth Century in Light of the Leninist Theses on Imperialism," R Roum Etudes, 2, no. 7 (1970), 25-42.
A discussion of Lenin's belief that the 1898-1903 conflicts between France and England, the United States and Germany, the United States and Spain, and various Western nations and China were proof that capitalist imperialism was nearing a world war.

1289 Rai, Lala Lajpat. "Lenin Exposed Imperialist Designs of the Allies," in LHIII (anthology), 27-28.
A positive review of Lenin's disclosure of Allied plans to divide the small nations among themselves after World War I.

1290 *Roberts, James W. "Lenin's Theory of Imperialism in Soviet Usage," Sov St, 29, no. 3 (July 1977), 353-72.

1291 *_____. "The Soviet Use of Lenin's Theory of Imperialism," University of North Carolina at Chapel Hill, 1973 (dissertation).

1292 *Rochester, Anna. Lenin on the Agrarian Question. New York: International Publishers, 1942; 224pp.
A chronological survey of Lenin's thought and policies on the agrarian question, with most attention given to the 1917-1923 period. Rochester first discusses Lenin's views on the development of capitalism in rural Russia and his creation of a revolutionary program to appeal to the lower and middle class peasants. She then reviews his assessment, both of the peasants' role in the 1905 Revolution and the Stolypin land reforms which followed the revolution, before presenting a general discussion of his agrarian program as Soviet leader. Rochester states throughout her study that Lenin's policies toward and programs for Russian agriculture were all indicative of his keen interest in the agrarian problem and were not only a chief source for his dispute with rival socialists, but also were important in determining his success as both a revolutionary and political leader. [HD715.R6]

1293 *Rodney, Walter. "The Imperialist Partition of Africa," in LT (anthology), 103-14.
A defense of Lenin's theory of imperialism against the

critics who claim it does not apply to the case of imperialism in Africa. Rodney states that simply because
Lenin had little to say about Africa does not mean his
theory of imperialism is not applicable there. The
author presents several instances of imperialism in
Africa that he sees as being completely consistent with
Lenin's conclusions. He also defends Lenin against the
critics who claim his economic definition of imperialism
overlooks the political, psychological, strategic, and
humanitarian motives behind imperialism.

1294 Rosenberry, William. "Rent Differentiation, and the Development of Capitalism among Peasants," Am Anthro,
78, no. 1 (Mar. 1976), 45-58.

1295 Roshchin, S. K. "Lenin and Mongolia's Non-Capitalist
War," in LANLIE (anthology), 151-78.
A discussion of Lenin's influence in Mongolia and of
Mongolia as "the first country of the East, outside the
Soviet republics, to implement Lenin's ideas of non-
capitalist development." Roshchin attacks "bourgeois
fibs" about the "export of Soviet revolution" while presenting Mongolia as an example confirming Lenin's principle that backward nations may bypass the capitalist
phase in route to a modern socialist economy and state.

1296 Rostovsky, S. N. "Lenin on the Question of Non-Capitalist
Development," in LANLIE (anthology), 83-112.
A positive presentation of Lenin's theory on backward
nations bypassing capitalism en route to modernization
as one consistent with Marxism and immensely influential on the national liberation movements of the world.
Rostovsky also discusses Lenin's implementation of the
principle that the various nationalities within the U. S. S. R.
must achieve complete cultural-economic-political equality
in the process of socialist construction. He presents
this principle as one having an essential link to Lenin's
theory of socialist revolution in backward nations and
as being vitally influential among third world nations.

1297 Rymalov, V. "Imperialism without Empires," in LVI (anthology), 89-115.
A Soviet examination of the effect on imperialist nations
of the collapse of colonial empires, and how this development is consistent with Lenin's theory of imperialism. Rymalov also defends Lenin's theory against critics who claim that its conclusions and methodology are
inapplicable to modern capitalism.

1298 _____. "Lenin's Doctrine of Imperialism and Our Age,"
Int Aff, 15, no. 9 (Sept. 1969), 36-45.

1299 *Santamaria, Ulysses and Alan Manville. "Lenin and the

Problem of Transition," Telos, no. 27 (Spring 1976), 79-96.
An assessment of the failure of the Bolshevik Revolution to achieve its ideals as due not to unfavorable historical conditions but to a type of "Economism" in Lenin's thought as exemplified by his ideas on the transition stage from capitalism-socialism and by his NEP.

1300 *Semmel, Bernard. "Arrighi's Imperialism," New Left R, no. 118 (Nov.-Dec. 1979), 73-80.
An assessment of Arrighi's critique, in Geometry of Imperialism, of Lenin's Imperialism.

1301 Sen, Bhowani. "Guidelines to Assess Agrarian Relations in India," in LAI (anthology), 36-56.
A discussion of Lenin's ideas on the peasant question for insight into the nature of the rural poor in India. Sen stresses that Lenin's The Development of Capitalism in Russia as well as his other writings on the peasant question helped to form the philosophical framework for understanding the agrarian problem in India. He concludes that the only solution to the Indian agrarian question is pursuit of a revolutionary non-capitalist path as outlined by Lenin.

1302 Serge, Victor. "Lenin and Imperialism," in From Lenin to Stalin. New York: Monad, 1973; 125-28.
A brief discussion of the affect on the author of Lenin's 1920 address to the Second Congress of the Communist International on the subject of imperialism. Serge gives a highly favorable assessment both of Lenin's qualities as a speaker and the content of his statement on imperialism. [DK266. S48] Originally in International Press Conference, (13 Sept. 1923), 659-60.

1303 *Shizirta, Hitoshi. "Imperialism as a Concept," Kyoto Un Ec R, 31, no. 1 (Apr. 1961), 1-13.
A critical assessment of Lenin's identification of imperialism with monopoly capitalism.

1304 *Silvermaster, Nathan G. "Lenin's Contributions to Economic Thought Prior to the Bolshevik Revolution," University of California, 1933 (dissertation).

1305 Singh, V. B. "Lenin as an Economist," Mainstream, 7, no. 47 (26 July, 1969), 25-27.

1306 *Smith, D. G. "Lenin's Imperialism: A Study in the Unity of Theory and Practice," J Pol, 17, no. 4 (Nov. 1955), 546-69.

1307 *Smolinski, L. "Lenin and Economic Planning," St Comp Com, 2, no. 1 (Jan. 1969), 96-114.

An examination of Lenin's Imperialism, State and Revolution and, especially, NEP to illustrate his support for economic planning.

1308   *Solodovnikov, V. and V. Bogoslovsky. "Lenin's Elaboration of the Conception of Non-Capitalist Development," in Non-Capitalist Development. An Historical Outline. Moscow: Progress Publishers, 1975; 38-51.

1309   Starushenko, G. B. "Progressive Africa Consults with Lenin," in HDASPIA (anthology), 25-33.
A description of the current (1970), state of African awareness and appreciation of Lenin, his works and accomplishments. Starushenko emphasizes the impact in Africa of Lenin's theory that economically backward nations could bypass the capitalist stage en route to a modern socialist economy.

1310   Steiger, Martin. "Imperialism, the Highest Stage of Capitalism," Prob Peoples USSR, no. 10 (1961), 20-23.

1311   *Stenson, M. R. "The Economic Interpretation of Imperialism: A Comment on Some Recent Writings," New Z J Hist, 10, no. 2 (1976), 178-88.
An exploration of the analytic gulf between Marxists and liberals.

1312   Stock, Noel. "Is Lenin's Face Red?" National R, 16 (14 Jan. 1964), 25.
An argument that Lenin and Hobson were entirely wrong in connecting imperialism with the increase in overseas investments. In fact, Stock states, most British investment was in America, South America, and Canada.

1313   *Strachey, John. Lenin's Theory of Imperialism Reconsidered. London: Today Publications, 1963; 11pp.
A review of Lenin's Imperialism arguing that it is correct in asserting that imperialism developed as capitalists sought new investment opportunities, but errs in concluding that capitalism would collapse if deprived of its colonies. In fact, Strachey argues, Britain is more prosperous since dissolving its empire because capitalism has restructured itself and is now able to invest at home with profit. He also criticizes Lenin for failing to see that ex-colonial areas can become truly independent without revolution, giving as an example modern India. [HC54. S77]

1314   Sumbatain, Y. "Lenin on the Non-Capitalist Path of Development," New Times, no. 42 (2 Oct. 1969), 14-16.

1315   Swedberg, R. "Lenin's Critique of Narodnik Sociology," Insurg Soc, 8, no. 4 (Winter 1979), 52-64.

1316   *Szymanski, Al.   "Capital Accumulation on a World Scale
           and the Necessity of Imperialism," Insurg Soc, 7, no.
           2 (Spring 1977), 25-53.
           An examination of the views of Lenin, Marx, and Luxem-
           burg on the relation between imperialism and the ac-
           cumulation of capital.

1317   *_____.   "Even Mountains Are Moved: A Response to
           Magdoff," Monthly R, 30, no. 1 (May 1978), 48-57.
           A discussion of the author's differences with Harry
           Magdoff over the Leninist theory of imperialism.   Reply
           by Magdoff, 57-61.

1318   *Tanaka, Masaharu.   "The Controversies Concerning Capital-
           ism: An Analysis of the Views of Plekhanov and Lenin,"
           Kyoto Un Ec R, 36 (Oct. 1966), 21-55.

1319   Toivonen, Timo.   "Aristocracy of Labour: Some Old and
           New Problems," Acta Soc, 21, no. 3 (1978), 217-28.
           Includes a review of Lenin's concept of aristocracy of
           labor.

1320   Tuchanska, B.   "A Phenomenon, the Essence of the Phe-
           nomenon, a Theory," Poznan St, 2 (1976), 65-79.
           In part, an examination of Lenin's Imperialism.

1321   *Ulyanovsky, R. A.   "Lenin's Concept of Non-Capitalist De-
           velopment," Pol Aff, 49, no. 10 (Oct. 1970), 41-52
           and 49, no. 11 (Nov. 1970), 41-52.

1322   *Vygodsky, S. L.   "Lenin's Contribution to the Political
           Economy of Capitalism," in LGT (anthology), 81-103.
           A Soviet discussion of Lenin's thought on the Marxist
           theory of production, the development of capitalism in
           Russia, imperialism, and the agrarian question.   Vygod-
           sky commends Lenin for his creative approach to and
           accurate assessment of the growth of capitalism within
           specifically Russian historical conditions.   He claims
           that Lenin was the first to define both the limits of
           capitalist development in backward Russia and the pre-
           cise nature of the changing class structure.   Vygodsky
           also reviews Lenin's theory of imperialism for insights
           into "the general laws of capitalism under monopoly
           capitalism domination. "

1323   *Willetts, Harry.   "Lenin and the Peasants," in LMTL (an-
           thology), 211-34.
           An assessment of Lenin's pre-1917 writings on the
           "peasant question" and his post-revolutionary policies
           dealing with the peasants.   Willetts praises Lenin's
           early writings (New Economic Trends in Peasant Life,
           1893, and The Development of Capitalism in Russia,
           1899) for their thorough, scholarly research stating that

"if Lenin had given up politics in 1900 we would remember him as an expert on agrarian relations in Russia." Willetts contends that as Lenin became more involved in politics, he wrote less scholarly studies of the agrarian situation and restricted himself to polemical retorts to specialists or to statements wholly political in content. The author concludes that Lenin was consistent throughout his work on the peasant question in the sense that his writings and policies under War Communism and NEP reflect the concerns of a Marxist trying to seize and maintain power in a backward nation.

1324   Wirth, Adam. "The International Factor in Lenin's Theory of Revolution," W Marxist R, 20, no. 3 (Mar. 1977), 76-85.
An exploration of the influence of imperialism both on the world revolutionary movement and Lenin's theory of revolution.

1325   Wirth, Margaret. "Towards a Critique of the Theory of State Monopoly Capitalism," Ec Soc, 6 (1977), 284-313.
Includes an assessment of Lenin's Imperialism.

1326   Wolfe, Betram D. "Lenin, Stolypin and the Russian Village," Rus R, 6, no. 2 (1947), 44-54.

1327   Zarodov, Konstantin. Leninism and Contemporary Problems of the Transition from Capitalism to Socialism. Moscow: Progress Publishers, 1972. [HX518.S8Z3413]

B. Practice

1328 *Achminov, Herman F. "Lenin's Conception of the Workers'
Movement," St Sov Un, 10, no. 1 (1970), 37-51.
An attack on Lenin for pursuing a manipulative and
hypocritical policy towards Russian labor.

1329 Alexandrov, P. P. "Story about Withheld Wages," in LCAM
(anthology), 119-22.
An account of Lenin's assistance to workers having dif-
ficulty obtaining back-wages due them.

1330 Avdeyev, S. F. "A Visit to Lenin," in LCAM (anthology),
136-37.
A brief account of financial aid given by Lenin to the
workers of the Doskin Shipyard who had not received
their wages in some time.

1331 Avrich, Paul. "The Bolshevik Revolution and Workers'
Control in Russian Industry," Slav R, 22, no. 1 (Mar.
1963), 47-63.

1332 Babayants, A. A. "Pointing the Way to Socialism," in LR
(anthology), 187-211.
A Soviet examination of Lenin's policies and guidance
in constructing a socialist state once the internal and
external enemies of the revolution had been repulsed.
Babayants praises Lenin's NEP as an essential step
towards rehabilitating the Russian economy after the
Civil War, and defends it against critics who depict it
as a retreat from principle instead of the consolidation
of socialism which it actually represented.

1333 Balabanoff, Angelica. "The New Economic Policy--Lenin
on Compromise and Retreat," in L (anthology), 170-72.
Excerpt from her Impressions of Lenin, 62-67.

1334 Barker, Tom. "Lenin Inspired Us--A Veteran's Reminiscences," Labour Mo, 52, no. 4 (Apr. 1970), 158-62.
Reminiscences of experiences at the Kuzbas Project.

1335 Barnett, J. "Leninism and Practical Work among the
Farmers," Communist, 13 (Jan. 1934), 39-46.

1336 Bell, Daniel. "One Road from Marx: On the Vision of

Socialism, and the Fate of Workers' Control in Socialist Thought," W Pol, 11, no. 4 (July 1959), 491-512.
Includes a criticism of Lenin's simplistic conception of the function of both the state and economic apparatus.

1337 *_____. "Two Roads from Marx: The Themes of Aliena-tion and Exploitation and Workers' Control in Socialist Thought," in End of Ideology. New York: Free Press, 1967; 355-92.
In part, a critical analysis of Lenin's State and Revolu-tion as a work which naively presents workers' control as a "magic phrase" which "promises to solve all ad-ministrative difficulties in operating the state." Bell also discusses how the breakdown or workers' control led to the establishment of centralized, bureaucratic control over the economy, the emasculation of the trade unions, and the elimination of democracy within the Bolshevik Party. [HN57.B45]

1338 Belov, Alexander. "A Lesson for Life," in LIOL (anthol-ogy), 221-39.
An account of the life and work of engineer Pyotr Yakob-son, and how Lenin suggested to him that he construct diesel trains for a new Soviet transportation system.

1339 "The Bolsheviks and the Peasants," Contemp R, 119, no. 164 (May 1921), 680-83.
A summary of Lenin's peasant policy under War Com-munism and, especially, NEP.

1340 *Bonch-Bruyevich, Vladimir. "How Vladimir Ilyich Wrote the Decree on Land," in AL (anthology), 49-54.
A recollection of both the atmosphere in which Lenin drafted the 1917 decree granting land to the peasantry and of Lenin's clear recognition that this draft would erode peasant support for the Socialist Revolutionary Party while increasing Bolshevik popularity. The author also recounts publication and distribution details con-cerning the decree. Also in OL (anthology), 103-06.

1341 _____. "Lenin and the Peasants," in NBPA (anthology), 227-31.
An account of Lenin's reception of peasants to hear their problems and complaints, and of his creation of a special office to deal with such matters.

1342 Borko, Lev. "Lenin and the Socialist Economy," Sov Life, 11, no. 158 (Nov. 1969), 20-21, 34, 35.
A general discussion of Lenin's economic views and policies.

1343 *Brinton, Maurice. The Bolsheviks and Workers' Control 1917 to 1921. The State and Counter-Revolution. Lon-don: Solidarity Press, 1970; 89pp.

A short introduction to the question of workers' control in Bolshevik theory and practice, followed by a detailed chronology, in outline form, of the leading developments (1917-1921) associated with this question. In the process, Brinton presents scattered but significant information on Lenin's policies toward organized labor and workers' control.

1344 Brown, Tom. Lenin and Workers' Control. London: Syndicated Worker's Federation, 1968, 14pp.
Unavailable for annotation.

1345 Bryant, Louise. "Interview with Lenin," in LIOUS (anthology), 76-77.
An excerpt from an October 13, 1920 interview (never before published in English) dealing with Lenin's desire to trade with the United States and his assessment of the agricultural labor movement in America.

1346 Buck, Tim. "Lenin and Today's Problems in the Trade Union Movement," in Lenin and Canada. Toronto: Progress Books, 1970; 115-19.
A Leninist approach to the question "How do we equip ourselves to give correct guidance to forward-looking members of the trade union movement?" [HX102.B8]

1347 *Carr, Edward H. A History of Soviet Russia. The Bolshevik Revolution 1917-1923, Volume II. New York: Macmillan, 1952; 400pp.
This highly acclaimed study does not have a separate chapter on Lenin, but contains significant information on his economic theory and practice. Carr first surveys the evolution of Bolshevik economic theory prior to 1917 before turning to his main concern--the economic order created by Lenin in the 1917-1923 era. He examines War Communism's origin, development, and impact as well as how and why Lenin replaced this system with the NEP. Carr concludes with a survey of the implementation of the NEP and an assessment of its success up to 1923. [DK266.C263]

1348 * _____. "The Russian Revolution and the Peasant," Proc Brit Acad, 49 (1963), 69-93.
In part, a discussion of Lenin's thought and policies (especially NEP) towards the peasantry.

1349 Ceausescu, Nicolae. "Lenin and Building Socialist Society," W Marxist R, 13, no. 5 (May 1970), 78-87.
A positive assessment of Lenin's theory and program of socialist construction.

1350 Chernov, Osip. "How I, a Non-Party Peasant from Siberia, Came to Vladimir Ilyich, and What Resulted," Sov Life, no. 3 (1970), 81-82.

An account of a 1921 meeting with Lenin over Bolshevik requisitioning of foodstuffs.

1351   "Conditioning Comrades; Lenin's Prohibition of Private Ownership," Time, 88 (2 Sept. 1966), 30.
A charge that the current Soviet leadership is not complying with Lenin's decree on private ownership.

1352   *Corrigan, Philip, Harvie Ramsay and Derek Sayer. "Lenin," in Socialist Construction and Marxist Theory. New York: Monthly Review Press, 1978; 53-65, bib. 191-222.
A scholarly analysis of a basic contradiction of Lenin's economic policies: "adherence to both capitalist productive forces and various socialist forms of political control." The authors state that this was a contradictory and short-sighted policy in that it failed to realize that capitalist techniques of production "cannot be copied neutrally. To follow them is to reproduce the appropriate ideological, cultural, political, and production relations which sustain them." They present various examples of the application of this contradictory policy to agriculture and industry from 1918-1923, and discuss Lenin's writings which show concern for its shortcomings. This study contains much additional and valuable information on the policies followed by Lenin as Soviet leader. [HX40. C76]

1353   *Daxton, Lawrence E. "Lenin and the New Economic Policy," University of Colorado, 1971 (dissertation).

1354   *DeMaris, E. J. "Lenin and the Soviet 'Control of the Ruble' System," Slav R, 22, no. 3 (1963), 523-29.
A examination of Lenin's ideas on the role of banks in capitalism and the utilization of banking as a means of establishing a socialist economy. Also included is information on the NEP and War Communism.

1355   *Demichev, P. N. The Great Truth of Our Epoch: Leninism--the Scientific Basis of the Party's Policy. Moscow: Novosti Press, 1965; 46pp.
A 1965 speech by the Secretary of the CPSU Central Committee, commemorating Lenin's 95th birthday. Demichev summarizes Lenin's teachings on and contributions to economic management (especially central planning), education of the workers, unity of the world revolutionary socialist movement, and the struggle against capitalist imperialism. [HX56. D4]

1356   *Dunayevskaya, Raya. "What Happens After," in Freedom and Marxism from 1776 until Today. New York: Twayne, 1964; 194-210.
An assessment of the relations that developed in the post-1917 period between the party, the workers, and

the dictatorship of the proletariat. Dunayevskaya examines the 1920-1921 debates within the Bolshevik Party over the role of the trade unions in the socialist state as a case study of the difficulties in determining the nature of these relations. She assesses the positions of Lenin, Trotsky, and Shlyapnikov, stressing Lenin's moderate posture between statifying the unions and unionizing the state, and emphasizes his growing dissatisfaction with the emerging bureaucratic tendencies of the state. She criticizes those who assert that in the 1917-1923 period Lenin became a dictator, arguing that he was opposed to the growing bureaucratic power of the party and urged that the party "be checked by non-party masses" not in a democratic sense but in the sense of voluntarily heeding their suggestions. Dunayevskaya concludes with a discussion of Lenin's will as an indictment of the party leadership and the direction in which it was heading. [HX36.D8]

1357   "Economic Work of the Revolution: Lenin's Personal Influence," Rus Info R, 4, no. 6 (9 Feb. 1924), 91-93.
A general survey of Lenin's influence on Soviet policy towards unions, industrialization, cooperatives, science and technology, electrification and the creation of a state bank.

1358   "Famine Testing Lenine," Lit D, 71 (19 Oct. 1921), 19-20.

1359   *Fetter, Frank W. "Lenin, Keynes and Inflation," Economica, 44 (Feb. 1977), 77-80.
A historical review of Lenin's supposed remark that the best way to destroy capitalism was through the promotion of severe inflation.

1360   Fofanova, Margarita. "Bait for the Peasants," in L (anthology), 159.
A recollection of Lenin's study of issues of the Peasant News (the organ of the All-Russian Congress of the Peasant Deputies) and materials on the Left Socialist Revolutionaries, as the prime sources of information for his Decree on Land issued immediately following the revolution. Excerpt from Petrograd, October 1917: Reminiscences. Moscow: Foreign Languages Publishing House, 1957; 15-16.

1361   _____. "Four Books," in LAB (anthology), 171-76.
A recollection of how Lenin, while staying at the author's flat, was greatly impressed by several books that he read on agriculture, the contents of which influenced his views on Soviet agricultural policies.

1362   Frantsov, G. P. "Lenin's Ideas about the Development of Communist Labour," in Philosophy and Sociology. Mos-

cow: Progress Publishers, 1975; 277-87.
A Soviet discussion of Lenin's views on communist labor
as a qualitatively new stage in the history of productivity.
Frantsov summarizes Lenin's teachings on the communist workers' efficiency, productivity, and class-
conscious approach to labor, and on the need to combine material incentives with moralistic ones as a means
of maximizing the workers' output. He also reviews
Lenin's criticism of capitalist labor. [HX542. F6613]

1363   Gak, Alexander. "Lenin and the Americans," New World
        R, 35 (9 Nov. 1967), 37-43.
        An account of Lenin's interviews with various Americans
        and his attempts to promote trade with the United States.

1364   *Garmash, Theodore. "Lenin and the Working Class," St
        Sov Un, 9, no. 1 (1969), 73-83.
        An argument that Lenin distorted Marxism to such a
        degree that the workers became exploited pawns of the
        Bolshevik Party rather than beneficiaries of the socialist
        revolution.

1365   *Garvy, George. "The Origins of Lenin's Views on the Role
        of Banks in the Socialist Transformation of Society,"
        J Pol Ec, 4, no. 1 (1972), 252-63.
        An examination of the influence of Saint-Simon, Marx,
        Hobson, and Parvus on Lenin's policies towards banks.

1366   *George, Francois. "Forgetting Lenin," Telos, 18 (Winter
        1973-1974), 53-88.
        An attack on Lenin for being solely a revolutionary
        technician who focused on the means but not the sub-
        stance of his actions. George states that effectiveness
        became the main criterion of action for Lenin and that
        such pragmatism led Lenin to establish an economy
        based on capitalist bureaucracy rather than one which
        liberated the workers or represented a new type of
        society.

1367   Gladkov, I. "Lenin's Plan of Peaceful Socialist Construction,"
        Prob Ec, 1 (Oct. 1958), 6-12.
        A review of Lenin's thought on the variety of forms of
        transition from capitalism to socialism.

1368   *Gordon, Manya. "Lenin Tames the Unions," in Workers
        Before and After Lenin. New York: Dutton, 1941;
        84-90.
        A critical account of Lenin's shift away from the "prim-
        itive anarchism" of State and Revolution to support for
        a centralized apparatus to administer the state and
        economy. Gordon discusses Lenin's position in the de-
        bate on the role of the trade unions in the Soviet state
        as an illustration of Lenin's new-found realism. She

states that his realization that the workers lacked the technical and administrative knowledge to govern the economy through trade unions and his awareness of the fact that the vast majority of workers were not communists led him to subjugate the unions to the control of the Communist Party and to relegate them to agencies concerned with protecting the local interests of the workers. [HD8526. G6]

1369 ———. "Lenin's Strategic Retreat," in Workers Before and After Lenin. New York: Dutton, 1941; 366-70.
A brief discussion of Lenin's abandonment of his long-held belief in the imminency of world revolution and his turn instead to the consolidation of socialism in Soviet Russia. Gordon surveys the accomplishments of the NEP under Lenin, especially his attraction of foreign capital to Russia. [HD8526. G6]

1370 Gubkin, Ivan. "The People's Trust Is Our Highest Reward," Sov Lit, no. 3 (1970) 62-67.
A recollection, by a Soviet geologist, of meetings with Lenin on the development of the Soviet energy industry.

1371 Guha, Amalendu. Lenin on the Agrarian Question. Calcutta: Indian School of Social Sciences, n. d.; 20pp.
An annotated bibliography of Lenin's writings on the agrarian question. In addition to very substantial annotations, Guha provides short introductions to and elaborations on Lenin's main writings in this field. [HD1992. G8]

1372 *Guroff, Gregory. "Lenin and Russian Economic Thought: The Problem of Central Planning," in LAL (anthology), 183-216.
An examination of Lenin's relationship to the development of Russian economic thought, especially in regard to industrialization and central economic planning. Guroff focuses on three topics: Lenin's economic thought before 1917, Russian economic development and thought before 1917, and Bolshevik policy in the immediate post-revolutionary period. He states that "the development of Soviet economic policies, and more particularly the origins of central planning, are more clearly understandable as outgrowths and adaptations of Russian economic thought and experience with the verities of the Russian economy, than as a product of Marxist-Leninist ideology...." Lenin's contribution to economic theory, Guroff claims, is paltry, whereas his ability to adapt effectively certain aspects of pre-revolutionary Russian economic policy is much more impressive.

1373 *Hammond, Thomas T. "Lenin on Russian Trade Unions under Capitalism, 1894-1904," ASEER, 8 (Dec. 1949), 275-88.

1374 * _____ . Lenin on Trade Unions and Revolution, 1893-
1917. New York: Columbia University Press, 1957;
155pp. , bib. 130-50.
A scholarly assessment of Lenin's views on the role
of unions in the revolutionary process. Hammond analyzes Lenin's ideas, writings, and actions in the 1893-
1917 period as a means of understanding Lenin's resolution of the following questions: are unions necessary
under capitalism; is the economic struggle more important than the political struggle; can unions replace
the party; do workers become socialist spontaneously;
what relationship should exist between the party and
the unions; and what is the relation between reform
and revolution. Hammond states that Lenin believed
the unions were necessary under capitalism, especially
in its early stages, both as a means of educating the
workers in the evils of capitalism and as a source of
mass support for the party's revolutionary program,
but that he believed the workers would follow a reformist
path unless guided by an organization of professional
revolutionaries separate from the labor movement.
[HX544. H3]

1375 * _____ . "Revolutionism and Vanguardism: Lenin on
Trade Unions under Capitalism, 1893-1917," Columbia
University, 1954 (dissertation).

1376 *Hindus, Maurice G. "The Bolsheviki and the Peasant Problem," in The Russian Peasant and the Revolution. New
York: Holt and Company, 1920; 251-77, bib. 325-27.
An examination of the evolution of Lenin's agrarian
policy through 1919 beginning with his position at the
3rd Party Congress in 1905. The author establishes
how Lenin, unlike European Marxists, came to recognize the peasants as a prospective ally of the proletariat
in the struggle against capitalism. Hindus examines
Lenin's appeal to the peasants in October of 1917 by
presenting, as the Bolsheviks' decree on land, a resolution drawn up by the pro-peasant Socialist Revolutionary
Party, even though this decree contradicted previous
Bolshevik views on the land question. Hindus concludes
with a critical survey of Bolshevik peasant policies in
1918 and 1919, arguing that since the peasants have so
firmly rejected Bolshevik agricultural policies, Bolshevism can never become a reality in Russia.
[DK265. H55]

1377 Hutira, Ervin. "The Creative Application by the Romanian
Communist Party of the Leninist Theory about the Building of a Many-Sidedly Developed Socialist Economy,"
in CFOLI (anthology), 77-101.
A discussion of Lenin's basic guidelines on socialist
construction and their faithful application by the Rumanian Communist Party.

1378 "Industrialization in the USSR," P Star, 4, no. 33 (Apr. 1970), 12-13, 14-17.
A positive account of Lenin's impact on Soviet industrialization.

1379 Iskrov, M. V. "Lenin on the Historic Role of the Working Class," in LGT (anthology), 249-74.
A Soviet discussion of Lenin's thought on the nature, organization and role of the proletariat in the contemporary world. Iskrov reviews Lenin's argument that the proletariat, as the most advanced and revolutionary class in society, was the only class capable of leading working peoples of both town and countryside in the struggle against capitalism. He restates Lenin's belief that the working class must be united, organized, and disciplined so as to lead effectively the liberation struggle, and that only the proletarian party could educate and guide the workers. Iskrov also discusses Lenin's views on the dictatorship of the proletariat, trade unions, and the international union of the workers' movement.

1380 Kaktyn, A. "How Ilyich Taught Us Revolutionary Tactics," in LIOR (anthology), 62-65.
A recollection of Lenin's work with the Central Council of Factory Committees in Petrograd over the question of workers' control of the factories.

1381 *Kaplan, Frederick I. Bolshevik Ideology and the Ethics of Soviet Labor. 1917-1920: The Formative Years.
New York: Philosophical Library, 1968; 521pp., bib. 462-503.
A comprehensive and scholarly assessment of the first three years of Bolshevik labor policy. Lenin is not the sole focus of this study, but it contains a great deal of valuable information on his views on and policies toward workers' control, the factory committees, trade unions, labor discipline, and the general relationship between labor and the party. Chapter one focuses specifically on Lenin's theory of knowledge as the root of Bolshevik ideology and has been annotated separately. [HD8526. K28]

1382 *Keep, John L. "Lenin's Land Decree," in The Russian Revolution. A Study in Mass Mobilization. New York: Norton, 1976; 385-93.
A discussion of Lenin's Decree on Land as an effective document which simultaneously subverted the popularity of the rival Socialist Revolutionary Party and won peasant support for the Bolshevik Party. Keep maintains, however, that, in spite of its short-term successes, Lenin's policy towards the peasantry turned out to be a disastrous one due largely to his misassessment of the peasants' basic mentality and of the nature of the

class struggle in the countryside. These miscalculations, Keep contends, forced the Bolsheviks to rely increasingly on coercion in their dealings with the peasantry which, in turn, accelerated the Bolsheviks' loss of popularity in the countryside. This study contains additional valuable, though scattered, information on Lenin's attempts to influence and control the peasantry. [DK165. K36]

1383   Kennell, Ruth E. "Lenin Called Us: Kuzbas Chronicle," New World R, 39, no. 4 (1971), 86-98.
Reminiscences of an American worker at the Kuzbas Project in the early 1920's.

1384   Kokashinskii, V. et al. "The Arithmetic of Socialism on the Land: A Leninist Class Lesson," in Sociology in the USSR. A Collection of Readings from Soviet Sources, Stephen P. Dunn, ed. White Plains: International Arts and Sciences Press, 1969; 244-54.
A report on a class held at a collective farm in the Kuban region on Lenin's theory of agricultural cooperatives. Originally in Sov Soc, 4 (1965), 32-42. [HN523. 5D83]

1385   Kollontai, Alexandra. "The Early Days of the Commissariat for Social Welfare," in LIOR (anthology), 81-88.
Reminiscences of Lenin's role in the establishment and early activities of the People's Commissariat for State Relief.

1386   Krassin, L. "Lenin and Foreign Trade," Rus Info R, 4, no. 6 (9 Feb. 1924), 88-89.
An account, by a member of the Commissariat of Foreign Trade, of Lenin's influence on the growth of foreign trade under the NEP.

1387   "The Kremlin Dreamer Proves Realistic," Sov Life, 11, no. 158 (Nov. 1969), 22-29.
An account of the implementation of Lenin's plans for electrification of the entire nation.

1388   Kucherov, Samuel. "Communism Versus Peasantry in the Soviet Union," Pol Sci Q, 70, no. 2 (June 1955), 181-96.
Includes a section on Lenin's views on the elimination of peasants as a separate social class.

1389   Kukin, D. Lenin's Plan for Building Socialism in the USSR. Moscow: Progress Publishers, 1974, 204pp.
A Soviet summary of the nature and impact of Lenin's teachings on socialist construction. Kukin concentrates on Lenin's argument for and implementation of the development of large scale industry, the electrification of the entire nation, the modernization of agriculture, and

the launching of a cultural revolution, especially in education. [HC335. K881413]

1390   Kulakov, Fyodor. "The Leninist Agrarian Policy and Its
        Implementation in the USSR," W Marxist R, 17, no. 10
        (1974), 15-27.

1391   Kuzminov, I. "Lenin and the Problems of the Economic
        Theory of Socialism," in LTCOA (anthology), 177-88.
        A short summary of Lenin's assessment of capitalist
        relations in the era of imperialism. Kuzminov devotes
        most attention to Lenin's views on planned economic
        management and the distinction between communist and
        socialist labor. He also discusses Lenin's policies in
        the construction of a socialist economy in Russia.

1392   *Laird, Roy D. "Lenin, Peasants and Agrarian Reform,"
        in LAL (anthology), 173-82.
        An assessment of Lenin's views on the peasant stressing
        the importance of his recognition of the world-shaking
        role to be played by the dissatisfied peasantry of the
        developing nations of the world. Laird examines the
        logic which led Lenin to merge Marxism with the pea-
        sant and colonial movements and to call for a two stage
        revolutionary process: the seizure of power by a united
        workers movement followed by the collectivization and
        industrialization of the countryside to 'revolutionize'
        agricultural production. He sees the first stage of this
        process as representing an important and profound his-
        torical development whereas the second stage has gen-
        erally remained as visionary as when Lenin conceived
        it.

1393   *Lawton, Lancelot. "Lenin's Zig Zags," Fortn R, (June
        1921), 911-20.
        A discussion of Lenin's NEP as an example of tactical
        flexibility as opposed to a betrayal of his socialist prin-
        ciples.

1394   _____. "Peasants under Lenin," N Cent, 88 (Sept. 1920),
        445-49.

1395   "Lenin and Steinmetz Correspond," Nation, 115 (19 July
        1922), 78.
        Steinmetz congratulates Lenin on the industrial regenera-
        tion of Russia.

1396   "Lenin and the Famine," Cur Op, 71 (Sept. 1921), 276-78.
        A statement that famine was hurting Lenin's relations
        with peasants more than anything else done by the
        Bolsheviks.

1397   "Lenin and the Work Process," Can Dim, 14 (Dec. 1979),
        19.

A critique of Lenin's plan to include aspects of capitalist production within a socialist system.

1398   "Lenin Preaches Capitalism to the Communists," Cur Op, 74 (Jan. 1923), 27-28.
A review of Lenin's speeches defending state capitalism as a necessary means of preserving socialism after the excesses of War Communism.

1399   "Lenin the Anti-Bolshevik," Liv Age, 313 (3 June 1922), 607-09.
A critical review of Lenin's justification for the NEP.

1400   "Lenine's 'Concessions' in True Light," B Rus Info Bur, no. 34 (23 Apr. 1921), 4-5.
A statement that Lenin's NEP does not represent a change in the party's political dictatorship nor its control of key industries.

1401   "Lenine's Economic Transformation," RR, 65 (Jan. 1922), 97-98.
A review of Lenin's NEP.

1402   "Lenine's Strategic Retreat," Lit D, 69 (4 June 1921), 21.
An assessement of Lenin's motives for launching the NEP.

1403   Liberman, Simon. "Origins of the New Economic Policy," in L (anthology), 168-70.
An excerpt from his Building Lenin's Russia, 192-94.

1404   Lomov, G. "How We Began to Build," in LIOR (anthology), 66-76.
An account of the 1917-1918 economic obstacles which faced Lenin as he sought to initiate the construction of a modern industrialized socialist economy.

1405   *Losovsky, A. Lenin and the Trade Union Movement. Chicago: Trade Union Educational League, 1925; 36pp.
A positive assessment of Lenin's revolutionary policies and tactics in the field of trade unionism. Losovsky reviews the evolution of Lenin's thought (from the writing of What Is to Be Done? through the early 1920's) on the role of the unions in the revolutionary movement and victorious socialist state. He maintains that Lenin saw the unions as playing an immense and positive role in the socialist movement, most notably as the means of education, mobilizing and leading the masses to proper action. Losovsky counters those critics who claim that after the revolution Lenin ruthlessly subordinated the unions to Bolshevik control by arguing that the unions were not capable of assuming responsibility for control of the economy and had to be fused with the broad apparatus of the dictatorship of the proletariat.

1406   Magnuson, Bruce. "Lenin and Workers' Control," Com V, 2, no. 2 (1970), 30-34.
A defense of Lenin's views on socialist management.

1407   *Manevich, Yefim. Lenin on Work under Socialism and Communism. Moscow: Novosti Press, 1969; 80pp.
A presentation of Lenin's views on the organization of labor under communism and a discussion of how these views have been put into practice in the Soviet Union. Manevich discusses, among many topics, Lenin's teachings on the universal character of labor, the socialist attitude to labor, democratic centralism and labor organization, labor productivity and how to increase it, distribution of labor, differentiation of wages, material incentives to labor, and the distinction between socialist and communist labor. [HX312.L43M3513]

1408   Manoharan, S. "Lenin on the Nationalization of Banks," Mainstream, 7, no. 43 (28 June 1969), 21-22.

1409   Meleshchenko, Yu. "Lenin and the Revolution in Science and Technology," in LTCOA (anthology), 189-201.
An account of Lenin's views on the nature and role of technical progress in the construction of socialism. The author presents the technical and scientific advances made in Soviet Russia as being consistent with Leninist teachings on the close relation between science and production, the political nature of technology, and on the advantages socialism has over capitalism in the full development and broad utilization of science and technology.

1410   *Meyers, George. "Lenin on Trade Unions," Pol Aff, 49, no. 4 (Apr. 1970), 14-23.

1411   Mikulsky, K. Lenin's Teaching on the World Economy and Its Relevance to Our Times. Moscow: Progress Publishers, 1975; 104pp. [HC244.M4913]

1412   Miliutin, V. "Lenin As an Economic Leader," Rus Info R, 4, no. 6 (9 Feb. 1924), 89-90.
A survey, by a member of the Supreme Economic Council, of the economic policies pursued by Lenin in the 1917-1921 period.

1413   Miller, Robert F. "Soviet Agricultural Policies in the Twenties: The Failure of Co-operation," Sov St, 27, no. 2 (1975), 220-44.
Includes a section on Lenin's reaction to the failure of Soviet experiments with agricultural cooperatives.

1414   "Millions Starving in Lenine's Paradise of Atheism," Lit D, 70 (6 Aug. 1921), 32-33.

1415   "Morality of Trading with Lenine," <u>Lit D</u>, 65 (15 May 1920), 28-29.
A discussion of the motives for the re-establishment of trade with Lenin's regime.

1416   Mustov, Alexei and Mikhail Lyashenko. "A Meeting that Never Took Place," in <u>LIOL</u> (anthology), 85-102.
An account of the life and work of Ivan Michurin, a skilled horticulturist whose work with scientific fruit farming was hampered by tsarist bureaucracy but flourished after the revolution because Lenin, who read Michurin's works, gave complete support to his experiments.

1417   *Nove, Alec. "Lenin and the New Economic Policy," in <u>LAL</u> (anthology), 155-71.
A scholarly examination of Lenin's reasons for proposing the NEP, followed by speculation on the economic policies Lenin would have pursued had he not died in 1924. Nove discusses Lenin's assessment of War Communism as a necessary and illuminating failure before turning to Lenin's immediate motives for launching the NEP. He identifies the roots of NEP as resting not in a fearful reaction to the Kronstadt Rebellion, but in Lenin's late 1920 recognition of the failure of his then current agricultural policy--a failure which threatened the continuation of Bolshevik political power. Nove cautions the reader to note that although the NEP retreat initially went farther than intended, Lenin, by 1922, set firmly the limits of the retreat and was aware of the dangers it posed to the party if maintained any longer than tactically necessary. In speculating on Lenin's economic policies had he lived longer, Nove states that although Lenin supported NEP up to the time of his death, both his traditional support of tactical flexibility in the face of any problem and his firm belief in the temporary nature of NEP make it impossible to claim that Soviet economic policy would not have gone the Stalinist route if Lenin had lived a full life.

1418   *Nutsch, James G. "Bolshevik Agrarian Policies, 1917-1921," <u>B Inst St USSR</u>, 17, no. 10 (Oct. 1970), 5-13.

1419   "Opening Lenine's Treasure-House," <u>Lit D</u>, 67 (4 Dec. 1920), 14-15.
A discussion of the reasons behind the increased trade with Lenin's regime.

1420   Ostroumov, G. "Realities and Prospects of Lenin's Cooperative Plan," <u>W Marxist R</u>, 13, no. 2 (Feb. 1970), 67-73.

1421   *Owen, Launcelot A. "Lenin and the Land Decree of October

26, 1917 (o. s.)," in The Russian Peasant Movement, 1906-1917. London: King and Sons, 1937; 239-47, bib. 251-57.
An assessment of Lenin's land decree as a return, for strategic reasons, "to the old earthen base of the earlier native Russian socialists." Owen states that the key to Lenin's power in 1917 was his adaptation of Bolshevik propaganda and policy to the moods and aspirations of the peasantry. Lenin realized that he must have the support of the peasantry and that the land policy which he adopted, though inconsistent with his ultimate goal, would secure that support for him. Lenin left to a later date, Owen concludes, the elimination of the petty bourgeois desire of the peasants to own land. [DK260.09]

1422   Pavlyuk, Mkhaylo. "The Financial Policy of the Kremlin and Gold," Ukr Q 11, no. 2 (1955), 118-27.
Includes a section on Lenin's contention that after the revolution gold would no longer be important.

1423   Polyanovsky, Valentin. "Lenin Keeps his Promise," Sov Life, 3, no. 162 (Mar. 1970), 44-45.
An account of Lenin's meeting with peasants to discuss collective farms, rural electricity and other matters.

1424   Pospelov, P. N. "Leninism and the Building of Communism in the USSR," in DORT (anthology), 9-53.
A positive presentation of Lenin's basic tenets and policies in the construction of socialism. Pospelov summarizes Lenin's NEP, especially his stress on heavy industry and electrification, and discusses the CPSU's pursuit of Lenin's policies since his death.

1425   *Prokhorov, Vasili. Lenin and the Trade Unions. Moscow: Novosti Press, 1971; 66pp.
A discussion, by the Soviet Secretary of the All-Union Central Council of Trade Unions, of Lenin's views on the trade unions, their role and place in a socialist society, and the influence of these views on the world trade union movement. Prokhorov surveys Lenin's pre-1917 thought on and policies toward unions, concentrating on Lenin's views on the place of the unions within the dictatorship of the proletariat. He also reviews Lenin's struggle against those (especially Trotsky) who opposed his policies. [HD6732.P7273]

1426   Radkey, Oliver H. The Sickle under the Hammer. The Russian Socialist Revolutionaries in the Early Months of Soviet Rule. New York: Columbia University Press, 1963; 525pp., bib. 497-510.
Lenin is not the focus of any one chapter in this study, but it contains many references to and short sections

on his peasant policies and relations with the Socialist Revolutionaries in the months immediately following the October Revolution.   [DK265.R228]

1427   *Raine, G. E.   "Lenin and Labour in Russia," in Bolshevik Russia.   London: Nisbet and Company, 1920; 66-93.
An attack on the policies pursued by Lenin towards the workers in the first two years after the revolution. Raine states that Lenin had never been a true friend of labor but only sought to use the workers, and especially their trade unions, as a means of gaining power and implementing his philosophy.   In examining Lenin's post-1917 policies toward labor, the author states that the code of labor laws introduced by Lenin failed to improve the material conditions of the worker and, in fact, led to the bondage of labor to a state authority more oppressive than that which existed before the revolution.   [DK265.R353]

1428   Ranadive, B. T.   "Lenin and the Working Class," Peo Dem, (22 Apr. 1970), 23-26.

1429   *Roberts, Paul C.   " 'War Communism': A Re-Examination," Slav R, 29, no. 2 (1970), 238-61.
The author's stated purpose is to present "a critical analysis of the prevalent interpretation of "War Communism" in Anglo-American literature that views the economic policies of that period as temporary expedients...."   Roberts draws heavily on Lenin's writings on War Communism for support.

1430   Rogov, Ye.   "Lenin and the Building of the Material and Technical Foundations of Socialism," in LTCOA (anthology), 201-18.
A discussion of Lenin's belief that heavy industry must first be established before socialism could be placed on a firm footing politically, socially, and economically.

1431   *Rubel, Maximilien.   "The Relationship of Bolshevism to Marxism," in Revolutionary Russia, Richard Pipes, ed. Garden City: Doubleday, 1969; 386-413.
Lenin is not the focus of this essay, but it contains interpretive information on the non-Marxist nature of the October Revolution and the regime created by Lenin. Rubel argues that Lenin's "socialist construction" was in fact "capitalist construction" necessitated by the fact that Lenin led his party to power in advance of the economic conditions which, according to Marx, should have produced a socialist revolution.   Lenin and the Bolsheviks, Rubel states, thus usurped the role Marx assigned to the bourgeoisie in establishing capitalism, and the dictatorship of the proletariat became just a socialist guise for a type of authoritarian industrializa-

tion/capitalism. There follows an assessment by Shlomo Avineri of Rubel's essay, and Rubel's response to Avineri's comments (413-425). [DK265.A135 1967aa]

1432   Rucker, R. D. "Workers' Control of Production in the October Revolution and Civil War," Sci Soc, 43, no. 2 (Summer 1979), 158-85.
        Includes an examination of Lenin's thoughts on and policies toward workers' control.

1433   "Russia in Reversion," Liv Age, 312 (7 Jan. 1922), 31-35.
        A review of Lenin's NEP and pursuit of peace with the West as the only policies conducive to settling Russia's economic problems.

1434   Sagaidachnaia, Z. A. "According to Lenin's Design: Socialist Reforms in Agriculture and the Training of Specialists," Sov Ed, 13 (Mar. 1971), 72-83.

1435   *Scheffer, Paul. "At the Pan-Russian Congress," Liv Age, 312 (Feb. 1922), 464-68.
        A discussion of Lenin's speech, at the Pan-Russian Congress, on the NEP and his policies toward the peasants.

1436   "Shades of Lenin," Newsweek, 63 (24 Feb. 1964), 40, 42.
        A statement on Khrushchev's citing of Lenin in regard to the need to learn from capitalist technology.

1437   Shelepin, A. N. "Lenin and Soviet Trade Unions," in International Trade Union Meeting on the Occasion of the Centenary Memorial of the Birth of V.I. Lenin. World Federation of Trade Unions. n.p., 1970; 9-24.
        A discussion of the great debt owed to Lenin by Soviet trade unions. The author states that the unions "appeared thanks to Lenin, were formed by Lenin ... and all their activities developed under the personal direction of Lenin." Shelepin traces Lenin's policies toward and thought on unions in the 1905-1923 period, stressing the crucial importance of the education and leadership roles assigned to unions by him during the period of socialist construction. [HD6475.A2W5132]

1438   Skrypnik, M. N. "Peasant Representatives Visit Ilyich in the Smolny," in LCAM (anthology), 124-28.
        An account of a visit to Lenin by peasants seeking advice on land they purchased (prior to the revolution) which was under consideration for redistribution.

1439   Smith, Jessica. "Some Memories of Russia in Lenin's Time," in LIOUS (anthology), 95-104.
        An account of the rapid social and economic progress in Russia under Lenin's leadership, and a note on Lenin's

correspondence with Charles P. Steinmetz concerning plans for the electrification of Russia.

1440   *Sorenson, Jay B.   The Life and Death of Soviet Trade Unionism, 1917-1928. New York: Atherton, 1969; 283pp., bib. 271-76.
Lenin is not the focus of any one chapter of this study, but it contains many references to and short sections on his views on and policies toward unions, labor, and labor-related issues in the 1917-1923 period.
[HD6732. S67]

1441   Sparks, Nemmy. "Lenin and the Americans at Kuzbas," New World R, 39, no. 4 (1971), 71-86.
Reminiscences of an American who worked at the Kuzbas project from 1921 to 1922.

1442   Stepanyan, T. A. "Lenin on the Objective Laws of the Building of Communism," in LGT (anthology), 60-80.
A discussion of the principles established by Lenin in regard to the economic priorities of newly established socialist states. Stepanyan isolates the following as Lenin's dictates: establish and continually develop the socialist mode of production; emphasize developing the means of production rather than consumer goods; combine centralized planning with maximum popular initiative; utilize all that modern-capitalist technology has to offer; and develop defense industries to protect against imperialist aggression while simultaneously working for peaceful coexistence.

1443   Stetsky, A. "The Ideas of Lenin in Actual Practice," Com Int, 14 (Mar. 1937), 230-41.
A discussion of the Leninist roots of the five-year plans and the Soviet Constitution.

1444   Turin, S. P. From Peter the Great to Lenin; A History of the Russian Labour Movement with Special Reference to Trade Unionism. London: King, 229pp.
Not available for annotation but listed as having information on Lenin.

1445   *Ugryumov, A. L. Lenin's Plan for Building Socialism in the USSR (1917-1925). Moscow: Novosti Press, 1976; 128pp.
A positive summary of Lenin's political, economic, and nationality policies as leader of the Soviet state. Ugryumov reviews Lenin's creation of the dictatorship of the proletariat as a representation of Soviet power; his establishment of centralized accounting and control of the economy; plan for the electrification of the nation; launching of the NEP; and his role in the creation of the U. S. S. R. as the fulfillment of his nationality pro-

gram. The author stresses the importance of Lenin's principle that socialism could triumph first in one country alone by establishing the industrial, agricultural, and cultural bases of socialism while maintaining peace with surrounding capitalist states. [JN6598.K7U37]

1446   Vaganov, B. "Lenin's Foreign Trade Policy," Int Aff, 15, no. 5 (May 1969), 49-53.

1447   Wells, H. G. "The Dreamer in the Kremlin," in Russia in the Shadows. London: Hodder and Stoughton, n.d.; 123-42.
An account of a conversation with Lenin in which the author notes Lenin's simple and frank manner, and recounts their discussion of the program for the socialist reconstruction of Russia, especially urban reconstruction, electrification of the countryside, and the education of the masses. [DK265.W37]

1448   Wilke, Wilhelm. Lenin on the Trade Unions and the Social Revolution in Africa. Bernau: College of the Confederation of Free German Trade Unions, 1968; 29pp.
Unavailable for annotation. [HD6857.W5]

1449   Williams, Harold. "The Prime Minister's Deal with Lenin," N Cent, (May 1921), 741-58.
A critical assessment of the 1921 trade agreement between England and Russia.

1450   *Williamson, John. "Lenin on Trade Unionism," Pol Aff, 52, no. 8 (Aug. 1974), 29-39.

1451   "Workers of the Tryokhogosnaya Textile Mill Recall Meetings with Lenin," in ROL (anthology), 89-96.
A group of over forty recollections by workers attesting to Lenin's genuine concern for all laborers.

1452   *World Federation of Trade Unions. International Trade Union Meeting on the Occassion of the Centenary Memorial of the Birth of V.I. Lenin. n.p., 1970; 25-82.
A series of thirty short extracts from speeches delivered by various international labor leaders in commemoration of the Lenin centennial. The speeches praise Lenin for his concern for the interests of both Soviet and international workers, his establishment of the Communist International, his principle of proletarian internationalism, and, especially, his policies toward organized labor. [HD6475.A2W5132]

1453   Zaboli, A. M. "Remembering Lenin," New Times, 24 (17 June 1970), 12-13.
A recollection of Lenin's 1921 speech on NEP.

1454   Zalamayev, I.   "A Letter from a Peasant," in LCAM (an-
        thology), 168-69.
        A recollection of a message sent by Lenin to a village
        committee demanding that a cow be returned to a pea-
        sant who had protested that the animal had been illegally
        confiscated.

1455   Zhitov, M.   "Lenin and the Planned Management of Industry,"
        in LIOR (anthology), 77-80.
        An account of a visit with Lenin to discuss plans for-
        mulated by the Council of Factory Committees for the
        development of a government organization to regulate
        industry and economic life.

1456   *Zile, Zigurds L.   "Lenin's Contribution to Law: The Case
        of Protection and Preservation of the Natural Environ-
        ment," in LAL (anthology), 83-100.
        An attack on the Soviet claim that Lenin played a prom-
        inent role in the foundation and maintenance of state
        protection of nature in Russia.   Zile examines Lenin's
        contributions to establishing the principles of environ-
        mental protection, devising specific environmental laws,
        and to supervising the enforcement of protective legis-
        lation.   He concludes that during Lenin's rule, environ-
        mental legislation was generally geared toward use and
        not protection, and the laws that were protective were
        technically deficient and poorly administrated versions
        of pre-revolutionary policies and concepts.   Zile sees
        no "creative involvement by Lenin personally" in even
        these meager environmental protective measures.

CULTURE AND THE CULTURAL REVOLUTION

A. General

1457   Aczel, G. "Lenin's Cultural Policy Principles," W Marxist
        R, 22, no. 11 (Nov. 1979), 35-42.

1458   Arnoldov, A. Leninism and the Cultural Revolution. Mos-
        cow: Novosti Press, 1975; 72pp.
        A positive review of Lenin's principles on the cultural
        revolution and their implementation under Lenin and his
        successors. Arnoldov stresses the importance of Le-
        nin's belief in assimilating all that was useful from the
        bourgeois cultural heritage and in waging a war against
        illiteracy as the first step towards developing a socialist
        culture. [HX523.A754]

1459   Bezmensky, L. "Notes on the Tampere Symposium," New
        Times, 17 (21 Apr. 1970), 33-35.
        A review of the proceedings at the Unesco international
        symposium on Lenin and the development of science,
        culture, and education.

1460   *Bullitt, Margaret M. "Toward a Marxist Theory of Aesthe-
        tics: The Development of Socialist Realism in the Soviet
        Union," Rus R, 35, no. 1 (Jan. 1976), 53-76.
        In part, a discussion of Lenin's role in the debate
        among Russian Marxists on the application of dialectics
        to problems of artistic production and analysis.

1461   *Claudin-Urondo, Carmen. Lenin and the Cultural Revolu-
        tion. Sussex, N.J.: Humanities Press, 1977. 134pp.
        A critical analysis, by a Spanish Marxist, of Lenin's
        concept of the cultural revolution and its relation to
        current cultural policy in the Soviet Union. Claudin-
        Urondo reviews Lenin's various writings on culture,
        and criticizes them for being based on a mechanical
        and non-dialectical approach to cultural change whereby
        the party "regulates the moments of transformation and
        decides the criteria by which it is to be judged."
        Lenin failed to consider that his centralized and re-
        strictive policies would defeat their very purpose and
        result in a sterile, passive, and conformist culture.
        [HX523.C5513]

1462   Gorbunov, V. "Lenin on Attitude Towards Cultural Heritage," Mainstream, 8 (18 Apr. 1970), 25-29+.

1463   *_____. "Lenin on the Class Character of Culture," in LTCOA (anthology), 133-56.
        A review of Lenin's teachings on the existence of two cultures (bourgeois and socialist) within national culture and their relation to each other. Gorbunov defends Lenin against those critics who argue that a nation's culture is above class allegiance, and argues, from Lenin, for the class character of all literature, art and religion. Abridged and translated from Voprsoy istorii KPSS, no. 6 (1966), 3-45.

1464   *_____. Lenin on the Cultural Revolution. Moscow: Novosti Press, 1969; 55pp.
        A positive portrayal of Lenin's plan for socialist construction as a "stupendous programme for the economic and cultural transformation of society." Gorbunov restates Lenin's argument for rapid industrialization as a material prerequisite for the cultural revolution, and then discusses Lenin's views on the nature of culture, the use of Russia's cultural heritage, the role of the intelligentsia in cultural development, the paramount importance of establishing a comprehensive educational system, and on the role both of the masses and party in the cultural revolution. [DK254. L46G633]

1465   Herzog, Marie-Pierre. "Lenin and Education, Science, Culture," UNESCO C, 23 (July 1970), 4-5.
        A summary of the papers presented at the Tampere (Finland) symposium on Lenin and culture.

1466   Iovchuk, Mikhail. "The Modern Age and Leninist Policy in Soviet Culture," Cult Life, 9 (Sept. 1969), 12-16.

1467   Kim, Maxim. "Cultural Revolution," Sov Life, 7, no. 154 (July 1969), 31, 35, 37.
        A restatement of Lenin's principles and policies on the cultural revolution.

1468   Korneichuk, Alexander. "An Inexhaustible Source of Inspiration," Cult Life, 6, (June, 1969), 10-13.
        An account of the positive influence on Soviet culture of Lenin's study of and concern for mass culture.

1469   *Krutkova, O. N. and N. N. Krutkov. "Lenin on the Independent Initiative and Creativity of the Personality in the Moral Sphere," Sov Ed, 12, nos. 3-5 (Jan.-Feb.-Mar. 1970), 153-73.
        An examination of Lenin's views on teaching communist ideals and moral standards in such a manner that the individual must be able to participate in a creative

fashion in both disseminating and depicting socialist values.

1470   Laing, Dave. "Culture and Art in Lenin," in The Marxist Theory of Art. Sussex, N.J.: Humanities Press, 1978; 20-25.
An appraisal of Lenin's influence on the role of artistic work in the cultural revolution, with most attention given to the impact on socialist realism of his concept of the partisan nature of art. [HX521.L32]

1471   *Lawson, John H. "Lenin's Impact on Culture," in LIOUS, (anthology), 202-20.
An attempt to counter those who contend that there must be a gulf between "the world of action and the realm of art" by illustrating the bridge between "Lenin and aesthetic sensibility." In support of this argument, Lawson examines Lenin's dramatic-artistic flair in his revolutionary writings, his theory of art, and the impact he has had upon American culture.

1472   Lukin, Iu. A. "Methodological Problems in the History of Soviet Esthetics," Sov St Phil, 8 (Spring 1970), 408-21.
In part, a review of Lenin's teachings on the cultural revolution and the partisan nature of culture.

1473   Lunacharsky, A. V. "Lenin at an Exhibition," in NBPA (anthology), 184-85.
A brief recollection of Lenin's love of art and the distress which he felt over the lack of time that he could devote to its study.

1474   _____. "Lenin on Art," Int Lit, no. 5 (May 1935), 66-71.

1475   Marten, John. "Lenin: Giant of Culture," New Masses, (26 Jan. 1943), 15-17.

1476   *Myashnikov, Alexander. "Foremost Aesthetics of the 20th Century," Sov Lit, no. 3 (1970), 143-50.
An examination of the relation between Lenin's theory of reflection and his aesthetics.

1477   Pismenny, Yuri A. "Lenin and the Arts," Thought, 22, no. 36 (5 Sept. 1970), 11-12.

1478   Poliakoff, V. "Leninism: Destroying Culture in Russia," N Cent, no. 522 (Aug. 1920), 209-16.

1479   Polonsky, Vyacheslav. "Lenin's View of Art," Mod Mo, 7 (1933), 738-43.

1480   *_____. "Lenin's Views of Art and Culture," in Artists in Uniform. A Study of Literature and Bureaucratism, Max Eastman. New York: Knopf, 1934; 217-52. A sympathetic account, by a Bolshevik literary critic, of Lenin's artistic tastes and views. Polonsky emphasizes the point that although Lenin never systematically developed a theory of art, he recognized and appreciated the power of art, and believed that since art belongs to the people it must therefore be intelligible to them. Translated and excerpted from Outline of the Literary Movement of the Revolutionary Epoch. Moscow, 1928. [DK267. E25]

1481 *Reeve, F. D. "Politics and Imagination," ASEER, 16, no. 2 (1957), 175-89.
A discussion of the conflicting positions of Lenin and Bryusov on the question of artistic freedom.

1482 Rumyantsev, A. "Lenin and Problems of the Development of Culture," Mainstream, 8, no. 33 (18 Apr. 1970), 22-24. Also in Com V, 2, no. 5 (Sept. -Oct. 1970), 42-45.

1483 *Ryurikov, Boris. "Lenin, Socialism and Culture," Sov Lit, no. 2 (1970), 135-47.
A summary of Lenin's theory of culture, with most attention given to his thought on the relation between ideology and culture.

1484 *Smirnov, G. L. "Lenin and Problems of Typification of the Personality," Sov Ed, 12, nos. 3-5 (Jan. -Mar. 1970), 174-96.
An assessment of Lenin's thought on the factors which shape personality and their utilization in creating the new Soviet man.

1485 *Tanase, Alexandru and Georgeta Todea. "V. I. Lenin and Some Problems of Socialist Culture," in CFOLI (anthology), 267-84.
A centennial presentation of Lenin's views on the cultural revolution and its role in the construction of socialism. The authors trace Lenin's support for universal education and artistic freedom as the means of creating the new Soviet man, and discuss his views on national and international culture and the problem of developing a socialist culture without infringing upon national cultural imperatives.

1486 Triumph of Lenin's Ideas of the Cultural Revolution in Uzbekistan. Tashkent: n. p. , 1970, 69pp.
A discussion of the economic and cultural development of the Uzbekistan SSR as a "direct result of the implementation of the cultural revolution in the Soviet Union, whose theory and practice was inspired by Vladi-

mir Lenin." The booklet acquaints the reader with the essence of Lenin's doctrine of cultural revolution and provides examples of it in practice from Uzbek policies on education, science, the economy and the rights of women and various nationalities. [DK946.A55]

1487   Weir, John. "Lenin--Science, Culture and Education," Com V, 2, no. 2 (Mar.-Apr. 1970), 45-49.

1488   *Wilson, A. C. "Lenin's Ideas on Art and a Discussion of Them," New Z Slavonic J, 12 (Summer, 1973), 130-41. A clarification of Lenin's artistic philosophy, with most attention given to his theory of reflection and concept of partiinost.

B. Literature

1489 Bhattacharya, Brenda K. "A Misconceived Seminar: Lenin's Impact on Indian Literature," Mankind, 14, no. 8 (Dec. 1970), 29-36.

1490 *Boiko, M. "Lenin on Leo Tolstoy," Mainstream, 8, no. 34 (25 Apr. 1970), 17-23+.

1491 *Brooks, Mary E. "Soviet Revisionist Distortions of Lenin on the Question of Partisanship in Literature," Lit Ideol, 14 (1972), 30-42.

1492 *Dasgupta, R. K. "Lenin on Literature," Indian Lit, 13, no. 3 (1970), 5-25.
An examination of Lenin's literary aesthetics and criticism (especially of Leo Tolstoy) as well as of his views on the purpose of literature in a socialist society.

1493 El-Sebai, Youssef. "Lenin and Literature," Lotus, 1, no. 4 (1970), 8-9.

1494 *Elwood, Ralph C. "Lenin as a Book Reviewer," Survey, 16, no. 1 (1970), 221-24.

1495 *Ermolaev, Herman. Soviet Literary Theories, 1917-1934. The Genesis of Socialist Realism. Berkeley: University of California Press, 1963; 261pp.
This scholarly study of socialist realism does not contain a separate chapter on Lenin, but presents significant information on his thought and policies toward literature. [PB13. C3]

1496 Essen, Maria. "Encounters with Lenin," in LAB (anthology), 176-77.
A recollection of Lenin's high regard for Chernyshevsky, Nekrasov, and literature in general.

1497 Gorky, Maxim. "A Letter to Nadezhda Krupskaya," in LAB (anthology), 159-60.
A brief excerpt from a letter indicating Gorky's feelings toward Lenin as a literary critic.

1498 * _____. "V. I. Lenin. A Literary Portrait," in LAB (anthology), 155-59.

246

Reminiscences of conversations with Lenin on literature and related matters.

1499   Haldar, Gopal. "Lenin's Impact on Indian Literature,"
        Contemp Ind Lit, 10, no. 2 (Apr.-June 1970), 6, 23.
        Also in New Age, (6 Sept. 1970), 4.

1500   *Harvey, Leon A. "Tolstoy and Lenin: A Study in Con-
        trast," Pan Am M, 31 (May 1920), 23-28; 31 (June
        1920), 66-74.

1501   *Krupskaya, N. "Ilyich's Favourite Books," in LAB (an-
        thology), 149-55.
        A recollection of Lenin's love of Russian classical lit-
        erature as well as of such foreign writers as Hugo,
        Balzac, Goethe, Barbusse, and London.

1502   *Kung, Tun. "Learn from Lenin's Theories on the Problem
        of the Critical Acceptance of the Literary Heritage,"
        Chin St Phil, 5 (Winter 1973-1974), 21-40.

1503   Kzhizhanovsky, G. M. "On Dostoevsky," in NBPA (anthol-
        ogy), 197-98.
        A note on Lenin's appreciation of Dostoevsky's Notes
        from the House of the Dead and dislike of The Possessed.

1504   *Lucid, Daniel P. "Preface to Revolution: Russian Marxist
        Literary Criticism, 1883-1917," Yale University, 1973
        (dissertation).
        In part, a discussion of Lenin as a representative of
        the Plekhanov school of literary criticism.

1505   *Lukacs, George. "Tolstoy and the Development of Realism,"
        in Studies in European Realism. New York: Grosset
        and Dunlap, 1974 (reprint of a 1964 publication); 126-
        205.
        In part, a discussion of Lenin's criticism of Tolstoy.
        [PN601. L8 1964]

1506   *Lunacharsky, A. V. "Lenin and Literature," Int Lit, 1
        (Jan. 1935), 55-83.
        A review of Lenin's philosophy of literature, literary
        criticism, and unpublished notes dealing with various
        literary matters, and an assessment of his impact on
        the Soviet theory of literature.

1507   _____. "Museum and Experimenting Youth," in NBPA,
        196.
        A recollection of Lenin's rejection of Lunacharsky's re-
        quest for financial assistance for the experimental the-
        ater.

1508   *Mjasnikov, Alexander S. "Aesthetics of a Struggle and
        Truth," Sov Lit, 8 (1969), 146-67.

A review of Lenin's article "Party Organization and Party Literature" as part of a discussion of his thought on the role of literature in the cultural revolution.

1509 *Morawski, Stefan. "Lenin as a Literary Theorist," Sci Soc, 29, no. 1 (Winter, 1965), 2-25.

1510 Morozov, B. "Lenin on Literature and Art," Cult Life, 2 (Feb. 1970), 19-21.

1510a Plomer, W. "Lenin's Favourite Novel," Spectator, (6 Aug. 1937), 248-49.
A note on Lenin's love for Balzac's A Country Doctor.

1511 *Reddaway, Peter. "Literature, the Arts and the Personality of Lenin," in LMTL (anthology), 37-70.
The stated purpose of this study is to explore through Lenin's attitude towards literature and the arts the sensitive side of his nature so often hidden by the dominant and intolerant side of his personality. Reddaway identifies a psychological dualism (emotionally pleasing but intellectually decadent) in Lenin's approach to literature and, especially, music which he loved but was disturbed by.

1512 Rühle, Jürgen. Literature and Revolution: A Critical Study of the Writer and Communism in the Twentieth Century. New York: Praeger, 1969, 520pp.
Lenin is not the focus of any one chapter in this study, but it contains useful information on his thought on the relation between art, revolution, and socialist culture.
[PN51. R813]

1513 Sajjard, Zaheer. "The Influence of Leninist Ideas on Indian Literature," New Age, (19 Apr. 1970), 27-29.

1514 Serafimovich, Alexander. "Visiting Lenin," LAB (anthology), 170-71.
A recollection of a conversation with Lenin on the common man's involvement in literature as both a reader and writer.

1515 *Shcherbina, Vladimir. Lenin and the Problems of Literature. Moscow: Progress Publishers, 1974, 396pp.
A comprehensive Soviet review of Lenin's thought on literature, its history and role in the cultural revolution. Shcherbina examines the relationship between Lenin's theory of reflection and concept of reality in literature; his principle of partisanship in literature; assessment of the role played by literature in the 19th century Russian revolutionary movement; criticism of Leo Tolstoy; relationship with Maxim Gorky; and, lastly, Lenin's views on socialist literature and his efforts to

promote a literature which the common man could both learn from and enjoy. Excerpt in Int Lit, 11 (1944), 2-7. [PG2975. S4713]

1516 Shneidman, Noah N. "The Russian Classical Literary Heritage and the Basic Concept of Soviet Literary Education," Slav R, 31, no. 3 (Sept. 1972), 626-38.
In part, a discussion of Lenin's thought on the relationship between Russia's bourgeois cultural heritage and socialist culture.

1517 Shukla, Yashvant. "The Impact of Lenin on Gujarti Literature," Bul Ch GV, 18 (Aug. 1974), 16-20.

1518 *Shurki, Ghali. "Lenin, Literature and Art," Lotus, 1, no. 6 (1970), 134-53.

1519 Somerville, John. "Lenin's View of Tolstoy," in Soviet Philosophy. A Study of Theory and Practice. New York: Philosophical Library, 1946, 129-131.
A brief review of Lenin's criticism of Tolstoy for recognizing the evils of capitalism but failing to do anything to eliminate them. [B4231. S6]

1520 *Sorokin, Boris. "Acute Conscience but Dulled Intelligence: A Famous Marxist Judges Tolstoy," No Dakota Q, 46 no. 1 (1978), 32-43.
A review of the different assessments of Tolstoy advanced by Lenin and Plekhanov.

1521 Srinivasa, Iyengar K. R. "Lenin and Indian Literature," Aryan P, 41, nos. 9-10 (Nov.-Dec. 1970), 357-63.

1522 Stassova, Helen. "Lenin and the World of Culture," Int Lit, 12, no. 1 (Jan. 1945), 2-4.
A discussion of Lenin's literary tastes, relationship with Gorky, and views on the role of literature in the cultural revolution.

1523 Valentinov, N. "Fine Pages of Russian Literature," in NBPA (anthology), 127-28.
An excerpt from a conversation between Lenin and Mikhail Olminsky debating the merits of a writing by Samsonov.

1524 Wilson, Edmund. "Marxism and Literature," Atlan Mo, 160 (Dec. 1937), 741-50.
In part, a review of Lenin's attitude towards literature in general and the works of L. Tolstoy and M. Gorky in particular.

1525 *Zaheer, Sajjad. "Influence of Leninist Ideas on Indian Literature," in GTSE (anthology), 61-77.

A sympathetic account of the penetration into India of Lenin's writings on literature, especially in regard to the partisan nature of literature. Zaheer states that Lenin's enthusiasm for the creation of a socialist paradise and his assigning of a paramount role to literature in this process impressed Indian writers.

1526   Zaitsev, N. "Lenin's Attitude toward the Theater," <u>Cult Life</u>, 8 (Aug. 1970), 18-19.

C. Education

1527 Andreyenko, Stepan. "Lenin's Concern for the Development of Science and Education," Cult Life, 10 (Oct. 1969), 6-9.

1528 Bereday, George and Joan Pennar. The Politics of Soviet Education. New York: Praeger, 1960, 514pp.
Lenin is not the focus of any one chapter in this study, but it contains useful information on his educational philosophy and policies.

1529 *Bibanov, T. P. "Lenin's Concern for the Growing Generation," Sov Ed, 12, nos. 3-5 (Jan.-Mar. 1970), 65-76.
An account of Lenin's pre-1917 concern for the lack of education for the poor of Russia, his work in countering illiteracy as Soviet leader, and his establishment of communist organizations for youth.

1530 Drozdov, V. "Lenin Rooms," Sov Mil R, no. 10 (Oct. 1978), 44-45.
A description of the Lenin rooms in the army and navy as extensions of Lenin's teachings on the need for propaganda and education both within and outside of the formal schools.

1531 *Fitzpatrick, Sheila. The Commissariat of Enlightenment. Soviet Organization of Education and the Arts under Lunacharsky, October 1917-1921. Cambridge: Cambridge University Press, 1970, 380pp; bib. 362-74.
This scholarly study of Soviet education does not contain a separate chapter on Lenin, but has many references to and short sections on his relationship with Lunacharsky and his views on education, literature, and the cultural revolution in general. [LA831.8F56]

1532 *Goncharov, N. K. "Lenin and Pedagogy," Sov Ed, 10 (Sept. 1968), 35-49.

1533 *Hayashida, Ronald H. "Lenin and the Third Front," Slav R, 28, no. 2 (June 1969), 314-23.
A critique of F. Lilge's article (see item 1540).

1534 Kachutin, P. A. "V. I. Lenin and People's Education," Convergence, 3, no. 1 (1970), 79-83.

1535   *Klarin, V. "Lenin and Krupskaya in the Struggle for Public
          Education," Sov Ed, 12 (Oct. 1970), 51-64.

1536   Kolesnikova, N. N. "He Taught Us to See the Future,"
          in LCAM (anthology), 157-61.
          A reminiscence of a discussion with Lenin on plans to
          establish village reading rooms for the education of
          illiterate peasants.

1537   *Korolev, F. "Lenin and Pedagogy," Sov Ed, 10 (Aug. 1968),
          3-19.

1538   *Landa, N. Lenin on Educating Youth. Moscow: Novosti
          Press, n. d. , 55pp.
          A positive presentation of Lenin's views on the impor-
          tance of education of youth for the success of socialist
          construction and the cultural revolution.   Landa reviews
          Lenin's thought on teaching communist morality, critical
          thinking and Marxism; on properly training teachers;
          and on developing fully a program of vocational educa-
          tion.   [LB775. L2824L33]

1539   *Lenin and Public Education. Moscow: Novosti Press, 1970,
          68pp.
          A general survey of Lenin's philosophy of education
          with most attention given to his role in implementing
          educational reforms.   The author discusses Lenin's
          formation of the People's Commissariat of Education
          as a means of replacing the educational apparatus of
          the bourgeois state; his inspirational role in winning
          the support of the majority of teachers for socialist
          principles; his insistence on the complete democratiza-
          tion of education; views on the class character of edu-
          cation; and, especially, his stress on the crucial role
          of the schools in determining the success of the cul-
          tural revolution.   [LB775. L2824L45]

1540   *Lilge, Frederic. "Lenin and the Politics of Education,"
          Slav R, 27, no. 2 (June 1968), 230-57.
          A positive assessment of Lenin's contributions to Soviet
          educational programs and policies, and a discussion of
          his views on the relation of education to politics and
          on the role of education in the cultural revolution.

1541   *_____. "Reply to Mr. Hayashida," Slav R, 28, no. 2
          (June 1969), 324-27.
          A response to Hayashida's critique (see item 1533).

1542   *McClelland, James C. "Bolshevik Approaches to Higher
          Education, 1917-1921," Slav R, 30, no. 4 (1971), 818-
          31.
          In part, a discussion of Lenin's active role, in 1921,
          in turning Bolshevik educational policy in a more con-
          servative direction.

1543 *_____. "Bolsheviks, Professors and the Reform of
       Higher Education in Soviet Russia, 1917-1921," Prince-
       ton University, 1971 (dissertation).

1544 *Panachin, F. G. "V. I. Lenin and the Formation of Teach-
       ing Cadres for the Soviet State," Sov Ed, 19, nos. 9-
       10 (July-Aug. 1977), 8-24.

1545 *Podgaetskaia, I. M. "Certain Forms of Lexical and Stylis-
       tic Analysis in Studying Literary Works on Lenin in
       the School," Sov Ed, 12, nos. 3-5 (Jan.-Mar. 1970),
       77-85.
       A discussion of the Soviet schools' use of literary works
       on Lenin, with most attention given to Mayakovsky's
       poetry.

1546 Ravkin, Z. "The Struggle for the Leninist Style of Work
       in the People's Commissariat of Education," Sov Ed,
       6 (Sept. 1964), 44-54.

1547 Sharma, K. D. "Lenin: Socialism and Education," in
       LAWC (anthology), 64-65.
       A brief statement on the importance assigned to educa-
       tion by Lenin in the construction of socialism.

1548 Singh, N. K. "Lenin on Socialist Education," in LACW
       (anthology), 97-100.
       A review of Lenin's support for combining in the schools
       the teaching of Marxist philosophy with academic and
       vocational education.

1549 *Skatershchikov, V. K. "Leninist Principles of Esthetic
       Education and the Contemporary Era," Sov Ed, 12,
       nos. 3-5 (Jan.-Mar. 1970), 101-29.
       A discussion of Lenin's opposition to a purely utilitarian
       approach to education on the grounds that it would stifle
       the creative and spiritual qualities of socialist culture.

1550 Stoletov, Vsevolod. "Education. The Key to Social Trans-
       formation," UNESCO Cr, 23 (July 1970), 12-15.
       A description of Lenin's lifelong love for learning and
       his efforts to advance education in Soviet Russia.

1551 *Widmayer, Ruth C. "The Communist Party and the Soviet
       Schools, 1917-1937," Radcliffe, 1953 (dissertation).

1552 Zetkin, Klara. "Illiteracy and Socialist Construction," in
       NBPA (anthology), 168-71.
       A recollection of Lenin's views on the benefits for art
       under a socialist system and his concern for illiteracy
       as an obstacle to the cultural revolution.

D. Libraries

1553   Bibliotecario (pseud.). "Lenin's Work and Ideas on Librar-
        ies," Herald Lib Sci, 9, no. 4 (Oct. 1970), 316-17.

1554   Bogachev, P. "Lenin--Reader in the British Museum," in
        LKAL (anthology), 63-65.
        An account of Lenin's great respect for the collection
        at the British Museum and the research he conducted
        there in 1902.

1555   *Bonch-Bruyevich, Vladimir. "A Contribution to the History
        of the Organisation of the Russian Central Book Cham-
        ber in Moscow," in LAB (anthology), 161-66.
        A recollection of a meeting with Lenin, immediately
        after the October Revolution, over the publication of
        the Russian classics, and the development of archives,
        libraries, and museums. Lenin felt that these matters
        were a top priority in the Bolsheviks' cultural program.

1556   _____. "Lenin's Marks on Knizhnaya Letopis," in LAB
        (anthology), 166-68.
        A note on Lenin's use of Knizhnaya Letopis (a chronicle
        of books) as a means of keeping abreast of those pub-
        lications which he believed were important to read.

1557   Danilov, N. "Lenin and Libraries," Indian Lib, 24, no. 4
        (Mar. 1970), 188-91.

1558   *Deviatov, V. I. "Books in Lenin's Life," Sov Ed, 12,
        nos. 3-5 (Jan.-Mar. 1970), 53-62.
        An account of Lenin's reading tastes, use of libraries,
        and research methods (especially in regard to his work
        on The Development of Capitalism in Russia).

1559   Gilenson, Boris. "American Books in Lenin's Library,"
        in LIOUS (anthology), 221-22.

1560   Karpinskii, V. A. "My Memoirs," in LKAL (anthology),
        58.
        A reminiscence, by a librarian who worked with Lenin,
        of Lenin's refusal, even as Soviet leader, to be treated
        any differently than an ordinary patron of the library.

1561   Krupskaia, N. K. "Lenin on Libraries," in LKAL (anthol-

thology), 9-10.
A recollection, by Lenin's wife, of Lenin's love for libraries and his efforts to promote their development after years of destruction during the Civil War.

1562 *_____. "Lenin's Work in Libraries," in LKAL (anthology), 58-63.
An account of Lenin's dependence, for lack of money and space, on various libraries for materials to assist him with his research on a wide range of topics. Krupskaya also records Lenin's opinions on the libraries of Paris, Geneva, Cracow, Bern, London, Berlin, Pskov, and Moscow. Also in LAB (anthology), 145-49.

1563 Kunetskaya, L. "Lenin's Personal Library in the Kremlin," Cult Life, 11 (Nov. 1970), 14-17.

1564 "Lenin on Libraries," Lib J, 89 (1 Nov. 1964), 4301+.
A review of Lenin's critique of various European libraries and of his work to improve the libraries of Russia, especially the Petrograd Public Library.

1565 Lunacharskii, A. V. "October Memories," in LKAL (anthology), 56-57.
A recollection of Lenin's statement, upon the author's appointment to the Commissariat of Education, on the need to create a library system that would be both comprehensive and easy to use so as to encourage the borrowing of books by all citizens.

1566 *Manucharyants, S. "Working in Vladimir Ilyich's Library," in LAB (anthology), 177-82.
An account, by Lenin's personal librarian, of Lenin's work habits and reading tastes.

E.   Art, Music, Science and the Press

1567   Armand, Inessa. "A Visit to a Students' Hostel," in NBPA
       (anthology), 188-91.
       An account of a visit by Lenin and the daughter of Ines-
       sa Armand to the students' dormitory of the Higher
       Art-Technical Institute of Moscow.

1568   Beeching, William C. "Lenin and the Role of the Press,"
       Com V, 2, no. 2 (Mar.-Apr. 1970), 50-54.

1569   Beletskaya, Wanda. "Unfinished Poem," in LIOL (anthology),
       287-302.
       A discussion of Lenin's great interest in science and
       technology and of his efforts to provide the best of fa-
       cilities and financial support for Soviet scientists.

1570   *Bowlt, J. E. "Russian Sculpture and Lenin's Plan of Monu-
       mental Propaganda," in Art and Architecture in Service
       of Politics, H. A. Millon and L. Nochlin, eds. Cam-
       bridge: M.I.T. Press, 1978; 182-93.
       A critical appraisal of Lenin's 14 April 1918 decree
       which called for the creation, throughout the cities of
       Russia, of monuments of revolutionary and popular
       heroes and the dismantling of those erected in honor of
       the tsars. Bowlt states that the distinct lack of sculp-
       tural talent in Russia and the absence of guidelines
       governing the creation of the monuments resulted in
       the production of works that were technically deficient
       and widely different in style. Although Lenin, other
       Bolshevik leaders, and many members of the general
       public were upset with the "monumental failure of the
       monumental plan," Bowlt asserts, Lenin's plan was a
       progressive one with much influence on the development
       of Soviet architecture and sculpture. [N8236. P5177]

1571   Fomin, A. A. "That Was the Kind of Man Our Leader
       Was," in LCAM (anthology), 142-44.
       An account of the assistance given by Lenin to the Puti-
       lov workers in organizing a music studio for their chil-
       dren.

1572   *Guback, Thomas H. and Steven P. Hill. The Beginnings of

256

Soviet Broadcasting and the Role of V. I. Lenin. Lexington, Kentucky: Association for Education in Journalism, 1972, 43pp.
A consideration of Lenin as "perhaps the only national leader of the time who saw in radio something more than a scientific toy for popular amusement.... Lenin's position in the party and government, his impassioned belief in the necessity of technical progress, and the priorities he attached to communication with the proletariat and peasantry, all contributed to the individual contact he made with scientists and to his personal encouragement in party and government circles for support of wireless." The authors examine carefully Lenin's actions and policies in the 1917-1923 period to support this contention. Also published as The Innovation of Broadcasting in the Soviet Union and the Role of V. I. Lenin. Urbana: University of Illinois Press, 1972. [PN4722.J6]

1573 *Konenkov, Sergie. "Guiding Star," in LIOL (anthology), 257-67.
A recollection, by the Chairman of the Moscow Sculptors' Union in 1918, of a meeting with Lenin on the creation of monuments in the Kremlin to commemorate the revolutionary movement.

1574 Korev, Yuri. "USSR: Achieving Lenin's Ideas in Music," W Mus, 14, no. 4 (1972), 32-47.
A restatement of Lenin's argument for a type of music that would be both enjoyable for and accessible to the common man.

1575 *Kostyukovsky, Boris. "Renewal," in LIOL (anthology), 33-51.
An account of Lenin's support for the rebuilding of damaged Kremlin monuments, the construction of new parks and an All-Russian Agricultural Exhibit, and the designing of a mass transportation system for Moscow.

1576 Lepeshinsky, P. N. "A Kind of Baritone," in NBPA (anthology), 54-55.
A statement on Lenin's love of music and song, and a description of his voice as being somewhat off-key and a combination of "baritone, bass, and tenor."

1577 Lunacharsky, A. V. "A Talk with Gorky," in NBPA (anthology), 181.
A review of Gorky's complaint to Lenin about searches and arrests of the Petrograd intelligentsia.

1577a _____. "Lenin on Cinema," (in NBPA (anthology), 205-05.

A recollection of Lenin's support for financial aid for film companies and his belief that "popular" as well as propaganda films should be produced.

1578   . "Lenin on Propaganda through Monuments," Int Lit, no. 1 (Jan. 1939), 88-90.

1579   . "On Monumental Propaganda," in NBPA (anthology), 200-02.
A restatement of Lenin's plan to have unemployed artists, sculptors, and poets design works and slogans to be placed all over the city with grand unveiling ceremonies as a rich source of propaganda.

1580   . "On Music," in NBPA (anthology), 207.
A reminiscence of Lenin's consistent refusal of invitations to concerts because, despite his great love of music, it affected him badly.

1581   *Montagu, Ivor. "Lenin on Film," in Anglo Sov J, 31, no. 1 (Sept. 1970), 15-30.
A discussion of Lenin's thoughts about film and a review of various films about Lenin.

1582   Platonov, Georgy. "Lenin and Timiryazev," Cult Life, 6 (June 1970), 12-13.
A brief note on Lenin's influence on Timiryazev's book Science and Democracy.

1583   *Resis, Albert. "Lenin on Freedom of the Press," Rus R, 36, no. 3 (1977), 274-96.
An investigation into how journalism fell under "draconian controls" inspired by Lenin in 1918 and 1919.

1584   Riordan, James. "Marx, Lenin and Physical Culture," J Sport Hist, 3, no. 2 (1976), 152-61.

1585   Ryabchikov, Yevgeny. "The Central Cosmodore," in LIOL (anthology), 307-19.
A description of Lenin's appreciation of science and of how the Soviet Union's first cosmonauts felt that their success was due to Lenin's support of science.

1586   Senkin, S. et al. "With Young Artists," in NBPA (anthology), 192-95.
Excerpts from talks between Lenin and young artists illustrating his artistic taste, especially his dislike of furturist art.

1587   Stetskevich, Marya. "On Music," in NBPA (anthology), 208.
An account of Lenin's love for music and how, upon listening to opera or a concert, he would become extremely tired from the intensity of his concentration and emotions.

1588   Sytin, Victor. "The Visionary from Kaluga," in <u>LIOL</u> (anthology), 107-21.
        A discussion of the career of aeronautical scientist K. Tsiolkovsky and of Lenin's support for his research.

1589   "Victory of the Moral Force," in <u>LHIII</u> (anthology), 117-19.
        A restatement of Lenin's views on freedom of the press and on political propaganda.

1590   Zholtovsky, Ivan. "In 1918," <u>Sov Lit</u>, no. 3 (1970), 60-61.
        A reminiscence of meetings with Lenin on plans to rebuild certain sections of Moscow.

7. NATIONALITY DOCTRINE AND PROGRAM

1591   Adamovich, Anthony. "Toward a Single Socialist Nation," St Sov Un, 1, no. 3 (1962), 33-40.
A discussion of the "fusing of nations" within the Soviet Union under Lenin and Stalin.

1592   *Barghoorn, Frederick C. "Nationality Doctrine in Soviet Political Strategy," R Pol, 3 (July 1954), 283-304.
An examination of Lenin's manipulation of national sentiment as part of Bolshevik revolutionary and political strategy.

1593   Batal, Georges. "Leninism and the National Question," W Marxist R, 13, no. 3 (Mar. 1970), 16-19.

1594   Bedriy, Anatole W. "Lenin for the Preservation of Russian Imperial Rule in the Ukraine," Ukr R, 17, no. 1 (1970), 61-66.
A charge that Lenin intended to preserve the Russian empire and give the Ukraine colony status, but once in power even colony status was denied.

1595   *Boersner, Demetrio. The Bolsheviks and the National and Colonial Question (1917-1928). Geneva: Libraire E. Droz, 1957; 285pp., bib. 277-85.
Lenin is not the focus of this study, but it contains significant information on his thoughts and policies on the national question and national liberation movements and his conflicts with the Austro-Marxist school of thought, Rosa Luxemburg, and the Left Bolsheviks in Russia. Boersner stresses the lack of attention by Marx and Engels to national liberation movements as the root of the wide range of twentieth-century Marxist interpretations of such movements and sees "the atmosphere of most intense social and national oppression" in tsarist Russia as the source of Lenin's insight into the revolutionary implications of the nationality problem. He discusses at length Soviet national policy as well as the policies pursued by the Comintern towards the national-colonial question. In the latter case, Boersner focuses on the "dual tactics" followed by Lenin as he similtaneously sought to promote revolution within capitalist states by uniting the world proletariat while in-

sisting on the right to self-determination by colonies of the capitalist nations. [JV151.B6]

1596 *Charachidze, G. "The Georgian Communist Party and the National Question," Cauc R, 1 (1955), 22-36.
A discussion of the difficulties encountered in Georgia by Lenin's nationality program.

1597 *Ciolkosz, Adam. "The Eclipse of Lenin's Ideas on the Nationality Program," Polish R, 21, no. 4 (1976), 59-68.

1598 *Ciuciura, Theodore B. "Lenin's Idea of a Multi-National Commonwealth," Ann Ukr Acad Arts Sci, 10, no. 1/2 (1962/63), 3-64.
A discussion of Lenin's nationality doctrine and its relation to the political needs of the Bolshevik Party before and after the revolution.

1599 Conquest, Robert, ed. Soviet Nationalities Policy in Practice. London: Bodley Head, 1967; 14-60, bib. 152-60.
Although this study does not have a separate section on Lenin it contains significant information on his nationality doctrine and program. [JN6520.M5C63]

1600 *Davis, Horace B. "Lenin and the Formulation of a Marxist Nationality Theory," in Nationalism and Socialism. Marxist and Labor Theories of Nationalism to 1917. New York: Monthly Review Press, 1967; 185-214., bib. 237-43.
A discussion of Lenin's pre-1917 thought both on nationalism as a historical phenomenon and on nationalities' movements. Davis examines Lenin's definition of nationalism, his assessment of Marx's ideas on nationalism and nationalities problems, and his views on self-determination of nationalities, the relation between the proletariat and nationalism, the changing nature of nationalism in the age of imperialism, and the place of nationalism in a socialist state. Davis states that prior to 1914 Lenin certainly underestimated the force of nationalism but afterwards adjusted his views and developed a deeper understanding and greater tolerance of nationalism, unlike his successor Stalin. [HX550.N3D3]

1601 * _____. "Lenin and Nationalism: The Redirection of the Marxist Theory of Nationalism, 1903-1917," Sci Soc, 31, no. 2 (1967), 164-85.
An examination of Lenin's application of dialectics to the nationality question, and a discussion of his support of self-determination only as a developmental stage in the evolution of the nation.

1602 d'Encausse, Helene C. "Party and Federation in the U.S.S.R.: the Problems of the Nationalities and Power

in the U. S. S. R. ," Gov Opp, 13 (Spring 1978), 133-50.
A balance sheet of Soviet nationality policy with a section
on Lenin's thought and policies.

1603 *Donzow, Dmytro. "Lenin as Theoretician of 'Proletarian'
Assimilation Policy," Ukr R, 18, no. 4 (1971), 39-55.
An attack on Lenin's nationality policy towards the Uk-
raine as one based on Russification.

1604 *Dzyuba, Ivan. "The Forces that Prepared the Revision of
the Leninist Nationality Policy," in Internationalism or
Russification? A Study in the Soviet Nationalities Problem. London: Weidenfeld and Nicolson, 1970; 34-39.
A short argument that the nationality policies pursued
by the C. P. S. U. (especially towards the Ukraine) since
Lenin's death are in opposition to Lenin's writings on
the national question. Dzyuba singles out Great Russian nationalism, clumsy bureaucratic centralization,
and flagrant hypocrisy as all being the product of a
perversion, began by Stalin, of Lenin's nationality guidelines. [JN6520. M5D943]

1605 *_____. Internationalism or Russification? A Study of
the Soviet Nationalities Problem. London: Weidenfeld
and Nicolson, 1970; 263pp.
Lenin is not the focus of this study, by a Ukrainian
scholar, but it contains significant interpretive and critical information on his nationality doctrine and program
and its relation to that which has been pursued by his
successors. [JN6520. M5D943 1970]

1606 *Eudin, Xenia. "Soviet National Minority Policies, 1918-
1921," SEER, 21 (1943), 31-55.

1607 *Fedenko, Boris. "Lenin and His 'Wise' Nationality Policy,"
Prob Peoples USSR, 23 (1964), 33-37.
An argument that Lenin kept the non-Russian countries
under Soviet control by stressing that their noncompli-
ance would "destroy social democracy."

1608 *Fedenko, Panas. "Lenin and the Nationality Question,"
St Sov Un, 3, no. 3 (1964), 59-79.
An argument that Lenin preached nationalism as a tactical revolutionary measure, but was a staunch enemy of
the concept of separate socialist nations.

1609 *_____. "Liberation Abroad and Colonialism at Home,"
St Sov Un, 1, no. 2 (1961), 5-22.
A critical discussion of the hypocritical qualities of
Lenin's nationality doctrine and programs.

1610 *Fedoseyev, P. N. et al. "Lenin's Leadership in the National State Question," in Leninism and the National
Question. Moscow: Progress, 1977; 240-58.

A Soviet account of Lenin's leadership within the Bolshevik Party in developing and implementing a nationality program.   Fedodeyev devotes most attention to
an elaboration of the factors which led Lenin to replace
the plan for a centralized, multi-national state with one
based on a federation of sovereign socialist states.
The author also examines the sources of the difficulties
that Lenin had in establishing and consolidating the
federated Soviet state.   [HX550. N3L48613]

1611   Fischer, Louis.   "Lenin's Legacy," Columbia U Forum,
7 (Fall 1964), 4-9.
An argument that Lenin left no clear guidelines on nationalism, hence the Soviets' inability to deal effectively
with both their own national peculiarities and nationalism in the modern world.

1612   Gaucher, Roland.   "Peoples, Believers; Peasants," in Opposition in the U. S. S. R. , 1917-1967.   New York: Funk
and Wagnalls, 1969; 155-82.
Lenin is not the focus of this chapter, but it contains
useful information on his nationality theory.
[DK266. 3G3413]

1613   Gomulka, W.   "Lenin's Approach to the National Question,"
W Marxist R, 13, no. 4 (1970), 77-84.

1614   *Goodman, Elliot R.   "The Issue of Centralism versus Federalism in the Leninist Era," in The Soviet Design
for a World State.   New York: Columbia University
Press, 1960; 190-238, bib. , 489-93.
A scholarly assessment of the issue of centralism versus federalism in the future world state which Lenin
and the Bolsheviks hoped to establish.   Goodman asserts that Soviet views on this issue "are largely a
projection of their attitude toward the centralist-federal-
ist issue as it arose in the building of the Russian
Party and state."   The author examines Lenin's writings
on and establishment of both a centralized political
party and national state as a means of illustrating that
Lenin, like his successors, was fundamentally opposed
to the concept of federalism.   Goodman argues that
neither Lenin's version of self-determination nor his
creation in 1922 of a Soviet federated socialist state
were concessions to federalism but rather were attempts
to subvert it en route to a truly centralized socialist
state.   The author concludes that if a world socialist
state ever did emerge, an eventuality which he doubts,
it certainly would be centralized if Lenin and the curren
Soviet leadership had their way.   [JC361. G66]

1615   Greenbaum, A. A.   "Soviet Jewry during the Lenin-Stalin
Period--I," Sov St, 16, no. 4 (Apr. 1965), 406-21.
Part II 17 (July 1965), 84-92.

1616　*Grover, D. C. "A Marxist Analysis of Lenin's Theory of Nationality," Krukshetra U Res J, 5, no. 1 (Apr. 1973), 165-73.

1617　*Hardy, Eugene N. "The Russian Soviet Federated Socialist Republic: The Role of Nationality in Its Creation, 1917-1922," University of California at Berkeley, 1955 (dissertation).

1618　*Holdsworth, Mary. "Lenin and the Nationalities Question," in LMTL (anthology), 165-96.
An analysis of Lenin's writings on and policies toward the national minorities in tsarist and Soviet Russia. Holdsworth examines Lenin's The Tasks of the Russian Social Democrats (1897), The National Question in Our Programme (1903), and Theses on the Nationalities Question (1913 and 1917) to determine how Lenin arrived at the conclusion that the party should align itself with the working class element in revolutionary nationalist parties, and support the right to self-determination while stressing the primacy of international proletarian solidarity over nationalist concerns. Holdsworth surveys Lenin's nationalities policy as Soviet leader and maintains that Lenin, with his careful attention to balancing the demands of revolutionary nationalism with those of revolutionary centralism, would not have supported the national policy followed by Stalin.

1619　*Horak, Stephen M. "Lenin's Policy of Non-Intervention and of World Revolution," Ukr R, 11, no. 1 (Spring 1964), 37-47.
An argument that Lenin's policies on non-intervention and world revolution were not antithetical to him (though they are to most people), and that he like his successors, consistently violated, especially in the Ukraine, the non-intervention principle.

1620　Humo, Avdo. "Lenin on the National Question," in LIPOY (anthology), 35-38.
A positive restatement of Lenin's belief that a voluntary association of socialist nations is dependent on the development of equality, epecially economic, among all nations.

1621　Ismagilova, R. N. "Lenin's General Democratic Programme on the National Question and Africa's Ethnic Problems," in HDASP (anthology), 57-85.
An account, based on a Soviet historian's conversations with African leaders, of how Africans are impressed not only by Lenin's doctrine of nationality but the concrete measures taken in the Soviet Union to implement it as a solution to ethnic problems. Ismagilova expounds on the nature of Africa's nationality problems while ar-

guing that Lenin's teachings on self-determination and equality of nations have great relevance to the African situation.

1622 Kerbabayev, Berdy. "Dreams Come True," in <u>LIOL</u> (anthology), 243-52.
A recollection of Lenin's influence on the life of the author, and, especially of the economic and cultural advances made in Soviet Turkestan under Lenin's nationality program.

1623 *Korol, Nestor. "Bolshevik Documents on the Conquest of the Ukraine," <u>Ukr R</u>, 16, no. 2 (1960), 164-76.
An examination of Lenin's negative reaction to the Ukrainian proclamation of independence.

1624 *Kreindler, Isabelle. "A Neglected Source of Lenin's Nationality Policy," <u>Slav R</u>, 36, no. 1 (1977), 86-100.
A discussion of the influence on Lenin's nationality doctrine of three individuals: Lenin's father, I. Iakolev (a family friend), and N. Ilminiskii (an orthodox missionary).

1625 Lebedinskaya, L. "The Nationality Question and the Formation of the Soviet State," <u>Int Aff</u>, 12 (1972), 10-15.
A positive assessment of Lenin's national doctrine and its implementation in the U. S. S. R.

1626 "Lenin-Founder of the Multi-National State of Working People," <u>News from USSR</u>, no. 36 (21 Dec. 1972), 1-10.

1627 <u>Leninism and the National Question</u>. Moscow: Progress, 1977; 540pp.

1628 Loewy, M. "Marxists and the National Question," <u>New Left R</u>, 96 (Mar. 1976), 81+.

1629 *Low, Alfred, D. <u>Lenin on the Question of Nationality</u>. New York: Bookman, 1958; 193pp., bib. 177-90.
An analysis of Lenin's views on the nationality question concentrating on the 1913 to 1917 period when he developed fully his national theory. Low emphasizes the consistency of Lenin's writings stating that Lenin did not change any basic conceptions during this period and that the continuity in this thought extended even through and beyond the October Revolution. Throughout, Lenin was convinced that "for the purpose of facilitating the 'proletarian' seizure of power and then perpetuating it" the party must support a program of full national equality in a multi-national state. Never, Low argues, did Lenin have true respect for the rights of the many small nationalities in Russia but rather always looked

upon them as pawns to be used to facilitate the proletarian revolution and the establishment of socialism. Lenin was in fact an enemy of nationalism and believed that "the right to self-determination not to be an encouragement of nationalism but rather a weapon to fight it" in that the socialist federation of equal nations would be a means of blunting national distinctions and establishing a truly international socialist culture. Low concludes that the many qualifications added by the Soviets since 1917 to the right of self-determination are not inconsistent with Lenin's views on this issue, though he certainly would be opposed for tactical reasons to the excesses of Stalin's national policy. [JC311. L75]

1630 *Mazlakh, Serhii and Vasyl' Shakhrai. "Questions for Comrade Lenin," in On the Current Situation in the Ukraine. Ann Arbor: University of Michigan Press, 1970; 170-79; bib. 214-17.
A 1919 attack, by two Ukrainian Bolsheviks, on the nationality program pursued in the Ukraine in Lenin's name. The authors expose the hypocrisy of the Bolshevik nationality policy and demand that Lenin answer a series of questions pertaining to it, especially in regard to the true meaning of his concept of self-determination. [DK265. 8. U4M383]

1631 Meissner, Boris. "The Soviet Concept of Nation and the Right of National Self-Determination," Int J, 35, no. 1 (Winter 1976/1977), 56-81.

1632 Menzhinsky, Victor. "Federation and Nation," Sov Life, 9, no. 156 (Sept. 1969), 40-41, 59.
A discussion of Lenin's theory of self-determination.

1633 *Metelitsa, L. and E. Tadevosyan. "Lenin on the National Question: the Implementation of His Principles in the U. S. S. R. ," in Leninist Solution to the National Question in the U. S. S. R. Moscow: Novosti, 1969; 29-56.
A discussion, as the basis of Soviet national policy, of Lenin's belief that the "unconditional recognition of the right of nations to self-determination, including secession ... leads to a genuinely profound and lasting solidarity and unity of nations--not their separation." The authors review the implementation of this principle in the Soviet Union in conjunction with the program to insure complete equality of all nationalities. [JN6520. M5L4]

1634 *Muradov, Gulam. "The U. S. S. R. Experience in Solving the National Question and the Liberated Countries of the East," Asian S, 14, no. 3 (1974), 289-306.
A discussion of Lenin's program for creating a multinational socialist state as a solution to the national question in Asia.

1635   The National Question and Leninism. New York: Interna-
        tional Publishers, 1952; 23pp.
        Not available for annotation.

1636   Nedasek, N. "National Self-Determination under the Soviets,"
        Belorus R, no. 8 (Sept. 1960), 3-16.
        An examination of Lenin's views and policies (1901-
        1924) on the nationality question and the program pur-
        sued by the party after Lenin's death.

1637   *Page, Stanley W. "Lenin and Self-Determination," SEER,
        28, no. 71 (1950), 342-58.

1638   *_____. "Lenin, the National Question and the Baltic
        States, 1917-1919," ASEER, 7 (Feb. 1948), 15-31.

1639   Paletskis, Justas, "Lenin and the National Question,"
        New Times, 15 (14 Apr. 1970), 6-8.
        A discussion of the implementation in Lithuania of Le-
        nin's nationality program.

1640   Pant, H. G. "Lenin, the Russian Revolution and National
        Boundaries," Mainstream, 9, no. 10 (Nov. 1970), 27-
        29 and 9, no. 11 (Nov. 1970), 26-28.

1641   *Pap, Michael S. Lenin and the Problem of Self-Determina-
        tion," in LAL (anthology), 137-151.
        A critical survey of Lenin's views on the nationality
        question in Russia from his first statement in 1894
        to his contributions to the December 1922 formation of
        the U.S.S.R. The author stresses that at first Lenin
        supported self-determination as a means of undermining
        tsarist authority and winning the support of national
        liberation movements, while believing that support of self-
        determination would not lead to the dismemberment of
        the Russian Empire, but rather to a voluntary union of
        nations in which the international proletarian struggle,
        not petty nationalism, would be the main concern. How-
        ever, once in power and confronted with separatist move-
        ments, Lenin followed a policy that independent, non-
        Russian states could exist only if they accepted the
        Soviet form of government. Pap states that only after
        the destruction of the national republics that opposed
        Soviet control did Lenin return to support of self-deter-
        mination, a principle which he incorporated into the
        1922 treaty which established the U.S.S.R. The author
        concludes by stating that this treaty also established
        the right of the central Soviet government to intervene
        in the affairs of its member states, a right which has
        been brutally applied, since Lenin's death, to Russify
        the U.S.S.R.

1642   *Pipes, Richard E. "Bolshevik National Theory before
        1917," Pro Com, 5, no. 2 (1953), 22-28.

1643 *_____ . "The Genesis of Soviet Nationality Policy," Harvard University, 1950 (dissertation).

1644 *_____ . "Lenin and the National Question before 1913," in The Formation of the Soviet Union. Communism and Nationalism 1917-1923. New York: Atheneum, 1968; 34-41. , bib. 305-28.
A discussion of the three stages in the development of Lenin's approach to the national problem: 1) 1897 to 1913, when he formulated his basic views; 2) 1913 to 1917, when he developed a plan to utilize for socialist revolution national minority movements; and 3) 1917 to 1923, when he abandoned previous plans in favor of one based on his practical experience as Soviet Russia's leader. In discussing Lenin's thought in the pre-1913 stage, Pipes stresses that Lenin developed here the fundamental belief that the national movements were a force suitable for Bolshevik exploitation in the struggle for power. Pipes also discusses the article Stalin wrote on this subject at the request of Lenin. In addition to the three chapters (annotated) in this study specifically on Lenin, there is much information on virtually every phase of the nationality question and Lenin's involvement with it. [DK266. P53 1964]

1645 *_____ . "Lenin's Change of Mind," in The Formation of the Soviet Union. Communism and Nationalism 1917-1923. New York: Atheneum, 1968; 276-293.
An examination of how, as evidence accumulated that Soviet nationality policy was ill-founded and unworkable, Lenin reappraised his position and began to formulate a revised program. Pipes discusses Lenin's negative reaction to the harsh centralist policies pursued in Georgia by Stalin and Ordzhonikidze, the policy revisions which Lenin devised, and how Lenin's failing health prevented him from implementing in an energetic fashion his new policies. Pipes states that Lenin's third stroke (March, 1923) removed the last obstacle to Stalin's establishment of centralized control over the Soviet nationalities. [DK266. P53 1964]

1646 *_____ . "Lenin's Theory of Self-Determination," in The Formation of the Soviet Union. Communism and Nationalism 1917-1923. New York: Atheneum, 1968; 41-49.
A discussion of Lenin's attempt, in the 1914 to 1917 period, to develop a theory on the nationality problem while at the same time waging a polemical war against the "rightists" (Renner and Bauer) and the 'leftists" (Luxemburg) on this issue. Pipes examines Lenin's theory of self-determination in the light of his attempt to steer a middle course between the rightist and leftist positions, and concludes that Lenin's theory was neither consistent nor practical. Lenin under-estimated the

power of nationalism in general, Pipes claims, and
failed to devise a feasible program for self-determination, but was able to harness for Bolshevik purposes
the national movements in Russia through skillfull propaganda. [DK266. P53 1969]

1647   Pittman, John. "Lenin on the National Question," New
        World R, 20 (Feb. 1952), 61-62.
        A review of Lenin's The Right of Nations to Self-Deter-
        mination.

1648   *Posti, Lauri A. "Lenin and the Cultural Rights of Minori-
        ties," UNESCO C, 23 (July 1970), 16-21.
        A discussion of Lenin's belief in and support of free
        and equal development of national cultures in the U. S. R.

1649   Rakhimov, T. R. "Great Hanist Chauvinism Instead of the
        Leninist Teaching on the National Question," in LIOL
        (anthology), 97-115.
        A Soviet critique of Maoism as a reversal of Lenin's
        principles on the national question, principles which
        the Chinese Communist Party had subscribed to in the
        1921 to 1949 period. Since gaining power, Rakhimov
        contends, the Maoists have, in particular, renounced
        self-determination and federal state organization in favor
        of Hanist chauvinism and returned to the imperialist
        policies followed by previous governments in China.
        Rakhimov provides examples of sinicization of non-
        Chinese areas, such as Tibet, Inner-Mongolia and Sin-
        kiang, to support the contention that Maoism is contra-
        dictory to Leninism.

1650   *Reshetar, John S. "Lenin on the Ukraine," Ann Ukr Acad
        Arts Sci, 9, no. 12 (1961), 3-11.

1651   Rysakoff, A. The Nationality Policy of the Soviet Union.
        London, 1931.

1652   Sasky, I. "Self-Determination in the U. S. S. R. ," Prob
        Peoples USSR, no. 4 (1959), 16-20.
        An examination of Lenin's support, for tactical reasons,
        of the principle of self-determination, and a charge
        that, once in power, he followed an imperialistic policy
        towards the Soviet nationalities.

1653   Sidelsky, R. "Formation and Development of the U. S. S. R.
        --a Triumph of Leninism," Int Aff, no. 1 (1973), 3-8.

1654   Stalin, Joseph. The National Question and Leninism. Mos-
        cow: Foreign Language Publishing House, 1950; 32pp.
        A defense of Soviet nationality theory and policy against
        those who argue that a nation cannot exist unless it has
        its own separate state. Stalin uses quotes from Lenin

to substantiate his own views and policies on the national question. [JC311. S76572]

1655 *Stercho, Peter G. "The Soviet Concept of National Self-Determination; Theory and Reality from Lenin to Brezhnev," Ukr Q, 29, no. 1 (1973), 12-17 and 29, no. 2 (1973), 158-68.

1656 *Suny, Ronald G. The Baku Commune 1917-1918. Class and Nationality in the Russian Revolution. Princeton: Princeton University Press, 1972; 412pp., bib. 363-95. Lenin is not the focus of this study, but it contains many references to and short sections on his nationality doctrine, support for the union of the socialist and national liberation movements, and assessment of revolutionary developments in Baku. [DK265. 8B3S85]

1657 *Thomas, Tony. "Lenin's Real Views on Nationalism," Int Soc R, 33, no. 1 (1972), 12-17, 34-38. A discussion of how Lenin supported nationalist movements by minorities within established countries and viewed nationalist demands as adaptable to Bolshevik views of history and revolution.

1658 Tobias, Henry J. "The Bund and Lenin until 1903," Rus R, 20, no. 4 (1961), 344-57.

1659 Topornin, Boris. "Lenin: Founder of the Soviet Multinational State," New World R, 40, no. 4 (1972), 79-83.

1660 _____. "Lenin--Founder of the U.S.S.R.," Sov Mil R, no. 11 (Nov. 1972), 6-8.

1661 _____. "V. I. Lenin--the Founder of the U.S.S.R.," Int Aff, 18, no. 5 (May 1972), 3-9.

1662 *Urban, Pavel. "The Nationality Question," St Sov Un, 9, no. 1 (1969), 56-72. A critical assessment of Lenin's nationality principles and the extent to which he adhered to them in practice.

1663 _____. "The Twentieth Party Congress and the National Question," Belorus R, no. 4 (1957), 83-95. In part, a discussion of Lenin's role in imposing socialism by armed force in Belorussia and of the hypocrisy behind the Leninist nationality policy.

1664 *Vaidyanath, R. "Lenin on National Minorities," India Q, 27, no. 1 (Jan.-Mar. 1971), 28-39. An exploration of Lenin's reasons for supporting the right of self-determination for non-Russian nationalities, and a restatement of the characteristics of the multinational voluntary union he envisioned.

1665   *＿＿＿＿＿. "The 'National Question' in Europe, with Special
        Reference to the Evolution of the Attitude of the Rus-
        sian Social Democratic Workers' Party," Int St, 4, no.
        4 (April 1963), 349-76.

1666   Voss, A. Lenin's Behests and the Making of Soviet Latvia.
        Moscow: Progress Publishers, 1970; 104pp.
        A centennial presentation of Lenin's writings and views
        on, involvement in, and policies toward Latvian com-
        munism, and a discussion of Latvian socialist and cul-
        tural development on the basis of Leninist principles.
        In addition, Voss defends Lenin and the Latvian Com-
        munist Party against Western critics who claim that
        revolution was imported into Latvia and did not reflect
        the true mood and aspirations of the Latvian people.
        [DK511. L18V613]

1667   *Vyshinsky, Pyotr. "V. I. Lenin's On the National Pride of
        the Great Russians," Int Lit, no. 4-5 (Apr.-May 1940),
        88-96.
        A review of Lenin's 1914 article on Russian national
        pride and its relation to World War I.

1668   *Wolfe, Bertram D. "The Influence of Early Military De-
        cisions upon the National Structure of the Soviet Union,"
        ASEER, 9, no. 3 (1950), 169-179.
        An argument, based on a series of excerpts from mili-
        tary correspondence between Lenin and other Bolshevik
        leaders, that military considerations of 1918-1919 had
        a pronounced affect on "the transformation of the Soviet
        Union from a federation of theoretically autonomous re-
        publics ... into a highly centralized state."

1669   Yesmeneyev, S. "Leninist Party Programme on the Na-
        tional Question," in Leninist Solution to the National
        Question in the U.S.S.R. Moscow: Novosti Press,
        1969; 5-28.
        A discussion of the evolution of the principles behind
        Lenin's program on the national question. Yesmeneyev
        reviews sympathetically Lenin's exposure of tsarist pro-
        motion of reactionary chauvinism and parochial national-
        ism, his linking the proletarian revolutionary movement
        with that of the nationalities, his theories of self-deter-
        mination and proletarian internationlism, and his strug-
        gles against opportunism within the socialist movement.
        [JN6520. M5L4]

1670   *Zhukov, B. Lenin on the Nationality Problem. Moscow:
        Novosti Press, 1968; 72pp.
        A summary, on the fiftieth anniversary of the October
        Revolution, of Lenin's nationality doctrine. Zhukov
        presents Lenin's views on the concept of the nation,
        the need for an international alliance of working people

against imperialism, the principle of self-determination as the basis of national structure, and on the need for both equality of all socialist nations and support for national liberation movements the world over. Zhukov concludes with a discussion of the present-day applicability of Lenin's nationality principles and policies. [HX550. N3Z43]

Cross-Reference: See also National Liberation Movements (IX-B-2).

8. FOREIGN POLICY

A. Theory

1671   *Achminov, Herman. "The Leninist Principle of Peaceful Coexistence," St Sov Un, 4, no. 1 (1964), 5. 19.

1672   *_____. "Lenin's Principles of Peaceful Coexistence," Majallah, no. 12 (1965), 3-26.

1673   Andreyev, G. "Lenin and Peaceful Soviet Foreign Policy," Int Aff, 16, no. 5 (May 1970), 3-14.

1674   Arsov, Ljupčo. "Lenin on War, Peace and Coexistence," in LIPOY (anthology), 39-42.
A brief discussion of Lenin as a revolutionary who saw war as the path to socialism in Russia but did not idealize war nor see it as the typical means of establishing a socialist state.

1675   Bestuzhev-Lada, I. and D. Yermolenko. "The Scientific Forecast of International Relations in the Light of Lenin's Teaching," Int Aff, 16, nos. 2-3 (Feb. -Mar. , 1970), 93-100.

1676   Browder, Earl. "The Party of Lenin and the People's Front," Communist, 15 (Feb. 1936), 120-29.
A Leninist justification of the Soviet Union's policy of allying with bourgeois parties opposed to fascism.

1677   _____. "The Study of Lenin's Teachings," Pol Aff, 24 (Jan. 1945), 3-10.
An argument for the study of Lenin's teachings on peaceful coexistence.

1678   Chandra, Romesh. "Lenin and the World Peace Movement," in GTSE (anthology), 57-60.
A presentation of Lenin as the main source of the contemporary world peace movement. Chandra maintains that from Lenin stem the principles of "peaceful coexistence, internationalism, the right of every people to sovereignty and liberty, the elimination of all forms of colonialism and racial discrimination, peace and national independence. "

1679   Chesnokov, D. I. "Peace and War as a State of Society,"
       in Historical Materialism. Moscow: Progress Pub-
       lishers, 1969; 550-63.
       A Soviet summary of Lenin's views on war and peace-
       ful coexistence. Chesnokov restates Lenin's views on
       the inevitability of wars in the imperialist era and their
       utilization to advance the cause of revolution, and his
       belief that, once established, a socialist state could
       peacefully coexist with capitalist states while still ex-
       ploiting the contradictions within the disputes between
       capitalist societies and encouraging national liberation
       and socialist movements around the world.
       [B809. 8. C57213]

1680   Dewhurst, Alfred. Lenin--Peaceful Coexistence and Social
       Progress," Com V, 2, no. 2 (Mar.-Apr. 1970), 25-29.

1681   *Djilas, Milovan. Lenin on Relations between Socialist States.
       New York: Yugoslav Information Center, 1950, 56pp.
       An examination of Lenin's teachings on relations between
       socialist states as a means of defending the Leninist
       course of the Communist Party of Yugoslavia against
       attacks by the Soviet regime. Djilas discusses Lenin's
       support for close military and economic cooperation
       among socialist states; the right of self-determination
       for all nations; unconditional and voluntary cooperation
       among socialist states; diverse forms in the construction
       of socialism; and for economic and political assistance
       of a non-profit bearing type by large socialist states
       to smaller ones. Djilas concludes that it is the Soviets
       who have violated Lenin's teachings on socialist rela-
       tions. [HX555. I5L44]

1682   Don, Sam. "Leninism in Foreign Policy," Communist, 23
       (Jan. 1944), 13-24.

1683   Frantsev, Yu. "Lenin--Founder of Soviet Foreign Policy,"
       Int Aff, 1 (Jan. 1955), 12-22.

1684   Gehlen, Michael P. The Politics of Coexistence. Soviet
       Methods and Motives. Bloomington: Indiana University
       Press, 1967. 334pp.
       Lenin is not the focus of any one chapter in this study,
       but it contains a discussion of his views on imperialism,
       war, and peaceful coexistence, and their relation to
       Soviet foreign policy. [DK63. 3. G4]

1685   No entry.

1686   Gorokhov, A. "Leninist Diplomacy: Principles and Tradi-
       tions," in POLFP (anthology), 76-96.
       A Soviet discussion of the tasks of modern Russian
       foreign policy as being similar to those faced by Lenin:

"thwarting the aggressive schemes of the imperialist
circles, rendering ... assistance to national liberation
movements, and preserving peaceful coexistence...."
Excerpt in Int Aff, 14, no. 4 (Apr. 1968), 38-44.

1687   *Gregor, Richard. "Lenin, Revolution and Foreign Policy,"
Int J, 22, no. 4 (Autumn 1967), 563-75.
A discussion of the adjustments, improvisations, and
contradictions in Lenin's foreign policy and their relation to the failure of his prediction that world revolution would follow the Bolsheviks' seizure of power.

1688   *Horak, Stephan M. "Heritage of Lenin's Coexistence,"
Ukr Q, 20, no. 2 (1964), 133-43.
An assessment of Lenin's and Khrushchev's support for
coexistence with the West as a policy motivated not by
any genuine concern for peace but rather as a means
of maintaining and strengthening communism in the
Soviet Union while still promoting world revolution.

1689   *_____. "Lenin on Coexistence: A Chapter in Soviet
Foreign Policy," St Sov Un, 3, no. 3 (1964), 20-30.

1690   *_____. "The United States in Lenin's Image," Ukr Q,
23, no. 3 (1967), 226-37.
An examination of the evolution of Lenin's thought on
America and its dogmatization by his successors.

1691   Igritsky, Yuri. "Revolution and Detente: How the Principles
of Soviet Foreign Policy Evolved," Sov Lit, no. 1 (Jan.
1979), 6-7.

1692   Imam, Zafar. "The Soviet View of Détente," Int St, 13,
no. 4 (1974), 609-33.
In part, an examination of the ideological significance
of Lenin's principle of peaceful coexistence for the contemporary Soviet policy of détente with America.

1693   Israelian, V. "The Leninist Science of International Relations and Foreign Policy Reality," Int Aff, 13, no. 6
(1967), 46-52.

1694   Ivanov, K. "Founder of Soviet Foreign Policy," New Times,
16 (21 Apr. 1970), 4-7.

1695   Ivanov, O. "Pursuing the Leninist Course of Peace," Sov
Mil R, 3 (Mar. 1977), 2-5.

1696   Kapchenko, N. "The Leninist Theory and Practice of Socialist Foreign Policy," in POLFP (anthology); 5-28.
A Soviet restatement of the basic principles of Lenin's
foreign policy and their relevancy to the contemporary
international political scene. In addition to reviewing

Lenin's thought on the relation between domestic and foreign policy, the foundations of imperialist diplomacy, and on proletarian internationalism, Kapchenko defends Lenin against the criticism of bourgeois historians. Abridgment in Int Aff, 14, no. 9 (1968), 53-60.

1697   Kaplin, A. "Lenin on the Principles of Socialist Diplomacy," Int Aff, 15, no. 6 (1969), 51-55.

1698   Khvostov, V. "Lenin on Principles of Soviet Foreign Policy," in LTCOA, 230-40.
A Soviet restatement of Lenin's teachings on peaceful coexistence, defense against capitalist encirclement, imperialism, national liberation movements and proletarian internationalism. Also in Kommunist, no. 9, 1969.

1699   _____. "The Leninist Principles of Foreign Policy," Int Aff, 3, no. 4 (1957), 18-26.

1700   Konstantinov, F. "The Principles of Internationalism and Peaceful Coexistence" in Leninist Approaches to Unity of the World Communist Movement, Yu. Frantsov et al., eds. Moscow: Novosti Press, 1970; 79-102.
A discussion of the basis of Soviet foreign policy as resting on the twin Leninist pillars of "the principle of proletarian, socialist internationalism in relations with other socialist countries and the working people of the capitalist world, and the principle of peaceful coexistence with bourgeois countries." [HX13. L45]

1701   Kroger, Herbert. "Leninism and Peaceful Coexistence," Ger For Pol, 9, no. 4 (1970), 263-81.

1702   *Kubalkova, V. "Marxism-Leninism and Theory of International Relations," University of Lancaster, 1975 (dissertation).

1703   Kudritsky, A. Leninist Principles of Foreign Policy in Action. Kiev: Politvidav Ukraini Publishers, 1977, 77pp.
A presentation, intended for the general public, of Soviet foreign policy as "the embodiment of the Leninist principles of proletarian internationalism and peaceful coexistence of states with different social systems."

1704   Kumaramangalam, S. M. "Lenin on Peaceful Coexistence," India Q, 27, no. 1 (Jan.-Mar. 1971), 57-64.

1705   Lebedev, N. "The Vital Power of Lenin's Foreign Policy Theory," Int Aff, 20, no. 12 (1974), 88-93.

1706   "Lenin and Peaceful Coexistence," Pol Aff, 34, no. 1 (1955) 1-3.

1707   "Leninist Foreign Policy of the Soviet Union," Sov Doc, 2,
        no. 47 (30 Nov. 1964), 3-5.

1708   Menon, K. P. S. "Lenin and Soviet Diplomacy," Link, 12,
        no. 36 (19 Apr. 1970), 27-29. Also in GTSE, 49-52.

1709   Modrzhinskaya, Y. "Lenin's Theory and Modern Interna-
        tional Relations," Int Aff, 16, no. 1 (1970), 56-62.

1710   Molchanov, Y. "The Leninist Policy of Peace," Int Aff,
        20, no. 2 (1974), 3-10.

1711   Murgescu, Costin. "International Collaboration and Cooper-
        ation in the Light of Leninist Ideas," in CFOLI (anthol-
        ogy); 136-54.
        A positive assessment of Lenin's creative application
        of Marxism to the question of relations between socialist
        and capitalist states. Murgescu emphasizes that, in
        spite of the hostile nature of world capitalism, Lenin
        successfully established peaceful coexistence and eco-
        nomic cooperation with capitalist states as the founda-
        tion of socialist-capitalist international relations, prin-
        ciples not antithetical to support of national liberation
        movements and pursuit of victory in the ideological
        struggle against capitalism.

1712   Nikolayev, Y. "The New Constitution: Continuity of the
        Leninist Policy of Peace," Int Aff, 11, no. 11 (1977),
        13-20.

1713   _____. "The Triumph of the Leninist Policy of Peace-
        ful Coexistence," Int Aff, 22, no. 2 (1976), 3-11.

1714   Pegov, Nikolai M. "Lenin on Peace and Peaceful Coexis-
        tence," For Aff Rep, 19, no. 3 (Mar. 1970), 25-31.
        Also in India Q 27, no. 1 (Jan.-Mar. 1971), 65-70.

1715   _____. "Lenin: Propounder of Peaceful Coexistence,"
        Times of India, 10 (22 Apr. 1970), 1-5+.

1716   Popov, V. "Lenin and Soviet Diplomacy," New Times, no.
        30 (29 July 1970), 18-20.

1717   _____. "Leninist Foreign Policy," New Times, no. 13
        (31 Mar. 1971), 6-9.

1718   Public Opinion in World Politics. Leninist Principles of
        Peaceful Coexistence. Moscow: Progress Publishers,
        1976, 152pp.

1719   Razmerov, V. "Leninist Foreign Policy--An Important Fac-
        tor in Contemporary World Development," Int Aff, no.
        5 (1974), 3-9.

1720   Rothstein, Andrew. "Lenin and International Relations Today," Labour Monthly 52, no. 4 (Apr. 1970), 177-81.

1721   Rozanov, G. "The Leninist Policy of Peace and Progress,"
Int Aff, 23, no. 5 (1977), 12-20.

1722   *Schuman, Frederick L. "The Legacy of Lenin," in Soviet
Politics at Home and Abroad. New York: Knopf, 1946,
184-94.
A general assessment of Lenin's foreign policy legacy
as representing an international version of the NEP,
namely to consolidate and strengthen the Soviet Union's
position before engaging in any radical policies to advance the cause of socialism internationally.
[DK266. S43]

1723   Semyonov, V. "The Leninist Principles of Soviet Diplomacy," Int Aff, 15, no. 4 (1969), 3-8.

1724   Sergiyev, A. "Leninism on the Correlation of Forces as
a Factor of International Relations," Int Aff, 21, no.
5 (1975), 99-107.

1725   Sevostyanov, I. "Leninist Scientific Foresight in Foreign
Policy," Int Aff, 17, no. 10 (1971), 60-67.

1726   Siskind, George. "Leninism--Guide to Unity for Peace,
Democracy, Socialism," Pol Aff, 29 (Jan. 1950), 4-13.

1727   Sovetov, A. "Leninist Foreign Policy and International Relations," Int Aff, 6, no. 4 (1960), 3-9.

1728   Tomashevsky, D. Lenin's Ideas and Modern International
Relations. Moscow: Progress Publishers, 1974, 288pp.
Not available for annotation. [D443. T5713]

1729   _____. "Some Questions of International Relations Research in Light of Lenin's Teaching," Int Aff, 16, no.
6 (1970), 72-79.
A comparison of Lenin's theories on imperialism, war
and peaceful coexistence with bourgeois theories.

1730   Tomashevsky, D. and V. Yefremov. "The Leninist Peace
Policy," Sov Mil R, no. 3 (Mar. 1975), 48-50.

1731   Trukhanovsky, V. "Leninist Policy of Peace and Cooperation
among Nations," Int Aff, 17, no. 4 (1971), 3-8.

1732   _____. "Lenin's Ideas and Contemporary International
Relations," Int Aff, 16, no. 4 (1970), 13-18.

1733   _____. "Proletarian Internationalism and Peaceful Co-
existence--Foundation of the Leninist Foreign Policy,"
in POLFP (anthology), 49-75.

A restatement of Lenin's foreign policy principles and a discussion of contemporary Soviet policy as being a response to the same general historical circumstances which Lenin faced. Abridged in Int Aff, 14, no. 11 (1968), 53-62.

1734 Vladimirov, V. and I. Orlov. "Socialist Foreign Policy Promoting Peace and Social Progress," in POLFP (anthology), 29-48.
A discussion of Lenin's principle that "socialism and peace are indivisible." The authors devote most attention to demonstrating that economic and military strength are essential, due to capitalist aggression, if the peaceful aspirations of the socialist nations are to be realized.

1735 Walsh, Sam. "Lenin--National and International Responsibilities," Com V, 2, no. 2 (Mar.-Apr. 1970), 40-44.

1736 Zisman, Georgi. "Peaceful Coexistence: Lenin's Concept, Today's Foreign Policy," Sov Life, 4, no. 209 (Apr. 1974), 4-5.

Cross-Reference: See also Proletarian Internationalism (IX-B-1).

B. Practice

1737   Akhramovich, R. T.   "Lenin and the Establishment of
        Friendly Soviet-Afghan Relation," in LANLIE (anthology),
        287-305.
        A positive account of Lenin's role in the 1919 recogni-
        tion, by the Soviet Union, of Afghanistan's declaration
        of independence and his efforts to develop close ties
        between the two nations as exemplified by the Febru-
        ary 1921 Soviet-Afghanistan Treaty of Friendship.

1738   *Akhtamzian, A. et al.   "Lenin's Foreign Policy Activity,"
        Int Aff, 15, nos. 1-12 (Jan.-Dec. 1969); 16, nos. 1-2
        (Jan.-Feb. 1970).
        A fourteen-part article surveying, in chronological order
        Lenin's foreign policy practice in the October, 1917 to
        March, 1918 period.

1739   *Andronov, I.   "Lenin's Ambassador in America," New
        Times, 17 (21 Apr. 1970), 28-32.
        A discussion of Lenin's contacts with Ludwig Martens
        who Lenin appointed in 1919 as an official representa-
        tive of the Soviet government commissioned to improve
        the Bolsheviks' image in America.

1740   Annenkov, Y. P.   "Lenin and the Deaf-Mutes: Some Un-
        published Notes," B Inst St USSR, 9, no. 5 (1962), 22-
        24.
        A commentary on notes by Lenin illustrating that his
        principle of peaceful coexistence was a scheme to dupe
        Western 'deaf-mutes' in regard to communism's real
        goals.

1741   *Aralov, S.   "On Lenin's Instructions," Int Aff, 6, no. 4
        (1960), 10-15.
        An account of how Lenin's support, in 1920, of peace
        between Russia and Poland was highly unpopular with
        Bolshevik military leaders who begrudgingly followed
        his instructions on this issue and later came to see
        their wisdom.

1742   *Babayants, A. A.   "Working for Peace and Defending the
        Revolution," in LR (anthology), 175-86.
        A discussion of Lenin's pursuit of peace with Germany

and other capitalist powers while building socialism in Russia. Babayants supports Lenin's argument that peace with Germany was essential since the continuation of war would only have played into the hands of the Bolsheviks' domestic and foreign enemies, and criticizes those (especially Trotsky) within the party who opposed Lenin's policy. He also reviews Lenin's military leadership during the Civil War in support of the claim that Lenin was "an expert in national defence, a military strategist and leader."

1743   Bailey, Sydney D. "Brest-Litovsk: A Study in Soviet Diplomacy," Hist Today, (Aug. 1956), 511-21.
In part, an assessment of Lenin's role in the negotiation of peace with Germany.

1744   * _____ . "Stalin's Falsification of History: The Case of Brest-Litovsk," Rus R, 14 (Jan. 1955), 24-35.
A critical review of Stalin's interpretation of his role and that of Lenin and Trotsky in the Brest-Litovsk negotiations with Germany.

1745   *Berzins, Alfred. "Lenin and Capitalism," in The Two Faces of Coexistence. New York: Speller and Sons, 1967; 1-40.
An exploration of Lenin's "cynical attitude towards capitalist nations and the methods he advocated for dealing with them." Berzins examines the policies pursued by Lenin in the years immediately after the October Revolution, and states that their success was due largely to Lenin's clever manipulation of the rivalries between capitalist nations. Lenin's manipulations, Berzins states, can be reduced to three dictates which he bequeathed to his successors: disseminate propaganda that Russia stands for peace and national independence, and that the capitalist nations stand for war and imperialism; conclude any treaty with any nation if by so doing the cause of communism will benefit; and use coexistence as a means of gaining economic assistance from the capitalist nations in the building of the Soviet economy and military machine. [DK63.3.B52] Excerpt in LDMORP (anthology), 45-51.

1746   Bezymensky, L. and N. Mtkovsky. "The Coexistence Policy--Early Beginnings," New Times, no. 11 (19 Mar. 1962), 6-17.
A discussion of Lenin's initiative (especially in regard to the Genoa Conference) in advancing peaceful coexistence with Western nations.

1747   *Bradley, J. F. N. "France, Lenin and the Bolsheviks in 1917-1918," Eng Hist R, 86, no. 341 (1971), 783-89.
An abridgment of a confidential report, to Georges

Clemenceau, assessing Lenin and the Bolshevik government so as to provide assistance to the Clemenceau government in determining French policy towards the Lenin regime.

1748   Browder, Earl. Lenin and Spain. New York: Workers'
        Library Publishers, 1937, 15pp.
        An address, delivered at a January 20, 1937 Lenin
        memorial meeting at Madison Square Garden, in which
        the speaker, an American communist leader, projects
        Lenin's feelings, if he were alive, both on the Spanish
        Civil War and Soviet policy towards it. [DP269.P25]
        Abridged in Communist, 16 (Feb. 1937), 112-19.

1749   Bullard, Arthur. "Lenin's Foreign Policy," in The Russian
        Pendulum. Autocracy-Democracy-Bolshevism. New
        York: Macmillan, 1919; 126-34.
        An examination of the dangers for Western nations posed
        by Lenin's policy of exporting revolution. Bullard sug-
        gests that the best way to counter this policy is not by
        military force, economic blockades, or propaganda
        campaigns, but rather by eliminating those conditions
        which make communism appealing. [DK265.B9]

1750   Bullitt, William C. "Lenin, a Living Legend," in LIOUS
        (anthology), 69-70.
        An excerpt, from a report to the U.S. Senate Commis-
        sion on Foreign Relations, by an emissary sent to Rus-
        sia in 1919, presenting a favorable image of Lenin.

1751   Buryakov, V. "Lenin's Diplomacy in Action," Int Aff, 18,
        no. 5 (1972), 92-97.
        A discussion of Lenin's role in determining Soviet policy
        at the Genoa Conference.

1752   *Carr, Edward H. A History of Soviet Russia. The Bol-
        shevik Revolution, 1917-1923, Vol. III. New York:
        Macmillan, 1953, 614pp., bib. 574-85.
        Lenin is not the focus of any one chapter in this widely
        acclaimed study of revolutionary Russia, but it con-
        tains significant discussion of the policy pursued by the
        Leninist regime towards the outside world.
        [DK266.C263]

1753   *Chicherin, Georgi. "Lenin and Foreign Policy," Sov Lit,
        no. 3 (1970), 72-78.
        A review, by the Commissar of Foreign Affairs under
        Lenin, of Lenin's involvement in foreign affairs, es-
        pecially his efforts to gain diplomatic recognition by
        Western nations.

1754   Chossudovsky, Evgeny. "Genoa Revisited: Russia and Co-
        existence," For Aff, 50, no. 3 (Apr. 1972), 554-77.
        In part, a discussion of Lenin's promotion of the Genoa
        Conference.

1755   *_____. "Lenin and Chicherin: The Beginnings of Soviet
       Foreign Policy and Diplomacy," Millennium, 3 (Spring
       1974), 1-16.

1756   *Clemens, Walter C. , Jr. "Lenin on Disarmament," Slav
       R, 23, no. 3 (Sept. 1964), 504-25.
       An assessment of Lenin's shifts in thought (1905-1923)
       on disarmament as tactical changes representing no real
       inconsistency in his foreign policy. Clemens states
       that Lenin always believed that peace and disarmament
       were strategies to be used to advance revolution.

1757   *Debo, Richard. "The Genesis of a Revolutionary Foreign
       Policy," in Revolution and Survival: The Foreign Policy
       of Soviet Russia, 1917-1918. Toronto: University of
       Toronto Press, 1979; 3-32.
       An analysis of Lenin's formulation, in 1917, of Bolshe-
       vik policy towards World War I, the Provisional Govern-
       ment, and the Western capitalist states. Debo states
       that Lenin developed the idea that the war should used
       to overthrow both the tsar and the bourgeoisie while in
       Swiss exile with little hope for its immediate applica-
       tion in Russia, but that with the February Revolution
       he quickly formulated a practical program of action
       consistent with this idea. Debo examines Lenin's at-
       tacks, upon returning to Russia, on the foreign policy
       of the Provisional Government and the moderate position
       of his fellow Bolsheviks, and outlines Lenin's thoughts
       on the foreign policy to be pursued after the revolution.
       Lenin is not the focus of any other chapter in this
       study, but it contains much additional information on
       his involvement in foreign affairs, especially in regard
       to his role in concluding peace with Germany.
       [DK265. D35]

1758   Dewhurst, Alfred. "Lenin--Peaceful Coexistence and Social
       Progress," Com V, 2, no. 2 (1970), 25-29.

1759   Fic, Victor M. "Lenin: Armed Exit," in The Bolsheviks
       and the Czechoslovak Legion. New Delhi: Abhinav
       Publications, 1978; 5-9.
       A brief review of Lenin's position on the 1918 exit from
       Russia of the Czech Legion.   [DK265.9. F52F5]

1760   *Fischer, Louis. "The Bolsheviks Make Peace," in The
       Soviets in World Affairs. A History of the Relations
       between the Soviet Union and the Rest of the World,
       1917-1929. New York: Vintage Books, 1960 (reprint
       of a 1930 publication); 3-49.
       Lenin is not focus of this chapter, but it includes a
       discussion of his role in the Brest-Litovsk negotiations.
       [DK63. F5]

1761   _____. "The Passing of Lenin," in The Soviets in World

Affairs. A History of the Relations between the Soviet
Union and the Rest of the World, 1917-1929. New
York: Vintage Books, 1960 (reprint of a 1930 publication); 341-44.
An estimate of Lenin's qualities as a statesman and
his legacy for Soviet foreign policy. Fischer states
that Lenin's basic foreign policy dictates were: to
exploit the divisions between the capitalist nations so as
to weaken the united front against Bolshevism; to appeal
to the capitalist powers in the name of economic advantage; to establish close ties with and assist national
liberation movements; and to maintain complete flexibility in tactics when pursuing any policy. [DK63.F5]

1762　"For a Talk with Lenin," W's Work, 43 (Feb. 1922), 348-
49.
A case for a conference with Lenin to consider establishing diplomatic relations between the Bolshevik regime and America.

1763　Gak, Alexander. "Lenin and the Americans," in A Symposium on the USSR. The First Fifty Years. New
York: National Council of American-Soviet Friendship,
1967; 37-43.
A general review of Lenin's interviews with various
Americans, his contacts with American workers, relationships with J. Reed and A. Williams, and his attempts to improve Soviet-American cultural, economic
and political relations. [DK266.A3F5]

1764　*Ginsburgs, George. "Neutrality and Neutralism and the
Tactics of Soviet Diplomacy," ASEER, 19, no. 4 (1960),
531-60.
An appraisal of the thought of Lenin and Stalin on the
place of neutrality in foreign policy as a means of
understanding better current Soviet diplomacy.

1765　Issaiev, V. I. "The Peril of Bolshevism: Why the Overthrow of Lenin is Necessary to Britain," RR, (June
1919), 199-219.

1766　*Jelavich, Barbara. "Lenin" in St. Petersburg and Moscow.
Tsarist and Soviet Foreign Policy 1814-1974. Bloomington: Indiana University Press, 1974; 291-332, bib.
458-64.
A useful general survey of Lenin's foreign policy principles and practices. Jelavich concludes that, in regard to the interests of the Russian state, Lenin's policies were a "complete disaster," but from the perspective of the Bolshevik Party's interests, they were highly
successful in defending the regime against foreign and
internal enemies and in developing the groundwork for
the spread of revolution in backward areas of the world.
[DK266.J4 1974]

1767   *Kennan, George F. Russia and the West under Lenin and
        Stalin. Boston: Little, Brown and Company, 1966;
        407pp.
        Lenin is not the focus of any one chapter in this schol-
        arly study of Soviet foreign policy, but it contains con-
        siderable and interpretive discussion of the policies he
        pursued toward Western nations. [DK63. 3. K38]

1768   Korablyov, Y. "Lenin's Decree," Sov Mil R, no. 2 (1971),
        34-37.
        A brief review of the importance and impact of Lenin's
        decree on peace.

1769   *Krasnov, Ivan. "Lenin, the U. S. A. and Peaceful Coexis-
        tence," in LIOUS (anthology), 12-24.
        A favorable survey of Lenin's efforts to promote normal
        and peaceful relations between Russia and America.

1770   Kulski, Wladyslaw W. Peaceful Coexistence. An Analysis
        of Soviet Foreign Policy. Chicago: Regnery, 1959,
        662pp.; bib. 623-38.
        The vast majority of this scholarly study of Soviet
        foreign policy deals with the years after Lenin's death,
        but it contains some discussion of his thought on na-
        tionalism, diplomacy, and world revolution as well as
        of the policies that he pursued as Soviet leader.
        [DK266. K8]

1771   "Lenin and His Socialist State," Cur Op, 65 (July 1918),
        9-11.
        A review of Lenin's relations with Germany, and specu-
        lation on the possibility of diplomatic recognition of
        Russia by President Wilson.

1772   "Lenin and Litvinov: First Steps of Soviet Diplomacy,"
        Sov Life, 2, no. 149 (Feb. 1969), 27.

1773   "Lenin in the Hour of His Greatest Peril," Cur Op, 68
        (June 1920), 753-55.
        An account of the difficulties facing Lenin over war with
        Poland.

1774   "Lenin on Peaceful Coexistence," USSR, 3, no. 4 (Apr.
        1960), 2-6.

1775   "Lenin on Poland," Ave Maria, 62 (18 Aug. 1945), 100.
        An attack on Lenin's statement that Russia had no in-
        terest in controlling Poland.

1776   "Lenin's Fight for Soviet Russia," Cur Hist M, 14 (July
        1921), 677-80.

1777   "Lenin's Peace Move," in LHIII (anthology), 49.
        A positive restatement of Lenin's decree on peace.

1778   Leonidov, A.   "Kremlin Documents," in LIOUS (anthology),
        223-24.
        A note on new documents which illustrate the difficul-
        ties encountered by Lenin in trying to establish relations
        with the United States.

1779   *_____.   "Lenin and Foreign Policy," New Times, no.
        1 (1 Jan. 1969), 3-6; no. 3 (22 Jan. 1969), 4-8; no.
        5 (5 Feb. 1969), 6-10; no. 7 (19 Feb. 1969), 10-13.
        A discussion of notes written by Lenin on foreign policy,
        most of which concern relations with America, the
        Genoa Conference, the Treaty of Rapallo, and the gener-
        al operation of the Foreign Affairs Commissariat.

1780   *Lubomirski, S.   "Lenin and Germany," Pol Ger, 11, nos.
        1-2 (1967), 14-20.
        An examination of Lenin's role in the peace talks which
        ended the war with Germany, and an attack on those
        who argue that Lenin was a German agent.

1781   Miller, A.   "The Origins of Leninist Eastern Policy," Int
        Aff, 18, no. 4 (1972), 68-75.

1782   "Our Hand or Fist for Lenine?," Lit D, 61 (12 Aug. 1919),
        9-11.
        A review of the pros and cons of American diplomatic
        recognition of Lenin's government.

1783   Pegov, N. M.   "Indo-Soviet Cooperation," LACW (anthol-
        ogy), 50-52.
        An address, by the Soviet Ambassador to India, to the
        All-India Youth Seminar paying tribute to Lenin's for-
        eign policy and discussing Soviet policy towards India
        as being consistent with Lenin's principles.

1784   *Petrov, V.   "Sources of Leninist Diplomacy," Int Aff, 21,
        no. 6 (1975), 107-14.
        A study of the relationship between ideological conflicts
        within the Bolshevik Party and the policies pursued dur-
        ing the months of negotiating the Brest-Litovsk Treaty.

1785   "Plight of the Allies between Lenin and Koltchak," Cur Op,
        67 (July 1919), 13-15.
        An account of how the equally negative images of Lenin
        and Kolchak led to a half-hearted Allied effort in sup-
        port of the White position during the Civil War.

1786   *Ponomarev, B. et al. , eds. "Lenin's Struggle for an Im-
        mediate Peace," in History of Soviet Foreign Policy,
        1917-1945. Moscow: Progress Publishers, 1969; 60-
        64.
        An account of the divisions within the Central Committee
        over whether to sign the Brest-Litovsk Treaty. The

editors summarize the positions of Trotsky, Bukharin,
and Lenin, and conclude that only Lenin's "unbending
will and insistence" prevented the Bolsheviks from
launching a disastrous revolutionary war against Germany. Lenin is not the focus of any other chapter in
this study, but it contains much information on his involvement in foreign affairs. [DK266.I7713]

1787   Radek, Karl. "Lenin as a Statesman," Rus Info R, 4, no.
4 (26 Jan. 1924), 52.

1788   Reed, John. "The War Is Ended! The War Is Ended!,"
in LIOUS (anthology), 51-55.
A restatement of Lenin's decree on peace, and a note on
its importance and impact. Excerpt from Ten Days
that Shook the World (see item 768). Also in Sov Life,
11 no. 158 (Nov. 1969), 33.

1789   *Reitzes, Robert S. "Marxist-Leninist Ideology and Soviet
Policies toward the United States, 1919-1939," Georgetown University, 1973 (dissertation).

1790   "Ring around Lenine," Lit D, 61 (10 May 1919), 14-15.
A statement on the 1919 opposition to Lenin's regime
by the White and Allied armies.

1791   Sayakh, H. "The Most Human of Men," Sov Mil R, no. 3
(Mar. 1970), 20-21.
A recollection of a December 1923 interview in which
Lenin criticized the Treaty of Versailles and the foreign
policies pursued by the major Western nations.

1792   *Schuman, Frederick L. Russia since 1917. Four Decades
of Soviet Politics. New York: Knopf, 1962, 508pp.
Lenin is not the focus of any one chapter in this study,
but it contains many references to his foreign policy
and its influence on that which was pursued after his
death. [DK266.S428]

1793   Spiro, George. "The Lenin-Caused 'Brest' Pogroms," in
Marxism and the Bolshevik State. New York: Red
Star Press, 1951; 801-14.
An attack on Lenin's Brest-Litovsk policy for causing
the Civil War and therein an "unprecedented anti-Jewish
terror." Spiro claims that Lenin was aware of the
fact that the Brest-Litovsk Treaty would lead to massive pogroms against the Jews who many believed were
responsible for Russia's plight, but did nothing to prevent or stop them except issue, in June of 1918, a
'hollow' decree against anti-Semitism. [JN6511.S6]

1794   Tilak, Lokmanya. "An Advocate of Peace," in LHIII (anthology), 4-5.

Support for Lenin's Brest-Litovsk policy, and a denial that he had any secret political dealings with Germany.

1795 "Trotzky and Lenin in Another Agony of Bolshevism," Cur Op, 64 (Mar. 1918), 167-69.
An attack on Lenin's support of the "disastrous" Treaty of Brest-Litovsk.

1796 Trush, M. "A Diplomat of the Leninist School (for the 100th Anniversary of the Birthday of G. V. Chicherin)," Int Aff, 18, no. 12 (1972), 66-72.
A review of Chicherin's relationship with Lenin and his pursuit of Leninist principles in Soviet foreign policy.

1797 * . "Lenin's Interviews with Foreign Correspondents," Int Aff, 13, no. 7 (1967), 62-67.
A discussion of the importance which Lenin attached to foreign public opinion, followed by a series of excerpts from some of his many interviews with foreigners, most of which concern the Civil War and foreign affairs.

1798 * . "Soviet American Relations as Viewed by Lenin," Int Aff, 20, no. 7 (1974), 13-21.
An account of Lenin's support for peaceful coexistence, economic cooperation and trade with the United States. Also in Sov Life, no. 1 (Jan. 1975), 52-53.

1799 *Ulam, Adam B. Expansion and Coexistence. The History of Soviet Foreign Policy, 1917-1967. New York: Praeger, 1968, 775pp.
Lenin is not the focus of any chapter in this study, but it contains many references to and short sections on his thoughts on and decisions in foreign affairs.
[DK266. U49]

1800 Von Wiegand, Karl H. "Lenin Urges Peace and Trade with the U.S.A.," in LIOUS (anthology); 24-26.
A recreation of an interview (1920), in which Lenin firmly indicated that he was opposed to the spread of communism through warfare and was in favor of peace and trade with America.

1801 *Warth, Robert D. The Allies and the Russian Revolution. From the Fall of the Monarchy to the Peace of Brest-Litovsk. Durham: Duke University Press, 1954, 294pp.
A scholarly study of wartime relations between Russia and the West which, though containing no separate chapter on Lenin, presents significant information on Western reactions to and assessments of Lenin and his relations with Germany. [DK265. W338]

1802 *Wesson, Robert G. "Lenin and Revolutionism," in Soviet Foreign Policy in Perspective. Homewood, Illinois: Dorsey Press, 1969; 21-93.

A scholarly examination of Lenin's early and simplistic approach to foreign relations and his gradual turn to a more traditional foreign policy as revolution failed to materialize in Europe. Wesson characterizes Lenin's initial concept of international relations as wildly naive in that he considered as unnecessary a foreign office or even official contacts with capitalist powers because world revolution was imminent, and reveled in making bold and crude statements about the West. Beginning with the Treaty of Brest-Litovsk, Wesson states, Lenin first demonstrated the characteristic which has become the mainspring of Soviet political behavior--interest in self-preservation, even at the expense of the world revolutionary movement, and a consequent desire for normal relations with the Western powers.
[DK63.3.W38]

1803   "What Lenine May Do at Genoa," Lit D, 72 (18 Feb. 1922), 12-13.

1804   *Williams, William A. American-Russian Relations, 1781-1947. New York: Rinehart and Company, 1952, 367pp.; 285-87.
This scholarly study does not contain a separate chapter on Lenin, but includes considerable discussion of his desire to normalize relations with America.
[E183.8.R9W63]

1805   *X. "Lenin: An Interpretation," Fortn R (Jan. 1920), 9-18. An assessment of Lenin with most attention given to his foreign policy. Lenin's foreign policy is seen as a militant one, but one which was opposed to spreading revolution by war, therefore making it possible for the Western nations to work with Lenin.

9. INTERNATIONAL SOCIALISM AND THE WORKERS',
REVOLUTIONARY, AND NATIONAL LIBERATION MOVEMENTS

A. Communist International

1806   *Aronowitz, Stanley. "Left-Wing Communism: The Reply
        to Lenin," in The Unknown Dimension. European Marx-
        ism since Lenin, Dick Howard and Karl E. Klare, eds.
        New York: Basic Books, 1972; 169-96.
        A defense of the "Council Communism" which Lenin
        attacked in Left-Wing Communism: An Infantile Dis-
        order. Aronowitz reviews the position of the Council
        Communists and Lenin's criticism of it, and concludes
        that the Council Communists were "direct descendants
        of the Marxian view of the proletariat as self-emanci-
        patory" and justified, from a Marxist perspective, in
        criticizing Lenin's voluntarism. He states that although
        Council Communist theory has its defects, particularly
        its simplistic view of workers' control and the opera-
        tion of social institutions, it nonetheless represents a
        healthy alternative to Lenin's perversion of Marxism.
        [HX36. H64]

1807   *Banchero, G. et al. "The Vanguard of the Masses," W
        Marxist R, 16, no. 10 (Oct. 1973), 25-39.
        A review of Lenin's Left-Wing Communism as part of
        a series of articles on the contemporary relevance of
        his major works.

1808   Banerjee, Subrata. "Lenin on Unity in the Struggle for
        Democracy and Socialism," Mainstream, 17, nos. 1-6
        (Jan. 1978), 109-14.

1809   *Beilenson, Laurence W. Power through Subversion. Wash-
        ington, D. C. : Public Affairs Press, 1972; 299pp. ;
        bib. 271-85.
        A critical presentation of Lenin as the world's "fore-
        most theorist-practioner of subversion. " Beilenson
        studies the similarities between Lenin's and past sub-
        version, and concludes that Lenin made three major
        changes in the opportunist and unsustained subversion
        of past centuries: he selected subversion rather than
        war as the chief tool to advance his ideology; he avoided

all offensive action that might jeopardize the security
of the subversive base; and he extended the horizons
of subversion to include every country on earth. Beilenson contends that "about general principles of political
power, Lenin was a mere imitator of Machiavelli,
Clausewitz and prior practitioners," but the extent of
his adaptation of subversion "virtually changed the tool."
[HX312. L43B43]

1810   Bloor, Ella R. "Lenin Is Here! Lenin Is Here!" in LIOUS
(anthology), 62-65.
A recollection, by an American communist, of Lenin's
great sympathy for the masses, as evidenced by his
address to an international labor conference in Moscow.

1811   Body, Marcel. "Reminiscences of the Third International,"
St Sov Un, 9, no. 1 (1969), 26-30.
A general account of Lenin's formation and leadership
of the Comintern.

1812   Childs, David. "Lenin's International," in Marx and the
Marxists. New York: Barnes and Noble, 1973; 109-14.
A brief review of the origins of Lenin's decision to
create a new international, and criticism of Lenin for
"his refusal to accept that his theories were, at very
best, products of Russian conditions, and relevant only
to those conditions." [HX36. C52]

1813   *Claudin, Fernando. "The Crisis of Theory," in The Communist Movement. From Comintern to Cominform.
New York: Monthly Review Press, 1975; 46-71.
An examination of the evolution of Lenin's thought on
the nature and imminency of world revolution. Claudin
discusses Lenin's belief that World War I should be
converted into a civil war bringing socialist regimes
to power in both Russia and the advanced capitalist nations, and then traces carefully his abandonment, after
1917, of faith in European revolution and his development instead of the theory that the world's backward
nations would be the scene of the next socialist revolutions while the capitalist states would have to wait for
a new world war to provoke revolution. Although this
study does not contain any other chapter on Lenin specifically, it does present valuable information on his
thought towards and influence upon world communism.
[HX40. C59813]

1814   *_____. "The October Revolution and the International
Communist Movement," Critique, 10 (Winter 1978), 5-
14.
An attack on Lenin's Bolshevization of the Comintern
as the cause of the world communist movement's failure
to serve as the vanguard of socialism.

1815   *Cliff, Tony. Lenin. Vol. IV. The Bolsheviks and World
        Communism. London: Pluto Press, 1979; 251pp.
        An analysis of "the efforts, the successes and failures
        of Lenin and the Bolsheviks in building a Communist
        International and in spreading revolution." Cliff ex-
        amines each of the major episodes in the 1919-23 course
        of the Comintern while tracing the ebbing of the revolu-
        tionary tide in the West and the "transformation of the
        Comintern into a mere appendage of the Kremlin's for-
        eign policy." Cliff notes a series of errors in assump-
        tion, theory, and policy made by Lenin in regard to
        European revolution, and argues that it is unlikely that
        Lenin made any more mistakes here than in dealing
        with Russian affairs but that whereas in the latter case
        his mistakes "were overcome by the sweep of the revolu-
        tion," in the former "each mistake ... was not made
        good by events, but accentuated by them."
        [DK254. L4C6]

1816   Deakin, F. W. and H. Shukman and H. T. Willetts. "Lenin
        and the War," in A History of World Communism.
        New York: Barnes and Noble, 1975; 43-45.
        A brief summary of Lenin's interpretation of World
        War I and his consequent disputes with the Second In-
        ternational. [HX40. D33]

1817   _____. "The Third International," in A History of World
        Communism. New York: Barnes and Noble, 1975;
        53-60.
        A non-interpretive account of Lenin's founding of the
        Third International and pursuit of ideological uniformity
        within it. [HX40. D33]

1818   *Dowson, Ross. "The Rise and Fall of the Third Interna-
        tional," in Fifty Years of World Revolution (1917-1967).
        An International Symposium, Ernest Mandel, ed. New
        York: Merit Publishers, 1968; 96-106.
        An examination of Lenin's creation and leadership of
        the Third International and of its degeneration, as an
        international organization, once the revolutionary tide
        subsided in Europe and the Bolshevik regime turned to
        consolidating its position at home. Dowson presents
        Lenin as the most ardent of internationalists in the
        Second International and as the spearhead of that group
        which sought to resurrect the revolutionary forces of
        Western Europe. He discusses Lenin's Comintern poli-
        cies, and stresses the point that Lenin's untimely death
        sapped the spirit of the Comintern and enabled Stalin
        to destroy it totally through pursuit of the policy of
        socialism in one country. [HX40. M256]

1819   *Dunayevskaya, Raya. "The Collapse of the Second Inter-
        national and the Break in Lenin's Thought," in Marxism

and Freedom from 1776 until Today. New York: Twayne, 1964; 167-76.

A discussion of the 1914 crisis in the Second International as the source for Lenin's break with the accepted interpretation of the Hegelian dialectic as a revolutionary process based upon the contradiction of "two units existing alongside of one another." Dunayevskaya states that this crisis led Lenin to redefine the dialectic as "the doctrine of the unity of opposites," a revision which became the philosophical basis of his reassessment of capitalist development as a means of explaining the chauvinistic behavior of the workers and their leaders. The author also discusses Lenin's application of his "new dialectics" to the question of self-determination of nations, using Lenin's interpretation of the 1916 Easter Rebellion in Ireland as a case study. [HX36.D8]

1820   *Fabsic, Jiri. "Lenin and the European Revolution, 1917-1920--a Re-interpretation," Manitoba, 1974 (dissertation).

1821   *Fainsod, Merle. "The Origins of the Third International, 1914-1919," Harvard University, 1932 (dissertation).

1822   *Florinsky, Michael. "Lenin and World Revolution," in World Revolution and the USSR. New York: Macmillan, 1933; 14-18.

An argument that Lenin, as early as 1914, was skeptical about the possibility of world revolution following a socialist revolution in Russia. Florinsky quotes from writings by Lenin prior to the October Revolution to prove that Lenin believed that the struggle between the world proletariat and capitalism would be "a slow and lengthy process" during which socialism would develop alone in Russia. [DK266.F56]

1823   Friis, J. "Lenin on Revolutionary Tactics Abroad," Liv Age, 306 (24 July 1920), 197-201.

1824   *Fuller, C. D. "Lenin's Attitude toward an International Organization for the Maintenance of Peace, 1914-1917," Pol Sci Q, 64 (June 1949), 245-61.

1825   Furnberg, F. "I Had the Pleasure of Seeing and Listening to Lenin," in WHML (anthology), 70-72.

A brief recollection of the impression made by Lenin's speech at the Fourth Congress of the Comintern.

1826   *Gankin, Olga H. "The Bolsheviks and the Founding of the Third International," SEER 20 (1941), 88-101. Also listed as Slavonic Yearbook, 1 (1941), 88-101.

1827   *Gankin, Olga H. and H. H. Fisher. The Bolsheviks and

the World War. The Origins of the Third International. Stanford: Stanford University Press, 1960 (reprint of a 1940 publication).
This collection of primary materials on the Bolsheviks' relations with the international communist movement does not contain a separate section on Lenin, but includes much information on his conflicts with various groups and individuals in the Second International. [HX11.I5G3]

1828 *Gruber, Helmut. International Communism in the Era of Lenin. A Documentary History. New York: Fawcett, 1967; 512pp.; bib. 499-502.
An introduction to Lenin's influence on international communism precedes a series of primary sources dealing with the creation of the Comintern, its role in promoting world revolution, and the establishment of Bolshevik control over the Comintern. An interpretive essay by a noted scholar accompanies each major section of documents. [HX40.G74]

1829 *Horton, John and Fari Filsoufi. "Left-Wing Communism: An Infantile Disorder in Theory and Method," Insurg Soc, 7, no. 1 (Winter 1977), 5-17.
A critique of the American left with much reference to Lenin's Left-Wing Communism.

1830 *Hulse, James W. The Forming of the Communist International. Stanford: Stanford University Press, 1964, 275pp.; bib. 251-64.
Lenin is not the focus of this scholarly study of the Comintern prior to its Second Congress, but it contains many references to and short sections on his writings and policies on international communism in the 1918-1920 period. [HX11.I5H83]

1831 *James, C. L. R. World Revolution 1917-1936. The Rise and Fall of the Communist International. Westport: Hyperion, 1973 (reprint of a 1937 publication); 118-40.
The major part of this study consists of a attack on the Comintern policies pursued by Stalin, but it contains significant information on Lenin's leadership in both Russia and the Comintern. James stresses that Lenin was able to exert a tremendous influence on the course of various events by way of the centralized political apparatus which he created. Unfortunately, this same apparatus which Lenin wielded in the cause of socialism served Stalin just as effectively in converting Lenin's international socialism into a perverted brand of national socialism. James concludes that the Third International, therefore, succumbed to the same disease which killed its predecessors--nationalism. [HX11.I5J25]

1832   Kalinin, M. I. "Lenin and Internationalism," in Marxism-
       Leninism on Proletarian Internationalism. Moscow:
       Progress, 1972; 277-79.
       A portrayal of Lenin as a leader who "while wholly
       absorbed in the Russian Revolution, never for a moment
       ceased to be an internationalist." [HX550.I5M3413]

1833   *Kautsky, Karl. "The Communist International," in Social
       Democracy versus Communism. New York: Rand
       School Press, 1946.
       A critical account, by a rival Marxist leader, of Lenin's
       motives in founding the Third International. Kautsky
       argues that Lenin's dictatorial party could not tolerate
       the democratic Second International and therefore Lenin
       devised an excuse for the creation of a new international
       organization to which would belong only parties that
       were Leninist. This new organization, Kautsky claims,
       won many supporters because of the prestige tempor-
       arily held by Lenin as the leader of the world's first
       socialist government, but that this popularity waned
       once the un-socialist nature of his regime became ap-
       parent and he began to extend his dictatorial methods
       to the Third International so as to make it a lifeless
       extension of the Bolshevik Party. [HX40.K35]

1834   Kolarov, V. "Lenin in Zimmerwald," in WHML (anthology),
       35-38.
       A recollection of Lenin's activities at and influence on
       the 1915 First International Socialist Conference against
       World War I.

1835   Kollontai, A. "The Voice of Lenin," in AL (anthology), 12-
       15.
       A recreation of Lenin's argument, amidst the collapse
       of world socialist opposition to World War I, that the
       war was an imperialist one that must be transformed
       into a civil war to advance the cause of socialism.
       Kollontai also discusses her actions in disseminating
       Lenin's interpretation of the war throughout Western
       Europe.

1836   Korsch, Karl. "Lenin and the Comintern," in Soviet Russia
       Masters the Comintern. International Communism in
       the Era of Stalin's Ascendancy. Garden City: Double-
       day, 1974; 44-48.
       A brief discussion of the difficulties Comintern mem-
       bers had in determining the true principles of Leninism
       amidst factional struggles within the Soviet Union and
       opposition to Leninism from European, especially Ger-
       man, Marxists. [HX11.I5G7]

1837   Landfield, J. "Lenin's Lying Legion," Review, 1 (13 Sept.
       1919), 380-81.
       An attack on Lenin's Comintern policies.

1838   *Lazitch, Branko and Milorad M. Drachkovitch. <u>Lenin and the Comintern</u>, Vol. I. Stanford: Hoover Institution Press, 1972; 683pp.
A comprehensive and scholarly study of the origins of the Comintern and the policies which it pursued under Lenin's direction in the 1919-1921 period. Beginning with Lenin's wartime disillusionment with the Second International, the authors trace the events that influenced him and the steps he followed in the creation of a new organization to promote the European revolutions which he believed would follow Russia's revolt. They examine carefully both Lenin's shift in Comintern strategy (once European revolution failed to materialize) away from stimulating proletarian revolution in the West and towards supporting national liberation movements in the East, and his 1921 shift from offensive to defensive, united-front tactics. Lazitch and Drachkovitch maintain that Lenin's Russification of the Comintern's organization and policies crippled its effectiveness as an international socialist agency, a claim which they support by demonstrating the incompatibility of Soviet national interests (as exemplified by the NEP) with those of the world revolutionary movement. [HX11.I5L338]

1838a   Reviewed in:
Am Hist R, 80 (Feb. 1975), 143-44, by T. T. Hammond.
Can Hist R, 55 (Mar. 1974), 117-18, by R. H. McNeal.
Can J Hist, 9, no. 1 (Apr. 1974), 106-08, G. D. Jackson.
Can J Pol Sci, 7, no. 4 (Dec. 1974), by R. Nordahl.
Can S P, 15, no. 3 (Fall 1973), 410-12, by W. Rodney.
Mod Age, 17, no. 1 (Winter 1973), 98-99, by G. P. Holman, Jr.
Pol Sci Q, 89, no. 1 (Mar. 1974), 238-39, by W. Lerner.
*Rus R, 32, no. 1 (Jan. 1973), by S. Hook.
Slav R, 32, no. 3 (Sept. 1973), 611-12, by H. Gruber.
SEER, 52 (July 1974), 476-77, by G. Stern.
Sov St, 26, no. 3 (July 1974), 453-55, by R. Kindersley.
TLS, (4 May 1973), 492.

1839   *Lindemann, Albert. "Lenin and the Problem of War," in <u>The "Red Years": European Socialism versus Bolshevism, 1919-1921.</u> Berkeley: University of California Press, 1974; 17-20; bib. 329-340.
A brief examination both of Lenin's analysis of the war and the polemics he launched against European socialists who he believed had betrayed the workers. In addition, this scholarly study contains many references to and

short discussions of Lenin's break with the Second International and his establishment and leadership of the
Comintern. [HX237.L54]

1840   *Lowe, Donald M. "Lenin," in The Function of "China" in
       Marx, Lenin, and Mao. Berkeley: University of Cali-
       fornia Press, 1966; 54-81, bib. 169-94.
       An analysis of the evolution of Lenin's thought on China
       from his early concept of a static, inferior nation, to
       his post-revolution concept of a revolutionary, demo-
       cratic one. Lowe identifies five phases in Lenin's
       thought, with Lenin's changing assessment of the nature
       of capitalism in Russia and Europe determining the
       nature of each stage. In general, the more Lenin ad-
       hered to classic Marxism, the less he was interested
       in China. [HX387.L6]

1841   *McInnes, Neil. "The Labour Movement. Socialists, Com-
       munists, Trade Unions," in The Impact of the Russian
       Revolution, 1917-1967. London: Oxford University
       Press, 1967; 32-133.
       Lenin is not the focus of this essay, but it contains
       significant discussion of his role in dividing the world
       labor movement by attempting to force it into a uniquely
       Russian mold characterized by his organizational prin-
       ciples and his dogmatic and "scientific" certitude on
       questions of practice and principle. [DK265.9.I515]

1842   McNally, Patrick. "Marxist Ideology and Soviet Economy,"
       St Sov Tho, 12 (Sept. 1972), 255-69.
       In part, a discussion of Lenin's internationalization of
       the class struggle as a means of having entire nations
       represent the bourgeoisie while others represent the
       proletariat so that the messianic role of savior is shifted
       from class to country.

1843   Minayev, L. M. "Lenin and Some Problems of the World
       Communist Movement," in LGT (anthology), 348-74.
       A Soviet survey of Lenin's various struggles against
       rival socialists in his attempt to create an effective
       international communist organization.

1844   *Nollau, Gunther. International Communism and World Re-
       volution. History and Methods. London: Hollis and
       Carter, 1961; 357pp.
       Although not specifically on Lenin, this scholarly study
       of international communism contains significant informa-
       tion on his leadership of the Comintern. [HX11.I5N514]

1845   Novack, George, et al. The First Three Internationals.
       Their History and Lessons. New York: Pathfinder
       Press, 1974; 207pp., bib. 205-07.

Lenin is not the focus of this study of the failure of
the first three internationals, but it contains considerable information on his involvement in the Second International and creation of the Comintern.   [HX11.I5N68]

1846   *Page, Stanley, W. Lenin and World Revolution. New York:
New York University Press, 1959; 252pp., bib. 245-48.
The author's stated purpose is to demonstrate that
Lenin, as "a revolutionary fanatic out to destroy the
existing order and build anew upon its ruins," was
possessed by "a demon-driven ego intent upon dominat-
ing the process of destruction and of rebuilding." Lenin's lifelong political behavior, Page argues, reveals
that he had "a compulsive need to dominate." Page
discusses Lenin's leadership of the international proletarian struggle in light of this contention. [HX40.P3]

1846a   Reviewed in:
Am Hist R, 65 (July 1960), 978, by R. Thompson.
Annals, 327 (Jan. 1960), 178, by R. Hare.
*Arch Eur Soc, 17 (1976), 366-83, by N. Harding.
Phylon, 21 (Winter 1960), 398, by J. B. McRae.
SEER, 4, no. 1 (Spring 1960), 85, by R. C. Tucker.
SEER, 18, no. 91 (June 1960), 578, by J. H. L.
   Keep.
W Pol, 12, no. 4 (July 1960), 621, by R. F. Byrnes.

1847   *_____. "Lenin's Assumption of International Proletarian Leadership," J Mod Hist, 26, no. 3 (1954), 233-
45.
A discussion of the evolution (1914-1917) of Lenin's
thought on the role to be played by himself and the
Bolshevik Party in Russian and world revolution.

1848   *_____. "The Russian Proletariat and World Revolution:
Lenin's Views to 1914," ASEER, 10 (1951), 1-13.
An examination of Lenin's belief that the Russian proletariat's "mission" was to spark and lead the world
revolution.

1849   Petrov, Andrei. "Lenin at the 3rd Party Congress of the
Comintern," Sov Life, 4, no. 151 (Apr. 1969), 34-39.

1850   *Plamenatz, John. "Leninism after the Revolution," in German Marxism and Russian Communism. New York:
Harper and Row, 1965; 261-66.
A brief examination of Lenin's thought on the failure of
communist revolutions to overturn European capitalism
in the years immediately following the Bolshevik Revolution.   Plamenatz states that Lenin never admitted that
his assessment of the European situation might be faulty
but instead blamed the European socialists for betraying
the cause. The author reviews Lenin's Left Wing Communism, an Infantile Disorder to illustrate both the na-

ture of Lenin's attack on social democracy and the tactics which he believed European communists should follow. [HX273. P45]

1851   Raja, C. Unni. "Lenin and the Comintern," in LAI (anthology), 179-91.
A sympathetic account of Lenin's founding of the Comintern, his struggles against opportunists within it, and his establishment of its general line and tactics on such issues as the national, colonial, and agrarian questions, relations with non-Marxist groups, and coexistence with bourgeois states.

1852   *Schlesinger, R. "Lenin as a Member of the International Socialist Bureau," Sov St, 16, no. 4 (1965), 448-58.
A critical appraisal of Lenin's role in the International Socialist Bureau (1907-1912), and an attack on Stalin's interpretation of Lenin's leadership of the Bureau.

1853   Sevryugina, N. Lenin's Struggle against "Leftism" in the International Communist Movement (1918-1922). Moscow: Novosti Press, 1966; 29pp.
A sympathetic presentation of Lenin's struggle within Russia and the Comintern against left opportunism. Sevryugina relies heavily on Lenin's works (especially Left-Wing Communism) to demonstrate the reckless, phrase-mongering nature of the leftists' position and to highlight the proper means to combat it. [HX11. I5S423]
Also in Lessons of History. Moscow: Novosti Press, 1965.

1854   *Skilling, H. G. "Permanent or Uninterrupted Revolution: Lenin, Trotsky, and Their Successors on the Transition to Socialism," Can S S, 5 (1961), 3-30.
An assessment of Lenin's thought on world revolution and of the applicability to world communism of the Bolshevik model of revolution.

1855   "Socialist Revolts against Lenin," Cur Op, 69 (Nov. 1920), 598-600.
A discussion of the havoc raised within the world socialist community by Lenin's Comintern policies and tactics.

1856   "Strategy of the World Communist Movement," in LAWRWM (anthology), 153-267.
A lengthy account of the Leninist policies and tactics being pursued by the contemporary international communist movement with less attention given to Lenin's founding and leadership of the Comintern.
[HX44. L39713]

1857   *Trotsky, Leon. "Lenin's Suppressed Speech on Ultra-Leftism," Int Soc R, 31, no. 3 (May 1970), 30-33.

A review of Lenin's June 17, 1921 speech on the ultra-leftism of Bela Kun, and an attack on Stalin's suppression of its publication. [HX11.I5T74]

1858 *_____. The Third International after Lenin. New York: Pathfinder Press, 1970; 346pp.
Lenin is not the focus of this study, but it contains numerous references to his Comintern policies for support for an attack on those pursued by Stalin. [HX11.I5T74 1970]

1859 Tyomkin, Y. "The Great Internationalist-Pages from Lenin's Life," Sov Mil R, no. 8 (Aug. 1969), 9-11.
A review of Lenin's anti-war policies and activities while in Swiss exile.

1860 Waltz, Kenneth N. "The Adjustment of Theory to Fact: Lenin," in Man, the State and War. A Theoretical Analysis. New York: Columbia University Press, 1969; 137-41, bib. 239-51.
A short assessment of Lenin's reaction to the failure of the European workers, at the outbreak of World War I, to behave in accordance with their class interests. Waltz maintains that Lenin believed that the workers had been duped by bourgeois patriots and betrayed by their own leaders and that the only possible way to set the workers' movement on the correct path again was through strong centralized leadership: "Lenin tended to emphasize ... the necessity for a leadership of inflexible will and to castigate the masses for failing to comprehend that their true interests lay in following it." [JX1308.W3]

1861 Weinstone, William. "Lenin and the Struggle against Opportunism," Pol Aff, 49, no. 4 (Apr. 1970), 24-35.
A review of Lenin's polemics against opportunism in the Second and Third Internationals in the 1915-22 period.

1862 *Weisbord, Albert. "The Third International under Lenin," in The Conquest of Power, Vol. 2. New York: Covici-Friede Publishers, 1937; 901-74.
An examination of the policies of the Third International against the background of the failure of socialist revolution to materialize in Europe. Weisbord discusses Lenin's motives in founding the Comintern as well as the problems which it faced in its infancy, and then turns to a detailed account of its Bolshevization at the Fourth Comintern Congress. [JA83.W4]

1863 West, James. "Lenin on Petty-Bourgeois Radicalism," Pol Aff, 49, no. 5 (May 1970), 19-27.
A positive assessment of Lenin's Left-Wing Communism.

1864 *Wilson, Edmund. "Lenin Identifies Himself with History,"
      in To the Finland Station. A Study in the Writing and
      Acting History. Garden City: Doubleday, 1953; 445-
      55.
      A discussion of Lenin's reaction to the collapse of Euro-
      pean socialism amidst the wave of patriotism which ac-
      companied the outbreak of World War I. Wilson states
      that although Lenin was at first incredulous and then
      bitter and disillusioned over the betrayal of the workers
      by their own leaders, he recovered his faith by identi-
      fying himself with what he believed to be an inevitable
      historical process leading to revolution in Russia and
      the rest of the world. [HX36.W5]

1865 *Wolfe, Bertram D. "A Party of a New Type. The Founda-
      tion Stone of the Communist International," in The
      Comintern: Historical Highlights. Essays, Recollec-
      tions, Documents, M. Drachkovitch, ed. Praeger,
      1966; 20-44.
      An examination of the Comintern's organizational prin-
      ciples as rooted in Lenin's 1900-1903 formation of "a
      party of a new type." Wolfe presents an image of
      Lenin as a virtuoso of organization and power: "Lenin's
      specialty was the how, rather than the why or what.
      Conspiracy, centralized organization, military discipline,
      the ability to stir, manipulate, and coalesce the sources
      of discontent for one's power purposes.... Here indeed
      was a revolutionist of a new type." The undemocratic
      system which emerged in both Soviet Russia and the
      Comintern, Wolfe states, were a consequence of Lenin's
      belief in the infallibility of his party, himself and the
      doctrine which he represented. [HX11.I5D65]

1866 *_____. "Life and Death of the Third International," in
      Marxism: 100 Years in the Life of a Doctrine. New
      York: Dell, 1967; 290-314.
      A critical examination of Lenin's Comintern arguing
      that it suffered from the same fatal flaw which had
      destroyed its predecessors--nationalism. Wolfe states
      that Lenin designed the Third International in the image
      of the Bolshevik Party (rigidly centralized, with con-
      cise organization and iron discipline) as a means of
      making it a more effective international organization,
      but that, in fact, this very design doomed it to failure
      because it was based on Lenin's narrowly Russian rev-
      olutionary experience. [HX40.W52]

1867 "World as Lenine's Oyster," Lit D, 67 (11 Dec. 1920), 26-
      27.
      An attack on Lenin's Comintern policies.

1868 Yaroslavski, E. "Lenin and the Struggle for the Communist
      International," Com Int, no. 3 (1939), 219-30.

1869   Yen-shih, Cheng, compiler. <u>Lenin's Fight against Revision-</u>
<u>ism and Opportunism</u>. Peking: Foreign Languages
Press, 1965; 275pp.; bib. 259-65.
A positive summary, by a Chinese Marxist, of Lenin's
many struggles against right- and left-wing deviations
from Marxism. Lenin's own writings constitute the
bulk of this volume, with the compiler providing historical background, introductions and short assessments.
[HX40. C5]

1870   Zetkin, Clara. "Lenin at the 3rd Congress of the Comintern," in <u>WHML</u> (anthology), 9-10.
A brief and favorable recollection of Lenin's address
to the Comintern's Third Congress.

B. Theory

1. Proletarian Internationalism

1871   Abdel-Hamid, Abu Aitah. "The Leninist Principle of Unity," W Marxist R, 15, no. 10 (1972), 32-34.

1872   *Azizyan, A. V. I. Lenin on Proletarian Internationalism. Moscow: Progress Publishers, n. d., 88pp.
A Soviet restatement of Lenin's teachings on the need for ideological unity within the world workers' movement; on cooperation among socialist states; coexistence between socialist and capitalist nations; and on support for national liberation movements around the world.
[HX40. A9513]

1873   Cunhal, Alvaro. "Proletarian Internationalism, a Policy and an Outlook," W Marxist R, 13, no. 5 (May 1970), 70-78.

1874   Fedoseyev, P. N., et al. "Leninism and Relations Between Socialist States," in Leninism and the National Question. Moscow: Progress, 1977; 259-70.
A Soviet summary of Lenin's principles on relations among sovereign socialist states stressing his belief that although the unity of socialist states is essential both to safeguard the gains of the revolution and to counter imperialism, this in no way justified interference in the internal affairs of a fellow socialist state.
[HX550. N3L48613]

1875   Henry, Ernst. "Lenin and the Fraternal Parties," W Marxist R, 15, no. 4 (1972), 33-42.
A tribute to Lenin as a great internationalist deeply concerned with world proletarian unity.

1876   Jespersen, Knud. "The Leninist Banner of Internationalism," in LITW-2, 131-39.
A restatement, by a Danish communist, of Lenin's principle of proletarian internationalism, and a discussion, in Leninist terms, of contemporary nationalism, workers' unity, and socialist military and economic cooperation.

1877   Konyukhovsky, V. N. "Proletarian Internationalism on the Line," in LR (anthology), 121-32.

A Soviet survey of the tactics pursued by Lenin in the
international workers' movement during World War I.
Konyukhovsky praises Lenin as the only Marxist leader
who remained faithful to proletarian internationalism by
way of his work in uniting the workers in a common
struggle against the imperialist war and for socialist
revolution.

1878   Manuilskii, D. Z.   Lenin and International Labor Unity.
          New York: Workers' Library, 1939, 31pp.
          Not available for annotation.

1879   *Marxism-Leninism on Proletarian Internationalism.   Mos-
           cow: Progress Publishers, 1972; 572pp.
          A short introduction to Lenin's views on proletarian
          internationalism and national liberation movements pre-
          cedes a collection of writings by Lenin and other Marx-
          ist leaders on international communism.
          [HX550.I5M3413]

1880   Moldovan, Roman.   "The Coordination of Plans--Main Method
          of Developing and Completing the Relation of Economic
          and Technical Cooperation Between the Socialist Coun-
          tries," in CFOLI (anthology), 155-64.
          A positive review of Lenin's teachings on international
          socialist cooperation and unity, and a discussion of the
          various political, economic, and cultural cooperative
          programs among contemporary socialist states.

1881   Nemes, D.   "Leninism and the Development of the Socialist
          World System," W Marxist R, 13, no. 1 (1970), 15-23.

1882   Nichamin, V. I.   "Leninist Principles on Relations Between
          the Socialist States and the Developing Countries," Ger
          For Pol, 9, no. 3 (1970), 22-33.

1883   Parsons, Howard L.   "Lenin and World Friendship," New
          World R, 38, no. 4 (1970), 86-91.

1884   Sedgwick, Peter.   "The Fate of Lenin's Isms," New Soc,
          15 (23 Apr. 1970), 693-94.
          A brief survey of the conflicting interpretations of Le-
          nin's teachings within the international Marxist community.

1885   *Semyonov, V. S.   "Lenin and Proletarian Internationalism,"
          in LGT (anthology), 375-91.
          A Soviet review of Lenin's principles on the relation
          between national and international revolutionary social-
          ism. Semyonov praises Lenin for steering world com-
          munism along a path between reckless adventurism and
          revisionist passivism; for opposing the export of revolu-
          tion by force; and for rendering to world revolution
          "every necessary material, political, ideological, cul-
          tural and military aid."

1886   Smitrenko, V. "Lenin's Idea of Internationalism," Sov Mil
        R, no. 3 (Mar. 1969), 12-16.

1887   Surovtseva, N. Lenin on Proletarian Internationalism. Mos-
        cow: Novosti Press, 1969; 46pp.
        A Soviet review of Lenin's teachings on proletarian in-
        ternationalism, and an argument for their relevancy for
        the contemporary international workers' movement and
        socialist world. [HD4854.S8713]

1888   Szydlak, Jan. "The Undying Leninist Ideas of Proletarian
        Internationalism," W Marxist R, 13, no. 2 (Feb. 1940),
        37-40.

1889   Tsedenbal, Iumzhagin. "Lenin's Ideas of Proletarian In-
        ternationalism Are Communists' Battle Standard," W
        Marxist R, 13, no. 4 (Apr. 1970), 73-77.

1890   Vlad, Constantin. "Internationalism, Sovereignty, and Pa-
        triotism," in CFOLI (anthology), 122-35.
        A positive assessment of Lenin's principles and policies
        on proletarian internationalism and the nationality ques-
        tion. Vlad stresses that although Lenin had great re-
        spect for national independence and cultures, he main-
        tained that nationalism was a temporary phenomenon
        which eventually would give way to a united, world so-
        cialist culture based on the equality of all peoples.

1891   *Weiss, Max. "Lenin and Proletarian Internationalism,"
        Communist, 20 (Jan. 1941), 18-34.

2.   National Liberation Movements

1892   *Adhikari, G. "Lenin on Roy's Supplementary Colonial
        Theses," in Marxist Miscellany. A Collection of Es-
        says, G. Adhikari, et al., eds. New Delhi: People's
        Publishing House, 1970; 1-30. [HX3.M34]

1893   Afanasyev, V., et al. "The Development of the National
        Liberation Revolution into the Socialist Revolution" in
        Fundamentals of Scientific Socialism. Moscow: Prog-
        ress Publishers, 1969; 153-59.
        A positive restatement of Lenin's views on permanent
        revolution, the alliance between the proletariat and the
        peasantry, and the relation between bourgeois-democratic
        revolutions and the national liberation and socialist move-
        ments. [HX44.A3613]

1894   *Agrawal, N. N. "Lenin on the National and Colonial Ques-
        tions," Indian J Pol Sci, 17, no. 3 (July-Sept. 1956),
        207-40.

1895   *Alexander, Robert J.   "Marx, Lenin and the Developing
         Countries," New Pol, 9, no. 2 (1971), 87-95.
         An analysis of Lenin's interpretation of Marxism as the
         root of Marxism's popularity among developing nations.

1896   Bagdash, Khalid.   "Lenin and the Struggle against Opportun-
         ism and Revisionism in the National Liberation Move-
         ment," W Marxist R, 13, no. 4 (1970), 92-97.

1897   Baratashvili, D.   "Lenin's Doctrine on the Self-Determina-
         tion of Nations and the National Liberation Struggle,"
         Int Aff, 16, no. 12 (Dec. 1970), 9-15.

1898   *Bender, Frederic L.   "Marxism East and West: Lenin's
         Revisions of Orthodox Marxism and Their Significance
         for Non-Western Revolution," Phil E W, 23, no. 3
         (July 1970), 299-313.

1899   Bhushan, Shashi.   "Lenin on the Anti-Imperialist Struggle,"
         in LACW (anthology), 24-27.
         A positive appraisal of the influence in Africa and Asia
         of Lenin's theory of imperialism.

1900   Bouhali, Larbi.   "The Lenin-Type Party and the Struggle
         for National and Social Liberation," W Marxist R, 13,
         no. 5 (May 1970), 4-11.

1901   Bryner, Cyril.   "Lenin and Three Worlds," Cur Hist M,
         20 (Feb. 1951), 65-69.
         A review of the place of Eastern and Western nations
         in Lenin's doctrine of revolution.

1902   *Duncanson, Dennis.   "The Triumph of Leninism," New Lu-
         gano R, 10 (1976), 2-16.
         An examination of the impact in Asia and Africa of
         Lenin's teachings on the national liberation movement.

1903   Dutt, R. P.   "Lenin on Colonial Liberation," in VILIL
         (anthology), 96-98.

1904   Dzaskoklov, A. and G. Kim.   "The Leninist Theory on the
         Unity of Revolutionary Currents," Int Aff, 15, no. 11
         (1969), 45-49.

1905   Fedoseyev, P. N., et al.   "Lenin Works on the Theory of
         the National and Colonial Questions in the Period after
         the October Revolution," in Leninism and the National
         Question. Moscow: Progress Publishers, 1977; 117-
         28.
         A Soviet summary of Lenin's theory that the national
         liberation and socialist movements must coalesce if
         they were to be successful in the backward areas of
         the world.   Fedoseyev also restates Lenin's argument

that socialist revolutions in the advanced imperialist nations would follow, not precede, revolutions in the colonial world. [HX550. N3L48613]

1906   Fyodorov, Vladimir. Newly Liberated Countries. Ways of Development. Moscow: Novosti Press, 1970; 125pp.
A Soviet discussion of Lenin's teachings on the reactionary nature of racism and colonialism; the fundamental characteristics of the national liberation movement; and the alliance between socialist and national liberation forces. Additionally, Fyodorov reconstructs Lenin's struggles against revisionist and opportunist interpretations of the national liberation movement and his war against neo-colonialist policy and ideology. [HX40. F35]

1907   Gafurov, B. G. "Lenin and the Liberation of the Peoples of the East," Int Aff, 16, no. 5 (May 1970), 35-40.

1908   _____. "V. I. Lenin, the October Revolution and the National Liberation Movement," in LARIE (anthology), 5-33.
A Soviet review of Lenin's doctrine on the national and colonial questions as one which ushered in "the era of the liberation of all peoples of the East from colonial oppression." Gafurov stresses the inspirational effect of Lenin's exposure of imperialism and his assertion that the national liberation and socialist movements must merge into one revolutionary current if they were to be successful.

1909   *Haithcox, John P. "The Roy-Lenin Debate on Colonial Policy--a New Interpretation," J Asian St, 23, no. 1 (1963), 93-101.

1910   Harmel, Michael. "Lenin and National Liberation Today," Labour Mo, 52, no. 4 (Apr. 1970), 182-83.

1911   Hutt, Allen. "Vital Spheres of Leninist Theory," Labour Mo, 14, no. 3 (Mar. 1932), 187-92.
A review of Lenin's teachings on the national and colonial questions.

1912   Iskrov, M. V. "Development of the Leninist Theory and Tactics of the International Working-Class Movement," in DORT (anthology), 293-327.
A Soviet restatement of Lenin's teachings on world revolution, national liberation movements, and proletarian internationalism, with much attention given to their impact in Third World nations.

1913   Jackson, James E. "Lenin and National Liberation," Pol Aff, 49, no. 5 (May 1970), 6-18.

1914   Karim, Ahmed. "Leninism and Some Problems of the National Liberation Movement," <u>W Marxist R</u>, 13, no. 3 (Mar. 1970), 62-65.

1915   Kartunova, A. I. "Lenin and the National Liberation Movement," <u>New Times</u>, no. 33 (1969), 13-15.

1916   Kharmis, S. and Y. Rozaliev. "Lenin and the National Liberation Movement," <u>W Marxist R</u>, 12, no. 12 (Dec. 1969), 20-25.

1917   Kim, G. F. "Lenin on the Strategy and Tactics of National Liberation Revolution," in <u>LANLIE</u> (anthology), 27-56. A positive survey of Lenin's views on and policies toward the national and colonial questions, and an attack on contemporary bourgeois interpretations of nationalism.

1918/9 *   . <u>Leninism and the National Liberation Movement</u>. Moscow: Novosti Press, 1970; 52pp. A Soviet survey of Lenin's teachings on the national liberation movement, its alliance with the world proletariat, and the various forms taken by its struggle for freedom. Kim also surveys the impact of these teachings among the backward nations of the world. [HX550. N3K5213]

1920   Lavrishchev, A. "The Soviet Union and the Developing Countries," in <u>LARIE</u> (anthology), 102-20. A discussion of Lenin's policy towards national liberation movements and newly created nations, and a review of Soviet faithfulness to it since his death.

1921   Lee, Vladimir. "Leninism and the National Liberation Movement," <u>Sov Mil R</u>, no. 4 (Apr. 1970), 44-46.

1922   <u>Lenin and Problems of the National Liberation Movement</u>. Moscow: Novosti Press, 1969; 133pp. Not available for annotation. [HX40. L38697]

1923   "Lenin on the Colonial Question," <u>Com R</u>, 1, no. 2 (Feb. 1929), 87-91.

1924   "Leninist Right of National Self-Determination," in <u>LHIII</u> (anthology), 54.

1925   Li, V. F. "Criticism of the Ideological Conceptions of Neocolonialism," in <u>LHIII</u> (anthology), 113-48. A defense of Lenin's doctrine on the national and colonial questions, and a critique of Western political scientists who attempt to counter it with " 'positive' conceptions of 'interpreting' present-day national liberation revolutions and of the 'revolution of growing expectations.' "

tions.'" Among the writers most criticized are C. Bowles, R. Emerson, C. Black, and G. Carleton.

1926   *Lowenthal, Richard. "Can Communism Offer an Alternative World Order? Some Lessons of 20th Century Politics," Encounter, 48 (Apr. 1977), 17-26.
A critique of the Leninist model for modernization of backward nations as one which is economically and militarily impressive but offers no equality or freedom.

1927   *Lunin, B. Lenin and the Peoples of the East. Moscow: Novosti, 1970; 110pp.
A positive report on Lenin's doctrine on the colonial question and its influence in on national liberation movements in Asian and Middle Eastern countries. As an example of the effectiveness of Lenin's teachings, Lunin discusses their role in the revolution, civil war, and construction of socialism in Soviet Central Asia. [DK254. L46L82]

1928   *Page, Stanley W. "Lenin: Prophet of World Revolution from the East," Rus R, 11, no. 2 (Apr. 1952), 67-77.
An examination of Lenin's replacement of Western Europe with the Eastern colonial world as the scene of socialist revolution. Excerpt in LDMORP (anthology), 37-44.

1929   Papawannou, E. "Lenin and Some Problems of the National Liberation Movement," W Marxist R, 13, no. 4 (1970), 26-32.

1930   *Pfeffer, Nathaniel. "Lenin and the Course of Colonial Communism," Yale R, 45, no. 1 (1955), 17-30.
An assessment of Lenin's support for Asian national liberation movements as a tactic to advance the appeal of communism.

1931   *Rashidov, S. R. Leninism--The Banner of Liberation and Progress of Nations. Moscow: Novosti Press, 1972; 109pp.
A report, to the International Scientific Conference on Socialist Transformations in the USSR and Their Significance, in which the speaker (First Secretary of the Uzbekistan Communist Party) discusses the worldwide impact of Lenin's teachings on imperialism, national liberation movements, self-determination of nations, proletarian internationalism, and the non-capitalist path to economic modernization. [HX312. L43R37]

1932   Reznikov, A. "How Lenin Fought Sectarianism in the National-Colonial Movement," in LARIE (anthology), 57-80.
A positive review of Lenin's 1920 struggle. at the Second Comintern Congress, against "petty-bourgeois views on the national liberation movement," especially those of Roy and Preobrazhensky.

1933 _____. "M. N. Roy's Deviation: Lenin's Fight against
Sectarianism in the National-Colonial Movement," Main-
stream, 8, no. 19 (10 Jan. 1970), 23-26; no. 20 (17
Jan. 1970), 22-24.

1934 Sehanavis, Chinmohan. "Lenin and the East," W Marxist
R, 13, no. 2 (Feb. 1970), 28-30.

1935 Shastitko, P. N. "Lenin's Struggle Against Sectarianism
and Dogmatism on the National-Colonial Question," in
LANLIE, (anthology), 57-82.
A sympathetic account of Lenin's struggle, at the Second
Congress of the Comintern, against "left-wing opportunism" and of the positive affect his polemics had upon
unity within the national liberation movement.

1936 Shatalov, I. "Leninist Foreign Policy and the National Liberation Movement," in LARIE (anthology), 81-101.
A brief summary of Lenin's teachings on imperialism,
national liberation, proletarian internationalism, and
peaceful coexistence, and a favorable account of the
spread of these principles throughout the world, in spite
of American opposition. Excerpt in Int Aff, 15, no.
(Jan. 1969), 70-76.

1937 Simoniya, N. "The October Revolution and National Liberation," Int Aff, 25, no. 12 (Dec. 1979), 60-67.

1938 Sobolev, A. "Lenin's Principles of Proletarian Internationalism and the Youth Struggle for Peace, Democracy, National Independence and Social Progress," in LYAWT
(anthology), 120-39.
An address to an international youth seminar calling
for the world's youth to follow Lenin's principle of proletarian internationalism as a means of promoting unity
among international progressive forces.

1939 Tyagunenko, V. "The Path Charted by Lenin," Sov Mil R,
no. 11 (Nov. 1969), 8-10.
A restatement of Lenin's principles on national liberation movements.

1940 Ulyanovsky, R. "Lenin and the National Liberation Movement," New Times, 16 (21 Apr. 1970), 8-11.

1941 _____. "Leninism, Soviet Experience and the Newly-
free Countries," Mainstream, 9, no. 43 (26 June 1971),
19-26.

1942 *Zevin, V. Y. "Lenin on the National and Colonial Questions,"
in LGT (anthology), 305-47.
A Soviet presentation of Lenin as the Marxist who made
the "most profound and all-round theoretical analysis"

of socialist, nationalist, and colonial revolutions. In particular, it is Lenin's uniting of the national-colonial movement with the socialist struggle against capitalism which Zevin sees as Lenin's single most important contribution to Marxist theory.

C. Influence

1. General

1943   Aluf, I. A. "Lenin on the Hegemony of the Proletariat and Present-Day Reality," Mainstream, 7, no. 32 (12 Apr. 1969), 32-36; no. 33 (19 Apr. 1969), 21-25.

1944   Andropov, Yu. V. Leninism Shows the Way Forward. Moscow: Novosti, 1964; 22pp.
A report, to the Central Committee of the CPSU commemorating the 94th anniversary of Lenin's birth, presenting Lenin as a beacon for world communism through his teachings on proletarian internationalism, national liberation movements, socialist construction and the leading role of the ideologically pure party.
[HX313.A6613]

1945   Bittelman, Alexander. "Lenin's Teachings and the Liberation of Humanity," Pol Aff, 31 (Jan. 1952), 1-11.

1946   *Bogdanova, K. F. and A. P. Yakushina, eds. Lenin through the Eyes of the World. Letters and Comments from Abroad. Moscow: Progress Publishers, 1969; 342pp.
A collection of nearly two-hundred letters, telegrams, notes and memoirs, the vast majority of which are from leaders and figures in the international workers' movement. The editors state that these writings represent "a minute fraction" of the worldwide documents on Lenin which "epitomize the great love felt by millions of people" for him. The writings typically illustrate Lenin's influence on the character, policies, and fortunes of various international workers' parties and organizations. Because of their brevity and vast number, these writings have not been listed individually.
[DK266.A3P5513]

1947   Danelius, G. "Leninism--Sharp Weapon of All Revolutionary Forces of Our Time," W Marxist R, 13, no. 4 (Apr. 1970), 9-13.

1948   *Desyalerik, V. and A. Latyshev. Lenin: Youth and the Future. Moscow: Progress Publishers, 1977; 241pp.
The authors' stated purpose is "to bring together, from

315

Lenin's works, unpublished material from archives and
numerous memoirs published in the U. S. S. R and abroad,
facts relating to Lenin's contacts with young foreign revolutionaries, to reveal the essence of the advice given
by the leader of the revolution to young fighters from
over twenty countries of the world. " The authors organize their selections under the following headings:
views on the revolutionary role of the younger generation abroad; contacts with young foreign revolutionaries
while in exile; work with the anti-militarist youth movement in Europe; advice to young revolutionaries on deviations from Marxism; and role in the formation of the
Young Communist International. [HX547. D4713]

1949 Fedoseyev, P. "Under the Banner of Unity of the Communist Movement," in Leninist Approach to Unity of
the World Communist Movement, Yu. Frantsov, et al.,
eds. Moscow: Novosti, 1970; 31-43.
A Soviet summary of the impact on world communism
of Lenin's founding of the Third International.
[HX13. L45]

1950 Hasan, Ziaul. "Lenin and the World Struggle," Link, 12,
no. 36 (19 Apr. 1970), 30.

1951 Henry, Ernst. "Lenin and Communists in Other Countries,"
Sov Lit, no. 4 (Apr. 1977), 28-30.

1952 Ho Chi-minh. On Lenin and Leninism. Moscow: Novosti
Press, 1971; 208pp. [DS557. A76H656]

1953 *Khvalebnova, O. A. and T. N. Sidorova. Lenin on Women's
Role in Society and the Solution of the Question of Wom-
en's Emancipation in Socialist Countries. Moscow:
Soviet Women's Committee, 1973; 375pp.
A collection of fifty speeches, delivered at a Moscow
international symposium dedicated to the centenary of
Lenin's birth, dealing largely with Lenin as a source
of guidance and inspiration for the international women's
revolutionary and liberation movements. Most central
to the speeches are Lenin's views on the role of women
in the revolutionary process; his attack on bourgeois
attitudes toward and treatment of women; his criticism
of those who saw the women's struggle as one against
the male sex instead of against the system which ex-
ploits them; and his policies as Soviet leader to advance
women's equality. [HQ1154. L4513]

1954 Labina, S. N. "Lenin on Socialism in Less Developed
Countries through the Non-Capitalist Path," Mainstream,
11, no. 11 (Nov. 1972), 26-28.

1955 Leninism and Modern Revisionism. Peking: Foreign Language Press, 1963, 20pp.

1956   "Leninism and the Historical Fallacy of Right and 'Left'
        Opportunism," in LAWRWM (anthology), 400-84.
        A general restatement, issued by the Institute of the
        International Working-Class Movement (Moscow), of
        Lenin's views on the basic qualities of the international
        revolutionary movement, and an attack on various con-
        temporary un-Leninist conceptions of this same move-
        ment.

1957   Leninism and the Revolutionary Transformation of the World.
        Moscow: Novosti Press, 1971; 256pp.
        Not available for annotation.

1958/9 "Leninist Concept of the World Revolutionary Process and
        the Bankruptcy of Its 'Critics,'" in LAWRWM (anthol-
        ogy), 127-52.
        A Soviet presentation of Lenin's principles, strategies
        and tactics as the foundation of the modern international
        working-class movement, and an attack on Lenin's critics
        and those socialists whose non-Leninist behavior has
        harmed the movement.

1960   Leninist Theory of Socialist Revolution and the Contemporary
        World.   Moscow: Progress, 1975; 448pp.
        Not available for annotation.   [HX44. L3975613]

1961   Leonidov, A.   "Lenin and the International Working-Class
        Movement," New Times, no. 17 (27 Apr. 1969), 3-5;
        no. 18 (1 May 1969), 11-14.

1962   Lesechko, M., et al.   Leninism and the Socialist Commu-
        nity.   Moscow: Novosti Press, 1969; 85pp.
        Not available for annotation.   [HC244. L44]

1963   Mathur, Girish.   "Lenin's 'Magic Way,'" Yojana, 21, no.
        10 (Nov. 1977), 9-11.
        A discussion of Lenin's immemse popularity throughout
        the world socialist community because of his belief that
        the socialist state and economy should be run by the
        workers themselves.

1964   Novoseltsev, E.   "Leninist Policy and the Revolutionary Re-
        newal of the World," Int Aff, 17, no. 5 (May 1971), 9-
        18.

1965   Offiong, Daniel.   "The Proletarian Revolution and the Inter-
        national Energy Crisis: A Third World View," West
        Geo Col R, no. 7 (1974), 11-19.
        In part, a discussion of Lenin's belief that the world
        socialist revolutionary movement would grow as a con-
        sequence of an energy crisis to be faced by the capital-
        ist nations in the near future.

1966   "Reliable Compass of the Revolutionary Movement," New

Times, no. 2 (13 Jan. 1970), 15-18.
A review of the symposium "Leninism and the World
Revolutionary Working-Class Movement."

1967   Ta-Chao, Li. "Lenin Is Immortal," in Marxism-Leninism
        on Proletarian Internationalism. Moscow: Progress,
        1972; 424-26.
        A tribute to Lenin as "the best friend of weak and small
        nations" and a devoted servant of the oppressed of the
        world. [HX550.I5M3413]

1968   Wilkinson, Paul. "Lenin's Antipolitik: A Centenary Re-
        appraisal of Lenin's Impact on the World Communist
        Movement," Contemp R, 217 (July 1970), 1-6.

1969   World Peace Council. Presidential Committee Meeting.
        Lenin Centenary. Helsinki: World Peace Council In-
        formation Center, 1970; 23pp.
        A review of the proceedings of the April, 1970 meeting
        of the World Peace Council which stressed the inter-
        national relevance of Lenin's teachings, especially in
        regard to imperialism, disarmament, and unity in the
        struggle for peace and national independence.
        [JX1907.W675 1970]

1970   Zaradov, Konstantin. "Leninism and the Revolutionary Re-
        newal of the World," W Marxist R, 21, no. 4 (Apr.
        1978), 17-26.

                    2.   Western World

a.   General

1971   Cogniot, Georges. "Lenin and the Communist Parties of
        the West," New Times, no. 17 (26 Apr. 1967), 13-16.

1972   _____. "Leninism and the Destiny of Europe," Int Aff,
        16, no. 5 (May 1970), 29-34.
        A contrast of the unity among those groups and nations
        following Lenin's teachings, with the disunity plaguing
        Western nations due to problems caused by imperialism.

1973   Hyde, Douglas. "The Eurocommunists and Lenin," Month,
        11 (June 1978), 207-08.
        A discussion of the Eurocommunists' abandonment of
        Leninism as a sign of its irrelevancy to societies with
        democratic traditions.

1974   *Jowitt, Kenneth. "Inclusion and Mobilization in European
        Leninist Regimes," W Pol, 28, no. 1 (Oct. 1975), 69-
        97.

An examination of the tasks, strategies, structures and ideological justification of Leninist-type regimes in Europe.

1975   "Lenin Yes, Moscow No!," Economist, 235 (18 Apr. 1970), 20.
An account of European communists' rejection, in Lenin's name, of the leadership of Moscow.

1976   Minor, Robert. "Lenin--His Meaning for Us Today," Communist, 18 (Jan. 1939), 25-31; (Feb.), 114-27.
A review of Lenin's teachings on imperialism and peaceful coexistence for support for the European communists' popular front against fascism.

1977   Norlund, I. B. "Leninism and Some Problems of the Labor Movement in Smaller Countries," W Marxist R, 13, no. 2 (Feb. 1970), 45-48.

1978   Weber, H. "Eurocommunism, Socialism and Democracy," New Left R, 10, no. 1 (July 1978), 3-14.
In part, a discussion of the revision, by European communists, of Lenin's theses on the state, bourgeois democracy, and the dictatorship of the proletariat.

b. Americas

1979   Allen, James S. "Lenin and the American Negro," Communist, 13 (Jan. 1934), 53-61.

1980   Alvarado, Huberto. "The Guatemalan Revolution and Lenin's Ideas," W Marxist R, 13, no. 12 (Dec. 1970), 26-31.

1981   Amis, B. D. "For a Strict Leninist Analysis on the Negro Question," Communist, 11 (Oct. 1932), 944-49.

1982   *Aptheker, Herbert. "Lenin, National Liberation, and the United States," in LIOUS (anthology), 159-67.
A favorable discussion of Lenin's views and writings on the conditions of Blacks both in America and under colonial rule.

1983   Arevalo, O. "Leninism and the Revolutionary Movement in Argentina," New Times, no. 12 (24 Mar. 1970), 16-18.

1984   Becerra, Longino. "Leninism and the Topical Problems of Revolutionary Struggle in Latin America," W Marxist R, 13, no. 3 (Mar. 1970), 44-46.

1985   Bittelman, Alexander. "For Leninism--For a Soviet America," Communist, 14 (Jan. 1935), 6-22.

1986   . "The Triumph of Lenin's Teachings," <u>Pol Aff</u>,
    30 (Jan. 1951), 38-53.
    A positive appraisal of Lenin's teachings on the leading
    role of the proletariat in democratic movements, and
    an argument that American workers should adopt Le-
    ninism.

1987 "Black Americans on Lenin," in <u>LIOUS</u> (anthology), 167-72.
    Comments by three Black Americans (W. E. B. DuBois,
    W. Domingo, and Claude McKay) on the favorable reac-
    tion to Leninism within the Black community.

1988 Boggs, James and Grace Boggs. "The Role of the Van-
    guard Party," in <u>LT</u> (anthology), 9-24.
    An argument that Lenin's organizational ideas are ap-
    plicable to the American Black revolutionary movement
    since it is plagued by the same ideological division and
    lack of discipline and professionalism which confronted
    Lenin in turn of the century Russia.

1989 Boldyrev, Sergei and Alexei Grechukhin. "Staunch to the
    End," in <u>LCIA</u> (anthology), 294-313.
    A description of the 1921 impression made by Lenin
    on American radical William Z. Foster, and how after-
    wards Foster was inspired to read all of Lenin's major
    works and to join the American Communist Party. The
    authors quote Foster as having said: "I am grateful
    to Lenin ... after my more than twenty years of search-
    ing, he put me on a solid revolutionary footing."

1990 Buck, Tim. "Lenin--A Man for All Time" in <u>Lenin and
    Canada. His Influence on Canadian Political Life.</u>
    Toronto: Progress Books, 1970; 93-113.
    A centennial address, to the Twentieth Convention of
    the Communist Party of Canada, reviewing Lenin's ac-
    complishments and discussing his lessons for the world
    revolutionary movement. [HX102. B8]

1991 *   . <u>Lenin and Canada. His Influence on Canadian
    Political Life.</u> Toronto: Progress Books, 1970; 133pp.
    A positive account of Lenin's influence on the formation
    and development of the Communist Party of Canada.
    Buck states that the Canadian workers' movement was
    divided and disillusioned prior to the October Revolu-
    tion, but as Lenin's successes and writings became
    known the movement became far better organized and
    more purposeful in its actions. Buck also discusses
    the disunity which returned to the party during its strug-
    gle against Trotskyism and the party's recovery through
    its adherence to Leninist teachings on party unity and
    ideological purity. Buck appends to this study several
    of his speeches and writings on Lenin. These have
    been annotated individually and listed under the proper
    subject heading. [HX102. B8]

1992   . "New Level of Struggle for Freedom, Peace and Socialism," in Lenin and Canada. His Influence on Canadian Political Life. Toronto: Progress Books, 1970; 120-26.
An argument that the North American Workers' movement is moving towards Leninist ideals as it becomes increasingly hostile to capitalism. Buck projects that the oppressed minorities, anti-imperialist and women's movements will coalesce into a revolutionary force following Lenin's principles, strategies, and tactics. [HX102.B8]

1993 Castro, Fidel. Lenin's Ideas--Our Lodestar. Moscow: Novosti Press, 1970; 44pp.
Not available for annotation. [F1788.2 1970.C38]

1994 Colman, Gustavo. "Lenin's Immortal Ideas and Our Guiding Star," W Marxist R, 13, no. 3 (Mar. 1970), 28-31.

1995 Dangulov, S. "Friend," in AL (anthology), 124-34.
A creative account, based on documents and recollections, of Lenin's relationship with and influence on American communist John Reed.

1996 *DeGrood, David H. "Lenin and the New Left," in Consciousness and Social Life. Amsterdam: Grüner, 1976; 57-94.
An attack on the American "New Left" for its unorganized and adventuristic nature, and an argument for the creation of a Leninist revolutionary movement in America. DeGrood examines the roots of the "New Left," isolates its leading deficiencies (anarchistic, chaotic, opportunistic, and fragmented), and provides a Leninist prescription for a cure for its many ills. [B804.D34]

1997 Dickman, Jose. "Lenin's Ideas Help the Working-Class People of Chile," W Marxist R, 13, no. 3 (Mar. 1970), 7-9.

1998 *Drabkina, Yelizaveta. "Poet and Chronicler of the Revolution," in LCIA (anthology), 204-33.
A review of John Reed's relationship with Lenin and a favorable assessment of Reed's writings on the October Revolution.

1999 Fendel, J. "Lenin and the American Labor Movement," Workers Mo, 5 (Apr. 1926), 256-58; (May 1926), 319-22.

2000 Foner, Philip S. "Lenin and the American Working-Class Movement," in LIOUS (anthology), 121-32.
A positive account of the impact on American laborers

of Lenin's teachings, especially on party organization,
unity, and the Black liberation movement.

2001   Foster, William Z. "The First Time I Saw Lenin," in
        LIOUS (anthology), 57-58.
        A recollection of the deep impression made by Lenin
        on the author at the Third Congress of the Comintern.

2002   _____. "Leninism and Some Practical Problems of the
        Post-War Period," Pol Aff, 25 (Feb. 1946), 99-109.
        An argument for the study, by American communists,
        of Lenin's teachings on party organization, imperialism
        and socialist unity.

2003   Franklin, R. "How Viable Is a Leninist Organization in
        Canada?," Can Dim, 7 (Dec. 1970), 51-54.

2004   Freeman, Harry. "Rockwell Kent on Lenin," in LIOUS
        (anthology), 91-92.
        An account of an interview, with the Chairman of the
        National Council of American-Soviet Friendship, on the
        Lenin Centenary and Lenin's influence on American
        youth.

2005   *Gardner, Virginia. "John Reed and Lenin: Some Insights
        Based on the Manuscript Collection at Harvard," Sci
        Soc, 31, no. 4 (1967), 388-403.

2006   *Geschwender, James A. "Marxist-Leninist Organization:
        Prognosis among Black Workers," J Black S, 8, no.
        3 (Mar. 1978), 279-98.
        A case study of the influence of Lenin's concept of
        party organization on the League of Revolutionary Black
        Workers.

2007   Glaberman, Martin. "Toward an American Revolutionary
        Perspective," Insurg Soc, 4, no. 2 (Winter 1974), 21-
        35.
        An argument that the misunderstanding, by American
        workers, of Lenin's What Is to Be Done? is a major
        cause of the lack of participation by laborers in the
        American radical movement.

2008   Hall, Gus. "Lenin's Letter to U.S. Workers," in LITW-2
        (anthology), 240-48.
        A review of Lenin's "Letter to American Workers,"
        and a claim that the letter has recently grown in stature
        among American laborers.

2009   Hansen, Joseph. The Leninist Strategy of Party Building.
        New York: Pathfinder Press, 1979; 608pp.
        Lenin is not the focus of this study of the strategy and
        tactics to be followed by the Latin American revolution-

ary movement (part of a debate, 1968-1978, within the Fourth International), but it contains considerable discussion of his theory of revolution and Trotsky's faithfulness to it. [HX110.5.A6H35]

2010   Haywood, Harry. "The Struggle for the Leninist Position on the Negro Question in the USA," Communist, 12 (Sept. 1933), 888-901.

2011   Hunter, Allen and Linda Gordon. "Feminism, Leninism and the U.S.: A Comment," Rad Amer, 13, no. 5 (Sept.-Oct. 1979), 29-36.

2012   Ivanov, Robert. "Lenin on America," Sov Life, no. 4 (Apr. 1970), 42-43.

2013   Jerome, V. J. "Lenin and Opportunism in the American Labor Movement," Pol Aff, 28 (Jan. 1949), 1-15.
A critique of the policies of the AFL-CIO with much reference to Lenin's struggle against Economism.

2014   Kashtan, William. "In the Light of Lenin's Teachings," in LITW-2 (anthology), 180-92.
A defense of Lenin, by a Canadian communist, against bourgeois critics who argue that his teachings are an out-dated, uniquely Russian philosophy.

2015   _____. "Lenin's Teachings--A Dependable Compass," W Marxist R, 13, no. 5 (May 1970), 11-16.
A report on the influence in Canada of Lenin's views on the peaceful path to socialism.

2016   *Klehr, Harvey. "Lenin on American Socialist Leaders and Samuel Gompers," Labor H, 17, no. 2 (1976), 265-70.
A survey of Lenin's opinion of Debs, Haywood, Gompers, and other American labor leaders. Klehr notes that Lenin was particularly critical of Gompers and, in fact, misrepresented many of Gompers' views and accomplishments.

2017   *_____. "Leninism, Lewis Corey, and the Failure of American Socialism," Labor H, 18, no. 1 (1977), 249-56.
A discussion of Corey's misassessment of the weaknesses of American radicalism as a consequence of his adherence to Lenin's teachings on the aristocracy of labor.

2018   *_____. "Leninism and Lovestoneism," St Comp Com, 7, nos. 1-2 (Spring-Summer, 1974), 3-20.
An argument that the influence of Lenin's ideas on monopoly capitalism upon American communist leader Jay Lovestone was responsible for the latter's faulty assessment of the American labor movement.

2019 *   . "Leninist Theory in Search of America," Polity, 9, no. 1 (Fall 1976), 81-96.
An examination of Lenin's shifting views of American capitalism, imperialism, and labor in the 1912-1920 period.

2020 Kryukov, Nikolay. "The Soviet Ship 'Shilka' in Seattle," in LIOUS (anthology), 132-40.
A history of the secret letter sent (1918) to Lenin by Seattle dockworkers requesting reliable information about the October Revolution and the Soviet political system.

2021/2 "Lenin on the Struggle for Genuine Political Consciousness: A Basic Lesson for American Labor Today: An Editorial," Pol Aff, 26 (Jan. 1947), 3-7.
A plea to American workers to abandon the leadership of the AFL-CIO and to follow Lenin's teachings.

2023 "Lenin's 'Free Tom Mooney' Demonstration," in LIOUS (anthology), 150-51.
An account of fearful American reaction to press releases about a rally in Petrograd, allegedly led by Lenin, in support of Tom Mooney who was under a death sentence in connection with a bombing in San Francisco.

2024 Losovsky, A. Lenin: The Great Strategist of the Class War. Chicago: Trade Union Educational League, 1924; 44pp.
An attempt to present the basics of Leninism in simple terms as a guide to American workers. [HD4676.Z49]

2025 McAfee, Kathy, et al. "Leninism and Forms of Organization," Rad Amer, 13, no. 1 (Jan. 1979), 52-59.
An application of Lenin's organizational precepts to the radical movement in America.

2026 Mason, Daniel. "He Changed the World," in LIOUS (anthology), 5-11.
A forward to the anthology Lenin's Impact on the United States.

2027 Menashe, Louis. "The Relevance of Leninism," Liberation, 14, no. 4 (July 1969), 22-25.
A positive appraisal of Leninism's relevancy for contemporary American radicalism.

2028 Minor, Robert. "With Lenin," in WHML (anthology), 63-69.
A recollection of conversations with Lenin, 1918-1921, on the Comintern and American communism. Minor also gives his impression of Lenin's character and personality.

2029   Nepomnyashchy, Karl.   "Workers' Heroine," in LCIA (an-
          thology), 280-93.
          An account of American communist Elizabeth Flynn's
          great admiration for Lenin and her pursuit of a Leninist
          course in the American workers' movement.

2030   North, Joseph.   "An American Reflects on Lenin," Pol Aff,
          48, no. 7 (July 1969), 17-31.
          A recollection, by an American Marxist, of first en-
          counters with Lenin through his writings and descrip-
          tions of him by J. Reed and E. Bloor, and a descrip-
          tion of Lenin as the most formative influence in the
          author's life.

2031   *O'Brien, Jim.   "American Leninism in the 1970's," Rad
          Amer, 11-12 (Nov.-Feb. 1977-78), 27-62.

2032   Petrov, Pyotr.   "Lenin's 'Letter to the American Workers,'"
          Sov Life, 12, no. 150 (Dec. 1969), 44-45.

2033   Powell, Angela.   "American Leninism," Rad Amer, 12,
          no. 4 (July 1978), 71-73.
          A description of the author's difficulties in attempting
          to apply Lenin's teachings on organization to the Ameri-
          can radical movement.   (A response to J. O'Brien's
          article, item 2031).

2034   Prestes, L. C.   "Lenin's Heritage and the Fight against
          Opportunism in the Brazilian Communist Party," W
          Marxist R, 13, no. 11, 10-17.

2035   Ramm, Hartmut.   "Che Guevara: Leninist," Soc Praxis,
          3, no. 3 (1975), 261+.

2036   *_____.   "Leninizing Guevara: Foquismo I," in
          The Marxism of Regis Debray. Lawrence: Regents
          Press of Kansas, 1978; 1-38, bib. 221-30.
          A critique of Debray's attempt to synthesize the thought
          and actions of Lenin and Che Guevara.   Ramm contends
          that Debray's "synthesis" is deficient in many respects:
          "Debray affirms Leninist methodology but ignores Lenin's
          class analysis; dilutes the objective conditions required
          by Lenin for beginning an insurrection" in order to ac-
          comodate Guevara's stress on subjective factors; dis-
          cards the Leninist party; and, as opposed to both Lenin
          and Guevara, allows for non-socialist participation in
          the revolutionary movement.   Ramm concludes that if
          the Cuban Revolution and Guevara are to be intergrated
          with Leninism, a better way must be found.
          [HX263.D38R35]

2037   *_____.   "Orthodox Leninism: No Foquismo II," in The
          Marxism of Regis Debray. Lawrence: Regents Press
          of Kansas, 1978; 127-46.

An examination of Debray's "rediscovery" of Leninism while in Bolivian imprisonment. Ramm contends that Debray began to make concessions to Leninism from the time of his Bolivian trial and that gradually he returned to Lenin's teachings on both party organization and the prerequisites for revolution (thereby repudiating Guevaraism) after three years of prison life.
[HX263.D38R35]

2038   *_____. "The Political Philosophy of Regis Debray: Between Lenin and Guevara," Florida State University, 1974 (dissertation).

2039   Reid, Willard S. "Lenin vs. Bernstein: The Peruvian Case," University of North Carolina, Chapel Hill, 1974 (dissertation).

2040   Schwarz, F. "Chile--Lenin's Tragic Triumph," Presb J (14 Nov. 1973), 10-11.

2041   *Shields, Art. "The Story behind Lenin's 'Letter to American Workers,'" Pol Aff, 46, no. 1 (Jan. 1970), 1-12.

2042   Travin, Pyotr. "How Lenin's Letter Was Delivered," in LIOUS (anthology), 118-20.
An account of the circumstances surrounding the delivery of Lenin's "Letter to American Workers."

2043   Vasquez, Alvaro. "Leninism and Colombia's Revolutionary Path," W Marxist R, 13, no. 2 (Feb. 1970), 18-21.

2044   Walsh, Sam. "Lenin--National and International Responsibilities," Com V, 2, no. 2 (1970), 40-44.
A Leninist assessment of the impact of the Quebec separatism on the Canadian workers' movement.

2045   Wolfe, Bertram D. "Towards Leninism," Workers Mo, 6 (Jan. 1927), 675-80.
A discussion of the progress made by American communists towards Leninism, especially in regard to party organization and cooperation with the labor unions.

2046   Wolfe, Bertram D. and Jack Stachel. "Lenin, the American Working Class and Its Party," Workers Mo, 5 (Feb. 1926), 154-60.

2047   *Wright, M. "The National Question: A Marxist Critique," Black Sch, 5, no. 5 (Feb. 1974), 43-52.
A positive appraisal of Lenin's doctrine on the national and colonial questions and its relevance for Afro-Americans.

c. British Isles

2048   Arnot, R. Page. "Lenin and British Labour Today," Labour Mo, 52, no. 4 (Apr. 1970), 173-76.

2049   Bell, Thomas. "Remembrance of Lenin," in WHML (anthology), 39-47.
A recollection of a 1921 conversation with Lenin on the
communist movement in England. Bell also includes
his impression of Lenin as a man and leader.

2050   Dutt, R. Palme. "Pointing the Way Forward," New Times,
17 (21 Apr. 1970), 22-24.
An account of Lenin's visits to and influence on Britain
and its communist movement.

2051   Fava, A. "Leninism and the International Aspect of the
Fight for Socialism in Britain," W Marxist R, 22, no.
1 (Jan. 1979), 28-36.

2052   *Fox, Ralph. Marx, Engels and Lenin on Ireland. New
York: International Publishers, 1940; 47pp.
A positive account of Lenin's interpretation of Irish
history and his support for and influence on the Irish
labor movement. Fox stresses the importance of Lenin's assertion that Irish national independence could
not be achieved through bourgeois "home rule," but
rather only by way of the establishment of a socialist
state, and that the national liberation and workers'
movements were natural allies and not enemies as pro-
claimed by the Second International. [DA913. F67]

2053   Gallagher, William. "Pages from the Past," in OL (anthology), 159-71.
A recollection of a 1920 meeting with Lenin which led
to the author's joining of the Communist Party of Great
Britain. Gallagher also describes Lenin's influence on
various members of the Comintern and Lenin's personality and conversational manner. Also in WHML (anthology), 28-34; excerpt in Int Aff, no. 2 (1959), 53-56.

2054   Hobsbaum, E. "Reflections on the Break Up of Britain,"
New Left R, 5 (1977), 1-23.
In part, a discussion of the influence of Lenin's doctrine
of colonial revolution on the disintegration of the British
Empire.

2055   Klugman, J. "Lenin, the Communist International and the
British Communist Party," in VILIL (anthology), 92-94.
An account of Lenin's speech at the Second Congress of
the Comintern and of his urging of the formation of a
British communist party.

2056   Matthews, Betty. "Lenin on Fight for Democracy in Capitalist Countries with Particular Reference to Britain," W Marxist R, 13, no. 3 (Mar. 1970), 38-41.

2057   *Mayer, Arno J. "Labour, UDC, and Lenin," in Political Origins of the New Diplomacy. New York: H. Fertig, 1969; 44-53.
An examination of the fusion in World War I Britain of radical and socialist groups into the Union of Democratic Control (UDC) as a means of influencing the government's wartime policies, and a review of Lenin's critique of the CDC in his article "English Pacifism and Dislike of Theory." [D610.M33 1969]

2058   O'Riordan, Michael. "The October Revolution, Lenin, and Ireland," W Marxist R, 29, no. 9 (Sept. 1977), 19-21.

2059   _____. "Lenin in Irish History," W Marxist R, 13, no. 4 (Apr. 1970), 66-70.

2060   Ramelson, B. "Leninism and the International Aspect of the Fight for Socialism in Britain," W Marxist R, 22, no. 1 (Jan. 1979), 28-36.

2061   Zhak, Luybov. "The Fighting Scotsman," in LCIA (anthology), 10-33.
A review of William Gallagher's conversion to Leninism in direct response to the impression made on him by Lenin, and a discussion of Gallagher's pursuit of Leninist policies in Britain and the Comintern.

     d.   Eastern Europe

2062   Andronov, I. "Lenin Lives in the People's Hearts," New Times, no. 5 (3 Feb. 1970), 12-15.
A description of Poland's high regard for Lenin.

2063   Belousov, N. and K. Yanev. "Bulgarians and Lenin's Iskra," New Times, no. 11 (17 Mar. 1970), 16-17.

2064   Ceausescu, Nicolae. "Rumania's Successes in Socialist Construction Confirm the Correctness of Lenin's Ideas," in LITW-2 (anthology), 19-34.
A positive review of the influence in Rumania of Lenin's principles and practices in the building of socialism.

2065   Davydov, Lev. "A Splendid and Dedicated Revolutionary," in LCIA (anthology), 130-61.
An account of how Hungarian revolutionary Bela Kun abandoned his "leftism" in response to a 1921 Comintern speech by Lenin which criticized Kun's position. Davydov also recreates various conversations between Lenin

and Kun on party organization, revolutionary commitment, propaganda, strategy, and tactics.

2066 *Deac, Augustin. "The Penetration of Leninism in Romania. The Influence of the Great October Socialist Revolution on Romania's Workers' Movement," in CFOLI (anthology), 29-48.
A centennial appreciation of Lenin and his influence on the Rumanian workers' movement. Deac discusses the first mentionings of Lenin in the Rumanian press, the spread of his Iskra writings in the early 1900's, the establishment of direct ties between Lenin and Rumanian Marxist leaders, and Rumanian support for Lenin's position and policies in both Soviet Russia and the Comintern.

2067 Dimitrov, Georgi. Under the Banner of Leninism. Sofia: Sofia Press, 1970; 95pp.
A collection of twenty-two articles dealing with various problems faced by Bulgarian communism. Although the majority of these writings deal with Lenin only in an indirect fashion, Dimitrov does describe his first (February 1921) meeting with Lenin, the influence of Lenin in the Balkans, and the uniformly high regard for Lenin as a man and leader. [HX314.Z7D513]

2068 Drizulis, A. V. I. Lenin and the Revolutionary Movement in Latvia. Riga: Latvian Society for Friendship and Cultural Relations with Foreign Countries, 1969; 30pp.
A positive review of Lenin's involvement in the Latvian workers' movement. Drizulis traces Lenin's work with Latvian revolutionaries in the early 1900's, discusses the impact in Latvia of his writings (especially What Is to Be Done?), and praises Lenin particularly for his role in the events which brought Soviet power to Latvia in 1919. [DK254.L4D74]

2069 Foitik, Jan. "To Fight Opportunism--Lenin's Behest," W Marxist R, 13, no. 3 (Mar. 1970), 46-49.

2070 Georgescu, Titu. "Vladimir Ilyich Lenin's Conception of the Party of a New Type. Setting Up of the Romanian Communist Party--An Embodiment of Leninism," in CFOLI (anthology), 49-76.
A centennial appreciation of Lenin, his party doctrine and its influence on the organization, discipline, strategy, and tactics of the Rumanian Communist Party.

2071 *Gitelman, Zvi. "Beyond Leninism: Political Development in Eastern Europe," Newsletter Comp St Com, 5, no. 3 (May 1972), 18-43.
An analysis of Lenin's views on the nature of political change and of the stagnant qualities of East European Leninist regimes.

2072   Husak, Gustav. "Confidently and Creatively Along the Le-
        ninist Road," W Marxist R, 19, no. 6 (June 1976), 3-
        14.
        A report on the Czech Communist Party's pursuit of
        a Leninist course in regard to socialist construction,
        proletarian internationalism, the nationality question,
        and party leadership.

2073   _____. "Lenin's Teaching on the Party and Czechoslovak
        Reality," W Marxist R, 13, no. 1 (Jan. 1970), 6-14.

2074   _____. "Leninism and the Communist Movement in
        Czechoslovakia," W Marxist R, 13, no. 5 (May 19-0),
        23-30.

2075   Johnson, Ross. "Is Yugoslavia Leninist?," St Comp Com,
        10, no. 4 (Winter 1977), 403-07.

2076   Kadar, Janos. "Lenin: Theorist and Organizer of Socialist
        Construction," in LITW-2 (anthology), 140-56.
        A positive appraisal, by a Hungarian communist, of
        Lenin's principles and policies on socialist construction
        and their influence in Hungary.

2077   Kocijanciv, Janez. "The Younger Generation and the Revo-
        lution," LIPOY (anthology), 43-45.
        A short summary of Lenin's qualities as a revolution-
        ary and a leader, and a statement on how the multitude
        of interpretations of Lenin and the cult of Lenin have
        partially obscured his true value for Yugoslav youth.

2078   Komocsin, Zoltan. "Lenin in Our Lives," W Marxist R,
        13, no. 2 (Feb. 1970), 52-56.

2079   Kostyukovsky, Boris. "An Indomitable Will," in LCIA (an-
        thology), 72-91.
        An examination of Lenin's positive influence on Bulgar-
        ian communist Georgy Dimitrov.

2080   Lenart, Jozef. "Leninism and the Lessons of the Slovak
        Uprising," W Marxist R, 17, no. 8 (1974), 20-29.
        A discussion of the Slovak national uprising of August
        1944 as being Leninist to the core: a combination of
        the national liberation, peasant and socialist movements
        under the leadership of the vanguard party.

2081   "Lenin Lives in Us--Or Does He?," E Eur, 11, no. 8 (Aug.
        1962), 39-40.

2082   Mujezinovic, D. "Lenin and the Revolutionary Movement in
        Yugoslavia," in LACW (anthology), 47-49.
        A presentation of Lenin as a source of strength and in-
        spiration for Yugoslav revolutionaries.

2083   Nemes, Deszo. "Some Results of Leninist Policy in Hungary," W Marxist R, 13, no. 3 (Mar. 1970), 10-13.

2084   Paleckis, Ustas. "The Most Important Thing in Life," in LIOL (anthology), 179-89.
A description of Lenin's influence on the author, a Lithuanian communist leader, who, though he never met Lenin, was much inspired by his writings and leadership.

2085   Popescu-Puturi, Ion. "The Victory of Socialism in Romania Stands Proof to the Vitality of Marxism-Leninism," in CFOLI (anthology), 285-305.
A review of Lenin's leading contributions to Marxism and their applicability to Rumania.

2086   Prymov, Ivan. "Lenin's Cooperative Plan in Bulgaria," W Marxist R, 13, no. 3 (Mar. 1970), 41-44.

2087   Radulescu, Ilie. "Leninism and the Experience of Building Socialist Society in Romania," W Marxist R, 13, no. 3 (Mar. 1970), 13-16.

2088   _____. "Leninism and the Romanian Communist Party's Experience in Leading the Revolution and the Construction of Socialism," CFOLI (anthology), 7-28.
A eulogy of Lenin precedes an account of how the Rumanian Communist Party has followed his teachings on dialectical materialism, party organization, strategy, and tactics, socialist construction, and proletarian internationalism.

2089   Rakowski, M. F. "Lenin and Poland," New Times, 17 (21 Apr. 1970), 25-27.
A discussion of Lenin's views on Polish independence and his influence on Poland's working class and construction of socialism.

2090   Roman, Valter. "The Activity of the Romanian Communist Party in Promoting Science and Technology in the Light of Leninist Ideas," in CFOLI (anthology), 206-27.
A summary of Lenin's views on the role of science in the construction of socialism and their influence on the development of a socialist economy in Rumania. Roman stresses the inspirational effect of Lenin's belief that, with the proper support, scientific achievement was almost limitless and would be the basis of man's attainment of freedom.

2091   *Samouilov, Itso. Ties of Bulgarian Revolutionaries with Lenin. Sofia: Sofia Press, 1970, 111pp.
An account of Lenin's contact with, views of, and influence on Bulgarian revolutionaries. Samouilov dis-

cusses Lenin's first contact with Bulgarian workers,
the spread of his Iskra articles, Bulgarian support of
Lenin's course in Soviet Russia and the Comintern,
and the opinions of scores of Bulgarian revolutionaries
on Lenin as a man, revolutionary, thinker, and leader.
[DR85. 5A1S313]

2092   *Stolte, Stefan. "The People's Democracies and Leninism,"
St Sov Un, 9, no. 1 (1969), 84-95.
A review of the varying interpretations of Leninism
prevalent in Yugoslavia, East Germany, Rumania, and
Czechoslovakia.

2093   Strokovsky, Nikolai. "The Pen as a Bayonet," in LIOL
(anthology), 55-81.
A discussion of Lenin's relationship with and influence
on Felix Kon, a Polish revolutionary, historian, and
ethnographer.

2094   "Tito Chooses Lenin," New Rep, 130 (25 Jan. 1954), 4.

2095   Vlahovic, Veljko. "Lenin and the Socialist Revolution," in
LIPOY (anthology), 21-24.
A consideration of the massive outpouring, in Yugoslavia
and elsewhere, of literature and sentiment on Lenin to
commemorate the centenary of his birth as yet "another
confirmation of Lenin's contemporary value and the
vigorous timeliness of his thinking."

2096   Voicu, Stefan. "The Influence of the Marxist-Leninist Ideology on Contemporary Social-Political Thought," in
CFOLI (anthology), 165-180.
A centennial appreciation of Lenin's influence on the
growth of socialist states, national liberation movements,
and the workers' struggle in capitalist nations. Voicu
presents examples from Rumanian communist experience
to substantiate his contentions.

2097   Zarodov, Konstantin. "Leninism--Banner of Our Movement,"
W Marxist R, 13, no. 3 (Mar. 1970), 68-71.

2098   Zhivkov, T. "Leninism and the Problems of Socialist Construction in Bulgaria," in LITW-2 (anthology), 223-39.
A positive survey of Lenin's influence on the formation
of the Bulgarian Communist Party and the policies it
has pursued.

2099   _____. Leninism Transforms the World. Sofia: Sofia
Press, 1970; 100pp.
A centennial appreciation of Lenin's influence on the
world workers' movement. Zhivkov praises Lenin for
both his theory of revolution and his guidance in the
construction of socialism, and provides examples from

Bulgarian communist history to illustrate the applicability of Lenin's teachings. [HX44. Z4913]

2100 _____. "Lenin's Principle of Unity of National and International Tasks," W Marxist R, 13, no. 4 (Apr. 1970), 14-22.

e. France

2101 Cachin, M. "Meetings with Lenin," in WHML (anthology), 48-58.
A recollection of a 1920 meeting with Lenin concerning the affiliation of the Socialist Party of France with the Comintern.

2102 Cogniot, G. "Lenin and France," New Times, no. 39 (30 Sept. 1930), 7-10.
A discussion of Lenin's influence on the founding of the French Communist Party and the policies which it has pursued.

2103 Cohen, F. "Lenin and French Communists' Struggle on Two Fronts," W Marxist R, 13, no. 8 (Aug. 1970), 84-86.

2104 Duclos, J. "Lenin and the French Communist Party," W Marxist R, 3, no. 4 (Apr. 1960), 14-18.

2105 _____. "Triumph of Lenin's Ideas," W Marxist R, 13, no. 4 (Apr. 1970), 37-42.
An account of the lessons provided by Lenin for the French Communist Party in its formative years.

2106 Isbakh, Alexander. "A Son of the People," in LCIA (anthology), 266-79.
A discussion of the influence on French communist Maurice Thorez of Lenin's works, especially State and Revolution and Left-Wing Communism.

2107 *Jefferson, Carter. "Communism and the French Intellectuals," Comp St Soc Hist, 11, no. 3 (1969), 241-57.
An argument that Soviet anti-intellectual policy began not with Stalin but with Lenin's distrust of the intelligentsia as exemplified by his support for increasing the percentage of worker-communists in the Comintern.

2108 Mironov, Georgy. "The Reward of a Lifetime," in LCIA (anthology), 110-29.
A description of French socialist Marcel Cachin's conversion to a Leninist position after being impressed by Lenin in a 1920 meeting. Mironov records how Cachin, after 1920, functioned as "a staunch and consistent com-

munist, follower of Lenin, and a true friend of the Soviet Union."

2109   Monmousseau, G. "My Interview with Lenin," WHML (anthology), 59-62.
A recollection of the favorable impression made by Lenin on the author in a 1921 meeting and how this led to Monmousseau's support for a Leninist position by the French Communist Party.

2110   *Rochet, Waldeck. "The Heritage of Lenin and Problems of the Revolutionary Working-Class Movement," in LAWRWM (anthology), 50-83.
A discussion of the problems faced by the French Communist Party and the lessons that can be learned from Lenin to help solve them. Rochet stresses Lenin's combining of tactical flexibility with inflexible goals thus teaching that there is more than one path to socialism. Cooperation with other parties and even a peaceful transition to socialism, Rochet states, are therefore consistent with the teachings of Lenin.

f.   Germany

2111   Becher, Johannes R. "The Path that Brought Me to Lenin," Int Lit, nos. 4-5 (Apr.-May 1940), 70-71.
A discussion of Lenin's deeds and writings as a source of inspiration for German workers and revolutionaries.

2112   Beyer, Heinz and Helga Kanzig. "Leninism and Its Application by the Socialist Unity Party of Germany," Ger For Pol, 9, no. 4 (1970), 282-96.

2113   Danelius, Gerhard. "Leninism--Militant Banner of Revolutionary and Progressive Forces," in LITW-2 (anthology), 108-15.
A general review of Lenin's thought on nationalism and the world communist movement, and a discussion of Leninism's relevancy for German communists and others.

2114   Fischer, Herbert. "Lenin and the Contemporary World," in LACW (anthology), 43-46.
A tribute to Lenin and an account of his influence on East German trade unions, socialist construction, and foreign policy.

2115   Heckert, Fritz. "My Meetings with V. I. Lenin," WHML (anthology), 16-27.
A recollection of conversations with Lenin on the difficulties being encountered by the German Communist Party.

2116 *Kellner, Douglas. "Korsch's Revolutionary Historicism,"
      Telos, 26 (Winter 1975-76), 70-93.
      In part, a discussion of Lenin's influence on Korsch
      after the collapse of German Marxism, and how Korsch
      later came to reject Leninism due to Soviet undemocratic
      policies in the Comintern.

2117 Lamberg, Werner. "Leninist Principles of Scientific Guid-
      ance of Socialist Construction and Their Application
      in the GDR," W Marxist R, 13, no. 2 (Feb. 1970), 21-
      24.

2118 Lowenthal, Richard. "The Bolshevisation of the Spartacus
      League," in International Communism, David Footman,
      ed. London: Chatto and Windus, 1960; 23-71.
      Lenin is not the focus of this essay, but it contains a
      discussion of the spread, by way of the Comintern, of
      his concept of party organization to the Spartacus Lea-
      gue. [HX40. F66]

2119 Munzenberg, Willi. With Liebknecht and Lenin. Moscow,
      1930.
      Not available for annotation.

2120 Norden, Albert. "Lenin and Germany." New Times, no.
      15 (14 Apr. 1970), 9-11.
      A survey of the assistance rendered by Lenin to the
      German Communist Party and of the Party's pursuit of
      Lenin's ideals.

2121 *Reichenbach, Bernhard. "Moscow 1921. Meetings in the
      Kremlin," Survey, no. 53 (1964), 16-22.
      An account of the author's gradual realization, through
      conversations with Lenin, that the Comintern was to be
      a tool to advance Russian interests.

2122 *Rotter, Seymour. "Soviet and Comintern Policy toward
      Germany, 1919-1923: A Case Study in Strategy and
      Tactics," Columbia University, 1954 (dissertation).

2123 Ryabchikov, Yevgeny. "Symbol of Ultimate Victory," in
      LCIA (anthology), 234-47.
      A report on the inspirational effect of Lenin and the
      October Revolution on German communist Ernst Thael-
      mann. Ryabchikov recreates Lenin's 1921 meeting with
      Thaelmann in which the latter was greatly impressed
      by Lenin's knowledge of German affairs and his concept
      of party organization and discipline.

2124 S., E. S. "New Policy Trends in Eastern Germany," W
      Today, 12 (May 1956), 173-81.
      An examination of the return to Leninism in East Ger-
      many as part of de-Stalinization policy.

2125 *Stepanov, A. "Vladimir Ilyich Lenin and Germany," Ger
For Pol, 9, no. 3 (1970), 205-220.
An examination of the influence on Lenin exerted by
various Germans and by German history, and a survey
of Lenin's effect on the German revolutionary movement.

2126 Ulbricht, Walter. "A Doctrine Transforming the World,"
in LITW-2 (anthology), 163-79.
A tribute to Lenin as a leader with immense influence
on the world revolutionary movement as well as on
those countries, such as East Germany, which have already overthrown capitalism.

2127 _____. "Lenin Always Stood Close to the German Labour
Movement," in Marxism-Leninism on Proletarian Internationalism. Moscow: Progress, 1972; 305-10.
A discussion of Lenin's keen interest in the German revolutionary movement and the immense influence of his
teachings in modern Germany. Ulbricht bemoans the
fact that Germany lacked an individual such as Lenin to
lead its revolutionary movement during World War I.
[HX550.15M3413]

2128 _____. "Lenin and the Socialist Unity Party of Germany,"
W Marxist R, 13, no. 4 (Apr. 1970), 42-46.

2129 _____. "Leninism and the Building of the Developed
Socialist Social System," in LAWRWM (anthology), 84-
110.
A report on the application of Lenin's leading principles
to the construction of socialism in the GDR. Ulbricht
states that in 1945, when Germany lacked the prerequisites for a socialist revolution, he took guidance from
Lenin's Two Tactics of Social Democracy in the Democratic Revolution and forged an alliance with all democratic forces in Germany which later made the transition
peacefully to a revolutionary dictatorship of the workers
and peasants. He goes on to discuss the GDR's pursuit
of Lenin's teachings on the cultural revolution, socialist
construction and peaceful coexistence.

g. Other

2130 Anderson, Perry. "The Antinomes of Antonio Gramsci,"
New Left R, 100 (Nov. 1976-77), 5-78.
In part, a discussion of Lenin's influence on Gramsci.

2131 Beckstrom, Knut. "Lenin and the Labor Movement in Swe-
den," W Marxist R, 13, no. 3 (Mar. 1970), 53-55.

2132 [No entry]

2133 *Davidson, Alistair. "Gramsci and Lenin, 1917-22," Social-
      ist Reg, 11 (1974), 125-50.

2134 Germanetto, Giovanni. "Long Live Lenin!," Int Lit, nos.
      4-5 (Apr.-May 1940), 73-78.
      A positive estimate of Lenin's influence upon Italian
      workers.

2135 Glezos, Manolis. "Sparks," in OL (anthology), 194-95.
      An account of the influence of Lenin, both through his
      written works and various secondary sources, upon the
      author as a youth.

2136 Golemba, Alexander. "Our Heart Is One," in LCIA (an-
      thology), 248-67.
      A discussion of Lenin's influence on Italian communist
      leader P. Togliatti who, though he never met Lenin,
      was deeply impressed by him as a theoretician and
      practical politician.

2137 Gunhal, Alvaro. "Reliable Beacon," in LITW-2 (anthology),
      58-67.
      A review, by a Portuguese communist, of Lenin's
      teachings on party organization and the class struggle,
      and an account of their influence on the policies followed
      by the Portuguese Communist Party in its struggle
      against fascism.

2138 Henry, Ernst. "Lenin and the Youth," Sov Lit, no. 4 (Apr.
      1978), 30-31.
      A favorable assessment of Lenin's impact upon the
      young radicals with whom he worked while in Swiss
      exile.

2139 Ibarruri, Dolores. "Compass and Battle-Standard in the
      Struggle for Democracy and Socialism," New Times,
      16 (21 Apr. 1970), 12-15.
      A presentation of Lenin as a great source of inspiration
      for Spanish communists.

2140 _____. "Leninism: Inspiration and Guide for Democracy
      and Socialism," W Marxist R, 13, no. 4 (Apr. 1970),
      85-91.

2141 _____. "Our Fighting Colours," in LITW-2 (anthology),
      82-89.
      An account of Lenin's influence on the formation of the
      Spanish Communist Party.

2142 *Karabel, Jeremy. "Revolutionary Contradictions: Antonio
      Gramsci and the Problem of Intellectuals," Pol Soc,
      6, no. 2 (1976), 123-72.
      In part, an appraisal of the influence of Lenin's princi-

ples of party orginization, discipline, and tactics on Gramsci.

2143   Khigerov, Raphail. "Mourn Not for the Fallen Fighter," in LCIA (anthology), 34-53.
A discussion of Lenin's formative influence on the thought and action of Antonio Gramsci.

2144   Koliyannis, Kostas. "Leninism and the Experience of the Communist Party of Greece," W Marxist R, 13, no. 4 (Apr. 1970), 48-53.

2145   Kornilov, Y. "Three Dutch Encounters," New Times, no. 7 (17 Feb. 1970), 16-18.

2146   Kuusinen, Otto. Triumphant March of Lenin's Ideas. London: Soviet Booklet No. 72, 1960; 17pp.
An April 22, 1960 address, to the Central Committee of the CPSU, outlining those teachings of Lenin that have greatly influenced Finland, the socialist community and the world in general. [DK254. L4K827]

2147   Lenin through Australian Eyes. Sydney: Communist Party of Australia, 1970; 47pp.
Not available for annotation.

2147a   Saarinen, A. "Lenin and Finland," W Marxist R, 13, no. 4 (Apr. 1970), 33-36.

2148   Silone, Ignazio. "How I Remember Lenin: An Interview," Dissent, 17, no. 5 (1970), 429-32.
An account of the great fascination with Lenin by Italian revolutionaries who saw him as a master teacher on how to seize and maintain power.

2149   Stringos, Leonidas. "Leninism and the Development of the Revolutionary Movement in Greece," in LITW-2 (anthology), 35-44.
A positive review, by a Greek communist, of Lenin's affect on the Greek Communist Party's policies, especially in regard to the struggle against imperialism and the pursuit of proletarian internationalism.

2150   Taft, B. "Selections from the Australian Communist Party/the Leninist Party," Socialist R, no. 21 (Jan. 1974), 85-100.

2151   *Togliatti, Palmiro. "Gramsci and Leninism," in On Gramsci and Other Writings. London: Lawrence and Wishart, 1979; 183-207.
A discussion of Lenin as the most decisive influence on Gramsci's "evolution as a thinker, and as a political man of action," and a survey of Gramsci's actions as he turned away from his early mistakes and towards a Leninist position. [JN5657. C63T53213 1979]

2152 *_____. "Lenin and Our Party," in On Gramsci and Other Writings. London: Lawrence and Wishart, 1979; 241-59.
A favorable account of the influence on the Italian Communist Party of Lenin's doctrines, practical policies, and general method of problem solving. Togliatti also reviews Lenin's writings and statements on Italy and its labor movement.

2153 _____. "Leninism in the Theory and Practice of Gramsci," in On Gramsci and Other Writings. London: Lawrence and Wishart, 1979; 161-81.
A presentation of Gramsci as a thorough and consistent Leninist who firmly grasped the basics of Lenin's theory of revolution, defended his teachings against left and right deviations, and implemented, in the Italian Communist Party, his doctrine on party organization. [JN5657. C63T53213 1979]

2154 Urbany, Dominique. "Lenin's Teaching and the Working Class," in LITW-2 (anthology), 157-62.
A tribute to Lenin, by a Luxembourg communist, as the inspirer of workers' unity in Luxembourg and the rest of Europe.

2155 _____. "Luxembourg Working Class and Lenin," W Marxist R, 13, no. 4 (Apr. 1970), 70-73.

2156 Wimmer, Ernst. "Leninism and the Perspectives of Our Struggle," W Marxist R, 21, no. 9 (Sept. 1978), 12-18.
A report on the impact on the Austrian Communist Party of Lenin's theory of revolution.

3. Non-Western World

a. Africa and the Middle East

2157 Africanus, Terence. "Lenin and Africa," W Marxist R, 38, no. 1 (Jan. 1970), 63-70.

2158 Chaoui, Nicolas. "Leninism and Problems of the Revolutionary Movement in Arab Countries," W Marxist R, 13, no. 5 (May 1970), 60-67.

2159 Davidson, Apollon. "Delegate from Transvaal," in LCIA (anthology), 54-71
An account of the 1919 trial of David Jones for writing what became known as the "Zulu Pamphlet" (a pro-Bolshevik tract) and of Jones' pre-1919 efforts to spread in South Africa a positive and accurate image of Lenin and the Soviet Union.

2160   Demir, Y. "Lenin and Some Problems of the Revolutionary
        Movement in Turkey," W Marxist R, 13, no. 4 (Apr.
        1970), 97-103.

2161   Ehrlich, Wolff. "Leninism and the Struggle against Chauvin-
        ism and for Proletarian Internationalism," W Marxist
        R, 13, no. 3 (Mar. 1970), 65-57.
        A note on the application of Lenin's teachings on prole-
        tarian internationalism to the struggle against Zionism.

2162   Harmel, Michael. "Lenin and African Liberation," New
        Times, 21 (26 May 1970), 22-23.

2163   Ivanova, M. N. "Leninist Foreign Policy and the Peoples
        of Iran in Their Fight for Independence and Social Pro-
        gress," in LANLIE (anthology), 306-27.
        A discussion of Lenin's assessment of the Iranian Revo-
        lution (1905-11), the impact of the October Revolution
        on Iran, and Lenin's role in the creation of the Soviet-
        Iranian Treaty of 1921, the first which Iran signed with
        a great power.

2164   Landa, R. G. "Lenin and the Revolutionary Process in the
        Arab Countries," in LANLIE (anthology), 433-60.
        A presentation of Lenin as a "true champion of the
        rights of the oppressed Arab peoples and an ardent op-
        ponent of the system of colonial slavery." Landa main-
        tains that Lenin's writings "opened up a qualitatively
        new stage in the Arab peoples' national liberation strug-
        gle."

2165   "Lenin and Africa," Polar Star, 4, no. 33 (Apr. 1970), 37-
        41.
        A discussion of Lenin's influence on African national
        liberation movements.

2166   Lightfoot, Claude. "Lenin Illuminates the Path to Black
        Liberation," Pol Aff, 49, no. 6 (June 1970), 29-39.

2167   Otegveye, T. "Leninism and African Revolution," W Marx-
        ist R, 13, no. 8 (1970), 78-83.

2168   Radmaneshe, Reza. "Lenin's Teaching in Our Life and
        Struggle," W Marxist R, 13, no. 4 (Apr. 1970), 59-65.
        A review of the impact on the Iranian revolutionary
        movement of Lenin's party doctrine.

2169   Sabri, Ali. Lenin Is with Us in Our Struggle. Moscow:
        Novosti Press, 1970; 7pp.
        A report on the influence on the Arab Socialist Union
        of Lenin's teachings on imperialism and the national
        liberation movement. [DK254. L447S25]

2170   Savvides, Georgos. "Leninism and the Struggle to Democ-
        ratize Society in Cyprus," W Marxist R, 21, no. 6
        (June 1978), 39-46.

2171   Shamsutdinov, A. A. "Lenin and Soviet-Turkish Relations,"
        in LANLIE (anthology), 328-57.
        A discussion of Lenin's keen interest in Turkish affairs,
        support for the Turkish revolutionary movement, and
        his leading role in the establishment of the Soviet-Tur-
        kish Treaty of Friendship and Brotherhood (1921).

2172   *Solodovnikov, V. G. "Africa in Lenin's Works," in HDASP
        (anthology), 12-25.
        An attack on the Western contention that the Soviet Union
        "turned to Africa out of purely pragmatic, political con-
        siderations, and that ... its policy towards the African
        peoples is of the moment, with no past history." Solo-
        dovnikov argues that Lenin's concern for national liber-
        ation movements was not limited to the East, but rather
        included all colonial areas, a contention which Solodovi-
        kov supports by providing quotes from Lenin's writings
        which mention or show concern for Africa.

2173   Tabari, Ehsan. "Lenin and the Problems of the Social
        Revolution in Iran," W Marxist R, 13, no. 3 (Mar.
        1970), 32-35.

2174   Vilner, Meir. "Leninism and Our Place in the Revolution-
        ary Struggle," W Marxist R, 13, no. 5 (May 1970),
        42-48.
        An account of the Communist Party of Israel's pursuit
        of Leninist policies in its struggle against Zionism.

        b. Asia

2175   Akatova, T. N. "Leninism and the Problems of the Chinese
        Revolution," in LANLIE (anthology), 179-210.
        A positive assessment of "Lenin's approach to the ques-
        tion of the Chinese revolution, ... the advances Lenin-
        ism has made in China, and the use and assimilation
        of Lenin's theoretical legacy and political experience by
        Chinese revolutionaries."

2176   Barkatullah, Maulvi. "Follow the Call of Brother Lenin,"
        in LHIII (anthology), 40.
        An appeal to the peoples of Asia to follow the teachings
        of Lenin in the fight against imperialism.

2177   Bogush, Y. "Leninist Foreign Policy," Int Aff, 19, no. 5
        (May 1973), 3-7.
        An attack on the Chinese Communist Party for its failure

to adhere to Lenin's principle of proletarian internationalism.

2178   *Brandt, Conrad. "Lenin and Asian Nationalism: Sources
       of an Alliance," in Stalin's Failure in China. New
       York: Norton, 1966; 1-17.
       An analysis of the Leninist roots of Stalin's policies in
       China. Brandt sees in Lenin's teachings on the rela-
       tion of revolutionary socialism to colonial liberation
       movements a rather ambiguous legacy for his successors
       in that Lenin failed to make clear the situations in
       which Asian communists should forge alliances with
       other groups opposed to the government. Consequently,
       both Stalin and Trotsky were able to claim to be "Le-
       ninist" in their assessments of the Chinese revolution-
       ary movement even though their positions were diamet-
       rically opposed. [DS740.5.R8B7]

2179   Budanov, A. G. "Leninism and the Vietnamese Revolution,"
       in LANLIE (anthology), 250-83.
       A positive description of Lenin's influence on the emer-
       gence and development of the Communist Party of In-
       dochina. Budanov stresses the impact of Lenin's ex-
       posure of contemporary imperialism's nature, his theory
       on merging the national liberation and socialist move-
       ments, and his belief that it was possible for backward
       nations to bypass the capitalist phase of development en
       route to modernization.

2180   Chên, Shao-yü. Lenin, Leninism and the Chinese Revolu-
       tion. Moscow: Novosti Press, 1970, 27pp.
       A sympathetic account both of Lenin's support for the
       Chinese revolutionary movement and of the importance
       of his teachings for contemporary China, and an attack
       on Maoist deviations from Leninism. [HX387.C52]

2181   Dmitriev, G. "Lenin on Socialist Economic Development.
       The Practice of Socialist Construction in China," in
       LAMCP (anthology), 166-38.
       A critical review of the Chinese Communist Party's
       deviations from its pre-1956 Leninist course in social-
       ist construction. In particular, Dmitriev asserts that
       the "unmitigated voluntarism" of the "Great Leap For-
       ward" and its dependence on the "decisive role of Mao"
       has replaced scientific Leninist principles of planning
       and therein wrecked the Chinese economy.

2182   Duan, Le. "Under the Party's Glorious Banner," in LITW-2
       (anthology), 193-211.
       A report on the influence in Southeast Asia of Lenin's
       writings on party organization, imperialism and socialist
       construction.

2183   "Forward along the Path of the Great Lenin!" in Long Live
        Leninism. Peking: Foreign Languages Press, 1960;
        57-85.
        An editorial on Lenin's doctrine of imperialism precedes
        a Leninist discussion of the three main tasks facing
        China: the construction of socialism, safeguarding of
        world peace, and maintenance of friendly ties with fellow
        nations.

2184   No entry.

2185   Hayward, J. E. S. "Leninizing China and Sinicizing Lenin,"
        Pol St, 14 (Feb. 1966), 95-99.
        A review article on several studies of Chinese commu-
        nism with much reference to Chinese interpretations of
        Lenin.

2186   "Ho Chi Minh on Lenin," Peo Dem, (22 Apr. 1970), 91-92.

2187   Katayama, Sen. "My Meetings with Lenin," Int Lit, nos.
        4-5.
        Recollections of conversations with Lenin, most of which
        concerned the Asian revolutionary movement.

2188   Kruchinin, A. "Proletarian Internationalism--The Basis
        of the USSR's Leninist Policy Towards China," in LAMCP
        (anthology), 233-53.
        A review of Lenin's principle of proletarian internation-
        alism and its application by the Soviet Union to the
        Chinese Communist Party, and a heated assault on "the
        Maoist ruptures" with it.

2189   *McMichael, Philip. "The Relations between Class and Na-
        tional Struggle: Lenin's Contribution," J Contemp Asia,
        7, no. 2 (1977), 200-12.
        A discussion of Lenin's merging of the national libera-
        tion and socialist movements and its effect upon the
        Asian revolutionary movement.

2190   Moses, Larry W. "Revolutionary Mongolia Chooses a Faith:
        Lamaism or Leninism," University of Indiana, 1972 (dis-
        sertation).

2191   North, R. C. and J. H. Paasche. "China in the World
        Revolution: Lenin's Extension of Marx," Far East S,
        18 (27 July 1949), 170-71.

2192   Nosaka, Sanzo. "What Has Assured Advancement of the
        Communist Party of Japan," W Marxist R, 13, no. 5
        (May 1970), 48-59.

2193   Roberts, Holland. "Lenin's Friends," New World R, 38,
        no. 4 (1970), 91-96.

A statement on the impact of a visit to Lenin's birth-place upon a Vietnamese delegation.

2194   Schwartz, Benjamin. "Marx and Lenin in China," Far East S, 18, no. 15 (27 July 1949), 174-78.
A consideration of the influence on Chinese Marxists of Lenin's ideas on party organization and backward nations bypassing the capitalist phase of development.

2195   Shabshina, F. I. "Leninism and the People's Democratic Revolution in Korea," in LANLIE (anthology), 211-49.
A discussion of the influence in Korea of the October Revolution and Lenin (especially his writings on national liberation movements), and a review of Lenin's notes on Korea and his contacts with various Korean revolutionaries.

2196   Shastri, S. N. "Lenin's Message to Asian People," in LHIII (anthology), 128-30.

2197   *Sladkovsky, M. I. "Lenin and China," in LAMCP (anthology), 9-31.
A positive examination of Lenin's assessment of and influence on the Chinese revolutionary movement. Sladkovsky emphasizes the importance of Lenin's teachings on the national liberation movement, party organization and the non-capitalist path of economic development.

2198   Sung, K. I. "The Triumph of Lenin's Great Ideas," in LITW-2 (anthology), 68-81.
A review of the influence in Korea, China, and Vietnam of Lenin's doctrine on the national and colonial questions.

2199   Ting-yi, L. "Unite under Lenin's Revolutionary Banner!" in Long Live Leninism. Peking: Foreign Languages Press, 1960; 86-107.
A praiseful report on Lenin's unmasking of imperialism and development of the theory of uninterrupted revolution, both of which were crucial to the success of the Chinese revolutionary movement.

2200   Trinh, N. D. "An Inexhaustible Source of Strength and Inspiration," Int Aff, 12 (Dec. 1977), 26-34.
A discussion of Lenin as a source of inspiration for Vietnamese revolutionaries.

2201   Tsedenbal, Y. "Always with Lenin's Land, the Land of the October Revolution," in LITW-2 (anthology), 3-18.
A favorable presentation of the influence in Mongolia of Lenin and his teachings on the national liberation movement.

2202   Velengurin, Nikolai. "Katayama: An Example of Firm Dedication," in LCIA (anthology), 92-109.

A survey of the activities of Sen Katayama in propagating in the Far East a favorable image of Lenin and the Soviet Union. Velengurin also recreates Katayama's 1921 meetings with Lenin which inspired the former to work vigorously for the union of all Asian revolutionary and anti-imperialist forces.

2203   Volzhanin, V. "Leninism and the Problems of Chinese Culture," in LAMCP (anthology), 166-92.
An attack on the un-Leninist policies followed in China during its "cultural revolution." In particular, Volzhanin argues that China's "vulgar, crudely utilitarian concepts about culture" are contrary to Lenin's teaching that culture must shape the spiritual side of man as well as prepare him for participation in socialist society.

2204   *Wittfogel, Karl. "The Influence of Leninism-Stalinism on China," Annals AAPSS, 277 (Sept. 1951), 22-34.

2205   Zakaznikova, Y. I. et al. "The Early Spread of Leninism in Some Countries of Southeast Asia," in LANLIE (anthology), 383-432.
A favorable account of Lenin's influence in Indonesia, the Philippine Islands, and Burma stressing the impact of his doctrine on the national liberation movement.

2206   Zoberi, Z. H. "Lenin and the Freedom Movement in Vietnam," Contemp R, 188 (Oct. 1955), 268-72.

1) Mao Tse-tung

2207   Astafyev, G. V. and M. V. Fomichova. "The Maoist Distortion of Lenin's Theory of the National Liberation Movement," in LAMCP (anthology), 206-32.
A restatement of Lenin's views on national liberation movements, and a sharp attack on those of Mao for abandoning Lenin's dictates on the leadership of the proletariat in its alliance with the peasantry; on flexibility in tactics and strategy in advancing liberation movements; and on ideological unity and purity within the world socialist camp.

2208   Chertkov, V. P. "Maoist Distortions of Lenin's Theory of the Socialist Revolution," in LAMCP (anthology), 32-54.
An attack on Mao for rejecting Lenin's principles on peaceful coexistence as an effective form of the class struggle; replacing the leadership of the proletariat in the revolutionary process with that of the peasantry; and for dividing the world revolutionary movement along nationalistic lines.

2209   Deutscher, Isaac. "Maoism--Its Origins, Background and
          Outlook," Socialist Reg, (1964), 11-37.
          In part, an examination of the similarities and differ-
          ences between Maoism and Leninism.

2210   Dubinsky, A. M. "The Maoist Distortions of Lenin's Views
          on War and Peace," in LAMCP (anthology), 193-205.
          An attack on Mao's portrayal of war as "an immutable
          and decisive motor of progress" as being at variance
          with Leninism. Dubinsky states that peaceful coexistence
          and proletarian internationalism were the principles
          established by Lenin as the basis of socialist foreign
          policy, and that the Maoists have fostered "a cult of
          crude violence" which not only contradicts Lenin's teach-
          ings but undermines socialist construction and the world
          revolutionary movement.

2211   Dunayevskaya, Raya. "The 'Philosophy' of the Yenan Per-
          iod. Mao Perverts Lenin," in Freedom and Marxism
          from 1776 until Today. New York: Twayne, 1964;
          304-08.
          A sharp critique of Mao's thought as being antithetical
          to Lenin's Philosophical Notebooks (which Mao cited)
          and as "insipid subjectivism" and "a perfect nest of
          thoughtless contradictions." [HX36. D8]

2212   Fang, William. "The Marxist-Leninist Components in the
          Political Thought of Mao Tse-tung," Southern Illinois
          University at Carbondale, 1977 (dissertation).

2213   Goodstadt, Leo. "Lenin: All Things to All Men," Far
          East Eco R, 88 (31 Apr. 1975), 27-30.
          An analysis of the Chinese Communist Party's campaign
          encouraging the study of Lenin as part of a move away
          from Maoism and towards the rehabilitation of Teng
          Hsiao-ping.

2214   Gudoshnikov, L. M. and B. N. Topornin. "Left Opportunist
          Revision of Lenin's Teachings on the State," in LAMCP
          (anthology), 69-96.
          An assault on Mao's cultural revolution as a destruction
          of China's Leninist state apparatus and a complete re-
          vision of Lenin's State and Revolution. The authors
          argue that Mao has substituted for the democratic people's
          organizations arbitrary and dictatorial rule; has re-
          placed the Chinese constitution and legal system with
          the will of Mao; and has subverted the Leninist concept
          of the dictatorship of the proletariat by denying the
          leading role of the workers in government.

2215   *Inoki, Masamichi. "Leninism and Mao Tse-tung's Ideology,"
          in Unity and Contradiction. Major Aspects of Sino-Soviet
          Relations. New York: Praeger, 1962; 103-21.

An analysis of Mao's various adaptations of Lenin's thought and policies. Inoki states that Mao followed Lenin's teachings in establishing an alliance of the proletariat and peasantry to lead both the bourgeois and socialist revolutions; in creating a centralized, vanguard party to lead the alliance; and in having the party lead the industrialization of the nation after the socialist revolution; but Mao strayed from Lenin by giving less attention to atheism and more to mind-training and by theorizing that contradictions can exist among the people. [DK68.7.C5155 1960]

2216 "Lenin and Mao," Thought, 22, no. 25 (June 1970), 4-5.

2217 *Lowe, Donald M. "The Idea of China in Marx, Lenin, Mao," University of California at Berkeley, 1963 (dissertation).

2218 *Pfeffer, Richard M. "Mao and Marx in the Marxist-Leninist Tradition: A Critique of 'the China Field' and a Contribution to a Preliminary Reappraisal," Mod China, 2, no. 4 (1976), 421-60.
An examination of Mao's thought for consistencies with Lenin's interpretation of Marxism, and a survey of various writings on this subject.

2219 *Roy, Asish K. "Lenin, Mao and the Concept of Peasant Communism," China Rep, 14, no. 1 (Jan.-Feb. 1978), 29-41.

2220 Schwartz, Harry. "If Lenin Were Alive Today," NY Times M (14 July 1963), 14, 36-37, 39.
Speculation on whether Lenin, if he were alive, would support Khrushchev or Mao in the Sino-Soviet rift.

2221 *Sharma, T. R. "From Marx to Lenin to Mao," Indian Pol Sci R, 12, no. 2 (July 1978), 179-93.
An assessment of the differences between the views of Marx and those of Mao and Lenin on peasant revolution, economic backwardness, the dictatorship of the proletariat, and the use of violence.

2222 *Thomson, George. "From Lenin to Mao Tse-tung," in LT (anthology), 115-25.
A discussion of Lenin's theory of the dictatorship of the proletariat and its further development by Mao both through his war against the same revisionism against which Lenin struggled and his adaption of it to the political and economic situation in China. Also in Monthly R, 21 (Apr. 1970), 115-25.

2223 *Van der Kroef, Justus M. "Indonesia: Lenin, Mao and Aidit," in Polycentrism. The New Factor in Interna-

tional Communism, Walter Laquer and Leopold Labedz, eds. New York: Praeger, 1962; 197-218.
An assessment of the thought of Indonesian communist leader D. N. Aidit as being rooted in the teachings of Mao and, especially, Lenin. Van der Kroef examines, in particular, Aidit's adaptation of Lenin's general theory of revolution and What Is to Be Done? as sources of guidance for determining the role to be played by the Indonesian Communist Party in the revolutionary process. [HX44. L3] Also in China Q, no. 10 (Apr.-June 1962), 23-44.

2224   Waller, Michael. "The Dialectic in Lenin and Mao," in The Language of Communism. A Commentary. London: Bodley Head, 1972; 32-35.
A brief review of Mao's On Contradiction with reference to his reliance more on Lenin than Marx or Hegel for research on dialectics. [HX44. W2]

2225   *Wittfogel, Karl. "Lenin and Mao Tse-tung," New Leader, 43, no. 15 (1960), 18-21.
An appraisal of the similarities in the views and policies of Lenin and Mao on peasant soviets.

2226   Yin, Ch'ing-yao. "From Marx to Lenin to Mao Tse-tung," Iss St, 9, no. 2 (1972), 11-18.
A discussion of the modifications of Marxism by Lenin and Mao.

        c. India

2227   Aruna, Asaf Ali. "Lenin and the Indian Freedom Movement," Sov Land, 23, no. 12 (June 1970), 26.

2228   Basu, Jyoti. "Lenin Teaches Us," Peo Dem, (22 Apr. 1970), 62-68.

2229   Begum, Hajrah. "How Indian Women Came to Know Him," in LAI (anthology), 134-59.
A favorable description of the impact of Lenin and the revolution on India in general and its women's movement in particular. Begum reports that in spite of British attempts to deny Indians accurate information on Lenin and the Soviet state, Indian women gradually came to see Lenin as a leader dedicated to eliminating inequality between the sexes as well as among social classes and nations.

2230   Bhopali, Aziz. "Fighter for Real Brotherhood, Equality and Freedom," in LHIII (anthology), 66.

2231   Bose, Subhas C. "Only Leninist Irreconcilability with Right-

ists May Save the Nation from Disaster and Tragedy,"
in LHIII (anthology), 25-26.
A comparison of India with pre-revolutionary Russia
stressing the need for organization and leadership of
the Leninist type.

2232 _____. "Unity of Struggle," in LHIII (anthology), 25.
A brief statement on Lenin's support for national liberation movements.

2233 "British Propaganda against the Bolsheviks," in LHIII (anthology), 73.
A critical commentary on the image of Lenin and the Bolsheviks advanced by the British press in colonial India.

2234 *Chandra, B. "Lenin on National Liberation Movements,"
India Q, 27, no. 1 (Jan.-Mar. 1971), 40-56.
A discussion of Lenin's teachings on national liberation
movements as the root of Marxism's appeal in India.

2235 Chattapadhyay, Gautam. "Lenin and Bengali Nationalists
(1921-1924), New Age, (19 Apr. 1970), 11.

2236 *_____. "Lenin in the Eyes of Contemporary Bengalis
(1917-1924)," in Lenin in the Contemporary Indian Press,
P. Joshi, et al., eds. New Delhi: People's Publishing House, 1970, 105-24.
An account of how, in spite of British attempts to block
news from Soviet Russia, Lenin became a source of
inspiration for Bengali revolutionaries, a claim which
the author supports by providing numerous excerpts
from speeches and writings by Bengali leaders.
[DK254. L46J68]

2237 Chaturvedi, Benarsi D. "What Lenin Has Meant to Me,"
in IAL (anthology), 22-24.
A recollection of the author's abandonment of his anar-
chist philosophy upon becoming familiar with the teachings of Lenin.

2238 Desal, Narayan. "Lenin and India," Mod R, 141, no. 5
(May 1977), 291-92.

2239 *Devyatkina, T. F. "Lenin and the National Liberation Movement in India," in LANLIE (anthology), 361-82.
A positive appraisal of Lenin's influence on the revolutionary and national liberation movements in India, and
a review of his involvement with Indian revolutionaries.

2240 "First Indian Delegation in Moscow--A Report," in IAL (anthology), 43-46.
A report on statements made by Lenin and others at
a 1918 meeting in Moscow on the national liberation
movement in India.

2241   Gafurov, B. et al. "Lenin and India," Sov Land, 23, no.
        8 (Apr. 1970), 41-45.

2242   Ghosh, A. "A Guide to Action," in LHIII (anthology), 41-42.

2243   Gorakh. "Educator and Inspirer of Youth," in LHIII (an-
        thology), 93-94.

2244   *Gupta, Manmathmath. "Indian Revolutionaries, Lenin and
        the Leninist Ideology," in GTSE (anthology), 87-85.
        A survey of the evolution in India of Lenin's influence
        after the 1917 revolution. Gupta states that Indian rev-
        olutionaries had, up to 1922, only "a very hazy idea
        of what Lenin stood for," largely because of British
        censorship of news from Soviet Russia, but in the decade
        following Lenin's death his writings and accomplishments
        became known throughout India and were influential in
        converting the Indian liberation movement into one with
        a mass revolutionary and socialist character.

2245   Gupta, Promode Das. "Lenin, Our Teacher," Peo Dem,
        (22 Apr. 1970), 45-50.

2246   Hussain, Syed. "Lenin, the Beacon of Light," in LACW
        (anthology), 53-54.

2247   "An Indian Present to Lenin--A Report," in IAL (anthology), 48.
        An account of how an item (a sandalwood walking stick)
        in the Lenin Museum in Moscow, which had been of
        unknown origin, was discovered to be a gift to Lenin
        from "the people of India."

2248   Jha, Shiv Chandra. "Lenin and the Indian Liberation Move-
        ment," Link, 12, no. 36 (19 Apr. 1970), 39-41.

2249   Joshi, Lakshman N. "Lenin's Hold on Workers," in LHIII
        (anthology), 65.
        A note on the impact on Indian workers of Lenin's views
        on self-determination.

2250   *Joshi, P. C. "Lenin--Contemporary Indian Image," in Lenin
        in the Contemporary Indian Press, P. C. Joshi et al., eds.
        New Delhi: People's Publishing House, 1970; 1-104.
        A historiographical survey of the evolution of Lenin's
        image in India. Beginning with the first (1921) Indian biog-
        raphy of Lenin, by S. Dange, and reviewing all major
        writings on him up to 1930, Joshi traces Lenin's growth in
        stature among Indian revolutionaries to the point where
        his influence became so great that it shaped the entire na-
        tional liberation movement as well as led to the founding of
        the Indian Communist Party. [DK254. L46J68]

2251   Kalyanasundaram, M. "He Illuminated Our Path," in

WLMTU (anthology), 16-21.
A report on the influence in Tamid Nadu of Lenin's teachings on party organization, the national liberation movement, and the language question.

2252   *Kaushik, Devendra. "Lenin in Hindi Literature and Press," in Lenin in the Contemporary Indian Press, P. C. Joshi, et al., eds. New Delhi: People's Publishing House, 1970; 125-32.
A historiographical survey of Hindi writings on Lenin illustrating the depth of his influence in India.
[DK254. L46J68]

2253   *_____. "Leninist Principle of National Self-Determination and the Indian National Movement," in GTSE (anthology), 67-77.
A discussion of Lenin's interest in and close ties to the Indian national liberation movement and of the impact in India of his nationality doctrine. Kaushik states that many Indian leaders became disillusioned with Allied war aims and Woodrow Wilson's half-hearted advocacy of self-determination, and turned to Lenin whose writings and policies contrasted sharply with those of Western leaders. Particularly influential were Lenin's nationality policies in Soviet Central Asia where the great advances made in "education, culture, medical care, and the emancipation of women ... impressed many people in India in all walks of life."

2254   Kidwai, S. M. H. "A Benefactor of Muslims," in LHIII (anthology), 141-42.
A eulogy to Lenin as a leader sincerely concerned with the plight of India's Muslims.

2255·   Komarov, E. N. "Lenin and India," Contemporary, 13, no. 4 (Apr. 1969), 35-36.

2256   *_____. "Lenin on India," in IAL (anthology), 72-96.
A favorable outline of Lenin's influence on and interest in India. Komarov discusses the impact of Lenin's writings on the national liberation movement and its alliance with those of the peasants and proletariat as well as his teachings on the non-capitalist path to economic modernization, and then reviews statements made by Lenin which illustrate his understanding of and sympathy with the Indian revolutionary movement.

2257   Krishnan, N. K. "Lenin and India," in Century, (2 May 1970), 13-14, 27.

2258   *_____. "Lenin and the Indian National Liberation Movement," in WLMTU (anthology), 9-15.
An account of the impact on India of the Russian Revolution and Lenin, especially his decree on land and doctrine on national liberation movements. Krishnan states

that Lenin gave Indian leaders the confidence to demand liberation and, in particular, influenced both Gandhi's non-cooperation movement of the 1920's and the formation of the Indian Communist Party.

2259   "Leaders of Indian Working Class Defend Leninism," in LHIII (anthology), 120-22.

2260   "Lenin and India," Sov R, (12 May 1970), 3-17.

2261   "Lenin: Meetings with Indian Patriots," New Age, 13, no. 17 (28 Apr. 1965), 13.

2262   Litman, A. D. "Lenin and Indian Social Thinking," Contemporary, 13, no. 7 (July 1969), 35-38.

2263   _____. "A Special Place for India," Link, 12, no. 36 (19 Apr. 1970), 43-45.

2264   Mehrotra, O. P. "Lenin and India's Struggle for Freedom," Sov R, (25 July 1972), 19-22.

2265   *Menon, K. P. S. Lenin through Indian Eyes. Delhi: Vikas Publications, 1970; 79pp.
        A positive assessment of Lenin as a revolutionary, political leader, and statesman with much attention given to his influence in India. Menon also discusses similarities between Lenin and Gandhi and reviews the celebration of the Lenin centennial throughout India. [DK254. L46M45]

2266   Menon, M. S. N. "India and Lenin," Mainstream, 8 (25 Oct. 1969), 13-15, 36.

2267   Mironov, Leonid. "Lenin and India," Illus Wk India, 90, no. 17 (27 Aug. 1969), 19-21.

2268   Mitra, Ashak. "Leninist Message Valid in the Indian Context," Yojana, 14, no. 7 (19 Apr. 1970), 7-8+.

2269   Mitrokhin, L. V. "Bengal's Impression of Lenin in the Early 1920's," Contemporary, 13, no. 10 (Oct. 1969), 49-50.

2270   Mukerjee, Hiren. "The Impact of Lenin on Jawaharlal Nehru," Link, 12, no. 36 (19 Apr. 1970), 21-22.

2271   _____. "Lenin and India," New Times, no. 51 (24 Dec. 1969), 6-9.

2272   _____. "Lenin and Indian Freedom," Sov Rev, (25 Oct. 1969), 44-56.

2273   Namboodiripad, E. M. S. "Leninism and the Indian Revisionists," Peo Dem (22 Apr. 1970), 37-41.

2274   Nehru, Jawaharlal. "An Advocate of Freedom of Nations,"
         in LHIII (anthology), 18-19.

2275   _____. "Founder of a New World Organization," in
         LHIII (anthology), 17-18.

2276   _____. "Hero of Hundreds of Millions," in LHIII (an-
         thology), 19-22.

2277   Panikkar, P. T. B. "To Be a Good Disciple of Lenin,"
         in WLMTU (anthology), 41-44.
         An account of Lenin's influence on the workers, students
         and intellectuals of Kerala and how the author turned
         to Lenin for guidance in organizing the Indian revolu-
         tionary movement in that region.

2278   "The Place of Lenin," in LHIII (anthology), 60.

2279   Pratap, Raja Mahendra. "My Meeting with Comrade Lenin,"
         in IAL (anthology), 32-34.
         A brief description of a conversation with Lenin on the
         author's book Religion of Love which Lenin criticized
         as an ineffective, Tolstoyan approach to solving India's
         problems.

2280   Prem, Singh. "Lenin and Militant Indian Nationalism,"
         Century, (2 May 1970), 25-27.

2281   Raikov, A. V. "India and Lenin," Commerce, 120, no.
         3075 (11 Apr. 1970), 3.

2282   Ranadive, B. T. "Lenin and the Indian National Movement,"
         in IAL (anthology), 10-19.
         A favorable review of Lenin's Imperialism and State and
         Revolution as his two works which most affected Indian
         revolutionaries in their struggle against British imperial-
         ism.

2283   Rao, C. Rajeswara. Lenin's Teachings and Our Tactics.
         New Delhi: Communist Party of India, 1974; 36pp.
         A discussion of the influence on the Indian Communist
         Party of Lenin's teachings on tactical flexibility as the
         key to success in revolution. Rao stresses the point
         that Indian communists should unite under their leader-
         ship all radical forces and selectively apply defensive
         and offensive tactics (short of insurrection) to promote
         the creation of a communist India. [JQ298.C6A23 1974]

2284   Saha, Panchanan. "Lenin in the Bengali Press," Main-
         stream, 6, no. 13 (25 Nov. 1967), 21-22.

2285   Saklatwala, Shapurji. "In Complete Accordance with Lenin,"
         in LHIII (anthology), 39.

2286 *Sankrityayn, Rahul. "Lenin and India," in IAL (anthology),
         20-26.
         A review of Lenin's speeches and writings on India,
         and a positive description of their impact upon the In-
         dian national liberation movement.

2287   Sardesai, S. G. "Lenin, Democracy and Patriotism," in
         GTSE (anthology), 53-56.
         A defense of Lenin's teachings on the socialist democ-
         racy, and an attack, in the name of Lenin, on those
         who "counterpose democracy, patriotism and nationalism
         to socialism."

2288   _____. "Lenin, the National Question and India," New
         Age, (19 Apr. 1970), 5, 21.

2289   * _____. "The National Question and India," in LAI (an-
         thology), 57-85.
         A restatement of Lenin's principles on nationalism,
         self-determination, and national liberation movements,
         and a positive estimate of their influence in India.

2290   _____. "What Lenin Means to Us Today," in WLMTU
         (anthology), 25-29.

2291   *Sehanavis, Chinmohan. "Lenin and India," Mainstream, 7,
         no. 51 (23 Aug. 1969), 26-32; no. 52 (30 Aug. 1969),
         17-23.

2292   Sen, Bhowani. "Lenin and Agrarian Relations in India,"
         New Age, (19 Apr. 1970), 7, 18.

2293   Sen, Mohit. "Lenin and India," Illus Wk India, 91, no. 17
         (26 Apr. 1970), 20-22.

2294   _____. "Leninism and India," Link, 12, no. 36 (19
         Apr. 1970), 33-37.

2295   Shastitko, P. "Lenin and the Indian Revolutionaries," Sov
         Land, 22, no. 7 (Apr. 1969), 10-11.

2296   Singh, Bhagat. "Follow Leninist Tactics and Strategy:
         Last Message for Indian Revolutionaries," in LHIII (an-
         thology), 29-30.

2297   _____. "Lenin's Name Will Never Die," in IAL (anthol-
         ogy), 42.

2298   *Singh, Gurbaksh. "Lenin's Significance for India," in
         WLMTU (anthology), 48-55.
         An argument that Lenin's success illustrates clearly the
         importance of organization, courage, and dedication in
         any mass movement and that if leaders of national lib-
         eration movements everywhere had not turned to Lenin,

they would still be under the yoke of imperialism.

2299   Sinha, Bejoy Kumar. "The Influence of Lenin on Bhagat Singh," Link, 12, no. 36 (19 Apr. 1970), 45-47.

2300   _____. "Lenin Inspired Indian Exiles," in LHIII (anthology), 144-45.

2301   Sohni, Brisham. "Lenin's Image Today," Link, 11, no. 37 (27 Apr. 1969), 25-26.

2302   Sri, Sri. "The Meaning, to Me, of Lenin," in WLMTU (anthology), 45-47.
      A definition of Leninism as meaning freedom from both imperialism and economic oppression.

2303   *Srivastava, N. M. P. "Lenin and Indian Revolutionaries," U Asia, 23, no. 5 (Sept.-Oct. 1971), 311-20.

2304   Sundarayya, P. "Lenin in My Life," Peo Dem, (22 Apr. 1970), 42-44.

2305   "Tribute to Lenin by Indian Personalities," in IAL (anthology), 50-51.

2306   Vafa, A. "Lenin's Ideas and Jawaharlal Nehru," Socialist Cong, (15 Sept. 1969), 17-18.

2307   Vasilyev, A. "Lenin and Indian Revolutionaries," Contemporary, 13, no. 8 (Aug. 1969), 51-52.

2308   Vidyalankar, Amar N. "What Lenin Means to Us," in WLMTU (anthology), 61-68.
      A discussion of Lenin as a leader with great influence upon Indian revolutionaries (Gandhi in particular) and as a revolutionary scientist who predicted that the socialist and national liberation movements would coalesce into one world-wide struggle against imperialism.

2309   Wickremasinge, S. A. The Rise and Growth of Leninism in Ceylon," W Marxist R, 13, no. 4 (Apr. 1970), 23-26.

2310   Yagnik, Indulal. "The Great Message of Lenin," in WLMTU (anthology), 56-60.
      A tribute to Lenin as a leader and an account of his influence on a 1924 strike in Bombay.

2311   Zaheer, Sajjad. "A Man Called Lenin," in IAL (anthology), 27-31.
      A recollection of early mentionings of Lenin in India and of British attempts to retard the spread of an accurate image of him.

1) <u>Gandhi</u>

2312   Achutan, R. "Lenin and Gandhi," <u>Link</u>, 12, no. 8 (5 Oct. 1969), 41-42.

2313   *Chand, Gyan. "Lenin's Accord with Gandhi," in <u>WLMTU</u> (anthology), 36-40.
        A discussion of the similarities between Lenin and Gandhi in their insistence on the need to organize the masses in order to change society. Chand also states that Lenin was in accord with Gandhi in his recognition that, when the situation permits, peaceful methods for revolutionary action should be employed.

2314   *Dange, S. A. <u>Gandhi vs. Lenin</u>. Bombay: Liberty Literature Company, 1921.
        Not available for annotation, but as an early Indian study of Lenin, this work has received considerable attention.

2315   *Fülöp-Miller, René. <u>Lenin and Gandhi</u>. New York: Garland, 1972; 343pp., bib. 321-39. (reprint of a 1927 publication).
        The author's stated purpose is "to describe the life and work of the two men whose personalities ... most forcibly embody the spirit of the present age ... which set itself the task of attaining the unattainable, the concrete realization of age-old utopias." Fueloep-Miller states that Lenin and Gandhi were possessed by utopian visions which "drove each to make his country an instrument for the redemption of all mankind; had similar characters (simple, ascetic); and were both sincere in their concern for the common man's welfare." Besides the obvious difference in the methods they favored for the promotion of change, the author asserts that they were poles apart in their assessment of the value of technology, views on religion, and their personal physiques. [DK254.L4F83]
2315a   Reviewed in:
        *Indian R, 24 (July 1928), 456, by M. Rathnaswamy.
        *<u>Liv Age</u>, 333 (15 Oct. 1927), 687-93, by E. Lothar.
        <u>Nat Ath</u>, 42 (10 Dec. 1927), 396, by L. Woolf.
        <u>New Rep</u>, 54 (16 May 1928), Sup. 402, by V. Sheean.
        *<u>Quar R</u>, 250 (Apr. 1928), 303-17, by S. Dark.
        <u>Sat R</u>, 144 (12 Nov. 1927), 668.
        <u>Sat R Lit</u>, 5 (8 Dec. 1928), 452, by J. B. MacDonald.
        <u>Spectator</u>, 139 (5 Nov. 1927), 776.
        <u>Survey</u>, 60 (1 May 1928), 187, by P. Gavit.
        <u>TLS</u>, (10 Nov. 1927), 799.

2316   "Gandhi and Nehru on Lenin," <u>Yojana</u>, 21, no. 19 (1 Nov. 1977), 14. Also in <u>Yojana</u>, 11, no. 22 (12 Nov. 1967), 11.

2317 Ganguli, B. N. "Lenin and Gandhi," India Q, 27, no. 1 (Jan.-Mar. 1971), 3-5.

2318 _____. "Lenin Centenary: Lenin and Gandhi," For Aff Rep, 19, no. 3 (Mar. 1970), 21-24.

2319 Gorakh. "Lenin and Mahatma Gandhi," in LHIII (anthology), 98-99.
A brief comparison of the ideas of Lenin and Gandhi on non-violence and modern technology.

2320 Kar, Paresh Chandra. "Gandhi Is Not Lenin," in Romantic Gandhi: A Search for Mahatma's Originality. Calcutta: W. Newman, 1933; 63-70.
Not available for annotation.

2321 Marla, Sarma. "Gandhi and Lenin," Sarvodaya, 21, no. 5 (Nov. 1971), 233-34.

2322 *Mazlish, Bruce. "Are We Ready for an American Lenin?," Horizon, 13, no. 4 (1971), 48-55.
An examination of the lives of Lenin, Gandhi, and Mao arguing that ascetics not aesthetics make revolutions.

2323 Menon, K. P. S. "Gandhi and Lenin," Bihar Info, 18, no. 8 (1 May 1970), 5-6.

2324 _____. "Gandhi and Lenin," Illus Wk India, 90 (5 Oct. 1969), 8-11, 55.

2325 "Non-Aligned between Gandhi and Lenin," Thought (14 Mar. 1970), 5-6.

2326 *Prasad, Devi. "Lenin and Gandhi: Contemporary Revolutionaries," Gandhi M, 14, no. 4 (Oct. 1970), 369-78.
Also in R Int Aff, (5 June 1970), 32-36.

2327 Rau, B. R. K. "Marx, Lenin and Gandhi," Janata, 33, no. 4 (26 Feb. 1928), 15-16; no. 5 (5 Mar. 1978), 15-16.

2328 Roy, M. N. "Lenin's Optimism about Gandhi and Indian Nationalism," in LHIII (anthology), 35-36.
A discussion of the opinions of Lenin and Chicherin on Gandhi's leadership of India's non-cooperation movement.

2329 Sardesai, S. G. "Centenary of Lenin and Gandhi," Contemp Ind Lit, 10, no. 2 (Apr.-June 1970), 11-13, 17.

2330 _____. "Evolution of Two Centenarians," Link (15 Aug. 1969), 35-36.

2331 Shastitko, P. "Lenin and Gandhi," Sov R, (30 Sept. 1969), 30-33.

2332   Singh, G. M.   "Lenin, Gandhi and Nehru: Master Minds
            of Great Revolutions," <u>Minor</u>, 7, no. 1 (Nov. 1967),
            16-19.

2333   Srivatsa, S.   "Gandhi and Lenin," <u>Swarajya</u>, 14, no. 23
            (6 Dec. 1969), 28.

2334   Vaswani, K. N.   "Gandhi and Lenin: Two Great Liberators,"
            <u>Sarvodaya</u>, 20, no. 1 (July 1970), 25-28.

2335   Ward, Harry F.   "Lenin and Gandhi," <u>W Tommorow</u>, 8
            (Apr. 1925), 111-12.

2336   "Where Are the Messiahs?," <u>Kurukshetra</u>, (May 1970), 1,
            36.

2337   *Acton, H. B.   "Lenin's Criticism of Phenomenalism," in
       The Illusion of the Epoch.   Marxism-Leninism as a
       Philosophical Creed.   London: Cohen and West, 1962;
       23-35.
       A discussion of the nature and historical roots of Le-
       nin's attack on phenomenalism in Materialism and Em-
       pirio-Criticism, Acton isolated Lenin's basic criticism
       as being similar to Feuerbach's argument that the
       idealist philosophy must be rejected because it denies
       what all of man's actions, senses, deeds, and daily
       dealings with the world tell him--that the materialist
       view of the world is correct.   In assessing the validity
       of Lenin's argument, Acton maintains that its polemical
       nature precluded comprehensive development of a sys-
       tematic philosophy by Lenin: "Lenin ... saw certain
       essential weaknesses of phenomenalism ... [but] he
       did not have the patience to probe them fully and un-
       excitedly. "   [B809.8A32]

2338   *_____.   "The Marxist-Leninist Theory of Religion,"
       Ratio, 1 (Dec. 1958), 136-49.
       A critical examination of Lenin's "anti-religious fury"
       as expressed in Socialism and Religion (1905) and his
       The Attitude of the Workers' Party Toward Religion
       (1909).

2339   *_____.   "The Marxist Outlook," Philosophy, 22 (Nov.
       1947), 208-30.
       A review of the world outlook of Marxism with much
       attention to Lenin's attack on phenomenalism in Mater-
       ialism and Empirio-Criticism.

2340   *Adler, Erwin.   "Lenin's View on Religion," St Sov Un, 10,
       no. 1 (1970), 61-69.
       An examination of the contradiction between Lenin's
       stated views on religion and the policies which he fol-
       lowed in attempting to weaken its appeal.

2341   Adoratsky, V.   Dialectical Materialism.   New York: Inter-
       national Publishers, 1934; 96pp.
       This work, by a Soviet Marxist philosopher, is not
       specifically on Lenin but contains many references to

and short sections on his dialectical materialism. In particular, Adoratsky reviews the main points Lenin presented in Materialism and Empirio-Criticism in his struggle against turn-of-the-century threats to Marxist dialectical materialism. In a concluding chapter, Adoratsky discusses "how to study Lenin," the contents of which have been annotated separately. [HX314.A35]

2342   Aleksandrov, A. D. "Space and Time in Contemporary Physics in the Light of Lenin's Philosophical Ideas," Sov St Phil, 10 (Winter 1970-1972), 257-62.

2343   *Althusser, Louis. "Lenin and Philosophy," in Lenin and Philosophy and Other Essays. New York: Monthly Review Press, 1971; 23-70.
An assessment not of Lenin's philosophy but rather of his views on philosophy. Althusser states that Lenin is "unacceptable" to philosophers because he viewed traditional philosophy as the domain of those who devoted their lives to rumination whereas his concern was to apply and practice a philosophy while continuing to develop it in the process. The author discusses Lenin's place in Marxist philosophy, and then analyzes in detail Materialism and Empirio-Criticism for insights into his views on philosophical practice and partisanship in philosophy. Althusser concludes that Lenin made a crucial contribution by illustrating that Marxism was not so important as a new philosophy but as a new practice of philosophy based on the proletarian class position. [B4249.L384A69]

2344   Aptheker, Herbert. "Lenin, Science and Revolution," Pol Aff, 49, no. 4 (Apr. 1970), 58-65.
A review of Lenin's thought on the partisan nature of science and science's crucial role in socialist construction.

2345   Ballestram, K. G. "Dialectical Logic," St Sov Tho, 5 (Sept. 1965), 139-72.
Includes a section on Lenin's application (in Philosophical Notebooks) of dialectics to the theory of knowledge.

2346   Barashenkov, V. S. "The Leninist Concept of the Inexhaustibility of Matter in Contemporary Physics," Sov St Phil, 10 (Winter 1971-1972), 263-68.

2347   Barton, William E. The Moral Challenge of Communism. Some Ethical Aspects of Marxist-Leninist Society. London: Friends Home Service Committee, 1966; 105pp.
This study does not center upon Lenin but contains references to and short critical sections on his views on religion, atheism, ethics, and morality. [BJ1390.B34]

2348   Berdyaev, Nicholas. "General Line of Soviet Philosophy,"
        Am R, 1 (Oct. 1933), 536-59.
        In part, on Lenin's contribution to the fundamentals
        which comprise the general line of Soviet philosophy.

2349   Bienstock, Gregory. "Lenin as a Philosopher," Nineteenth
        Cent, no. 754 (Dec. 1939), 723-28.
        An assessment of Lenin's metaphysics and dialectical
        materialism as part of a review article on volume twelve
        of Lenin's Collected Works.

2350   *Bitsakis, E. I. "Symmetry and Contradiction," Sci Soc,
        38 (Fall 1974), 326-46.
        An examination of the laws of physics on symmetry in
        view of Lenin's dialectics.

2351   Blakeley, Thomas J. "The Leninist Theory of Reflection,"
        in Soviet Theory of Knowledge. Dordrecht: Reidel,
        1964; 29-35.
        A non-critical review of Lenin's theory of reflection as
        the fundamental doctrinal tenet of the theory of know-
        ledge of contemporary Soviet dialectical materialism.
        [BD161. B47]

2352   *_____. "The Salient Features of the Marxist-Leninist
        Theory of Knowledge," Boston Coll St Phil, 1 (1966),
        155-74.

2353   *Bloor, David. "The Dialectics of Metaphor," Inquiry, 14
        (Winter, 1971), 430-44.
        An analysis of Lenin's theory of perception.

2354   *Bochenski, I. M. "The Russian Origins: Lenin," in Soviet
        Russian Dialectical Materialism. Dordrecht, Holland:
        Reidel, 1963; 20-30.
        A discussion of Lenin as the founder of contemporary
        dialectical materialism with much emphasis on the his-
        torical-cultural milieu from which he emerged. Boch-
        enski contends that Marxism was attractive to Russian
        revolutionaries and Lenin in particular because of its
        "doctrinaire, revolutionary, atheistic, and messianic
        character." The Marxist philosophy which Lenin de-
        veloped, Bochenski states, was geared towards practical,
        Russian realities; "Leninism has always been a cult of
        technical practice." In spite of his practical nature,
        Bochenski asserts, Lenin nonetheless made major the-
        oretical contributions to Marxism: he fused the doctrine
        of Marx and Engels; worked out an epistemology for
        Russian Marxists; elevated the importance of human
        will in the social evolutionary process; and developed
        the link between theory and the role of the party. Bo-
        chenski concludes that Lenin added to Marxism "a blend
        of typically Russian traits and features." [B809. 8. B613]

2355   *Bociurkiw, Bohdan R.   "Lenin and Religion," in LMTL (anthology), 107-34.
An analysis of the evolution of Lenin's views on religion contending that although in a relative sense religion occupies only a small section of Lenin's collected writings, it would be a serious error "to minimize either the importance of atheism in Leninist theory or the political significance ascribed by him to the role of religion in Russian society." Bociurkiw divides Lenin's concern with religion into three stages: pre-1905, during which he was concerned chiefly with exploiting religious dissent in Russia for revolutionary purposes; 1905-1917, when he expounded the Bolshevik program and tactics on religion; and 1917-1924, when as leader of the Soviet state he shifted from theorizing on the problem of religion to practical means of dealing with the hostile Orthodox Church while overcoming religious beliefs among the masses.

2356   Bociurkiw, Bohdan R. and John W. Strong, eds. Religion and Atheism in the U.S.S.R. and Eastern Europe. London: Macmillan, 1975; 412pp.
Lenin is not the focus of any chapter in this study, but it contains some discussion of his policies toward religion and their influence on the policies of his successors. [HX536. R437]

2357   *Brameld, Theodore B.   A Philosophic Approach to Communism. Chicago: University of Chicago Press, 1933; 242pp.
An analysis of communism in terms of the basic continuity in the thought of Marx, Engels, and Lenin. Brameld argues that although Marx and Engels stated their ideas more systematically than Lenin, the latter possessed a "deeply philosophic spirit" which permeates his work, a spirit which is at one with "the essential features of his predecessors in all important respects." In attempting to substantiate this contention Brameld structures his study dialectically by a series of paired chapters (Marx-Engels: Lenin) dealing with acquiescence and activity, on individual and world levels, as illustrated in the major philosophical works of the three men. He concludes that whether dealing with the individual as a passive agent of the world process, or as an active force giving this process its distinctive features, Lenin, Marx, and Engels were in agreement, and collectively their thought represents a consistent doctrine. [HX86. B782]

2358   Buick, A.   "Lenin as a Philosopher," Rad Phil, 14 (Summer 1976), 32-41.

2359   Caponigri, A. Robert.   "Nikolai Lenin," in A History of

Western Philosophy, Volume 5, Philosophy from the
Age of Positivism to the Age of Analysis. Notre Dame:
University of Notre Dame Press, 1971; 82-82.
A brief discussion of Lenin's Materialism and Empirio-
Criticism and Philosophical Notebooks as ambiguous and
somewhat shallow philosophic works motivated more by
polemics than legitimate concern for knowledge.
[B72. M32]

2360   Chambre, Henri. "Lenin's Conception of Matter," in From
        Karl Marx to Mao Tse-tung. A Systematic Survey of
        Marxism-Leninism. New York: Kennedy and Sons,
        1963; 230-32.
        A non-critical summary of Lenin's concept of matter.
        [HX39. C483]

2361   *Ch'en, Ho-ching. "Lenin on the Principle of Party Nature
        in Philosophy," Chin St Phil, 5 (Winter 1973-1974),
        4-20.

2362   Chou, Yang. "The Fighting Tasks of Philosophy and Social
        Science Workers," Chin St Phil, 3 (Spring 1972), 239-
        95.
        A discussion of philosophy and social science as im-
        portant parts of the ideological struggle. The author
        reviews Lenin's war against revisionists and opportunists
        (especially Bernstein and Kautsky) and discusses their
        relation to the contemporary struggle against revision-
        ism.

2363   Cohen, Robert S. "Dialectical Materialism and Carnap's
        Logical Empiricism," in The Philosophy of Rudolf Car-
        nap, Paul A. Sclipp, ed. La Salle, Illinois: Open Court
        Press, 1963; 99-158.
        Lenin is not the focus of this chapter, but it includes
        an examination of his Materialism and Empirio-Criticism.
        [B945. C164S3]

2364   Cornforth, Maurice. Materialism and the Dialectical Method.
        New York: International Publishers, 1960; 139pp.
        Lenin is not the focus of any chapter in this study,
        but it does contain a non-critical summary of his con-
        tribution to the philosophy of dialectical materialism.
        [B809. 8C67]

2365   Dallmayr, F. "Marxism and Truth," Telos, 29 (Fall 1976),
        130-59.
        In part, a critical assessment of Lenin's philosophy as
        a mere reiteration of the thought of Marx and Engels.

2366   *Daniels, Robert V. "Fate and Will in the Marxian Philosophy
        of History," J His Ideas, 21, no. 4 (1960), 538-52.

An analysis of the theories on free will and determinism as presented by Marx, Lenin, and Western scholars.

2367 *Dansoko, A. et al. "Scientific Analysis, Communist Partisanship," W Marxist R, 16, no. 3 (Mar. 1973), 8-23. A review of Lenin's Materialism and Empirio-Criticism as part of a series of articles on the contemporary relevance of Lenin's major works.

2368 Deborin, A. M. "Lenin and the Crisis in Contemporary Physics," in Otchet O Deiatel'nosti Akademii Nauk S.S.S.R. Za 1929g. Volume One (appendix). Leningrad, 1939.

2369 *De George, Richard T. "Lenin's Philosophical Legacy," in Patterns of Soviet Thought. Ann Arbor: University of Michigan Press, 1961; 161-78.
An examination of Lenin's philosophical writings after Materialism and Empirio-Criticism, and a short assessment of his impact on Soviet philosophy. De George reviews several essays written by Lenin in 1913-1914 before turning to an analysis of Philosophical Notebooks where he argues that Lenin's views on dialectics and theory of knowledge are far less suited to philosophical rigor and consistency than they are to "Lenin's vision of man as an active being who could change reality and objectively realize his goals"--a fact De George sees as consistent with Lenin's practical nature. There follows a discussion of the differences between Lenin's thought and Marxism (especially over imperialism, colonial revolutions, socialism in one country, and dictatorship of the proletariat), and of Lenin's conception of Marxism as a developing, not static, body of truth which party leaders, as the heirs to Lenin's custodianship of theory, can justifiably modify. [B809.8.D4]

2370 *_____. "Materialism and Empirio-Criticism," in Patterns of Soviet Thought. Ann Arbor: University of Michigan Press, 1961; 146-60.
A critical analysis of Lenin's Materialism and Empirio-Criticism: Critical Comments on Reactionary Philosophy (1908). De George states that as a major source of contemporary Soviet philosophy and as Lenin's fullest exposition of his theory of knowledge and of reality, this work requires careful consideration. He identifies Lenin's purposes for writing the book as threefold: to defend Marx against the neo-Kantian, idealist, and Machian threats; to develop a theory of knowledge; and to clarify the status of matter. De George summarizes Lenin's thought on each of these subjects, and reaches the following critical judgments: Lenin's arguments against idealism are impressive only for their polemics and vigor but not for precision or conclusiveness; his "copy" theory of knowledge is riddled with faulty sup-

positions and serious oversimplifications; and his attempt to resolve the debate on the precise nature of matter, in fact, raised only new questions on the issue. [B809. 8. D4]

2371 *Dolgov, K. "Artistic Creativity and Lenin's Theory of Reflection," in Marxist-Leninist Aesthetics and Life. A Collection of Articles. I. Kukikova and A. Zis, eds. Moscow: Progress Publishers, 1976; 30-40.
A discussion of Lenin's precept that "man's consciousness not only reflects the objective world, but creates it" as the key to understanding the nature of artistic creativity. Dolgov stresses that Lenin's theory of reflection transcends "vulgar materialism" by depicting reflection not as a totally passive process but as a consciously active and potentially creative one. In this way the artist may not only present the objective world but also reveal "the depth and nature of man's spiritual attitude to reality and that of the subject's to the object." [BH41. M3513]

2372 *Dunayevskaya, Raya. "Hegelian Leninism," in Towards a New Marxism, Bart Grahl and Paul Piccone, eds. St. Louis: Telos Press, 1973; 159-75.
An argument that Lenin, upon reading Hegel's Science of Logic, underwent a "totally new philosophical departure toward the self-development of thought." Dunayeskaya analyzes Philosophical Notebooks to illustrate that Lenin was deeply impressed by Hegel's "genius in the dialectic" and became convinced that a systematic and comprehensive analysis of Hegelian dialectics was a crucial task to be performed by Russian Marxist philosophers if Marx's materialism was to be understood fully. Dunayevskaya examines Lenin's application of his new found dialectics to the phenomena of imperialism and modern would revolution, and discusses the lack of understanding by his fellow Bolsheviks of his "dialectics of liberation." She contends that Russian philosophers have deliberately down-played and disregarded Lenin's Philosophical Notebooks in an attempt to hide the "philosophical revolution" which occurred in his thought as well as to cloak the current Soviet regime's diversion from Leninist dialectics. Originally a paper at the Proceedings of the First International Telos Conference (1970). [HX13. 1487]

2373 *_____. "The Shock of Recognition and the Philosophic Ambivalence of Lenin," Telos, 5 (Spring 1970), 44-57.
A discussion of the proletariat's desertion of socialism for patriotism upon the outbreak of World War I as the cause of a philosophical crisis necessitating a new assessment by Lenin of the relation between subjective and objective factors in shaping history. Dunayevskaya

illustrates how this led Lenin to a study of Hegel and, as <u>Philosophical Notebooks</u> shows, to a break with much of his previous philosophy as stated in <u>Materialism and Empirio-Criticism.</u>

2374   *Eastman, Max. "Lenin's Philosophy," in <u>Marx, Lenin and the Science of Revolution.</u> Westport, Conn.: Hyperion, 1973 (reprint of a 1926 publication); 169-74.
A discussion of Lenin's philosophy as being much closer to skepticism than to dialectical materialism. Eastman contends that Lenin, in his rigid assertion that all philosophy is essentially partisan in nature, undermined the truthfulness of the dialectical materialist philosophy which he supposedly was championing. He concludes that Lenin would have been far more consistent philosophically if he had "got rid of all metaphysics and become consciously and theoretically, what he was in actual fact, a revolutionary engineer." [HX56.E3]

2375   Fedoseyev, P. N. "Lenin and the Methodology of Modern Science," <u>Revolutionary World,</u> 1 (1973), 67-74.

2376   *Feenberg, Andrew. "Notes on Methodology and Ontology in Lenin's Thought," <u>Poznan St,</u> 1 (1975), 58-64.

2377   *Feuer, Lewis S. "Between Fantasy and Reality: Lenin as a Philosopher and Social Scientist," in <u>LAL</u> (anthology), 59-79.
A psychological analysis of the evolution of Lenin's philosophical thought as it moved away from scientific and materialistic foundations to one more metaphysical and utopian. Feuer states that Lenin's early works are permeated with a self-confident, factually based, scientific materialism in which philosophical idealism and the subjective method in sociology are ridiculed. He argues that Lenin's constant struggle to determine absolutely the nature of reality was psychologically crucial to him because he was plagued by the worry ("revolutionary anxiety") that his thought might be colored by fantasy. The author illustrates the depth of Lenin's anxiety, by analyzing his highly explosive and emotional reaction to rival theorists (especially E. Mach) whose ideas threatened his assessment of reality, and therein his sanity. Feuer goes on to argue that during the years of disillusionment and frustration while in exile, Lenin's rigid materialism was shaken and thus increasingly gave way to the very fantasies against which he had previously struggled, so that his latter works (especially <u>State and Revolution</u>) are characterized by utopianism not realism. He concludes that Lenin's "utopian fantasy and materialist harshness were a curious joint product, the two polarities of a personality racked with aggressions, toward self, toward others."

2378   *_____ . "Lenin's Fantasy: The Interpretation of a Rus-
       sian Revolutionary Dream," Encounter, 35 (Dec. 1970),
       23-35.
       An argument that Lenin alternated between materialism
       and utopian fantasy as evidenced by his 1894-1915 writ-
       ing.

2379   *Fitzpatrick, J. P. "Lenin, Heir to Marx," Thought, 12
       (June 1937), 211-24.
       A sharp attack on the mechanistic and atheistic view
       of man held by Lenin and Marx.

2380   *Fleischer, H. "The Materiality of Matter," St Sov Tho,
       2 (Mar. 1962), 12-20.
       In part, a discussion of Lenin's contribution to the theory
       of matter.

2381   *Flew, Antony. "Lenin and the Cartesian Inheritance," in
       A Rational Animal. Oxford: Clarendon Press, 1978;
       196-221.
       A critical analysis of Lenin's Materialism and Empirio-
       Criticism as an illustration of how "false assumptions
       embodied in The (Cartesian) Problem of the External
       World both presuppose and support ... an equally er-
       roneous view of the nature of man." Flew criticizes
       Lenin for neglecting to carry his argument against ideal-
       ism far enough: Lenin was "not interested in the in-
       tellectual sources of the idealist error. He therefore
       never attempts to isolate and examine the Cartesian
       starting point" but tries "to dispose of idealism by im-
       petuous appeals to practice and to ... the materialist
       theory of knowledge." Flew states that Lenin had a
       simplistic and contradictory concept of perception at
       the heart of his theory of knowledge, and chose to rely
       on this in his attack on idealism instead of challenging
       directly its Cartesian foundations. [BD450. F55]

2382   *_____ . "A Linguistic Philosopher Looks at Lenin's Ma-
       terialism and Empirio-Criticism," Praxis, 3 (1967),
       98-111.

2383   *Franklin, M. "Professor Topolski on Lenin's Theory of
       History," Poznan St, 2 (1976), 79-88.

2384   Frolov, Ivan. "Lenin's Philosophical Testament," W Marx-
       ist R, 15, no. 3 (1972), 101-05.
       An analysis of Lenin's On the Significance of Militant
       Materialism as a representation of his political testa-
       ment. Frolov states that Lenin's argument for alliance
       of the Marxist philosophy and the natural sciences is
       not a distortion but an important extension of Marxism.

2385   Frostin, P. "Modern Marxist Critique of Religion. A

Survey," Luth World, 20, no. 2 (1973), 141-53.
Includes a section on Lenin's revision of Marx's views
on religion.

2386   Fu, Charles Wei-Hsun. "Marxism-Leninism-Maoism as an
        Ethical Theory," J Chin Phil, 5 (Dec. 1978), 343-62.

2387   *Fueloep-Miller, Rene. "Bolshevism in the Light of Sectar-
        ianism," in The Mind and Face of Bolshevism. An
        Examination of Cultural Life in Soviet Russia. New
        York: Harper and Row, 1965 (reprint of a 1926 pub-
        lication); 71-88.
        An interpretive examination of Lenin's Bolshevism as
        a new religion and not a scientific doctrine. The author
        states that the furious nature of Bolshevism's assault
        on religion is alien to the scientific approach to truth
        and that Lenin's adherence to materialism had all the
        blind fanaticism of the old religious sects in Russia.
        Fueloep-Miller further carries the parallel between the
        thought of Lenin and that of various Russian sectarian
        groups, and sees similarities in tone, language, and
        their communal goals. He concludes that "Bolshevism
        is, therefore, in many respects to be regarded as the
        political embodiment of the old Russian hope of the ad-
        vent of the millenium of the 'man-god'...." and that
        its Marxist ideology is "merely an attempt to conceal
        the religious and sectarian foundation of Bolshevism."
        [DK265. F785]

2388   *_____. "The Philosophy of Bolshevism," in The Mind
        and Face of Bolshevism. An Examination of Cultural
        Life in Soviet Russia. New York: Harper and Row,
        1965 (reprint of a 1926 publication); 50-70.
        An analysis of the materialist philosophy, its develop-
        ment by Lenin and other Russian Marxists, and the
        struggle waged by the Bolsheviks against all forms of
        philosophical idealism. Fueloep-Miller examines Lenin's
        assertion that all philosophies are partisan in nature
        and that the idealist philosophy is representative of "a
        class remote from the direct process of production."
        He discusses the Bolsheviks' application of the material-
        ist philosophy to Russian culture of the 1920's, espe-
        cially to the universities, art, literature, religion, and
        psychology, and concludes with a summary of Lenin's
        thought on the dialectical process in the natural sciences
        and the need to cleanse Russian science of idealistic
        philosophy. [DK265. F785]

2389   Gedo, Andras. "Philosophical Relevance of Leninism,"
        W Marxist R, 13, no. 12 (Dec. 1970), 96-103.
        A positive account of the value of Lenin's philosophical
        ideas in countering contemporary philosophical idealism.

2390 *Glezerman, G. E. "Lenin and the Problem of Scientific
Prediction," Sov St Phil, 9 (Summer 1970), 3-27.
An analysis of Lenin's thought on historical determinism
and its relation to practical decision making.

2391 *Gontarev, G. A. "The Treatment of Problems of Marxist
Ethics in the Post-Revolutionary Works of Lenin," Sov
St Phil, 6 (Winter 1967-1968), 34-41.

2392 Gotshalk, D. W. "The Paradox of Naturalism," J Phil, 43
(Mar. 1946), 152-56.
A critique of Lenin's theory of reflection and his general
naturalistic doctrine as being crude and anti-humanistic.

2393 Graham, Loren R. Science and Philosophy in the Soviet
Union. New York: Knopf, 1972; 584pp., bib. 455-84.
Lenin is not the focus of any chapter in this study, but
it contains, in many instances, significant information
on his dialectical materialism, definition of matter, and
views on physics. Graham includes in an appendix an
essay by H. J. Muller on "Lenin's Doctrines in Relation to Genetics" (item 2449). [Q127.R9G72]

2394 Gregor, A. James. "Changing Concepts of Logic in Soviet
Philosophy," Duquesne R, 11 (Fall 1966), 87-100.
Includes a discussion of Lenin's interpretation of the
logic of Hegel.

2395 * _____. "Lenin on the Nature of Sensations," St Left,
3, no. 2 (1963), 34-42.

2396 * _____. "The Philosophy of V. I. Lenin," in A Survey
of Marxism. Problems in Philosophy and the Theory
of History. New York: Random House, 1965; 73-110.
A critical assessment of Lenin's Materialism and Empirio-
Criticism and Philosophical Notebooks, and an examination of the problems faced by contemporary Soviet Marxists who attempt to synthesize Lenin's ambiguous and
sometimes contradictory ideas. Gregor reviews Lenin's
thought on the nature of matter, knowledge, and truth,
and asserts that major "epistemological difficulties at-
tend each of these three fundamental elements of Lenin's
Marxism as a philosophy of nature." Gregor provides
numerous illustrations of what he sees as errors in
Lenin's logic, assumption and deduction, oversimplifications, and, most importantly, conclusions which fully
seem to refute many of the very points Lenin hoped to
prove. To make matters worse, Gregor argues, Lenin,
as he became more sophisticated in his philosophical
thought recorded views in his Philosophical Notebooks
which are inconsistent with those expressed in Materialism and Empirio-Criticism especially in regard to
his theory of reflection. [B809.8G65]

2397 * _____ . "V. I. Lenin and the Materialist Conception of
History," in A Survey of Marxism. Problems in Philosophy and the Theory of History. New York: Random House, 1965; 205-55.
A scholarly examination of Lenin's concept of the role
of consciousness in history as a significant departure
from the classical Marxist conception of history. Gregor links Lenin's belief that "some men were possessed
of the gift of class consciousness while others were
not" to Lenin's general inversion of classical Marxism
through reduction to a minimum the part played by objective historical conditions while maximizing the role
played by exceptional leaders and their organizations.
[B809.8G65]

2398 Gulian, Constantin I. "Leninist Principles in the Philosophical Research Carried on in Romania," in CFOLI (anthology), 349-66.
A discussion of various disputes and developments within Rumanian Marxist philosophy with much reference to
Lenin's Materialism and Empirio-Criticism and Philosophical Notebooks for theoretical support.

2399 *Gurian, Waldermar. "Partiinost and Knowledge," in Continuity and Change in Russian and Soviet Thought, Ernest J. Simmons, ed. Cambridge: Harvard University
Press, 1955; 298-306.
A discussion of Lenin's Materialism and Empirio-Criticism as the basis of the CPSU's belief that all knowledge "ought to be determined by partiinost," meaning,
it must serve the party and its policies. Gurian devotes most of his essay to showing the practical and
negative consequences of partiinost. [DK263.3J6]

2400 Hoffman, John. Marxism and the Theory of Praxis. A
Critique of Some New Versions of Old Alliances. New
York: International Publishers, 1975; 239pp.
This study does not focus on Lenin or have a separate
chapter on him but has many critical references to and
short sections on his philosophical views as expressed
in Materialism and Empirio-Criticism. [B809.8H564]

2401 *Hogan, Homer. "The Basic Perspective of Marxism-Leninism," St Sov Tho, 7 (Dec. 1967), 297-317.
A positive assessment of Lenin's theory of reflection
as presented in Materialism and Empirio-Criticism.

2402 * _____ . "On Interpreting Lenin, a Rejoinder to S. A.
Jordan," St Sov Tho, 8 (Mar. 1968), 68-71.

2403 *Holmes, Larry E. "Science as Fiction: The Concept of
'History as Science' in the U.S.S.R. 1917-1930," Clio,
3 (Oct. 1974), 27-50.

Includes a section on Lenin's contribution to the Soviet concept of history as an exact science.

2404 *Il'in, A. and P. V. Alekseev. "Lenin's Idea of the Union of Marxist Philosophy and Natural Science," Sov St Phil, 12 (Summer 1973), 86-97.

2405 *Iovchuk, Mikhail. Philosophical Traditions Today. Moscow: Progress Publishers, 1973; 317pp.
A comprehensive Soviet discussion of the contributions made by Lenin to Marxist philosophy and to the Marxist history of philosophy. Iovchuk also reviews favorably Lenin's impact on the Soviet philosophy of science, the reception in the communist world of the Leninist philosophical tradition, and the relevance of Leninism to the current ideological struggle against capitalism and revisionism. [B4249. L38415513]

2406 Jaworskj, Michael. "Lenin's Interpretation of Dialectical Laws," in Soviet Political Thought. An Anthology. Baltimore: J. Hopkins Press, 1967; 12-15.
A brief analysis of Lenin's thought on dialectical laws and dialectical materialism. Jaworskj contends that "Lenin's contribution to the clarification of the problems that fall within the scope of dialectical materialism is not very impressive" and that Lenin's theory of the struggle of opposites is, in fact, incompatible with the idea that communism will be a society without opposite classes and hence without struggle. [JA84. R9J3]

2407 Joja, Athanase. "Reflections about Ideology and Science," in CFOLI (anthology), 197-205.
A positive presentation of Lenin's ideas on the relation between ideology and the pure and social sciences. Joja summarizes Lenin's views on the partisan nature of philosophy and on the cognition of matter and stresses the importance of Lenin's assertion that the nature of matter is a scientific not an ideological concern.

2408 *Jordan, Z. A. "The Dialectical Materialism of Lenin," Slav R, 25, no. 2 (June 1966), 259-86.

2409 * _____. "The Dialectical Materialism of Lenin," in The Evolution of Dialectical Materialism. A Philosophical and Sociological Analysis. London: Macmillan, 1967; 108-49.
A critical discussion of the basic elements of Lenin's dialectical materialism as a doctrine distinctly different from that of Engels who Lenin often claimed to be defending against revisionism. Jordan carefully surveys Lenin's epistemological determinism, (discussing the roots of his views as well as their inadequacies) and his principle of partisanship in philosophy. In compar-

ing Lenin's and Engel's dialectical materialism, the author states that Lenin rejected the absolute materialism of Engels, reduced Engels' three laws of dialectics to one, lacked Engels' deep concern for natural science (a concern which tempered Engels' views on the laws of dialectics), and had a much more practical approach to dialectical materialism than the more philosophical Engels. [B809.8J6]

2410 * _____. "Engels' Representative Realism and Lenin's Theory of Perception," in Philosophy and Ideology. The Development of Philosophy and Marxism-Leninism in Poland Since the Second World War. Dordrecht, Holland: Reidel, 1963; 322-34.
A highly critical analysis of Lenin's theory of perception for inconsistencies with the thought of Engels. Jordan establishes that in Engels' conception of philosophy there is no place for a theory of knowledge, and that Engels' own writings on this subject never went beyond the adoption of "the common sense, naively realistic" point of view. Jordan summarizes the principal points of Lenin's theory of knowledge, especially his copy theory of perception, and then systematically criticizes it for not progressing beyond a critical review of rival philosophers. He provides numerous examples of facts that cannot be accommodated within Lenin's copy theory, and concludes with an assessment of contemporary Polish Marxist-Leninist attempts to smooth out its inconsistencies. [B4681.P6J6]

2411 Kaplan, Frederick I. "Berkeleian Arguments against the Theory of Reflection," in Bolshevik Ideology and the Ethics of Soviet Labor. 1917-1920: The Formative Years. New York: Philosophical Library Press, 1968; 895-97, bib. 426-503.
A three point critique, from the perspective of Berkeley, of Lenin's theory of reflection. [HD8526.K28]

2412 * _____. "Bolshevik Ideology: Lenin's Theory of Knowledge and Lenin's Theory of History," in Bolshevik Ideology and the Ethics of Soviet Labor. 1917-1920: The Formative Years. New York: Philosophical Library Press, 1968; 9-42.
An assessment of Lenin's materialist philosophy as the foundation of Bolshevik ideology and, in turn, the source of Bolshevik reasoning and policy towards labor in the 1917-1920 period. Kaplan outlines Lenin's philosophical thought and develops an argument that Lenin's epistemology is the basis of his theory of history and political actions. More particularly, Kaplan states that Lenin's theory of reflection "functions politically and psychologically both to reinforce the authoritarian principle by which there can be only one view of the world and

at the same time to engender doubt and uncertainty concerning the knowledge that can be acquired of that world. "

2413 *Katkov, George. "Lenin as Philosopher," LMTL (anthology), 71-86.
A discussion of Lenin's lack of concern with the purely philosophic aspects of Marxism as compared to his attention to Marxism's revolutionary principles. Katkov studies Lenin's Philosophical Notebooks and concludes that Lenin added nothing of significance to any of the philosophers that he read. Lenin's attacks on Marxist philosophers (especially Bogdanov) who deviated from his interpretation of Marx, Katkov claims, are abusive and show little insight into philosophical knowledge. He discusses Lenin's Materialism and Empiro-Criticism, as a plagiarized version of a work by Akselrod (1904), the sole merit of which rests in the insights it provides into Lenin's infatuation with the theory of reflection.

2414 Katvan, Zeev. "Reflection Theory and the Identity of Thinking and Being," St Sov Tho, 18, no. 2 (May 1978), 87-109.
Includes a section on Lenin's theory of reflection.

2415 *Kedrov, B. M. "Lenin's Doctrine of Dialectics," W Marxist R, 22, no. 7 (July 1979), 37-43.

2416 * . "On the Distinctive Characteristics of Lenin's Philosophical Notebooks," St Sov Phil, 9, no. 1 (Summer 1970), 28-44. Translated from Voprosy Filosofii, no. 12 (1969).

2417 * . "V. I. Lenin on the Dialectics of the Development of Natural Science," Sov St Phil, 10 (Winter 1971-1972), 231-39.

2418 *Keldysh, Mstislav. "Lenin and Science," Cult Life, 7 (July 1970), 16-18.
A positive assessment of the influence of Lenin's dialectical materialism on the development of physics.

2419 * . "Lenin and the Development of Science," UNESCO C 23 (July 1970), 6-11.
A discussion of Materialism and Empirio-Criticism as a Marxist response to turn of the century developments in physics, and a review of Lenin's efforts to advance science as a point of socialist construction.

2420 *Kelle, V. Zh. "The Leninist Conception of Scientific Ideology and Its Critics," Sov St Phil, 9 (Fall 1970), 99-120.
A review of Lenin's belief that Marxist ideology is scientific not philosophical.

2421   Kharchev, A. G. and B. D. Iakolev. "The Development of
        Marxist-Leninist Ethics in the Period of Socialist Con-
        struction in the U. S. S. R. ," Sov St Phil, 7 (Winter 1968),
        21-29.
        In part, on Lenin's views on ethics and the cultural
        revolution.

2422   Kirschenmann, Peter P. "Lenin's Influence on the Doctrine
        of Reflection," in Information and Reflection. On Some
        Problems of Cybernetics and How Contemporary Dialec-
        tical Materialism Copes with Them. Dordrecht, Hol-
        land: Reidel, 1969; 97-99.
        A short statement on Lenin's Materialism and Empirio-
        Criticism as being the source of the epistemological
        stress placed by Soviet philosophers on the doctrine of
        reflection in their study of matter and consciousness.
        [B809. 8K5213]

2423   *Kolakowski, Leszek. "Philosophy and Politics in the Bol-
        shevik Movement," in Main Currents of Marxism. Its
        Rise, Growth and Dissolution. Vol. 2. The Golden
        Age. Oxford: Clarendon, 1978; 413-66, bib. 529-36.
        Lenin is not the focus of this chapter, but it contains
        an assessment of his Materialism and Empirio-Criticism,
        Philosophical Notebooks, and his thought on religion.
        [HX36. K61813]

2424   Kolman, E. "Modern Natural Science Confirms Lenin's
        Prevision," W Marxist R, 3, no. 4 (Apr. 1960), 28-34.
        A discussion of how Lenin's general laws of natural
        science, as expressed in Materialism and Empirio-Cri-
        ticism, have been confirmed empirically by modern
        science.

2425   Konstantinov, F. "The Leninist Stage in the Development
        of Histomat," in Blakeley, T. J. Themes in Soviet
        Marxist Philosophy. Selected Articles from the 'Filo-
        sofskaja Enciklopedija. ' Dordrecht, Holland: Reidel,
        1975; 169-73.
        A Soviet restatement of Lenin's basic thoughts on his-
        torical materialism, and a defense of Lenin against
        Western critics who claim he deviated from Marx.
        [B809. 8T47]

2426   *Konyukhovsky, V. N. "Lenin and Philosophy," in LR (an-
        thology), 13-34.
        A Soviet review of Lenin's contributions to the philosoph-
        ical basis of Marxism. Konyukhovsky discusses Le-
        nin's views on the partisan nature of philosophy, ma-
        terialism and the natural sciences, and the materialist
        conception of history. He gives particular attention to
        Lenin's theory of reflection.

2427 Kopnin, Pavel. "Lenin's Approach to Dialectical Materialism," Revolutionary World, 2 (1973), 1-9.

2428 Laszlo, Ervin. "Marxism Leninism versus Neurophysiology,"
St Sov Tho, 9 (June 1969), 104-11.
Includes an analysis of Lenin's views on objective reality
as reflected by the senses.

2429 *Lefebvre, Reginald R. "Lenin's Materialism; An Evaluation
of the Philosophical Basis of Communism," St. Louis
University, 1936 (Dissertation).

2430 *Lenin and Modern Natural Science. Moscow: Progress
Publishers, 1978; 422pp.

2431 "Leninism and Philosophy," in LTCOA (anthology), 106-22.
A defense of Lenin as a philosopher against those who
maintain that he was only effective in practical politics.
The author reviews Lenin's main philosophical contributions to Marxism (Materialism and Empirio-Criticism,
Philosophical Notebooks and On the Significance of Militant Materialism) concentrating on his theories of knowledge and reflection.

2432 *Levine, Norman. "Lukacs on Lenin," St Sov Tho, 18 (Feb.
1978), 17-31.
A survey of the evolution of Lukacs' attitude toward
Leninism as a philosophy and political creed.

2433 *Lowy, Michael. "From the 'Logic' of Hegel to the Finland
Station in Petrograd," Critique, no. 6 (1976), 5-15.
An assessment of the Hegelian foundations of Lenin's
philosophical break with the Marxism of the Second International and his theoretical transformation to the
revolutionary dialectics of the April Theses of 1917.

2434 Lupinin, Nikolai. "Introduction to and Commentary on an
Unpublished Letter of V. I. Lenin to the Members of
the Politburo," Trans Asso Rus-Am Sch, 5 (1971), 187-89.
A 1922 letter which the author presents as an illustration of Lenin's belief in use of force as a means of
crushing religion.

2435 McGill, V. J. "Notes on Theory and Practice in Marxist
Philosophy," Phil Phen Res, 5 (1944-1945), 217-241.
Includes an assessment of Lenin's Materialism and Em-
pirio-Criticism.

2436 McInnes, Neil. "From Marx to Marcuse," Survey, 16, no.
1 (1971), 138-55.

2437 *Mackinnon, D. "Lenin and Theology," Theology, 74 (Mar.
1971), 100-11.

2438 *McKown, Delos B. "The Classical Marxist Critiques of
          Religion: Marx, Engels, Lenin, Kautsky," Florida
          State University, 1972 (Dissertation).

2439 *_____. "Lenin's Critique of Religion," in The Classical
          Critiques of Religion: Marx, Engels, Lenin, Kautsky.
          Hague: Martinus Nijhoff, 1975; 94-121, bib. 163-67.
          A critical assessment of Lenin's theoretical views on
          religion asserting that while he was aware on a practi-
          cal level of the complexity and vitality of religion, his
          philosophical thought on religion is very simplistic.
          McKown summarizes Lenin's writings on the etiology
          of religion and criticizes Lenin for seeing religion's
          roots as resting only in "the socially downtrodden con-
          dition of the proletariat," while ignoring the many other
          sources of religion. McKown states that Lenin was
          even more superficial in his study of the history of re-
          ligion and its various functions, and contented himself
          with mouthing familiar Marxist themes as opposed to
          studying scientifically the complexities of religion. The
          author concludes with a discussion of Lenin's views on
          agnosticism, his opposition to presenting socialism as
          a religion, and criticism of contemporary religious
          movements. [HX536. M314]

2440 *Marcu, Valeriu. "Dogma and Dialectic in Lenin," in Men
          and Forces of Our Time. Freeport: Books for Li-
          brary Press, 1968 (reprint of a 1931 publication); 51-
          72.
          A critique of Lenin as a Marxist philosopher stressing
          the overly practical and polemical nature of his thought.
          Marcu discusses Lenin's attack on philosophical ideal-
          ism, his spirited debates with fellow Marxists, and his
          narrow-minded self-confidence in all that he professed
          as being polemically impressive but not based on any
          carefully conceived philosophy. The author sees this
          pragmatic approach to philosophy as the root of the
          "thousand contradictions" in Lenin's writings, and con-
          cludes that Lenin simply adjusted his dialectical ma-
          terialism "plastically to all vicissitudes" and then meas-
          ured the validity of these adjustments in terms of how
          successfully they could be practiced in the real world
          of twentieth-century Russia. [D412. M313]

2441 *Mare, Calina. "Lenin's Presence in Contemporary Philosoph-
          ical Thought," in CFOLI (anthology), 228-41.
          A positive assessment of Lenin as a philosopher. Mare
          compares Lenin's Materialism and Empirio-Criticism
          and Philosophical Notebooks, and stresses the less rigid
          approach to the reflection theory in the latter work,
          where Lenin argued "human consciousness does not only
          reflect the objective world but it also creates it." Mare
          concludes that the polemical nature of Materialism and

Empirio-Criticism dictated the extreme position taken
by Lenin in this work, where-as in Philosophical Notebooks Lenin demonstrated more tolerant and sophisticated philosophical thought with greater relevance to
contemporary philosophy.

2442   *Marek, Jiri. "Lenin's Relationship to the Ideas of Physi-
cists," St Sov Tho, 17, no. 1 (May 1977), 63-80.
A critical examination of Materialism and Empirio-
Criticism.

2443   *Maxey, Chester C. "The Proletarian State," in Political
Philosophies. New York: Macmillan, 1938; 640-53,
bib. , 652-53.
A discussion of Lenin as a political philosopher of
power, depth, and importance who was no opportunist
but rather based his revolutionary actions on a cohesive
political philosophy. Maxey contends that Lenin consistently and faithfully applied dialectical materialism
to Russian circumstances of 1917-1923 as a means of
determining the nature of the proletarian state, and
that his dialectical assessment of the dangers posed by
the extremes of revolutionary anarchism and bourgeois
democracy led him to the construction of a centralized
dictatorial revolutionary regime as the best means of
socialist government. [JA81. M35]

2444   Merleau-Ponty, Maurice. "Pravda," in Adventures of the
Dialectic. Evanston: Northwestern University Press,
1973); 59-73.
In part, a critique of Lenin's theory of knowledge as
expressed in Materialism and Empirio-Criticism.
[B809. 8M4413]

2445   *Mikulak, M. W. "Lenin on the 'Party' Nature of Science
and Philosophy," in Essays in Russian and Soviet History in Honor of Geroid Tanquary Robinson, John S.
Curtiss, ed. New York: Columbia University Press,
1973; 164-76.
A discussion of Lenin's ideas on the partisan nature of
philosophy and science and the historical context within
which these ideas were developed. Mikulak reviews
the "crisis in physics" which developed at the turn of
the century, and how various materialist philosophers
sought to rationalize the new discoveries in physics with
the materialist conception of matter. He discusses
Materialism and Empirio-Criticism as an attempt to
resolve this crisis, and then surveys the impact of
Lenin's concept of partiinost' on Soviet policies towards
the sciences, especially physics and biology. [DK4. C8]

2446   *Milovidov, A. S. "The Leninist Style of Scientific Creativity," in PHVIL (anthology), 268-86.

A Soviet account of the blend of creative, dialectical, and ethical elements in Lenin's philosophy. Milovidov begins by stating that Lenin believed the "definiteness of political position is the most important element for the investigator." From this fundamental propostion Lenin proceeded to enumerate the most effective means for specific scientific-theoretical investigation as being scrupulous study of all related facts, careful combination of dialectical flexibility with definite concepts, and maintenance of complete humility, honesty, and dedication as a firm ethical foundation. Milovidov stresses that throughout all of Lenin's career he exhibited complete unity of thought and action and always insisted that science be approached in a creative fashion rather than treated as formulas and lessons to be memorized.

2447   *Moore, Stanley. "Marx and Lenin as Historical Materialists," Phil Pub Aff, 4, no. 2 (Winter 1975), 171-94.

2448   Mshvenieradze, V. V. "Lenin as Philosopher," in Marxism, Revolution and Peace, Howard L. Parsons and John Somerville eds. Amsterdam: B. R. Gruner B. V., 1977; 197-204.
A short summary of the basics of Lenin's philosophy as expressed in Materialism and Empirio-Criticism and Philosophical Notebooks, and a positive review of his contribution to the history of philosophy. [B809.8S557]

2449   *Muller, Hermann J. "Lenin's Doctrines in Relation to Genetics," in Science and Philosophy in the Soviet Union, Loren R. Graham, ed. New York: Knopf, 1972; 453-69, bib. 555-84.
A positive assessment of Materialism and Empirio-Criticism based primarily on the contention that Lenin placed natural science on firm philosophical foundations by showing that "true science could only be unequivocally materialistic." Following Lenin's example in his assault on the Machian school in physics, Muller attacks various geneticists and biologists (especially T. H. Morgan) for interjecting idealism (cloaked as empiricism) into science. [Q127.R9G72]

2450   *Mussachia, M. M. "On Contradiction in Dialectical Materialism," Sci Soc, 41, no. 2 (Summer 1977), 257-80.
A discussion of the views of Marx, Engels, and Lenin on logic, dialectics, and contradiction, with much reference to Hegel. Criticism by M. Colman, Sci Soc, 42, no. 2 (Summer 1978), 185-91 with a reply, 191-98.

2451   Novikov, A. I. "The Historiography of Philosophy: Subject Matter and Aims," Sov St Phil, 3 (Fall 1964), 24-34.

Includes a section discussing Lenin's history of philosophy as expressed in Philosophical Notebooks.

2452   Okulov, A. F. "How Lenin Developed the Philosophy of Marxism," in LGT (anthology), 30-59.
An examination of Lenin's positive contributions to the materialist conception of history, the dialectical process of history, and the history of Marxist philosophy. Okulov pays most attention to Lenin's works: The Development of Capitalism in Russia, Imperialism, the Highest Stage of Capitalism, The State and Revolution, Philosophical Notebooks, and Materialism and Empirio-Criticism as he praises Lenin's thought for depth, clarity, and boldness, and for providing guidance in the struggle against revisionism.

2453   *Olgin, Constantine. "Lenin's Philosophical Legacy: The Reconstruction of Dialectical Materialism," St Sov Un, 4, no. 4 (1965), 62-74.
An assessment of Lenin's thought on dialectical materialism and partiinost', and a review of the post-1955 attempts by Soviet philosophers to develop systematically Lenin's thought.

2454   *_____. "The Philosophy of V. I. Lenin," St Sov Un, 3, no. 3 (1964), 31-58.
A review of the strengths and weaknesses of and inconsistencies between Lenin's Materialism and Empirio-Criticism and his Philosophical Notebooks.

2455   *_____. "Soviet Philosophy," St Sov Un, 2, no. 3 (1963), 146-65.
An examination of Soviet philosophers' attempts to adapt Lenin's philosophy to present day realities.

2456   Omel'ianovskii, M. E. "V. I. Lenin and Problems of Dialectics in Contemporary Physics," Sov St Phil, 10 (Winter 1971-1972), 240-51.

2457   *O'Rourke, James J. "Lenin," in The Problem of Freedom in Marxist Thought. Dordrecht, Holland: Reidel, 1974; 69-78.
An analysis of Lenin's conception of human freedom and to what degree his understanding is decidedly deterministic in nature. O'Rourke examines Lenin's early defense of Marxism against the charge of fatalism; his adaptation and interpretation of the Engelsian view on freedom and necessity; his conception of the relation between objective laws and human activity as found in the Philosophical Notebooks; and the importance of his alleged voluntarism. He asserts that "Lenin's early rejection of free will and his stumbling interpretation of relations between freedom and necessity did not enrich

the Marxist tradition," but some of his "cryptic jottings
in the Philosophical Notebooks on freedom and subjec-
tivity" are at least somewhat innovative and interesting.
He concludes that Lenin's greatest "legacy to the Soviet
view of freedom was his own revolutionary action which
demonstrated quite clearly that a single individual can
... exert extraordinary influence on that social reality
of which he is alleged to be a product." [B824. 4. 076]

2458　*Pakhamov, V. Ia.　"Contemporary Physics and Lenin's
Conception of Objective Truth," Sov St Phil, 9 (Summer
1970), 60-80.

2459　*Pannekoek, Anton.　Lenin as Philosopher.　A Critical Examination of the Philosophical Basis of Leninism.　New
York: New Essays, 1948; 80pp.
A defense of E. Mach and R. Avenarius against the
criticisms advanced by Lenin in Materialism and Empirio-Criticism, and a sharp attack on Lenin's philosophy.
Pannekoek examines Lenin's polemic against Mach, and
states that Lenin assigned to Mach opinions different
from Mach's real ones: "Lenin ... manifestly does
not care about what Mach really thinks, but about what
he should think if his logic were identical to Lenin's,"
thereby rendering Mach in an "entirely wrong and mean-
ingless way." Pannekoek asserts that Lenin followed
the same tactic in criticizing Avenarius. He characterizes Lenin's thought on materialism and natural science as being simplistic, short-sighted and contradictory,
and far more a reflection of a practical mind than one
steeped in philosophy. Pannekoek concludes that "Lenin
never knew the real Marxism" so his "Russian bolshevism cannot be reproached for having abandoned the
way of Marxism, for it was never on the way."
[B4249. L384. P2713]

2460　Pantazi, Radu.　"Leninist Criteria for Interpreting the
Trends of Contemporary Thought," in CFLOI (anthology),
242-48.
A favorable discussion of Lenin's belief that philosophical questions should be considered from a historical
viewpoint and in relation to the other philosophical questions so that Marxism would be a broad-minded, flexible, and realistic philosophy. Pantazi maintains that
this capacity for critical self-development makes Leninism superior to any contemporary philosophy.

2461　*Park, Desiree.　"Lenin and Berkeley: Origins of a Contemporary Myth," St Int Folosof, 2 (Fall 1970), 11-28.

2462　*Parsons, Howard L.　"The Influence of Lenin's Thought on
U. S. Philosophers," in LIOUS (anthology), 181-201.
An historiographical essay on the assessment by Ameri-

can philosophers of Lenin's philosophy stressing the
direct connection between interpretations of Leninism
and the status of American-Soviet relations. Parsons
distinguishes five main periods in Soviet-American relations (1917-1928, 1941-1945, 1945-1960, 1960-1970)
and illustrates how assessments of Lenin during World
War II and the era of peaceful coexistence were both
more numerous and favorable than those during the
periods when hostility towards the Soviet Union was more
pronounced in America. He provides capsule reviews
of nearly one hundred books, essays, and articles which
either focus on or in part deal with Lenin's philosophy.

2463 *_____. "Lenin's Theory of Personality," in East-West
Dialogues, Paul K. Crosser, David H. DeGrood and
and Dale Riepe, eds. Amsterdam: Gruner, 1973; 79-
86.
A positive assessment of Lenin's theory of personality
as one which is "practical, active and optimistic." Parsons discusses the dialectical materialist roots of Lenin's
theory of personality and asserts that such roots in no
way led Lenin to a dogmatic and deterministic concept
of personality. The author reviews how Lenin reconciled
freedom and creativity with determinism by calling for
men to utilize the "objective, collective, creative power
within them ..." to "free themselves from exploitive
conditions and create a humane socialist order." Originally an address to the Seventh World Congress of
Sociology, Varna, Bulgaria. [HX542. C75]

2464 "Patriarch's Letter to Lenin and Trotzky," Cur Hist M,
11, part 2 (Feb. 1920), 299-301.
An encyclical critique (later revised), by Patriarch
Tikhon, of Lenin's undemocratic policies.

2465 *Paul, G. A. "Lenin's Theory of Perception," in Philosophy
and Analysis, Margaret MacDonald, ed. Oxford: B.
Blackwell, 1954; 278-86.
A critical assessment of Lenin's theory of perception
in terms of whether or not it can provide either a
"simple description of how something works" or "of how
the human perceiving apparatus works." Paul finds
Lenin's theory to be wholly inadequate as it yields only
an indirect comparison of an object's reflection and the
object itself with no way of determining in practice or
independently if there was a reflection or not.
[B808. A5] Also in Analysis, 5, no. 5 (Aug. 1938), 65-
73.

2466 Pavlov, Todor. "Marxism-Leninism and the Copernican
Revolution in Philosophy," Sov St Phil, 13 (Summer
1974), 4-23.
Includes a section on Lenin's theory of reflection.

2467   Petrovic, Gajo. Marx in the Mid-Twentieth Century. A
        Yugoslav Philosopher Considers Karl Marx's Writings.
        Garden City: Doubleday, 1967; 237pp.
        This work does not have a separate chapter on Lenin
        but contains numerous references to and several short
        sections on various points of his philosophy, theory of
        reflection, and views on the nature of matter, truth,
        and reflection. [HX39.5P47]

2468   Philipov, Alexander. Logic and Dialectic in the Soviet
        Union. New York: Research Program in the U.S.S.R.,
        1952; 89pp.
        Lenin is not the focus of any one chapter in this study,
        but it contains many references to his philosophy, most
        of which deal with its logical inconsistencies.
        [B809.8F48]

2469   *Piccone, Paul. "Towards an Understanding of Lenin's Phi-
        losophy," Rad Amer, 4, no. 7 (Sept. 1970), 3-20.
        A review of Lenin's philosophy as expressed in Mater-
        ialism and Empirio-Criticism and Philosophical Note-
        books.

2470   Protasenko, Z. M. "Partisanship (Partiinost') in Philosophy
        and Political Parties," Sov St Phil, 9 (Fall 1970), 121-
        40.

2471   *Rozhin, V. P. "Lenin and Problems of the Marxist Theory
        of Development," Sov St Phil, 9 (Summer 1970), 45-59.
        A favorable assessment of Lenin's contribution to the
        growth of materialist dialectics as a science of develop-
        ment in opposition to the metaphysical notion of develop-
        ment.

2472   *Ruben, David-Hillel. "Lenin and His Critics," in Marxism
        and Materialism. A Study in Marxist Theory of Know-
        ledge. Sussex, New Jersey: Humanities Press, 1977;
        165-99.
        A positive assessment of Lenin's theory of reflection
        as expressed in Materialism and Empirio-Criticism,
        and a defense of this theory against its critics. Ruben
        isolates as the main strengths of Materialism and Em-
        pirio-Criticism "Lenin's clear perception of the intimate
        connection between materialism and a reflection theory
        of knowledge" and his linking of "the choice between re-
        flective and interpretive (a priori) roles with the choice
        between materialism and idealism respectively." Ruben
        discusses at length this strength and argues that what-
        ever defects exist in Materialism and Empirio-Criticism,
        they "do not outweigh this important virtue, which has
        been systematically overlooked" by critics, especially
        Pannekeok and Valentinov. [B809.8R76]

2473 *Sabine, George H. "The Ethics of Bolshevism," Phil R,
      70 (July 1961), 299-319.
      An argument that Lenin created a code of ethics for
      Russian revolutionists by drawing on the moral ideas
      current in Russian literature (Goncharov, Dostoevsky,
      Chekhov, Tolstoy) for purposes different than the authors
      intended.

2474 Saha, Meghnad. "Lenin's Deep Knowledge of Science," in
      LHIII (anthology), 45.

2475 *Schedler, George. "A Defense of the Lenin-Engels View
      of Dialectical Materialism and Class Consciousness,"
      Revol World, 33 (1979), 40-70.

2476 *Schneider, Eberhard. "Lenin as a Philosopher," St Sov Un,
      9, no. 1 (1969), 37-55.

2477 Sellars, Roy W. "Reflections of Dialectical Materialism,"
      Phil Phen Res, 5, no. 2 (Dec. 1944), 157-79.

2478 *Selsam, Howard. "Some Comments on Lenin's Philosophical
      Notebooks," St Left, 3, no. 2 (1963), 43-53.

2479 *Shteppa, Konstantin, et al. Russian Historians and the
      Soviet State. New Brunswick: Rutgers University
      Press, 1962; 436pp.
      Lenin is not the focus of any one chapter in this study,
      but it contains many references to and several short
      sections on his views on history and historians and
      their relation to culture. [D16.4R9S45]

2480 Sidikhmenov, V. Y. "Against Distortions of the Leninist
      Philosophical Heritage," in LAMCP (anthology), 36-68.
      A critical review of the main aspects of the Maoist
      philosophy as being inconsistent with Lenin's teachings
      and heavily tainted with subjectivism. Sidikhmenov
      stresses the Maoists' exaggerations of the role of man
      in isolation from objective material factors, and pro-
      vides as examples Maoist views on nuclear war, the Great
      Leap (1958-1960), and the "earth moving force" of the
      ideas of Mao. On a philosophical level, Sidikhmenov
      labels the Maoists' interpretation of dialectical mater-
      ialism as "subjectivist idealism" and a direct contra-
      diction of Lenin's law of the unity of conflict of op-
      posites. He also argues that the Maoists have "falsi-
      fied" Lenin's theory of cognition by reviving the meta-
      physical approach to knowledge.

2481 *Smeveskiy, B. N. Lenin's Contributions to the Development
      of Geography. New York: American Institute for Marx-
      ist Studies, 1973; 37pp.

A positive assessment, by a Soviet geographer, of Lenin's Materialism and Empirio-Criticism as an effective critique of idealism and mysticism and a work which greatly advanced the science of geography. Smeveskiy contends that geography has been aided by Lenin's principles on matter and motion, the unity and struggle of opposites, transformation of quantitative to qualitative change, and the law of the negation of the negation. He also discusses Lenin's theory of economic regionalization, as stated in The Development of Capitalism in Russia, as opening up "a new epoch in the development of economic geography." [HF1028. S4313]

2482　*Somerville, John.　"Lenin on Partiinost' in Sociology," in East-West Dialogues, Paul K. Crosser, David H. DeGrood and Dale Riepe, eds.　Amsterdam: Gruner, 1973; 170-78.
A discussion of Lenin's belief that personal neutrality in the class struggle is, in fact, the same as support of the system and is thus as much of a political decision as is the conscious selection of sides in the class struggle.　Somerville applies this belief to the discipline of sociology, and argues that the very selection by a sociologist of problems to analyze is an example of partiinost' in that the results may advance the "specific power of a specific social group, relative to the power of others." [HX542. C75]

2483　Spirkin, A.　"The Leninist Stage in the Development of Diamat," in Themes in Soviet Marxist Philosophy.　Selected Articles from the 'Filosofskaja Enciklopedija,' T. J. Blakeley.　Dordrecht, Holland: Reidel, 1975; 11-15.
A Soviet review of Lenin's "defence of dialectical materialism against revisionism, exposure of bourgeois ideology and creative development of dialectical materialism."　Spirkin restates Lenin's definition of matter, theory of knowledge, and basic thoughts on the dialectical process. [B809. 8T47]

2484　*Szczesniak, Boleslaw, ed.　The Russian Revolution and Religion.　A Collection of Documents Concerning the Suppression of Religion by the Communists, 1917-1925.　South Bend: University of Notre Dame Press, 1959; 289pp., bib. 253-69, intro. 1-26.
This collection of documents (resolutions, decrees, letters, telegrams, memos, articles, etc.) does not include much direct information on Lenin (only twelve documents), but it presents valuable materials concerning the reaction of the Russian and world religious community to his religious policies. Also useful is a lengthy introduction by Szczesniak in which he discusses the various stages of the suppression of religion in Russia under Lenin's leadership. [BR936. S94]

2485   *Topolski, Jerzy. "Lenin's Theory of History," Poznan St,
        1 (1975), 72-85.

2486   *Topolski, Jerzy and F. J. Fleron. "Comments on Lenin's
        Theory of History," Poznan St, 2 (1976), 89-91.

2487   *Traina, Michael J. "Lenin, Religion, and the Russian
        Orthodox Church: an Analysis of Theory and Practice,"
        Kent State University, 1970 (dissertation).

2488   *Vavilov, S. I. Lenin and the Philosophical Problems of
        Modern Physics. Moscow: Foreign Languages Pub-
        lishing House, 1953; 32pp.
        A positive presentation of Lenin's thought on the con-
        nection between the new physics and philosophy as ex-
        pressed in his Materialism and Empirio-Criticism.
        Vavilov reviews Lenin's main points in the attack on
        those (especially Mach) who sought to "utilize the newly
        discovered facts of physics to revive idealism," and
        stresses the scientific impact of Lenin's freeing of
        physics from the quagmire of metaphysical materialism.
        [QC6.V3513]

2489   No entry.

2490   Wallace, Kyle. "Dialectical Materialism and the Problem
        of Knowledge," J Crit Anal, 2, no. 3 (Oct. 1970), 23-
        35.
        Includes an assessment of Lenin's Philosophical Note-
        books and Materialism and Empirio-Criticism.

2491   *Wetter, Gustav A. "The Leninist Concept of Matter," in
        Dialectical Materialism. A Historical and Systematic
        Survey of Philosophy in the Soviet Union. New York:
        Praeger Press, 1960; 286-95.
        An analysis of Lenin's definition of the concept of mat-
        ter as part of his attempt to overcome the crisis in
        philosophical materialism sparked by the new discover-
        ies in physics. Wetter asserts that Lenin sought an
        escape from this crisis by postulating a purely philo-
        sophical concept of matter as objective reality reflected
        by our senses and not dependent on the inner structure
        of matter. He criticizes Lenin's concept of matter for
        arbitrarily limiting all reality to material reality and
        for not defining matter itself. [B809.8W433]

2492   *_____. Soviet Ideology Today. New York: Praeger,
        1966; 334pp.
        Although not specifically on Lenin, this study has many
        passing references to him which illuminate and analyze
        his thought on philosophical Marxism. [B809.8W4213]

2493   *_____. "Vladimir Ilyich Lenin," in Dialectical Material-
        ism. A Historical and Systematic Survey of Philosophy

in the Soviet Union. New York: Praeger, 1960; 110-27.

An analysis of Lenin's contributions to Marxist philosophy, dividing his philosophical career into three periods: pre-1905, 1906 to World War I (1914), and 1914 to 1916. Wetter states that in the first period Lenin exhibited an interest in philosophical problems but failed to study them directly and seriously, and concentrated instead on party organization and disputes. In the second period, he produced his most important philosophical work Materialism and Empirio-Criticism (1909) which addressed two central problems: the relation of theory of knowledge to dialectical materialism and the nature of matter in light of new discoveries in the sciences. In the third period, he studied philosophy intensively and compiled detailed notes, especially on Hegel and the dialectic process of history, but due to the pressing practical concerns of war and revolution, failed to produce any written work. Wetter concludes with a survey of the different definitions of Leninism, and a discussion of Lenin's contribution to Marxism as being his deepening of the concept of matter, establishment of the "copy theory," emphasis on the unity of theory and practice, and his stressing the partisan nature of philosophy. [B809. 8W433]

2494   *Wolfe, Bertram D. "Lenin as Philosopher," Partisan R, 14, no. 4 (July-Aug. 1947), 396-413.

2495   *_____. "Party Histories from Lenin to Khrushchev," in Contemporary History in the Soviet Mirror, John Keep, ed. London: Allen and Unwin, 1964; 43-60; discussion of essay, 61-68.
Lenin is not the focus of this essay, but it contains a short and provocative account of him as the founder of the Soviet policy of re-writing history to suit party purposes. Wolfe states that "it was Lenin who set the example of harnessing Clio to his chariot every time he changed tactics, got into a fight with his own movement, or in the revolutionary movement as a whole, started another split, or celebrated the anniversary of one of those innumerable schisms in his life and that of his movement." Wolfe also sees Lenin as the source of Soviet historians' obsession with periodization. [DK16. 4R9C6]

2496   *Yakhot, I. "The Leninist Stage in Soviet Philosophy," St Sov Tho, 20 (Oct. 1979), 303-08.
A survey of the 1930-1939 attempts, by Soviet philosophers, to elaborate Lenin's philosophy so as to counter the pre-occupation with him as practical revolutionary and politician. Yakhot concludes that there has been no such underestimation of Lenin as a philosopher and this

sham exercise was part of the development of the Stalin cult.

2497　*Zawasky, John P.　"The Sources of Dialectical Materialism: Hegel, Marx, Engels and Lenin," Harvard University, 1965 (dissertation).

2498　*Zenkovsky, V. V.　"V. I. Lenin.　His Philosophic Views," in A History of Russian Philosophy, Volume 2.　New York:　Columbia University Press, 1953; 744-53.
A critical examination of the nature of Lenin's thought and writings in philosophy.　Zenkovsky asserts that Lenin's thought from the very beginning, followed the extremely narrow-minded tack that "everything that corresponds to the position of dialectical materialism ... is accepted without reservations; everything that fails to correspond to it is rejected for this reason alone." He argues that Lenin's version of dialectical materialism was, in fact, a radical departure from the classical determinism of Marx, and was permeated "with revolutionary Zusammenbruch, the 'leap' into the dictatorship of the proletariat."　By definition, Lenin believed that all that hindered this leap was false, while all that helped it was true.　Zenkovsky concludes that Lenin's philosophy "consists of a return to highly oversimplified naive realism" which "if it were not so tragic would be ridiculous."　There follows a short account of the negative influence of Lenin's philosophy upon Soviet philosophy and science.　[B4201. Z4213]

11. LENINISM

2499   Aarons, Eric. Lenin's Theories on Revolution. Sydney:
Young, 1970; 95pp.
A restatement, by an Australian Marxist, of Lenin's
basic teachings on revolution, the party, state, dictatorship of the proletariat, imperialism, self-determination,
and the building of socialism. Lenin's own words constitute the bulk of this work. [HX312.L43A25]

2500   Adoratsky, V. "How to Study Lenin," in Dialectical Materialism. New York: International Publishers, 1934;
86-93.
An argument that Leninism can only be understood properly by studying it in conjunction with Lenin's activities
and the historical environment within which he functioned.
Adoratsky states that just as Lenin approached Marxism
as a guide to action rather than as a sterile dogma, so
must those who study Lenin approach his thought.
[HX314.A35]

2501   Afanasyev, V. G. "The Leninist Phase in the Development
of Scientific Communism," in Fundamentals of Scientific
Communism. Moscow: Progress Publishers, 1977;
39-48.
A praiseful commentary on Lenin's enrichment of Marxism through his writings on revolution, imperialism,
the dictatorship of the proletariat, socialist construction,
and international communism. [HX314.A35]

2502   Andropov, Yu. Leninism: Science and Art of Revolutionary
Creativity. Moscow: Novosti Press, 1976; 29pp.
A report, to a Moscow meeting commemorating the
106th anniversary of Lenin's birth, on Lenin's "creative
effort in theory, in politics, in organizing class struggle, and in building party and state." [HX44.A55513]

2503   Arismendi, R. "Leninism Gives the Key to Understanding
the Modern Epoch," W Marxist R, 22, no. 3 (Mar.
1979), 41-45.

2504   Belkina, G. L. "Marxism and Bourgeois Marxicology:
Historical Stages of the Struggle," St Sov Phil, 16 (Fall
1977), 89-113.
In part, an attack on Western interpretations of Leninism as narrowly Russian and/or un-Marxist.

2505   Bender, Frederic L. The Betrayal of Marx. New York:
        Harper and Row, 1975; 452pp. , bib. 436-444.
        An anthology of the writings of the disciples of Marx
        presented by the editor as an illustration of the be-
        trayal of Marx through the transformation of his theory
        from a humanistic to a despotic one. In a lengthy in-
        troduction, Bender asserts that Lenin betrayed Marx by
        establishing an elitist and ruthless movement of pro-
        fessional revolutionaries to execute the revolution and
        dictatorially govern the socialist state. As examples
        of this betrayal, Bender presents a series of excerpts
        from Lenin's writings on the party, state, revolution,
        imperialism, philosophy, and international communism.
        [B809. 8. B47]

2506   Bittelman, Alexander and V. J. Jerome. "Leninism Is the
        Only Marxism of the Imperialist Era," Communist, 13
        (Oct. 1934), 1033-56.

2507   *Black, Cyril E. "Marxism, Leninism and Soviet Commu-
        nism," W Pol, 9, no. 3 (1957), 401-12.
        A review article on seven books which deal with the
        relationship between Marxism and Leninism.

2508   Bubnov, Andrei S. Leninism. Moscow: Cooperative Pub-
        lishing Society, 1932; 32pp.
        Unavailable for annotation. [HX314. B78]

2509   *Bukharin, Nikolai. Lenin As a Marxist. London: Com-
        munist Party of Great Britain, 1925; 64pp.
        An attempt to counter those who argue that Lenin's
        theoretical works were insignificant in comparison to
        his practical revolutionary and political activities. Bu-
        kharin restates Lenin's thought on imperialism, revolu-
        tion, the state, dictatorship of the proletariat and the
        peasant and national questions, and states that this body
        of thought must not be looked upon as a rigid theory but
        rather as a guide to practical action. Bukharin pre-
        dicts that in the future "Lenin will appear before us
        in his real height not only as a genius practitioner of
        the labour movement, but also as a genius theoretician."
        [HX314. B83]

2510   *Catlin, George. "Kautsky, Lenin, Trotsky, Stalin," in
        The Story of the Political Philosophers. New York:
        McGraw-Hill, 1939; 609-33, bib. 647-48.
        A review of Lenin's political and philosophical thought
        and his career as a revolutionary and a political leader.
        Catlin criticizes Lenin for having a contradictory and
        simplistic approach to philosophical materialism, and
        labels him "a reactionary from the empiric standpoint,"
        but states that Leninism as a whole represents a highly
        effective combination of the revolutionary elements of

the "early Marx" with the radical tradition of 19th-century Russia. [JA81. C3]

2511 Chambre, H. "Soviet Ideology," Sov St, 18, no. 3 (Jan. 1967), 314-27.
A discussion of Lenin's contributions to Marxism and of Soviet attempts to systematize his ideological legacy.

2512 Charles, K. T. "The Marxism of Lenin," So Eco, 9, no. 22 (15 Mar. 1971), 7-8.

2513 *Cornforth, Maurice. Readers' Guide to the Marxist Classics. London: Lawrence and Wishart, 1953; 114pp.
A useful introduction to the fundamentals of Leninism. Cornforth lists Leninism's main points in outline form so as to help students "find their way among the many works available, to decide what to tackle and where to begin." [Z7164. S67C6]

2514 D'Arcy, Martin C. "Lenin and Stalin," in Communism and Christianity. New York: Devin-Adair Company, 1957; 41-55; bib. 241-42.
A discussion of the leading principles of Leninism with many parallels made to religion. D'Arcy asserts that Lenin approached and defended Marx's writings as if they were "canonical scriptures"; created a party which resembles a consecrated elite in dedicated pursuit of a faith; and launched a holy "crusade" against world capitalism. In support of these assertions, D'Arcy discusses several of Lenin's major works, as well as his leadership of the party in and after the October Revolution. Although titled "Lenin and Stalin" there is scant information on Stalin. [HX246. D17 1957]

2515 Dutt, R. P. Leninism. London: Lawrence, 1941.
Not available for annotation.

2516 Fedenko, Panas. "The Soviet Brand of Marxism," B Inst St USSR, 15, no. 10 (1968), 14-24.

2517 *Fedoseyev, P. N. "Lenin, the Great Theoretician," in LGT (anthology), 5-29.
A positive account of Lenin's contributions to Marxist theory through his establishing that socialism could triumph in a single, backward country before triumphing in the West; unifying the national and international factors in the struggle for socialism; and establishing the leading role of the vanguard party before, during, and after the revolution. [HX40. M2935] Also in LTCOA (anthology), 54-83; Marxist Leninist Teaching on Socialism and the World Today. Moscow: Progress Publishers, 1978; 51-97.

2518   Fellman, David. "Leninism," in The Soviet Polity. Government and Politics in the USSR. New York: Dodd, Mead and Company, 1971; 91-94.
A brief overview of the leading tenets of Leninism stressing the practical nature of Lenin's thought.

2519   For Unity and Cohesion. Marxism-Leninism--A Single Internationalist Teaching. Moscow: Novosti Press, 1969; 327pp.
A series of editorial statements and speeches by Soviet and European communist party leaders on the basic points of Leninist thought and their relevance for today. [HX40. M2893]

2520   Frantsov, G. P. "Lenin's Work on the Problems of Scientific Communism," in Philosophy and Sociology. Moscow: Progress Publishers, 1975; 153-65.
A positive review of Lenin's teachings on revolution and socialist construction. Frantsov states that Lenin's assessment of the uneven development of capitalism in the age of imperialism accurately foreshadowed the revolutionary events of 1917, while his writings on the explosive effect of the first socialist revolution on national liberation and socialist movements around the world have also turned out to be correct. [HX542. F6613]

2521   Hall, Gus. "Marxism-Leninism: The Star of Revolutionary Transition," New World R, 38, no. 1 (1970), 176-80.
A centennial appreciation of Lenin's influence on Marxist revolutionary theory and practice.

2522   Hansen, Joseph. "Is Marxism-Leninism Obsolete?," Int Soc R, 28 (July-Aug. 1967), 1-25.
A half-century favorable estimate of Lenin's contribution to the adaptation of Marxism to 20th-century conditions.

2523   Hecker, Julius F. "Dialogues X-XII," in Moscow Dialogues. Discussions on Red Philosophy. London: Chapman and Hall, 1936; 108-46.
An attempt to present, in a readable and popular form, the development and nature of Lenin's thought against the background of Russian social, political and economic history. Hecker presents his views in dialogue form with "Socrates" serving as the spokesman for Leninism in conversations with various mythical critics. [DK265. H338]

2524   *Hunt, R. N. Carew. "Leninism and Stalinism," in The Theory and Practice of Communism. New York: Macmillan, 1957; 139-93.
An examination of Lenin's contribution to Marxist theory in six main areas: strategy and tactics of revolution,

dictatorship of the proletariat, role of the party, strategy and tactics of the world communist movement,
doctrine of capitalist imperialism, and Marxist philosophy. Hunt maintains that although Lenin was not a
serious theoretician and was certainly concerned more
with revolutionary practice than theory, it is wrong to
underestimate the depth of his Marxist convictions.
The fact that Marx offered fundamental principles without practical guidelines for their application, Hunt argues, led Lenin to the adaptations that he made and has
also led critics to brand him (unfairly) as un-Marxist
or being concerned only with practical matters.
[HX36. H8 1957a]

2525 *_____. Marxism. Past and Present. London: Geoffrey Bles, 1954; 180pp.
This scholarly study of Marxism does not have a separate chapter on Lenin, but it contains considerable
discussion of his writings on dialectics, materialism,
theory of knowledge, the state, dictatorship of the proletariat, revolution, democracy, and the future socialist
society. [HX36. H77 1954]

2526 Jerome, V. J. "Lenin's Method--Guide to the Grasp of
Reality," Pol Aff, 25 (Jan. 1946), 3-17.
An attack on George Browder's "dogmatic interpretation"
of Leninism, and a discussion of Lenin's teachings as
a flexible guide to revolutionary theory and practice.

2527 Konstantinov, F. "Leninism. Philosophy of the Contemporary Epoch," in LTCOA (anthology), 95-105.
A presentation of Leninism as the only philosophy ade-
quately reflecting and expressing the revolutionary
spirit and character of the modern era. Konstantinov
criticizes Lenin's Marxist rivals (Kautsky, Bernstein,
Struve, Trotsky, Mao) and those bourgeois ideologues
who claim that Leninism is an out-dated, uniquely Russian theory.

2528 *Krasin, Y. Lenin, Revolution and the World Today. Moscow: Progress Publishers, 1971; 320pp.
The author's stated aim is "to show the connection between Lenin's theory of the socialist revolution and the
present day, to show that Lenin's ideas, which developed
along with the international revolutionary movement,
cannot be interpreted abstractly and scholastically."
To this end, Krasin restates Lenin's teachings on socialist and bourgeois revolution, the dictatorship of the
proletariat, international revolution, peaceful coexistence, and the ideological struggle between socialism
and capitalism. Krasin links Lenin's teachings to the
present world by presenting the essence of Leninism
as being a guide to action as opposed to an inflexible
theory. [HX314. K713]

2529 * _____ . Leninism and Revolution. Reply to Critics.
Moscow: Novosti Press, n. d.; 93pp.
A defense of Leninism against Western critics who
charge that Lenin's approach to Marxism was opportunistic and stressed voluntarism at the expense of the
deterministic essence of Marxism. Krasin singles out
for particular criticism the works of R. Carew Hunt,
S. Hook, H. Marcuse, A. Ulam, R. Daniels, G. Sabine, and M. Lipset. [HX44. K673]

2530 *Kuusinen, Otto, ed. Fundamentals of Marxism-Leninism.
Moscow: Foreign Languages Publishing House, 1961;
891pp.
An official revision of the Stalinist presentation of Marxism-Leninism. The authors restate Lenin's teachings
on dialectical and historical materialism, political economy of capitalism, the theory and practice of the international communist movement, and the construction
of socialism. [HX56. F813]

2531 *Laird, Roy D. "Leninism," in The Soviet Paradigm. An
Experiment in Creating a Monohierarchical Polity. New
York: Free Press, 1970; 50-69.
A discussion of Leninism as part of the Soviet "myth
complex" which is at the base of the communist state.
Laird restates the basics of Leninism, and concludes
that in spite of Lenin's extreme authoritarianism, he
added much to the understanding of imperialism and
nationalism, while providing an ideological rationaliza-
tion for the Soviet "monohierarchical polity."
[JN6515 1970. L35]

2532 *Lawler, James. "Existential Politics and Marxism-Leninism: Lenin," in The Existential Marxism of Jean-Paul
Sartre. Amsterdam: Gruner, 1976; 265-88.
A critique of Sartre's existential interpretation of Leninism contending that Leninism has a coherent theoretical basis ("a definite reality") and does not exist only
in the eye of the beholder. Lawler isolates the essence
of Lenin's thought on the party, revolution and the proletariat, and demonstrates through numerous examples
how Sartre misinterpreted and distorted Leninism to
such an extent that Sartre's "existential Marxism" can
be said to bear little resemblance to the materialistic
theory of political action. [B2430. S34L38]

2533 Leff, Gordon. The Tyranny of Concepts: A Critique of
Marxism. University, Ala.: University of Alabama
Press, 1969; 256pp.
Lenin is not the focus of any one chapter in this study,
but it contains many references to and short sections
on his thought on Marxist philosophy, revolution, the
state, and the dictatorship of the proletariat.
[B809. 8. L36]

2534   *Leonhard, Wolfgang. "The First Transformation: Leninism," in Three Faces of Marxism: The Political Concepts of Soviet Ideology, Maoism, and Humanist Marxism. New York: Holt, Rinehart and Winston, 1974;
47-94, bib. 438-45.
An exploration of Lenin's place in the evolution of the
political aims and concepts of Marxism by assessing
his answers to two groups of questions. The first
group concerns revolution, and consists of questions
such as: what class is to perform the transformation
of society; to what extent are other classes necessary
allies; what forms of struggle are to be used; how should
the party be organized and what tactics should it employ; and can the revolution be accomplished in one
country alone? The second group concerns the construction of socialism and includes such questions as:
what are the roles and characteristics of the dictatorship of the proletariat; what types of relations will exist
between capitalist and socialist nations; and how long
will it take to establish a communist society.
[HX44. L39813]

2535   Leninism, an Effective Ideological Weapon. Moscow: Novosti Press, 1969; 72pp.
Not available for annotation. [B844. L415]

2536   Leninism and the Revolutionary Process. Prague: Peace
and Socialism Publishers, 1970.
Not available for annotation.

2537   Leninism. The Science of Revolution. Prague: Peace and
Socialism Publishers, 1974; 189pp.
Not available for annotation. [HX312. L43L467]

2538   *Lichtheim, George. "Lenin," in Marxism: An Historical
and Critical Study. New York: Praeger, 1961; 325-51.
An analysis of Leninism stressing that, from 1903 onwards, it represented "a profound revision of Marxist
doctrine" in that Lenin maintained only Marxist aims
while he used wholly un-Marxist means to realize these
aims in a society uniquely unsuited for socialist revolution. In line with this thesis, Lichtheim discusses
Lenin's concept of party organization and his general
theory of revolution. To Lenin's credit, Lichtheim
states, he correctly assessed the opportunity for a revolution in Russia, an opportunity which he was able to
capitalize on largely because of the centralized character
of the Bolshevik organization. [HX36. L48]

2539   Lieberstein, Samuel. "Leninism: A Study in the Sociology
of Political Alienation," University of California at
Berkeley, 1967 (dissertation).

2540   *Liebman, Marcel. Leninism under Lenin. London: J.

Cape, 1975; 477pp., bib. 9-17.
A comprehensive examination of the origins, leading
principles, and policies of Leninism, with much attention given to the historical circumstances which shaped
Lenin's thought. Liebman states that the success of
Leninism as a doctrine of revolution was due primarily
to the organized, disciplined and tactically flexible qualities of the party which Lenin created. He believes that
Lenin did not intend for the party to rule in an authoritarian fashion, but that the chaotic and hostile environment in which the Bolsheviks found themselves after
1917 encouraged the development of the authoritarian
qualities latent within the party. Leninism must be
seen as a failure, Liebman concludes, in that it has
not created an instrument to bring about world revolution, nor has it succeeded in building a truly socialist
democracy and culture on the ruins of the old capitalist
system. What it has bequeathed is a highly effective
model for the conquest and maintenance of power.
[HX312. L43L5313]

2541   "Long Live Leninism," in Long Live Leninism. Peking:
        Foreign Languages Press, 1960; 1-56.
        A restatement of the main principles of Leninism on
        revolution, imperialism, and the state, and a Leninist
        attack on contemporary revisionism, especially that of
        Tito.

2542   *Lukacs, Georg. Lenin. A Study on the Unity of His Thought.
        Cambridge: M.I.T. Press, 1971 (reprint of a 1924
        publication); 104pp.
        A positive assessment of Lenin as a theorist depicting
        him as "the greatest thinker to have been produced by
        the revolutionary working-class movement since Marx."
        Lukacs discusses Lenin's concept of the revolutionary
        alliance of the proletariat and peasantry; his creation
        of a disciplined organization to accelerate, plan, and
        lead the revolution; articulation of the theory of im-
        perialism; theory of the proletarian state as a repres-
        sive and powerful weapon of the class struggle; and
        consistent application of Marxism to all problems con-
        fronted by the Soviet state. Lukacs concludes that
        Leninism does not represent a revision of Marx's teach-
        ings but rather a faithful adaptation of them to the con-
        temporary age and the building of socialism. A post-
        script, written in 1967, provides some interesting re-
        assessments of Leninism in view of the developments
        that occurred in Russia after Lenin's death.
        [HX312. L43L813]

2543   McCullagh, Francis. "Leninism: The Design of the Bol-
        sheviks," N Cent, (Aug. 1920), 199-208.
        A discussion of Leninism as a doctrine which could only
        appeal to a country such as Russia.

2544   McDonald, Lee Cameron. "Lenin," in Western Political
        Theory: The Modern Age. New York: Harcourt,
        Brace and World, 1962; 412-29.
        A survey of Lenin's major writings and political career
        arguing that he was a great organizer and activist but
        not a major theorist. McDonald writes that because
        Lenin was skillful with words, a great polemicist, and
        "adept at fitting Marxist categories to his own position,
        we can call him a theorist of influence. But inasmuch
        as he failed to push beyond the urgent to the enduring
        issue ... he was no theorist at all." [JA71. M15]

2545   McLellan, David. "Lenin," in Marxism after Marx. An
        Introduction. New York: Harper and Row, 1979; 86-
        114, bib. 110-14.
        A general introduction to the fundamentals of Lenin's
        thought and their relation to Marxism. McLellan re-
        views Lenin's doctrine on the party, revolution, im-
        perialism, the state, and the national question, and in-
        cludes a short section on Lenin's philosophy.
        [HX36. M23]

2546   Mayo, Henry B. Democracy and Marxism. New York:
        Oxford University Press, 1955; 364pp., bib. 339-54.
        This study of the foundations of Marxist philosophy does
        not have a separate chapter on Lenin, but it contains
        many references to and short discussions of his thought
        on dialectics, history, democracy, dictatorship, revo-
        lution, imperialism, and the state. [HX86. M36]

2547   Menashe, L. "Methodology of Leninology," Socialist Rev,
        5, no. 1 (Apr. 1975), 89-99.
        A critique of Carmen Sirianni's approach to studying
        Leninism as one which neglects developments after
        Lenin's death.

2548   Merkl, Peter H. "The Theory of Leninism," in Political
        Continuity and Change. New York: Harper and Row,
        1967; 468-72.
        A brief, non-interpretive outline of Leninism.
        [JA81. M444]

2549   *Meyer, Alfred G. Leninism. New York: Praeger, 1967
        (reprint of a 1957 publication); 324pp., bib. 295-98.
        A scholarly and critical study of Leninism within the
        context of the historical conditions which shaped Lenin's
        thought. Meyer examines Lenin's views on the pro-
        letariat's tasks, revolution, nationalism, the state, and
        imperialism, as well as Lenin's practical application
        of his beliefs as leader of the Soviet state. In assess-
        ing Leninism as a doctrine, Meyer maintains that, al-
        though Marxist theory provides little guidance on the
        many and crucial practical questions of revolution,
        "Lenin firmly maintained that there was such a thing

as a correct solution to every problem of strategy,"
a belief which accounts for Leninism's "combining with
blindness, doctrinaire rigidity with opportunistic adaptability." Meyer also states that Lenin's faith in "organization and centralization as rational methods of decision making" both ignored the human fallibilities of party
leaders and betrayed his pessimistic estimate of the
abilities of the social class he supposedly was championing. [HX314]

2550   Modrzhinskaya, Yelena. Leninism and the Battle of Ideas.
        Moscow: Progress Publishers, 1972; 363pp.
        Unavailable for annotation. [HX44.M56213]

2551   *Niemeyer, Gerhart. "Lenin and the Total Critique of So-
        ciety," R Pol, 26, no. 4 (Oct. 1964), 473-504.
        An analysis of Lenin's critique of society as expressed
        in four works: What Is to Be Done?, Two Tactics of
        Social Democracy in the Democratic Revolution; State
        and Revolution, and Left-Wing Communism: An In-
        fantile Disorder.

2552   Plamenatz, John. "Deviations from Marxism," Pol Q, 21
        (Jan. 1950), 40-55.
        In part, a discussion of Lenin's revision of Marx's
        teachings.

2553   *Ponomarev, Boris N. Marxism-Leninism. A Flourishing
        Science. A Reply to Critics. New York: International
        Publishers, 1979; 121pp.
        An attack on Western critics who assert that Leninism
        is an out-dated theory. Ponomarev states that such
        attacks are motivated by the desire to de-revolutionize
        Leninism and, thereby, subvert the working class move-
        ment and save capitalism. The most effective counter
        to these critics, he maintains, is to restate the funda-
        mental truths of Leninism and to emphasize that the
        theory is a living, creative one which serves as a
        flexible guide to interpreting and solving the problems
        which confront the contemporary world. [HX40.P684513]

2554   Reichenbach, B. "Are the Russians Marxists: From Marx
        to Lenin," Socialist Com, 15 (Feb.-Mar. 1951), 32-36,
        62-65, 88-91.

2555   *Roley, Paul. "Flexibility and Dogmatism: The Ambiguous
        Legacy of Leninism," in On the Road to Communism.
        Essays on Soviet Domestic and Foreign Politics, Roger
        E. Kanet and Ivan Volgyes, eds. Lawrence: Univer-
        sity of Kansas Press, 1972; 6-14.
        An examination of two strands of Leninism, revolution-
        ary Marxism and tactical pragmatism, as the prime
        sources of the ambiguous nature of Lenin's ideological

legacy. Roley states that the Leninist organizational principle is not, as is often argued, the central element of Leninism, but rather "was a consequence of an outlook that was fundamental to his whole approach to politics ... a willingness to compromise on the tactical level." It would be equally erroneous, he argues, to assert that pragmatism is the essence of Leninism, because Lenin's doctrinal rigidity was only slightly less central to his creed than tactical flexibility. While Lenin was able to maintain the delicate balance between pragmatism and principle, his heirs have allowed the former to triumph over the latter, and have pursued "the most blatant and unprincipled opportunism, sacrificing ideological commitment to minute considerations of policy, prestige and power...." [DK266.047]

2556   *Sabine, George H. "Communism," in A History of Political Theory. New York: Holt, Rinehart and Winston, 1961; 805-83, bib. 882-83.
A critical analysis of Lenin's main writings and policies. Throughout his analysis, Sabine discusses Lenin's various adaptations of Marxism in the light of a definition of Leninism as "a version of Marxism applicable to an industrially underdeveloped society with an agrarian economy." The prime connection between Marxism and Leninism, he argues, is not a logical one but a moral one: "what tied Lenin to Marx was not cogency of argument but dedication to social revolution as the sole and certain means of human progress." Consequently, "what Lenin bequeathed to communism was a moral attitude far more important than its intellectual content." [JA81.S3 1961]

2557   Schmalhauser, Samuel D. "The Logic of Leninism," Mod Q, 2, no. 4 (Winter 1930-1931), 454-66.

2558   *Selucky, Radoslav. "Leninism," in Marxism, Socialism, Freedom. Towards a General Democratic Theory of Labour-Managed Systems. New York: St. Martin's Press, 1979; 98-109.
An assessment of Leninism as a major revision of Marxism. Selucky particularly criticizes Lenin's concept of the dictatorship of the proletariat as an organization that "reminds one of a prison or the barracks rather than of the 'free association of free individuals' as demanded by Karl Marx." In identifying the roots of Lenin's revisionism, Selucky dismisses traditional interpretations, and argues instead that "the concept of a market-free, commodity-free and money-free socialist economic organization along the principles of one nation, one factory, and subject to command social planning, leads inevitably to the Leninist dictatorship of the proletariat exercised by the party structure according

to the principles first suggested by Lenin."
[HB97. 5. S42]

2559   *Stalin, Joseph. Foundations of Leninism. New York:
International Publishers, 1939; 127pp.
A series of lectures, delivered in 1924, defining the
term "Leninism" and elaborating its main precepts.
Stalin defines Leninism as the "Marxism of the era of
imperialism and of the proletarian revolution," and discusses its historical roots, methodology, and its theory
on proletarian revolution, the dictatorship of the proletariat, the national and peasant question, party organization, and the strategy and tactics of revolutionary
leadership. As an early, Soviet elaboration of Leninism and a major contribution to the rise of the "cult
of Lenin," this work is an important one. [HX314. S8173]
Also in Problems of Leninism. Moscow: Foreign
Languages Publishing House, 1940; 1-85; Leninism.
Moscow-Leningrad: Cooperative Publishing Society,
1934; Vol. I, 11-102.

2560   *_____. "Interview with the First American Labour Delegation," in SOL (anthology), 55-64.
A concise outline of the basics of Leninism, in response
to questions raised, in a 9 September, 1927 interview,
by members of the American workers' delegation. Excerpt in LDMORP (anthology), 9-12.

2561   *_____. Leninism, 2 Vols. Moscow-Leningrad: Cooperative Publishing Society, 1934; 421pp.; 405pp.
A compilation of Stalin's major writings on Leninism,
and a discussion of a wide range of topics and issues
from the "Leninist perspective." Included in these
volumes are Stalin's Foundations of Leninism, Problems
of Leninism, and Lenin on the Alliance with the Middle
Peasant. [DK254. L4S74]

2562   *_____. Problems of Leninism. Moscow: Foreign Languages Publishing House, 1940; 667pp.
A compilation of Stalin's major writings on Leninism,
and a series of other writings which largely use Lenin
for scriptural support for Stalinist policy.
[DK254. L4S75]

2563   Suslov, M. A. "Leninism and the Revolutionary Transformation of the World," in Marxism-Leninism--The International Teaching of the Working Class. Moscow:
Progress Publishers, 1975; 39-76.
A summary of Lenin's application of Marxism to 20th-
century historical conditions and a review of the "Leninist course" pursued by the CPSU since Lenin's death.
Suslov, a Politburo member, also defends Leninism
against critics who assert that it is a purely Russian

philosophy by providing examples of the relevance of
Lenin's teachings on imperialism, national liberation
movements, and proletarian internationalism.
[HX44.S93513] Also in LAWRWM (anthology), 13-49;
excerpt in W Marxist R, 12, no. 5 (May 1969), 3-17.

2564   Utechin, S. V. "Leninism," in Russian Political Thought.
        A Concise History. New York: Praeger, 1964; 215-33,
        bib. 279-306.
        A general introduction to Lenin's main writings and
        leading practices as a revolutionary and a political
        leader. [JA84.R9U8]

2565   What Is Leninism? New York: International Publishers,
        1936; 124pp.
        A collection of excerpts from the writings of Stalin and
        Lenin as a means of presenting the fundamentals of
        Leninism. Implicit throughout this work is that Stalin
        has faithfully applied the teachings of Lenin and has
        continued to develop Leninism as a theory. [HX314.W46]

2566   "What Is Leninism?," Tablet, 184 (Oct. 1944), 295.

2567   *Wolfe, B. D. "Leninism," in Marxism in the Modern World,
        Milorad M. Drachkovitch, ed. Stanford: Stanford Uni-
        versity Press, 1966; 47-89.
        An interpretive essay on the basic points of Lenin's
        thought and their relation to the teachings of Marx.
        Wolfe criticizes Lenin's acceptance of Marxism as "a
        unitary, monolithic system" since Marxism is "full of
        contradictions and ambiguities." Wolfe see two distinct
        phases in Marx's thought, and asserts that Lenin chose to
        accept as "his Marx" the radical, pre-1851 Marx charac-
        terized by centralism, voluntarism, and conspiracy, char-
        acteristics which Wolfe goes on to discuss in Lenin's
        thought on class war, party organization, and the dictator-
        ship of the proletariat. [HX40.D72]

2568   *_____. Marxism: 100 Years in the Life of a Doctrine.
        New York: Dell, 1967; 404pp.
        In addition to its two chapters (annotated individually)
        on Lenin, this scholarly study of Marxism has many
        references to and short discussions of Lenin's inter-
        pretation of the ambiguous legacy of Marx on war, rev-
        olution, party organization, the dictatorship of the pro-
        letariat, and nationalism. [HX40.W52]

2569   Zhilin, Yu. "Creative Essence of Leninism," in LTCOA
        (anthology), 83-95.
        A discussion of Leninism's creative essence as resting
        in Lenin's approach to Marxism as a guide to action
        and a means of forecasting the future rather than as a
        rigid set of theoretical prescriptions.

12. COMPARISONS AND PERSONAL RELATIONSHIPS

A. N. BUKHARIN

2570 *Buchanan, H. Ray. "Lenin and Bukharin on the Transition
from Capitalism to Socialism: The Meshchersky Controversy, 1918," Sov St, 28, no. 1 (1976), 66-82.

2571 *Cohen, Stephen F. Bukharin and the Bolshevik Revolution.
A Political Biography, 1888-1938. New York: Knopf,
1973; 495pp. , bib. 479-95.
Lenin is not the focus of any one chapter in this study,
but it contains significant information on him, his relationship with Bukharin, and their ideological ties.
[DK268. B76C63 1973]

2572 * . "Bukharin, Lenin and the Theoretical Foundations
of Bolshevism," Sov St, 21, no. 4 (1970), 436-57.
An estimate of Bukharin's influence on Lenin's Imperialism and State and Revolution, and a discussion of his
relationship with Lenin.

2573 *Day, R. B. "Dialectical Method in the Political Writings
of Lenin and Bukharin," Can J Pol Sci, 9, no. 2 (June
1976), 244-60.

2574 *Heitman, Sidney. "Between Lenin and Stalin: Nikolai Bukharin," in Revisionism: Essays on the History of Marxist Ideas, L. Labedz, ed. New York: Praeger, 1962,
77-90.
Lenin is not the focus of this essay, but it contains a
discussion of Bukharin as the forerunner of Lenin's
views both on imperialism and the state. Heitman states
that although Bukharin borrowed from Lenin, he carried
Lenin's ideas further and integrated them more completely with Marxism. [HX40. L14]

2575 *Hook, Sidney. "Case of Comrade Bukharin," Encounter,
43 (Dec. 1974), 81-92.
An analysis of Cohen's thesis (Bukharin and the Bolshevik Revolution) that Bukharin, not Trotsky or Stalin,
was the rightful heir to Lenin.

2576 * . "Rethinking the Bolshevik October Revolution,"

403

in Revolution, Reform and Social Justice. New York:
New York University Press, 1975, 182-207.
An analysis of Stephen Cohen's Bukharin and the Bolshevik Revolution. A Political Biography, 1888-1938
serves as a point of departure for an assessment of
"the relation between Lenin and Stalin and of both to
the thought of Marx." Hook agrees with Cohen's contention that had Bukharin become Lenin's heir, Soviet
Russia would have developed on a far more humane
path, but disagrees that "Bukharin's policies were Lenin's and that he, not Stalin or Trotsky, was the true
heir of Lenin's revolutionary legacy." [HX36.H65]

2577 *Kresl, Peter K. "Nikolai Bukharin on Economic Imperialism," R Rad Pol Ec, 5, no. 1 (1973), 3-12.
A comparison of the theories of imperialism of Lenin
and Bukharin.

B. M. GORKY

2578 *Andreyeva, M. "Encounters with Lenin," in LAG (anthology), 334-39.
An account of various meetings between Lenin and Gorky
illustrating their close relationship and admiration for
each other.

2579 *Bonch-Bruyevich, Vladimir. "Gorky and the Organisation
of the S.W.C.," in LAG (anthology), 364-371.
A recollection of how Gorky's work in the "founding
of the Scientists' Welfare Commission led to the re-
establishment of friendly relations with Lenin which
had been strained by Gorky's participation in an un-
official society to aid writers and scientists.

2580 *Byalik, Boris. "Lenin and Gorky. Notes on Their Correspondence," Sov Lit, no. 3 (1970), 110-14.

2581 Fedin, Konstantin. "From Reminiscences of Gorky," in
LAG (anthology), 358-61.
A recollection of the powerful influence Lenin had upon
Gorky.

2582 Glyasser, M. "Lenin and Gorky," in LAG (anthology), 349-
50.
Reminiscences, by Lenin's secretary, of meetings between Lenin and Gorky illustrating Lenin's willingness
to see Gorky at any time and support for him in various
personal and professional matters. Reprint in Sov Lit,
no. 3 (1970), 79-80.

2583 Ivanov, Vsevolod. "Meetings with Maxim Gorky," in LAG
(anthology), 362-63.

A brief reminiscence illustrating the dynamic affect
Lenin had on Gorky and the strong nature of their
friendship.

2584　*Kaun, Alexander. "Gorky and Lenin," in Maxim Gorky and
　　　His Russia. New York: J. Cape and H. Smith, 1931;
　　　405-514.
　　　A detailed discussion of the relationship between Gorky
　　　and Lenin from the 1907 London Conference of the
　　　RSDLP until Lenin's death. Kaun establishes that while
　　　Gorky accepted Lenin's views on proletarian revolution
　　　and Lenin admired Gorky as a talented writer of fiction,
　　　the two men had many differences, mainly concerning
　　　Gorky's "political vagueness" and philosophical devia-
　　　tions, and Lenin's cultural policies after the October
　　　Revolution. Kaun makes thorough use of Lenin's cor-
　　　respondence with Gorky and the latter's memoirs to
　　　illustrate the nature of their relationship, and provides
　　　valuable insights into Bolshevik Party affairs and Le-
　　　nin's personal make-up. [PG3465.K3]

2585　Krupskaya, N. K. "Lenin and Gorky," in LAG (anthology),
　　　329-31.
　　　An account of Lenin's high regard for Gorky and his
　　　works and of Gorky's respect and love for the common
　　　people.

2586　Lunacharsky, A. V. "Maxim Gorky," in LAG (anthology),
　　　347-48.
　　　A brief note on Lenin's affection for Gorky and willing-
　　　ness to forgive him when he "veered from the straight
　　　path" in either word or deed.

2587　*Malkin, B. "V. I. Lenin and M. Gorky," in LAG (anthol-
　　　ogy), 351-55.
　　　An account of the relationship between Lenin and Gorky
　　　discussing Lenin's friendly concern for Gorky even when
　　　the latter associated with Lenin's rivals. The author
　　　also recollects how Lenin involved Gorky in various
　　　decisions on books and book publishing.

2588　*Mathewson, Rufus W., Jr. "Lenin and Gorky: The Turning
　　　Point," in The Positive Hero in Russian Literature.
　　　New York: Columbia University Press, 1958; 200-26.
　　　An analysis of Lenin's 1905 article Party Organization
　　　and Party Literature and Gorky's novel Mother as
　　　marking a watershed in the history of Russian litera-
　　　ture. Mathewson states that Gorky's application, in
　　　Mother, of Lenin's call for political partisanship in
　　　literature represented a crucial break with Russia's
　　　classical literary heritage and set the stage for the
　　　rigid application by the current Soviet regime of the
　　　principle of literary partisanship. [PG2989.H4M3]

2589   Peshkova, Y. P. "Vladimir Ilyich Visits A. M. Gorky in
        October 1920," in LAG (anthology), 356-57.
        A recollection of a conversation between Lenin and
        Gorky both on the financial support for young writers
        and on plans to preserve the country's scientific, liter-
        ary, and artistic heritage.

2590   Ulyanova, M. "Lenin and Gorky.   From Reminiscences,"
        in LAG (anthology), 332-33.
        A brief reminiscence of Gorky's role in promoting the
        publication of Lenin's writings.

2591   Voronsky, A. K. "Meetings and Talks with Maxim Gorky,"
        in LAG (anthology), 372-77.
        An account of Lenin's work with Gorky in attempting to
        establish Krasnaya Nov, a monthly literary magazine.

2592   *Wolfe, Bertram D.   The Bridge and the Abyss.   The Trou-
        bled Friendship of Maxim Gorky and V. I. Lenin.   New
        York: Praeger, 1967; 180pp., bib. 166-74.
        An examination of the long and frequently stormy re-
        lationship between Gorky and Lenin stressing that in
        spite of the vast differences between the two men they
        retained a mutual admiration for each other.   Wolfe
        discusses the differences between Lenin and Gorky in
        temperment, attitude towards politics and organization,
        and feelings on artistic freedom and the role of litera-
        ture in shaping life and their basic conception of man,
        and examines their personal relationship up to and in-
        cluding their 1922 split over the Bolshevik trial of 12
        Socialist Revolutionary leaders.   In an epilogue, Wolfe
        compares Gorky's three (1917-1918, 1920, and 1924)
        portraits of Lenin, written respectively upon Lenin's
        seizure of power, 50th birthday, and death.
        [PG3465. Z9L48]
2592a   Reviewed in:
            Am Hist R, (June 1968), 1584, by S. W. Page.
            Annals AAPSS, (July 1968), 152, by A. Rabinowitch.
            J Mod Hist, (June 1969), 288, by S. Monas.
            Listener, (23 May 1968), 674, by H. Gifford.
            Nation, (18 Mar. 1968), 382, by D. Levin.
            NY R Books, (27 Mar. 1969), 20, by H. Muchnic.
            New Yorker, (3 Feb. 1968), 111.
            Rus R, (July 1968), 361, by I. Weil.
            Spectator, (23 May 1968), 674, by R. Hingley.
            TLS, (11 July 1968), 724.

2593   *Zhak, Lydia. "Gorky," in LIOL (anthology), 11-32.
        A description of the relationship between Gorky and
        Lenin relying upon numerous direct quotes from both
        men as a means of illustrating their mutual admiration,
        respect and friendship for each other.

C. N. KRUPSKAYA

2594   Ageloff, H. "Meet Mrs. Lenin," Outlook, 159 (25 Nov.
        1931), 398-9, 414.
        In part, a discussion of Krupskaya's relationship with
        Lenin.

2595   Casey, Jane B. I Krupskaya. My Life with Lenin. Bos-
        ton: Houghton Mifflin, 1974, 327pp.
        A semi-fictionalized account of the Lenins' lives to-
        gether written as if the author were Krupskaya. Casey
        tampers little with major historical facts restricting
        her creativity to projecting herself into the personality
        and thought of Krupskaya to provide a living account
        of the Lenins. [PZ4. C3393]

2506   Deich, Genrikh. "Krupskaya and Lenin," Sov Life, 6, no.
        153 (June 1969), 30-31+.
        An account of the relationship between Lenin and his
        wife including their courtship and years in exile.

2597   Dridzo, V. "Krupskaia's Meeting with Lenin," in LKAL
        (anthology), 54-56.
        A description of the first meeting between Lenin and
        Krupskaya, their correspondence while awaiting trial
        and exile, and Lenin's proposal of marriage to her by
        way of a letter in invisible ink.

2598   *McNeal, Robert H. Bride of the Revolution. Krupskaya
        and Lenin. Ann Arbor: University of Michigan Press,
        1972; 326pp. , bib. 298-301.
        Although the focus of this study is Lenin's wife, it con-
        tains a great deal of information, from mainly Russian
        sources, on Lenin's personal Life. McNeal examines
        the early contacts between Krupskaya and Lenin, their
        marriage and "honeymoon" period while in Siberian
        exile, their years together as exiles in Western Europe,
        and their lives during the years of Lenin's leadership
        of the Soviet state. He discusses Lenin's concept of
        ideal love (lofty, controlled and subservient to the cause)
        as well as the more mundane aspects of the Lenins'
        marital affairs. The author also examines the nature
        of Lenin's relationship with Inessa Armand, Krupskaya's
        many contributions to Lenin's work, her care for Lenin
        as his health declined, and her efforts to preserve his
        legacy after death. [DK254. K77M3]
2598a   Reviewed in:
            Am Hist R, 79, no. 2 (Apr. 1974), 544-45, by R.
                Thompson.
            Annals AAPSS, 407 (May 1973), 214-15, by F. A.
                Miller.
            Can S P, 15, no. 3 (Fall 1973), by S. Page.

*Encounter, 40, no. 4 (Apr. 1973), 74-77, by L.
Schapiro.

History, 50 (June 1974), 300.

Hist Today, 23, no. 2 (Mar. 1973), 216-17, by J.
Richardson.

Lib J, 97 (1972), 2590, by R. H. Johnson.

New Sta, 85 (12 Jan. 1973), 59-60, by P. Lewis.

NY Times Bk R, (19 June 1972), 35, by C. Simmons.

Rus R, 32, no. 3 (July 1973), 324-25, by B. Farns-
worth.

*Sci Soc, 38, no. 2 (Summer 1974), 251-53, by A.
T. Rubinstein.

Slav R, 33, no. 1 (Mar. 1974), 141-42, by C. Shul-
man.

Sov St, 26, no. 2 (Apr. 1974), 294-95, by R. Pethybridge.

TLS, no. 3701 (9 Feb. 1973), 144.

2599   Sevidova, Sofya. "Nadezhda Krupskaya: Lenin's Wife,
        Friend and Colleague," Sov Life, no. 7 (July 1976), 35-
        37.

D. R. LUXEMBURG

2600   Brand, P. "Lenin Versus Luxemburg," Campaigner, 4, no.
        3 (Fall 1971), 27+.

2601   *Davis, Horace B., ed. "Introduction: The Right of Na-
        tional Self-Determination in Marxist Theory-Luxemburg
        versus Lenin," in Selected Writings of Rosa Luxemburg.
        New York: Monthly Review Press, 1976; 9-48.
        A review of the debate between Lenin and Luxemburg
        on the national question. Davis outlines the main dif-
        ferences that separated Lenin and Luxemburg, discusses
        the historical setting within which the debate took place,
        and examines their various writings on the national
        question. Davis also assesses Lenin's attempt to apply
        his theory of self-determination, and concludes that
        Lenin and his successors have only been able to pay
        lip service to self-determination and that it is Luxem-
        burg's position on this issue that has contemporary
        validity, especially her statement that "when the term
        (self-determination) is not defined with exactitude, adop-
        tion of the slogan may not be a solution of the problem
        but a means of avoiding it." [HX276. L84328]

2602   *_____. "The Theory of Nationalism: Luxemburg, Stalin,
        Lenin, and Trotsky," in Toward a Marxist Theory of
        Nationalism. New York: Monthly Review Press, 1978;
        54-87, bib. 263-78.
        An examination of the evolution of a Bolshevik theory
        of nationalism through the interplay between the ideas
        of Luxemburg, Lenin, Stalin and Trotsky. Davis out-

lines the major points of difference between Luxemburg and Lenin as revealed in their pre-World War I debates (especially over the concept of the "right of self-determination"), and assesses the validity of their respective arguments. He discusses the difficulties which prevented Lenin from implementing successfully his theory of self-determination and which led Lenin to bequeath to his successors an ambiguous and contradictory nationality policy. Davis parallels this discussion with an analysis of Stalin's Marxism and the National Question (1913) and states that although Lenin generally accepted the essay his thought on nationalism continued to change so that by the early 1920's he opposed Stalin's nationality practices in regard to the issue of autonomy for the republics and the use of coercion against national minorities. [HX550. N3D33]

2603 *Elliott, Charles F. "Lenin, Rosa Luxemburg and the Dilemma of the Non-Revolutionary Proletariat," Midwest J Pol Sci, 9, no. 4 (Nov. 1965), 327-38.

2604 * _____. "'Quis Aistodiet Sacra?' Problems of Marxist Revisionism," J Hist Ideas, 28, no. 1 (1967), 71-86.
A review of the differing treatments of the revision of Marx by Luxemburg, Bernstein, and Lenin. Elliott sees Lenin's alterations of Marxism as being the least extensive of the three.

2605 Frölich, Paul. "Lenin and Luxemburg," in Rosa Luxemburg. Her Life and Work. New York: Howard Fertig, 1969; 106-108.
A brief review of the differences between Luxemburg and Lenin over party organization. [HX273. L83F713 1969]

2606 *Geras, Norman. "Rosa Luxemburg after 1905," New Left R, no. 89 (Jan. 1975), 3-46.
A review of the respective positions of Luxemburg, Trotsky, and Lenin in the 1905-1917 period on party organization, revolution, and imperialism.

2607 *Jacoby, Russell. "Lenin and Luxemburg: The Negation in Theory and Praxis," Rad Amer, 4, no. 7 (1970), 21-32.

2608 *Jha, Shiva Chandra. Marxist Theories of Imperialism: Lenin, Rosa Luxemburg, and Fritz Sternberg. Calcutta: Bookland Private Limited, 1959, 79pp.
Unavailable for annotation.

2609 *Nettl, J. P. Rosa Luxemburg. Volume II. London: Oxford University Press, 1966; 533pp.
Lenin is not the focus of any one chapter in this study, but it contains considerable discussion of his relationship with Luxemburg. [HX273. L97N4]

2610   *Nicholls, A. J. "Rosa Luxemburg and Lenin," History,
        51, no. 173 (Oct. 1966), 331-35.
        A discussion of Lenin and Luxemburg's relationship as
        part of a review of J. P. Nettl's Rosa Luxemburg and
        Possony's Lenin: The Compulsive Revolutionary.

2611   *Schurer, H. "Some Reflections on Rosa Luxemburg and the
        Bolshevik Revolution," SEER, 40, no. 95 (1962), 356-
        72.
        An assessment of Luxemburg's essay on the Russian
        Revolution and of her relationship with Lenin.

2612   Shachtman, Max. "Lenin and Rosa Luxemburg," New Int,
        2, no. 2 (Mar. 1935), 60-64.

2613   _____. "Lenin and Rosa Luxemburg," New Int, 4, no.
        5 (May 1938), 141-44.

2614   _____. Lenin. Liebknecht. Luxemburg. Chicago:
        Young Workers League, n. d.
        An introduction for young American workers to Lenin,
        Liebknecht, and Luxemburg as "three great figures
        whose example is a beacon light." Shachtman reviews
        the careers of each and discusses Liebknecht and Luxem-
        burg as "great disciples of Lenin." [DK254. L42S43]

2615   *Smith, Ross. "The Debate between Lenin and Rosa Luxem-
        burg in 1917," Flinders J Hist Pol, 3 (1973), 22-25.

2616   *Winslow, Earl M. "Later Developments: Lenin and Some
        Others," in The Patterns of Imperialism: A Study in
        Theories of Power. New York: Columbia University
        Press, 1948; 178-88.
        A comparative discussion of the theories of imperialism
        advanced by Hilferding, Luxemburg, Lenin, and Kautsky.
        Winslow sees the interpretations of Luxemburg and Hil-
        ferding as being original whereas Lenin's is interesting
        only for its polemics and exposition. The author dis-
        cusses Lenin's links to Hobson and Hilferding and the
        nature of Lenin's assault on Kautsky's interpretation of
        imperialism. [JC359.W55]

2617   *Wolfe, Bertram D. "Rosa Luxemburg and V. I. Lenin;
        The Opposite Poles of Revolutionary Socialism," Antioch
        R, 21 (Summer 1961), 209-26.
        A critical review of the differences between Lenin and
        Luxemburg on party organization and leadership.

        E. J. STALIN

2618   Avtorkhanov, A. "Khrushchev, Leninism and Stalinism,"
        B Inst St USSR, 3 (Nov. 1956), 13-20.

2619   *Basseches, Nikolaus. "Leninism," in Stalin. London:
        Staples Press, 1952; 111-17.
        An examination of Stalin's concept of "Leninism" as
        expressed in the Foundations of Leninism. Basseches
        summarizes the main points advanced by Stalin, and
        states that Stalin was the only Bolshevik leader to elab-
        orate Lenin's ideas because the others regarded them-
        selves as original thinkers quite competent to formulate
        their own theories. Basseches also discusses Stalin's
        various other efforts to surround Lenin's legacy with
        an official halo. [DK268. S8B]

2620   *Bentley, W. "The Contribution of Lenin and Stalin to Com-
        munist Theory," Cahiers B, 2 (July 1952), 84-107.

2621   Burnham, James. "Lenin's Heir," Partisan R, 12, no. 1
        (Winter 1945), 61-72.
        A review of Trotsky's biography of Stalin with informa-
        tion on the relations of Stalin and Trotsky with Lenin.
        Burnham sees Stalin, not Trotsky, as Lenin's heir.

2622   _____. "Politics for the Nursery Set," Partisan R, 12,
        no. 2 (Spring 1945), 188-90.
        A reply to Macdonald's criticism (item 2639) of Burn-
        ham's article on Stalin as Lenin's heir.

2623   *Chamberlin, William H. "From Leninism to Stalinism,"
        in The Russian Enigma. An Interpretation. New York:
        Scribner's and Sons, 1943; 92-116.
        A ten point comparison of the policies pursued by Stalin
        and Lenin stressing that Stalin "veered towards a more
        moderate, sometimes a definitively more conservative
        standpoint, by the standards of the original challenges
        of the Revolution." The points of comparison used by
        Chamberlin are property, religion, family, patriotism,
        methods of education, privileges for industrial workers,
        culture, rank and subordination, attitude towards Russia's
        past, and Pan-Slavism. He concludes that Stalin's
        changes from the policies of Lenin are significant enough
        collectively to label his rule as "the Russian Thermidor."
        [DK265. C428]

2624   _____. "The Three Eras of Soviet Communism," Rus R,
        24, no. 1 (Jan. 1965), 3-12.
        A discussion of Lenin, Stalin, and Khrushchev as each
        having placed his stamp on the era in which he ruled.

2625   *Cohen, Stephan F. "Bolshevism and Stalinism. New Re-
        flections on an Old Problem," Dissent, 24 (Spring 1977),
        190-205.
        An assessment of the continuity between Leninism and
        Stalinism.

2626   Crankshaw, E. "Again the Battle for Lenin's Mantle,"
        NY Times M (25 June 1950), 5, 25.
        In part, on Lenin's relations with Stalin, and Stalin's
        perversion of Lenin's image and teachings.

2627   *Dadrian, Vahakn N. "The Development of the Soviet Pos-
        ture on the Nationalities: A Reappraisal of the Roles
        of Lenin and Stalin," Indian Soc B, 6, no. 1 (1968),
        18-38.

2628   Delbars, Yves. "Lenin as Stalin's Teacher," in The Real
        Stalin. London: Allen and Unwin, 1953; 78-85, bib.
        419-22.
        A discussion of Stalin's 1917 shift from a conservative
        to a radical position on the question of socialist revolu-
        tion as a response to Lenin's April Theses. Delbars
        claims that Stalin's "sixth sense, which guided him with
        the certainty of radar, convinced him of the practical
        strength of Lenin's argument. He felt that Lenin's ex-
        hortations would exert a decisive influence in the whirl-
        wind" of 1917. Delbars also states that Lenin was im-
        pressed with Stalin's courage and boldness and that
        Stalin, in supporting Lenin at every turn in the summer
        of 1917, learned much about how to lead the masses.
        [DK268.S8D454]

2629   Dennis, Eugene. "Lenin, Stalin and the Mid-Century,"
        Pol Aff, 29 (Mar. 1950), 1-6.
        A comparison of the paths and policies (1917-1950) of
        socialism and capitalism with much reference to Lenin
        and Stalin.

2630   *Deutscher, Isaac. Stalin. A Political Biography. New
        York: Random House, 1960; 600pp., bib. 571-76.
        Lenin is not the focus of any one chapter in this widely
        acclaimed biography of Stalin, but it contains a great
        deal of information on virtually every aspect of Stalin's
        relationship with Lenin. A comprehensive subject index
        listing subheadings beneath Lenin's name facilitates lo-
        cation of information on Lenin. [DK268.S8D48]

2631   *Ellison, Herbert J. "Stalin and His Biographers: The
        Lenin-Stalin Relationship," in Reconsiderations on the
        Russian Revolution, Ralph C. Elwood, ed. Cambridge,
        Massachusetts: Slavica, 1976; 256-69. [DK265.A138 1974]

2632   Fischer, Louis. "Russia, 22 Years after," Nation, 150
        (10 Feb. 1940), 182-84, 186.
        A contrast of Lenin and Stalin, with an assessment of
        Bolshevism as developed by Stalin.

2633   Foster, W. Z. "Lenin and Stalin as Mass Leaders," Com-
        munist, 18 (Dec. 1939), 1120-29.

2634   *Gerratano, Valentino. "Stalin, Lenin and Leninism," New
       Left R, 103 (May-June 1977), 59-71.
       An attack on Stalin for using Leninism for his own pur-
       poses and for retarding the development of the revolu-
       tionary movement.

2635   *Gurian, W. "From Lenin to Stalin," R Pol, 12 (July 1950),
       379-88.
       A discussion of the Leninist roots of Stalin's expansion-
       istic foreign policy.

2636   *Hopkins, Mark W. "Lenin, Stalin, Khrushchev: Three Con-
       cepts of the Press," Journalism Q, 42, no. 4 (Autumn
       1965), 523-31.

2637   "Leninism versus Stalinism," Fourth Int, 6, no. 7 (July
       1945), 195-96.
       An attack on American Stalinists Foster and Browder
       as betrayers of Leninism.

2638   *Luck, David. "A Psycholinguistic Approach to Leader Per-
       sonality. Imagery of Aggression, Sex and Death in
       Lenin and Stalin," Sov St, 30, no. 4 (Oct. 1978), 491-
       515.

2639   *Macdonald, Dwight. "Stalin and Lenin's Heritage: A Con-
       troversy," Partisan R, 12, no. 2 (Spring 1945), 181-87.
       A critique of Burnham's article "Lenin's Heir" (item
       2621). Answered by Burnham, item 2622.

2640   *Medvedev, Roy A. "Conclusion: Leninism and Stalinism,"
       in On Stalin and Stalinism. Oxford: Oxford University
       Press, 1979; 183-98.
       An assessment, by a Soviet historian and dissident, of
       the elements of continuity and divergence between Le-
       ninism and Stalinism. Medvedev states that there are
       apparent similarities between Leninism and Stalinism
       because many of Stalin's practices were a continuation
       of centralist and anti-democratic trends began by Lenin.
       He does not, however, believe that such continuity can
       be accepted as proof of the similarities of the two isms
       since Lenin's undemocratic practices were due to his-
       torical circumstances while Stalin's were motivated by
       personal gain. Medvedev sees distinct differences be-
       tween the two leaders both in regard to the substance
       of the policies they pursued (especially towards the
       party, nationalities and the economy) and their personali-
       ties. [DK267. M416]

2641   Molotov, Vyacheslav. "Stalin as the Continuer of the Cause
       of Lenin," Int Lit, no. 12 (Dec. 1939), 32-41.

2642   Munby, D. L. and D. M. Mackinnon. "Leninism and Stalin-

ism," in Christian Faith and Communist Faith. London. 1953.
Unavailable for annotation.

2643 *Phillips, William. "The Lions and the Foxes," Partisan R, 12, no. 2 (Spring 1945), 190-98.
A discussion of Burnham's and Macdonald's articles on whether Stalin's regime represents a break with that of Lenin. (see items 2621, 2622, and 2637.)

2644 Rubinstein, N. "A Great Friendship," Com Int, 15 (May 1938), 476-86 and 15 (June 1938), 583-94.
A claim that Lenin and Stalin were great friends who cooperated throughout the 1901-1923 period.

2645 *Scheffer, Paul. "From Lenin to Stalin," For Aff, 16, no. 3 (Apr. 1938), 445-54.

2646 *Smith, Edward E. "Lenin Rediscovers Dzhugashvili," in The Young Stalin. The Early Years of an Elusive Revolutionary. New York: Farrar, Straus and Giroux, 1967; 235-66, bib. 423-56.
An account of how Stalin came to Lenin's attention in 1911 through a politically indiscreet and abrasive letter sent by Stalin to the Moscow Bolshevik organization and of how, in spite of this, Lenin appointed him to the Bolshevik Central Committee membership less than a year later. Smith examines the factors (including the role of the police-agent Malinovsky) which influenced Lenin in this appointment, and discusses the impact of this impressive appointment on Stalin's early career.
[DK268. S8S52]

2647 Spratt, P. "Stalin or Lenin," Swarajya, 12, no. 16 (14 Oct. 1967), 5+.

2648 *Trotsky, Leon. Stalin. An Appraisal of the Man and His Influence. New York: Stein and Day, 1967; 516pp.
This important study of Stalin does not contain a separate chapter on Lenin, but has a vast amount of information on his revolutionary and political career, and, especially, his relationships with Stalin and Trotsky. An excellent index makes for easy location of information on Lenin.
[DK268. S817 1967]

2649 *Tucker, Robert C. "The Appeals of Lenin," in Stalin as a Revolutionary, 1879-1929. New York: Norton, 1974; 122-30.
An examination of those aspects of Lenin's thought and policies which appealed to Stalin in his first few years as a Marxist. Tucker advances the thesis that the type of party organization outlined by Lenin in What Is to Be Done? was uniquely suited to Stalin's martial mentality,

rebellious nature, and need to belong to a cohesive
group. This book contains many small sections and
references which provide additional and valuable information on Stalin's involvement with Lenin.
[DK268. S8T85]

2650   *Ulam, Adam B. "The Uses of Revolution," in <u>Revolution-</u>
        <u>ary Russia</u>, R. Pipes, ed. Garden City: <u>Doubleday,</u>
        <u>1968</u>; 426-52.
        An assessment of how "both the maker of the revolution
        (Lenin) and his successor (Stalin) have tried to sooth
        their ideological conscience and to fit the Bolshevik Rev-
        olution into the Marxist scheme of things." Ulam main-
        tains that Lenin and Stalin sought a vindication of the
        non-Marxist beginning of the revolution in the Marxist
        content of the continuing revolution after 1917. In the
        process, Ulam states, they "projected in their retro-
        spective view of the revolution their self-image: Lenin
        in that of a liberator who tried to lead Russia out of
        oppression and 'unculturedness' and save her from a
        pseudo-revolution; Stalin in that of a builder of a new
        civilization who rescued communism from theoretical
        and personal wranglings that threatened it with dissolu-
        tion on Lenin's death." There follows a critique by
        H. Arendt and a panel discussion of Ulam's article.
        [DK265. A135 1967aa]

2651   *Vishniak, M. "Lenin's Democracy and Stalin's," <u>For Aff</u>,
        24, no. 4 (July 1946), 610-21.

2652   *Volgyes, Ivan. "Myth and Man: In Search of the Real
        Lenin and Stalin," <u>Choice</u>, 6 (Dec. 1969), 1347-56.
        A historiographical essay on leading studies of Lenin
        and Stalin.

2653   Vyshinsky, A. Y. <u>Lenin and Stalin. The Great Organizers</u>
        <u>of the Soviet State.</u> Moscow: Foreign Languages Pub-
        lishing House, 1952; 68pp.
        A Soviet discussion of Lenin's thought and policies on
        the state and the nationalities question, and how, in
        the author's estimate, Stalin faithfully continued Lenin's
        work. [DK267. V936]

2654   _____. <u>The Teachings of Lenin and Stalin on Proletarian</u>
        <u>Revolution and the State.</u> London: Soviet News, 1948;
        120pp.
        An account, by a Soviet leader, of the role played by
        both Lenin and Stalin in leading the October Revolution,
        establishing the Soviet state and building socialism.
        Vyshinsky summarizes the standard writings, actions,
        and policies followed by Lenin in October and afterward
        and, at every turn, asserts that Stalin was Lenin's
        principal assistant who has followed his teachings since
        his 1924 death. [DK267. V938]

2655   Wilson, F. M. "Lenin's Shoes and Stalin's Boots," New
        Rep, 134 (30 Apr. 1956), 12.
        A comparison of Stalin's harsh policies to the more
        humane ones of Lenin.

        F. L. TROTSKY

2656   Bachman, Jon E. Lenin and Trotsky. Woodbury, New
        York: Barron's Educational Series, 1976.
        Unavailable for annotation.

2657   *D'Agostino, A. "Ambiguities of Trotsky's Leninism," Sur-
        vey, 24, no. 1 (Winter 1979), 178-203.
        A discussion of Trotsky's defeat at the hands of Stalin
        as resting in the nature of his Leninism, especially his
        differences with Lenin on party organization and rela-
        tions with the workers.

2658   *Deutscher, Isaac. The Prophet Armed. Trotsky: 1879-
        1921, Volume I. New York: Random House, 1965;
        540pp. , bib. 523-28.
        This scholarly and comprehensive biography of Trotsky
        does not have a separate chapter on Lenin but contains
        much information on virtually every aspect of Trotsky's
        relationship with him in the 1903-1921 period. A de-
        tailed index listing sub-headings beneath Lenin's name
        makes for convenient location of information on him.
        [DK254. T6D4]

2659   Fischer, L. "Lenin versus Trotzky," Nation, 120 (21 Jan.
        1925), 61-63.
        An assessment of Lenin as a pragmatist and Trotsky
        as an orthodox Marxist.

2660   Leach, H. "Lenin and Trotsky," Chambers J, 9 (26 Apr.
        1919), 321-25 and 9 (31 May 1919), 401-05.

2661   London, Kurt. "Leninism, Trotzkyism, Stalinism," in
        Backgrounds of Conflict: Ideas and Forms in World
        Politics. New York: Macmillan, 1947; 265-69.
        A brief discussion of the views of Lenin, Trotsky, and
        Stalin on whether it was best to concentrate on building
        socialism within the Soviet Union or to promote world
        revolution. [D443. L57]

2662   Russell, Bertrand. "Lenin, Trotsky, and Gorky," in Bol-
        shevism: Practice and Theory. New York: Arno,
        1972; 35-43.
        An account of a 1920 conversation with Lenin. Russell
        describes Lenin's appearance and mannerisms (stress-
        ing his simplicity) and then recounts their discussion of
        the likelihood of revolution in England, the problem of

establishing socialism in a peasant country, and economic relations with capitalist countries. Russell concludes with a comparison of the impression made on him by Trotsky (brighter and more personable than Lenin, but having less character) and Gorky ("the most lovable and ... sympatheitc of Russians").
[DK265. R82] Excerpt in Nation, 27 (17 July 1920), 493-4.

2663 Ryss, P. "Lenin and Trotsky: A Parallel," New Rus, 2, no. 24 (15 July 1920), 332-35.
An examination of the similarities and differences in the background and personalities of Lenin and Trotsky.

2664 Sarel, Benno. "Lenin, Trotsky and Stalin," Dissent, 4 (Winter 1957), 76-87.
A discussion of Lenin's views on the party, socialist democracy and revolution, and an assessment of his relationship with Stalin and Trotsky.

2665 Shapiro, William E. , ed. Lenin and Trotsky. New York: F. Watts, 1967; 66pp.
A general account (prepared for the CBS series The 20th Century) of the revolutionary events in modern Russia through the roles played by Lenin and Trotsky.

2666 Stewart, William. "Lenin--Anarchism and the Ultra Left," Com V, 2, no. 2 (Mar.-Apr. 1970), 55-59.
A comparison of Lenin's teachings on revolution and socialist construction to those of Trotsky.

2667 *Warth, Robert D. "The Iskra Period and the 'Majestic Prologue of 1905,'" in Leon Trotsky. Boston: Twayne, 1977; 26-47.
Lenin is not the focus of this chapter, but it contains much information on his relationship and conflicts with Trotsky in the 1903-1905 period. [DK254. T6W37]

2668 *Wistrich, Robert. "The Break with Lenin," in Trotsky. Fate of a Revolutionary. London: Robson Books, 1979; 24-36.
An examination of Trotsky's 1903 break with Lenin over the RSDLP's organization and relation to the workers' movement. Wistrich states that Trotsky interpreted Lenin's centrist political philosophy as a crude attempt to gain personal control of the revolutionary movement and the Social Democratic Party, and that consequently Trotsky's attack on Lenin assumed a very personal and derogatory tone. Wistrich also discusses possible emotional and psychological motives for Trotsky's assault on Lenin: "Trotsky's revolt against paternal, social and institutional authority was still too fresh to allow him to submit readily to Lenin's authority."
[DK254. T6W57]

2669   *Wolfenstein, E. Victor. The Revolutionary Personality.
        Lenin, Trotsky and Gandhi. Princeton: Princeton
        University Press, 1967; 330pp., bib. 319-26.
        An examination of the lives of Lenin, Trotsky, and
        Gandhi as a means of developing some preliminary ob-
        servations on the "psychological characteristics of revo-
        lutionists." Wolfenstein develops a personality model
        for each man, and then employs it as a means of ex-
        plaining the respective political behavior of the three
        men while at the same time developing a hypothesis
        about the revolutionary personality in general. He
        divides his study into four main sections: childhood and
        adolescence, young manhood, adulthood I, and adulthood
        II. In the first two parts, he discusses various episodes
        in Lenin's life which shaped his personality, while in
        the last two parts he abandons the chronological approach
        for a case study of some of the events which best yield
        insight into Lenin's mind and the psychological attributes
        of revolutionary leadership. Wolfenstein also evaluates
        the influence of Lenin's personality on Bolshevik party
        organization and tactics as well as on his preoccupation
        with minute details as leader of Russia after 1917.
        [HX312.L36W6]

        G. WOODROW WILSON

2670   Araquistain, Louis. "As the Actors Leave the Stage," Liv
        Age, 320 (22 Mar. 1924), 541-42.
        A discussion of the deaths of Lenin and Wilson and the
        similarities in their careers. Araquistain states that
        both were deeply concerned with the redemption of hu-
        manity, failed to achieve their goals, and had their
        health desert them when it was most needed.

2671   Eastman, Max. "Lenin and Wilson," in Russia. New York:
        The Liberator Publishing Company, 1919.
        Unavailable for annotation. [DK265.R87]

2672   Hofer, W. "Lenin and Wilson in 1917. The Dominant Ten-
        dency of Our Century," Mod W, 6 (1968), 67-74.
        A discussion of the conflict between democracy and
        totalitarianism as represented by Wilson and Lenin re-
        spectively.

2673   *Lukacs, John. "Wilson Is Overtaking Lenin," National R,
        26 (15 Feb. 1974), 199-203.
        A comparison of Wilson and Lenin as failures in changing
        civilization in the direction they intended, but as being
        responsible for launching their nations on the road to
        world power.

2674   *Mayer, Arno J. "Wilson versus Lenin," in Political Origins

of the New Diplomacy. New York: Howard Fertig,
1969; 368-94, bib. 395-420.
An examination of the interrelationship between the positions of Lenin and Woodrow Wilson on war aims, nationalities and self-determination. Mayer asserts that
Lenin's radical stance, especially on self-determination,
forced the Allied leaders to clarify their position on
the national question. He discusses the similarity between the views of Lenin and Wilson as well as the
radically different instruments (world revolution versus
the League of Nations) advanced by the two leaders to
solve the national question. [D610. M33 1969]

2675　*Victorson, H. S. "Wilson and Lenin," Strat Mo, n. s. 1
(1924), 263-68.
An estimate of the careers of Wilson and Lenin with
most attention devoted to the failures of both men:
Wilson with his "new political order" and Lenin with
his "new economic order."

2676　"Wilson and Lenin," Chris Cent, 41 (14 Feb. 1924), 197-99.

H.　OTHERS

2677　Äikiä Armas. "Red Pine of the North," in LCIA (anthology), 162-83.
An account of the close relationship between Lenin and
the Finnish communist Otto Kuusinen and of Lenin's
influence on Kuusinen and the Communist Party of Finland.

2678　*Althusser, Louis. "Lenin and Hegel," in Lenin and Philosophy and Other Essays. New York: Monthly Review
Press, 1971; 107-26.
An assessment of the reasons for Lenin's reading of
Hegel. Althusser states that Lenin turned to Hegel in
response to historical circumstances which demanded
a comprehensive review of the dialectical process. To
this end, Lenin analyzed Hegel not in terms of inverting
Hegel's thought but in hope of separating the mass of
Hegel's faulty philosophy from that which was both insightful and acceptable. Althusser asserts that Lenin
was most particularly interested in Hegel's criticism
of Kant, especially in regard to the concept of "the
absolute idea," part of which Lenin adapted for his own
philosophy. [B4249. L384A69]

2679　*Anin, D. "Lenin and Malinovsky," Survey, 21 (Autumn
1975), 145-56.

2680　Ascher, Abraham. Pavel Axelrod and the Development of
Menshevism. Cambridge: Harvard University Press,
1972; 420pp.

Lenin is not the focus of this study, but it contains many references to him and his relations with Axelrod. [DK254. A49A9]

2681   Aukrust, T. "Luther and Lenin," Luth Stand, 7 (22 Aug. 1967), 2+.

2682   *Avtorkhanov, A. "Khrushchev, Leninism and Stalinism," B Inst St USSR, 3, no. 11 (Nov. 1956), 13-20.
        An assessment of Khrushchev's use of Lenin in his 1956 speech attacking Stalin at the 20th CPSU Congress.

2683   *Bailes, Kendall E. "Lenin and Bogdanov: The End of an Alliance," in Columbia Essays in International Affairs. Volume II. The Dean's Papers, 1966, Andrew W. Cordier, ed. New York: Columbia University Press, 1966; 107-33.
        A discussion of the roots of Lenin's split (1908-1909) with Bogdanov as resting in philosophical differences between the two Bolshevik leaders. Bailes dismisses the interpretation that Lenin and Bogdanov split over Bolshevik finances, and instead asserts that with the 1907 end of the revolutionary ferment in Russia the philosophical differences between Lenin and Bogdanov, which had existed since their 1904 alliance, came to the surface. He analyzes Lenin's Materialism and Empirio-Criticism as a distorted critique of Bogdanov's dialectical materialism, and evaluates the significance of the split within Bolshevik ranks caused by the Lenin-Bogdanov schism. [JX1395. C6 1966]

2684   Balabanoff, Angelica. "Death and Funeral," in NBPA (anthology), 121.
        A brief reminiscence concerning Lenin's grief at the funeral of Inessa Armand.

2685   *Ballestrem, Karl G. "Lenin and Bogdanov," St Sov Tho, 9, no. 4 (1969), 283-310.
        An assessment of differing interpretations of Marx advanced by Lenin and Bogdanov, and a critique of Lenin's attack on Bogdanov in Materialism and Empirio-Criticism.

2686   *Banaji, Jairus. "Chayanov, Kautsky, Lenin: Considerations Towards a Synthesis," Ec Pol W, 11, no. 40 (2 Oct. 1976), 1594-1607.
        An appraisal of the influence on Lenin and Kautsky of Chayanov's analysis of peasant production.

2687   Baron, Samuel. "Between Marx and Lenin: George Plekhanov," in Revisionism: Essays on the History of Marxist Ideas, Leopold Labedz, ed. New York: Praeger, 1962; 40-54.

This essay does not focus on Lenin, but it contains a discussion of Plekhanov's opposition to Lenin's brand of Marxism. Originally in Sov Sur, no. 32 (1960), 94-101. [HX40. L14]

2688   Basu, Chitta. "Lenin and Netaji Bose," Link, 12, no. 36 (19 Apr. 1970), 31-33.

2689   Bedriy, Anatole W. "Mikhnovskyi and Lenin," Ukr R, 18, no. 2 (1971), 58-75.
A discussion of Lenin and the Ukrainian leader Mikhnovskyi as leaders of two separate nations in conflict with each other. Bedriy depicts Lenin as a Russian imperialist hiding behind internationalism, and Mikhnovskyi as a Ukrainian nationalist championing freedom.

2690   _____. "The Year of Chuprynka versus the Year of Lenin," Ukr R, 17, no. 2 (1970), 2-12.
An attack on Soviet nationality policy by way of a comparative discussion of Lenin and the Ukrainian nationalist Taras Chuprynka.

2691   Body, Marcel. "Alexandra Kollontay Remembers," in NBPA (anthology), 122.
Short excerpts from the writings of Kollontay on the close relationship between Lenin and Inessa Armand, and on the possibility that Armand's death contributed to the deterioration of Lenin's health.

2692   Bonch-Bruyevich, V. D. "Kropotkin's Death," in NBPA (anthology), 82-84.
An account of Lenin's provision of medical care for Kropotkin.

2693   _____. "Meeting with Kropotkin," in NBPA (anthology), 74-81.
An account of Lenin's discussion with Kropotkin on anarchism and cooperatives.

2694   Brophy, Liam. "From Luther to Lenin via Liberalism," Irish Mo, 74 (May 1946), 192-97.
A comparison of the characters of Lenin and Luther, linking Lenin to the secularization process which Luther began.

2695   Burtsev, Vladimir. "Lenine and Malinovsky," Strug Rus, 1, nos. 9-10 (17 May 1919), 138-40.
An account of Malinovsky's exposure and trial as a tsarist police agent.

2696   *Carlsnaes, W. E. "The Concept of Ideology and Political Analysis: A Critical Examination of Its Usage by Marx, Lenin and Mannheim," Oxford University, 1977 (dissertation).

2697   *Cassidy, Frank P.   "Revolutionary Politics and Normal
            Politics: Rousseau, Marx and Lenin," Stanford Uni-
            versity, 1973 (dissertation).

2698   Chambre, Henri.   "Lenin and Clausewitz," in From Karl
            Marx to Mao tse-Tung.   A Systematic Survey of Marx-
            ism-Leninism.   New York: Kennedy and Sons, 1963;
            216-17.
            A short summary of the points of Clausewitz's military
            theory which appealed to Lenin.   [HX39.C483]

2699   *Charlesworth, N.   "Russian Stratification Debate and India,"
            Mod Asian St, 13 (Feb. 1979), 61-95.
            A comparison of the views expressed by A. Chayanov
            and Lenin (The Development of Capitalism in Russia)
            on the functioning and evolution of peasant economies.

2700   *Claudin, Fernando.   "Democracy and Dictatorship in Lenin
            and Kautsky," New Left R, no. 106 (Nov.-Dec. 1977),
            59-76.

2701   *Davies, D. R.   "Cromwell and Lenin: A Comparison and
            Contrast," Congreg Q, (Oct. 1939), 459-66.

2702   *Deich, Alexander.   "Lunacharsky," in LIOL (anthology),
            125-41.
            A discussion of the personal relationship between Lenin
            and Lunacharsky with most attention given to Lenin's
            influence on and admiration for the work of Lunacharsky
            as Commissar of Education.

2703   *Elwood, R. C.   "Scoundrel or Saviour?   Solzhenitsyn's view
            of Roman Malinovskii," Can S P, 19, no. 2 (June 1977),
            161-66.
            In part, a discussion of Lenin's relationship with Mal-
            inovsky.

2704   Fischer, Gerhard.   " 'The State Begins to Wither Away....':
            Notes on the Interpretation of the Paris Commune by
            Bakunin, Marx, Engels, and Lenin," Aust J Pol Hist,
            25, no. 1 (1979), 29-38.

2705   Fischer, Louis.   "Lenin to Franklin D. Roosevelt," Nation,
            137 (20 Dec. 1933), 698-99.
            A consideration of Lenin's critique of the problems fac-
            ing the Russian economy under Kerensky's regime as
            being similar to Roosevelt's assessment of the 1933 ills
            of the American economy.

2706   *Frankel, Jonathan.   "Martov and Lenin," Survey J, 70/71
            (1969), 202-26.
            A review of I. Getzler's Martov: A Political Biography
            of a Russian Social Democrat discussing Martov's love-
            hate relationship with Lenin.

2707 *_____ . "The Polarization of Russian Marxism (1883-1903) Plekhanov, Lenin and Akimov" in Vladimir Akimov on the Dilemmas of Russian Marxism 1895-1903. Cambridge: Cambridge University Press, 1969; 1-98.
A comprehensive and scholarly examination of the nature and significance of the clash between Akimov and the Economists, on the one hand, and Plekhanov and Lenin, on the other. Frankel establishes that both Lenin and Akimov were attracted to Plekhanov because of his interpretive application of Marxism to Russian conditions. The author argues that Plekhanov's interpretation of Marx, in fact, failed to resolve many questions, most notably those concerning the nature of the revolutionary party and its relation to the workers and the bourgeois revolution, and, as a result, his disciples (Akimov and Lenin) were able to advance rival elaborations of Plekhanov's ideas. Frankel concludes that although those who later became Mensheviks sided initially with Lenin against Akimov's deterministic and gradualistic interpretation, Akimov's critique of Lenin's radical voluntarism accurately foreshadowed those aspects of Lenin's thought which later split the Social Democratic movement. [HX312. M233]

2708 *Getzler, Israel. Martov. London: Cambridge University Press, 1967; 246pp.
This study does not contain a separate chapter on Lenin but it includes significant information on his relationship with Martov. [HX312. M2764]

2709 Globerman, Martin. "Lenin versus Althusser," Rad Amer, 3, no. 5 (1969), 19-24.

2710 *Gortat, Radzislawa and Piotr Marciniak. "The Attitude of Lenin and Plekhanov towards the Russian Revolution," Dialec Hum, 4 (Summer 1971), 25-36.
An appraisal of the different interpretations of the Russian Revolution advanced by Plekhanov and Lenin, with most attention given to the question of whether revolution was to be a spontaneous product of conditions or needed to be stimulated by the workers' party.

2711 Gvishiani, Ludmila. "Lenin and Robins," Sov Life, no. 4 (Apr. 1970), 43-44.

2712 *Harvey, Mary Kate McCarty. "The Political Views of Lenin and Nasser on State and Trans-State Politics: A Comparative Analysis," University of Southern Mississippi, 1973 (dissertation).

2713 *Henry, Maureen D. "The Development of Civil Theologies in the Philosophies of Hobbes, Rousseau, Saint-Simon, Comte, and Lenin," Notre Dame University, 1974 (dissertation).

2714   Kline, George L. "Hegel and the Marxist-Leninist Critique
        of Religion," in Hegel and the Philosophy of Religion,
        Sarrell E. Christensen. Hague: M. Nijhoff, 1970; 187-
        202.
        Lenin is not the focus of this essay but it contains a
        short, interpretive section on his views on religion as
        being totally at odds with and of much less depth and
        soundness than those of Hegel. Some additional infor-
        mation can be found in the comments on Kline's essay
        and his response to the comments (203-15).
        [B2949R3W6 1968]

2715   *Kruger, Daniel H. "Hobson, Lenin, and Schumpeter on
        Imperialism," J Hist Ideas 16, no. 2 (Apr. 1955), 252-
        59.

2716   *Laski, Harold J. "Lenin and Mussolini," in The Foreign
        Affairs Reader, Hamilton F. Armstrong, ed. New
        York: Harper and Brothers, 1947; 43-56.
        A comparison of the rise to power, philosophy, and
        political practices of Lenin and Mussolini, and a survey
        of the vastly different receptions the two regimes re-
        ceived internationally. Laski sees marked similarities
        in Mussolini's and Lenin's willingness to use any end
        to advance the philosophies they respectively believed
        to be superior to all others. The more popular inter-
        national reception received by Mussolini, Laski states,
        was due to his less radical views on private property.
        The author concludes with a sharp condemnation of the
        un-democratic policies of both leaders. Originally in
        For Aff, 2 (Sept. 1932), 43-54. [D844. F6]

2717   "Lenin and Churchill," New Sta, 15 (19 June 1920), 296-97.

2718   "Lenin and Kerenski," New Eur, 15 (Nov. 1917), 129-32.

2719   "Lenin and Loyola: Parallels Real and Unreal," America,
        56 (6 Mar. 1937), 515.

2720   "Lenin's Proposal and Roosevelt's," New Rep, 75 (17 May
        1933), 3-4.
        Parallels between Lenin's pre-October Revolution ideas
        on how to improve the Russian economy and those an-
        nounced by Roosevelt in 1933.

2721   *Lerner, Warren. "Radek and Lenin: Collaboration and
        Conflict," in Karl Radek. The Last Internationalist.
        Stanford: Stanford University Press, 1970; 31-53, bib.
        221-33.
        An assessment of the factors which brought Lenin and
        Karl Radek together during World War I. Lerner states
        that differences "over revolutionary organization, the
        role of party leadership, and the question of national

self-determination had prevented any close association between Lenin and Radek," but that they set aside these differences because of their mutual belief that, in 1915, the major goal of socialism was the formation of a new socialist international organization committed to revolution and opposition to the war. Lerner discusses the temporary collapse of their collaboration due to a dispute over the issue of self-determination of nationalities, and how the same opportunistic considerations which led to their initial cooperation triumphed over this difference of opinion. [HX312. R3L4]

2722 *Levi, Albert W. "Society in Distress: V. I. Lenin and Thorstein Veblen," in Philosophy and the Modern World. Bloomington: Indiana University Press, 1966; 198-243. An examination of the differences between Lenin and Veblen as social philosophers defending freedom. Levi states that whereas "Lenin tested his freedom in the realm of thought always with an ambiguous reference to the realm of social and political activity ... Veblen realized his freedom in the act of autonomous thinking, in ironic and detached understanding of the organization of modern industrial society." Levi traces the roots of their thinking to the writings of Marx, and, in Lenin's case, asserts that Marx's materialistic interpretation of the world led to the conclusion that "ideas are not to be judged primarily according to their theoretical truth or falsity, but according to their social role." Such a conclusion, Levi maintains, accounts for the functional and purposive quality of Lenin's thought, and for Lenin's assault, in Materialism and Empirio-Criticism, on those who indulged in philosophy for philosophy's sake. [B803. L45]

2723 *Lewin, Rhoda G. "Some New Perspectives for Social Change," University of California at Los Angeles, 1979 (dissertation). An assessment of the works of Blanqui, Marx, and Lenin.

2724 *Lozinski, Jerzy. "On the Problems of the Relation between Marxism and Phenomenology; Truth and Revolution; Husserl and Lenin," Dialec Hum, 3 (Winter 1976), 121-33.

2725 *McCullagh, Francis. "Peter the Great and Lenin," Studies, 19 (Dec. 1930), 564-76.

2726 McNeal, Robert H. "Lenin and 'Lise de K ... ' a Fabrication," Slav R, 28, no. 3 (Sept. 1969), 471-74, An attack on the claim that Lenin had an affair with a woman only known as 'Lise de K.'

2727   Menon, K. P. S. "Emperor Asoka and Comrade Lenin:
        Two Decrees of Peace," Illus Wk India, 91, no. 17
        (26 Apr. 1970), 30-31.

2728   *Pavlov, Todor. "Kant and Hegel, Marx and Lenin," Dar
        Int, 18, no. 1 (Jan. 1978), 12-18.

2729   *Pipes, Richard. "The Encounter with Lenin," in Struve--
        Liberal on the Left, 1870-1905. Cambridge: Harvard
        University Press, 1970; 121-43.
        A scholarly examination of the origins and nature of
        Lenin's relationship with P. Struve in 1895. Pipes
        establishes that Lenin and Struve were distinctly dif-
        ferent in their values, level of education and tempera-
        ments, and that these differences colored their respec-
        tive interpretations of Marxism and capitalism. He
        illustrates, through a discussion of Lenin's review of
        Struve's Critical Remarks, the clash between Lenin's
        impatient, simplistic and revolutionary Marxism and
        Struve's more evolutionary, non-violent and scholastic
        Marxism. In spite of their differences, Pipes states,
        Lenin and Struve were able to collaborate closely from
        1895 to 1900 largely because each felt he needed the
        other. Lenin believed he needed Struve as an ally in
        order to forge an effective power base for himself,
        while Struve, in a less manipulative sense, favored an
        alliance with Lenin because he believed that the only
        way to wage war against autocracy was through a broad
        coalition of all groups opposed to the government. Later
        chapters in this study contain references to and short
        sections on the collapse of Lenin's relationship with
        Struve and his bitter assaults on Struve as a revisionist.
        [DK254. S597P5]

2730   Rothschild, Richard. Jefferson, Lenin, Socrates; Three
        Gods Give an Evening to Politics. New York: Ran-
        dom House, 1936; 216pp.
        A presentation of the principal views of Jefferson, Lenin
        and Socrates by way of a creative and informal, after-
        dinner discussion among them on such topics as free-
        dom, history, philosophy, and man's destiny and future.
        Rothschild has Jefferson represent the individualist posi-
        tion, Lenin the collectivist point of view, and Socrates
        a position between the two extremes. [JC252. R6]

2731   Russell, B. "Gladstone and Lenin," Atlan Mo, 187 (Feb.
        1951), 66-68.

2732   *Rutko, Arseny. "A Heart of Faith and Courage," in LCIA
        (anthology), 184-203.
        A discussion of Fritz Platten's relationship with Lenin
        stressing Platten's assistence to Lenin in the negotia-
        tions with the German government which led to Lenin's
        April 1917 return to Russia from Switzerland.

2733   *Salvadori, Massino. Karl Kautsky and the Socialist Revolution, 1880-1938. London: NLB, 1979; 375pp.
        Lenin is not the focus of any one chapter in this study, but it contains many references to and short sections on his dispute with Kautsky over differing interpretations of imperialism, revolution, the state, the dictatorship of the proletariat, and international communism.
        [HX273. K34S2413]

2734   *Samchuk, Ulace. "Dostoevsky on Leninism," Ukr Q 6 (1950), 299-309.
        An application to Leninism of Dostoevsky's portrayal of radicalism in The Possessed.

2735   *Schapiro, Leonard B. "Rationalism and Nationalism in the Political Thought of P. B. Struve, G. V. Plekhanov and V. I. Lenin," in Rationalism and Nationalism in Russian 19th Century Thought. New Haven: Yale University Press, 1967; 128-39.
        A comparison of the varying interpretations advanced by Struve, Plekhanov, and Lenin on the development of capitalism in Russia. Schapiro states that whereas Struve and Plekhanov saw capitalism as a slowly developing and beneficial stage for Russia, Lenin saw capitalism as already in existence and needing to be destroyed. Lenin thus believed that Russian capitalism developed along uniquely national lines, whereas Struve and Plekhanov believed it developed the same way in all countries. Schapiro identifies two other elements in Lenin's thought which gave a national character to Bolshevism: his view of revolution as an aim not a process (hence his sense of urgency), and his belief in the need for a professional revolutionary elite to lead the workers' revolt. [JA84. R9S353]

2736   *Schapiro, Leonard B. and John W. Lewis. "The Roles of the Monolithic Party under the Totalitarian Leader," China Q, 40 (1969), 39-64.
        A comparative analysis of the roles played by five leaders (Lenin, Stalin, Hitler, Mao, and Mussolini) in four totalitarian systems to illustrate the Tucker thesis on the classification of totalitarian states.

2737   *Schedler, George. "Justice in Marx, Engels and Lenin," Sov St Tho, 18 (Aug. 1978), 223-33.

2738   *Scheibert, Peter. "Lenin, Bogdanov and the Concept of Proletarian Culture," LAL, (anthology), 43-58.
        A discussion of the varying conceptions of proletarian culture in the years immediately following the October Revolution. Scheibert examines both Bogdanov's "universal theory of organization" as a source of guidance for those (especially in the Prolekult) who sought to establish an autonomous proletarian culture and Lenin's

opposition to the ideas of Bogdanov with whom he had long standing philosophical differences. Although Prolekult was absorbed by the People's Commissariat of Education and Bogdanov fell into disfavor, Scheibert states, Bogdanov's ideas have to some extent influenced the Soviet theory of management, but because of the still effective tyranny of Lenin's condemnation of Bogdanov, he remains an outcast except in Russia's subculture.

2739   *Schurer, H. "Anton Pannekoek and the Origins of Leninism," SEER, 41, no. 97 (June 1963), 327-44.
A examination of Pannekoek's influence on Lenin's views on the aristocracy of labor and the possibility of a socialist revolution in a backward nation.

2740   Serebryakova, Galina. "By Right of Seniority," in LCIA (anthology), 314-37.
A survey of Clara Zetkin's revolutionary career and, to a lesser extent, her relationship with Lenin. Serebryakova presents most information on Zetkin's 1921-1923 contacts with Lenin and Krupskaya, recounting a number of their conversations.

2741   Settembrini, Domenico. "Mussolini and the Legacy of Revolutionary Socialism," J Comtemp Hist, 11, no. 4 (1976), 239-68.
In part, an assessment of the similarities between the methods and philosophy of Mussolini and Lenin.

2742   *Shizirta, Hitoshi. "Reconsideration of Lenin's Criticism of Kautsky's Ultra-Imperialism Theory," Kyoto Un Ec R, 85, no. 5 (May 1960), 1-19.

2743   *Shub, David. "Kropotkin and Lenin," Rus R, 12, no. 4 (Oct. 1953), 227-34.

2744   *_____. "Lenin and Vladimir Korolenko," Rus R, 25, no. 1 (1966), 46-53.

2745   *Sinclair, Keith. "Hobson and Lenin in Johore: Colonial Office Policy Towards British Concessionaires and Investors, 1878-1907," Mod Asian St, 1, no. 4 (1967), 335-52.

2746   *Sochor, Zenovia A. "Modernization and Socialist Transformation: Leninist and Bogdanovite Alternatives of the Cultural Revolution," Columbia University, 1977 (dissertation).

2747   *Steigerwald, Robert. "Lukacs and the Theory of the Working Class Party in Marx, Engels and Lenin," Rev W, 13 (1975), 267-86.

2748   *Struve, Peter. "My Contacts and Conflicts with Lenin," Slavonic R, 12 (Apr. 1934), 573-95 and 13 (July 1935), 66-84.

2749   *Traub, Rainer. "Lenin and Taylor: The Fate of Scientific Management in the (Early) Soviet Union," Telos, 37 (Fall 1978), 82-92.

2750   *Trotzky, L. "H. G. Wells and Lenin: The Philistine Discourseth on the Revolutionary," Labour Mo, 6 (July 1924), 411-20.
A critique of the image of Lenin advanced by Wells in Russia in the Shadows.

2751   *Turner, Ruth Spriggs. "Violence and Nonviolence in Confrontation: A Comparative Study of Ideologies; Six Historical Cases (Paine, Lenin, Hitler, Gandhi, Luthuli, King)," University of Massachusetts, 1979 (dissertation).

2752   *Ulyanovsky, Rostislov. "Marx, Engels and Lenin on the National and Colonial Questions," in National Liberation. Essays on Theory and Practice. Moscow: Progress Publishers, 1978, 7-35.

2753   *Urban, G. R. "Mussolini and Lenin: A Conversation with Domenico Settembrini," Survey, 23, no. 3 (Summer 1977-1978), 87-117.
A discussion of the similarities between the views of Mussolini and Lenin on party organization, opposition to syndicalism, and attitude towards World War I. Urban concludes that both men revised Marxism because they believed it was a sterile doctrine. Also in Eurocommunism, G. Urban, ed. London: 1978.

2754   Warde, William F. "From Lenin to Khrushchev," Int Soc R, 22 (Fall 1961), 107-14.
A comparison of Khrushchev's new program of the 22nd Congress of the CPSU to Lenin's program announced at the 8th Congress.

2755   *White, James. "From Karl Marx to Bogdanov," Co-existence, 15, no. 2 (1978), 187-206.
An evaluation of the clash between Lenin and Bogdanov as one based on fundamentally opposite views on revolution. White states that Bogdanov's starting point was the workers' needs, while Lenin began with only abstract concepts of socialism and the historical process.

2756   Williams, W. C. "Abraham Lincoln and Nicolai Lenine; a Contrast," Cur Op, 72 (Mar. 1922), 320-23.

2757   Wilson, H. W. "Napoleon and His Modern Parodists. Trotsky and Lenin: Inquiry into the Alleged Napoleonic Precedents for Their Methods," National R, (June 1921), 514-23.

2758 *Wolfe, Bertram D. "Lenin and Inessa Armand," Slav R, 22, no. 1 (Mar. 1963), 96-114.
A survey of the relationship between Lenin and Armand speculating on the possibility of a love affair. Also in Encounter, 12 (Feb. 1964), 83-91.

2759 * _____. "Lenin and the Agent Provocateur Malinovsky," Rus R, 5, no. 1 (Autumn 1945), 49-69. Also in Three Who Made a Revolution. New York: Dell, 1964; 535-57.

2760 * _____. "Lenin Has Trouble with Engels; A Heretofore Unanalyzed Source of Lenin's Theory of Imperialism," Rus R, 15, no. 3 (July 1956), 196-203.

2761 *Wright, Erik O. "Bureaucracy and the State," in Class, Crisis and the State. London: Lowe and Brydone, 1978; 181-225, bib. 255-60.
An exploration of the question "how should we understand the relation between class struggle and the internal structure of the state?" through comparing the analysis of bureaucracy and the state formulated by Lenin (State and Revolution, 1917) and Max Weber (Parliament and Government in a Reconstructed Germany, 1917). Wright presents, in semi-outline form, the leading propositions of Lenin and Weber, juxtaposes their main arguments, and then draws several conclusions on their similarities and differences. He states that although Lenin and Weber differ substantially in their assumptions and conclusions, a general theory of the state can be formulated by synthesizing Weber's concept of the state as an organization manipulated by elites with Lenin's contention that the state is an organization which classes rule through a particular kind of structure.
[HX541.5.W75]

2762 * _____. "To Control or to Smash Bureaucracy: Weber and Lenin on Politics, the State and Bureaucracy," Berkeley J Sociol, 19 (1974), 69-108.

2763 Yakhontoff, Victor A. "Dr. Sun-Yat-sen and Lenin," in Russia and the Soviet Union in the Far East. London: Allen and Unwin, 1932; 148-49.
A brief statement on how Sun-Yat-sen, due to unsuccessful appeals to the Western powers for assistance in his revolutionary work, turned to Lenin, became an ardent admirer of his, and reorganized the Kuomintang along Leninist lines. [DK246.Y3]

Cross-References: For personal influences on Lenin, see Revolutionary Movement, Precursors (II-A).

For Lenin's influence on other people, see International Socialism, Influence (IX-C).

For Lenin's influence on and comparison to Gandhi,
see International Socialism, Influence (IX-C-3-c-1);
Mao-Tse-tung, (IX-C-3-b-1).

13. LENINIANA

A. Cult of Lenin

2764   Altman. "Sculpturing Lenin," Liv Age, 340 (Aug. 1931), 603-04.

2765   Bakunshinski, A. "Lenin in Soviet Sculpture," Int Lit, no. 1 (Jan. 1935), 90-100.
A description of the work of N. A. Andreyev in sculpting Lenin.

2766   Bakunts, A. "Legend of Lenin," Liv Age, 346 (May 1934), 245-48.

2767   *Bonch-Bruyevich, V. D. "Cult of Personality," in NBPA (anthology), 88-89.
A brief account of Lenin's dismay over the tremendous concern shown for his welfare by the many newspaper articles written about the attempt on his life. Lenin was particularly upset over the "mystique" with which they surrounded his name.

2768   Brewster, Dorothy. "Lenin and the Prize Pig; All-Russian Agricultural Exposition," Nation, 117 (7 Nov. 1923), 510-11.
A report on how the "presence" of Lenin was everywhere at the All-Russian Agricultural Exposition of 27 September 1923 by way of posters, pins, pamphlets, "Lenin corners," etc.

2769   Byron, R. "Lenin's Mausoleum in Red Square," Arch R, 71 (May 1932), 177-78.

2770   *Central V. I. Lenin Museum. A Guide. Moscow: Progress Publishers, 1979; 109pp.
An annotated guidebook for the Lenin Museum in Moscow.

2771   *Chamberlin, W. H. "Why Russia Loves Lenin," W Tomorrow, 7 (July 1924), 207-210.
An account of Lenin's funeral and the national mourning over his death. Chamberlin states that Lenin was es-

pecially loved for his sincerity, simplicity, and willingness to talk with the common man.

2772 Cholerton, A. T. "Lenin Today," Liv Age, 353 (Jan. 1938), 448-50.
An account of the embalming of Lenin's body, and a description of his mausoleum and the procedures that are followed there by visitors.

2773 Clinchy, Everett R. "I Saw Lenin," Chris Cent, 49 (14 Sept. 1932), 1099-1100.
A recollection of a visit to Lenin's tomb, and a discussion of Lenin as Russia's 'messiah.'

2774 Cummings, Edward E. "The Tomb of Lenin," Hound and Horn, 6, no. 1 (Oct.-Dec. 1932), 20+.

2775 "Daily March Past Lenin," Lit D, 115 (14 Jan. 1933), 15.

2776 Dandavate, M. R. "Lenin--An Inspiration and a Warning," Janata, 25, no. 14 (26 Apr. 1970), 3-5.
A warning against turning Lenin's teachings into a holy scripture, and a positive appraisal of Lenin's thought and great humanism.

2777 Dangulov, S. "Artists Great Achievement," Sov Lit, no. 4 (1974), 173-82.
A review of Nikolai Zhukov's drawings of Lenin.

2778 Dean, Robert. "The Idol of Russia," New R, 8 (1938), 516-19.
An account of the embalming of Lenin's body and the construction of his mausoleum.

2779 Demirjian, Derenik. "Lenin. Hero of Folklore," Int Lit, no. 6 (June 1935), 46-48.

2780 "Drive to Make Lenin a Secular Saint," Time, 95 (13 Apr. 1970), 27.

2781 *Duranty, Walter. "Lenin's Death," in Reports from Russia. New York: Viking, 1934; 121-50.
A collection of reports, by an American journalist and observer, dealing with the deterioration of Lenin's health, his death and, especially, its impact throughout Russia. Duranty describes the immediate public reaction to news of Lenin's death, the vast procession of people who passed his body, and the week of eulogies, testimonials, and public mourning that swept the country. [DK266.D8]

2782 *Fosburg, Nina T. "The Lenin Cult: Its Origin and Early Development," Harvard University, 1975 (dissertation).

2783   Foust, C. M. "Lenin," High Sch J, 46 (Jan. 1963), 135-
        41.
        A discussion of the cult of Lenin as one based upon a
        very bland and improbable hero. Foust sees Lenin's
        true claim to greatness as resting in his being the
        greatest modern theorist of socialism.

2784   Glagoleva, N. "The First Film about Lenin," Sov Film,
        no. 212, (1975), 40.

2785   "God of the Communists Lies for His First Entombed Por-
        trait," Life, 8 (5 Feb. 1940), 68-69.

2786   "God under Glass; the Preservation of Lenin's Body," Time,
        26 (9 Sept. 1935), 34.

2787   Hart, A. B. "Is Lenin among the Prophets?," Cur Hist M,
        33 (Dec. 1930), 415-18.

2788   Kapler, Alexei. "My Work on the Film 'Lenin in 1918,'"
        Int Lit, no. 3 (Mar. 1939), 107-110.

2789   Kapler, Alexei and T. Zlatogorova. "Lenin in 1918," Int
        Lit, no. 3 (Mar. 1939), 3-44.
        A restatement of the main dialogue of the film "Lenin
        in 1918."

2790   *Karaganov, A. "Leniniana Continues," Sov Lit, no. 4
        (1977), 160-72.
        A discussion of Lenin's image as presented in a series
        of documentary and creative films.

2791   "Kremlin Waxworks," Time, 59 (19 May 1952), 42+.

2792   Kunitz, J. "Lenin, a Legend in the Making," Nation, 126
        (8 Feb. 1928), 147.

2793   Lebedev, Nikolai. "Shchukin's Work on the Scenario 'Lenin
        in 1918,'" Int Lit, no. 1 (Jan. 1941), 105-08.

2794   Lenin. A Collection of Photographs and Stills. Moscow:
        Progress Publishers, 1970.

2795   "Lenin: Icon or Idea?," Yojana, 21, no. 19 (1 Nov. 1977),
        11-12.
        A review of Lenin's impact on the world through his
        ideals and the glorified image of him constructed and
        disseminated by his disciples.

2796   "Lenin in Documentary Film," Sov Life, 2, no. 162 (Feb.
        1970), 48-49.

2797   "Lenin Legend," Newsweek, 39 (21 Apr. 1952), 48-49.

An attack on the cult of Lenin which has presented "a liar and a bigot" as a saint.

2798   "Lenin: The Myth that Lives On," <u>US News W Rep</u>, 83 (24 Oct. 1977), 51-52.

2799   "Lenin's Anniversary," <u>B Inst St USSR</u>, 2, no. 2 (Feb. 1955), 29-30.
A description of the great fanfare for the 31st anniversary of Lenin's death as having far surpassed that for the anniversary of Stalin's death.

2800   "Lenin's Mummy Rules in Moscow," <u>Lit D</u>, 85 (11 Apr. 1925), 42-44.
An account of the embalming of Lenin and the construction of his mausoleum.

2801   "Lenin's Tomb a Rival of Lourdes," <u>Lit D</u>, 86 (19 Sept. 1925), 49.

2802   "Lenin's Week," <u>Time</u>, 49 (3 Feb. 1947), 24.
A description of the proceedings in Moscow in commemoration of the 23rd anniversary of Lenin's death.

2803   "Loved One; Mausoleum Closed for Repairs," <u>Time</u>, 86 (19 Nov. 1965), 48.

2804   Lyons, E. "Body in Lenin's Tomb," <u>National R</u>, 26 (15 Feb. 1974), 203-05.

2805   *McNeal, Robert H. "Krupskaya: The Feminine Subcult," in <u>LAL</u> (anthology), 219-28.
In part, a discussion of Krupskaya's role as a propagator of the Lenin cult. McNeal relates the possessive nature of Krupskaya's guardianship of Lenin's image (for both personal and political reasons) and her many efforts, written and otherwise, to preserve his legacy. He also examines Krupskaya's temporary eclipse, following her death, by Stalin as the guardian of Leninism, as well as the post-Stalin revival of her writings about Lenin.

2806   *"Madame Lenin's Request," <u>Rus Info R</u>, 4, no. 6 (9 Feb. 1924), 84.
A restatement of Krupskaya's plea that no monuments be built to Lenin, but rather people should only work more vigorously to achieve his goals.

2807   Magidenko, R. "Lenin in Uzbek Legend," <u>Asia</u>, 34 (May 1934), 319-20.

2808   Magidoff, Robert. "Lenin in Folklore," <u>Int Lit</u>, no. 1 (Jan. 1939), 96-100.
A general review of songs and tales about Lenin.

2809   "Memorials to Lenin," Rus Info R, 4, no. 10 (8 Mar. 1924),
        158.
        A note on the creation of a state depository for Lenin-
        related materials, and a description of six memorials
        to Lenin.

2810   *Miller, Jacob.   "Lenin and Soviet Mythology," in LAL (an-
        thology), 229-36.
        An analysis of the inadequacies of official attempts to
        propagate the Lenin myth.   Miller states that a study
        of the Leniniana issued just prior to the 1970 centennial
        reveals that the Lenin myth lacks many of the qualities
        possessed by a thriving myth, a development due largely
        to the fact that, over the past fifty years, Soviet leaders
        have become less sophisticated than the population which
        they rule and, consequently, issue Leniniana too primi-
        tive and oafish for the tastes of contemporary Soviet
        society.   To revitalize the Lenin myth, Miller suggests
        that Lenin be divested of his infallibility, that materials
        for the open study of his life and work be made public,
        and that the attempt to link him with everything be
        abandoned.

2811   Nexo, Martin A.   "Lenin's Influence on the Artists of the
        West," Int Lit, nos. 4-5 (Apr.-May 1940), 72-73.
        A note on Lenin as depicted by Western poets.

2812   "90th Anniversary of Lenin's Birth," W Marxist R, 3, no.
        4 (Apr. 1960), 60-62.

2813   Pieck, Wilhelm.   "At Lenin's Funeral," in WHML (anthol-
        ogy), 73-75.
        A brief note on popular reaction in the Soviet Union to
        Lenin's death.

2814   Plotnikov, Nikolai.   "The Role of My Lifetime," Sov Lit,
        no. 3 (1970), 173-79.
        An actor's account of his study of Lenin's character in
        preparation for playing the role of Lenin on the stage.

2815   _____.   "A Playwright on Lenin," W Marxist R, 3, no.
        4 (Apr. 1960), 35-38.
        A discussion of the importance and difficulties in re-
        creating, in the arts, the image of Lenin.

2816   "Resolutions of the Union Congress," Rus Info R, 4, no. 6
        (2 Feb. 1924), 84.
        A restatement of the resolution announcing plans to
        construct Lenin's mausoleum, erect monuments to him
        in the capital city of each republic, and to change the
        name of Petrograd to Leningrad.

2817   Rokotov, Timofei.   "Lenin on the Screen," Int Lit, no. 1
        (Jan. 1939), 90-95.

2818   Russell, F. "Mummy of Red Square," National R, 23 (10
          Aug. 1972), 865-66.

2819   "Saint Lenin," Lit D, 89 (26 Jan. 1926), 29-30.

2820   *Schwartz, Harry. "The Lenin Cult and Its Uses," in LAL
          (anthology), 237-42.
          An analytical review of the use of the cult of Lenin by
          Lenin's principal successors. Schwartz discusses Sta-
          lin's manipulative use of the Lenin cult (as the sole in-
          terpreter and protector of Lenin's heritage) against
          various political opponents, and then notes the decline
          of the cult's usage under Khrushchev, and its revival
          by Khrushchev's successors who, as "political pygmies,"
          sorely need the status given to them through identifica-
          tion with Lenin. In assessing the cult's future,
          Schwartz maintains that the increasingly profuse, crude,
          and narrowly nationalistic nature of the cult limits its
          appeal, while Lenin's many shifts in tactics and phi-
          losophy make his legacy ambiguous and a questionable
          one as a model worthy of emulation.

2821   *Seinenskii, A. E. "Lenin Musuem in the School," Sov Ed,
          15 (Aug. 1973), 37-55.

2822   Simonov, Vladimir. "A Museum for a Revolutionary," Illus
          Wk India, 87, no. 17 (24 Apr. 1966), 27.
          A description of the Moscow Central Lenin Museum's
          holdings.

2823   Singh, Iqbal. "Glimpses of Lenin in Moscow," in IAL (an-
          thology), 35-41.
          A description of the collection of the Central Lenin
          Museum, and a note on the great affection and admira-
          tion for Lenin shown by the museum's many visitors.

2824   Sokolov, Alexander. "A History of Lenin Sculpture," Sov
          Life, no. 4 (Apr. 1970), 45-47.

2825   *Souvarine, Boris. "The Cult of Lenin," Mod Q, 2 (Summer
          1939), 16-25.

2826   "Tattooed Mummy," Time, 48 (29 July 1946), 83.

2827   *Thompson, Dorothy. "Leninism: A Power and a Faith,"
          in The New Russia. New York: Holt and Company,
          1928; 89-120.
          A discussion of the foundation of the party's power as
          resting in the cult of Lenin rather than in its organiza-
          tional structure or the instruments of force at its dis-
          posal. Thompson (an eye-witness, American journalist-
          observer), states that since Lenin's death, the reverence
          for him has grown to such proportions that Leninism has

assumed many of the qualities of a dynamic, religious faith. [DK267. T5]

2828   "Throughout the Soviet Union," Rus Info R, 4, no. 6 (9 Feb. 1924), 86-88.
A review of the demonstrations, mourning, and commemorative plans in the weeks following Lenin's death.

2829   Tobenkin, E. "Lenin's Homecoming, a Russian Thanksgiving Day," Cur Hist M, 21 (Oct. 1924), 88-92.

2830   "Tribute to Lenin," Sov Life, 11, no. 206 (Nov. 1973), 6.
A note on the Lenin Mausoleum as the national monument of the Soviet Union.

2831   "Tributes to Lenin," Rus Info R, 4, no. 8 (23 Feb. 1924), 125-26.
An account of various plans to build Lenin memorials, and a sampling of the tributes to Lenin upon his death.

2832   *Tucker, Robert C. "Lenin as a Revolutionary Hero," in Stalin As a Revolutionary. 1879-1929. A Study in History and Personality. New York: Norton, 1974; 18-63.
A scholarly examination of the origin of the leader-centered qualities of the Bolshevik Party. Tucker states that from its theoretical foundation in What Is to Be Done?, to its development in the years of exile before 1917, and rise to and exercise of power, the Bolshevik Party was centered about the heroic image of Lenin. Lenin's "unusual powers of discourse and persuasion," the compelling quality of his writings, and his deep faith in the righteousness of his cause, all exerted a remarkable and hypnotic influence on his followers. In particular, his highly effective leadership of the Soviet state, Tucker maintains, confirmed his heroic image in the eyes of his disciples who, in spite of Lenin's protests began to glorify him even before his death. [DK268. S8D85]

2833   * _____. "The Rise of Stalin's Personality Cult," Am Hist R, 84 (Apr. 1979), 347-67.
In part, a discussion of the origins of the cult of Lenin.

2834   *Ulam, Adam B. "The Marxist Pattern," in Philosophers and Kings. Studies in Leadership. New York: Braziller, 1970; 95-111.
A study of the reasons behind the exaltation of the leader-figure in Marxism in general and Russia in particular. Ulam asserts that from its very beginnings Russian Marxism "was extraordinarily influenced by the qualities and characteristics of a few men," most notably, Plekhanov, Martov, and Lenin. This fact, coupled with the doctrinaire nature of Marxism and the fanatic

devotion to the cause characteristic of the 19th-century Russian revolutionary movement, led to a leader such as Lenin being viewed as an infallible hero and prophet and the source of all truth. [HM141. R83]

2835   V. I. Lenin. Album. Moscow: Bookniga, 1939.

2836   Vaprakhovsky, Leonid. "An Inexhaustible Subject," Sov Lit, no. 3 (1970), 171-72.
A description of the opportunities and difficulties facing actors who seek to portray Lenin on the stage.

2837   *Voronitsyn, Sergei. "The Lenin Cult and Soviet Youth," St Sov Un, 9, no. 1 (1969), 31-36.

2838   Wesson, Robert. "Leninism and Prussianism," in The Soviet Russian State. New York: Wiley and Sons, 1972; 149-54.
A brief inquiry into the nature and extent of the glorification of Lenin that has taken place in the Soviet Union since his death and, especially, during the 1970 celebration of the 100th anniversary of his birth. Wesson also examines the transferral of this glorification from Lenin to the party and then to the state, thus leading to a "wholehearted devotion to the collectivist, socialist fatherland."

2839   *White, W. C. "Hero for Russia," Scrib M, 81, no. 5 (May 1927), 489-94.
An account of the growing reverence for Lenin in the first few years after his death.

2840   Wilson, Jack. "Around the Corner from Red Square," Int Lit, nos. 4-5 (Apr.-May 1940), 97-106.
A description of the collection of the Central Lenin Museum.

2841   Wolfenden, J. "What They Say As They Wait to See Lenin," NY Times M, (13 Dec. 1964), 26-27+.

2842   Zhukov, Nikolai. "A Great Theme," in LIOL (anthology), 271-82.
An account, by an artist who painted portraits of Lenin, of the personal characteristics of Lenin that artists must seek to capture.

B. Lenin Centenary

2843   Bezymenskii, L. "Unesco and the Lenin Year," <u>New Times</u>,
       no. 3 (20 Jan. 1970), 10-12.

2844   "Birthday for Lenin and a Boost for Brezhnev," <u>Time</u>, 95,
       (27 Apr. 1970), 30-31.

2845   Blokh, A. et al., comps. <u>Lenin Centennial</u>. Moscow:
       Progress Publishers, 1970.
       An annotated centennial album.

2846   Castro, Fidel. "Lenin's Centennial and the Cuban Revolu-
       tion," <u>New World R</u>, 38, no. 3 (1970), 15-24.

2847   "Centenary Preparations," <u>New Times</u>, 14 (7 Apr. 1970),
       21.

2848   "Centenary Selection of Lenin Photographs," <u>Labour Mo</u>, 52,
       no. 4 (Apr. 1970), 165-72.

2849   *Chou, Yu-kuang. "Kremlin Prepares Elaborate Programs
       to Mark Lenin's Centennial of Birth," <u>Iss St</u>, 6, no. 7
       (1970), 26-34.

2850   Guillen, N. "The Lenin Centenary," <u>Eyewitness</u>, 2, no. 4
       (Apr. 1970), 4+.

2851   "If He Had a Grave He'd Be Turning in It," <u>Economist</u>,
       234, (10 Jan. 1970), 32.

2852   "In Commemoration of Lenin Centenary," <u>Peo Dem</u>, (22
       Apr. 1970), 1-22.

2853   "Jubilee Publications," <u>Cult Life</u>, (May-Dec. 1969).
       A series of 21 articles on the Lenin Centenary.

2854   Kirko, V. M. "The Lenin Jubilee in Africa," in <u>HDASP</u>
       (anthology), 137-50.
       A praiseful review of the various ways in which the
       centenary was celebrated in Africa and by whom.

2855   *Kutsenko, T. "The Komsomol and the Schools in the Lenin
       Year," <u>Sov Ed</u>, 12, nos. 3-5 (Jan.-Mar. 1970), 130-52.

Advice on how to prepare the Komsomol for an effective role in the Lenin Centenary.

2856   "Lenin Birth Centenary Calendar," Sov Lit, no. 3 (1970),
        attached as a supplement.

2857   "Lenin Centenary; Editorial," Call, 21, no. 11 (Apr. 1970),
        3-8.

2858   "Lenin Centenary Preparations in Fraternal Parties," W
        Marxist R, 13, no. 1 (Jan. 1970), 24-26.

2859   "Lenin Centenary Preparations in Fraternal Countries,"
        W Marxist R, 13, no. 2 (Feb. 1970), 57-67.

2860   "The Lenin Jubilee," New Times, 17 (28 Apr. 1970), 1-2.

2861   "The Lenin Year," W Marxist R, 13, no. 1 (Jan. 1970),
        3-5.

2862   "The Lenin Year," W Marxist R, 13, no. 12 (Dec. 1970),
        3-4.

2863   "The Lenin Year," Cult Life, (Jan.-Aug. 1970).
        A series of tributes to and reminiscences of Lenin,
        and accounts of the celebration of the Lenin Centenary.

2864   "Leninism: Any Number Can Play," Newsweek, 75 (27 Apr.
        1970), 39.
        A discussion of the fanfare surrounding the Lenin Cen-
        tenary as a diversionary tactic by the Soviet regime in
        regard to internal dissent over economic and other con-
        ditions.

2865   "Lenin's Birthday," in LHIII (anthology), 116.

2866   Lopatin, Y. "From Cavriago to Palermo," New Times, 15
        (14 Apr. 1970), 12-13.
        A survey of centennial preparations in those towns in
        Italy which Lenin visited or stayed.

2867   Mowrer, E. A. "Nixon and Lenin's Birthday," Hum Events,
        30 (1970), 13.

2868   Naumov, Pavel. "The Lenin Year," New Times, no. 1
        (Jan. 1970), 3.

2869   "One Prophet They'll Stand by," Economist," 233 (22 Nov.
        1969), 43-44.
        A review of centennial preparations in the Soviet Union
        and Eastern Europe.

2870   *Panachin, F. "On Reading the Theses of the Central Com-

mittee of the CPSU: The Party's Words on Lenin,"
Sov Ed, 12, nos. 3-5 (Jan.-Mar. 1970), 8-15.
A positive reaction to the Communist Party's call for
a campaign to highlight all that is great about Lenin,
and a discussion of the opportunities this presents for
educators.

2871   "Preparations for Lenin Centenary," USSR Info B, no. 10
        (Oct. 1969), 3-4.

2872   "Preparing for the Centenary of Lenin's Birth," Cult Life,
        (Apr. 1968-May 1969).
        A fifteen part series of articles on centennial prepara-
        tions.

2873   *"Quarterly Notes: Lenin's Centenary," Survey, 16, no. 1
        (1970), 290-310.
        An examination of the Lenin Centenary in the Soviet
        Union and its manipulation for various purposes by
        Soviet leaders.

2874   "Saint Lenin; Honored by U.N. ," Chris Today, 14 (8 May
        1970), 26.

2875   *Sarafannikova, G. P.   "Improving the Work of the School
        Lenin Museums," Sov Ed, 12, nos. 3-5 (Jan.-Mar.
        1970), 197-218.
        An account of the increased efforts in Soviet schools to
        familiarize students with Lenin's life and work as part
        of the Lenin Centenary.

2876   *Shnekendorf, Z. K.   "Toward the Glorious Anniversary,"
        Sov Ed, 12, nos. 3-5 (Jan.-Mar. 1970), 16-28.
        A report on the 19-20 June 1969 Moscow educators'
        conference resolutions on how best to prepare Soviet
        schools for the Lenin Centenary.

2877   "Soviet Union: Leadership at the Crossroads," Time, 95
        (4 May 1970), 33-36.
        In part, a discussion of the celebration of the Lenin
        Centenary.

2878   Spratt, P.   "The Lenin Centenary," Swarajya, 14, no. 47
        (23 May 1970), 1-3.

2879   "UN Observes Lenin Centenary," UN Mo Chron, 7 (May
        1970), 62-64.

2880   Unni, Raja C.   "Towards the Lenin Centenary: India,"
        W Marxist R, 12, no. 6 (June 1969), 61-62.

2881   "Vladimir Lenin's Birth Centennial," Sov Life, 8, no. 167
        (Aug. 1970), 30-34.

2882   Weaver, Kitty D.   Lenin's Grandchildren.   Preschool Edu-
        cation in the Soviet Union.   New York: Simon and
        Schuster, 1971; 254pp.
        Lenin is not the focus of any one chapter in this study,
        but it contains a discussion of the stories about him
        which circulated within Soviet preschools as part of the
        Lenin Centenary celebration.   [LB1140. 2. W4]

2883   Zagladin, V.   "Triumphant Advance of Lenin's Ideas," W
        Marxist R, 13, no. 6 (June 1970), 5-8.
        A consideration of the Lenin Jubilee as a sign of Lenin's
        tremendous impact on the modern world.

2884   *Zviagintseva, A. P.   "The Lenin Corner in the School,"
        Sov Ed, 12, nos. 3-5 (Jan.-Mar. 1970), 29-35.
        A review of the purpose of the Lenin corners in the
        schools, and suggestions on how to utilize them effec-
        tively during the Lenin Centenary.

14. MISCELLANY

A. Introductions to Lenin's Written Works

2885   Allen, James S. Lenin on the United States. New York: International Publishers, 1970; 674pp. [DK254. L3A546]

2886   Block, Russell. Lenin's Fight against Stalinism. New York: Pathfinder, 1975; 160pp. [HX313. L4135]

2887   Christman, Henry M. Essential Works of Lenin. New York: Bantam Books, 1966; 372pp. [HX312. L27]

2888   Connor, J. E. Lenin on Politics and Revolution: Selected Writings. New York: Pegasus, 1969; 375pp. [DK254. L3A515]

2889   Fraina, Louis. The Proletarian Revolution in Russia. New York: Communist Press, 1918; 453pp. [DK265. L4P7]

2890   Gafurov, B. G. and Kim, G. F. Lenin and National Liberation in the East. Moscow: Progress Publishers, 1978; 468pp. [DK254. L46. L39213]

2891   Hall, Gus. Letter to American Workers by V. I. Lenin. New York: New Outlook Publishers, 1970; 39pp. [DK254. L3P4813]

2892   Krupskaya, Nadezhda K. Lenin on the Emancipation of Women; from Writings. New York: International Publishers, 1969; 135pp. [HQ1663. L3913]

2893   Kurella, A. Speeches of V. I. Lenin. New York: International Publishers, 1928; 94pp. [DK254. L3S7]

2894   Lieteisen, C. The National Liberation Movement in the East. Moscow: Progress Publishers, 1969; 363pp. [DK254. L3A5723 1969]

2895   _____. On Peaceful Coexistence. Moscow: Foreign Languages Publishing House, 1963; 255pp. [DK254. L304563]

2896 Lumer, Hyman. "Introduction," to Lenin, on the Jewish Question. New York: International Press, 1974; 155pp. [DS135. R9L37313]

2897 Mitzkovitch-Kapsukas, V. Lenin on Organization. Chicago: Daily Worker Publishing Company, 1926; 235pp. [DK254. L3L44]

2898 Pollitt, Harry. Lenin on Britain; a Compilation. New York: International Publishers, 1934; 316pp. [HC255. L55]

2899 Possony, Stefan T. The Lenin Reader. Chicago: Regnery, 1969; 528pp. [DK254. L3A576]

2900 Rust, William. Lenin on the I. L. P. London: Modern Books, 1933; 55pp.

2901 S. , M. The Suppressed Testament of Lenin. New York: Pioneer Publishers, 1935; 47pp. [DK254. L3S9]

2902 Sevryugina, N. G. Lenin on Petty-Bourgeois Revolutionism. Moscow: Novosti Press, 1970; 174pp. [HX518. R4L4115]

2903 Stalin, Joseph. Marxism and Revisionism. New York: International Publishers, 1946; 64pp. [DK254. L3A56]

2904 Tarasenko, A. Letter to American Workers by V. I. Lenin. Moscow: Novosti, 1973; 53pp. [HD854. L4413]

2905 Trachtenberg, Alexander. Lenin Speaks to the Youth. New York: International Publishers, 1936; 22pp. [HQ799. R9L42]

2906 _____. A Letter to American Workers. New York: International Publishers, 1934; 23pp. [DK254. L3L5]

2907 _____. The Soviets at Work. Seattle: Seattle Union Record Publishing Company, 1918; 61pp. [DK254. L3S6]

2908 _____. What Is to Be Done? New York: International Publishers, 1929; 175pp. [DK254. L4A203]

2909 Ushakov, A. V. V. I. Lenin on Bourgeois-Democratic Revolution. Moscow: Novosti Press, 1975; 135pp. [DK263. 16. L462 1975]

2910 Utechin, S. V. What Is to Be Done? Oxford: Clarendon Press, 1963; 213pp. [HX314. L342]

B. Historiography/Lenin's Writings

2911   Ashukina, Marina. "Apt, Colorful and Concise," <u>Sov Life</u>, 3, no. 162 (Mar. 1970), 48-49.

2912   Bandyopadhyay, P. "A Bibliography of Lenin's Theoretical Works," <u>Com V</u>, 3, no. 6 (1971), 61-64.

2913   Beard, C. A. "Lenin and Economic Evolution," <u>New Rep</u>, 75, (17 May 1933), 22-24.
A review article on Lenin's <u>The Revolution of 1917</u>.

2914   *Brookes, R. H. "The Editions of Lenin's <u>Sochineniia</u>," <u>Pol Sci</u>, 6, no. 2 (Sept. 1954), 68-76.
A comparative analysis of four Russian editions of Lenin's works.

2915   *Elwood, Ralph C. "How Complete Is Lenin's <u>Polnoe Sobranie Sochinenii?</u>," <u>Slav R</u>, 38, no. 1 (Mar. 1979), 97-105.

2916   Fedoseyev, P. "New Lenin Documents," <u>W Marxist R</u>, 13, no. 6 (June 1970), 8-11.

2917   *Kamenev, L. B. "The Literary Legacy of Ilyitch," <u>Com Int</u>, no. 1 (1924), 54-69.
A chronological survey of Lenin's writings during the 1893-1917 period, and a review of the first compilation of his works.

2918   *Keep, John L. H. "Lenin's Letters As an Historical Source," in <u>LAL</u> (anthology), 245-68.
An analysis of the historical value of Lenin's correspondence, as published in the 5th edition of his <u>Collected Works</u>. Using Vol. I of the <u>Trotsky Papers</u> (J. Meijer, editor) as a non-Soviet source of comparison, Keep examines the letters for accuracy and reliability, and concludes that, although some of Lenin's letters are missing, the editors have removed most of the falsifications of the Stalin era and presented a reasonably complete and accurate set of documents of great value to researchers. Keep also discusses the letters for insights into Lenin's mind and his approach to solving the various problems which confronted him in the 1917-

1920 period. Condensed version in <u>Rus R</u>, 30, no. 1 (Jan. 1971), 33-42.

2919   *Lacquer, Walter. "Lenin: for and against," in <u>The Fate of the Revolution. Interpretations of Soviet History</u>. New York: Macmillan, 1967; 59-82.
A scholarly, historiographic essay on fifty years of writings about Lenin. Lacquer reviews: the early mis- information on Lenin; the gradual shift of public opinion (1917-1921) towards him as favorable accounts of his character, personality, and goals were published by Western interviewers; the devotional literature which began to appear immediately following his death; the first comprehensive Western biographies; and the second wave of Western scholarship which came after World War II with the growth of interest in the Soviet Union. Lacquer provides most depth on this last group of writ- ings, singling out the works of Shub, Wolfe, Fischer, and Ulam for individual review. He concludes with a survey of "the cardinal questions that have a direct bearing on the historical assessment of Lenin's ideas and policies." [DK265.9.H5L3]

2920   "New Lenin Documents," <u>W Marxist R</u>, 17, no. 3 (Mar. 1974), 3-16.
A discussion of six new documents (speeches, reports and articles) by Lenin. The documents, which deal with various aspects of the revolutionary movement, are appended to the article.

2921   Paul, W. "Lenin, the Pathfinder," <u>Labour Mo</u>, 18 (Nov. 1936), 703-06.
A review article on volumes 3-6 of Lenin's <u>Selected Works</u>.

2922   Peresvetov, Roman. "The Original: Where Is It?," <u>Sov Life</u>, 6, no. 153 (June 1969), 38-40.
Speculation on the whereabouts and contents of missing pages from Lenin's <u>What the 'Friends of the People' Are: How They Fight the Social Democrats</u>.

2923   Price, M. P. "Lenin in History; Based on a Biography Prepared by the Marx-Engels-Lenin Institute," <u>Spectator</u>, 171 (3 Sept. 1943), 212+.

2924   Rosen, V. "Depository of Lenin Documents," <u>New Times</u>, 15, (14 Apr. 1970), 16-17.
A survey of the Institute of Marxism-Leninism's collec- tion of Lenin documents, and a discussion of its efforts to locate all Lenin-related materials.

2925   *Schapiro, Leonard. "Lenin after 50 Years," in <u>LMTL</u> (an- thology), 3-22.

A survey of primary materials available for the study
of Lenin, and a discussion of the characteristics of
Lenin most often stressed by his biographers.   The
primary materials reviewed by Schapiro are: 5th edition
of Lenin's complete writings (55 vols.); a chronological
bibliography of Lenin's writings; his annotation of the
Marx-Engels correspondence; the catalogue of his Kremlin library; and his annotation of Steklov's biography of
Chernyshevsky.   The characteristics of Lenin most discussed by biographers, Schapiro states, are his dedication, lack of personal vanity or ambition, and his combination of kindly and ruthless behavior.   Schapiro criticizes two additional judgments often made about Lenin:
that he was a universal genius and that he founded a
new type of society.

2926   *Shub, David.   "New Light on Lenin," Rus R, 11, no. 3
(July 1952), 131-37.
A review of the 35 volume edition of Lenin's collected
works.

(for editors of anthologies, see pages xix-xxvi)

Note: Since many of the general studies listed in section I-A (entries 1-57) contain information on the vast majority of the subjects listed below, no attempt has been made to index them here. The user must consult the indexes of these studies to determine their value in researching a particular subject.